PROMOTING FAMILY WELL
PREVENTING CHILD MALTREATMENT

Fundamentals for Thinking and Action

Based on extensive research over many years, with a broad range of Canadian and international contributors, this collection of essays is an important addition to the child welfare agenda. It deals with the promotion of emotional well-being in families and the prevention of child maltreatment. Values, policies, and resources are examined as both facilitators of and barriers to effective action.

The authors interviewed nearly one hundred and fifty people, including researchers, policymakers, social workers, and clients of the child welfare system. Both theoretical and practical issues emerge, as the authors discuss the social context of abuse and the scientific context wherein policy is made. They conclude that the following social conditions are essential in effectively reducing abuse: upheld values of self-determination and the health of children; sufficient material and psychological resources for children and families; family-friendly parental leave and child support policies; and empirically grounded and tested prevention programs.

Contained within the work is extensive examination of current issues in Aboriginal child welfare. The authors advocate certain collective approaches to childrearing, inspired by current and historical Aboriginal practices.

Promoting Family Wellness is relevant to all those involved in child welfare and to researchers and students too. It is readable and clear enough to appeal to the general reader who is interested in this intellectually complex and emotionally fraught topic.

ISAAC PRILLELTENSKY teaches in the Department of Psychology at Victoria University, Melbourne, Australia.

GEOFFREY NELSON and LESLEA PEIRSON teach in the Department of Psychology at Wilfred Laurier University.

Promoting Family Wellness and Preventing Child Maltreatment

Fundamentals for Thinking and Action

Edited by
ISAAC PRILLELTENSKY,
GEOFFREY NELSON,
AND LESLEA PEIRSON

UNIVERSITY OF TORONTO PRESS
Toronto Buffalo London

© University of Toronto Press Incorporated 2001
Toronto Buffalo London
Printed in Canada

ISBN: 0-8020-4861-7 (cloth)
ISBN: 0-8020-8383-8 (paper)

Printed on acid-free paper

National Library of Canada Cataloguing in Publication Data

Main entry under title:

Promoting family wellness and preventing child maltreatment :
  fundamentals for thinking and action

Includes bibliographical references and index.
ISBN 0-8020-4861-7 (bound)   ISBN 0-8020-8383-8 (pbk.)

1. Child abuse – Canada – Prevention. 2. Social work with children –
Canada. 3. Family social work – Canada. 4. Child welfare – Canada.
I. Prilleltensky, Isaac, 1959– . II. Nelson, Geoffrey B. (Geoffrey Brian).
III. Peirson, Leslea, 1968– .

HV745.A6P76 2001   362.76′7′0971   C2001-930747-0

The University of Toronto Press acknowledges the financial assistance to its publishing program of the Canada Council for the Arts and the Ontario Arts Council.

University of Toronto Press acknowledges the financial support for its publishing activities of the Government of Canada through the Book Publishing Industry Development Program (BPIDP).

Contents

Preface vii

Acknowledgments xi

The Family Wellness Project Team xiii

Section I: Context

1 Mapping the Terrain: Framework for Promoting Family Wellness and Preventing Child Maltreatment 3
 ISAAC PRILLELTENSKY, LESLEA PEIRSON, and GEOFFREY NELSON

2 Context, Contributing Factors, and Consequences 41
 LESLEA PEIRSON, MARIE-CLAIRE LAURENDEAU, and CLAIRE CHAMBERLAND

3 Vision and Values for Child and Family Wellness 124
 ISAAC PRILLELTENSKY, MARIE-CLAIRE LAURENDEAU, CLAIRE CHAMBERLAND, and LESLEA PEIRSON

Section II: Interventions

4 Social Policies for Promoting the Well-Being of Canadian Children and Families 177
 RAY DE V. PETERS, JESSICA E. PETERS, MARIE-CLAIRE LAURENDEAU, CLAIRE CHAMBERLAND, and LESLEA PEIRSON

5 A Review and Analysis of Programs to Promote Family Wellness and Prevent the Maltreatment of Preschool and Elementary-School-Aged Children   220
GEOFFREY NELSON, MARIE-CLAIRE LAURENDEAU, CLAIRE CHAMBERLAND, and LESLEA PEIRSON

6 Programming for Distressed and Disadvantaged Adolescents   273
GARY CAMERON, JAN O'REILLY, MARIE-CLAIRE LAURENDEAU, and CLAIRE CHAMBERLAND

7 Program Implementation and Diffusion   318
GARY CAMERON, JEFF KARABANOW, MARIE-CLAIRE LAURENDEAU, and CLAIRE CHAMBERLAND

Section III: Aboriginal Context and Interventions
8 A Circle of Healing: Family Wellness in Aboriginal Communities   349
ED CONNORS and FRANK MAIDMAN

Section IV: Conclusion
9 Beyond the Boundaries: Themes for Thinking and Action in the Promotion of Family Wellness and the Prevention of Child Maltreatment   419
GEOFFREY NELSON, ISAAC PRILLELTENSKY, and LESLEA PEIRSON

References   449

Index   531

Preface

To promote family wellness and prevent child maltreatment we must be sensitive to three separate but related contexts: the social, the scientific, and the pragmatic. First, we have to attend to the *social* context in which wellness and maltreatment take place. We need to know what cultural norms contribute to well-being or to abuse, and we must have a clear reading on what roles communities and governments are willing to play in these issues. In order to understand the social context, we studied, researched, and talked to people about their values and their vision, and about current opportunities and threats to family wellness. We found that the Canadian social context presents both threats and opportunities. Whereas opportunities exist because of the renewed interest in prevention and community-based approaches to health, threats are omnipresent because federal and provincial/territorial governments are dramatically decreasing their role in supporting people in need. Although our book was finished in the first half of 1999, and some changes have taken place in the policy arena since then, we believe that more vigorous changes have to take place to promote child wellness in Canada.

Second, we have to locate our efforts in the *scientific* context. It was our job to research published and unpublished literature concerning risk and protective factors and proven methods of promoting family well-being and preventing abuse and neglect. Our team effort, as well as our international contacts and access to multiple databases, permitted us to review hundreds of studies and policies in several countries. What we found is that family wellness is a multilayered and ecological concept, brought about by the synergy of positive forces at the individual, parent, family, community, and societal levels. Maltreatment, in turn, is the result of accumulated risks and vulnerabilities at all these levels. In the absence of protective factors, vulnerabilities predispose families to abuse; in the presence of protective factors and supports, there is a chance that families and children will develop resilience.

We also found that for successful policies and programs to thrive, the social and political contexts have to be ripe. Not only in affluent European countries, but also in poor countries with communitarian philosophies, such as Cuba, governments assume a more active role in prevention and promotion than those in Canada and the United States. Within Canada, we note that First Nations communities invoke collective responsibility more often than peoples of European descent. This shows us that not only money and material resources are needed to launch policies and programs of social responsibility, but also a culture of care, interdependence, and intergenerational justice. This, however, should not absolve governments from their responsibility to provide adequate funding. European countries have committed large amounts of money to universal child care and to generous child and family policies. In their view, it is worth it.

The implementation of effective policies and programs is determined, to a large extent, by society's model of responsibility. In individualistic societies like Canada and the United States, governments are retreating from their role in supporting families. Instead, more and more responsibility is being ascribed to and expected of individual parents. We also found that even with the best intentions, and perhaps even with adequate funding, effective programs are difficult to implement. Human factors and organizational dynamics have to be delicately handled for all the players to collaborate and for all the pieces of the puzzle to fall into place. Challenges notwithstanding, we offer guidelines for the successful implementation and diffusion of effective initiatives.

Third, we need to address the *pragmatic* context. This refers to the ability of professionals, politicians, and citizens involved in child and family wellness to generate positive changes on behalf of children. For positive changes to take place, everyone involved in the well-being of children has to collaborate and take a stance. The pragmatic realm relies on the social and scientific contexts to help us understand the cultural climate and the empirical bases of problems and solutions. Without social and scientific clarity, none of us would know how to channel our efforts. But without pragmatic clarity, all of our knowledge would, frankly, go to waste. Practically speaking, there is no one way to achieve family wellness; the methods are numerous and parallel. The key to pragmatic clarity is to ask ourselves what we can do, in our role as professionals and citizens, about wellness and maltreatment in the short and long terms and with whom we should partner to promote children's development. All of us, professionals and citizens, political as well as grass-roots organizations, have a role to play. We offer in this book points of entry into the arena of wellness and maltreatment for everyone. If you are a child care worker, a social worker in the field of child welfare, a manager of children's services, an elected official, a child activist, a child psychologist, a public health practitioner, a nurse, a physician, a parent, or a graduate of the child welfare system, there are things you can do. This book offers recommendations for: (1) a better understanding of *wellness, maltreatment, prevention,* and *promotion*; (2) value-based actions; and (3) successful policies and programs. We have come to the conclusion that it is not enough to limit our efforts to work-related initiatives, either as professionals or volunteers. We believe that there is a need to join social movements that promote child-friendly cultures and policies. Social pressure has as much legitimacy as scientifically proven social programs. Without pressure and public demand, governments are bound to attend to other interests. Children need not only professional helpers, but also social activists.

Our claims to legitimacy in the social, scientific, and pragmatic contexts derive from our extensive efforts to consult with people like you, the reader. We read about and talked to people like you throughout Canada and several other countries. We talked to youth, parents, workers, volunteers, managers, policy advisers, and researchers. We engaged in discussions with people within the welfare system and people critical of it. We talked to people who received formal and informal services.

To make this research representative of our country, our team consisted of researchers from English and French Canada and from First Nations. The information concerning First Nations is captured in a separate chapter, while the research from English and French Canada is incorporated throughout the remaining sections.

So far we have described the various contexts of our work and the input we used for the project. Now about the output. All of our efforts would be in vain if there was no meaningful output stemming from this work. Our commitment to make this research relevant and meaningful led us to produce short and informative summaries about each chapter of the book. (These summaries may be found on the Child Welfare League of Canada website, in the resources section, http://cwlc1.cwlc.ca/live/E/resc/dwn.shtm.) In addition, we made an effort to write in language that is understandable and useful, and we used formats that facilitate communication and action. Our collective challenge, ours as authors and yours as readers, is to find a piece of wellness and maltreatment that we can work on. If you are a manager in a child welfare, family services, or health services agency, we invite you to ask yourself what you can do to launch effective prevention programs. If you are a child welfare director, we ask you what you can do to implement some of the child and family policies we discuss in this book. If you are a front-line worker, we ask what you can do to enact values that promote child and family wellness. If you are a citizen concerned with the well-being of children, we ask what organizations or movements you can join to make children a priority for our country. Whoever you are, we ask what you can do to advance values and visions of wellness. We hope you use this book to ask yourself these questions and to act on the answers.

The Editors
6 April 2000

Acknowledgments

This research was made possible by funding provided by Human Resources Development Canada through its Social Development Partnerships Program (SDPP), and as part of the Federal/Provincial Child Welfare Research Agenda. We would like to acknowledge our partnership with the provincial, territorial, and regional (in Quebec) Directors of child welfare. Our thanks in particular go to our federal liaison at SDPP, Évariste Thériault, and our provincial liaison, Phil Goodman, who were most helpful in guiding our efforts. Their financial assistance facilitated the publication of this volume as well as the production of research bulletins. Financial support was also provided through several grants from Wilfrid Laurier University that funded, in part, the qualitative components of this study.

We extend our profound appreciation to all those people who participated in the consultation processes, in Canada and abroad, who were extremely generous in helping us to understand their realities, their work, their research, and their dreams.

We are also very grateful to our many colleagues who aided in the editorial process by reviewing draft manuscripts and summaries: Merle Beedie, Gary Cameron, Claire Chamberland, Else Christensen, Ed Connors, Bob Glossop, Barbara Hearn, Nena LaCaille-Johnson, Marie-Claire Laurendeau, Louise Lefort, Frank Maidman, Greg McGregor, Gary Melton, Virginia Murphy-Berman, Geoffrey Nelson, Leslea Peirson, Joyce Pelletier, Ray De V. Peters, Mike Pratt, Isaac Prilleltensky, Danetta Restoule, Colin Wasacase, and David Wolfe. We appreciated all the feedback received, even critical observations, as all the comments helped in some significant way to raise the level of accuracy, readability, and insight of our products.

Our many research assistants – Isaac Asante, Salinda Horgan, Rolando Inunza, Jeff Karabanow, Laura Keily, Louise Lefort, Jennifer MacLeod, Cameron Norman, Jan O'Reilly, Jessica Peters, Dan Salhani, Laura Sanchez, Monique Shapiro, Holt Sivak, James Taylor, and Barb Zupko – were invaluable in bringing this project to fruition. Clerical assistance and support for various project needs were competently provided by Valerie Angus, Marlene Cox, Donna Connors, Philomene Kocher, Josée Lacombe, Annick Landreville, Judith Lavoie, Lois Logan, Alan Kirker, Linda Potter, Elma Schweigert, Monique Shapiro, and Ramona Teichroeb. Special thanks to Tara Pocket for designing our logo. Many other people contributed to the project in a variety of ways, for example, by sharing research or program materials, providing technical information and support, and organizing site visits and interviews. To all of you we offer our sincere gratitude.

The Family Wellness Project Team

Gary Cameron (co-investigator) was the director of the former Centre for Social Welfare Studies from 1986 to 1996 and is currently an associate professor at the Faculty of Social Work, Wilfrid Laurier University, Waterloo, Ontario. He has been the principal investigator on several major research and demonstration projects focusing on interventions with vulnerable children and families, for example: 1983–5 investigation of family support measures in Ontario children's aid societies; 1988–92 Parent Mutual Aid Organizations in Child Welfare Demonstration Project; 1993–7 investigation of intensive family preservation services in five child welfare and children's mental health settings; 1994–5 Promising Programs and Organizational Realities: Protecting Children and Supporting Families Project; 2000–3 Partnerships for Children and Families Project. A particular area of interest for Dr Cameron has been program implementation issues. He has authored numerous research reports and is the co-author of two volumes on interventions with high-risk families. He is the primary author of a recent comprehensive review of support programming in child welfare.

Claire Chamberland (co-investigator) has a Ph.D. in experimental child psychology. She is a full professor at the School of Social Work, University of Montreal. Her teaching and research interests include child development, prevention and promotion practices, ecological approaches, and violence toward children and women. Since 1995 she has directed the Institute of Research for Social Development of Children and Youth. This research organization is connected with a social agency working on child maltreatment, conduct disorder, and delinquency issues.

Ed Connors (co-investigator) is a psychologist registered in the provinces of Ontario and Saskatchewan. He is of Mohawk ancestry and is a band member of Kahnawake First Nation. He has worked with First Nations communities across Canada during the past fifteen years in both urban and rural centres. His work during the past seventeen years includes clinical director for an infant mental health centre in the city of Regina and director for the Sacred Circle, a suicide prevention program developed to serve First Nations communities in northwestern Ontario. While developing the latter service, Dr Connors worked with the elders and apprenticed in traditional First Nations approaches to healing. Today his practice incorporates knowledge about healing. He and his wife Donna manage Onkwatenro'shón:'A, a health planning firm that provides health consultation to First Nations communities from his offices at Rama First Nation in Ontario. Dr Connors was a board member and vice-president of the Canadian Association for Suicide Prevention between 1990 and 1998. He is currently on the advisory council for the Ontario Suicide Prevention Network. His publications have been in the area of health and healing in First Nations with an emphasis on understanding and preventing self-destructive and abusive behaviour.

Marie-Claire Laurendeau (co-investigator) holds a Ph.D. in psychology from the Université du Québec à Montréal. From 1983 to 1992 she was the coordinator of the Mental Health Program at the Montreal General Hospital's Community Health Department. In this context she developed and implemented many prevention and health promotion programs in the areas of family support and children's and adolescents' mental health. In 1988, Quebec's Minister for Health and Social Affairs named Dr Laurendeau a member of the Comité de la Santé Mentale du Québec, a major planning and evaluation body responsible for the development of the province's mental health policy. Between 1992 and 1994 she temporarily left public health to take charge of the psychology service at the Université de Montréal. Since 1994 she has headed the Human and Social Ecology Unit of Montreal's Directorate of Public Health.

Frank Maidman (co-investigator) is a consulting sociologist specializing in the social development of Aboriginal communities in Ontario. Over the last fifteen years, he has conducted policy research in social services, conducted community needs assessment studies in Aboriginal communities, facilitated the design and development of family support services, and evaluated Aboriginal prevention programs in child welfare. Other projects include research and development in community mental health, education, adult education, family life and adolescence, school helping professions, voluntarism, and women in nontraditional work. Before commencing his private consulting practice, Dr Maidman was a research scientist at the Clarke Institute of Psychiatry and assistant professor at the Ontario Institute for Studies in Education in Toronto.

Geoffrey Nelson (co-investigator) is a professor of psychology and former director of the M.A. program in community psychology at Wilfrid Laurier University, Waterloo, Ontario. He has served as senior editor of the *Canadian Journal of Community Mental Health* and chair of the Com-munity Psychology Section of the Canadian Psychological Association. Professor Nelson was the site researcher for the Highfield Community Enrichment Project, which is one of the sites for the Better Beginnings, Better Futures Project in Ontario. Some of his research and writing has focused on community and school-based prevention programs for children and families.

Leslea Peirson (project manager/co-investigator) holds a graduate degree in community psychology from Wilfrid Laurier University and is currently enrolled in a doctoral program in community health at the University of Toronto. Since receiving her M.A. in 1993, Leslea has worked consistently in applied research settings where she has been involved in evaluations of child welfare and children's mental health services and several organizational change processes in child welfare, children's mental health, education, and community services. Her primary research interests include prevention and promotion practices focusing on children, youth and families, and the realities of policy and program implementation. Leslea currently volunteers with several community-based organizations that are devoted to improving the quality of life for all children and families.

Ray De V. Peters (co-investigator), Ph.D., is a professor of psychology at Queen's University in Kingston, Ontario. Dr Peters is also the research director of the Better Beginnings, Better Futures Project, which is a large, multi-site longitudinal study in Ontario on the prevention of social, emotional, health, and cognitive problems in young children from birth to age eight. He was a visiting scientist with the Oregon

Social Learning Center in 1979–80 and with the Mental Health Division of the World Health Organization in Geneva, Switzerland, in 1986–7. Since 1982 he has served on the executive committee of the Banff International Conference on Behavioral Science. His primary research interests are in the areas of promotion, prevention, and early intervention in child and family development.

Isaac Prilleltensky (principal investigator) is research professor in the Department of Psychology at Victoria University in Melbourne, Australia. Until the completion of the family wellness project, he was in the Department of Psychology at Wilfrid Laurier University in Waterloo, Ontario. He is the author of *The Morals and Politics of Psychology: Psychological Discourse and the Status Quo* (State University of New York Press, 1994) and co-editor with Dennis Fox of *Critical Psychology* (Sage, 1997). Until his departure to Australia in December 1999, he was chair of Action for Children, a children's rights group that seeks to eliminate child abuse and neglect and to improve the social and economic wellness of children. Isaac is a fellow of the Division of Community Psychology of the American Psychological Association and a former director of the graduate program in community psychology at Wilfrid Laurier University. He is interested in the promotion of value-based practice and interventions in community mental health. He believes that social justice is a key value in the prevention of psychological problems and in the promotion of personal and collective wellness.

SECTION I
Context

CHAPTER ONE

Mapping the Terrain: Framework for Promoting Family Wellness and Preventing Child Maltreatment

Isaac Prilleltensky, Leslea Peirson, and Geoffrey Nelson

INTRODUCTION

We know that prevention is better than cure, but provincial ministries of health in Canada devote less than 1 per cent of their budgets to the prevention of mental health problems. Most of the money goes toward treatment (Nelson, Prilleltensky, Laurendeau, & Powell, 1996). The situation is much the same in the United States (Goldston, 1991).

We want teenagers who are unprepared for parenthood to stop having children, but we are unwilling to invest in family planning, educational, and preventive services (Harris, 1996; Mitchell, 1998a; Simone, 1995). We know that about 26 per cent of Canadian children experience behavioural, learning, emotional, or social problems, but nobody seems to panic (Offord, Boyle, & Szatmari, 1987; Statistical profile of Canada's children, 1997). We understand that brain malleability is greatest during the first years of life (Bertrand, 1996; Keating & Mustard, 1996; Ramey & Ramey, 1998), but we spend most of our economic and social resources on adults and seniors. We have social funds for unemployed people and pension plans for the retired, but there is no comparable fund for disadvantaged children (Campaign 2000, 1996, 1997a, 1997b).

We hear economic deficits are going down, but the number of at-risk children goes up all the time. While provincial and federal budgets are being balanced, children continue to suffer, perhaps more than before. A child is reported missing in Canada about every nine minutes, for a total of more than 56,000 cases a year. These are children who often leave their homes to escape abuse (Mitchell, 1998b). Close to a million and a half, or about one-quarter, of Canada's children live in poverty, half a million more than in 1989, when the entire House of Commons voted to end child poverty by the year 2000 (Campaign 2000, 1997b; Canadian Council on Social Development [CCSD], 1997, 1998).

We are aware that health is determined by multiple factors, but our interventions focus on single solutions. Population health frameworks, widely known in Canada, show that health outcomes depend on five key determinants: social and economic environment, physical environment, personal health practices, individual capacity and coping skills, and services needed for health (Canadian Public Health Association, 1996; Federal, Provincial and Territorial Advisory Committee on Population Health, 1994, 1996; Hamilton & Bhatti, 1996; National Forum on Health, 1996; Standing Committee on Health, 1997). Despite our sophisticated ecological notions of health, interventions typically focus on the person and fail to change pernicious environments (e.g., Albee & Gullotta, 1997a; Institute of Medicine, 1994; Weissberg, Gullotta, Hampton, Ryan, & Adams, 1997).

We want communities to contribute to the well-being of children and youth, but instead of supporting formal and informal services we cut their funding. Recently, the National Forum on Health (1996), the Standing Committee on Health of the House of Commons (1997), Health Canada (1996b), the National Crime Prevention Council (1996), and the Canadian Public Health Association (1996), to name but a few partners, affirmed the importance of strong communities for children's health. These claims are at odds with prevailing policies of social disinvestment.

We are proud of Canada's international reputation in promoting children's rights, but the country has higher rates of child poverty than most industrialized nations (CCSD, 1998). In a report entitled *Towards Well-Being*, the Standing Committee on Health of the House of Commons (1997) stated that

> poverty among children in Canada is especially troublesome when compared with the rate in other industrialized countries. The rate of child poverty in Canada after government redistribution is four times the rate in Sweden, twice as high as in France and Germany, and 1.4 times the rate in Great Britain. Only in the United States is the rate higher than in Canada. (p. 7)

We require a licence to fish but have no standards to ensure that parents know how to treat their children. 'So what,' you might say, 'life is full of contradictions, and besides, we're not perfect.' True, we're not perfect, but unless like Rip Van Winkle, we've been sleeping peacefully for the past twenty years, we must be disturbed by these contradictions.

Child maltreatment happens every day, in every community. Yet public concern is only sporadic, elicited mainly by reports of brutal assaults against children. Child maltreatment, however, is not just about brutality or neglect; it is also about subtle but protracted and piercing pain, about feeling lonely, abandoned, betrayed, rejected, and unworthy.

Chances are that one in four people you know have been physically abused. Perhaps you were abused yourself. What about children you know? While one in four of them may be the subject of physical abuse, countless others are treated with disrespect, made to feel ashamed and psychologically terrified (Brown, 1997; Emery & Laumann-Billings, 1998; Morrison, 1997; Trocmé, McPhee, & Tam, 1995). In Ontario, a survey of 9,953 randomly selected residents aged 15 and older found high rates of abuse. The research, led by child psychiatrist Harriet MacMillan, and summarized in a recent issue of the *Canadian Medical Association Journal*, revealed that

> 31 per cent of men and 21.1 per cent of women reported having been abused physically while growing up. Childhood sexual abuse was reported by 12.8 per cent of women and 4.3 per cent of men. Severe abuse was reported by 10.7 per cent of men and 9.2 per cent of women, and severe sexual abuse was reported by 11.1 per cent of women and 3.9 per cent of men. (Brown, 1997, p. 867)

Maltreatment is about trust betrayed, love warped, and opportunities lost; it is about stealing happiness and depriving joy; it is about exploiting power and denigrating others. Abuse and neglect are about a vicious cycle that affects victims, their offspring, and society at large. Victims of maltreatment require expensive remedial services that take money away from preventive programs. With scarce resources, the private tragedy of abuse and neglect also presents an economic and social concern. While some children develop resiliency and overcome abusive and neglectful backgrounds to become loving, caring, and productive citizens, many others succumb under the weight of the trauma and develop psychological problems. Crime and delinquency, which cost Canadians approximately $46 billion annually, have been linked to histories of abuse. 'Today's child victim often becomes tomorrow's criminal offender' (National Crime Prevention Council, 1996, pp. 9–10). The enormous price of punitive and rehabilitative services drains our social wealth to the point that little is left for preventing abuse and neglect from occurring in the first place.

The answer: Address the root causes of the problem and interrupt the vicious cycle. The barrier: Cynicism about governments' and communities' abilities to stop abuse and neglect. The evidence: Many emotional, cognitive, behavioural, and social problems, including child maltreatment, can be significantly prevented. As veteran preventionists Albee and Gullotta put it, 'the evidence is clear that primary prevention of mental disorders works and that it is the only hope for reducing incidence' (1997b, p. 14). Indeed, research shows that some prevention programs are highly effective and save governments considerable amounts of money. The early-intervention High/Scope Perry Preschool Program saved $7.16 US for each dollar invested (Weikart & Schweinhart, 1997). The savings in the home visitation Prenatal/Early Infancy Project were also impressive:

> By the time the children were 4 years old, low-income families who received a nurse during pregnancy and through the second year of the child's life cost the government $3,313 [US] less than did their counterparts in the comparison group. When focused on low income families, the investment was recovered with a discounted dividend of about $180 per family within two years after the program ended. (Olds, 1997b, p. 61)

Unless we are determined to eradicate child maltreatment, we can expect the cost of remedial and therapeutic services associated with it to go up endlessly. The more maltreatment there is, the stronger the call for reactive services, and the fewer the dollars for proactive interventions. In 1995, for example, the number of children aged 0 to 16 in the care of the state in Canada was almost 40,000 (CCSD, 1997). In 1998, there were not enough foster homes in Toronto to place children in need. Children were being sent to other cities while agencies were desperately trying to find new facilities.

It is only by a serious reorganization of services and reallocation of resources into prevention that we can reasonably expect less suffering and reduced expenditures. Such an investment, while costly at first, will more than pay for itself in dollars saved for remedial services in special education, welfare, health, and the criminal justice system. In human terms, the savings simply defy calculation.

As authors, we see ourselves as liaison officers between the academic and the policy worlds, between the realm of science and the realm of practice, between the sphere of ideas and the ground of action. Our task is not just to point to best policies and practices, but to generate lasting efforts, efforts that will promote family wellness and prevent child maltreatment.

Our main challenge is to contribute to the well-being of children and families by synthesizing what we know about wellness and maltreatment, and translating this knowledge into morally sound, technically effective, and enduring social interventions. By interventions we mean policies, programs, and practices designed to enhance wellness and reduce risk factors and disempowering processes. The job of translation and interpretation is crucial. Unless we make sense of the literature and present it in such a way that it can be applied, the vast research base that exists is not put to good use. Hence, we place emphasis on deriving user-friendly lessons from the research and from our own data gathering.

CONCEPTUAL FRAMEWORK

There are three components to the conceptual framework that guides the material presented throughout this book: (1) an ecological perspective on wellness and maltreatment, (2) the promotion–prevention–protection continuum, and (3) the notion of partnership. We begin by considering the ecological perspective on wellness and maltreatment.

Ecological Perspective on Wellness and Maltreatment

'Wellness is not the same as the absence of disease. Rather it is defined by the presence of positive marker characteristics that come about as a result of felicitous combinations of organismic, familial, community, and societal elements' (Cowen, 1996, p. 247). According to Cowen (1991, 1994, 1996), wellness can be further defined as:

> the positive end of a hypothetical adjustment continuum – an ideal we should strive continually to approach ... Key pathways to wellness, for all of us, start with the crucial needs to form wholesome attachments and acquire age-appropriate competencies in early childhood. Those steps, vital in their own right, also lay down a base for the good, or not so good, outcomes that follow. Other cornerstones of a wellness approach include engineering settings and environments that facilitate adaptation, fostering autonomy, support and empowerment, and promoting skills needed to cope effectively with stress. (Cowen, 1996, p. 246)

In order to promote wellness and prevent maltreatment we require an ecological framework that can help us understand the issues and improve children's lives. We define wellness as *a favourable state of affairs brought about by the combined presence of cogent values, satisfactory psychological and material resources, effective policies, and successful programs. Basically, family wellness is a state of affairs in which everybody's needs in the family are met.* Family wellness is more than the absence of discord; it is the presence of supportive, affectionate, and gratifying relationships that serve to promote the personal development of family members and the collective well-being of the family as a whole. Family wellness comes about through the satisfaction of psychological, material, and economic needs (Basic Behavioral Science Task Force of the National Advisory Mental Health Council, 1996a; Moore et al., 1996; Standing Committee on Health, 1997; Stinnett & DeFrain, 1985; Stinnett, DeFrain, King, Knaub, & Rowe, 1981).

Wellness is an ecological concept. According to Cowen (1996), 'optimal development of wellness ... requires integrated sets of operations involving individuals, families, settings, community contexts, and macrolevel societal structures and policies' (p. 246). In *Mental Health for Canadians: Striking a Balance*, wellness is defined as:

> the capacity of the individual, the group and the environment to interact with one another in ways that promote subjective well-being, the optimal development and use of mental abilities (cognitive, affective, and relational), the achievement of individual and collective goals consistent with justice and the attainment and preservation of conditions of fundamental equality. (Epp, 1988, p. 7)

These definitions of wellness are predicated on the presence of a healthy and just society that affords citizens opportunities for growth and development (Albee, 1986; Canadian Public Health Association, 1996).

For the purpose of this study, we identify wellness at four key ecological levels: child, parent and family, community, and society. Figure 1.1 shows the ecological and hierarchical structure of wellness, whereby smaller units rely on progressively larger constructs. Thus, child wellness relies on the fulfilment of basic needs at the levels of parental and family, community, and societal wellness.

Table 1.1 provides an overview of the values, resources, policies, and programs required to bring about child, parental and family, commu-

Figure 1.1 The Ecological and Hierarchical Structure of Wellness

TABLE 1.1
An Ecological Conceptualization of Wellness

	Societal Wellness	Community Wellness	Parent and Family Wellness	Child Wellness
Selected resources	Economic security; housing; health insurance; democratic institutions; culture of peace, harmony, and sustainability	Safety, formal and informal support, solidarity, cohesion, social services, high-quality schools, recreational facilities	Affective bonds; intimacy; communication; conflict resolution; quality time; personal space; support from spouse/extended family; interdependence; health; opportunities for personal growth, job satisfaction, recreation	Love, nurturance, self-esteem, cognitive, physical/emotional development, psychological/physical health, acceptance, social skills
Selected values	• Social justice in provision of resources • Support for strong community structures • Respect for human diversity	• Collaboration and respect for the community • Support for strong community structures • Respect for human diversity	• Caring and protection of health • Opportunities for education and personal development • Self-determination	• Caring and protection of health • Opportunities for education and personal development • Self-determination
Selected policies	• Policies to reduce child poverty • Initiatives that evaluate impact of policies on child wellness • Fair taxation • Universal health care • Legislation against discrimination	• Public services that support families • Accessible and universal well-baby clinics	Flexible working hours and parental leaves that take family needs into account; adequate child allowance; employers and government to provide affordable daycare, recognize financial value of house work	Office of ombudsperson that protects children's rights; free or affordable access to education and child care
Selected programs	Adequate financial support and outreach programs to the poor	Leisure and recreation, community development, help phone lines, self-help groups, family resource centres	Self-help groups for parents, home visitation programs, parenting courses	Educational programs to prevent abuse; social skills training; early stimulation programs

nity, and societal wellness. Our book is structured in such a way that each chapter offers a comprehensive review of the four key components of wellness. The chapter dealing with family wellness and child maltreatment in Aboriginal communities incorporates this framework into its analysis of special circumstances affecting this unique population.

We are invested not only in promoting wellness but in preventing maltreatment as well. According to Wolfe (1998), child maltreatment is:

> broadly defined as the physical or mental injury, sexual abuse or exploitation, negligent treatment, or maltreatment of a child under the age of 18 years by a person who ... is responsible for the child's welfare. The behaviour must be avoidable and non-accidental ... Based on these general criteria, *physical abuse* usually includes scalding, beatings with an object, severe physical punishment, slapping, punching and kicking; acts constituting *neglect* include deficiencies in caretaker obligations, such as failure to meet the educational, supervisory, shelter and safety, medical, physical, or emotional needs of the child, as well as physical abandonment. (pp. 108–109)

Like wellness, maltreatment is an ecological construct. 'Child maltreatment is now widely recognized to be multiply determined by a variety of factors operating through transactional processes at various levels of analysis (i.e., life-course history through immediate-situational to historical evolutionary) in the broad ecology of parent–child relations' (Belsky, 1993, p. 413). So varied are the sources of influence on children and families that we require an ecological perspective to understand their lives and to devise useful programs. An ecological and contextual approach considers multiple levels of analysis. Thus, mental health problems are viewed in the context of characteristics of the individual (e.g., coping skills, personality traits); the microsystem (e.g., the family); the mesosystem, which mediates between the individual and his or her family and the larger society (e.g., work settings, schools, religious settings, social networks, neighbourhoods); and the macrosystem (e.g., economic policies, social safety net, social norms, social class).

Each of the smaller levels is nested within the larger levels (e.g., person in the family in the community in society). Thus, for example, the problem of child maltreatment is viewed as being influenced by characteristics of the individual (e.g., whether or not the person committing the abuse was abused himself or herself as a child, lack of practice in the parenting role), microsystem (e.g., marital conflict, coercive family interactions), mesosystem (e.g., job loss, work-related stress, neighbourhood isolation), and macrosystem (e.g., the level of violence in society, social norms that sanction corporal punishment for disciplining children) (Belsky, 1993; Garbarino, 1992a; Wolfe, 1998). As Belsky (1993) put it:

> Although most child maltreatment takes place in the family and thus 'behind closed doors,' this immediate and even developmental context of maltreatment itself needs to be contextualized. Cultural attitudes, values, and practices, as well as the economic circumstances of a society and its cultural history, play an important role in the etiology of child maltreatment. (p. 423)

The example of child maltreatment illustrates the presence of risk factors at different levels of analysis. At the same time, there are protective factors at the individual (e.g., coping skills), microsystem (e.g., a supportive relationship with one parent), mesosystem (e.g., neighbourhood cohesion, a supportive employer), and macrosystem (e.g., economic safety net) levels.

The Promotion–Prevention–Protection Continuum

We can draw a continuum that represents our concern with promotion, prevention, and protection. Figure 1.2 shows families along a continuum that ranges from adequate functioning to the need for intensive protective services. Our review of policies and programs deals with the various points along this continuum, reinforcing the view that interventions only at the right end of the line are too little too late. The spheres denote the population the policy or program is designed to reach. Proactive, universal policies and programs are for everyone in the population. Proactive, high-risk approaches, however, focus only on a subset of the population, those deemed to be at high risk for maltreatment. Finally, reactive, indicated approaches deal with an even smaller subset of the population, those who have already experienced maltreatment.

As the nested spheres in Figure 1.2 demonstrate, all families, even those at most risk, can benefit from proactive universal interventions. Indeed, numerous calls have been made to allocate more resources to strengthen families, as the current and dominant focus of child welfare is the protection of children at risk. That is the situation in Canada (Armitage, 1993; Wharf, 1993), the United States (Emery & Laumann-

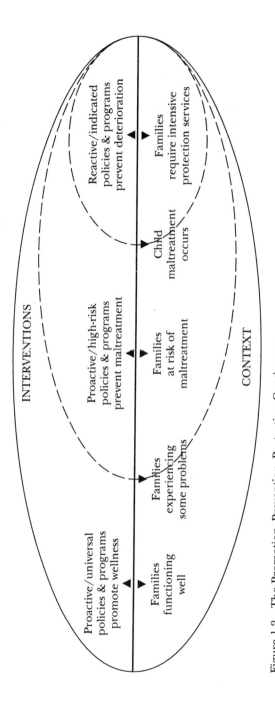

Figure 1.2 The Promotion–Prevention–Protection Continuum

Billings, 1998; Melton & Barry, 1994b; Schorr, 1997), and the United Kingdom (Burton, 1997; Hearn, 1995).

Despite what we know about the impact of various systems and levels on families, most preventive and reactive interventions in child welfare and mental health deal with individuals or dyads, such as parent–child or marital relationships. Our actions seriously lag behind our understanding of wellness. An enormous body of evidence points to the powerful impact of socioeconomic, cultural, and contextual factors in shaping the lives of children and families (Basic Behavioral Science Task Force of the National Advisory Mental Health Council, 1996a; Bronfenbrenner & Neville, 1994; Garbarino, 1992a; McLoyd, 1998; National Forum on Health, 1996; Ramey & Ramey, 1998), yet in apparent disregard for this knowledge, organizational and bureaucratic structures continue to focus on counselling and therapy as the main vehicles for the promotion of wellness (Albee, 1990; Fox & Prilleltensky, 1997; Prilleltensky, 1994a; Prilleltensky & Nelson, 1997; Wharf, 1993).

Partnerships for the Promotion of Family Wellness and the Prevention of Child Maltreatment

The third key concept guiding our review and analysis is that of partnership. The concept of partnership implies that no one individual, group, or agency is sufficient to promote family wellness and prevent child maltreatment. Rather, the collaboration of multiple and diverse stakeholder groups is necessary for a coordinated and comprehensive approach. The concept of partnership guided our approach to this project. We did not want to simply review the literature to determine the state of the art of how to promote family wellness and to prevent child maltreatment. We also wanted to know about the ideas and experiences of diverse stakeholders who have professional and experiential knowledge about the issues surrounding child maltreatment. To this end, we engaged in an extensive consultation process with youth who have been maltreated, parents who have maltreated their children, direct service providers, agency managers, provincial and territorial child welfare directors, and research and policy advisers. We believe that it is important to 'hear the voices' of people most affected by an issue.

Also, it is important to be aware that many partnerships are unbalanced with respect to power (Lord & Church, 1998). For example, professionals have considerably more power than families at risk for child maltreatment. Given this power imbalance, we believe that partnerships should ultimately benefit those stakeholders with the least power, which, in this case, is disadvantaged children and families who are at risk for child maltreatment. Elsewhere (Nelson, Prilleltensky, & MacGillivary, in press), we have defined partnership as:

> value-based relationships between human service-providers and/or researchers and disadvantaged people; relationships that should strive to advance the values of caring, compassion, community, health, self-determination, participation, power-sharing, human diversity, and social justice for disadvantaged people, both in the processes and the outcomes of the partnership, and in multiple contexts. (p. 5)

For us, partnership implies that all stakeholders, and in particular those who are most vulnerable, have a democratic right to participate in the analysis and proposed solutions to the particular problem under study.

Partnership is also a key concept in best policies and programs to promote family wellness and to prevent child maltreatment. There has been a shift in policy and practice away from exclusively professional or expert-driven approaches to child maltreatment in which it is presumed that the professional 'knows best' and the service recipient should follow the advice or direction provided by the professional. Many parenting programs, which we describe in later chapters, follow this approach. More recently, there is a recognition that service recipients need to be actively engaged in the intervention process and that the role of the professional is more of a resource, collaborator, or facilitator (Tyler, Pargament, & Gatz, 1983). This is very much the case in self-help/mutual aid and community development approaches to the prevention of child maltreatment, as we will show in subsequent chapters. Also, case management approaches, such as home visitation and intensive family preservation services, also emphasize the 'therapeutic alliance' between the interventionist (who can be a professional or a nonprofessional) and the family (Olds, Kitzman, Cole, & Robinson, 1997). Thus, in practice, partnership means voice, choice, and respectful relationships between different stakeholders (Constantino & Nelson, 1995; Lord & Church, 1998; MacGillivary & Nelson, 1998).

Summary of Conceptual Framework

To summarize, complete wellness can be attained only in the synergy that comes from meeting needs at the levels of child, parent and family, community, and society. Wellness at only one or two levels is not sufficient to obtain our goals of promoting family wellness and preventing child maltreatment. Wellness needs at each ecological level are fulfilled by the presence of satisfactory resources, cogent values, effective policies, and successful programs. The combined effect of these elements will determine where families are placed along a continuum that ranges from adequate functioning to serious risk of maltreatment. Finally, broad-based, ecological approaches to promotion and prevention are based on the concept of partnership. Relationships between diverse stakeholder groups must be formed for a comprehensive, coordinated, community-based approach to this problem.

Our book is organized according to the three main constructs of ecological wellness, the continuum of interventions, and partnership. Readers will find in the following chapters how interventions at various ecological levels impact families along different points of the promotion–prevention–protection continuum, and the types of partnerships and relationships that are formed between different stakeholders to make these policies and programs happen.

OBJECTIVES

The main purpose of this book is to identify and recommend policies and programs that are successful in promoting family wellness and in preventing child maltreatment. To achieve this goal, the team investigated four key areas related to wellness and maltreatment: context and etiology, vision and values, interventions (policies and programs), and implementation and diffusion. As can be seen in Figure 1.3, context and etiology and vision and values serve as the basic building blocks for research and action.

The first area we examine is context and etiology – we have to understand children's and families' realities before we suggest interventions. Vision and values, the second pillar of the project, are needed to provide a clear picture of what we wish for children and families – without them, we do not know what to promote. Whereas context and etiology constitute the scientific base, vision and values provide the ethical foundation of the project. Science and ethics complement each other. To foster a good life for children we require a thorough understanding of their life circumstances. To devise helpful interventions we need to know what values will guide our actions.

Once we have grasped the context of the problem, formulated a clear

Framework for Promoting Family Wellness 17

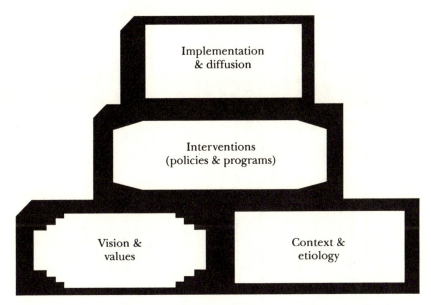

Figure 1.3 Building Blocks for Research and Action on Promoting Family Wellness and Preventing Child Maltreatment

vision, and articulated compelling values, we are in a position to study and recommend interventions. Interventions have to be assessed in light of the context of the problem, vision, and values. We have to ascertain that interventions reflect families' realities and challenges and that they are congruent with vision and values. Once we have identified successful interventions and their key ingredients, another empirical foundation of the project, we are ready to study and recommend implementation and diffusion procedures. The job is not complete until we implement programs that will promote family wellness and prevent child maltreatment. While automatic transfer of programs from one site to another may result in failure, starting programs from scratch is like reinventing the wheel. Careful analysis of implementation and diffusion issues is essential. These building blocks parallel Sections I and II of the book. Section III attends to the four building blocks in dealing with family wellness and child maltreatment in Canada's Aboriginal communities.

Table 1.2 describes the rationale, helpful paradigms, implications for action, and unique contributions of each module or building block of our research. The main goal of our project was to study in depth the

TABLE 1.2
Research Framework for Promoting Family Wellness and Preventing Child Maltreatment

Modules	Rationale	Helpful Paradigms	Implications for Action	Unique Contributions
Context & etiology	• Need to learn about lives of vulnerable families and examine gap between their present and desired state of affairs. • Need to understand factors that help families maintain their well-being, global factors that place families at-risk in general, and specific factors that bring them in contact with child welfare system.	• Quantitative and qualitative inquiries into unique circumstances of diverse populations of vulnerable families. • Risk and protective factors and processes, including family stress and coping, living conditions, and longitudinal studies. • Empowering and disempowering processes and circumstances.	• Create interventions that are sensitive to unique needs of diverse types of vulnerable families in the population. • Create interventions grounded in thorough understanding of risk, disempowering conditions, and successful coping.	• This approach promotes interventions that differentiate among diverse realities of vulnerable families. • Best interventions are judged on the extent to which they successfully modify antecedents and negative processes, and lead to empowering outcomes.
Vision & values	• Need to describe desirable state of affairs for children and families. • Need to clarify values that should guide interventions with children and families.	• Philosophy of wellness and empowerment. • UN Charter of Rights for Children. • Comprehensive philosophy of health. • Rationales for prevention policies and programs.	• Incorporate vision of health, wellness, and empowerment in policies and practices. • Develop questions to guide implementation of values in interventions.	• Value orientation clarifies principles and objectives and questions interventions that foster a deficit approach and perpetuate an unjust state of social affairs.

TABLE 1.2 (*concluded*)
Research Framework for Promoting Family Wellness and Preventing Child Maltreatment

Modules	Rationale	Helpful Paradigms	Implications for Action	Unique Contributions
Policies & programs	• Need to identify successful policies that promote healthy functioning of families in general and of vulnerable families in particular. • Need to identify best programs.	• Preventive policies and programs at universal, high-risk, and indicated levels. • Promotion and growth-oriented interventions leading to health and empowerment.	• Creation of effective interventions based on documented best policies and practices.	• Policies and programs are based on best practices and address entire population, from low-risk to very high-risk groups.
Implementation & diffusion	• Need to study how to implement and diffuse sustainable best practices on a large scale with maximum impact.	• Organizational analyses of human and systemic factors promoting and inhibiting implementation and diffusion of enduring interventions. • Studies of projects successfully implemented and diffused.	• Engage in processes to understand community contexts. • Elimination of barriers impeding wide-scale diffusion of enduring, successful interventions.	• Ensure follow-up and longevity of proven policies and programs.

four modules. This led to six main objectives, each of which contributes to knowledge and has practical significance for preventing child maltreatment and promoting child and family wellness.

Describe Context and Etiology

Contributions to Knowledge
Provide a synthesis of factors and dynamics leading to family wellness and to child maltreatment.

Practical Significance
Use the best information available about the lives of strong and vulnerable families to guide the development of policies and programs.

Social interventions need to be grounded in the daily realities of children and families. We need to know what pathways contribute to family wellness and what mechanisms lead to maltreatment. In particular, we need to understand the factors that are causing families to seek help as well as the dynamics that empower them to cope and to prosper independently.

Throughout the book we deal with values, policies, and programs that affect families along the entire continuum of wellness, from those families who are doing very well to those who require intensive help. It is important to study not just risk factors but also protective and promoting factors. We need to understand what mechanisms promote wellness and resilience and what dynamics lead to maltreatment.

Chapter 2 examines the factors that contribute to wellness, resilience and risk, and maltreatment. The mental and physical health of children can be considered the result of the relation between risk, protective, and promoting factors. Incidence – the number of new cases of a problem or illness in a population in a specific period of time – can be decreased by reducing risk factors, strengthening protective factors, and/or enhancing conditions that promote wellness. *Risk and protective factors* may be defined as circumstances, events, or characteristics of a person or their environment that respectively increase or reduce the likelihood of problems (Muñoz, Mrazek, & Haggerty, 1996; Reiss & Price, 1996; Rolf, Masten, Cicchetti, Nuechterlein, & Weintraub, 1990). Examples of risk factors are poor physical health; stressful life events such as separation, divorce or death; sexual, physical, or emotional abuse; and economic exploitation. Some protective factors include high self-esteem, competent coping skills, sufficient social supports, and ample material resources. *Conditions that promote wellness* tend to exist at broader levels of the ecological hierarchy – for example, supportive social policies such as public education and health care, social norms that respect children, and cohesive community environments.

The dynamic interplay between risk and protective factors has led to the concept of *protective mechanisms*. Rutter (1987) has identified four key protective processes. These are: (1) the reduction of risk impact, (2) the reduction of negative chain reactions stemming from stressful life events, (3) the enhancement of self-efficacy, and (4) the creation of opportunities for educational and personal development. The reduction of risk impact may be attained through the gradual exposure of the child to stressful situations, for example, taking children to visit the hospital prior to surgery, or having them go to kindergarten only for an hour during the first week of classes. The potential negative chain reaction stemming from the loss of parents may be averted by ensuring sustained and adequate care for the children. Self-efficacy can be fostered in children through the promotion of feelings of mastery and control. Finally, opportunities for personal development may be created by teaching youth social skills and by providing early stimulation that prepares them for academic success. This last mechanism may be conceptualized as the promotion of positive chain reactions: Adequate social skills lead to friendships, which translate into social supports that have the effect of buffering stress (Gore & Eckenrode, 1994).

Risk and protective factors are moderated and mediated by personal and contextual variables and processes. In other words, a particular stressful life event will have a differential impact on people depending on their psychological make-up, availability of external resources, and ability to enact protective mechanisms (Rutter, 1994). It follows from this that the mental and physical health of children can be improved by the *reduction of risk*, the *strengthening of protective factors and mechanisms*, and the *enhancement of wellness-promoting influences* (Haggerty, Sherrod, Garmezy, & Rutter, 1994; Rolf et al., 1990; Rutter, 1987, 1988).

Formulate a Vision and Values

Contributions to Knowledge
Articulate a coherent vision and a comprehensive statement of values for policy and practice in child and family wellness.

Practical Significance
Establish desirable outcomes and guide processes of policymaking and practice in child and family wellness.

Our second objective was to formulate a vision and values for child and family wellness. The clarification of goals and values that should guide research and action is a basic step in efforts to promote wellness and prevent maltreatment. The task of improving children's lives begins with knowing in what direction we wish to change their lives. Unless we explicitly articulate the desired state of affairs we pursue, we risk tinkering with minor changes in their lives and leave detrimental and stressful circumstances unaltered. The values we propose in Chapter 3 serve to elucidate not only the end state envisioned for children and families, but also the very process of helping them.

By vision we refer to a desirable state of affairs for children and families. A vision may include opportunities for children to develop their potential, or a family atmosphere of cohesion and mutual support. A positive vision is an end state in which abuse and neglect no longer occur. Values, in turn, are the principles that guide our actions toward a vision; they inform our personal, civic, and professional actions to promote children's rights. Values are instrumental in guiding thinking and action, setting priorities, avoiding contradictions, and evaluating policies and programs.

The values we choose to promote child and family wellness should derive from the needs and lived experience of children, parents, and community members, as much as from moral thinking. Our selection of values is based on the following criteria:

- Values should be complementary and not contradictory.
- Values should be comprehensive enough to cover the essential needs of families.
- Values should sustain the holistic development of children.
- Values should inform processes and actions.
- Values should point to desirable outcomes or end states.

A content analysis of our data reveals the presence of seven main values that can be classified into three categories: (1) *values for personal wellness* (self-determination, education and personal development, caring and protection of health), (2) *values for collective wellness* (social justice, support for strong community structures), and (3) *values for relational wellness* (collaboration and respect for the community, respect for human diversity). These categories reflect well the need for balance between individual and social benefits, as well as the necessity of having mediational values for people to co-exist peacefully. Our findings show that there is a dialectic between personal and collective values, and that one kind cannot exist without the other. What is often missed in the literature and nicely captured in our findings is the absolute necessity to have the third kind of values – relational values – which ensure the pursuit of private goals in harmony with social aims.

Values should both reflect and meet certain needs. In Chapter 3 we elaborate on the needs that are addressed by each value. Values can promote the needs of individuals, groups, and communities, but they can also inform policies and programs. We provide in Chapter 3 examples of how personal, collective, and relational values can be actualized in policies and programs. That chapter concludes with a practical checklist (see Table 3.6) to examine the extent to which personal and professional actions reflect the values of child and family wellness. Practitioners and policymakers are encouraged to ask questions such as *Whose interests are primarily served by a certain policy? What kind of mechanisms are in place to allow meaningful participation of consumers?* and *Do programs and policies support community structures that facilitate the pursuit of personal and collective goals?*

Identify and Recommend Essential Factors of Successful Policies

Contributions to Knowledge
Provide an integrative review and analysis of essential factors of successful policies.

Practical Significance
Facilitate incorporation of essential features into existing and new policies.

Family wellness and child maltreatment depend, to a large extent, on prevailing social policies. Government policies can do much to alleviate and avert negative family outcomes, such as placement of children in alternative care. Successful prevention programs flourish only with the support of comprehensive social policies designed to reduce certain risks in the population. Isolated efforts that are not embedded in overall government strategies are likely to fail. It is very important to know not just which programs are effective, but also what policies support and reinforce these initiatives. This fact underscores the importance of examining promising prevention and promotion approaches in conjunction with general schemes for improving the welfare of families. Consequently, we will explore in Chapter 4 relevant policies in Canada, and other industrialized countries, with a view toward documenting their contribution to promotion and prevention.

At present, the field of social policy is marked by serious tensions. On one hand, there is a major thrust toward implementing social policies that prevent health and social problems. Community-based approaches are promoted as promising vehicles for reducing health-related problems. The idea of prevention has a lot of appeal because of its human and economic benefits. Effective preventive policies improve health and welfare and save money. However, on the other hand, the general safety net is being dramatically weakened. The welfare state is being eroded and government is pressured by interest groups to withdraw from its involvement in helping disadvantaged citizens (Barlow & Campbell, 1995). As a result, the appeal of preventive policies remains largely conceptual but not necessarily practical. Government officials understand the importance of early intervention, income supplements, child care, and child benefits, but they are under the influence of political leaders who respond to the pressure to cut spending by reducing investment in children (Griffin Cohen, 1997).

The chapter on policies compares Canada's efforts to support children and families with initiatives undertaken in other Western and European nations. Attention is drawn to issues of child benefits, child support, parental leave, family time, and child welfare. These issues are analysed in the overall context of child poverty. We return to these issues in Chapter 4 and in the concluding section of the volume.

Identify and Recommend Essential Factors of Successful Programs

Contributions to Knowledge
Provide an integrative review and analysis of essential factors of successful programs.

Practical Significance
Facilitate the incorporation of essential features into existing and new programs.

The concepts of prevention and, more recently, promotion, have evolved since they were first introduced in the field of public health in the 1950s (Nelson, Prilleltensky, & Peters, 1999). Initial discussions of prevention focused on three types: (1) primary (the reduction of the incidence of a disorder), (2) secondary (the reduction of the duration of a disorder through early intervention), and (3) tertiary (the reduction of disability arising from a disorder) (Caplan, 1964). More recently, the U.S. Institute of Medicine (IOM, 1994) has introduced a new typology of prevention: (1) universal (which is aimed at everyone in a particular geographic area or setting), (2) selective (which is aimed at a subgroup of the population who are deemed to be 'at risk' of developing a disorder), and (c) indicated (which is aimed at 'at-risk' groups that already manifest some type of behavioural or emotional problem).

One of the problems with the typologies described above is that there is often 'definitional slippage' as to what truly constitutes prevention and promotion (Cowen, 1977). According to Cowen (1980, 1996), true prevention and promotion programs are characterized by the following attributes: (1) a focus on people who are well (i.e., the problem to be prevented is not already present), (2) a population-wide approach, and (3) a proactive, intentional emphasis on promoting wellness and preventing problems. These characteristics make it clear that proactive prevention/promotion is synonymous with what has previously been defined as primary prevention. Moreover, there are two major approaches to proactive prevention/promotion: universal and high-risk (Nelson et al., 1999). Reactive approaches are synonymous with what has been called secondary and tertiary prevention or indicated prevention and do not fit Cowen's (1980, 1996) qualities of prevention/promotion.

In our review of prevention programs for children and youth, our major focus is on proactive programs that strive to promote wellness (at one or more ecological levels) and/or prevent child maltreatment. We also review some reactive programs that aim to reduce the reoccurrence of child maltreatment, prevent out-of-home placement of children and youth, or prevent maltreatment of the sibling(s) of children who have been maltreated. Treatment-oriented programs may have long-term preventive impacts by ending the cycle of maltreatment in a family. We know that people who have been physically and/or sexually abused or neglected when they were children or adolescents have an increased risk of maltreating their own children or other children. Thus, a treatment intervention that helps in the healing process of children, adolescents, or adults who have been maltreated may have a preventive impact on the next generation.

Our review of programs builds on earlier reviews. In the mid-1980s, two different groups reviewed the literature on primary prevention and mental health promotion: the Prevention Task Force of the American Psychological Association (APA) and the Technical Advisory Group to the Ontario Ministry of Community and Social Services. The APA Prevention Task Force reviewed nearly 1,000 prevention programs in the United States and profiled fourteen programs that met their criteria as exemplars of the most promising approaches in prevention (Price, Cowen, Lorion, & Ramos-McKay, 1988). At roughly the same time, the Technical Advisory Group in Ontario reviewed the literature on promising prevention approaches for preschool and school-aged children. Their review was widely circulated in Ontario and was used by service providers and community residents as reference material for the development of proposals for the *Better Beginnings, Better Futures Primary Prevention Program* for children in Ontario (*Better Beginnings, Better Futures*, 1989). More recently, Durlak and Wells (1997, 1998) have completed meta-analyses of both prevention programs and reactive (indicated) programs for children and adolescents.

While these reviews are excellent starting points for examining promising approaches and best practices in prevention, they are already out of date and they do not focus specifically on the prevention of child and adolescent maltreatment. Moreover, none of the previous reviews examined the research on intensive family support programs, which serve families in crisis and have as their primary goal the prevention of placement of children in foster families or alternative care (Cameron & Vanderwoerd, 1997a). Thus a more comprehensive and up-to-date review of the literature is needed to inform policymakers, practitioners, and community residents of the most promising approaches and best practices in the prevention of problems and the promotion of children's well-being.

Several reviews and studies have identified a number of features of effective prevention programs (*Better Beginnings, Better Futures*, 1989; Blanchet, Laurendeau, Paul, & Saucier, 1993; Chamberland et al., 1996; Dryfoos, 1990; Price, Cowen, Lorion, & Ramos-McKay, 1989; Schorr, 1997). It is important to note that the Technical Advisory Group criticized existing prevention programs for having single foci, for lacking citizen participation, and for being too short in duration. In other words, successful prevention/promotion programs should be comprehensive in addressing wellness at several different ecological levels of analysis, should involve and empower citizens and service recipients, and should be of sufficient duration to have meaningful long-term effects.

Identify and Recommend Essential Factors for the Implementation and Maintenance of Successful Interventions

Contributions to Knowledge
Develop a framework and guidelines for the expansion, diffusion, and preservation of successful interventions.

Practical Significance
Increase the likelihood of implementation and diffusion of successful programs.

Information about promising programs is no doubt growing (*Better Beginnings, Better Futures*, 1989; Cameron & Vanderwoerd, 1997a; Price et al., 1988; Ramey & Ramey, 1998; Schorr, 1989, 1997). However, it is striking how little impact these promising approaches have had on decisions about how to allocate resources and devise helpful responses. Ways of helping that differ markedly from established ways of working encounter formidable obstacles in being adapted for everyday use (Rothery & Cameron, 1985). More often, established systems change promising programs rather than the other way around (Cameron & Vanderwoerd, 1997a; Weissberg & Elias, 1993).

While there have been a few analyses of expansion and institutionalization of effective prevention programs (e.g., Clabby & Elias, 1990; Commins & Elias, 1991; Schorr, 1997), by and large, the most successful programs remain unreplicated and underutilized (Schorr, 1997). The resources required for new programs cannot simply be added onto existing child welfare or mental health systems. Without serious consideration of implementation, diffusion, and replication issues, most of what we learn about best practices with vulnerable children and families will remain marginal to child wellness practice. Our hope is to help translate good ideas into practical and effective policies, programs, and organizations that help vulnerable children and families. These pivotal issues will be discussed in Chapter 7.

The move from demonstration to institutionalization of successful programs has proven incredibly difficult. Chapter 7 draws attention to the importance of articulating a program model, fostering community ownership, selecting receptive settings, allowing sufficient time for program implementation, and providing adequate support. These guidelines facilitate diffusion and adaptation of successful programs in other communities.

Identify and Recommend Essential Factors of Successful Programs and Implementation Procedures in Aboriginal Communities

Contributions to Knowledge
Provide a synthesis of historical and current factors and dynamics leading to family wellness and to child maltreatment in Aboriginal communities. Provide an integrative review and analysis of essential factors of successful, culturally appropriate programs. Provide a review of factors that facilitate or inhibit implementation of effective programs in Aboriginal communities.

Practical Significance
Use the best information about the lives of strong and vulnerable Aboriginal families to guide the development of programs. Facilitate incorporation of essential features into existing and new programs. Increase the likelihood of implementation and diffusion of successful, culturally appropriate programs.

Our sixth objective was to examine family wellness promotion and child maltreatment prevention in Aboriginal communities in Canada. This is the specific focus of Chapter 8.

First Nations children and youth are disproportionately represented in child welfare statistics compared with non-Native children. Earlier reports estimated that Native children accounted for more than 20 per cent of children in substitute care in Canada, even though Aboriginal people represented only about 6 per cent of the Canadian population (Hepworth, 1980; Ross & Shillington, 1989). Many of the informants we spoke with, particularly in the western parts of Canada, echoed concerns about the disproportionately high number of Aboriginal children on child welfare caseloads. In one province with about 4 per cent Aboriginal population, it is estimated that 37 per cent of child welfare services are directed at Native families; while in another province about 65 per cent of the children in care are First Nations and Métis.

The need to address issues of Native child welfare is fuelled not only by concerns about the overrepresentation of Aboriginal children in care, but also by the devastating impacts of removing these children from their communities and their culture. As will be discussed in Chapter 8, Aboriginal children who are removed from their communities and placed in substitute care arrangements are likely to be socialized within the dominant non-Native culture. These children often lose contact with their cultural heritage and some even come to devalue their own Native background. The loss of Aboriginal children through such processes consequently contributes to the continued disintegration and destruction of Native communities.

It is important to examine child welfare practice and its interaction with Aboriginal people from a perspective that recognizes the historical significance of colonialism and acculturation as well as the current realities facing Native children and families. In the last 25 years Aboriginal communities have begun to reclaim their role in protecting children and supporting families through the establishment of their own systems of child welfare and the restoration of traditional holistic healing practices. It is our goal to facilitate the sharing of Native teachings for enhancing wellness in Aboriginal communities. However, we also view the discussion in Chapter 8 as an important resource for those people working in mainstream Canadian child welfare since there are many lessons to be learned from the struggles and successes of promoting family wellness and preventing child maltreatment in Native communities.

One of the main lessons we derive from Chapter 8 is the importance ascribed to community involvement in child wellness. We note that communities are enlisted to provide both pressure and support. Positive pressure is exerted on parents by friends and relatives to engage in the best possible and most child-centred parenting practices. But pressure is accompanied by support and compassion. The dual role of community as promoter of both positive norms and support is a very important lesson. It is not just one role or the other that helps families cope with adversity and foster wellness, but the combined effect of enforcing proper child care and affording support. We return to this lesson in the concluding chapter.

PLAN OF ACTION

The conceptual plan for addressing the four key areas of research and action in the Family Wellness Project is depicted in Figure 1.4. The main stages of the project move through the figure in a left-to-right hierarchy where each step builds on what comes before. The objectives reviewed earlier in this chapter are present throughout the model.[1]

As illustrated on the left-hand side of the diagram, the enterprise of

---

1 The sixth objective is reflected at a number of stages within the model. Chapter 8 presents information on context, values, programs, and implementation issues pertaining to child maltreatment prevention and family wellness promotion in Aboriginal communities.

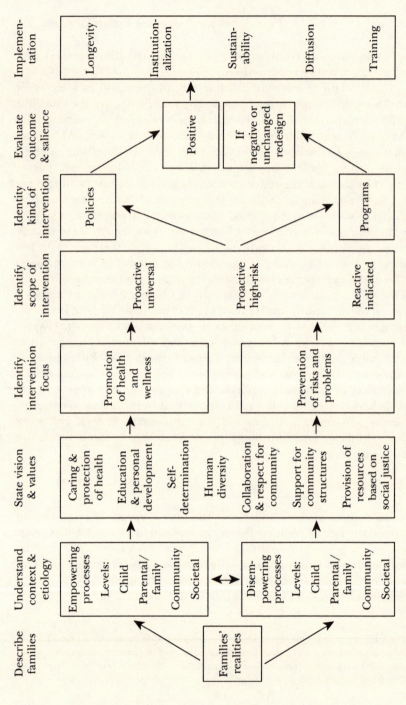

Figure 1.4 Stages and Main Tasks in Promoting Family Wellness and Preventing Child Maltreatment

prevention and promotion should begin with an examination of the context and etiology of child maltreatment and family wellness, which is in turn based on an understanding of families' realities. It is important to document the diverse types of families that fall along the prevention continuum in order to suggest interventions that are sensitive to their unique needs. The etiology of child maltreatment and family wellness is based on the balance of power between *empowering* and *disempowering processes*, as illustrated by the double-headed arrow connecting the two boxes in the second column. The dynamic interplay of empowering and disempowering forces determines families' abilities to cope with stressors and maximize advantages. As can be seen in the figure, empowering and disempowering processes can occur: on the micro level with the child, parent, and family; on the meso level, in the community (in schools, workplaces, neighbourhoods, and other settings); and on the macro level in terms of culture and society.

Disempowering processes have been described in studies exploring risks. Risks may be defined as sociopolitical and psychological circumstances or characteristics of persons and families that are conducive to negative outcomes. This approach is based on research documenting the risks, stressors, and vulnerabilities encountered by families (Haggerty et al., 1994; Rolf et al., 1990; Rutter, 1988). Sociopolitical sources of distress include poverty, exclusion, and lack of resources (Febbraro, 1994; McKnight, 1989; Schorr, 1989). Empowering processes include elements such as positive social integration, personality characteristics, and access to resources and supports (Cameron & Vanderwoerd, 1997a; Lord & Hutchison, 1993; Vaux, 1988). In understanding families' realities and their position along the continuum, there is a need to investigate factors related to these processes and how they interact to create risk, protective, or promoting conditions that may lead to child maltreatment, resilience, or family wellness.

We move next to the third column in the figure, and our second main objective, which is to describe a coherent vision of the desired state of affairs for children and families, and of the values to be enacted in the process of helping or supporting them. Unless this is properly done, we run the risk of contributing to the plight of many families. Many traditional forms of help are based on deficit models that preclude the possibility of citizen empowerment (Durkin, 1990; Fox, 1981; Hasenfeld & Chesler, 1989; Rappaport, 1981, 1987). Furthermore, these interventions often tend to dissociate families' problems from the social context where they occur, focusing most of their attention on intrapsychic or micro-level treatments provided by professional experts (Prilleltensky, 1994a). As suggested by the arrow linking columns two and three, our model holds that vision and values must be informed by contexts existing at all ecological levels and by the realities faced by families all along the range of the promotion–prevention–protection continuum.

Together, the fourth, fifth, and sixth columns in the figure represent the next main tasks in the research, which focus on the third and fourth objectives of the project: to *identify and recommend essential factors of successful policies and programs*. As can be seen in the fourth column, interventions may be oriented toward the prevention of risks and problems or toward the promotion of health and wellness. According to Dunst, Trivette, and Thompson (1990), the former seeks elimination of or reduction in the prevalence or incidence of negative outcomes, while the latter facilitates competence by enhancing capabilities that strengthen functioning. The two are complementary and are not mutually exclusive; hence the double-headed arrow joining the two boxes in the fourth column. Children's welfare and mental health can be enhanced by the reduction of risk factors, including disempowering conditions, by strengthening protective aspects such as positive social integration and better income (Cameron & Vanderwoerd, 1997a; Commission on Prevention of Mental-Emotional Disabilities, 1987; Werner, 1985) and by enhancing promoting influences such as social justice and community development.

Another important dimension of this stage, as depicted in the fifth column, is to identify the level of intervention: proactive (universal or high-risk) or reactive. Identifying the kind of intervention is also important, as suggested in column six. Despite the many effective programs that have been designed to prevent child maltreatment and promote healthy family functioning, research indicates there are still many vulnerable children and families in neighbourhoods across our country (CCSD, 1997; National Longitudinal Survey of Children and Youth, 1996, 1998; Statistics Canada, 1998). Macro-level conditions are taking a toll.

The final set of tasks for the project are illustrated in the two columns on the far right of the diagram. Sustainability, longevity, institutionalization, diffusion, and training are crucial components of the preventive enterprise, yet they have not received the attention they merit, for very few programs survive past the demonstration stage (Weissberg & Elias, 1993). Our fifth objective in the project is to *identify and recommend essential factors for the implementation and maintenance of successful interventions*.

METHOD

The Project Team

The Family Wellness Project Team is made up of nine key investigators.[2] All members of the team have an established record of scholarship in prevention research, policy, and practice. In various combinations, the investigators have collaborated on many previous and current studies. However, this is the first opportunity all nine co-investigators have had to work together. All investigators have been integral in designing the project, gathering and analysing stakeholder data, reviewing literature and chapter drafts, and preparing this volume. While the project has been a full team effort, chapters in this volume are authored by subgroups of the team. Although we had many discussions conceptualizing the issues under a common framework, chapter authors exercised liberty to express their own interpretations in their respective contributions to the volume. In general, however, we believe the reader will note the cross-fertilization that has taken place. We all commented on the chapter drafts, and many revisions have been done to maximize coherence across chapters. Nevertheless, the chapters reflect the opinions of their authors and do not necessarily reflect consensus. The work of the team was facilitated by sixteen research assistants who contributed in excess of 3,500 hours to the project.

Methodology

We have accessed three main sources in conducting our research: published and unpublished literature, original data gathered through stakeholder interviews and focus groups, and the grounded field-based experiences of the investigators. Our review and analysis of the literature serve to inform all chapters within the volume. The data we collected through our stakeholder consultation process have been integrated into the chapters to validate, enhance, and build on the information found in the literature. Finally, all chapters, particularly Chapter 8 ('A Circle of Healing: Family Wellness in Aboriginal Communities') are grounded in the practical experiences of the team members who work, or have worked, as consultants and/or in front-line and

---

2 A short biographical statement on each team member is provided on page xiii of this volume.

managerial positions in child welfare agencies and community-based organizations.

Document Review

A number of different search strategies were employed and a variety of sources were consulted to locate relevant materials for review. Although the methods and materials used for each chapter differ somewhat, in general our research included: contacting clearinghouses, research institutes, and project offices for published and unpublished documents; accessing computerized databases (e.g., CHILD ABUSE AND NEGLECT, ERIC, PSYCHLIT, SOCIOFILE, FAMILY STUDIES, IRIS, and MEDLINE), Internet websites, and existing data sets about specific programs and policies in child welfare systems; performing manual searches through relevant academic journals; obtaining trade and academic books, conference materials and papers, inquiry reports, pamphlets, newsletters, and reports from agencies, NGOs, and government ministries; and maintaining a scrapbook of current newspaper and magazine articles.

Stakeholder Consultation Process

The purpose of this initiative was to gather data from key informants in order to validate the information found in the literature, to enhance our understanding of the main areas of the project, and to sensitize us to the realities of our stakeholder groups. Between June and October 1997 a series of 62 interviews and focus groups were conducted with 114 participants (all in Canada except one in the United States) representing three main stakeholder groups: Consumers, Service Providers, and Advisers. The Consumers group is made up of 24 parents and 25 youth, most of whom are, or have been, clients of the child welfare system and/or have accessed community services such as family resource centres. The Service Providers group is made up of 33 people including 11 agency managers or program planners, and 22 direct-service practitioners in child welfare agencies or other organizations that serve children and families such as child guidance clinics and Centres Locaux Services Communautaires (CLSCs) in Quebec. The Advisers group is made up of 32 participants, including informants from policy institutes, advocacy groups, and health and social services; educators; nationally and internationally known researchers; provincial and territorial child welfare directors; and regional child welfare directors in Quebec.

Information on the four main foci of the project (see Figure 1.3) was gathered during focus groups, in-person interviews, and telephone interviews. Three people were responsible for conducting the interviews and focus groups: Louise Lefort, a graduate student in community health who also has a DESS (Diploma in Specialized Higher Studies) in community health, led all 32 French interviews and focus groups; Holt Sivak, a graduate of a Master's program in community psychology, completed eleven telephone interviews with child welfare directors or their representative(s); and Leslea Peirson, the Family Wellness Project manager, conducted the remaining nineteen English interviews and focus groups. Before beginning the discussions, all participants were asked to read an information letter and complete a consent form. Consumer participants were given a stipend, up-front, for their involvement. All key informants were asked if they would like to receive feedback on the project in the form of chapter summaries.

A series of interview guides, tailored to the different stakeholder groups, were used to direct discussions with informants. Some of the questions posed to participants are listed below. To help us better understand the Context and Etiology of child maltreatment and family wellness we asked:

- In the current context, what are the realities and challenges facing children and families in general, and at-risk children and families in particular?
- What are some of the factors that place families at risk of accessing child welfare services?
- What are some of the protective factors or strengths that children and families have, develop, or use to enhance family wellness?

Under the heading Vision and Values we asked:

- What are the most important values and priorities that should underlie programs and policies to support families at risk?
- To what extent are these values and priorities reflected in practice?

Under the Policy heading we asked:

- What current policies can you identify that have a beneficial effect on promoting child and family well-being or preventing child maltreatment?

- What policies can you identify that might, could, or should be put in place that would have a beneficial effect on promoting child and family well-being or preventing child maltreatment?

Finally, for the section on Programs we asked:

- What programs can you identify that have a beneficial effect on promoting child and family well-being or preventing child maltreatment?
- What are the essential factors contributing to effective programs?
- What challenges are associated with implementing effective programs into everyday ways of working?

All sessions were tape-recorded with the participants' permission and later transcribed. Transcripts were reviewed for common themes, and the information was organized according to the main areas of the project and other important issues that were identified by informants (e.g., intersectoral cooperation, social marketing for child welfare). A technical report of this consultation process was prepared as a working document for the Family Wellness Project researchers (Peirson, Laurendeau, Chamberland, & Lefort, 1998). The authors of chapters in this volume have selected quotes from the technical report to highlight their discussions. The 'voices' of our participants can be identified throughout the volume by the use of italic script.

With the goal of learning more about the promotion of family wellness and the prevention of child maltreatment from an international perspective, a second phase of stakeholder consultations occurred between July and December 1998. While on sabbatical leave, the principal investigator conducted eleven interviews and two focus groups with Advisers and Service Providers in Belgium (1 interview with an Adviser), Denmark (1 interview with an Adviser), England (2 interviews with Advisers; 1 focus group with 4 Service Providers), Holland (1 interview with an Adviser), Israel (2 individual interviews with Advisers; 1 interview with 2 Advisers), and Sweden (1 interview with an Adviser; 1 interview with 2 Advisers; 1 interview with 2 Service Providers; 1 focus group with 4 Service Providers). During a teaching exchange in Cuba, the principal investigator conducted an additional interview with two Advisers and held discussions with a group of approximately 40 faculty, students, and community-based professionals. The international lessons were further expanded by graduate student research in Ghana. In collaboration with Isaac Asante, a graduate student from Ghana studying at Wilfrid Laurier University, and with the assistance of a community psychologist in Ghana, Charity Akotia, we conducted interviews with ten directors or policy advisers from the National Ghanaian Committee on Children. These key informants represented different regions across the country. This research took place between October 1998 and January 1999.

The interview guide used for these international efforts contained a number of questions pertaining to the four main areas of the project that were selected from the interview guides described earlier. As above, all international participants were given an information letter, a consent form to complete, and the opportunity to request feedback on the project. Like the data collected during the Canadian consultation process, the information gathered during these interviews has been integrated where appropriate throughout the volume.

Selected key informants from our consultation processes and other specialists identified by team members and provincial/territorial contacts were asked to provide feedback on draft materials.[3] In particular, reviewers were asked to identify gaps in our examination of the literature and to point out where concepts and discussions required refinement to enhance the presentation of information. Wherever appropriate and/or possible, we have incorporated this feedback through further investigation and revisions.

ORGANIZATION OF THIS BOOK

In this first chapter we have attempted to 'map the terrain' of the volume; we have described the problem of child maltreatment, presented the conceptual framework and main objectives of the project, traced our plan for addressing the key areas of research and action, and described the project team and our methods. In the remainder of the chapter we have presented an outline of the volume's contents, which parallel the flow of Figure 1.4.

The second chapter in Section I, 'Context, Contributing Factors, and Consequences,' describes the incidence and prevalence and consequences of child maltreatment and examines the relationship between disempowering and empowering processes and how these conditions contribute to child maltreatment and family wellness. Vulnerabilities, protective mechanisms, and wellness-promoting influences at the

---

3 In Chapter 8, the term 'key informant' is used to refer to someone who reviewed draft materials, not to a participant in the qualitative study.

macro, meso, and micro levels are presented along with a discussion concerning the interplay between these forces.

In the third chapter of Section I, 'Vision and Values for Child and Family Wellness,' the authors examine a series of questions dealing with vision and values, and challenge the reader to rethink his or her priorities. Sources of values for family wellness are explored and the basic values for the promotion of family wellness are shared. The authors articulate how personal, collective, and relational values can be applied to personal, professional, and civic interactions with children and families, and how they can inform policies and programs.

Section II contains four chapters focusing on interventions. In Chapter 4 the authors present a review and analysis of social policies for promoting the well-being of Canadian children and families. This chapter examines social policies that have been studied extensively, those that are currently at the centre of the public policy debates in Canada, and those that show some promise of being modified to increase child and family wellness in Canada in ways that have direct ties to child welfare. The discussion is organized into four categories, each category representing a unique domain of social policy that independently and/or collectively impacts child and family functioning: (1) family benefits, child support, and economic security; (2) maternal and parental leave; (3) child care; and (4) child welfare. Canadian policies in each of these domains are described and compared with policies from several other industrialized countries. Permeating the discussion in each of the four areas is the issue of family poverty.

Chapter 5 reviews and analyses programs to promote family wellness and prevent the maltreatment of children in preschool and elementary-school. The overarching goal of this review is to describe and interpret 'state-of-the-art' programs that are designed to promote family wellness and prevent child maltreatment. With this broad goal in mind, the authors address four main objectives. First they describe different types of programs that have been developed to prevent child maltreatment, sometimes noting exemplary programs and key components of innovative approaches. Second, they present a comprehensive review of the research evidence pertaining to the effectiveness of these programs. Third, the authors provide a critique of the conceptual, empirical, and practical aspects of the programs. Finally, they note the common elements of programs that are effective in preventing child maltreatment. The authors conclude with a message about the importance of a social policy context for effective programs.

Framework for Promoting Family Wellness 39

We continue our look at programs in Chapter 6 with a review and analysis of programming for distressed and disadvantaged adolescents. The emphasis in this chapter is on five program models that hold the promise of fostering better outcomes for adolescents and their families: (1) adolescent competence and skill development programs, (2) family- and parent-focused programs, (3) social integration programs, (4) multiple-component programs, and (5) neighbourhood transformation programs. The authors also consider the relationships among various promising program strategies and the implications of organizing efforts to help adolescents who come into contact with child welfare organizations. The authors conclude with a call to 'move beyond programs' and to invest in service system transformation.

The last chapter in Section II, 'Program Implementation and Diffusion,' is organized around five themes that focus on the implementation requirements for single programs as well as the challenges of diffusing successful programs to diverse settings or bringing them into established service organizations. These five themes are: (1) balancing clarity and adaptation; (2) time, complexity, resource, and expertise requirements; (3) the centrality of support and management; (4) the power of established procedures; and (5) crossing boundaries and fostering innovation.

The sole chapter in Section III, 'A Circle of Healing: Family Wellness in Aboriginal Communities,' examines the four main project areas (context and etiology, vision and values, interventions, and implementation and diffusion) with a focus on Aboriginal people in Canada. The chapter begins with an overview of traditional tribal family life and a description of child care and child development in tribal communities. The authors then recount the history of Native child welfare, from the establishment of reserves in the 1850s to the development of residential schools in 1879 to agreements signed in the past 25 years resulting in the creation of locally controlled child welfare agencies in First Nations communities. Models of prevention initiatives in Aboriginal communities are described, followed by a discussion of features unique to First Nations' prevention approaches. The challenges of program implementation in these communities are also examined. The authors conclude with suggestions for action for a variety of stakeholders including funders, planners, and consultants.

The volume concludes in Section IV with an integration of the material presented in the preceding eight chapters. The purpose of this final chapter is to reflect on what we have learned regarding the promotion of family wellness and the prevention of child maltreatment (fundamentals for thinking) and what we suggest for the future to enhance Canada's ability to promote children's well-being (fundamentals for action). In so doing, the authors consider key themes that have been identified throughout the book as well as other themes that emerged over the course of the project. In suggesting directions for the future, we, the research team, do not so much propose changing what we do, as we propose going beyond the boundaries of current practice.

CHAPTER TWO

Context, Contributing Factors, and Consequences

Leslea Peirson, Marie-Claire Laurendeau, and Claire Chamberland

INTRODUCTION

Prevention begins with understanding. The question is, how much do we need to understand before we begin to act? Citing an example from public health history, Gerald Caplan (1964) reminds us that while full knowledge of a phenomenon's etiology would be valuable, there is still much that can be done in prevention with a partial understanding:

> The history-making preventive action of Snow in removing the handle of the Broad Street pump to halt the London epidemic of cholera in the nineteenth century was not based on knowledge of the existence of the cholera organism in the polluted water or of the significance of this microorganism in the etiology of the epidemic ... [Snow] relied on the best current judgements of factors which seemed to be associated with the presence or absence of illness in various segments of the population. [He] based [his actions] on personal observation ... Snow carefully listed the addresses of persons contracting cholera and demonstrated that they all drew their water from the Broad Street pump, whereas those who obtained water from some other source were not infected. (pp. 29–30)

In the case of child maltreatment, researchers have spent many years investigating and documenting the scope of this problem, its consequences, and its etiology. The volume of data that has been gathered to date clearly reveals the complexity of this phenomenon. There are many more sources of child maltreatment than there are for a single contaminated well; the problem is not geographically confined to a single town; and the solutions are not so simple as removing the handle from a pump. While the challenge of understanding child maltreatment is great, it should not be considered impossible. Through research and practical experience we have learned a great deal about the etiology of this problem.

But understanding the nature of the problem is only the beginning. We must also learn what it takes to keep children and families from succumbing to the vulnerabilities that place them at risk for experiencing or inflicting maltreatment. How do we explain that many children who are challenged by disadvantage and adversity grow up to be competent and well-functioning adults/parents? How do we explain that many families who experience crises and persistent stress are still able to provide healthy, safe, and nurturing environments for their children? The prevalence of positive outcomes for so many at-risk children and families (e.g., Werner & Smith, 1992) suggest we can learn something about the protective mechanisms that help them to counteract vulnerabilities and become resilient (Chamberland & Fortin, 1995; Cicchetti, Rogosch, Lynch, & Holt, 1993; Garmezy, 1991; Rutter, 1985; Steinhauer, 1998). This is exactly one of the messages put forward in *Turning Points*, a document released by Health Canada (1996b) that contains eight national goals for fulfilling a mission 'to safeguard and improve the health and well-being of all children and youth in Canada' (p. 3).

Reflecting on the promotion–prevention–protection continuum presented in Figure 1.2 in Chapter 1, we realize that there is another important sphere to consider – that is, examining and understanding child and family wellness. It is essential that we learn more about what it takes to promote wellness in children and families. We should not be satisfied only with the idea of prevention, of alleviating problems and circumventing risks. An emerging realization in the literature is that we must place more emphasis on enhancing, enriching, and optimizing the development of all children and families, and building the capacities of all communities and societies to meet the needs of their members (Bond, 1984; Danish & D'Augelli, 1984; Guy, 1997; Steinhauer, 1996).

In this chapter we present current knowledge regarding the context and etiology of child maltreatment, resilience, and family wellness. Our review is informed by both published and unpublished sources, as well as by the voices of stakeholders interviewed for the qualitative component of this project (see Chapter 1 for a description of this research). We begin by presenting some epidemiological information about the scope of child maltreatment. While rates, percentages, and statistics can show us the extent of child maltreatment, an examination of the effects of abuse and neglect can give us an appreciation for the seriousness of this problem. One section of this chapter deals specifically with the consequences of maltreatment. We move next into a review of the literature on etiology. In this section we identify some of the many vulnerabilities that have been found to place children and youth at risk for maltreatment and we describe some of the protective and promoting mechanisms that have been found to reduce the likelihood of maltreatment and/or enhance child and family wellness. We have organized the information in both discussions according to the ecological and hierarchical structure of wellness presented in Figure 1.1 (i.e., societal, community, family/parental, and child levels). As the authors of *Our Promise to Children* point out, it is essential to consider the evidence at all levels since 'all the places where children live, learn, grow and play affect their development. Families come first, but families thrive or flounder within a wider context that includes neighbourhoods, workplaces, voluntary organizations, schools, communities and government' (Guy, 1997, p. v). Finally, we conclude with some questions for readers to consider as they explore other areas of this volume.

SCOPE OF THE PROBLEM

There is reason to suspect that estimates of the incidence (the number of new cases of child maltreatment during a specific time period, usually one year) and prevalence (the number of existing cases during a given time period or the proportion of the population who were maltreated at any point during childhood) of child maltreatment are conservative and underestimate the scope of the problem. Studies that seek to determine incidence and prevalence rates are plagued by many limitations. Estimates typically have been extracted from official reports to child protection services or from clinical samples. These sources are based on disclosed incidents of maltreatment, which do not account for the many cases not included in official reports or that never come to the attention of the authorities due to: social stigma and fear of consequences; the failure by professionals to recognize and report child maltreatment (Zigler & Hall, 1989); the large number of children who were abused who never tell anyone (Bagley & Thurston, 1998); small samples and/or samples that are not representative of the general population (Wolfner & Gelles, 1993) and often exclude First Nations people living on reserves, residents of extremely remote locations, people in institutions, and the homeless (MacMillan et al., 1997; Ross, Scott, & Kelly, 1996b);

difficulties with complete and consistent record-keeping, variability in definitions and criteria, and misidentification of cases (Coulton, Korbin, Su & Chow, 1995; National Center on Child Abuse and Neglect, 1994); and the lack of attention paid to children and families experiencing less serious problems, but who are still at risk (Fortin, 1992; Straus, Gelles, & Steinmetz, 1980). In fact, as Chamberland and Fortin (1995) point out, 'it could be argued that these rates are but the tip of the iceberg and that they include only the most serious of abusive family situations' (p. 145).

One of the central complications in the literature is the variation that appears across studies with respect to the definition of child maltreatment and the criteria used to identify types of maltreatment. For example, in the U.S. National Incidence Studies of Child Abuse and Neglect (Sedlak & Broadhurst, 1996), the reported rate of abuse in 1993 ranged from 1.5 million (23 of every 1,000 children) to 2.8 million (42 of every 1,000 children). Comparatively, the results of a 1994 Gallup poll (Gallup, Moore, & Schussel, 1995) suggest approximately 4 million children in the United States were victims of maltreatment in that year. Part of the variation in findings between the National Incidence Study (NIS) and the Gallup poll may be attributed to the fact that the definition used in the NIS for severe abuse was based on whether there was a need to provide the child with immediate medical attention to prevent long-term disability, whereas the definition used in the Gallup poll was based on specific behaviours listed under the categories of aggressive acts (e.g., spanked on bottom, pinched, shook lightly) and abusive acts (hit child with fist, kicked child under 2, hit child with object somewhere other than on their bottom) and not on the consequences of the abuse. Furthermore, the data compiled for the Gallup poll's estimate of child maltreatment did not include incidents of physical neglect or psychological maltreatment, information which was gathered and included in the NIS estimate (for a detailed comparison between studies, see Emery & Laumann-Billings, 1998).

The literature on sexual abuse provides another example of definitional variation. A 1983 national survey conducted in Canada reported 8.2 per cent of boys and 17.6 per cent of girls experienced incidents of sexual abuse before age 17 (Badgley et al., 1984). Different rates of sexual abuse (3.9 per cent for boys and 11.1 per cent for girls) were reported in the Ontario Health Supplement (MacMillan et al., 1997). As MacMillan and her colleagues point out, the Badgley Report statistics were based on much broader definitions of victims and perpetrators than were designated in the Ontario Health Supplement. The inconsistent use of definitions and criteria leads to evidence which may not be comparable and findings which may not be generalizable.

In spite of different definitions and methods in the research, even conservative estimates of the incidence and prevalence of child maltreatment leave no question that children are being mistreated. Cases of maltreatment reported to child welfare agencies in Canada and the United States have risen dramatically over the last two decades (Canadian Council on Social Development, 1997; Coulton et al., 1995). Table 2.1 provides some estimates of Canadian, U.S., and international rates of maltreatment as reported in recent literature. Due to the limitations described above and the variation in data sources (e.g., research studies, agency reporting systems, judicial figures), these estimates should not be compared. Presently few data are available on national rates of child maltreatment in Canada. However, an ambitious study is underway in which researchers are examining reported cases of child abuse and neglect in order to ascertain national incidence levels for various forms of child maltreatment (Trocmé, Michalski, McPhee, Tam, & Scarth, 1995).

The most current resource available that documents child welfare involvement in families in nine Canadian provinces (Quebec is excluded) and the territories is the *Statistical Report* compiled by the Federal–Provincial Working Group on Child and Family Services Information (FPWG) (1998). This document provides data for three fiscal years, from 1994–5 to 1996–7. Since the reporting system varies across provinces/territories, 'there are extensive variations in the types of data collected and the manner in which they are reported ... Therefore *data for a given province or territory cannot and should not be compared across jurisdictions*' (p. 3; emphasis in original). In Table 2.2 we present selected data from this report, not for comparative purposes, but to provide the reader with a general idea of the involvement of child welfare services in Canadian families. The data reporting child maltreatment rates in Quebec have been taken from the 1997–8 *Rapports statistiques annuels des Centres Jeunesse* (Ministère de la Santé et des Services Sociaux, 1998) and reflect 17 of the 18 regions in this province (Grand Nord region is missing; data for 7 of the 24 Centres Jeunesse in the 17 included regions are missing).

Of all the forms of maltreatment, neglect tends to be the most common. Selected provincial and territorial data suggest about twice as many reports, investigations, substantiated cases, or placements are connected to neglect compared with physical abuse and sexual abuse combined (FPWG, 1998; Ministère de la Santé et des Services Sociaux,

TABLE 2.1
Incidence and Prevalence Estimates Reported for Various Forms of Maltreatment in Canada, the United States, and Internationally

Type of maltreatment	Province or country	Date	Incidence per 1,000 or %	Prevalence per 1,000 or %	# Children, cases, or reports	Source
Maltreatment in general (unspecified forms or multiple forms)	Ontario	1993	21			Trocmé, McPhee, Tam, & Hay, 1994
	United States	1990	43			National Center on Child Abuse & Neglect (NCCAN), 1993
		1993	23.1		1,554,000	Sedlak & Broadhurst, 1996
		1994			4,273,000	Gallup et al., 1995
		1995	15		996,000	Lung & Daro, 1996
	Germany	1993	0.7		11,733	Concerted Action on the Prevention of Child Abuse in Europe (CAPCAE), 1997
	Italy	1993	1			CAPCAE, 1997
	Spain	1994	0.6			CAPCAE, 1997
	Belgium	1995	2		2,417	CAPCAE, 1997
	England	1995	3.2			CAPCAE, 1997
	France	1995	4.1		65,000	CAPCAE, 1997
	Ireland	1995	1.7		2,276	CAPCAE, 1997
Physical abuse	Ontario	1990–1		Boys 31% Girls 21%		MacMillan et al., 1997
		1993	9			Trocmé et al., 1994
	Quebec	1992–3	27%			Bouchard & Tessier, 1996
	United States	1990	2.6			NCCAN, 1993
		1993	5.7		382,000	Sedlak & Broadhurst, 1996
		1994	49		3,000,000	Gallup et al., 1995
	Germany	1991		94		CAPCAE, 1997

TABLE 2.1 (concluded)
Incidence and Prevalence Estimates Reported for Various Forms of Maltreatment in Canada, the United States, and Internationally

Type of maltreatment	Province or country	Date	Incidence per 1,000 or %	Prevalence per 1,000 or %	# Children, cases, or reports	Source
Neglect	Ontario	1993	6			Trocmé et al., 1994
	United States	1990	4.6			NCCAN, 1993
		1993	3.2		339,000	Sedlak & Broadhurst, 1996
		1995			540,000	Lung & Daro, 1996
Psychological maltreatment	Ontario	1993	2			Trocmé et al., 1994
	Quebec	1992–3	48%			Bouchard & Tessier, 1996
	United States	1986	6.9			Starr, Dubowitz, & Bush, 1990
		1990	0.7			NCCAN, 1993
		1990		257		Vissing, Straus, Gelles, & Harrop, 1991
Sexual abuse	Ontario	1990–1		Boys 4% Girls 13%		MacMillan et al., 1997
		1993	5			Trocmé et al., 1994
	Canada	1979–95		Boys 5% Girls 7%		Bagley & Thurston, 1998
		1983		Boys 8% Girls 18%		Bagley et al., 1984
		1994		Boys 4% Girls 28%		Canadian Institute of Child Health, 1994
	United States	1990	1.7			NCCAN, 1993
		1993	3.2		218,000	Sedlak & Broadhurst, 1996
		1994			1,273,000	Gallup et al., 1995
		1995			110,000	Lung & Daro, 1996
	International	1984–93		Boys 3–11% Girls 20%		Finkelhor, 1994b
	France	1993			10,717	CAPCAE, 1997
	Spain	1994		190		CAPCAE, 1997

TABLE 2.2
Selected Allegations, Investigations, and/or Substantiated Cases of Child Maltreatment in Canadian Provinces and Territories

Type of Maltreatment	Province or Territory	Number of Allegations, Investigations, and/or Substantiated Cases	Time Frame
Physical abuse	Nfld.	806 children investigated	04/96–03/97
	NS	26 cases recorded in Child Abuse Register	1995
	NB	1,618 families reported, investigated, and/or found to have a child in need of protection	04/96–03/97
	Quebec	3,472 reports; 560 substantiated cases	04/97–03/98
	Sask.	194 families had children deemed in need of protection	as at 31/03/97
	Alberta	2,374 investigations had primary outcome assessment related to physical abuse	04/96–03/97
	BC	398 investigations conducted	March 1997
	Yukon	40 children considered in need of protection; 20 more being investigated	as at 31/03/97
	NWT	12 intake reports filed	March 1997
Neglect	NB	2,851 families reported, investigated, and/or found to have a child in need of protection	04/96–03/97
	Quebec	11,642 reports; 3,860 substantiated cases	04/97–03/98
	Sask.	627 families had children deemed in need of protection	as at 31/03/97
	Alberta	4,028 investigations had primary outcome assessment related to neglect	04/96–03/97
	BC	278 investigations conducted	March 1997
	Yukon	167 children considered in need of protection; 32 more being investigated	as at 31/03/97
Psychological maltreatment	Nfld.	551 children investigated	04/96–03/97
	Sask.	14 families had children deemed in need of protection	as at 31/03/97
	Alberta	1,459 investigations had primary outcome assessment related to psychological abuse	04/96–03/97
	Yukon	5 children considered in need of protection	as at 31/03/97
Sexual abuse	Nfld.	728 children investigated	04/96–03/97
	NS	178 cases recorded in Child Abuse Register	1995
	NB	1,487 families reported, investigated, and/or found to have a child in need of protection	04/96–03/97
	Quebec	2,500 reports; 372 substantiated cases	04/97–03/98
	Sask.	163 families had children deemed in need of protection	as at 31/03/97
	BC	121 investigations conducted	March 1997
	Yukon	50 children considered in need of protection; 24 more being investigated	as at 31/03/97
	NWT	233 intake reports filed	1996

Sources: Federal–Provincial Working Group on Child and Family Services Information (1998); Ministère de la Santé et des Services Sociaux (1998).

1998). The Ontario Incidence Study (Trocmé, McPhee, Tam, & Hay, 1994) lends some support to this observation, though with less magnitude. Substantiated cases in this research involved neglect more often (34 per cent) than any other distinct form of maltreatment. Our qualitative study participants support the overall trend of these data:

Neglect represents 55 per cent of cases taken into the care of youth protection. (Adviser)

Neglect is still our largest single category that we serve. (Adviser)

The incidence and prevalence estimates presented in Table 2.1, including the Canadian-based data, seem to indicate that physical abuse is about twice as common as sexual abuse. However, a review of the provincial/territorial service data (FPWG, 1998) suggests these forms of maltreatment occur with about the same frequency. For provinces/territories that provided applicable data, physical abuse and sexual abuse each account for roughly one-fifth to one-third of the reports, investigations, substantiated cases, or placements. In some jurisdictions the numbers for physical abuse are somewhat higher than for sexual abuse, in other jurisdictions the pattern is reversed, and in some areas the figures are very similar. When *substantiated* cases of maltreatment were considered in the Ontario Incidence Study, Trocmé and his colleagues (1994) found physical abuse and sexual abuse were connected with about the same percentage of cases (34 per cent and 28 per cent respectively).

Disentangling data on psychological maltreatment can be difficult given that this form of maltreatment is often subsumed under the category of neglect. Psychological maltreatment, which involves overt psychological acts committed against children including spurning, terrorizing, isolating, corrupting, and exploiting, as well as omissions in caregiving such as emotional, cognitive, or educational neglect, is purported by Hart, Binggeli, and Brassard (1998) to be the core component of child maltreatment. Contrary to Vondra's (1990) claim that neglect is the single most predominant form of child maltreatment, some researchers argue that psychological maltreatment is the most frequent type of violence inflicted upon children within the family setting (Garbarino, Guttman, & Seeley, 1986; Hart, Gelardo, & Brassard, 1986). However, the evidence available to date does not support this argument. There have been few attempts to investigate the incidence and prevalence of this form of maltreatment and service statistics often do not include specific data relevant to psychological (or emotional) maltreatment. Yet the available research indicates that this area deserves more attention. The Canadian Incidence Study of Reported Child Abuse and Neglect (Trocmé et al., 1995), which is currently in progress, includes an examination of reported cases of emotional abuse.

As mentioned above, researchers are sceptical of the accuracy of current incidence and prevalence statistics for all forms of child maltreatment, suggesting in fact, that the actual rates are much higher. These concerns serve to strengthen the position that advocates for more prevention in the area of child maltreatment, for the magnitude of the underestimates is sufficiently alarming to warrant serious attention. The situation becomes more dire, and the need for prevention becomes indisputable, when these statistical signals are considered in conjunction with the consequences of maltreatment.

CONSEQUENCES OF MALTREATMENT

The consequences of child maltreatment go far beyond bruises and hurt feelings. Child abuse and neglect have been connected to a wide range of adverse outcomes for victims, affecting physical, emotional, psychosocial, cognitive, and behavioural functioning. While it is true that these problems have been found in samples of children who have not experienced maltreatment, research shows they are more commonly exhibited by children who have been abused and neglected (MacMillan & Finkel, 1995). The effects of multiple forms of maltreatment are cumulative and it can be difficult to distinguish which outcomes are connected to specific subtypes of maltreatment (Bagley & Thurston, 1998). However, due to the distinctive focus of some research, consequences may be described by authors only in relation to the particular form of maltreatment under study. Tables 2.3a through 2.3e present some of the consequences for children's functioning that have been found to be associated with child abuse and neglect in general and in relation to the various subtypes of maltreatment.

While the research demonstrates that there is an abundance of children who suffer a wide range of negative outcomes, many victims of child maltreatment exhibit no overt symptoms (Bagley & Thurston, 1998; Institute of Medicine, 1994; Kendall-Tackett, Meyer Williams, & Finkelhor, 1993; MacMillan & Finkel, 1995). For example, in their review of the literature on sexual abuse, Kendall-Tackett and her colleagues (1993) found between 21 and 49 per cent of sexually abused

TABLE 2.3a
Consequences of Maltreatment on Children's Functioning (Unspecified Forms of Maltreatment or Multiple Forms)

Functioning	Consequences	Sources
Physical	Somatic ailments (e.g., abdominal pain, headaches), self-inflicted injuries, death	Gove, 1995; Lung & Daro, 1996; MacMillan & Finkel, 1995; McClain, Sacks, Frohlke, & Ewigman, 1993
Emotional	Anxiety and depression, nightmares, high levels of negative emotions, restlessness, lack of affect control, problems with empathy, symptoms of posttraumatic stress	Cicchetti & Toth, 1995; Egeland, Sroufe, & Erickson, 1983; Éthier & Piché, 1989; Hoffman-Plotkin & Twentyman, 1984; Lewis, 1992; MacMillan & Finkel, 1995; Straker & Jacobson, 1981
Psychosocial	Disruption of attachment formation, difficulties in social interaction with peers	Aber & Allen, 1987; Cicchetti & Toth, 1995; Drotar, 1992; Howes & Espinosa, 1985
Cognitive	Declining school performance, lack of competence in problem solving, diminished ability to cope with new or stressful situations	Aber & Allen, 1987; MacMillan & Finkel, 1995; Main & George, 1985
Behavioural	Aggression, conduct disorders, delinquency, criminal behaviour, violent acting out in adulthood	Egeland et al., 1983; Éthier, Palacio-Quintin, & Jourdan-Ionescu, 1991; Éthier & Piché, 1989; Herrenkohl, Herrenkohl, & Egolf, 1994; Lane & Davis, 1987; Malinosky-Rummell & Hansen, 1993; Rogeness, Amrung, Macedo, Harris, & Fisher, 1986; Vanier Institute of the Family, 1996

TABLE 2.3b
Consequences of Physical Abuse on Children's Functioning

Functioning	Consequences	Sources
Physical	Bruises, burns, abrasions, fractures, head and abdominal injuries, severe disabilities, death	Baladerian, 1991; Emery & Laumann-Billings, 1998; Lung & Daro, 1996; MacMillan & Finkel, 1995
Emotional	Low self-esteem, depression, hopelessness, posttraumatic stress disorder	Allen & Tarnowski, 1989; Famularo, Fenton, Kinscherff, Ayoub, & Barnum, 1994; Kazdin, Moser, Colbus, & Bell, 1985; Kiser, Heston, Millsap, & Pruitt, 1991
Cognitive	Lower levels of attention, less perseverence, academic underachievement	Cryan, 1985; Egeland et al., 1983
Behavioural	Aggression, delinquency, criminal behaviour	Cicchetti & Carlson, 1989; Dodge, Bates, & Pettit, 1990; Malinosky-Rummell & Hansen, 1993; Widom, 1989a, 1989b

TABLE 2.3c
Consequences of Neglect on Children's Functioning

Functioning	Consequences	Sources
Physical	Nonorganic failure to thrive, malnutrition, rashes, infections, poor muscle tone, injuries suggesting inadequate supervision such as ingestions or near drownings	Emery & Laumann-Billings, 1998; MacMillan & Finkel, 1995; Tower, 1993
Emotional	Anger, negative affect, apathy, depression	Egeland & Sroufe, 1981; Egeland et al., 1983
Psychosocial	Difficulty establishing relationships to peers, withdrawal, less social interaction, anxious attachment	Crittenden, 1992; dePaul & Arruabarrena, 1995; Egeland et al., 1983; Hoffman-Plotkin & Twentyman, 1984; Prino & Peyrot, 1994; Schneider-Rosen, Braunwald, Carlson, & Cicchetti, 1985
Cognitive	Lags in development, academic delays, language delays and disorders, poor problem-solving skills	Allen & Oliver, 1982; Crittenden, 1985; Crittenden & Ainsworth, 1989; dePaul & Arruabarrena, 1995; Egeland et al., 1983; Katz, 1992; Kurtz, Gaudin, Wodarski, & Howing, 1993; MacMillan & Finkel, 1995
Behavioural	Aggression, school disciplinary problems, passivity, conduct disorders, delinquency	Brown, 1984; Crittenden, 1985, 1992; Crittenden & Ainsworth, 1989; dePaul & Arruabarrena, 1995; Rivera & Widom, 1992; Rogeness et al., 1986

TABLE 2.3d
Consequences of Psychological Maltreatment on Children's Functioning

Functioning	Consequences	Sources
Physical	Poor appetite, encopresis, enuresis, failure to thrive, suicide	Fortin & Chamberland, 1995; Hart et al., 1998; Hart, Germain, & Brassard, 1987
Emotional	Low self-esteem, guilt, depression, emotional instability or emotional maladjustment, reduced emotional responsiveness, habit disorders, neurotic traits	Fortin & Chamberland, 1995; Hart et al., 1998; Hart et al., 1987
Psychosocial	Dependency, withdrawal, inability to trust others, difficulty forming or maintaining satisfying interpersonal relationships	Fortin & Chamberland, 1995; Hart et al., 1998; Hart et al., 1987
Cognitive	Incompetence, academic under-achievement, lags in development	Fortin & Chamberland, 1995; Hart et al., 1998; Hart et al., 1987
Behavioural	Stealing, lying, aggression, prostitution, homicide	Fortin & Chamberland, 1995; Hart et al., 1998; Hart et al., 1987

TABLE 2.3e
Consequences of Sexual Abuse on Children's Functioning

Functioning	Consequences	Sources
Physical	Sexually transmitted diseases, genital trauma, chronic vulvovaginitis, pregnancy, enuresis, encopresis, deliberate self-harm	Bagley & Thurston, 1998; Kendall-Tackett, Meyer Williams, & Finkelhor, 1993; MacMillan & Finkel, 1995
Emotional	Guilt and self-blaming, depression, low self-esteem, anxiety, post-traumatic stress disorder, eating disorders, borderline personality, neurotic mental illness, fear, nightmares, feelings of traumatization, betrayal, stigmatization, and powerlessness	Allard-Dansereau, Hebert, Tremblay, & Bernard-Bonnin, 1998; Bagley & Thurston, 1998; Finkelhor & Browne, 1985; Kendall-Tackett et al., 1993; Kiser et al., 1991; McLeer, Deblinger, Hentry, & Orvaschel, 1992; Wolfe, Sas, & Wekerle, 1994
Psychosocial	Withdrawal, confusion about psychosocial identity	Allard-Dansereau et al., 1998; Bagley & Thurston, 1998; Kendall-Tackett et al., 1993
Behavioural	Sexually inappropriate behaviour, cruelty, delinquency, running away	Allard-Dansereau et al., 1998; Bagley & Thurston, 1998; Kendall-Tackett et al., 1993

children show no symptoms. A few explanations have been offered to account for this phenomenon: (1) studies may not include measures, or sensitive-enough measures, of all outcomes (Kendall-Tackett et al., 1993); (2) consequences may not be manifested until a later stage in victims' development (Berliner, 1991; Finkelhor & Browne, 1985; Gomes-Schwartz, Horowitz, Cardarelli, & Sauzier, 1990; Institute of Medicine, 1994; Kendall-Tackett et al., 1993; MacMillan & Finkel, 1995); and (3) 'the asymptomatic children may be those with the least damaging abuse ... the most resilient children, the ones with the most psychological, social, and treatment resources to cope with the abuse' (Kendall-Tackett et al., 1993, p. 170). For whatever reasons, these children do not appear to be adversely affected. However, it is important to recognize that these children exist, and that it is equally important to prevent the incidents of violence that are inflicted upon them.

The consequences of maltreatment go beyond problems in functioning. Many children and youth who are deemed in need of protection by the systems of child welfare are placed into care. In the United States, in 1994 alone, estimates suggest over one-quarter million children were placed in foster care primarily as a result of abuse or neglect (Tatara, 1994). In Canada it is estimated that approximately 40,000 children and youth are in out-of-home placements[1] (Ross, 1996) and statistics indicate a rise in the number of children in care in recent years (Canadian Council on Social Development, 1997). The provincial/territorial statistics presented in Table 2.4 provide some indication of the number of children in care in various Canadian jurisdictions during the 1996–7 fiscal year[2] (FPWG, 1998).

While out-of-home placements can have the positive outcome of removing children from abusive caregivers and inappropriate environments or providing much-needed respite in situations where parents are too ill to look after their children, there are also negative consequences. Children who are placed in care are often also separated from their nonabusing caregivers, their siblings, their homes, their possessions, their schools, their friends, and their communities.

1 Not all placements are due to child maltreatment. Other conditions, such as the death of the caregiver(s) or parental illness, may precipitate the need to place children in care.
2 Data from Quebec are not provided in source. All figures are as of 31 March 1997 except for New Brunswick, which was as of 26 March 1997, and Ontario, which was as of 31 December 1996. As in Table 2.2, the data presented in Table 2.4 cannot and should not be compared across jurisdictions.

TABLE 2.4
Number of Children in Care in Canadian Jurisdictions

Jurisdiction	# Children	Jurisdiction	# Children
Nfld	721	Manitoba	5,203
PEI	204	Sask.	2,416
NS	1,767	Alberta	5,543
NB	1,083	BC	8,232
Quebec	n/a	Yukon	185
Ontario	10,379	NWT	345

Beyond the consequences to victims of maltreatment, there are additional practical consequences in terms of the extensive fiscal expenditures required to provide treatment and residential services through child welfare systems, not to mention costs incurred in other sectors such as justice, health, and education.

We turn next to a review of the factors that have been found to contribute to maltreatment, to protect at-risk children from maltreatment, and to promote child and family wellness. Before doing so, however, we caution that much of the research that does attempt to chart the course of maltreatment, resilience, or wellness is retrospective or cross-sectional in nature (Belsky, 1993; Luthar & Zigler, 1991). These research designs do not allow for examination of the dysfunctional or healthy processes through which maltreatment, resilience, and wellness develop. Deriving definitive causation for these outcomes then becomes impossible since it is not clear, for example, whether children's disruptive behaviour is one of the factors leading to maltreatment (Anderson, Lytton, & Romney, 1986; Brunk & Henggeler, 1984) or whether it occurs as a result of maltreatment (Engfer & Gavranidou, 1988). Many prospective investigations, though better at identifying antecedents of abuse and neglect, are limited in their predictive ability due to relatively short durations of study.

Longitudinal prospective studies seem to hold more promise for untangling cause and effect. However, due to the tremendous investments and conditions required to conduct this form of research, there are few examples of these investigations reported in the literature (for a rare exception, see Werner & Smith, 1992). Yet only through prospective longitudinal research will we be able to accurately discern which particular behaviours or conditions precipitate maltreatment and which ensue from it. Whether cause or consequence, what seems clear from the literature is that many factors become part of a cyclical pattern of maltreatment.

CONTRIBUTING FACTORS

It is clear that child maltreatment occurs at an alarming rate and that the consequences of child maltreatment are dire. The need to prevent this form of violence, and indeed to promote child and family wellness, is indisputable. So how does it happen? Neither states of wellness nor the maltreatment of children occur in vacuums. There are contributing factors that serve to foster wellness and resilience or induce maltreatment; contexts that do or do not meet needs. However, there is no single path to maltreatment and there is no magic formula that guarantees wellness.

Since no definitive causes for maltreatment or resilience have been found, the task is to identify factors associated with an increased probability of these outcomes. *Vulnerabilities* may be defined as conditions, circumstances, or characteristics of a person or his or her environment that heighten the likelihood of problems such as abuse and neglect (Muñoz, Mrazek, & Haggerty, 1996; Reiss & Price, 1996; Rolf, Masten, Cicchetti, Nuechterlein, & Weintraub, 1990). Examples of vulnerabilities are poor physical health; stressful life events, such as separation, spousal conflict, or death; and economic deprivation. In vulnerable situations, *protective mechanisms* (which may also be described as conditions, circumstances, or characteristics of a person or his or her environment) serve to enhance the potential for resilience. Some examples of protective mechanisms are self-esteem, coping skills, social supports, and material resources.

A useful formula for attempting to determine the probability of child maltreatment, as well as other problems, has been proposed by Albee (1980, 1985) and further elaborated by Werner (1985), Elias (1987), Gullotta (1997), and ourselves. In the outcome equation, shown below, the numerator consists of vulnerabilities, and the denominator of protective mechanisms.

$$\text{likelihood of maltreatment} = \frac{\text{vulnerabilities}}{\text{protective mechanisms}} = \frac{\text{organic causes} + \text{stress} + \text{exploitation} + \text{deprivation}}{\text{coping skills} + \text{self-esteem} + \text{support systems} + \text{opportunities} + \text{adequate living conditions}}$$

Maltreatment is more likely to occur when the burden of vulnerabilities in the numerator outweighs any existing protective mechanisms. The probability of resilience as an outcome is increased when the number or significance of protective mechanisms in the denominator is sufficient to counteract presenting vulnerabilities. In other words, 'resilient' individuals and/or families are able to maintain 'adaptive functioning in spite of serious risk hazards' (Rutter, 1990, p. 209).

In Chapter 1 we defined wellness as *a favourable state of affairs brought about by the combined presence of cogent values, satisfactory psychological and material resources, effective policies, and successful programs; a state of affairs in which needs are met.* Although not depicted in the above equation, wellness is characterized by the absence of identifiable vulnerabilities and the presence of significant and stable promoting mechanisms that satisfy psychological, material, and economic needs (Basic Behavioral Science Task Force of the National Advisory Mental Health Council, 1996a; Moore et al., 1996; Simmons, 1997; Stinnett & DeFrain, 1985; Stinnett, DeFrain, King, Knaub, & Rowe, 1981). Promoting mechanisms tend to exist at broader levels of the ecological hierarchy – for example, supportive social policies such as public education and health care, social norms that respect children, and cohesive community environments. At the same time, conditions, circumstances, or characteristics existing at the micro levels – that is, within the family, the parent or the child – can also contribute to optimal functioning. Examples of mechanisms at these levels that can help to maintain states of wellness include: quality family time, positive communication between parents and children, strong marital relationships, children's involvement in social activities, connections to supportive adult role models, and strong feelings of self-worth.

Certainly there are similarities between what would be considered protective and promoting mechanisms; however, the difference between these concepts lies in the position of families along the promotion–prevention–protection continuum (see Figure 1.2). Mechanisms that promote wellness are enacted for and by families that are found on the left side of the continuum, families that are functioning well. The same mechanisms may be available to families at the middle and to the right side of the continuum, but when they work to prevent maltreatment or further harm, these mechanisms are considered to be protective in nature.

We can argue, then, that children's mental and physical health is determined by the presence or absence of vulnerabilities and protective factors, by the extent to which the child and his or her caregivers successfully engage protective mechanisms in coping with stress, and by the presence of conditions that promote wellness. It follows from this that the mental and physical health of children can be improved by the *reduction of vulnerabilities*, the *strengthening of protective mechanisms*, and the *enhancement of wellness-promoting influences*.

Theorists and researchers have increasingly adopted dynamic, multifactoral, interactive, ecological models in their examinations of maltreatment, resilience, and wellness (Belsky, 1980, 1993; Chamberland, 1996; Chamberland & Fortin, 1995, Emery & Laumann-Bllings, 1998; Institute of Medicine, 1994; Korbin & Coulton, 1996; Krishnan & Morrison, 1995; Mayer-Renaud, 1993; National Crime Prevention Council, 1996; Walsh, 1996; Wolfe, 1998). This approach, which is based on Bronfenbrenner's (1979) ecological model of human development, looks for combinations of contributing factors at multiple levels of analysis, that is from within the nested contexts of the macrosystem (e.g., social class, norms, and beliefs), the mesosystem (e.g., neighbourhoods and communities, schools, workplaces, religious settings, social networks), and the microsystem (e.g., the individual and the family). While the act of child maltreatment is played out at the parent–child level, the stage is set by conditions existing, or not existing, at all levels. The approach also reflects on how contributing factors work in concert to heighten vulnerability to child maltreatment, to enhance resilience, or to promote wellness. Further, dynamic application of the model at varying points throughout childhood and adolescence allows for the recognition of the shifting balance of contributing factors that comes with a child's entry into a new developmental stage, life transitions, changing social trends, and so on, which inevitably affect the probability of maltreatment or the propensity for resilience and wellness.

Figure 2.1 represents the combination of the outcome equation and the ecological model. As indicated by the arrow on the left side of the diagram, vulnerabilities occurring at one or more of the ecological levels, unchecked by relevant and/or sufficient protective mechanisms, lead to an increased probability of maltreatment. When relevant and sufficient protective mechanisms are enacted at one or more of the levels, the impact of existing vulnerabilities may be buffered, resulting in resilient children and families and the prevention of maltreatment. The arrow in the middle of the figure that joins the two sets of circles represents this interaction between vulnerabilities and protective mechanisms which may lead to the positive outcome of resilience. As

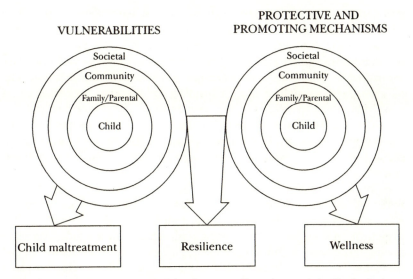

Figure 2.1 The Combination of the Outcome Equation and the Ecological Model

illustrated by the arrow on the right side of the diagram, in the absence of identifiable vulnerabilities, promoting mechanisms serve to facilitate functioning and enhance wellness. The specific vulnerabilities and protective and promoting mechanisms that fit within each of the ecological levels are likely to be different for each individual or family and to vary over time. Furthermore, while multiple vulnerabilities or protective and promoting mechanisms may exist concurrently, some will contribute more significantly to an outcome than others. For example, social norms that tolerate violence may have a distal relationship to the incidence of maltreatment, while the existence of strong support networks may have a proximal connection to resilience. In other words, a particular contributing factor will have a differential impact on people depending on their unique context. This is why it is difficult to predict with certainty the outcome of specific negative life events on particular children and families. Some will cope better than others.

Certainly in this chapter we do not purport to present an exhaustive examination of all the contributing factors to maltreatment, resilience, or wellness. Instead, what we have done is provide information on those factors that are more consistently identified within the literature in relation to each of the outcomes. Furthermore, we do not engage in a detailed examination of various theories that have been proposed to explain the incidence of abuse and neglect (e.g., attachment theory [Bowlby, 1969], self-efficacy theory [Bandura, 1977]). We recognize that a great amount of careful thought and research have gone into establishing connections between maltreatment and certain contextual factors. However, we believe that by framing the evidence according to an ecological and hierarchical structure and along the promotion–prevention–protection continuum (see Figures 1.1 and 1.2), we can consider the variables contained in these theories and offer perhaps a more pragmatic review of the complex processes through which maltreatment, resilience, and wellness ensue.

In both the 'Vulnerabilities' and 'Protective and Promoting Mechanisms' sections we begin by looking at factors within the macrosystem level, and move the discussion toward smaller levels of analysis. This organization flows from the ecological model, in which smaller levels of analysis are nested within larger levels. However, in this review we found that while there is a plethora of information available, it is for the most part narrow in focus and lacking in diversity. Although the literature advocates that an ecological perspective is essential for understanding child maltreatment, resiliency, and wellness, much of the research in these areas has been conducted at the microsystem level with a focus on individual children, parents, and families. Attention to meso- or macrosystem levels has been limited, though there is evidence of a growing interest in broadening the level of investigation (see Coulton et al., 1995; Garbarino & Kostelny, 1992; Vondra, 1990 – mesosystem focus; Tolan & Guerra, 1998; Willis & Silovsky, 1998 – macrosystem focus).

Even within the largely microsystemic examination of child maltreatment there is a narrowing of focus. For example, most of the evidence is based on investigations of mothers' contributions to and involvement in the mistreatment of their children (Belsky, 1993; Mayer-Renaud, 1990b). We know comparatively little about the role of fathers.

There are further limitations to the literature in relation to the lack of generalizability and relevance to the diversity of families in contemporary society. Families today take many different forms and function under diverse circumstances. Consider that there are 'blended families, single parent families, homosexual families, cohabitating families, reconstituted families ... grandparent and grandchildren families, and other alternative family types' (McCoy, 1996, p. 244) such as shared-home families, teen-parent families, mixed ethnicity or religion families, immigrant families, poor families, dual-earner families, biologically intact families, foster families, and the list goes on. In Canada one in three children are born out of wedlock (1994 data; Canadian Council on Social Development, 1997) and in at least one province (i.e., Quebec) the rate is closer to one in two children (1993 data; Marcil-Gratton, 1995). Although 'recent studies have expanded the data base to many cohorts ... diverse families still tend to be evaluated in comparison to one standard' (Walsh, 1996, p. 268).

Vulnerabilities Associated with Child Maltreatment

The concept of vulnerability, which is often referred to as risk, denotes possibilities of misfortune or harm, not certainties. Having one or more of the vulnerabilities or risk factors associated with child maltreatment does not confirm that abuse will occur; it implies that there is only a possibility. In fact, as many researchers candidly and sometimes vehemently note, most families in risk situations do not mistreat their children; the majority of parents who were abused as children do not go on to perpetrate violence against their own children; most children living in poor families are neither abused nor neglected; the majority of premature or low-birth-weight infants do not become victims of maltreatment; and so on. Research has not been able to conclusively identify specific or sufficient antecedents for any form of maltreatment, although it has produced an extensive inventory of contributing factors. For example, one group of researchers suggests that there are over 100 variables associated with an increased probability of child physical abuse (Muir et al., 1989). What research has shown, however, is that the risk of negative outcomes for children is compounded by the presence of multiple concurrent vulnerabilities. A British study (Rutter, 1979) found that children with one risk factor did no better or worse than children with no risk factors. However, when two risk factors were present, the risk increased by four times, and when a child experienced four or more vulnerabilities, the probability of distress increased tenfold.

Although more effort is being made to disentangle the different forms of abuse from one another (e.g., Fortin & Chamberland 1995; Hart et al., 1998; MacMillan, Niec, & Offord, 1995), many studies still combine physical abuse and neglect, which makes it difficult to differentiate between these two forms of maltreatment (or three forms if neglect is further subdivided into physical neglect and components of psychological maltreatment as we have done in this chapter) (Belsky, 1993). Part of the difficulty in separating out forms of maltreatment is their co-morbidity. Many children concurrently experience multiple forms of maltreatment (Mash & Wolfe, 1991; McGee & Wolfe, 1991; McGee, Wolfe, Yuen, Wilson, & Carnochan, 1993; Pianta, Egeland, & Erickson, 1989; Zuravin, 1988), thus making it difficult to tease out the contributing factors and effects of particular subtypes. While a few factors have been repeatedly identified, such as poverty, social support, and parental history of childhood maltreatment, the literature is replete with debate about the contribution of these and other factors to child maltreatment. Replication of findings is not consistent across studies; the predictive power of individual variables is tenuous; and while the regression equations for some research are complex, there are certainly no studies that exhaustively examine the pathways to maltreatment.

Vulnerabilities at the Societal Level

> *Whether the presenting problem is unemployment, child abuse, or crime, the nature of these problems suggests their embeddedness in society. While solutions may lie with one individual or family at a time, there are structural factors which indicate the real causes lie beyond the individual level.* (Adviser)

'To understand the challenges facing families ... it is important to create a context for viewing prevailing social, cultural, and economic pressures. Today's families are under siege as they attempt to adapt to these pressures' (Weick & Saleebey, 1995, p. 142). At the societal level, factors such as poverty, unemployment, and norms and values that support violence and disregard children combine to create highly stressful living conditions for families (Chamberland & Fortin, 1995; Wolfe, 1998). Laying blame solely on at-risk families fails to recognize the debilitating and demoralizing impact of these and other social conditions that exist far beyond their personal control. As illustrated in Figure 2.2, in this section we examine the literature that links pernicious social conditions of poverty, unemployment, and immigration, as well as the social norms of tolerating violence, protecting family privacy, devaluing caregivers, and gender stereotyping, with the problem of child maltreatment.

Poverty or Low Income

Many studies have demonstrated a relationship between poverty or low income and maltreatment, particularly in the form of neglect (Burgdoff, 1980; Garbarino, 1976, 1989; Garbarino & Kostelny, 1992; Garbarino & Sherman, 1980; Gelles, 1992; Hampton, 1987; MacMillan et al.,

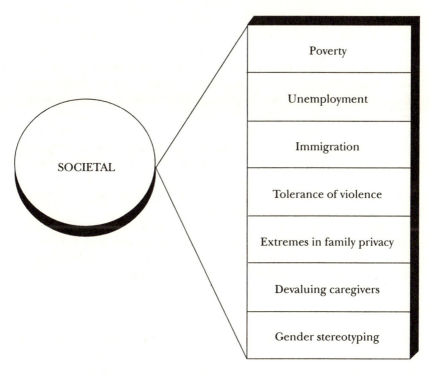

Figure 2.2 Societal-Level Vulnerabilities Associated with Child Maltreatment

1995; Maden & Wrench, 1977; Martin & Walters, 1982; Mayer-Renaud, 1991; McLoyd, 1990; Oxman-Martinez, 1993; Pelton, 1978, 1981; Polansky, Gaudin, Ammons, & Davis, 1985; Schorr, 1989; Spearly & Lauderdale, 1983; Trocmé et al., 1994; Wolfe, 1998; Zuravin, 1989). There is further evidence that suggests that maltreatment becomes chronic and more severe the longer a family lives in poverty (Kruttschnitt, McLeod, & Dornfeld, 1993).

Although exact numbers are difficult to obtain, researchers and practitioners alike agree that poor or low-income families are disproportionately represented in the population served by provincial/territorial child welfare and protection systems (*A Choice of Futures*, 1989). Figures for 1986 indicate that between 54 and 75 per cent of children in the care of child welfare systems in Canada came from low-income families (*A Choice of Futures*, 1989). Current estimates are comparable. In 1996, 75 per cent of the children served by the Metropolitan Toronto Children's Aid Society (MTCAS) were considered to be at or below the poverty line and 55 per cent of families on the MTCAS caseload were receiving some form of social assistance (Canadian Council on Social Development, 1997). One of the advisers in our qualitative study estimates that in New Brunswick *'60 to 70 per cent of the families [they] deal with through [their] child protection program are either receiving social assistance or unemployment insurance.'* Moving westward, the trend is similar. Another of our advisers reports about 50 per cent of the child protection families in Saskatchewan are receiving social assistance, though this figure varies according to geographic location. *'In some [child welfare] offices in northern Saskatchewan, which again have a higher percentage of Aboriginal people living in those areas, the percentage could go as high as 90 or 95 per cent of families [on the caseload] ... receiving social assistance.'*

Poverty or low-income status is not necessarily a precursor to child welfare involvement and child welfare clients are not exclusively poor. In fact, many of our qualitative-study participants revealed that an increasing number of families with moderate to high incomes are experiencing problems, particularly related to parent–teen conflict, and are becoming involved with child welfare services.

However, it certainly appears that there is an increased risk of maltreatment for children living in poor or low-income families. The term 'feminization of poverty' was introduced about twenty years ago to describe the increase in the number of women in the ranks of the poor (Pearce, 1978). Today the term 'juvenization of poverty' is better reflective of our current situation (Dooley, 1994). Despite a decline in the child population (Ross et al., 1996b), the number of children living in poverty has risen. In fact, children make up the single largest group of poor people in Canada. In 1989, when the entire House of Commons passed a resolution to end child poverty by the year 2000, there were 934,000 poor children, representing 14.5 per cent of the child population (Campaign 2000, 1997b). As the year 2000 target drew closer, the situation got worse, not better. Figures for 1995 and 1996 indicate approximately 1.5 million children, or 21 per cent of the child population in Canada, were living in poverty (Campaign 2000, 1997b; Canadian Council on Social Development, 1998). The most striking increases have occurred in British Columbia (85 per cent) and Ontario (99 per cent) (Campaign 2000, 1997b – figures represent comparison between 1989 and 1995 data).

The term 'child poverty' is somewhat of a misnomer. Although some youth work to supplement household earnings (Ross, Shillington, &

Lochhead, 1994), typically children are not expected to be financially responsible for their families (Ross, Scott, & Kelly, 1996a). Hence a more accurate term for what we are looking at is 'family poverty.'

There is no official poverty line in Canada. Instead, poverty rates are often based on the Statistics Canada low-income cut-off (LICO) levels (35 different levels across Canada calculated according to family and community size). Poor families are considered to be those who spend more than 55 per cent of their before-tax income on food, housing, and clothing (Campaign 2000, 1997b, Clarke, 1992; Ross et al., 1994). In 1995 the National Council of Welfare estimated there were 2.6 million poor households in Canada (Canadian Council on Social Development, 1997). At a provincial level (excludes territories), using LICO grades and data for children ages zero to 11 in 1994–5, Newfoundland showed the highest percentage of children in poor families (33.1 per cent) followed by Manitoba with 28.9 per cent; British Columbia posted the lowest rate of all the provinces at 22.1 per cent (Ross et al., 1996b). However, figures based on statistical levels or cut-offs can be misleading, failing to provide an accurate picture of the intensity and extent of the problem. Ross, Scott, and Kelly (1996a) provide a practical example that demonstrates how poverty or low-income levels lack sensitivity to intensity:

> In 1996: a non-poor family of two persons living in a large city should have a gross annual income of no less than $21,700; in rural areas they should have no less than $15,000 per year. However, based on Statistics Canada surveys, we know that the 'average' poor family in Canada actually lives far below this poverty line – by as much as $9,000 for a single-parent mother with a child. (p. 2)

The extent of the problem is masked since families who exist just above the LICO levels are not included in the counts, yet they experience many of the same obstacles and difficulties as 'officially' poor families (Clarke, 1992).

So who are these poor and low-income families? In many ways they are just like other families in Canada. The majority of poor families live in Ontario or Quebec (31 per cent and 29 per cent respectively, of Canada's total poor – 1992 data) (Ross et al., 1996a), particularly in large urban centres such as Montreal and Toronto (Campaign 2000, 1997b; Lochhead & Shillington, 1996; Ross et al., 1996a). The Canadian Council on Social Development's (Ross et al., 1994) calculations of the distribution of low-income households for 1991 show more two-parent families at low income levels than lone-parent families (34.4 per cent versus 22.9 per cent). However, when the rates within different types of families are considered, poverty rates for single parents with children under age 18 reach 56 per cent, and climb higher to 76 per cent when the lone parent is a mother with children under age 7, and even higher to 81 per cent when the mother has never been married (Ross et al., 1996a). Zyblock's (1996) analysis of family market income inequality in Canada also shows that lone-parent families are clearly at an economic disadvantage compared with other family types. 'What distinguishes poor families, however, is their low level of formal education ... and their low level of employment ...' (Ross et al., 1994, p. 39). Finally, First Nations families are highly overrepresented in Canada's poor population. In fact they are the most economically disadvantaged group in the country (*A Choice of Futures*, 1989; Ross et al., 1994; Shillington, 1990).

'Poverty creates stresses that compound the already difficult task of raising children. Low-income parents run a greater risk of encountering problems that erode their capacity to parent competently' (*A Choice of Futures*, 1989, p. 6).

In 1995 'poverty in full-time employed families hurt 433,000 children ... The problem is that [some] parents just can't earn enough, even working full-time to raise a family. These children of the "full-year working poor" make up 29% of all poor children' (Campaign 2000, 1997b, p. 7).

For many children, youth, and parents from poor or low-income families, it is not enough that they cannot always afford what they need; they also experience negative social impacts (Robichaud, Guay, Colin, Pothier, & Saucier, 1994; Steinhauer, 1998). One informant speaking to the Standing Committee on Health (Simmons, 1997) said:

> We know that growing up in poverty – and it isn't just the economic deprivation, it's the psychosocial deprivations that are highly clustered in a poor population – doubles the rate of just about every poor outcome for children except conduct disorder, which is the forerunner of delinquency, and it more than triples the rate of that. (p. 12)

Poor families are also criticized, ridiculed, excluded, ostracized, and discriminated against because they do not fit in or they cannot participate at the same level as their non-poor peers. As noted by one service provider, *'the price paid for being poor, for children in some ways especially ... is even greater than it used to be. The need to conform to the up-to-date stuff to fit in requires more money than it ever used to.'* There can be humiliating consequences for not being able to afford what it takes to fit in, as one parent told us: *'The kids that do have more money, they are calling [poor children] "sleaze buckets"... and "welfare cases"... They are always stuck in that stigma.'*

Unemployment

Related to poverty and low income is the problem of unemployment. Researchers have found lack of work, limited employment, and unstable work conditions to be associated with an increased risk for child maltreatment (Claussen & Crittenden, 1991; Gabinet, 1983; Galdston, 1965; Gelles, 1975; Gelles & Hargreaves, 1981; Jones & McCurdy, 1992; Krugman, Lenherr, Betz, & Fryer, 1986; Oxman-Martinez, 1993; Whipple & Webster-Stratton, 1991; Wolfe, 1998; Young, 1964). A few studies provide evidence supporting unemployment as a causal link or true risk factor (MacMillan et al., 1995) for maltreatment (Bycer, Breed, Fluke, & Costello, 1984; Lichtenstein, 1983; Steinberg, Catalano, & Dooley, 1981), as opposed to merely identifying it as a concurrent vulnerability. 'Gil (1971) has shown, for example, that nearly half of the fathers of the 13,000 cases of abuse he analyzed in his national survey experienced joblessness in the year that immediately preceded the abusive incident' (Belsky, 1980, p. 327). However, caution should be used when interpreting Gil's findings since the rate of maltreatment before unemployment was not reported.

Unemployment is currently one of the primary issues of concern to Canadians (Canadian Council on Social Development, 1997). Parental joblessness is the main cause of poverty in families with children. The number of children in families experiencing long-term unemployment (defined as more than six months) increased from 570,000 in 1989 to 835,000 in 1995 (Campaign 2000, 1997b). Informants in our qualitative study from across the country identified unemployment as a key issue facing many of the families involved in child welfare services.

The reasons for unemployment are varied (Maxwell, 1993). With globalization and the North American Free Trade Agreement, many jobs are leaving the country. In some provinces employment levels fluctuate with changes in primary industries such as mining or fishing. The shift from manual labour to high-tech computer-based business has left many parents untrained for positions in today's job market.

Immigration

Migration and integration processes may also contribute to societal-level vulnerability, primarily because of the lack of accessible family support services to immigrant families, particularly when they arrive in Canada. Children and youth in recently immigrated families have been found to be at high risk for neglect (Bouchard, 1991) and parent–child/teen conflict (Messier & Toupin, 1994). Separation from parents during the migration process is a problem which has been linked to broken family ties and children being abandoned or left in the care of social services. Cultural and generational conflicts between parents and children/youth become aggravated when problems of integration or of daily survival are not shared by the family at large and when extended family supports become geographically scattered (Messier & Toupin, 1994). (Native-born Canadians who migrate interprovincially/territorially can experience the loss of support networks, and the diversity of context across the country may also pose integration difficulties for some of these families.)

The influx of immigrant families into Canada is a major phenomenon. The 1996 census recorded 5 million immigrants living in this country, comparatively representing 17.4 per cent of Canada's population (Statistics Canada, 1998). Our informants talked about issues related to parents raised in other countries who do not know or who do not espouse acceptable norms for childrearing in Canada. Furthermore, we were told that language barriers prevent many immigrant families from learning about available resources and from understanding what is going on when they enter child protection systems. Comments from two of our participants capture the essence of this contributing factor for maltreatment and/or involvement in child welfare:

> *We have a large Vietnamese population, Cambodian, Laotian, Filipino. And those families would not have had previous child welfare contact, for the most part, and a lot of their contact is around physical abuse issues. They need to learn what is culturally acceptable in Canada, and be able to translate that.* (Service provider)

> *One issue that probably isn't unique to Ontario ... might be the level of immigration that Ontario experiences. It's not to say that all these families are at risk, but coming to a new country and struggling with a different cultural experience, and the family tensions between parents brought up in one value system and children who are trying to acclimatize to an Ontario context, all those things can lead to stresses.* (Advisers)

Tolerance of Violence and Acceptance of Physical Punishment

We are witness to acts of violence every day, whether on the news, in the headlines, at the movies or in popular song lyrics, in playgrounds, on ice rinks, and in grocery store checkouts. Unwittingly, we accept violence as part of life, and what we learn from it shapes our values, our behaviour, and our approach to conflict resolution (Fortin & Chamberland, 1995; Gouvernement du Québec, 1991). 'Numerous observers have drawn attention to the fact that enduring and recent aspects of [North] American society create a cultural context in which the maltreatment of children can flourish' (Belsky, 1993, p. 422). The tolerance for, and identification with, violence has been identified as a major social contributor to child maltreatment (Belsky, 1980, 1993; Besharov, 1996; Bouchard, 1991; Finkelhor & Dziuba-Leatherman, 1994; Garbarino, 1977a; Gelles, 1976; Vissing et al., 1991; Vondra, 1990).

The prevalence of child maltreatment indicates that we are not merely a society of bystanders; we allow children to suffer, and some of us inflict the harm. In some countries there are laws against striking a child; spanking is not tolerated as a form of discipline (Ziegart, 1983). In our culture however, the use of physical punishment is still a generally accepted means of controlling children's behaviour (Belsky, 1980, 1993; Bouchard, Tessier, Fraser, & Laganière, 1996; Chamberland & Fortin, 1995; Finkelhor & Dziuba-Leatherman, 1994; Garbarino, 1977a; Gil, 1970; Straus et al., 1980; Vondra, 1990). 'The implicit sanction of parental violence in our culture is also interwoven with the idea that the parent owns the child' (Chamberland & Fortin, 1995, p. 148 – also see Bouchard et al., 1996; Garbarino, 1977b; Garbarino, Stocking, & Associates, 1980; Gil, 1970, 1976; Straus et al., 1980; Vondra, 1990).

Extremes in Family Privacy

Many observers argue that the broad cultural belief that family matters are private also contributes to child maltreatment (Belsky, 1993; Bouchard, 1991; Finkelhor & Dziuba-Leatherman, 1994; Garbarino, 1977a; Vondra, 1990). One adviser we spoke with commented, *'we still tend to treat families as private units expected to go about their own business.'* As such, society's averted glance or turned head leaves children open to victimization behind a veil of closed doors and covered windows. A lack of public scrutiny in family settings means observation and reporting of maltreatment is limited and thus restricts interventions to mitigate the problem (Chamberland & Fortin, 1995; Fortin & Chamberland, 1995).

Devaluing the Role of Caregivers

As noted above, the lack of importance given to children, indeed the tendency to consider them mere possessions, has been identified as a major social contributor to child maltreatment (Belsky, 1993; Bouchard, 1991). Likewise, the denigration of the role of child care provider, as demonstrated by poor pay for early childhood education workers, the low status of teachers and child protection workers, the feminization of poverty, and the widespread exodus of parents from the primary caregiving role, minimizes the need to care well for children and places children in potentially unsafe situations (Belsky, 1993).

Traditional Gender Roles
For both women and men, traditional gender roles, on their own and in contention with current living realities, can impede the ability to parent effectively and increase the potential for child maltreatment (Vondra, 1990). Women have traditionally been given the responsibility to provide for the care and well-being of children. At one time many mothers were able to remain in the home, looking after their families' needs on a full-time basis. Now, the precarious financial situation faced by numerous two-parent families and the majority of single-parent, mother-led families has forced many women into the workforce, though typically into lower-paid and lower-status jobs than men. 'At the same time, it is expected that the full-time employed mother should continue to function as the full-time housekeeper and childcare provider' (Vondra, 1990, p. 26). Although individual fathers may be more involved in looking after children, at a societal level, we still do not expect fathers to assume equal responsibility for childrearing or household chores (Vondra, 1990). In cases where fathers are absent due to separation or divorce, and cannot provide practical assistance with housekeeping and child care, society also excuses them from their obligations to provide financial aid to their families by not enforcing child support payments (Baker, 1997; Vondra, 1990).

While placing the burden of child care on mothers, gender stereotypes serve to limit the role of fathers in the lives of their children (Bouchard, 1991). Fathers who work are particularly restricted in this sense (Dulac, 1993). Though parental leaves of up to ten weeks are available, only 4.2 per cent of the leaves are taken by fathers, and only 2.5 per cent of these men use the full ten weeks (Moisan, 1997).

Vulnerabilities at the Community Level

'Child maltreatment is a symptom of not just individual or family trouble but neighborhood and community trouble as well' (Garbarino &

Kostelny, 1992, p. 463). Empirical study and observation have led some researchers to identify a relationship between pernicious neighbourhood conditions (e.g., lack of social cohesion, increased unemployment rates, high levels of mobility, inaccessible services and resources, inferior housing, and inadequate child care settings) and rates of maltreatment (Belsky, 1980; Bouchard, Le Bossé, & Dumont, 1995; Cicchetti & Lynch, 1993; Coulton et al., 1995; Garbarino, 1977a; Garbarino & Kostelny, 1992; Garbarino & Sherman, 1980; Korbin & Coulton, 1996; U.S. Advisory Board on Child Abuse and Neglect, 1993). While there is some indication that interest in the area is growing (e.g., Coulton et al., 1995; Korbin & Coulton, 1996), there has been limited examination of the influence of neighbourhood and community conditions on child maltreatment (Korbin & Coulton, 1996), and prevailing models that attempt to explain the etiology of maltreatment fail to adequately account for the impacts of changing community conditions (Coulton et al., 1995; Garbarino & Kostelny, 1992). Citing Kasarda and Janowitz (1974) as their source, Coulton et al. (1995) define community social organization as 'patterns and functions of formal and informal networks and institutions and organizations in a locale' (p. 1263). Based on the recognition that structural properties of neighbourhoods and communities can affect the level of social organization or disorganization (Sampson, 1991; Sampson & Groves, 1989; Shaw & McKay, 1942; Suttles, 1968), we present the evidence linking child maltreatment to a number of community dimensions, as illustrated in Figure 2.3.

Impoverishment

In a community context the term impoverishment refers to conditions such as poverty and unemployment levels, and percentage of female-led and racial minority families. In a cross-sectional study of the ecology of child maltreatment rates in Cleveland's urban neighbourhoods, Coulton et al. (1995) found impoverishment, which included the four variables listed above as well as the level of vacant housing and population loss, had the greatest effect on maltreatment rates. Zuravin (1989) found two components of impoverishment – low income and the amount of vacant housing – were the most powerful predictors of maltreatment rates. Bouchard, Chamberland, and Beaudry (1988) confirm studies by Garbarino and his colleagues (Garbarino & Crouter, 1978; Garbarino & Sherman, 1980) that report a high correlation between neighbourhoods' economic and social poverty and the incidence rate of child maltreatment. In their Montreal-based study, Bouchard et al.

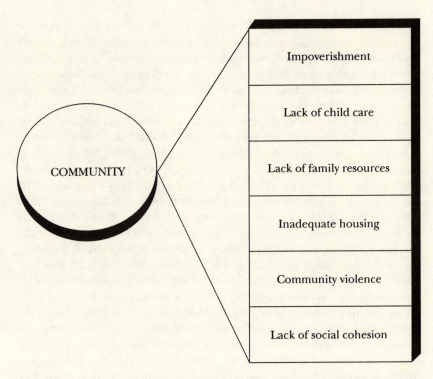

Figure 2.3 Community-Level Vulnerabilities Associated with Child Maltreatment

(1988) found two factors were the strongest indicators of maltreatment in the residential sectors surveyed: (1) a high percentage of poor families, and (2) a high percentage of families with mothers as the only wage earners. Mayer (1997) also found high levels of poverty in surveyed sectors to be associated with greater incidence of various types of maltreatment, but more so with the rate of neglect than the rate of physical abuse. Community unemployment levels have also been found to be related to the incidence of maltreatment. Following a decline in the employment rate, Steinberg, Catalano, and Dooley (1981) noted an increase in county-based maltreatment rates.

Lack of Child Care Options

In some areas daycare facilities and other child care options are inadequate to serve the individual and collective needs of the community

(Vondra, 1990). Some researchers have identified a connection between this lack of resources for child care and rates of child maltreatment (Wolfe, 1998). Second to impoverishment, Coulton and her colleagues (1995) found that the level of child care burden in Cleveland's urban communities explained a large portion of the variance in child maltreatment rates. In this study child care burden was measured by examining the ratios of children to adults and males to females, and the percentage of the population who were elderly. The researchers believe that the combination of these variables represents the 'amount of adult supervision and resources that may be available for children in the community' (p. 1270).

A consultation on services for young children conducted among approximately 100 parents with children from birth to age 6 shows that child care services represent a real need for families all over Quebec. Parents count on government support and community resources to compensate for weak or nonexistent family networks. Parents believe that all of the services available to children have a major influence on children's social integration and the prevention of problems during childhood and adolescence. Most parents surveyed wished child care services would be preserved and further developed to help them reconcile their work and family obligations and to meet their needs for respite (Conseil de la famille, 1996).

According to the Canadian Council on Social Development's *The Progress of Canada's Children* (1997), 'less than one-third of the 1.5 million children under age 12 who needed child care in 1994 were in regulated programs, including home-based child care facilities' (p. 30). In five provinces, spaces in regulated child care facilities have been reduced. Standards of care and the enforcement of such have also been curtailed in some provinces. Government expenditures on child care have decreased. Grants to providers have been cut, frozen, or cancelled in the majority of provinces/territories. Conversely, the cost of child care has increased. In 1997 the average cost per month for child care ranged from $350 to $1,200 (Canadian Council on Social Development, 1997). As reported in the Canadian Council on Social Development's 1998 report *The Progress of Canada's Children*, child care represents the largest single expenditure associated with raising a child, at 33 per cent of the total costs.

Parents face many barriers to obtaining child care services. For many low- and moderate-income families, the cost of high-quality care is simply beyond their means (Conseil de la famille, 1996; Pharand, 1995;

Schorr, 1989). Even for those who can afford to pay, the number of spaces available is often not flexible enough to meet the needs of parents who have irregular work schedules, who work mornings, evenings, weekends, or during busy holiday seasons (Conseil de la famille, 1996; Pharand, 1995). Of further concern to parents is the quality of care and lack of programs that include substantial educational components as opposed to simply custodial supervision (Pharand, 1995; Schorr, 1989). For many working parents these barriers mean they must rely on informal sources of child care and for some it means they end up leaving their children unattended.

Our qualitative-study participants had a lot to say about the lack of and need for accessible, affordable, high-quality child care in their communities as well as programs that are geared toward older children. They said these resources are necessary for working parents, but they also emphasized their importance for parents pursuing educational opportunities and for those parents who do care for their own children full-time but need some time to themselves.

Most people are paying well over $100 a week just to have one of their children in daycare. And if you have three kids, you are working for nothing. You are basically paying to have your children in daycare while you are busting your butt and getting no further ahead than you were before you started working. (Parent)

I think that there is a big gap. There aren't many programs for kids who are 7, 8, 9, 10. Like my brother is 10 years old, he can't go to daycare and his dad starts work at 7:30 in the morning and it's really really difficult for him. Half of what he earns goes into paying somebody else to take care of [my brother], especially at those extreme hours. (Youth)

Absent or Inaccessible Family Resources

In addition to child care services, many high-risk communities lack other supportive resources such as recreational facilities, job training programs, libraries, schools, physicians, and substance abuse centres (Coulton et al., 1995; Vondra, 1990). Investigators have noted that the inadequacy or nonexistence of supportive resources in communities is a major influence on child maltreatment (Bouchard, 1991; Harvey, 1991; Jasmin, 1992; Schorr, 1989; Wolfe, 1998). Smaller, impoverished, or geographically isolated communities may be unable to attract or sustain a comprehensive selection of support services and/or personnel. In some larger urban centres the growth of supportive resources has not kept pace with the influx of population. Reflecting on the community where he works, one service provider noted *'the population expanded and the infrastructure has never caught up at all. So there are more opportunities for kids to get support than there were, but it's not nearly what's needed.'*

Some researchers suggest that there are resources available in communities, but that parents who mistreat their children do not use them (Corse, Schmid, & Trickett, 1990; Giovannoni & Billingsley, 1970; Polansky et al., 1985; Trickett & Susman, 1988). Irrespective of the validity of this observation, other researchers have examined why families may not access resources within their communities. Parents in a Quebec survey mentioned they have difficulty finding information on existing general services (Conseil de la famille, 1996). Some of our qualitative study participants agreed:

> *I'm finding sometimes it's hard to find the information you want. Unless you go through a lot of bother yourself, you don't know that a lot of services are available ... They should advertise the programs bigger, and not so complicated wording.* (Parent)

> *That's what always amazes me in talking to families. You mention things like the XXX Hospital and they have child and family counselling, or XXX Children's Centre. And over and over people have never heard of these places. Why? Why have they never heard of a major community hospital having a child and family clinic? Why does nobody know that? Because they don't advocate, they don't advertise.* (Service provider)

Where resources are located, when programs are offered and how they are delivered can restrict access or place burdens on families. Some services may be out of reach of families with limited access to transportation (Vondra, 1990). Several of our informants said the process of getting to appointments and community activities is made difficult by unreliable vehicles and public transportation systems that are often expensive, unavailable (particularly in rural communities), and unmanageable for parents with several children, strollers, and other items to mind. Families may also be turned off of particular resources because they are not nice places to be. Participants in Garbarino and Kostelny's (1992) study of the ecology of child maltreatment in selected Chicago communities described the physical spaces in which programs were offered as dark and depressing. The timing of programs and services is not always opportune. Participants in our study said many services are offered at inconvenient times, which means parents miss work, children must be excused from school, or resources just are not used. Another barrier that prevents children and families, particularly those in lower income levels, from accessing resources or engaging in community activities is the cost of participating (Canadian Council on Social Development, 1998). As one service provider observed, there may be plenty of resources offered in a community, but they are likely to be accessible only to those who can pay:

> *There are lots of recreational opportunities for children and youth, but there are financial barriers in terms of registration, transportation, equipment. The community at one time would subsidize some children and youth to participate in recreational activities, but that has disappeared ... The grants have gone. Recreation that used to be rather easy to obtain and do, isn't that way anymore.*

Finally, supportive resources for families may be too overwhelmed and too underfunded to adequately serve the individual and collective needs of the community (Canadian Council on Social Development, 1997; Schorr, 1989; Vondra, 1990). Parents we spoke with voiced their frustration with waiting lists that are too long:

> *Where we were, there was nothing, there were no groups. And to get into a group out of town you were waiting 8 to 10 months, and by then your child is already placed and is beyond help.*

Unaffordable and Inadequate Housing

Unaffordable or inadequate housing has a major influence on rates of child maltreatment and other negative outcomes for children (Cohen-Schlanger, Fitzpatrick, Hulchanski, & Raphael, 1995; Doyle, 1992; Macpherson, 1984; McLaughlin, 1988; Schorr, 1989; Wolfe, 1998). In some areas the amount of available low-cost housing may not be sufficient to meet the needs of the community (Canadian Council on Social Development, 1998; Vondra, 1990). The stock of social housing in Canada is the second smallest in the twelve largest industrialized countries, followed only by the United States (Canadian Council on Social Development, 1997). In 1994 Quebec's Ombudsman estimated that 20,000 people were waiting to get into low-cost housing in that province; among those, 80 per cent were families with children (Bouchard, 1995).

According to the Canada Mortgage and Housing Corporation, rent is considered to be affordable if it costs less than 30 per cent of a family's gross income (Doyle, 1992). Figures for 1992 indicate one-quarter of poor families living in rental housing spent at least half, if not more than half, of their gross income on shelter, though on average poor families spend about 45 per cent of their income on housing (Ross et al., 1996a). Data from the 1996 census indicate that 25 per cent of Canadian households spent more than 30 per cent on shelter costs (Statistics Canada, 1998). Affordable housing tends to be most problematic for lone parents, urban residents, and renters (Statistics Canada, 1998). In one of the communities where we spoke to people, a service provider noted: *'It's hard to be poor in this community. There is very limited low-cost housing. It's very expensive to find accommodation.'* Given the shortage of social housing and the high costs of other forms of shelter, many families 'find it increasingly difficult to afford safe, clean, and healthy home environments in which to raise their children' (Canadian Council on Social Development, 1997).

Cost is only one important dimension of housing. Just as critical is the adequacy of housing. 'A child's housing must provide shelter from the elements. It must be warm and dry, in basic repair and have necessary sanitary and cooking facilities. It also must be large enough for the number of people living in it' (Doyle, 1992, p. 1). In 1991, 500,000 children lived in housing that did not meet federal standards for affordability or for adequacy (Canadian Council on Social Development, 1996), housing that was inferior, cramped, infested, and in need of major repairs and basic safety features such as smoke alarms (Doyle, 1992; Simmons, 1997). Families living in rural and northern communities and especially those who live on reserves are at particular risk for poor-quality housing. Problems facing these families include inadequate water supplies, lack of basic sanitation and waste disposal, inefficient heating systems, overcrowding, lack of fire protection services, and the need for major structural repairs (Doyle, 1992; Marsden, 1991; McLaughlin, 1988).

Community Violence

The issue of housing adequacy goes beyond conditions existing within the walls of individual homes. It also includes the ability of neighbourhoods and communities to provide children and families with protection from violence (Doyle, 1992). Marginalized neighbourhoods with problems such as crime and substance abuse can impair the healthy functioning of families (Garbarino, Dubrow, Kostelny, & Pardo, 1992; Richters & Martinez, 1993; Steinhauer, 1998). In their cross-sectional study of the ecology of child maltreatment rates in urban neighbourhoods, Coulton and her colleagues (1995) found maltreatment to be 'embedded within a set of forces in the community that also produces deviant behavior such as violent crime, drug trafficking, juvenile delinquency, and teen childbearing' (p. 1274). One of the youths we spoke with said going to school was for her an escape from the violence in her neighbourhood:

Where you live matters ... People around with drugs, whatever ... The people aren't necessarily bad who live there, but the area attracts bad things. So when you live there you always feel like you're going to be in some fight, probably get shot, drugs, whatever.

Lack of Social Cohesion and Social Isolation

Communities with high rates of reported maltreatment are often characterized by a lack of social cohesion and mutual caring and interaction among residents. A number of investigations have shown effective parenting and healthy functioning to be compromised by limited social ties to extended family, neighbours, and informal community resources (Coulton et al., 1995; Furstenberg, 1993; Garbarino & Crouter, 1978; Garbarino & Kostelny, 1992; Garbarino & Sherman, 1980; Korbin, 1994; Thompson, 1994). In addition, numerous investigators report a strong connection between parents' social isolation and rates of child maltreatment (Chamberland, Bouchard, & Beaudry, 1986; Chamberland & Fortin, 1995; Colletta, 1983; Coohey & Braun, 1997; Crittenden, 1985; Egeland, Jacobvitz, & Sroufe, 1988; Garbarino, 1976; Gelles, 1992; Hampton, 1987; MacMillan et al., 1995; Massé & Bastien, 1995; Oxman-Martinez, 1993; Pelton, 1981; Polansky et al., 1985; Schorr, 1989; Vondra, 1990; Whipple & Webster-Stratton, 1991; Wolfe, 1998; Zuravin, 1989), though some researchers debate this finding (Seagull, 1987; Thompson, 1994). The emotional support and concrete assistance provided by social networks are essential to general healthy functioning of parents both as individuals and as care givers to their children (Colletta, 1983; Levitt, Weber, & Clark, 1986; Whittaker & Garbarino, 1983). Our qualitative study participants said a lack of social connectedness is a prevalent reality for families who come into contact with child welfare systems, particularly in cases where parents are neglecting children. One mother told us, *'I don't have family support. They couldn't help me with any of this stuff. They really don't care.'* Another mother described the turmoil she experienced when the neighbourhood support network she relied on was no longer available:

> *Sometimes things just get so crazy in my house, I just want to crawl into a hole or just run away or something. And coming here on Fridays was the best, best thing. And when our centre closed for renovations, I fell apart. I fell apart. I got so depressed and I couldn't function. So now I finally went to the doctor and now I see a psychiatrist and I'm taking medication. And it's like I was doing okay when the centre was here, and when it was gone, I got lost.*

Several authors (Korbin & Coulton, 1996; Stack, 1974; Vondra, 1990) point out that when social networks are limited, families can come to depend on a select few people to provide supports. However, the ability of neighbours to lend their support may be mediated by the fact that they too are dealing with problems and are also in need. When such informal sources of support are lacking, the alternative for many families is to turn to formal community resources. Unfortunately, in many impoverished communities where cohesion levels are often low, the availability of formal supports is also limited (Bouchard et al., 1988; Coleman, 1987; Coulton et al., 1995).

Some of our informants explained families' lack of social connectedness to their communities as a consequence of the transience of many high-risk families and the increased mobility of the population in general, a rationale that is supported within the literature (Belsky, 1980, 1993; Bouchard et al., 1988; Coulton et al., 1995; Peterson & Brown, 1994; Wolfe, 1998).

Vulnerabilities at the Family and Parental Level

The family is the immediate context in which child maltreatment occurs. Research has identified certain structures, dynamics, and realities at this level that have been found to increase the potential for maltreatment. Research has also identified certain characteristics that 'individual parents who mistreat their offspring bring with them to the family setting and to the parenting role' (Belsky, 1980, p. 321). These characteristics range in nature from personal history to age, from parental knowledge to level of intelligence, from habits to personality, and from mental health to innate responses. As illustrated in Figure 2.4, in this section we report the evidence on factors contributing to child maltreatment occurring at the family and parental level.

Family Size and Structure

Child maltreatment has been found to occur in greater frequency in

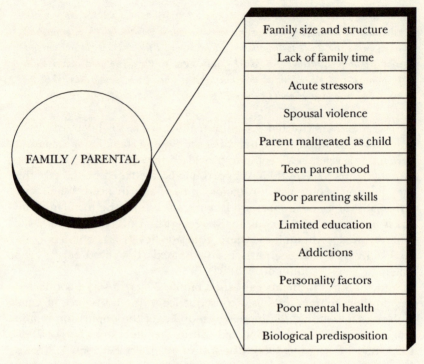

Figure 2.4 Family/Parental-Level Vulnerabilities Associated with Child Maltreatment

large families (Altemeier et al., 1979; Bouchard & Tessier, 1996; Connelly & Straus, 1992; Creighton, 1985; Gaines, Sandgrund, Green, & Power, 1978; MacMillan et al., 1995; Polansky, Chalmers, Buttenwieser, & Williams, 1981; Wolfe, 1998; Zuravin & Grief, 1989). Household crowding (Peterson & Brown, 1994) and overextended economic and human resources (Belsky, 1980) may contribute to the elevated levels of abuse and neglect reported in such families. Rates of maltreatment are also disproportionately higher in families in which children are born in rapid succession (Altemeier, O'Connor, Vietze, Sandler, & Sherrod, 1984; Benedict, White, & Cornely, 1985; Furstenberg, Brooks-Gunn, & Morgan, 1987; Schorr, 1989; Zuravin, 1988, 1989).

Children today are being raised in a broad range of family structures. While data from the 1996 census (Statistics Canada, 1998) indicate that most children still live in married-couple families (73 of every 100 children), this proportion is down from 78 per 100 children recorded five years earlier in the 1991 census. Coinciding with this decrease, the census recorded an increase in the proportion of children living in both common-law and lone-parent families. In 1996 there were 735,565 children living in common-law families, a figure 52 per cent higher than in the 1991 census. Quebec is home to almost half of these children and this province has experienced the most substantial increase in this population since 1991 (up 69 per cent). Almost 1.8 million children lived in a lone-parent family in 1996. Statistics Canada says this figure translates into one in four children living with a single parent, a ratio that is again greater than the one in six figure reported five years earlier. The majority of these children (84 per cent) lived in female-led families. More subtle distinctions about the types of family structures that include children are not made within the census. However, the General Social Survey for 1995 did find that 10 per cent of all couple-families (now-married and common-law) were blended families. As part of the National Longitudinal Survey of Children and Youth, David Cheal (1996) looked more closely at children under age 12 who were members of step-families in 1994–5. Based on the survey's data, Cheal reports that 8.6 per cent of children under age 12 in Canada were living in a step-family during this time period. Step-children made up about half of this group, and the remaining children were either born or adopted into these families.

In terms of composition, both the literature and our consultation process reveal that maltreatment occurs more often in lone-parent families and in blended or step-families. Children living in single-parent families are at greater risk for physical abuse and neglect, but particularly for neglect (Chamberland et al., 1986; Furstenberg et al., 1987; MacMillan et al., 1995; Mayer-Renaud, 1990b; Polansky et al., 1981; Trocmé, McPhee, & Tam, 1995; Wolfe, 1998). A number of sources, including some of our qualitative-study informants, claim that over half of the families served in many child welfare agencies across Canada are headed by single parents, usually mothers (Canadian Council on Social Development, 1997; *A Choice of Futures*, 1989). Clearly, the state of lone-parenthood in and of itself is not what places children in these families at higher risk for maltreatment. Concurrent realities common to single-parent families such as poverty (48 per cent of female-led and 24 per cent of male-led lone-parent families live below the Statistics Canada low-income cut-off levels [Statistics Canada, 1998]) and fewer resources and supports to assist with parenting responsibilities can exacerbate the stress of raising a child alone.

Research also provides evidence that step-children are at greater risk for child maltreatment, particularly for physical and sexual forms of abuse (Bagley & Thurston, 1998; Burgess, Garbarino, & Gilstrap, 1983; Charbonneau & Oxman-Martinez, 1996; Creighton, 1985; Daly & Wilson, 1980, 1985, 1988, 1994; Gil, 1970; Martin & Walters, 1982; Wilson & Daly, 1987; Zuravin, 1989). However, this finding is somewhat controversial and has not been consistently replicated (Gelles & Harrop, 1991; Giles-Sims & Finkelhor, 1984; Malkin & Lamb, 1994; McCloskey, Figueredo, & Koss, 1995).

Lack of Family Time

Many families today lack quantity and quality time together. Over the last fifteen years there has been a significant increase in the number of children living in two-parent families in which both parents are working. In 1996, 60 per cent of children under age 15 and 56 per cent of children under age 6 who lived in dual-parent families were in this situation (Statistics Canada, 1998). Many children living in single-parent families were in a similar position. Slightly less than 50 per cent of children living with a lone mother and almost 73 per cent of children residing with a single father had a parent who worked in 1996 (Statistics Canada, 1998). For many, longer work hours and more jobs means parents are exhausted and overwhelmed and have less time and energy to dedicate to their children (Pharand, 1995; Simmons, 1997; Steinhauer, 1998). Reconciling work and family priorities becomes increasingly difficult. Escalating rates of separation and divorce (Ross et al., 1996b) and a high rate of mobility (between 1991 and 1996, 43 per cent of Canadians moved (Statistics Canada, 1998])) also mean that extended-family members are less able and/or less available to share time with children (Steinhauer, 1998).

Acute Stressors

Rates of child maltreatment have been found in greater proportion in families experiencing higher levels of acute stress, particularly when environmental supports available to such families are concurrently limited (Bouchard & Defossé, 1989; Chamberland & Fortin, 1995; Coohey & Braun, 1997; Egeland, Breitenbucher, & Rosenberg, 1980; Éthier & LaFrenière, 1991; Éthier, Palacio-Quintin, & Jourdan-Ionescu, 1991; Schorr, 1989; Williamson, Borduin, & Howe, 1991.) Children are more at risk for maltreatment during times of family instability and stressful transitions and following the loss of supports and services (Wolfe, 1998).

Authors suggest acute stress develops in families as a result of a variety of situations and circumstances, including: economic insecurity; inadequate housing; unstable employment, loss of employment, or the transition back into the workforce; transitions into and out of school; changes in residence; serious health problems; death of family members or close friends; separation and divorce; spousal conflict and violence; pregnancy and birth; and neighbourhood violence (Bouchard et al., 1996; Chamberland et al., 1986; Coohey & Braun, 1997; Jones, 1990; Schorr, 1989; Steinberg et al., 1981). Some of our consultation participants commented on the impact of multiple acute stressors on family functioning:

> *If you have a family that is really stretched financially, they don't have enough food, they can hardly clothe their kids, they are worried about accommodation, and they don't have any way of really improving their situation. That creates incredible stress within the family, and you know that somehow that is going to be displaced on the children.* (Service provider)

However, in most families experiencing stress, children are not mistreated. Successful coping styles and alternative supports moderate stress to help families weather the storms of instability, transition, and loss.

Spousal Violence

Research has documented a significant association between spousal conflict and violence and the incidence of all forms of child maltreatment (Belsky, 1980; Chamberland & Fortin, 1995; Emery & Laumann-Billings, 1998; Levinson, 1989; MacMillan & Finkel, 1995; MacMillan et al., 1995; McCloskey et al., 1995; Palacio-Quintin, 1995; Vondra, 1990; Wolfe, 1998). Estimates of child maltreatment range from 40 to 78 per cent in families in which mothers are victims of domestic violence (Bouchard & Tessier, 1996; Chénard, Cadrin, & Loiselle, 1990; Layzer, Goodson, & DeLange, 1986; Straus et al., 1980). Children in such families are mistreated by both mothers and fathers. One-third to one-half of physically abusive mothers in several studies had been assaulted by their partners (Coohey & Braun, 1997; Gayford, 1975; O'Keefe, 1995; Stark & Flitcraft, 1988). Some men who commit violence against their wives or common-law partners also inflict harm on children in the family. In their survey of 365 mothers and one of their children (166 battered women recruited through shelters and community sources and 199 comparison mothers recruited through community advertisements for participants in a study on the family), McCloskey and her colleagues (1995) discovered either social or biological incest (male partner to child) occurring in almost 10 per cent of families experiencing spousal violence; only one case of within-family sexual abuse was reported in comparison families. Reports from mothers and children in this study also indicate that children who were living in violent family conditions were more likely to be slapped, hit with objects, beaten, and burned by their fathers (or mothers' partners) than children in the comparison sample. Children may be intentionally or unintentionally injured as they try to interrupt parents' fighting or attempt to escape from violent situations (Jaffe, Wolfe, & Wilson, 1990). They may also be harmed when parents use them to assert power and control or in retribution against their partner. In one study (Williams-Meyer & Finkelhor, 1992), 9 of the 100 incestuous fathers who were interviewed admitted their primary motivation for sexually abusing their daughters was to retaliate against their wives. Some of the mothers we spoke to in our consultation process, who admitted to mistreating their children, said they had been abused by their husbands, common-law partners, or boyfriends:

The father was ... a drug addict ... when I moved back, it was all over again. He started the needles, he started the drinking. And I was living in a hotel room and the last thing he did was push me and my baby.

However, children do not have to be 'caught in the crossfire' of spousal abuse to be adversely affected. Children are harmed simply by witnessing violence or threats of violence against significant individuals such as their mothers. In the McCloskey et al. (1995) study, children reported seeing or hearing their mothers being assaulted by their husbands or partners in numerous ways ranging from being yelled at, to being slapped, kicked, beaten, choked, and threatened with weapons. In addition to being traumatized by this experience (Graham-Bermann & Levendosky, 1998), there is growing evidence that suggests children who observe spousal violence exhibit many of the same consequences as children who are themselves targets of maltreatment (Holden, 1998; Jaffe, Wolfe, Wilson, & Zak, 1986; Sternberg et al., 1993). However, not all children exposed to spousal violence experience negative effects; many children in these families are found to function within normal parameters. Whether or not there are effects to witnessing abuse, advocates are spreading the message that 'to witness violence is child abuse'

(Davy, 1997) and they are pushing for the inclusion of children witnessing domestic violence as sufficient grounds for child welfare involvement under provincial/territorial legislation.

Parental History of Child Maltreatment

A childhood history of maltreatment in parents has been found to be a good predictor of those same parents victimizing their own children (Altemeier et al., 1984; Charbonneau & Oxman-Martinez, 1996; Coohey & Braun, 1997; Dubowitz, Hampton, Bithoney, & Newberger, 1987; Herrenkohl, Herrenkohl, & Toedtler, 1983; Kempe, Silverman, Steele, Broegemueller, & Silver, 1962; MacMillan et al., 1995; Steele & Pollack, 1968). While much of the evidence is based on retrospective research, prospective studies have demonstrated similar findings (Egeland, Jacobvitz, & Papatola, 1987; Hunter, Kilstrom, Kraybill, & Loda, 1978). The data we gathered in our qualitative study strongly support this evidence as well. A number of the service providers and advisers talked about the cyclical nature of abuse and neglect and the generational involvement of child welfare services in many families. *'For some families it is cyclical. [Parents] have learned the inappropriate behaviours in terms of discipline and childrearing, and I think in some instances they are passing on that to their children, which often leads to us ... intervening'* (Adviser). *'In neglect, abuse or abandonment situations, very often the parents themselves had been placed'* (Service provider). Even some of the parents we spoke with, who admitted to having mistreated their own children, revealed that they had been raised in abusive or neglectful situations. One mother said, *'I came from a very dysfunctional family ... I didn't know what normal children were like.'*

There is some indication that parents are more likely to perpetrate particular subtypes of maltreatment depending on their own histories. A study by Éthier, Palacio-Quintin, and Couture (1992) showed that violent mothers were more often victims of child physical, psychological, or sexual abuse, whereas neglectful mothers were more often neglected as children. In a controlled study Delozier (1982) found that mothers who were physically abusive toward their children were much more likely to have histories of psychological maltreatment. Ney (1989) reported that patterns of verbal abuse are likely to be repeated in subsequent generations. Reported rates of intergenerational transmission of child maltreatment range from a low of 7 per cent (Gil, 1973) to a high of 70 per cent (Egeland & Jacobvitz, 1984), though reviews of this literature suggest a more realistic estimate would be that about one-third of the children who are maltreated become abusive or neglectful parents themselves (Kaufman & Zigler, 1987; Malinosky-Rummell & Hansen, 1993; Widom, 1989b).

Teen Parenthood

Pregnancy and birth rates among adolescents may be lower than they were a few decades ago, but Canada's teen pregnancy rate has risen sharply since 1987 (Canadian Council on Social Development, 1998; Kennedy, 1998; Mitchell, 1998a, 1998b) and today's reality is that more and more teenage girls who follow through with their pregnancy are choosing to keep and raise their babies (Canadian Council on Social Development, 1997). There are currently about 20,000 teen mothers in Canada (Canadian Council on Social Development, 1997). Young maternal age has been noted by several authors to increase the probability of maltreatment for children (Furstenberg et al., 1987; MacMillan & Finkel, 1995; MacMillan et al., 1995; Oxman-Martinez, 1993; Schorr, 1989; Wolfe, 1998). Many of our qualitative-study informants talked about the issue of teen pregnancy as it relates to child maltreatment. One service provider said child welfare is seeing *'a deluge of teen pregnancies'* and a number of participants said it is not uncommon for agencies to provide services to both mother and child as minors (i.e., both as victims of maltreatment). We heard from several participants about the generational nature of teen pregnancy, that is, children born to teen mothers becoming pregnant in their teens. A 37-year-old grandmother, who was rather passionate about this issue, stated:

> *The problem in most of the neighbourhoods like this, is the adults are just children themselves. You've got 14-, 15-year-old girls that are pregnant and mothers. And all they are doing is their mother got pregnant at 15 and they are on 'the system.' 'Oh, when you get 16 you can get pregnant and start getting money too.' It's children having children. There should be a law.*

We also heard from some service providers about young women getting pregnant because they did not get what they needed from their parents while growing up and they have made the assumption that a baby will fill their need to be loved.

The report of a study on teen mothers living in readaptation centres in Quebec describes the multiple problems and challenges faced by these young parents. Many pregnant girls were abandoned by their families, left without resources or supports, and forced to raise their children on their own. They suffered from a lack of affection and had difficulties accepting the presence of a child in their lives. These teenage mothers were also less likely to have finished high school or to have gone on to postsecondary education, and were more likely to be unemployed or to work in low-paying jobs (Association des centres d'accueil du Québec, 1991).

Poor or Undeveloped Parenting Skills

Participants in our qualitative study said many families on child welfare caseloads are there primarily because parents need help to develop better knowledge and skills related to childrearing. Discipline, interaction, and expectations are three areas of parenting that maltreating parents seem to have difficulty with.

The potential for physical and psychological abuse increases when parents rely on punitive discipline strategies such as yelling, threatening, slapping, pushing, and grabbing to control their children (Bousha & Twentyman, 1984; Disbrow, Doerr, & Caulfield, 1977; Loeber, Felton, & Reid, 1984; Pransky, 1991; Whipple & Webster-Stratton, 1991; Williamson et al., 1991) rather than reasoning and problem solving (Azar, Robinson, Hekimian, & Twentyman, 1984; Chilamkurti & Milner, 1993; Oldershaw, Walters, & Hall, 1986; Trickett & Kuczynski, 1986; Trickett & Susman, 1988). Several of the youths we spoke with said their parents or caregivers routinely used abusive disciplinary tactics:

> *[Parents] think you should take care of yourself, and if you do something bad, they want to beat the shit out of you. If you do something you shouldn't have done, they would rather beat you than sit down and tell you the right way or talk to you ... I didn't have anyone to talk to. I was always getting beat up on for something.*

However, some research has not been able to replicate findings that maltreating parents practise higher rates of negative or punitive discipline than nonmaltreating parents (Burgess & Conger, 1978; Evans, 1980; Starr, 1982; Susman, Trickett, Iannotti, Hollenbeck, & Zahn-Waxler, 1985; Webster-Stratton, 1985).

Parents reported to child welfare agencies for maltreatment have also been found to demonstrate low levels of competence in their interactions with their children (Wolfe, 1985) and to lack wellness in parenting. In studies with comparison groups, physically abusive parents demonstrated fewer positive behaviours toward their children. They were involved in less mutual engagement and they communicated, verbally and visually, less frequently with their children (Bousha & Twentyman, 1984; Browne & Saqi, 1988; Burgess & Conger, 1978; Dietrich, Starr, & Weisfield, 1983;

Disbrow et al., 1977; Frodi & Lamb, 1980). These parents displayed fewer responses to child initiation (Kavanagh, Youngblade, Reid, & Fagot, 1988) and were less likely to praise children for good behaviour or demonstrate affection (Bousha & Twentyman, 1984; Lahey, Conger, Atkeson, & Treiber, 1984; Schmidt & Eldridge, 1986; Susman et al., 1985). Neglectful mothers have also shown similar difficulties with parent–child interactions. Crittenden (1981, 1985) and Disbrow, Doerr, and Caulfield (1977) found such mothers to be indifferent to their children, neither engaging them nor responding to their attempts to initiate interaction. The neglectful mothers in Bousha and Twentyman's (1984) study showed fewer social interactions with their children than comparison and physically abusive mothers, as well as lower rates of verbal and nonverbal instructional behaviour. Compared with the physically abusive mothers, neglectful mothers showed similar rates of verbal and nonverbal affection and play behaviour but rates for both groups were significantly lower than for nonmaltreating comparison group mothers.

Observations of numerous investigators indicate that parents who mistreat their offspring often overestimate the rate at which their children should develop (Azar et al., 1984; Blumberg, 1974; Pransky, 1991; Steele & Pollack, 1968; Twentyman & Plotkin, 1982; Williamson et al., 1991; Wolfe, 1991, 1998). Theory (Elder, 1977) and research (Whiting & Whiting, 1975) suggest that this contributing factor may play more of a part in the etiology of maltreatment for children born to first-time parents or for the oldest of siblings since the development of responsive, informed, and nurturing parenting behaviour is considered to be partially attributed to practice in this role.

Limited Education

Several of our qualitative-study participants and a number of authors suggest limited parental education (e.g., high-school dropout, weak academic performance history, no schooling, illiteracy) is associated with rates of maltreatment (Belsky, 1993; Egeland & Brunnquell, 1979; MacMillan et al., 1997; Oxman-Martinez, 1993; Schorr, 1989; Zuravin & Grief, 1989). Parents with limited education may be less able to compete for employment and have fewer personal resources to deal with the stress associated with unfavourable socioeconomic conditions (Chamberland & Fortin, 1995; Fortin & Chamberland, 1995). These parents may also have limited problem-solving skills to assist them in childrearing (Wolfe, 1987). Though not overly strong, findings from the MacMillan et al. (1997) community survey of approximately 10,000 Ontario residents provide some support for including limited parental education as a contributing factor for child maltreatment. Male participants raised in families in which the primary wage-earning parent had not completed high school reported higher rates of physical abuse (35 per cent) than male respondents who were raised in families in which this parent had completed a secondary-school education (26.2 per cent).

Addictions

Alcohol and drug dependency are often cited as contributing factors for child maltreatment and other forms of family violence (Kantor & Straus, 1990; Kelleher, Chaffin, Hollenberg, & Fischer, 1994; Leonard & Jacob, 1988; Pan, Neidig, & O'Leary, 1994; Widom, 1992; Wolfe, 1998). In the opinion of an adviser in our qualitative study, alcohol and drug usage leads to *'neglect issues in the family where the parent is just not able or competent to supervise the children adequately.'* According to practitioners in Metropolitan Montreal, drug addiction appears to be a more common problem for neglectful mothers (Mayer-Renaud, 1990b). One group of youths we spoke with became incensed when the issue of parental alcohol abuse was raised, many of them blaming their involvement in child welfare on their parents' drinking. Even those youths who had been quiet during the rest of the focus group spoke up at this point:

It's got a lot to do with the parent too. It's the parents' fault, just the things that they do.

Like drink.

Yeah, drinking. And they lose their kids to alcohol because the alcohol is more important than their family is. They'd rather drink and leave their kids at home by themselves than to be home with them.

I don't think it's ever going to stop if people keep drinking and ruining their lives, and their kids are always going to need help from someone. It's the parents' fault. If they had a stable home and if drinking wasn't a big problem, then their kids wouldn't have to be somewhere, they could look after them themselves.

I went into care 'cause my mom was drinking too much.

I was one of the lucky ones. I had grandparents that were willing to take us 'cause my parents were drinking too much. (Youths)

However, the evidence for causal links between substance abuse and maltreatment is inconclusive (Epstein, 1977; MacMillan et al., 1995; Orme & Rimmer, 1981). In their 1985 community survey of family violence in the United States, Wolfner and Gelles (1993) found no significant differences in rates of abuse between participants who reported using alcohol and those who did not use alcohol. In this same survey, compared with non–drug users, drug users reported 20 per cent more minor family violence and 46 per cent more severe violence. One of the advisers we interviewed cautioned that *'while it is not in children's best interests to be raised in home where there is alcohol and drug abuse, people seem to put an overemphasis on that as having a strong relationship with abuse.'*

Although not discussed in the literature, a number of our qualitative-study participants talked about the negative impacts of gambling addictions on family functioning and their role in contributing to child maltreatment. This is a particular concern in provinces where gambling laws are already fairly open, and it may prove to be an issue in other jurisdictions where casinos and various forms of gambling are becoming more established.

Personality Factors

Gelles (1973) and Wolfe (1985) both concluded that research has failed to demonstrate a consistent relationship between caregivers' personality attributes or traits and child maltreatment. Only four of the nineteen different traits Gelles discerned through his review of the literature were reported in more than one study. Other researchers take a different position. They maintain that associations have been noted between personality and child maltreatment (Friedrich & Wheeler, 1982) and they include personality factors as a component in ecologically based approaches to understanding child maltreatment (Belsky, 1993; Emery & Laumann-Billings, 1998; Wolfe, 1998).

Research shows some maltreating parents experience elevated levels of emotional arousal and negative affect and demonstrate problems with aggression, hostility, and anger management in interactions with their children (Bauer & Twentyman, 1985; Egeland et al., 1980; Frodi & Lamb, 1980; Lyons-Ruth, Connell, Zoll, & Stahl, 1987; Milner, Halsey, & Fultz, 1995; Pianta et al., 1989; Susman et al., 1985; Trickett & Kuczynski, 1986; Wolfe, Fairbank, Kelly, & Bradlyn, 1983). In contrast, some maltreating parents, particularly neglectful parents, have been described in the literature as less nurturing (Egeland et al., 1988) and unresponsive toward their children (Crittenden, 1981, 1985; Disbrow et al., 1977). There is also evidence to suggest that some maltreating parents manifest an external locus of control, attributing responsibility for their abusive and neglectful behaviour to their children or to other mitigating factors such as the family's financial difficulties (Azar, 1986, 1989; Bradley & Peters, 1991; Bugental, Blue, & Lewis, 1990; Bugental, Mantyla, & Lewis, 1989; Larrance & Twentyman, 1983; Milner, 1993; Wolfe, 1987). Maltreatment is more than a function of whether parents project responsibility outward. Research has found this outcome is also connected to parents' heightened response and negative reactivity to stress (Chamberland & Fortin, 1995; Conseil permanent de la jeunesse, 1993; Mayer-Renaud, 1990b; Oxman-Martinez, 1993; Pianta et al., 1989; Wolfe, 1991).

Poor Mental Health

Early research attempted to demonstrate that child maltreatment was the result of mental illness or pathological personality on the part of abusive caregivers (Melnick & Hurley, 1969; Steele & Pollack, 1968). Subsequent evidence that the majority of parents who mistreat their children do not suffer from psychological disorders (Dubowitz & Newberger, 1989; Mayer-Renaud, 1990b; Wolfe, 1985) has led researchers to broaden their investigation of perpetrator typologies (Belsky, 1993; Emery & Laumann-Billings, 1998; MacMillan et al., 1995). However, while the psychological profile of the parent is no longer the central focus of etiological study regarding child maltreatment, it is still of interest as a contributing factor.

Results of a recent study involving 812 women in Quebec showed a connection between mothers' psychological distress or suicidal tendencies and violent behaviour directed at their children (Bouchard & Tessier, 1996). Parents who mistreat their children have also been found to suffer from low self-esteem (Altemeier, O'Connor, Vietze, Sandler, & Sherrod, 1982; Culp, Culp, Soulis, & Letts, 1989; Evans, 1980; Melnick & Hurley, 1969; Milner, 1988; Oates & Forrest, 1985; Pianta et al., 1989; Rosen, 1978; Shorkey & Armendariz, 1985), depression (Lahey et al., 1984; Mayer-Renaud, 1990b; Milner & Robertson, 1990; Oxman-Martinez, 1993; Whipple & Webster-Stratton, 1991; Zuravin, 1989), and anxiety (Aragona, 1983; Egeland et al., 1988; Lahey et al., 1984; Meier, 1985; Reid & Kavanagh, 1985).

Biological Predisposition

In their reviews of the literature, Belsky (1993) and Emery and Laumann-Billings (1998) highlight evidence suggesting a biological predisposition of parents to mistreat (some of) their offspring. 'A variety of studies indicate that humans ... are prone to respond to a variety of unpleasant stimuli, including stressful family interactions, with aggression (Berkowitz, 1983). From this perspective, frustration and anger in close family relationships is expected' (Emery & Laumann-Billings, 1998, p. 127). Although they note that the evidence is inconclusive, both sets of reviewers report an association between biological relatedness and maltreatment. As mentioned in an earlier section, children who are genetically unrelated to one of their parents have been found to be at greater risk for maltreatment than children who do share such a connection with both parents. According to an evolutionary perspective, step-children (Bagley & Thurston, 1998; Charbonneau & Oxman-Martinez, 1996; Daly & Wilson, 1985, 1994; Martin & Walters, 1982; Wilson & Daly, 1987), along with children in large families (Bouchard & Tessier, 1996; Creighton, 1985; MacMillan et al., 1995; Wolfe, 1998), children of unplanned pregnancies (Altemeier et al., 1982; Daly & Wilson, 1988; Egeland & Brunnquell, 1979; MacMillan et al., 1995; Murphy, Orkow, & Nicola, 1985; Schorr, 1989; Zuravin, 1988, 1989, 1991), and ill or disabled children (Chamberland et al., 1986; Bouchard, 1991; Schorr, 1989) are all at particular risk for maltreatment especially when the economic resources of a family are limited.

Vulnerabilities at the Infant/Child/Adolescent Level

At the top of the ecological and hierarchical structure we find the victims of maltreatment: infants, children, and adolescents. Research has also identified factors at this level that are associated with increased risk for abuse and neglect. As illustrated in Figure 2.5, in this section we review evidence pertaining to children's physical health, mental health and cognitive functioning, behaviour, gender, developmental stage, and cultural background.

Prematurity and Low Birth Weight
Premature birth and low birth weight (less than 2,500 grams) are conditions associated with extremes in maternal age (i.e., <20 and >45), multiple births, poor maternal diet and alcohol and drug abuse, maternal smoking during pregnancy, maternal health, and genetics (McIntyre, 1996; Ross et al., 1996a, 1996b; Steinhauer, 1998), the effects of which may be compounded by low income (Campaign 2000, 1997b; Ross et al.,

Context, Contributing Factors, and Consequences 95

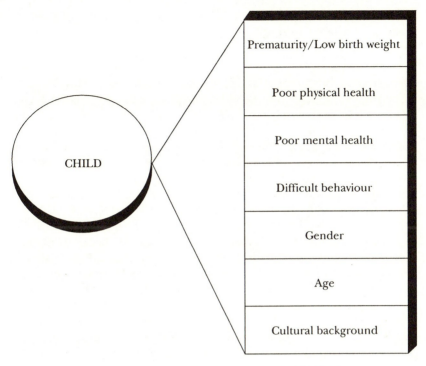

Figure 2.5   Child-Level Vulnerabilities Associated with Child Maltreatment

1996a; Wilkins, Sherman, & Best, 1991). The findings of a number of studies, including some prospective research, support the inclusion of prematurity and low birth weight as components in the etiology of child maltreatment (Chamberland et al., 1986; Elmer, 1977; Herrenkohl & Herrenkohl, 1979; Hunter et al., 1978; Klein & Stern, 1971; Lynch & Roberts, 1982; Oxman-Martinez, 1993; Starr, 1982).

There is, however, some disagreement in the field regarding premature and low-birth-weight infants and child maltreatment. According to some researchers these child characteristics may instead be antecedents of factors contributing to maltreatment such as a lack of a true attachment between parents and children due to parents' feelings of anxiety or rejection (Bourassa & Couture, 1986) and the fact that many premature or low-birth-weight babies are physically unattractive, and cry in a distressing, high-pitched manner (Frodi, 1981). Other researchers have concluded that there is no relationship between these two conditions and an outcome of child maltreatment (Corey, Miller, & Widlak, 1975; Egeland & Vaughn, 1981; Kotelchuck, 1982; Leventhal, 1981).

Poor Physical Health

According to some authors, children who are born handicapped (Chamberland et al., 1986) or who experience poor physical health in infancy and childhood (Bouchard, 1991; Schorr, 1989) are at greater risk for maltreatment. Other researchers concede that while physical health problems may contribute to maltreatment, they do so in the context of an interaction with additional factors such as a lack of attachment or other parental characteristics (Bourassa & Couture, 1986; Sherrod, O'Connor, Vietze, & Altemeier, 1984). One of the advisers in our qualitative study noted *'being a disabled child is a risk factor for child protection because it's harder for the parents to cope and those children can be rejected and seen as different.'* A mother we spoke with said she became involved with child welfare services after the birth of her disabled son. *'My son was born with spina bifida and I didn't know how to handle him because I was only 17.'* Considering the retrospective nature of much of the research, another group of authors contend there is insufficient evidence that physical disability precedes physical abuse and suggest that disability may instead be an outcome of maltreatment (MacMillan et al., 1995). In reference specifically to psychological maltreatment, Fortin and Chamberland (1995) note the absence of physical factors among precursors of this form of maltreatment.

Poor Mental Health and Cognitive Functioning

Though limited, there is some evidence to suggest that children who are mentally challenged or who demonstrate limited intellectual capacity are at greater risk for maltreatment (Bouchard, 1991), particularly for physical abuse (Chamberland et al., 1986). Though as Bourassa and Couture (1986) point out, the relationship between these child characteristics and maltreatment may have more to do with intervening variables such as a lack of attachment between parents and children with mental or cognitive difficulties.

Difficult Behaviour and Temperament

The role of child behaviour in provoking coercive or unresponsive parental behaviour has been considered within the literature. Some researchers have found that maltreatment, particularly in the form of physical abuse, can be precipitated by incidents of difficult child behaviour (Brooks, 1994; Herrenkohl, Herrenkhol, & Egolf, 1983; Wolfe, 1998). However, neglected children, as found in one study (Wolfe, 1985), do not seem to differ from comparison children in terms of their rates of aversive behaviour, though Belsky (1980) points out that these children may elicit neglect through a lethargic demeanour that does not demand attention from caregivers.

Other researchers (Belsky, 1993; MacMillan et al., 1995) question the role of child behaviour in the etiology of child maltreatment, arguing that while maltreated children have been found to exhibit more difficult behaviour than comparison children (Bousha & Twentyman, 1984; Lahey et al., 1984; Trickett & Kuczynski, 1986; Wolfe, 1985), this finding is not replicated when the observer is more objective than the maltreating parent (Mash, Johnston, & Kovitz, 1983; Reid, Kavanagh, & Baldwin, 1987; Whipple & Webster-Stratton, 1991). Further, due to the cross-sectional, nonexperimental, and retrospective design of many studies, it is difficult to determine whether child behaviour is really an antecedent of maltreatment or whether it is a consequence of abuse or poor parenting (Belsky, 1993; MacMillan et al., 1995).

Service providers and advisers voiced their concern about the increasing number of children born with fetal alcohol syndrome (FAS) and drug addictions who are coming into the child welfare system.

Gender

There is disparity in the literature regarding the influence of children's gender on maltreatment. While some researchers observe that violent behaviour against children does not appear to be associated with gender (Bouchard & Tessier, 1996), others have found relationships (MacMillan et al., 1997; Wolfner & Gelles, 1993). In their random sample of approximately 10,000 Ontario residents aged 15 years and over, MacMillan and her colleagues (1997) found a history of physical abuse was reported more often by male participants (31.2 per cent) than by female participants (21.1 per cent). Conversely, data from the Canadian Institute of Child Health (1994) suggest girls are twice as likely to experience physical abuse. Research on sexual abuse prevalence clearly shows girls are at higher risk for this form of maltreatment than boys (Badgley, 1984; Bagley, 1989; Bagley & Thurston, 1998; Canadian Institute of Child Health, 1994; Finkelhor, 1994a, 1994b; MacMillan et al., 1997). The most recent report containing provincial/territorial child welfare statistics (FPWG, 1998) does not yield conclusive evidence about relationships between gender and different forms of abuse, or even between gender and maltreatment in general. However, in jurisdictions that provided applicable figures (i.e., Nova Scotia, Northwest Territories), there is some indication that more girls are involved in cases of sexual abuse than boys.

Age

Our review of the relevant literature suggests that child maltreatment, at least that which is reported, does not occur at the same rate across developmental periods. There is however some divergence in the evidence. Several sources allege that younger children are victims more often of physical forms of abuse and neglect (Daro & McCurdy, 1990; Direction de la santé publique, 1996; MacMillan et al., 1995; Mayer-Renaud, 1990a; Straus et al., 1980), the effects of which may be magnified since they are physically more susceptible to injury (Lung & Daro, 1996). In addition to their physical vulnerabilities, Belsky (1993) submits that young children might be more at risk for maltreatment because: (1) they have more contact with and are more dependent on their caregivers, and (2) difficulties with emotion regulation during this early developmental phase (e.g., the 'terrible twos') may elicit coercive parental behaviour.

Egley (1991), on the other hand, found rates of physical abuse and neglect were highest for children between the ages of 3 and 8 years. A Quebec survey of 812 women found 48 per cent of children aged 3 to 17 were verbally or symbolically victimized at least once during the previous year and 31.4 per cent of children in this age range were victims of physical violence (27 per cent minor incidents; 4.4 per cent serious abuse). Rates for minor physical abuse declined as children got older (Bouchard & Tessier, 1996). In terms of sexual abuse, children over the age of 6 seem to be at higher risk (Tourigny, Péladeau, & Bouchard, 1993). Statistics from some Canadian jurisdictions suggest peak involvement with child welfare services occurs with school-age children and young adolescents, followed by infants and preschool children and older teens (FPWG, 1998).

While some evidence suggests the risk of maltreatment, particularly in the form of physical abuse, declines for children as they get older (American Association for Protecting Children, 1987; Benedict et al., 1985; Bouchard & Tessier, 1996; Creighton, 1985; Powers & Eckenrode, 1988), other studies reinforce the fact that preteen youth and adolescents are still at risk for maltreatment (Canadian Institute of Child Health, 1994; Trickett & Weinstein, 1991). In fact, a national incidence study in the United States found, when compared with younger children, adolescents demonstrated higher rates of physical abuse (National Center on Child Abuse and Neglect, 1988). Further, Bouchard and Tessier (1996) found that older children were more likely to suffer from psychological forms of maltreatment. The variation in these findings may be attributed to a variety of factors such as: (1) the fact that preschool and school-age children are more likely than infants or toddlers to come into contact with community resources (e.g., child care and elementary school) where maltreatment may be recognized and reported, and (2) recent recognition of adolescent maltreatment and increased reporting to child protection services by and on behalf of teens (Belsky, 1993).

Cultural Background

Aboriginal children and youth appear to be more at risk for maltreatment (Bouchard, 1991) and are disproportionately represented in child welfare statistics compared with non-Native children. It is estimated that Native children account for more than 20 per cent of children in substitute care in Canada (Hepworth, 1980; Ross & Shillington, 1989), even though they represent only 4 per cent of the child population (Statistics Canada, 1998). The most recent statistical report on child and family services from the Federal–Provincial Working Group (1998) also contains skewed data with respect to the status of Aboriginal children. In Alberta during the 1996–7 fiscal year, 37.5 per cent of the children considered to be in need of protection and 48.1 per cent of children in care were Aboriginal, though 1996 census information indicates only 4.6 per cent of Alberta's population was Aboriginal (Statistics Canada, 1998). Similarly, in the Yukon, 32.6 per cent of children deemed in need of protection and 51.9 per cent of children in care were Native, though only 20.1 per cent of the Yukon's population in 1996 was Aboriginal (Statistics Canada, 1998). Many advisers, particularly in the western parts of Canada, echoed concerns about the disproportionately high number of Aboriginal children on child welfare caseloads.

Vulnerabilities Related to Sexual Abuse

The etiology literature for sexual abuse is not well developed. However, researchers have noted that there seem to be different contributing factors for sexual abuse than for physical abuse and neglect. Our review of the literature and information provided by our qualitative-study participants point to a few contributing factors for sexual abuse at the child and the family/parental levels, as illustrated in Figure 2.6. Vulnerabilities at the broader levels of ecological analysis were not identified through this review, through they may in fact exist.

Girls tend to be more at risk for sexual abuse than boys (Badgley, 1984; Bagley & Thurston, 1998; Canadian Institute of Child Health, 1994; MacMillan et al., 1997), and children over the age of 6 are more at risk than younger children (Tourigny et al., 1993). Sexual abuse tends to be more common in families with marital conflict and family dysfunction, poor parent–child relationships, distant or punitive parents, in families with an absent maternal figure (MacMillan & Finkel, 1995), in cases of diminished supervision, and in 'families with disordered patterns of communication, tension of interchange, mental illness or alcoholism in a parent, and distorted roles, such as expecting a child to perform duties ... that are normally adult tasks' (Bagley & Thurston, 1998, pp. 142–3). Compared with biological fathers, step-fathers are five times more likely to perpetrate sexual abuse on a child in their household (Bagley & Thurston, 1998; MacMillan & Finkel, 1995). Unlike physical abuse and neglect, there is no evidence of relationships between sexual abuse and the level of parents' education or poverty. The bottom line, however, is that researchers have not been able to make reliable predictions of which children are at risk for sexual abuse and which adults are likely to perpetrate this form of maltreatment (MacMillan & Finkel, 1995). Our practitioner participants were equally unable to identify specific contributing factors for sexual abuse or to suggest a profile for people who sexually abuse children.

Protective and Promoting Mechanisms Associated with Resilience and Wellness

Although a great deal has been learned over the years, the study of child maltreatment is relatively new. Interest in researching this phenomenon began about four decades ago, around the time Kempe's seminal article was published in the *Journal of the American Medical Association* (Kempe, Silverman, Steele, Broegemueller, & Silver, 1962). Most efforts and investments in the study of abuse and neglect have been directed toward risks and problems in children and families. The study of resiliency and wellness is much newer. Only recently has research turned to the protective factors and empowering processes related to preventing maltreatment and promoting wellness (Anthony, 1987; Cohler, 1987; Dugan &

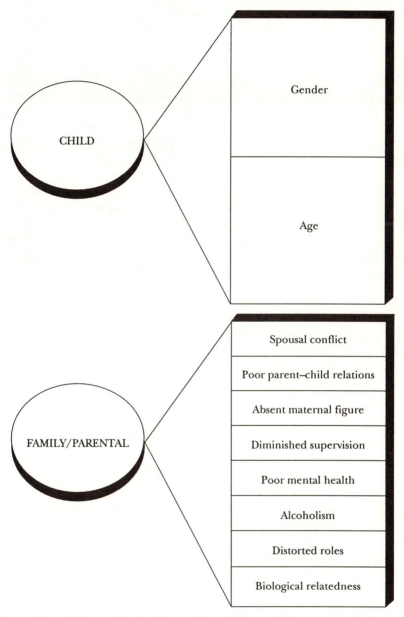

Figure 2.6　Child- and Family/Parental-Level Vulnerabilities Associated with Child Sexual Abuse

Coles, 1989; Farber & Egeland, 1987; Garmezy, 1987, 1991; Herrenkohl et al., 1994; Luthar & Zigler, 1991; Masten, Best, & Garmezy, 1990; Rutter, 1985, 1990; Simeonsson, 1995). But as one of the advisers in our study noted, *'the literature ... tells you precious little about the so-called protective factors.'* There are no comparable statistics that tell us how many families are faring well, nor have we extensively looked at the concepts of strength, capacity, and resilience in children, parents, families, and communities. Other than a few exemplary initiatives (e.g., Werner, Bierman, & French, 1971; Werner & Smith, 1977, 1982, 1992), there are not many longitudinal prospective studies that explore the pathways to wellness.

When they do appear in the literature, protective factors, capacities, and strengths are often defined as the absence of, or the opposite to, risks and vulnerabilities. However, we can't assume that there is an inverse relationship between the conditions that precipitate family disadvantage or dysfunction and the conditions that foster resilience and healthy family functioning (Cowen, 1996). Risk mechanisms do not operate in the same manner as protective mechanisms or promoting mechanisms (Garmezy, 1991; Rutter, 1990). Protection and promotion efforts should not be based solely on the premise that by creating and reinforcing conditions opposite to those that contribute to risk and vulnerability we will cultivate resilient and healthy families.

What does it take to protect children and families against identifiable risk factors? What does it take to promote wellness in families in general, in the absence of identifiable risk factors? Generally, protective and promoting mechanisms are conditions, circumstances, and characteristics that assist children, parents, families, organizations, and communities to deal effectively with challenges and stresses (Institute of Medicine, 1994; Rutter, 1985); yet a distinction should be made. As mentioned earlier in the chapter, protective and promoting mechanisms are enacted at different points along the promotion–prevention–protection continuum; the difference between these two concepts is in their relationship to risk. When we enact protective factors, we *counteract* risk. When we promote wellness, we *prevent* risk. It is expected that even well children and families will experience the challenges and stresses of normal living (e.g., death of a close family member, transition into adolescence, the formation and breaking of intimate ties). However, a stable and sufficient complement of promoting mechanisms surrounding these children and families will help them to successfully manoeuvre through situations and cope with or adapt to changing contexts without placing them at risk. At the same time, just as children and families may move in and out of states of vulnerability, they may also move in and out of states of wellness as the nature and availability of promoting mechanisms fluctuates with conditions like transitions to new developmental phases and changing social and economic contexts (Herrenkohl et al., 1994).

In her discussion of the need to shift attention in the field of prevention from a focus on risk to a focus on resilience, Chess (1989) puts forward several questions for consideration:

> What are the features of children who, in the presence of known potentials for disaster, have managed nevertheless to sustain healthy development? What are the features of the environment that have potentiated these healthy outcomes? What interactions and mutual influences of child and environment have provided protective and buffering effects? (p. 180)

These questions draw our attention to the fact that, just like maltreatment, resilience and, we would also argue, wellness are multidetermined phenomena influenced by interacting conditions occurring at the various ecological levels. However, similar to the literature on vulnerabilities, most of the focus has been on protective and promoting mechanisms occurring at a micro level within the family or the individual parent or child, though some researchers have attempted to move the discussion to broader ecological levels (e.g., Coulton et al., 1995; Garbarino & Kostelny, 1992; Garmezy, 1991; Vondra, 1990). Also consistent with the literature on vulnerability, scholars and researchers have engaged in debate over what should be included in inventories of protective and promoting mechanisms. We next present certain themes that appeared in the literature and in our discussions with key informants.

Protective/Promoting Mechanisms at the Societal Level

Although many researchers have pointed to the seriously destructive impacts of societal conditions on child and family functioning, few sources have focused on protective and promoting mechanisms occurring at the societal level. As illustrated in Figure 2.7, most of what is discussed in the literature has to do with the provision of supportive social policies, the promotion of strong social values, and growing social awareness about the need to intervene on behalf of children who are at risk of maltreatment.

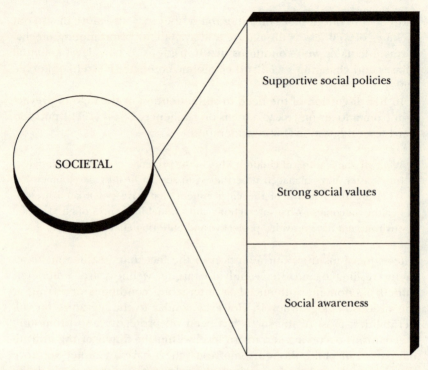

Figure 2.7 Societal-Level Protective/Promoting Mechanisms

Supportive Social Policies
The literature tells us that the presence of supportive social policies can play a significant role in promoting child and family wellness. Such policies include: universal health care, education, child care, and prenatal and postnatal supports; housing benefits, guaranteed minimum incomes, child allowances, and tax laws that support parents to care for their own children (as parents who get tax credits for child care); as well as job sharing, flextime, compressed work weeks, and parental leaves of absence after birth or adoption of a child. Policies that support these opportunities enhance the capacity of families to invest in the future of their children and have been shown to influence a range of positive outcomes for families and children (Belsky, 1993; Glossop, 1996; Guy, 1997; Schorr, 1997; Simmons, 1997; Steinhauer, 1998; Wekerle & Wolfe, 1993).

Canada does not have explicit family policies; rather, it has a series of independent federal and provincial/territorial policy initiatives that are aimed at improving some aspects of children's and families' well-being. Chapter 4 provides a detailed review of child and family policies in Canada, and provides comparative information on social policies in place in other OECD (Organization for Economic Co-operation and Development) countries. What seems clear from the review in Chapter 4 is that there are many examples of social policies that have been proven to support healthy, strong, and resilient children and families but that many of these policies tend to be present in countries other than Canada and/or they are implemented on targeted as opposed to universal levels.

Strong Social Values
As described in an earlier section, the acceptance and actualization of some societal values (e.g., tolerance of violence and physical punishment, extremes in family privacy, and traditional gender roles) have been associated with an increased risk of maltreatment. In Chapter 3 the authors address how values such as social justice in the provision of resources, support for strong community structures, and respect for human diversity can be applied and practised at a societal level for the purpose of promoting child and family wellness.

Social Awareness
Some authors question whether increasing rates of reported child maltreatment reflect not higher levels of abuse and neglect, but rather greater public awareness of maltreatment, a lower tolerance for what constitutes mistreatment, and the recognition that children need to be treated well to be healthy children and to grow up to be competent and contributing adults (Coulton et al., 1995; Emery & Laumann-Billings, 1998). With more eyes and ears open to how parents treat children and to the environments in which children live, with more reporting of risky situations, and with more offers to assist parents in childrearing or to correct inappropriate parenting behaviours, children stand a better chance of faring well.

Protective/Promoting Mechanisms at the Community Level

Imagine a community that is effective in supporting families to raise healthy and resilient children with promising futures. What are the characteristics of such a community? What features are necessary for

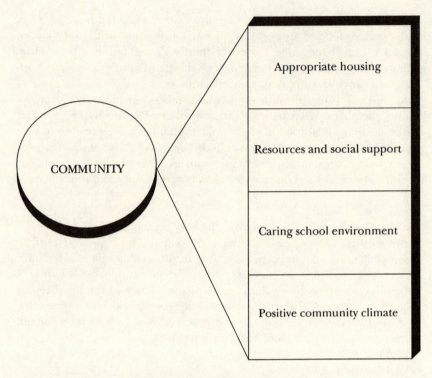

Figure 2.8 Community-Level Protective/Promoting Mechanisms

fostering positive outcomes? As for factors at the societal level, research has not focused extensively on community-level conditions that protect children and promote child and family wellness. However, blaming individuals for their misfortunes and trying to 'fix' them, criticizing single organizations for not effectively redressing problems such as maltreatment, and forsaking optimism in light of ominous social trends has minimal positive impact for children. Given these realizations, interest in exploring the potential of community-level contributions to supporting families is growing (e.g., Benson, 1997; Blyth & Roehlkepartian, 1993; Guy, 1997; Melton & Barry, 1994a; Schorr, 1997; Steinhauer, 1996). As illustrated in Figure 2.8, in this section we look at four important community conditions that are reported in the literature, and by our consultation participants, to protect children from maltreatment and to promote child and family wellness.

Appropriate Housing
An early study of child neglect among low-income families revealed that the treatment of children is influenced by a variety of conditions, including the quality of housing (Giovannoni & Billingsley, 1970). Based on extensive research on the housing situation of single-parent, mother-led families, Klodawsky and Spector (1988) report on a number of features of appropriate housing for families with children that are important in giving people a sense of control over their lives and are pivotal to efforts to maintain and enhance wellness. These aspects include: (1) accessibility to resources and services, schools, work, and child care; (2) the planning of neighbourhoods for children's physical play; (3) opportunities for mutual sharing and support; (4) privacy; and (5) opportunities for residents to participate in decisions that affect their housing.

Accessible and Available Resources and Social Supports
Access to networks of community resources, professional services, and social supports has been found to moderate the impacts of daily stress and to enhance physical and psychological wellness when stressors are not present (Egeland et al., 1988; Gottlieb, 1987; Mitchell, Billings, & Moos, 1982; Ratcliffe & Wallack, 1985/86; Schorr, 1989; Walsh, 1996; Wekerle & Wolfe, 1993). In addition, communities need to provide opportunities for the social engagement of children, that is, opportunities for children to participate and contribute (Baumrind, 1989).

As important as formal resources are to some families, what is suggested within the literature, and by our informants, is that informal networks of support may in fact play more central roles in preventing child maltreatment and promoting family wellness. Extended family, friends, neighbours, and religious, mutual aid, or other community group affiliations can provide people with practical assistance, social supports, and a basic sense of connectedness through which problems may be prevented and positive social contexts can be promoted (Guay, 1984; Korbin & Coulton, 1996; Walsh, 1996; Werner, 1989).

I think the biggest thing for families is having a support network around them. They are probably the healthiest families ... I think families can sometimes be more direct and more nurturing than any service provider could be because that link is always going to be there. (Service provider)

It's community supports, that they are connected with people, whether it's extended family or friends ... that really helps [families]. They aren't there alone, isolated with their children, their stress, and their frustration ... The families, I think, that do well are the ones that are connected in the community somehow. (Service provider)

In their study of child neglect among low-income families, Giovannoni and Billingsley (1970) found that treatment of children was influenced by various conditions including church attendance and the existence of a network of family and friends. Likewise, the presence of social supports was one of the significant factors Hunter and Kilstrom (1979) identified as differentiating parents who repeated the cycle of abuse with their own children from parents who did not. Residents of Cleveland, Ohio, who were interviewed by Korbin and Coulton (1996) said that they were more optimistic that child maltreatment in high-risk families could be effectively prevented through neighbour-to-neighbour intervention (79.3 per cent) than through government strategies (59.6 per cent). When asked what neighbours can do, one of the primary responses given by participants was that neighbours can intervene and help one another by talking supportively, confronting abusers, volunteering to care for children, and watching for incidents of maltreatment.

For children and youth, parents are not the only possible source of support. One of the most significant positive influences for children that is consistently found in the literature, and reported by our consultation participants, is the presence of at least one adult role model in a child's life, an extended family or community member, someone with whom the child can identify with, who will act as an advocate for him or her, who thinks he or she is wonderful, and who accepts him or her unconditionally (Ainsworth & Marvin, 1995; Brooks, 1994; Gottlieb, 1998; Grizenko & Pawliuk, 1994; Herrenkohl et al., 1994; Katz, 1994; Rutter, 1987; Segal, 1988; Simmons, 1997; Walsh, 1996; Werner, 1993; Werner & Smith, 1982). Just that one person, whether he or she is a grandparent, an aunt, an uncle, a neighbour, a teacher, a coach, a member of the clergy, or an older peer, can build a lot of resilience into a child's ability to cope.

Having a mentor. Having one person believe in them somewhere along the line in their life makes a huge difference. One person who stuck with them, who gave them hope that they were better than they were, or could be better than they were. This is an extremely strong protective factor. (Adviser)

The influence of a supportive adult role model has been demonstrated in a number of studies. Beardslee and Podorefsky (1988) studied eighteen youths 15 to 18 years old whose parents had serious psychiatric disorders. They found that the resilient adolescents had a relationship with a significant adult, family member, or friend. According to a group of researchers in Quebec (Cloutier, Champoux, Jacques, & Chamberland, 1994), the overall situation regarding family and social relationships for teenagers aged 15 to 19 is a positive one. Most of them are satisfied with their social life, have friends, people to confide in, and a large network of people to show them affection and are ready to help them whenever they need it. In their review of several studies (Beardslee & Podorefsky, 1988; Cowen, Wyman, Work, & Parker, 1990; Garmezy, 1991; Lipsitt, 1991; Norman & Turner, 1991; Rhodes & Brown, 1991), Zunz and her colleagues (1993) determined that one of the commonly cited protective factors for children is a relationship with a significant, positive adult role model who is not necessarily a parent. Longitudinal data from the Kauai, Hawaii, study showed that all of the resilient children had 'at least one person in their lives who accepted them unconditionally, regardless of temperamental idosyncracies, physical attractiveness, or intelligence' (Werner, 1993, p. 512). Finally, in their study of over 350,000 students in grades 6 through 12, in communities across the United States, the Search Institute found that the presence of at least three adult relationships, other than with parents, was a significant asset in the lives of young people (Benson, Galbraith, & Espeland, 1998a, 1998b). Forty-one per cent of the students surveyed said they knew other adults they could turn to for advice and support.

Caring School Environments
It could be argued that no one community institution plays a larger role in the lives of children and youth than school, a place where they spend a great amount of time, where they learn, and where they socialize. Many authors have described schools as primary structures that can provide children and youth with experiences that can enhance their self-esteem and develop intellectual and social competence, thereby strengthening resilience (Brooks, 1991, 1992, 1994; Curwin, 1992; Gribble et al., 1993; Guy, 1997; Rutter, 1980, 1985; Rutter, Maugham, Mortimore, & Ouston, 1979; Zunz et al., 1993). School environments in which children feel secure, respected, cared for, and challenged by high but achievable expectations can help reduce the likelihood or impact of adversity and foster academic and social success (Gribble et al., 1993; Rutter et al., 1979; Steinhauer, 1998). In their extensive research of students across the United States, the Search Institute found that a caring

school climate was an important asset in children's lives (Benson et al., 1998a, 1998b). Unfortunately, only 24 per cent of the young people surveyed thought this asset was present in their lives.

Positive Community Climate

> A sense of community is a sense of the common good. It is what animates collaborative action. It is shared involvement and responsibility. Community becomes a determinant of healthy development when it works to provide quality environments for children and families. (Guy, 1997, p. 105)

Whereas a lack of cohesion and negative community dynamics have been attributed to higher rates of child maltreatment and family stress, positive community climates have been associated with lower rates of abuse and neglect and an increased sense of belonging. In communities in which maltreatment rates were lower than expected ('West') (based on socioeconomic indicators) Garbarino and Kostelny (1992) found more positive community climates, as compared with communities with higher rates of abuse and neglect ('North'). Evidence of a stronger social fabric and better outcomes for children in these 'West' communities was demonstrated by a number of characteristics:

> In 'West,' people were eager to talk about their community. While they listed serious problems, most of them felt that their communities were poor but decent places to live. 'Poor but not hopeless' was the way one respondent described it ... In 'West,' there were more services available, the subjects knew more about what was available, and there were very strong formal and informal social support networks. The subjects in 'West' also reported strong political leadership from a local political leader ... There were 19 child maltreatment deaths reported for the four community areas we studied during the period 1984–1987. Eight of these deaths occurred in 'North,' a rate of 1 death for each 2,541 children. For 'West,' the rate was 1 death for each 5,571 children. (pp. 461, 463)

Protective/Promoting Mechanisms at the Family and Parental Level

> *The family is still society's place for children to grow up in. We haven't found, as a society, any alternative to a family that can provide such levels of nurturance.* (Service provider)

Context, Contributing Factors, and Consequences 111

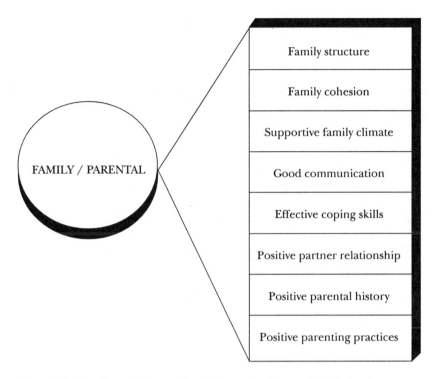

Figure 2.9 Family- and Parental-Level Protective/Promoting Mechanisms

The structural and functional aspects of families, the nature of interactions between family members, and parental characteristics can offer protective and promoting mechanisms that enable families to surmount crises, deal effectively with stress, and function well. In this section, as illustrated in Figure 2.9, we provide a review of the literature and present some findings from the qualitative study in relation to family- and parental-level factors that contribute to resilience and wellness.

Family Structure
The potential for children's healthy functioning and development is significantly affected by family structure. For example, evidence from the National Longitudinal Survey of Children and Youth (NLSCY) (Lipman, Offord, & Dooley, 1996) has shown that living in a family with two parents can give a child certain advantages that make favourable educa-

tional and social outcomes more likely. Compared with children from single-mother families, children from two-parent families demonstrated significantly lower rates of all the emotional and behavioural problems (e.g., hyperactivity, conduct disorder, emotional disorder) and academic and social difficulties (e.g., repetition of a grade, current school problems, social impairment) examined in the NLSCY research. Furthermore, in terms of economic assuredness, two-parent families are better off than lone-mother families (Lipman et al., 1996).

Family Cohesion
Based on her review of assessment models addressing mutidimensional processes that distinguish well-functioning families from dysfunctional families, Walsh (1996) concluded that cohesion is one of the essential processes promoting basic family functioning and family wellness. One of the service providers we spoke with also talked about the protective nature of family cohesion:

> *Certainly there are families that are raised in the middle of all the worst conditions you can have. If there has been in that family a history of family togetherness, and tightness, and everybody supports everybody, and everybody is cared about [then they can do well].*

Three main dimensions of family cohesion that act as protective and promoting mechanisms can be discerned in the literature and in the data gathered for our qualitative study: (1) attachment and strong family bonds, (2) shared beliefs and culture, and (3) shared activities and family time.

According to Steinhauer (1998), 'probably the strongest single familial factor protecting the potential for resilience during [the period between birth to toddler years] is anything that supports the establishment of a secure attachment to a primary caregiver' (p. 57). As a protective factor, a secure attachment with at least one parental figure has been found to counteract the risks associated with family conflict (Rutter, 1979) and child maltreatment (Hunter & Kilstrom, 1979). Cowen and his colleagues (1990) have also shown that attachment to a primary caregiver can buffer the effects of significant life stresses for children. In their study of demographically matched fourth through sixth graders in Rochester, New York, who had experienced four or more significant life stresses and who participated in the Rochester Child Resilience Project, Cowen et al. (1990) found that, unlike the children who were affected by stress, the stress-resilient children did not experience early separation from their primary caregiver, and/or they received ample child care including the involvement of a father figure.

For children, a pathway to wellness begins, as many authors have argued (Cowen, 1991, 1994, 1996; Guy, 1997; Schorr, 1989; Wekerle & Wolfe, 1993), with the formation of secure attachments and positive relationships with their parents and caregivers. The premise is that individuals who have made secure attachments to adults early in life will fare well in later life. In Quebec, a survey of students aged 15 to 19 showed that those youth who had a positive relationship with their mother and father, and who had a strong feeling of family belonging, felt better about themselves and were less anxious, more at ease in school, and more optimistic about their future (Cloutier et al., 1994).

Shared beliefs among family members can foster a sense of connection and a spirit of cooperation, and instil confidence, all of which are vital in coping with adversity and daily challenges (Walsh, 1996). The way in which crisis situations are interpreted and explained shapes how families respond and is critical for family resilience (Antonovsky & Sourani, 1988; Carter & McGoldrick, 1989; Reiss, 1981; Reiss & Oliveri, 1980; Rolland, 1994). According to Beavers and Hampson (1990), families with shared spiritual values and a strong sense of cultural heritage can find broader meaning and purpose in their lives. This theme is particularly relevant to the discussion in Chapter 8, which addresses family wellness in Aboriginal communities.

Some of our qualitative-study participants also addressed the importance of shared beliefs and cultural connections as a protective and promoting mechanism. Based on their experiences, many of the youth we spoke with said that, in situations in which children must be placed into care, it is extremely important that they be placed with families who share, or support, the same beliefs and culture as the children.

Family members spending time together and participating in shared activities is another important dimension of family cohesion. In the Search Institute's study (Benson et al., 1998a, 1998b) 'family time – being together, interacting, getting serious, having fun' (Benson et al., 1998b, p. 160) was found to be an important asset for children and youth, and 50 per cent of the students surveyed said they had this asset in their lives. McCoy (1996) looked at healthy family functioning in nontraditional shared-home families (twenty families including 52 adults and 26 children) in California, Texas, and Florida. After housing and a shared sense of commitment and responsibility, the strength most often mentioned by these families was shared activities. The participants' concepts of healthy family life included time for members to do things together. Sharing leisure time and fostering family table time and conversation are also two of the fifteen traits of a healthy family identified in Curran's (1983) research.

The importance of parents and children spending time together as a protective and promoting factor was a prominent theme in the data we gathered for the qualitative study:

[It is important] to talk to your family every day. Don't just come home and don't talk to anyone. You need interaction.

Family time.

You should all go out together once a month or every so often. The whole family should go out together.

Set a time to have fun and play.

Spend time together. (Youths)

Positive and Supportive Family Climate
One determinant that has been found to contribute to strong and resilient children is a positive and supportive family climate (Cloutier et al., 1994; Gribble et al., 1993; Rutter, 1985; Schorr, 1989; Simmons, 1997; Werner, 1989, 1993). These home environments tend to be characterized by warmth, affection, respect, trust, emotional support, involvement, and explicit yet reasonable structures and limits. Evidence from the National Longitudinal Survey of Children and Youth (1996, 1998) seems to suggest that caring and supportive family climates can significantly reduce the likelihood of difficulties, even for children whose history and circumstances would otherwise put them at risk. A key family strength identified by the nontraditional shared-home families interviewed by McCoy (1996) was *help and support.* Included in their lists of traits of healthy families, McCoy's participants mentioned, first and foremost, *family members help and support one another,* followed by a number of other qualities including *family members validate and affirm one another,* and *family members show respect and consideration to one another.*

Feeling loved and supported within their family was a primary asset identified for children and youth who participated in the Search Institute's study (Benson et al., 1998a, 1998b). Sixty-four per cent of the students surveyed thought they had this asset in their lives. Another important feature of a supportive family climate is parents' involvement in children's education and social activities. Having parents actively involved in helping their children succeed in school, talking about school, helping with homework, and attending school events was an asset identified in the Search Institute research, although only 29 per cent of the students surveyed thought this asset was present in their lives (Benson et al., 1998a, 1998b). Another asset identified by the Search Institute that is related to supportive family climates is the presence of family boundaries, that is, clear rules and reasonable and logical consequences. Forty-three per cent of the participating students said their families had defined boundaries, and in their review of other research, the Search Institute found that teens actually want more family boundaries (Benson et al., 1998b).

Participants in our qualitative study also had a lot to say about what they thought were qualities of caring and supportive family environments and the importance of these factors for preventing problems and promoting wellness:

Acceptance. Love. Belonging. (Parent)

Love ... Encouragement from your family. (Youth)

Love. Affection. Caring. Commitment. (Service provider)

Respect is a big factor ... I think if [parents or caregivers] show they respect you as much as you respect them, then conversation, or anything, would be much easier. (Youth)

Good Communication

Positive and open communication between parents and children has been found to be essential in facilitating family functioning and enhancing the well-being of family members (McCoy, 1996; Walsh, 1993). The Search Institute describes positive family communication as a key asset in helping children and youth to succeed: 'Kids turn to their parents for advice and support. They have frequent, in-depth conversations with each other on a variety of topics. Parents are approachable and available when kids want to talk' (Benson et al., 1998a, p. 33). However, in their study the Search Institute found that only 26 per cent of the children and youth who were surveyed had this asset in their lives. Many of our informants also talked about the need for good communication within the family and how this can improve family functioning:

> *[It is important] that parents offer an environment that the child is able to speak when they want to, to have their views, and not feel threatened.* (Youth)

> *Good communication, to be able to talk things out without yelling and screaming. That's a big thing in our house. If you have a problem, not to keep it in, to sit down and talk about it and everybody in the house try to work it out.* (Parent)

Effective Coping and Problem-Solving Skills

A protective factor for many families is the strength to cope, adapt, and endure in spite of recurrent crises or chronic stress (McCubbin, McCubbin, & Thompson, 1992). Participants in McCoy's (1996) study identified modelling of problem-solving skills by adults and the flexibility to change family processes to reflect current societal realities as two key traits of a healthy family. Likewise, in her review of the research, Walsh (1993) found that two of the features distinguishing well-functioning families from dysfunctional families were their effective use of problem-solving skills and their flexibility. Although most of the discussions centred on the lack of coping and problem-solving skills in families at risk, some of our consultation participants mentioned that the ability to deal constructively with conflict and change is an important protective factor for families.

Positive Partner Relationship

A positive and supportive relationship between partners can foster the capacity for resilience and wellness in all family members (Belsky, 1993; Egeland et al., 1987, 1988; Steinhauer, 1998).

> One of the central hypotheses of ecologic theory is that the capacity of the parent–child relationship to function effectively as a context for development depends on the nature of other relationships that the parent may have. The parent–child relationship is enhanced as a context for development to the extent that each of these other relationships involves mutual positive feelings and that the other partners are supportive of the parent–child relationship. (Bronfenbrenner, 1979, p. 77)

A number of research studies have demonstrated protective influences of supportive intimate relationships or marital support on the quality of mothers' parenting, in particular for mothers who are considered to be at risk of mistreating their children (Belsky, Youngblade, & Pensky, 1990; Brown & Harris, 1978; Caliso & Milner, 1992; Crockenberg, 1987; Parker & Hazdi-Pavlovic, 1984; Quinton, Rutter, & Liddle, 1984; Rutter & Quinton, 1984). There is also some evidence to suggest that harmony between partners can have a promoting influence, moderating negative parenting practices in the case of mothers not considered to be at risk (Belsky et al., 1990).

Parental History of Positive Relationship with Parent(s)
While much more research has been done that examines the relationship between growing up with an abusive and/or neglectful parent and later maltreatment of one's own children, there is some evidence that suggests a close relationship with at least one supportive, nonmaltreating parent can act as a protective factor against perpetuating the cycle of harm. Although limited to the time frame of the studies, two different research teams (Egeland et al., 1987; Hunter et al., 1978) conducting prospective studies with new mothers found that one of the factors that differentiated parents with childhood histories of abuse and/or neglect who did not mistreat their own children from parents with the same background who did mistreat their children was the experience of a positive relationship with one of their parents while growing up.

Positive Parenting Practices
Whereas a lack of, or ineffective, parenting skills has been associated with poorer outcomes for children, positive parenting practices such as consistency, appropriate discipline, respect for children's individuality, emotional support, encouragement of exploration and learning, and an understanding of, and responsiveness to, children's developmental needs, have been found to act as protective influences in the lives of children at risk (Guy, 1997; Laurendeau, Gagnon, Desjardins, Perreault, & Kischuk, 1991; Rutter, 1989; Wekerle & Wolfe, 1993; Werner & Smith, 1982). Using Cycle 1 (1994–5) data from the National Longitudinal Survey of Children and Youth, Landy and Tam (1996) found that even for children whose family context included at least four risk factors (e.g., lone-parent, low income, low social support, prenatal problem), high-quality parenting made a significant difference in their developmental prospects (Rutter, 1979).

> Children in at-risk situations who enjoyed positive parenting practices achieved scores [on measures of helping behaviour, motor and social

118   Section I: Context

development, language development, getting along with peers, and satisfaction with primary caregiver relationships] within the average range for children in Canada. Sometimes their outcomes even surpassed those of children who were living in more favourable sociodemographic conditions but who were exposed to less positive parenting practices or to more hostile/ineffective parenting. (Landy & Tam, 1996, p. 109)

Protective/Promoting Mechanisms at the Infant, Child, and Adolescent Level

Although they may be shaped and influenced by forces existing at broader levels of the ecological hierarchy, infants, children, and adolescents also have inherent and acquired qualities and capacities that can help them to cope with life's challenges and to optimize opportunities for healthy functioning (Steinhauer, 1998). Research has identified factors at this level that are associated with increased potential for resilience and wellness. As illustrated in Figure 2.10, in this final section we review evidence pertaining to children's behaviour, intellectual functioning, problem-solving abilities, social competence, and resilient perspective, which includes the dimensions of self-esteem and a sense of optimism.

Positive Behaviour and Temperament
Much of the research has focused on the contributions of children's negative behaviour in the etiology of child maltreatment and other adverse outcomes. However, positive, prosocial behaviour has been identified by some researchers as an important protective characteristic that fosters the development of children's self-esteem and coping styles. Based on a measure of prosocial behaviour, data from the National Longitudinal Survey 'strongly suggests that most children [ages 10 and 11] adopted a caring attitude toward others. Less than 10 per cent had scores under 10, indicating that they had more of an "antisocial" attitude to others than the vast majority of children this age' (Ross et al., 1996b, p. 27). Similarly, children who have a positive temperament – that is, they are happy and easy-going – have been found to elicit more positive responses from their caregivers and to have enhanced problem-solving skills and coping styles (Grizenko & Pawliuk, 1994; Quinton & Rutter, 1988; Walsh, 1996).

Intelligence
There is some research that suggests average to above-average intelli-

Context, Contributing Factors, and Consequences 119

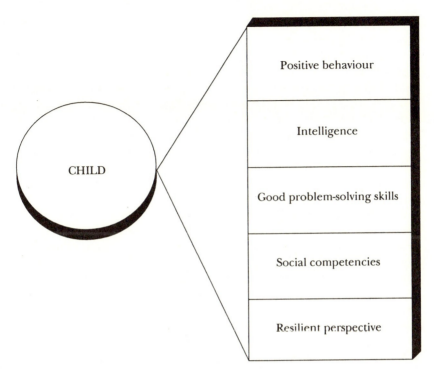

Figure 2.10 Child-Level Protective/Promoting Mechanisms

gence can have a protective effect for high-risk children (Kandel et al., 1988; Masten et al., 1988; Werner, 1989; Werner & Smith, 1982). In their longitudinal study of children from infancy through late adolescence, Herrenkohl and her colleagues (1994) found at least average intelligence to be connected with academic success for abused and neglected children. By the final phase of the study, of the 23 participants from child welfare families who were considered to be high-functioning children, all 14 of the adolescents who had graduated or were still in high school had average or above-average IQ. Although not conclusive, the results of Radke-Yarrow and Sherman's (1990) study that focused, in part, on protective factors discriminating between children 'who seem to be surviving multirisk conditions of genetic and environmental origins' (p. 100) and children who did not seem to be surviving, suggest that above-average intelligence was an important characteristic of 'survivors.'

Despite these positive findings, some studies have not found intelligence to play a significant role in counteracting risk and preventing problems (White, Moffitt, & Silva, 1989). In fact, there is other research that suggests, for some children, high levels of intelligence can actually act as a vulnerability. Based on a study of ninth grade students in an inner-city school, Luthar (1991) found that while intelligence was found to be a protective factor in low-stress situations, it became more of a vulnerability as the levels of stress increased for the youth. The explanation given for this finding is that more intelligent children tend to have an increased sensitivity to high-stress environments, which in turn can exacerbate their susceptibility to risks and reduce the otherwise protective nature of this trait.

Good Problem-Solving Skills
Researchers have found that resilient children often have advanced problem-solving abilities (Garmezy, 1991; Steinhauer, Santa-Barbara, & Skinner, 1984; Werner & Smith, 1982). Compared with children who were considered to be stress-affected, the stress-resilient children identified in the study conducted by Cowen et al. (1990) were those children who had effective problem-solving skills and who had developed personal coping strategies. Likewise, the resilient adolescents who participated in Beardslee and Podorefsky's (1988) research were characterized as having good problem-solving abilities.

Social Competence
Strong, resourceful, and resilient children have been described in the literature as demonstrating high levels of social competence (e.g., good interpersonal skills, assertiveness, sense of humour) (Brooks, 1994; Garmezy, 1991; Luthar, 1991; Masten, 1982; Simmons, 1997; Werner, 1989; Werner & Smith, 1982). These personal skills help children and youth make positive choices, establish relationships, and develop into independent and capable adults. Five of the twenty internal assets identified in the Search Institute's research were related to social competence: (1) planning and decision making; (2) interpersonal skills such as empathy, sensitivity, and the ability to make friends and maintain these relationships; (3) cultural competence – accepting and appreciating diversity in culture, race, and ethnic backgrounds; (4) resistance skills that help kids withstand peer pressure and avoid dangerous situations; and (5) peaceful conflict-resolution skills (Benson et al., 1998a, 1998b). However, only about one-third to two-fifths of the students surveyed thought these assets were present in their lives.

Resilient Perspective

One factor that stands out in the literature as having a protective and promoting influence on children and youth is a resilient perspective. Our review of the literature suggests there are four key dimensions of a resilient perspective: (reasonable) internal locus of control, high self-esteem, sense of meaning and purpose, and optimism.

Having an internal locus of control – that is, believing that one can control or influence events in one's life – has been linked to resilience in children and youth and to positive developmental outcomes (Kobasa, 1985; Luthar, 1991; Moran & Eckenrode, 1992; Murphy & Moriarty, 1976). In the longitudinal study of stress resistance in the children of Kauai, Hawaii, researchers found that the resilient children strongly believed that they had personal power over their circumstances, rather than relinquishing themselves to unpredictable environments (Werner, 1989; Werner & Smith, 1982). The stress-resilient children in Cowen, Wyman, Work, and Parker's (1990) study also demonstrated a realistic sense of what they could and could not control in their environments.

According to some authors, one of the most significant personal traits characterizing resilient children is high self-esteem (Brooks, 1994; Moran & Eckenrode, 1992; Walsh, 1996). In explaining the importance of self-esteem as a cornerstone of resilience, Rutter (1985) wrote: 'A sense of self-esteem and self-efficacy makes successful coping more likely while a sense of helplessness increases the likelihood that one adversity will lead to another' (p. 603). In their study of primary-school children who had experienced four or more significant life stresses, Cowen et al. (1990) found that the stress-resilient children demonstrated higher levels of self-esteem and feelings of self-worth than the children who were considered to be stress-affected. Self-esteem was also identified as an asset for children and youth through the Search Institute research, although only 47 per cent of the students surveyed said they felt good about themselves.

In his review of the literature, Steinhauer (1998) found that having a sense of purpose and believing that their life has meaning are important personal characteristics that act as a protective factor for some children. Similarly, the Search Institute listed having a sense of purpose as one of the internal assets of successful children and youth (Benson et al., 1998a, 1998b).

Optimism, hope, and confidence in the future are key features of a resilient perspective and are key determinants of children's healthy development (Brooks, 1994; Guy, 1997; Murphy, 1987). Reflecting on the longitudinal study conducted in Kauai, Werner (1993) wrote: 'The central component in the lives of the resilient individuals ... that contributed to their effective coping in adulthood appeared to be a feeling of confidence that the odds can be surmounted' (p. 512). Researchers with the Centres Jeunesse in Quebec (Cloutier et al., 1994) report that even though teens living in youth centres experience major problems, their hopes for the future are well defined. Most of them feel they have good chances of leading successful adult lives and believe it will be easy to earn a living and find a job that they like later on. The idea of starting a family is very important to them; they intend to have a stable relationship and have children, and they believe they can be good parents. One of the advisers we spoke with in the qualitative study said an important protective factor for high-risk children and youth is *'having a sense that there was something ... something as nebulous as hope that things could be better in the future, a belief that they could do something that would make things better for themselves.'*

FINAL THOUGHTS

While it is true that we do not know everything there is to know about the etiology of child maltreatment or about promoting wellness, we do know a lot. Like Snow in the public health example cited in the introduction of this chapter, we have valuable information at hand to help us continue the tasks of removing the pump handle from the well of children's suffering and tapping the springs of wellness. We should take Caplan's (1964) advice and work toward these goals even without absolute knowledge. This is not to say that researchers should stop gathering information on the context and etiologies of maltreatment, resilience, and wellness; rather, we need to put what we do know to use. What we know, from this and similar reviews (e.g., Belsky, 1993; Emery & Laumann-Billings, 1998), is that child maltreatment and family wellness are determined by multiple, interacting vulnerabilities and protective and promoting mechanisms occurring at various levels of the ecological hierarchy. The implications of this knowledge are incorporated in the discussion in Chapter 9.

The following chapters in this volume focus on vision and values, and on interventions that attempt to prevent child maltreatment and promote family wellness. As you explore these other sections of the volume, we invite you to consider a number of questions. Are discussions of vulnerabilities and interventions targeting high-risk groups balanced with discussions of wellness and universal strategies for promotion? Are issues of diversity in families (e.g., in structure, cultural background, economic status, opportunities) adequately addressed? Do interventions respond to the range of families' needs, abilities, and contexts? Are community- and societal-level structures considered and/or involved in efforts to prevent maltreatment and promote wellness?

CHAPTER THREE

Vision and Values for Child and Family Wellness

Isaac Prilleltensky, Maire-Claire Laurendeau, Claire Chamberland, and Leslea Peirson

INTRODUCTION: MORE THAN JUST WORDS

Historically, children have suffered because they have no social movement to advance their cause. Unlike other groups claiming their legitimate rights, such as seniors, labour, women, and ethnic minorities, children are political orphans. Consider the following examples: Austria, 1940s, doctors kill children with disabilities to examine their brains (Silvers & Hagler, 1997); Brazil, 1980s, off-duty police execute street children because they are considered a public nuisance (Scheper-Hughes & Hoffman, 1997); United States, 1990, the U.S. Advisory Board on Child Abuse and Neglect declares society's lack of response to the crisis of child abuse a national moral disaster (Melton & Barry, 1994a); Canada, 1989, the House of Commons passes a resolution which seeks 'to achieve the goal of eliminating poverty among Canadian children by the year 2000'; Canada, 1997, the number of children living in poverty reaches almost a million and a half, 500,000 more than in 1989 and an increase of 58 per cent (Campaign 2000, 1997b). Children's rights are violated because children have no vote and no power.

Clearly we need to invest effort and resources to prevent these tragedies from occurring, in the present and in the future. Adults invest in pension plans to avert poverty in old age. Employees contribute to unemployment insurance to guard against harsh economic times. Even the government contributes to these funds because it recognizes that citizens need protection. But this protection is afforded only to those who vote: adults and seniors. Children have no vote and no comparable social fund.

I don't know if we really value children as we should, and the importance of these early childhood years to children. We don't put any resources into children. (Adviser)

The United Nations Convention on the Rights of the Child, or UNCRC (United Nations, 1991), stipulates that children's rights depend on our ability to provide them with protection, health care, education, and adequate resources. But to fulfil these goals we need more than just words; we need to translate values into action. This chapter is concerned with this crucial act of translation.

In this chapter we present a series of values that can guide our concerted efforts to promote family wellness and prevent child maltreatment. Without a lucid set of values we cannot be clear about our objectives. We need to be sure that we are promoting sound values for children and for society at large. This chapter explores a series of questions dealing with vision and values. The first section discusses the historical context of values. The second part offers basic values for the promotion of family wellness, while the third section shows how we can use these values in policies and programs. The fourth part specifies roles for citizens and professionals concerned with child and family wellness. The last part of the chapter presents a practical checklist all of us can use in our dealings with children and families. The checklist is designed to evaluate how well we are implementing the values we believe in when we work with children and families.

Vision and Values in Historical Context

Vision is an ideal state of affairs. In this chapter we are concerned with a vision for children and families in which children grow up with opportunities to develop their potential and in which families resolve conflicts peacefully. Our vision is of a state in which child abuse and neglect no longer occur.

If a vision is the end point of a journey, then values are the roads and vehicles to get there. Values are the principles that guide our actions; they inform our personal, professional, and civic behaviour (Schwartz, 1994). Values bring us closer to the vision. However, we do not espouse values like caring, compassion, and democracy just because they lead toward a vision, but also because they have merit on their own (Kane, 1994; Kekes, 1993). In fact, 'values may be defined as enduring prescriptive or proscriptive beliefs that a specific mode of conduct (instrumental value) or end state of existence (terminal value) is preferred to another mode of conduct or end state' (Mayton, Ball-Rokeach, & Loges, 1994, p. 3). Briefly stated, values are 'humanly caused benefits that human beings provide to others ... By way of illustration, we may say that love and justice are moral goods' (Kekes, 1993, p. 44).

Some key ideals for children include a state of complete health, respect for children's rights, and family harmony and cohesion. Central values to guide practice include collaboration and participation of families in children's services, respect for diversity, and distributive justice. These are some of the values we wish to uphold in research, practice, and policy – values that are intrinsically good and extrinsically beneficial. But throughout history societies have emphasized different values for children and families. As Levine and Levine (1992) have demonstrated, during conservative times there is an emphasis on individualistic values such as personal responsibility, whereas during progressive times there is an emphasis on collective values such as social justice and community support. Conservatives expect that individuals will help themselves out of negative situations, whereas progressives claim that improved health and welfare will derive from social changes. They claim that there are two primary modes of help, the situational and the intrapsychic (see also Prilleltensky, 1994a). The situational is the preferred mode of help during periods of social reform; the intrapsychic, on the other hand, flourishes during periods of political conservatism.

> The situational mode assumes that people are basically 'good' but have been exposed to poor conditions and therefore have not reached their full potential. Improving their situation thus should improve their psychological states. Improving people's situations may mean creating new services or new community facilities or modifying existing community agencies to better serve human needs. On the other hand, the intrapsychic mode assumes that people are in difficulty not because of the situation but because of personal weaknesses and failings; it assumes that the situation is more or less irrelevant, that what must be changed is not the circumstance but the person. (Levine & Levine, 1992, p. 8)

Although the intrapsychic and the situational modes of helping coexist, the dominant ideology of the times determines which one receives more attention. During conservative times, like ours, intrapsychic help is favoured because it supports the 'status quo by placing the onus of both the problem and the change on the mind and emotions of the individual' (Levine & Levine, 1992, p. 8). Our position is that we need to reach a balance between the various modes of helping, and that if one modality is being ignored, then we should try to restore its importance. If the current political environment works against social change and places excessive demands on personal change, we need to address this imbalance by reminding ourselves that both helping modalities are useful.

Across societies and across different historical periods we see a range of values, from individualistic to collective values, that parallel the modes of helping identified by the Levines. Societies with highly individualistic values expect people to solve their own problems. Societies that are high on collectivism expect more government interventions. There are many signs that North American societies are currently in a period of conservatism that promotes individualistic values and intrapsychic interventions (Novick, 1994). These attitudes lead to a blame-the-victim mentality. We witness this in particular in the way welfare recipients are treated. There is a pervasive discourse that contributes to the 'continued demonization of welfare recipients' (Wilson, 1996, p. 193). People receiving state support are 'at the receiving end of continuous moral condemnation' (Leonard, 1997, p. 52). This attitude simplifies the complexity of child abuse.

> Child neglect and abuse are attributed solely to the failure of parents rather than being recognized as emanating from a complicated web of factors including the powerlessness of women, the lack of status and adequate rewards for care giving roles, and the effect of other social policies that condemn one-sixth of Canada's children to live in poverty. (Wharf, 1993, p. 211)

Political, economic, and societal factors challenge intrapsychic notions that if you have a problem it is always your fault and your sole responsibility to fix it (Allahar & Côté, 1998). It is crucial not to jump to conclusions and blame the victim when dealing with delicate matters of social policy affecting disadvantaged children and families (Kamerman, 1996a, 1996b; Novick, 1994; Woodward, 1996). We should be careful not to reproduce stereotypical assumptions about disadvantaged people (Docherty, 1997). One of our advisers pointed out:

> *There is diminished appreciation and respect for difficult circumstances. There is an increased sense to attribute personal failing to the individual who is in that at-risk family, and that is what allows us to rationalize cutbacks to various services and*

supports and probably leads to a heightened degree of isolation on the part of these families at risk.

A mother who used protective services commented:

> We were always the ones that were wrong. Just because we have problems doesn't mean that we are always wrong ... We always had to accept being confronted and criticized.

The prevailing ethos in society is that personal conviction is sufficient to overcome personal misfortune. This idea emanates from our belief in a supreme self, an inner force capable of coping with adverse consequences, whatever these might be. Such belief is rooted in rugged individualism, in survival of the fittest, and in competition, values that characterize Canadian and North American society (Allahar & Côté, 1998). We can choose to accept these values as immutable, as part of our unquestioned common sense, or we can choose to question their usefulness for child and family wellness. We, the authors of this chapter, chose the latter. We chose not to accept the prevailing values of individualism at face value. We believe that we need a more balanced approach to social interventions, one that pays as much attention to social factors as to individual factors.

Today, most interventions cater to individual goals. We seek to promote autonomy and to enhance personal wellness. We endeavour to foster healthy lifestyles. No doubt these are worthy causes. But the problem is not investing in individuals. Rather, the problem lies in neglecting situational strategies of change. Balancing personal with collective interventions is crucial because strong communities are vital in supporting private citizens to achieve their goals. A poor medical system blocks the attainment of health, a prerequisite for autonomous functioning. A stagnant educational system prevents us from reaching scholastic excellence. High-quality public institutions help citizens to pursue their private goals in life (Etzioni, 1996). Two advisers, key informants in our research, commented on the need to go beyond the individual level in helping children and families at risk:

> Not all problems are amenable to solutions at the family level, the local or community level. We do have to address structural issues in our society and economy. We may not be able to resolve these issues, but we should recognize them for what they are. Our response has to be on a society-wide basis. Hence we need a nation-wide health program and policies.

Unless we reflect on our own beliefs with respect to personal and situational interventions, we risk promoting contradictory notions that really do not make sense (see also Chapter 4). For instance, while some policies dictate that we invest in prevention, others order the elimination of social programs designed to do just that (Campaign 2000, 1996; Gadd, 1996; Goodwin, 1997; Mackie, 1998). Child welfare and mental health workers know that child abuse derives from family dynamics as well as from social and economic factors, yet most of their interventions focus on the mother and leave systemic forces largely untouched (Febbraro, 1994; Pelton, 1994). As an adviser put it

> *If you are a single parent, already have two children, have less than a grade 9 education, live in an underprivileged neighbourhood where living conditions are unhealthy, then you will receive services. We don't target the fact that you live in an underprivileged neighbourhood where living conditions are unhealthy ... we don't target that. We target people who present all of those risk factors. According to this way of thinking, people are made to carry problems that aren't theirs and for which neither the individual nor the field practitioners have solutions ... We have to stop believing that we can solve problems with individual interventions and start targeting collective risk factors.*

This is why we need time to reflect on comprehensive, value-based solutions. Such an undertaking begins with vision and values.

Sources of Values

The vision and values that guide this chapter derive from three main sources: (1) moral and political philosophy, (2) grounded and lived experience, and (3) practical philosophy. The synergy of these three sources provides a firm basis for the promotion of family wellness.

Moral and political philosophers debate what constitutes the good life, what makes a good society, and how we get there. They explain the merits and drawbacks of diverse tenets, the conditions under which one value may supersede another, potential contradictions among competing conceptions of the good life, and the like. These philosophers spend considerable time trying to formulate coherent visions of the good society. But convincing philosophical positions are insufficient to create social policy that meets the needs of families and children. We should remember that the process of value implementation is arduous at best. Conflict among values, conflicts among people, and personal conflicts all pose serious challenges to value-driven practice. Subjective motives, organizational dynamics, interpersonal disagreements, power differences, political climate all have a bearing on our ability to enact values and policies. There is not a ready-made formula to obtain 'value-neat' interventions or 'value-perfect' conduct. It would be a mistake to pretend that just because we have clarity with respect to vision and values people will readily embrace them (Wharf & McKenzie, 1998).

What good is it to have an internally consistent set of values that cannot be applied? The corollary of this question is that *moral philosophy is not enough*. Any attempt to implement values has to take into account the context of application. Otherwise, we can end up with notions that are theoretically flawless but practically useless. This is a serious risk, for as Bowden (1997) contends, in grand theories of ethics, 'attention to the messy contingencies of concrete situations is set aside in favour of the theoretical project of organizing moral knowledge under general principles and rules of conduct that exhibit the exactness and formality of mathematics' (p. 3) but that forget about people's struggles, aspirations, conflicts, and frustrations. Bowden made us fully aware of the situatedness of values. When dealing with values, she said, it is important not to forget the 'dynamic complexity and diversity of specific situations, and the particular needs, desires, intellectual and emotional habits of the persons participating in them' (Bowden, 1997, p. 3).

Moral philosophy and grounded experience are complementary. Philosophical theories have to be validated with lived experience. Qualitative studies of people's struggles, aspirations, conflicts, and frustrations provide a picture of the context of applied ethics. Researchers ask parents and children what they want from each other, what they wish for each other. In our work we considered this line of questioning essential. This is why we conducted an extensive consultation process with a variety of stakeholders. We asked service planners, providers, and consumers of child welfare services what their vision of healthy and happy families was, and what values they deemed essential for child and family wellness. Our project strove to integrate philosophical reflection with grounded and lived experience (see Chapter 1 for a description of our methodology).

To translate the visions of philosophers and families we need practice, we need practical philosophers. Practical philosophers are the people who translate moral values and grounded input into action. These are the professionals, paraprofessionals, volunteers, and citizens who combine philosophical values with human experience to improve the welfare of children. These citizens bridge the gap between the abstract notions of philosophers and the lived experiences of families. They promote values for children and youth. They try to adapt ideals of the good society to specific contexts. In that sense, all of us who work on behalf of children are practical philosophers. We are philosophers of a kind because we have values that guide our work, and we are practical workers because we strive to apply what we know to improve family wellness. Front-line workers, child advocates, government officials, program managers, academics, policymakers, and politicians concerned with the welfare of children should be practical philosophers. None of us can afford to advance legislation, policies, programs, or interventions that discount families' voices.

The act of combining values with lived experience often starts with mission statements and policy papers. Task forces exploring child issues usually engage in practical philosophy. A paradigmatic example of practical philosophy in child wellness is the United Nations Convention on the Rights of the Child (UNCRC, United Nations, 1991). The Convention is an amalgam of universal values and needs required for the promotion of healthy development. In the remainder of this chapter we engage in very practical philosophy. We articulate basic values and concrete tasks for family wellness.

BASIC VALUES FOR THE PROMOTION OF CHILD AND FAMILY WELLNESS

Values are guidelines for thinking and acting in ways that benefit others. By following certain values we confer benefits on individuals and communities (Kekes, 1993). In our case, we are interested in personal values that promote child and family wellness and in collective values that promote community and societal wellness. In this section we offer criteria for the selection of values; explain what each value means; discuss the connection between values, needs, and wellness; present a value-based vision for child and family wellness; and show how values can influence policies and programs.

Choice and Definition of Values

The values we choose should meet the following criteria:

1. Values should be complementary and not contradictory.
2. Values should be comprehensive enough to cover the essential needs of families.

3. Values should sustain the holistic development of children.
4. Values should inform processes and actions.
5. Values should point to desirable outcomes or end states.

The complementarity of values and goals is illustrated in Health Canada's (1996b) national goals for healthy child and youth development:

> No single goal stands in isolation from the others. Each is interrelated, and builds on and reinforces the others. The impact of achieving these goals will be cumulative in children's lives. For example, babies who get a good start in life will be more likely to have a healthy infancy and early childhood. Early childhood experiences have an important influence on learning and coping later in life. Families who are supported in their communities and receive the help they need with parenting will be more likely to raise healthy children. (p. 8)

Based on the criteria of complementarity and holistic development, we can construct a framework of values for the promotion of family wellness. Our framework relies on the UNCRC and on extensive consultations we conducted with stakeholders of the child welfare system, primarily across Canada, but in other countries as well, including Belgium, Cuba, Denmark, England, Ghana, Holland, Israel, Sweden, and the United States. The composition of our values is informed by other sources as well; these deal with the lived experience of families and with statements of practical philosophy produced by policymakers, child advocates, practitioners, and academics.

In this section we present the findings of the qualitative study on vision and values within the context of the literature and the UNCRC. Upon examination of the categories emerging from the data, we realized that they fit quite well with the main tenets of the UNCRC. As a result, we decided to integrate the findings of the qualitative study with the values contained in the Convention. Although our data supported all the principles stated in the Convention very well, our participants placed more emphasis on certain values than did the accord. This was the case with the values of social justice and support for strong communities. Consequently, we go beyond the UNCRC in our presentation of key values. In order to present a holistic picture, we complement the discussion with relevant literature.

We rely on the UNCRC because it is a comprehensive document of what children all over the world need. The Convention, which was ten years in the making, is a major accomplishment. Writers of the UNCRC managed to incorporate input from diverse cultures into one manifesto of children's rights. The legitimacy of the document is demonstrated in the weight it carries in nations across the globe. Governments use it to measure progress in health, education, and social development; while professionals adopt it for promoting children's mental health, legal entitlements, and basic securities (Avard, 1995; Goulet, 1995; Health Canada, 1996b; Levesque, 1996; Limber & Wilcox, 1996).

The Convention is a convincing tool for advancing children's wellness, and it has been invoked as a mission statement in various fields of practice. In his presidential address at the 10th International Congress on Child Abuse and Neglect, Krugman (1995) stated that 'the United Nations Convention on the Rights of the Child provides an excellent infrastructure for the development of ... child protection policy' (p. 275). Melton (1991) has drawn on the Convention's implications for the field of child abuse and neglect, while Prilleltensky (1994b) has shown that its values can be translated into prescriptions for children's mental health. In this chapter, we illustrate how it can be applied to wellness in general.

A content analysis of our data reveals the presence of seven main values compatible with the UNCRC. These are briefly presented in Table 3.1. As the table shows, the values can be classified into three categories: (1) values for personal wellness (caring and protection of health, education and personal development, and self-determination); (2) values for collective wellness (social justice in provision of resources, support for strong community structures); and (3) values for relational wellness (respect for human diversity, collaboration and respect for the community). These categories reflect well the need for balance between individual and social goods, as well as the necessity of having partnership values for people to co-exist peacefully. Values for personal wellness have been the primary concern of liberal philosophers, whereas the issue of collective wellness has been championed by communitarian thinkers. Our findings show that there is a dialectic between these two types of values, and that one kind cannot exist without the other. What is often missed in the literature and nicely captured in our findings is the absolute necessity to have the third kind of values, partnership values, which ensure the pursuit of private goals in harmony with the objectives of others. Relational values point to the necessity to have democratic processes whereby citizens negotiate their differences in amicable ways. Neither personal nor collective wellness can exist without mechanisms for bridging the gap between conflicting interests.

TABLE 3.1
Basic Values for the Promotion of Child and Family Wellness

	Definitions	Needs Addressed
Values for Personal Wellness		
Caring and protection of health	Expressing care, empathy, and concern for the physical and emotional health of children	Empathy, nurturance, emotional and physical well-being
Education and personal development	Providing children and adults opportunities for education and personal growth	Cognitive, emotional, physical, and spiritual growth; autonomy
Self-determination	Promoting the ability of children and adults to pursue chosen goals without undue frustration and in consideration of other people's needs	Mastery, control, self-efficacy, voice, choice
Values for Collective Wellness		
Social justice in the provision of resources	Promoting the fair and equitable allocation of bargaining powers, obligations, and resources in society	Economic security, shelter, clothing, nutrition, access to vital health and social services
Support for strong community structures	Promoting vital community structures that facilitate the pursuit of personal and communal goals	Sense of community, cohesion, formal support
Values for Relational Wellness		
Respect for human diversity	Promoting respect and appreciation for diverse social identities and for people's ability to define themselves	Identity, dignity, self-respect, self-esteem, acceptance
Collaboration and respect for the community	Fostering partnerships whereby children and adults can have meaningful input into decisions affecting their lives	Solidarity, mutuality, peace, involvement, participation, belonging

Informed by grounded input and practical philosophy, our findings alleviate the tension between polarized liberal and communitarian philosophies. Liberal philosophers, who emphasize autonomy, self-determination, and the rights of the individual, are reluctant to promote too much state intervention in the lives of families because they are afraid that governments will end up dictating to private citizens how to run their lives. Communitarian thinkers, on the other hand, claim that we have gone too far in meeting the needs of individuals and that we have sacrificed our social obligations in the pursuit of private satisfaction (Etzioni, 1993, 1996; Lerner, 1996; Mulhall & Swift, 1996; Sandel, 1996; Shapiro, 1995). Communitarian philosophers argue that for citizens to fulfil their dreams they need one another. A vision of mutual help and commitment to the welfare of the collective benefits the individual, for the attainment of one's aims depends on collaboration with others.

Each position poses risks as well as benefits (Kymlicka, 1990; Sandel, 1984). Liberals deserve recognition for promoting the liberation of individuals from oppressive social norms and regulations. This school of thought advances the right of the citizen to pursue his or her dreams without undue interference from others. However, in excess, the pursuit of private goals can lead to unmitigated individualism, selfishness, and materialism (Allahar & Côté, 1998; Leonard, 1997). 'When people pursue private goals, the risk is that they may never acquire an ennobling sense of a purpose beyond the self' (Damon, 1995, p. 66). A creed that sanctions personal advancement above all can easily deteriorate, as has happened in our society, into rampant individualism. 'Looking out for number one' translates into fierce competition and disregard for the welfare of others (Kohn, 1986). Autonomy, voice, and choice have to be closely monitored, lest they turn into a selfish preoccupation with one's own power. This risk is very apparent in market societies in which state intervention is minimal.

Communitarian thinking is based on the assumption that without cooperation individuals cannot achieve their private goals. Like liberals, they endorse the fulfilment of personal goals and the liberation from oppressive social forces; but unlike liberals, they think that we should strengthen social and communal institutions because personal happiness is not possible without them (Etzioni, 1996; Haste, 1996). Liberals freed us from coercive institutions, but along the way they weakened even those institutions we really need to promote not only the good society, but also the good life (O'Neill, 1994; Sandel, 1996). Hence, communitarian thinking strives to restore a balance between the pursuit of private and collective aims. We know that strong communities provide a better environment for children than weak communities. Essential public programs, sufficiently funded and effectively managed, can have long-lasting and beneficial effects for all children (Schorr, 1989, 1997).

But communitarian thinking is not without risks either. Collectivist societies are known for expecting great sacrifices from their members for the benefit of the public good. Citizens feel coerced to do things they do not like and they experience state intervention as oppressive. The Israeli kibbutz, for instance, used to expect a great deal of personal sacrifice from its members. While this demand was reasonable in the early stages of the kibbutz, when communal effort was essential to the survival of the collective, it became too onerous in later years. Members denounced expectations for heavy personal concessions and started to request more personal freedoms. This realization led to more liberal policies regarding employment, family practices, and opportunities for personal development.

The values we uncovered in our research call for a balance between personal and collective wellness. These two sets of values have to be mediated by relational and partnership values. As we saw in Chapter 1, relational or partnership wellness can be defined as value-based relationships that strive to advance caring, compassion, community, health, self-determination, participation, power sharing, human diversity, and social justice for everyone concerned. In the case of child and family wellness, the personal values of parents have to be in harmony with the personal values of children. The personal values of any one individual have to be in harmony with the collective values of society. Personal values have to respect collective values of health and safety. Killing others while driving intoxicated or affecting a baby's health while smoking in his or her presence are examples of personal acts that interfere with collective well-being. In turn, community norms can deprive individuals of basic values. This is the case when the state censors personal freedoms or does not support poor children. These potential conflicts require the presence of partnership values to mediate the conflicting interests of individuals or groups.

Personal and collective values need to be harmonized, for they are complementary and interdependent; they cannot be pursued in isolation. The interdependence of self-determination and social justice provides a good example. Without affording people sufficient resources to further their choices, self-determination is quite meaningless. Partnership values strive to meet the needs of individuals with the needs of the community as a whole.

Shared values between partners are perhaps the most important factor for partnerships (Gray, 1989; Labonté, 1993). This is how social workers and families gain mutual trust. This is how policymakers and child advocates work toward the same goals (Wharf & McKenzie, 1998). The values of the partnership should resonate with the values of the individual partners (Curtis & Hodge, 1994). Building shared values and principles requires extensive prenegotiation work. Commitment to consensually agreed upon goals is important for facilitating a successful partnership (Boudreau, 1991; Butterfoss, Goodman, & Wandersman, 1993; Wharf & McKenzie, 1998). When there is substantial value incongruence between the partners, a successful partnership is unlikely. Researchers, community agencies, and disadvantaged people often have divergent perspectives and priorities. Strong interpersonal relationships, skills in collaboration, and respectful dialogue facilitate partnerships (Putnam, 1996). This is the essence of what Habermas (1990) calls communicative ethics. Key aspects of collaborative processes and respectful dialogue include clear and open communication, open-mindedness and sensitivity, on-going learning, mutual respect, caring, and, ultimately, trust (Nelson, Prilleltensky, & MacGillivary, in press). Our findings affirm the positive contributions of liberal thinking to personal values, of communitarian thinking to collective values, and of communicative ethics to partnership and relational values. The definitions provided in Table 3.1 combine the precepts embodied in the United Nations Convention with the grounded input obtained in our own investigation. The table further shows the needs addressed by each value. As wellness is defined as a state of affairs where certain needs are met, the table shows the role of values in promoting personal, collective, and relational needs. The values depicted in Table 3.1 address the needs reviewed in Chapter 2.

The UNCRC appropriately embeds the wellness of the child within the wellness of the family. The dual commitment to the child and the family unit is clearly spelled out. The preamble states that

> the family, as the fundamental group of society and the natural environment for the growth and well-being of all its members and particularly children, should be afforded the necessary protection and assistance so that it can fully assume its responsibilities within the community.

The next paragraph discerns the role of family environment in children's wellness. It proclaims that 'for the full and harmonious development of his or her personality,' a child 'should grow up in a family environment, in an atmosphere of happiness, love and understanding.' This was echoed by an adviser who told us that *'children should be with their families, wherever possible, provided the environment is safe for them.'*

The Convention is clear in its support of a family wellness model (Melton, 1996; Weisz & Tomkins, 1996). The child's future is linked to a prosperous family climate. This should be a climate in which children's needs are met by caring adults who possess sufficient resources to provide opportunities for educational and personal development. The child should grow up in an atmosphere of appreciation for his or her views, an atmosphere that respects diversity of opinions and that fosters the peaceful resolution of conflict. The family is portrayed as a setting where collaboration and personal responsibility should be nurtured. The Convention's approach to child development is clearly ecological in nature; it binds the health of the child to the well-being of caregivers whose welfare, in turn, depends on the level of social progress.

After a careful examination of the Convention's articles and our own data, we believe that the seven principles presented below provide a reliable synopsis of the accord and of the voices of our participants. We combine in our presentation text from the Convention, quotes from our participants, as well as pertinent literature.

Values for Personal Wellness

Caring and the Protection of Health

Children have evolving capacities. For these capacities to mature, children need warmth, secure attachments, protection, and adequate health care. Infants' vulnerability and inability to care for themselves underscore the importance of providing them with the basic necessities of life in an affirming environment. Given the vulnerable condition of the newborn, it is imperative that efforts be directed to nurture the infant and to prevent long-lasting harm. This is why programs seek to establish secure bonds between the immediate caregiver and the infant. Advice, support, and tangible help are offered in order to ensure a healthy start for children (Broussard, 1997; Caruso Whitney, 1997; Olds, 1997a, 1997b).

The heavy responsibility of parents or alternate caregivers for creating a positive environment cannot be denied. Although this is a responsibility that falls directly on caregivers, the state also has an obligation to attend to children, not only in the form of protection from harm, but in securing sufficient material resources as well. The Convention is explicit in its emphasis on parental and state responsibility in pursuing children's best interests. The role of the state in protection is clearly articulated in Article 19 of the UNCRC: 'States Parties shall take appropriate legislative, administrative, social and educational measures to protect the child from all forms of physical or mental violence, injury or abuse, neglect or negligent treatment, maltreatment or exploitation, including sexual abuse.'

Achieving health is another explicit concern of the Convention. Article 24 asserts 'the right of the child to the enjoyment of the highest attainable standard of health.' Looking after children in nurturing ways, protecting them from harm, and procuring the best available health care are essential values of the Convention, values that are eloquently articulated by children. Hample (1979), in a book entitled *Hugging, Hitting and Other Family Matters: Children Talk about Their Families*, reports children's desire for care and protection. The following passages, written by two children (hence the spelling errors), reflect their wishes:

> We need families to be taken care of. To be loved by. To get breckfast. And dress you. To put you to bed. And all that. And thats parents.

> I would not like to be all alone or not be healthy. This world really needs familys so much. I feel sorry for the children who are not cared for and have no family. (no page numbers provided)

In another book, entitled *Children's Reflections on Family Life* (Moore et al., 1996), a 15-year-old had this to say about caring:

> Interviewer: ... Tell me all the words that come into your head, when you think of the word 'family.'
> Meena: Close, loving, supportive, listening.
> Interviewer: ... What is it like to live in a family?
> Meena: It's nice to have people always around you. To know people care, people want you around, lots of love and bonding. They are there when we need each other. (p. 107)

Participants in our own study stressed how vital it is for children to enjoy a bright start in life, a beginning marked by affective devotion and diligent caring. This is what youth consumers of the child welfare system had to say in our focus groups:

> *I was a very unhappy child. I was really quiet, depressed ... Anything I heard from my mother was toward discipline instead of any love and affection.*

> *It's supposed to be understood that parents will love you no matter what. But they don't say that, and you need to hear it.*

Opportunities for Education and Personal Development

Article 28 of the Convention enshrines the 'right of the child to education' by asking signatory States to 'make primary education compulsory and available free to all,' while Article 29 proclaims that 'the education of the child shall be directed to the development of the child's personality, talents and mental and physical abilities to their fullest potential.'

Next to the provision of basic material and emotional essentials such as food, clothing, shelter, and love, the Convention recognizes the crucial role that education plays in the lives of children. According to the charter, wellness entails the formation and unfolding of spiritual, artistic, technical, and scholastic aptitudes. Securing autonomy and mastery in life requires the acquisition of intellectual, manual, and social skills. It is up to the state and the adults in charge of the child to furnish meaningful opportunities for personal and educational development.

Self-efficacy, a key component of a healthy personality, derives from coping successfully with demands that are calibrated to the child's level of abilities. These challenging experiences are to be provided in the home, at school, and in the community. The sense of mastery derived from engaging competently in meaningful tasks is of inestimable value; it promotes a child's sense of worth and prepares him or her for work and for civic and family life (Damon, 1995).

Children's Rights and Self-Determination

Rights and self-determination are linked because they pertain to the preservation of dignity, voice, and choice. In essence, this value upholds the integrity of the child; it recognizes that children are largely powerless and that they require special moral and legal protection. Historically, children have been silenced – their needs marginalized, their wishes neglected. The UNCRC procures a voice for children. Article 12.1 declares that

> States Parties shall assure to the child who is capable of forming his or her

own views the right to express those views freely in all matters affecting the child, the views of the child being given due weight in accordance with the age and maturity of the child.

Health Canada (1996b) identified the meaningful involvement of children and youth in decisions affecting their health as a national priority:

> Young people want to have a say about the things they see as important. Too often, the adult world dismisses their point of view. Their voices need to be heard, particularly on issues that affect their own well-being. Young people should be enlisted to help shape policies and programs that affect them. (p. 15)

Children appreciate signs of trust. They value opportunities to exercise their autonomy. This is how an 11-year-old girl expressed it:

> My parents, each in their own ways, let me be independent. I get responsibilities that I can handle, and I'm very thankful ... And they listen to me – it helps so much that they listen. They let me make decisions for myself, even if they think it's not a good idea. What's more, they're very patient – they help, but they don't push. Most important, they respect me. (Delisle, 1984, p. 96)

The obligation to listen to children and to parents did not escape our key informants.

Values for Collective Wellness

Social Justice in the Provision of Resources

While based on the spirit of the Convention, this value goes beyond the text of the accord. We decided to include the value of social justice because the Convention talks mainly about supplying resources, not distributing them according to principles of justice. Authors make a distinction between retributive, procedural, and distributive justice (Tyler, Boeckmann, Smith, & Huo, 1997). We concentrate here on the last kind, that is, on the fair and equitable allocation of bargaining powers, resources, and obligations in society. We cannot afford to neglect social and distributive justice. To do so would be to turn a blind eye to all we know about the risks of social disadvantage (Canadian Council on Social

Development, 1997; Pelton, 1994; Zill, Moore, Wolpow Smith, Stief, & Coiro, 1995).

The fulfilment of a vision of wellness is predicated on the synergy of essential values. Health, protection, and nurturance depend on the psychological state of the caregiver; on proper nutrition, shelter, and clothing; and on access to medical facilities, regardless of ability to pay. Opportunities for growth and educational advancement depend on access to educational institutions. Self-determination depends on the value we place on human diversity and on our ability to collaborate on mutually acceptable goals. Such collaboration means sharing the social resources we have in a manner that is just and fair.

Children need resources to enjoy good health, to reach their potential, and to nurture their identity. This is why the pursuit of social justice is so decisive. Without it, the prospects of a bright future for all children remains elusive. Two service providers emphasized the importance of meeting basic needs before families can devote energies to the development of children's potential:

Families need enough material resources to allow people to get along with their developmental tasks, so energies are devoted to that end rather than to acquiring the things you need to survive, like food, housing, basic needs.

I think you have to look at a really basic level initially ... I think finances within the family and a kind of safety net within the family, you need to address those issues first ... If you have a family that is really stretched financially, they don't have enough food, they can hardly clothe their kids, they are worried about accommodation, and they don't have any way of really improving their situation; that creates incredible stress within the family. And you know that somehow that is going to be displaced on the children. I think that is the place you have to start. That somehow there needs to be the resources and safety nets in place to address those kinds of issues. And going to any other level without making sure those issues are covered, to me is kind of senseless.

'States Parties recognize the right of *every* child to a standard of living adequate for the child's physical, mental, spiritual, moral and social development' (UNCRC, Article 27.1, emphasis added). The same Article insists that countries 'shall take appropriate measures to assist parents and others responsible for the child to implement this right and shall in case of need provide material assistance and support programmes, particularly with regard to nutrition, clothing, and housing' (Article 29.3).

Justice may be defined as the fair and equitable allocation of bargaining powers, resources, and obligations in society. For children to get their fair share they require strong-willed advocates. If we are serious about promoting family wellness, we should devote as much energy to the value of social justice as we do to other values. Perhaps we should devote even more energies to this value than to others, for in the current social context it is the one that is most neglected. Challenging structures of inequality is a primordial task in the promotion of child welfare; it should be a pillar of our covenant with children. Unfortunately, we live in a culture that promotes acquiescence and compliance as opposed to resistance to an unjust status quo (Tappan & Brown, 1996).

Support for Strong Community Structures

Although the Convention makes reference to the indispensable role of publicly funded agencies, we believe that more emphasis could have been placed on supporting these vital institutions. Neoconservative and neoliberal thinkers alike insist on reducing the functions of the state in helping disadvantaged children and families. Publicly funded institutions perform a critical role in preventing disempowering chain reactions for people at risk. But their virtue goes beyond supporting the needy, for these organizations enhance the health and welfare of the population at large. Strong community structures afford us clean water, sewage systems, child care (in countries where it is publicly funded), recreational opportunities, libraries, unemployment insurance, pension plans, free primary and secondary education, access to health care, and many other social goods. Taking these structures for granted is not a choice. There are fierce forces wishing to privatize these services (Novick, 1994).

Promoting strong community structures for children and families should be a guiding value for family wellness. Preserving worthy institutions and creating new ones should be part of our vision for children. If child tax benefits rescue families from falling below the poverty line, then we should maintain them. If children's services prevent abuse from occurring, then we should praise them. If innovative programs reduce the incidence of abuse and neglect, then we should implement them. But these initiatives require active support of community structures. Implicit or tacit endorsement is not sufficient, for there are those who are committed to dismantling what we have (O'Neill, 1994).

An appreciation for what community structures do should be part of our social values. A good society cannot flourish in the absence of supporting institutions. Private dreams require public playgrounds. Personal and common aspirations thrive on material and spiritual grounds. Community structures afford tangible aid and a sense of community that are essential for nourishing the physical and the psychological (O'Neill, 1994; Schorr, 1997). Without instruments of public help, those at risk slide further down toward despair.

At a time when in North America 'privileged sectors of market society conceive of contracting out from the provision of civic staples by the purchase of marketized services' and when 'forces abound that weaken governments, communities, and families, that put at high risk children and single mothers, [and] that aggravate racism, sexism, and ageism' (O'Neill, 1994, p. 35), we should support structures that work for the common good.

Parents, advisers, and service providers in our research commented on the loss of vital community resources:

There are not always the things available that are required to address the problems. Particularly with cutbacks. There has been a drastic change recently regarding what's available in communities, particularly in terms of people being able to meet their basic needs. (Service provider)

I miss community health. Let me give you an example. If we had young kids in care and if the plan was to return them to parents, then during the visits they would come and teach these parents, these young moms. And right now I have one case and I called and they said we don't do things like that anymore. And I have gone to six different places in the community for somebody to come in and teach this mom. (Service provider)

Values for Relational Wellness

Respect for Human Diversity

Children embody diverse cultural and personal characteristics that define who they are. Appreciation of their distinct qualities helps to consolidate their identities, while disapproval or condemnation lessens their dignity. From a moral point of view, recognition of and respect for children's unique identities are ethical obligations equivalent to according them the right for self-determination (Taylor, 1992). Respect for a person's identity is, according to Canadian philosopher Charles Taylor (1992), 'not just a courtesy we owe people. It is a vital human need' (p. 26). When we affirm people's identities, we help them affirm themselves. When we respect their defining human qualities, we help them respect themselves. Conversely, Taylor says, 'a person or group of people can suffer real damage if the people or society around them mirror back to them a confining or demeaning or contemptible picture of themselves. Nonrecognition or misrecognition can inflict harm, can be a form of oppression' (p. 25).

From a mental health perspective, studies have shown the beneficial effects of granting children and adults an opportunity to define their own personal identity without fear of oppression or discrimination. On the other hand, when people's identities are disparaged or diminished, there are negative effects on their self-esteem and overall mental health (for reviews of research, see Gardner & Esses, 1996; Prilleltensky & Gonick, 1996; Trickett, Watts, & Birman, 1994). Appreciation for diverse social identities serves as a protective factor, whereas lack of respect constitutes a definite risk factor.

Arising from the collaborative effort of countries with diverse cultures and traditions, the Convention is highly sensitive to issues of human diversity. It confirms that services and resources are to be rendered to all children who need them, 'irrespective of the child's or his or her parent's or legal guardian's race, colour, sex, language, religion, political or other opinion, national, ethnic or social origin, property, disability, birth or other status.'

Our consultations revealed that people are in fact very sensitive to issues of diversity in skills, marital status, social class, background, abilities, and gender orientation. A parent who had been involved with the child welfare system talked about acceptance as the main antidote for discrimination. She expressed the need to accept '*that I am doing the best I can.*' With regards to her kids, she lamented: '*I always thought that my kids needed to be better than they were.*' '*Accepting who they are,*' she said, is vital for their self-esteem.

Collaboration and Respect for the Community

Whereas self-determination and respect for human diversity deal primarily with the child as beneficiary of principles enacted by others, the value of collaboration and respect for the community calls on the developing young person to respect the rights of others and of the community as a whole. The Convention recognizes the dual role of the child, as recipient and agent of values at the same time.

Growth and maturity bring with them obligations toward the community. Youth have the duty to respect other persons and democratic norms. The charter encourages communal, national, and international cooperation in achieving mutually beneficial goals; it invokes a spirit of solidarity among nations. As children mature, they become themselves moral agents; they have the capacity to enact virtues or vices, to serve or to harm.

The values of tolerance and peaceful co-existence are subsumed under the principle of collaboration and respect for the community. It is here that the Convention balances rights with responsibilities, an equilibrium that is hard to attain. As Damon (1995) has argued, our society has swung from demanding too much from children to expecting too little. His study of societal expectations of children demonstrates that youngsters not only need but also enjoy helping others. Many positive outcomes accrue from altruistic and generous behaviour, not only to the community but to the youngsters themselves (Berman, 1997; Coles, 1997; Damon, 1995; Pritchard, 1996; Yates & Youniss, 1998; Youniss & Yates, 1997). These include an enhanced sense of self-efficacy, a strong personal identity, an enriched moral and spiritual life, and a sense of purpose in the creation of a better society. 'Youth ought to be given direct opportunities to experience themselves in the history-making process. Youth would thereby develop confidence in their own agency, accept social responsibility, and advance their political–moral socialization' (Youniss & Yates, 1997, p. 154).

Programs that involve youth in volunteer work show that teenagers gain self-respect and valuable life skills through these activities. Not to be discounted is the construction of their civic identity:

> Community service offers opportunities for this crucial self–society linkage in identity construction. In working to help other persons in need, adolescents can begin to experience their own agency. They can also begin to ask why people in our society live in such different conditions and do not possess similar resources. They may also begin to ask about the political bases of variations in conditions and to question the moral positions that would support either the status quo or reasons for changing it. Most importantly, adolescents who start reflecting in this manner would necessarily consider how they as individuals want to take stands on existing ideologies and so decide whether they might simply live though the present moment of his-

Vision and Values for Child and Family Wellness   147

tory or take responsibility in the actual making of history. (Youniss & Yates, 1997, p. 3)

The Relationship between Values, Needs, and Wellness

We saw in Table 3.1 how values promote personal, collective, and relational wellness. In a similar vein, we can see how these values promote child, family, community, and societal wellness.

Table 3.2 marks the connection between the needs for child and family wellness identified in Chapter 2 and the values required to achieve wellness at different ecological levels. At the level of child wellness, needs for love, nurturance, identity, and self-esteem are promoted by values such as self-determination, opportunities for education and personal development, and caring and protection of health. At the level of family wellness, parental needs for growth and support are similarly advanced by personal values of self-determination, opportunities for personal development, caring, and compassion. Family wellness is possible when the needs for income security, good communication, mutual respect, belonging, and acceptance are met. The values of respect for diversity, social justice, collaboration and respect, and caring and protection of health feature prominently in meeting family wellness needs. Community wellness is premised on needs such as economic prosperity, health, safety, and access to services and resources. These needs are facilitated by the presence of collective values such as support for strong public institutions and distribution of resources based on social justice. Finally, societal wellness is defined as a state of affairs in which there is sufficient employment and the population has access to decent housing and enjoys high-quality services such as universal health and child care. These needs are met by social policies premised on values such as distribution of resources based on social justice, support for strong civic institutions, respect for human diversity, and the provision of opportunities for personal development and self-sufficiency.

Children's Evolving Role as Beneficiaries and as Agents of Values

By virtue of their vulnerability and relative helplessness, we do not expect infants to worry about others. For as long as infants and children depend completely on others for their survival, they are primarily, as they should be, only beneficiaries of values. They are not yet in a position to contribute to the well-being of others. But this situation changes

TABLE 3.2
The Relationship between Selected Values, Needs, and Ecological Levels of Wellness

Societal Wellness	Community Wellness	Family/Parental Wellness	Child Wellness
Selected Needs			
Economic security, housing, health insurance, democratic institutions, culture of peace, harmony, and sustainability	Safety, formal and informal support, solidarity, cohesion, social services, high-quality schools, recreational facilities	Affective bonds, intimacy, communication, conflict resolution, quality time, personal space, support from spouse/extended family, interdependence, health, opportunities for personal growth, job satisfaction, recreation	Love, nurturance, self-esteem, cognitive, physical and emotional development, physical and psychological health, acceptance, social skills
Selected Values			
• Social justice in provision of resources • Support for strong community structures • Respect for human diversity	• Collaboration and respect for the community • Support for strong community structures • Respect for human diversity	• Caring and protection of health • Opportunities for education and personal development • Self-determination	• Caring and protection of health • Opportunities for education and personal development • Self-determination

as the child matures. Gradually, children learn skills that enable them to help others and to think about others' needs. Slowly, children and youth become moral agents themselves; their actions affect the well-being of relatives, friends, and the community at large, and they possess the ability to evaluate the impact of their behaviour on others.

With age, children become full moral agents. Cognitive and emotional development facilitate children's consideration of other people's needs. Hence, children evolve from mere beneficiaries of care to providers of care. It is unfortunate that North American society has neglected its duty to prepare children for civic obligations (Berman, 1997; Damon, 1995; Youniss & Yates, 1997). Our failure to view children not only as beneficiaries but also as agents of values has fed right into the prevalent culture of individualism. When we drop expectations that children will be of help in the house and in the community, we reinforce the message that they are the centre of the world and that they deserve all they get, without a duty to reciprocate.

Children will become teenagers and adults with responsibilities toward themselves and others. Unless we prepare them, and expect from them responsibility from a young age, they may engage in risky behaviours that are detrimental to the well-being of others. Teaching responsibility toward fellow human beings from a young age may prevent acts that will harm others. Fostering responsibility toward oneself and others may be a great public health act. Expecting children and youth to be moral agents from a young age can promote their own wellness and the welfare of the community at large (Damon, 1995; Harris, 1996).

A Value-Based Vision of Child and Family Wellness

A comprehensive vision of wellness requires an ecological perspective. To talk meaningfully about child wellness we need to address family wellness. That is, we need to attend to the needs of parents as individuals and to the needs of the family as a whole, as a unit. In turn, to ensure family wellness we need to secure community and societal wellness, for the family is nested within these two larger ecologies. In this case, community refers to meso-level structures such as schools, health and human services, churches, recreational clubs, boys and girls clubs, and other meeting places where people congregate to pursue common interests or needs. Societal wellness is defined as the capacity of social and cultural norms and policies to advance the well-being of the population. Societal wellness is the larger and more encompassing ecological definition of welfare. Social policies set by the government of the day dictate, to a large extent, the social services to be rendered to families in need. Cultural norms are also important in that they influence public attitudes toward disadvantaged children. Tax laws and benefits distribute wealth among the population. These are some examples of macro-level regulations that impinge on the ability of various sectors of the community to pursue and attain life objectives.

Within an ecological frame of reference, as can be seen in Table 3.3, child and family wellness are defined in the context of child, family, communal, and societal wellness. The various levels of analysis are intimately connected. Within each level or context, individuals or entities can be recipients or providers of values. People can be beneficiaries as well as agents of social goods. As noted in the previous section, children gradually mature into a dual role of recipients and providers of care. The same moral duty applies to parents as individuals, as well as to the entire family unit. Communities and social structures welcome and confer values all the same. Social groups and agencies do not have a life of their own; they come to life through the actions of their elected officials and paid or volunteer staff. Every person at the different ecological levels has a right to enjoy certain privileges and a duty to reciprocate.

Table 3.3 offers an operational definition of child and family wellness based on moral values, principles inscribed in the UNCRC, and our research. What we see in Table 3.3 is a vision for child and family wellness based on seven fundamental values for human welfare. The table denotes the main values that apply to each ecological unit. In the proposed conceptualization of wellness, we illustrate in concrete terms what each value means for that particular unit. Thus, caring and protection of health mean, for children and youth, getting the love and nurturance they need, and acting responsibly toward self and others. In the case of parents, self-determination means being supported to pursue personal goals and helping spouses and children to achieve theirs. In this fashion, we define child and family wellness as the outcome of certain values at various ecological contexts in which each person or entity is entitled to enjoy certain rights and obliged to contribute to others. We may say that wellness is measured by the presence and strength of values in both the 'shipping and receiving' gates. In a society in which everyone expects goods but nobody reciprocates, the state of collective welfare is woeful. In a community in which everyone is expected to give but nobody can get anything, the state of individual welfare is dismal.

THE ROLE OF VALUES IN CHILD AND FAMILY WELLNESS

Sound values can provide us with concrete benefits in our pursuit of child wellness. There are six important benefits to adopting a value-based approach to family wellness.

Guide Thinking and Action in Policies and Programs

Values can promote the needs of individual children and parents, of groups like families and communities, and of entire societies. But in addition to that, values can inform policies and programs designed to promote wellness. Table 3.4 provides examples of how personal, collective, and relational values can be actualized in policies and programs to advance child and family wellness.

Personal values like self-determination play an important role in the design of both policies and programs for family wellness. This value points to the need to involve children and parents in the creation of initiatives to address their needs. Children, youth, and parents should be empowered to have a voice in programs and services offered them. Caring and protection of health is a value expressed in programs like home visitation, where the objective is not just to deliver medical information but to establish a bond with parents as well. Programs that foster secure attachments between parent and child do much to promote nurturance for the child. The values of education and personal development are expressed in policies and programs that offer the population opportunities for training, academic growth, civic involvement, and artistic expression.

Relational values are advanced in programs that foster social skills, family cohesion, assertiveness, and conflict resolution in families and schools. Support for community structures is a value that needs to be promoted in educational policies designed to enhance civic and political consciousness. Programs that teach a balance between the rights of the individual and obligations toward the community illustrate the values of solidarity and respect for the community.

Collective values like social justice are reflected in policies that distribute goods and resources in a fair and equitable way. Taxation policies and child benefits are governmental vehicles used in many countries to support the disadvantaged. Policies that distribute social resources not just on the basis of merit but also on the basis of need do much to eliminate child poverty.

TABLE 3.3
A Value-Based Vision of Child and Family Wellness

A Vision of	Entails Individuals or Entities as	
	Recipients of Following Values	Agents of Following Values
Child and youth wellness	**Caring and protection of health:** Loving and safe environment, nurturance and interest in their lives, psychological development. **Education and personal development:** Support and expectations of progress; growth opportunities are present. **Self-determination:** Children's rights are respected; voice and independence are promoted. **Respect for human diversity:** Free of stigmas, recognition of strengths. **Collaboration and respect:** Children have chance to participate in decisions affecting their lives. **Resources based on social justice:** Basic material, psychological and spiritual needs are met.	**Caring and protection of health:** Responsibility for personal health, and prevention of risky behaviours such as teen pregnancy or substance abuse. **Education and personal development:** Responsibility for personal and academic growth. **Self-determination:** Develop independence. **Respect for human diversity:** Respect differences and avoid demeaning others. **Collaboration and respect:** Enact value of reciprocity with peers and adults. **Support for community:** Contribute to community structures; assume developmentally appropriate civic duties; learn about role of community structures in meeting personal and collective needs.
Parental and family wellness	**Caring and protection of health:** Personal emotional needs met; time for personal nourishment; support from extended family, friends, and community resources; strong family bonds; belonging. **Education and personal development:** Support for self-advancement; growth opportunities.	**Caring and protection of health:** Consistent and nurturing parenting; support for spouse and community. **Education and personal development:** Support for children in school and extra-curricular activities; children expected to perform well according to their abilities.

TABLE 3.3 *(continued)*
A Value-Based Vision of Child and Family Wellness

A Vision of	Entails Individuals or Entities as	
	Recipients of Following Values	Agents of Following Values
	Self-determination: Able to work towards personal goals; families are afforded opportunities for meaningful involvement in helping processes.	**Self-determination:** Provide spouse and children meaningful opportunities to pursue their goals; families assert their needs and actively participate in helping processes.
	Respect for human diversity: Unique identity valued; self-acceptance; diverse families are accepted by society and not discriminated against.	**Respect for human diversity:** Acceptance of spouse and child and models acceptance of others as well; promotion of tolerance within the family and in the community.
	Resources based on social justice: Stable and sufficient income; basic needs met; family time.	**Resources based on social justice:** Allocates burdens and benefits within the family in equitable form; parents and children are concerned with distribution of societal burdens and benefits.
	Collaboration and respect: Both spouses participate in parental decisions; spouses treat each other with respect; conflict always resolved peacefully; physical or psychological violence never used; good communication among family members; parents collaborate with educators and service providers in decisions affecting children.	**Collaboration and respect:** Affords others in family chance to participate in decisions; physical or psychological violence never used; parenting is shared; as a group, families respect neighbours and others in the community and engage in constructive cooperation with teachers and other social agents; supports extended family.
		Support for community: Models for children appreciation for community resources that enhance collective health and well-being; parents and children contribute to vital community agencies and initiatives.

TABLE 3.3 *(continued)*
A Value-Based Vision of Child and Family Wellness

A Vision of	Entails Individuals or Entities as	
	Recipients of Following Values	Agents of Following Values
Community wellness	**Support for community:** Well-resourced agencies and supports; advocacy to preserve institutions that work for common good. **Resources based on social justice:** Prosperous neighbourhoods that enjoy good health, safety, educational and recreational facilities.	**Caring and protection of health:** Support for families in need; compassion in service delivery. **Resources based on social justice:** Services and resources allocated on fair basis and without discrimination. **Education and personal development:** Adults encouraged to participate in personal growth programs. **Collaboration and respect:** Clients and consumers of services participate in decision-making processes affecting their lives; meaningful public participation in administration of social agencies. **Respect for human diversity:** Recognition of strengths in diverse groups.
Societal wellness	**Support for community:** Civic institutions receive active support from public and government; children and adults educated about vital role of public institutions in promoting the common good; public is not cynical about politics but engaged in social change.	**Support for community:** Adequate funding of agencies and supports; public appreciation of human service sector. **Caring and protection of health:** Family wellness values are a social priority; compassion toward disadvantaged is a national value; vision of child wellness is promoted via UN Convention on the Rights of the Child or equivalent standard.

TABLE 3.3 *(concluded)*
A Value-Based Vision of Child and Family Wellness

	Entails Individuals or Entities as	
A Vision of	Recipients of Following Values	Agents of Following Values
		Collaboration and respect: Respect for parenting role; involve stay-at-home parents in policies affecting their parenting.
		Resources based on social justice: Political will to allocate resources for disempowered children and families; high-quality child care is a national priority; universal programs to help entire population; corporate responsibility toward community well-being.
		Respect for human diversity: Parents with problems are not stigmatized; no prejudice against poor, same-sex couples, or single-parent families.
		Education and personal development: Accessible educational and recreational programs for all children and adults.

TABLE 3.4
The Actualization of Values in Policies and Programs

	Policies	Programs
Values for *Personal Wellness*		
Caring and protection of health	Facilitate access to health-care services through universal and outreach programs.	Establish networks of support for parents and foster in them ability to empathize with child.
Education and personal development	Establish national policies for accessible and affordable child care and job training for parents.	Build into programs competency-enhancing components for personal and occupational growth.
Self-determination	Devise child and family policies in consultation with children, families, and communities.	Promote voice and choice of children and adults in selection and administration of programs.
Values for *Collective Wellness*		
Social justice in the provision of resources	Implement policies that provide adequate family benefits in order to decrease child poverty.	Provide families with comprehensive supports to meet needs for housing and economic security.
Support for strong community structures	Promote policies that decrease work–family conflicts and that promote more-integrated community-based services.	Create awareness and support for the creation and preservation of effective formal and informal supports.
Values for *Relational Wellness*		
Respect for human diversity	Promote inclusive family policies that do not discriminate on basis of marital status, gender, ability, sexual orientation, class, culture, or any other source of social power.	Consult with diverse groups of stakeholders and develop inclusive and culturally sensitive programs based on partnerships.
Collaboration and respect for the community	Balance policies for personal responsibility with policies that promote obligations toward the community at large.	Foster climate of respect and develop skills for meaningful and democratic participation in programs.

Vision and values serve as our moral compass; they set the direction of our actions. Once we are clear about the goals and objectives we want to reach, and about the principles that should inform the process, then we have a blueprint for action.

Values can also help in conflict resolution. If members of a program agree that collaboration and respect for diversity are moral precepts to be upheld, then they can develop peaceful forms of conflict resolution. By referring back to a list of key values, participants can see where they may have gone wrong and what can be done to repair the situation.

Set Priorities

Policymakers, practitioners, and private citizens can address family wellness in many different ways, ranging from individual therapy to parenting groups to economic support. Having an explicit vision and accompanying values can help us set priorities. We can compare the ideal vision with the current state of affairs of families and see what is missing to achieve the desired outcome. This can translate into actions to fill the gaps.

Similarly, a comparison between dominant and preferred values can tell us what values we should be promoting and what beliefs we should be tempering. When faced with multiple possibilities, agents of change need guidelines to set priorities, parameters that will tell them this course of action is better than that one. Referring back to the vision and the values facilitates the decision-making process.

Assume a program planner wishes to empower service recipients. She is planning an intervention designed to improve family wellness. The program will include parenting courses, budgeting lessons, and coordination of services with other local organizations. She wishes to grant participants voice and choice in the matter, so she invites them to express their needs. By doing so she is granting them a measure of self-determination and autonomy in that they are collaborating on program planning. Their voices are being heard. The value of self-determination is being activated. This is fine. However, after a while she realizes that participants need more than an expression of opinions; they also need concrete resources such as economic assistance and food supplements. This is when she discovers that distributive justice, or the fair and equitable allocation of resources in society, is a key value, for without it people can recite their needs and wants but will not get what they need. The planner then tries to incorporate this realization into her program and looks for ways to address the dearth of resources. Distributive justice becomes a priority.

In Canada, children's advocacy groups like Campaign 2000 (Campaign 2000, 1996; Hughes, 1995), the Child Welfare League of Canada (Woollcombe, 1996), the Canadian Council on Social Development (Ross, 1996), the Caledon Institute (Torjman & Battle, 1995), the Laidlaw Foundation Children at Risk Program (O'Neill, 1994; Shields, 1995), and Voices for Children (Canada Health and Social Transfers, 1997) all agree that in the current context financial support to poor families is essential. While these organizations recognize the need for direct services to families in need of psychological intervention, they also consider distributive justice a national priority. Research consistently shows that economic deprivation is a primary risk factor for neglect or abuse of children (Pelton, 1994). There is little doubt that in the current social context, priority should be given to economic justice (Kitchen, 1995). Empowering participants to have a say in program planning is a desirable but not a sufficient condition to meet the needs of children. Early intervention programs that enrich the educational environment of children and families is another desirable but insufficient component of a comprehensive strategy to improve the lives of vulnerable families (Barnett & Boocock, 1998; Bertrand, 1996). Conversely, programs that merely give money to poor parents but do not address their isolation are equally insufficient. Material resources, in the absence of psychological meaning and social support, are not enough (Wolfe, 1998).

Avoid Contradictions

In the absence of a template of values, it is entirely possible to hold contradictory or incompatible tenets. Many people respect human diversity in the abstract, but when it comes to employment policies such as affirmative action they adamantly oppose giving people from disadvantaged groups a better chance at a job. In another case, we may promote the value of health and good nutrition for infants and babies, but again, when it comes to allocating benefits to poor families and children, many people object on the basis that this will increase their taxes. If people are really serious about helping others in need, then it follows that they should be willing to distribute societal resources in a more fair and equitable fashion, and that they should be willing to contribute to national health and social programs. On the other hand, it is conceivable that members of society would be willing to pay more taxes and donate more money to charity but behave in cruel ways toward their own children and never do an hour of volunteer work in their entire lives.

Cutting poor parents from welfare on the basis that it will promote the value of self-sufficiency can result in increased levels of family stress and in higher risks for children (Rickel & Becker, 1997; Torjman & Battle, 1995). While desirable, economic self-sufficiency has to be introduced in ways that do not hurt children. Otherwise, the attainment of one goal undermines the achievement of another.

Challenge Myths and Misconceptions

'We could never invest in social programs as much as other countries do!' 'We do not know enough yet to eliminate risk factors for children and families!' 'Values are a private matter and the state should not intervene in family matters!' 'If children act out, rigid discipline will teach them to behave!' Notions such as these gain currency in society without much reflection. In most cases, misconceptions serve the status quo. In other words, they exist to protect the current state of affairs and those who are opposed to change.

By applying a set of values, we can challenge received wisdom. We could show, for instance, that Canada or the United States has more comparative national wealth than Sweden but has less regard for the value of distributive justice (Campaign 2000, 1997a; Kitchen, 1995). It is not a matter of having the resources, but rather of setting value priorities. By examining the first statement in the paragraph above in light of a set of values, we can discern whether it is truly impossible to invest in lone-parent families as much as Sweden does (Kamerman & Kahn, 1988, 1991) or whether it is just a matter of priorities (Loizou, 1996).

The same reasoning applies to the second statement, that we don't know enough yet to improve the lives of children and families. Knowledge is a relative term, and while it is certainly true that we do not know everything about children and families, we could argue that we know a great deal to justify much higher investment in children and families. High-quality prevention and early intervention programs have tremendous humanitarian and economic benefits, yet social investment in prevention in Canada and the United States is meagre (Harris, 1996; Nelson, Prilleltensky, Laurendeau, & Powell, 1996). Pondering the lack of social action to help children and families, Schorr (1997) noted that 'we deluded ourselves into thinking we didn't know enough, when what actually has kept us from going to scale was an unwillingness to invest the necessary resources or a reluctance to disturb the status quo' (p. 25).

Let's examine the third statement, 'Values are a private matter and the state should not intervene in family matters!' People opposed to state interventions may use this argument to reject any type of help, for themselves or for others (Garbarino, 1996; Rodger, 1995). But the sanctity of family privacy may need to be violated if children's rights are being violated within the family. The merit of privacy has to be weighed against the protection of children.

The last statement of the opening paragraph concerns children's discipline. Sure enough, tough measures can bring children into compliance with social norms, but the question is, at what cost? The values of tradition and respect for authority have to be assessed in light of the damage that rigid discipline can cause. Emotional apathy, depression, decreased self-esteem, increased aggression, and a potential for abusing others are all likely outcomes of a punitive upbringing (Azar, 1997; Belsky, 1993; Browne & Herbert, 1997; Mattaini, McGowan, & Williams, 1996; Wolfe, 1994).

Evaluate Policies and Programs

Knowing the desired outcomes and processes of policies and programs is a precondition for their evaluation. Without clarity of aims and values, there is no background against which to assess progress. By gauging the distance between our ideals and program outcomes, we know how far we are from our target. By reviewing the values of policies and programs against our own, we learn about possible changes we need to make. A value-based evaluation asks not only what we have achieved, but also how we have achieved it. Have we offered parents resources in a cool and detached way or have we also given them emotional support? Have we informed teenagers about the risks of early pregnancy in ways that are engaging and empowering or in threatening terms that lead to further alienation? Vision and values remind us to ask ourselves where are we going and how are we getting there.

Overcome Passivity and Challenge the Status Quo

Values of justice, compassion, and empowerment can wake up a society that is too accustomed to hearing horror stories about child abuse and too complacent to do anything about it. There is ample reason to challenge a societal status quo that has failed vulnerable children and families. Having coherent visions and values can invigorate citizens to overcome the current passivity that exists in matters of child welfare. We need to restore the discourse of hope and possibility (Freire, 1997; Hernández, 1997). Our values can reflect and nurture this commitment.

We live in a society of conflicting values. For those of us whose priority is to reduce the incidence of child maltreatment and promote family wellness, we need a set of values that will help us choose options for children. We need to know where to position ourselves with respect to personal and collective values, and we need to know what criteria to use to make good decisions.

THE ROLE OF CHANGE AGENTS IN PROMOTING VALUES FOR CHILD AND FAMILY WELLNESS

Seeking a Balance between Personal and Collective Values

Identifying values is important, but it is only the first step in promoting child and family wellness. Establishing an equilibrium between personal and collective values is the next step. This task requires an analysis of our culture. Once we realize what moral principles we favour and what values we ignore, we can take corrective action. If we have veered too far in the direction of personal values, we can take action to recover collective ideals. If we have neglected personal freedoms, we should moderate collectivist tendencies that suppress individual liberties (Etzioni, 1996). The moment one principle takes too much space, others shrink proportionately. Applied to North American society, this means that collectivist values such as solidarity, sharing, cooperation, and social justice have shrunk in reverse proportion to the increase in individualism. This trend is reflected in preventive policies and programs that concentrate on person-centred approaches.

To reach a balance of values that is sensitive to the social context, it is our task to evaluate the salience of each desirable value. In our social environment, the eminence of individualism has led to the obscurity of collectivism. What is the solution? A full swing toward the collectivist end of the spectrum is not advisable, for we would confront another conundrum. A creative equilibrium that would foster the rights of the individual *and* the needs of the community is a more tenable approach. Entitlements and duties do not have to be mutually exclusive.

Like it or not, the fulfilment of the self is linked to the contentment of the group. Violent neighbourhoods constrain personal well-being. Poorly resourced communities limit opportunities for health and development. Change agents need to appreciate the interaction between psychological and sociological forces. Accordingly, solutions to family and social problems should include strategies that change personal and interpersonal dynamics as well as societal factors (Kraemer & Roberts, 1996).

Using Values to Promote Child and Family Wellness

Values should be guides for action. Improving child and family wellness entails the reduction of risk and the enhancement of protective factors, the promotion of empowering processes and the elimination of disempowering processes, and the pursuit of a balance between personal and collective values. These tasks are carried out by parents, teachers, school administrators, cultural workers, professionals, community helpers, employers, policymakers, legislators, and advocates, to name but a few. Virtually every member of society, perhaps with the exception of highly dependent individuals, has the potential to act as an agent of prevention and promotion.

Child-friendly cultures evolve as a result of the combined efforts of multiple players. A society that values children benefits from the collective efforts of people in many quarters. It is hard to identify the one value-driven intervention that can make a difference in the lives of children at risk. All of us who work with or on behalf of children have a role to play. It is the synergy created by a common vision that has the potential to radically alter social agendas in favour of children. The changes we need to pursue should take place in homes, schools, the media, religious congregations, community clubs, social agencies, neighbourhoods, and legislative bodies. These are all legitimate and required arenas for the pursuit of children's rights.

We examine next how the value-based and ecological conceptualization of child wellness can be translated into action (see Table 3.5). This is by no means an exhaustive coverage of players or values. Table 3.5 offers a synopsis of interventions, while the text that follows explains how citizens can advance a set of values in their different social roles. In the table, each intervention suggested at each level represents the seven values guiding child and family wellness.

Person: The Role of Youth and Adults

We begin our discussion with the smallest unit of analysis: the individual.

TABLE 3.5
Value-Driven Actions to Promote Child Wellness

Change Agents	Sample of Value-Driven Actions to Promote Child Wellness
Parents and extended family	• Foster secure attachments with children. • Become involved in child's education. • Promote child's empowerment and self-efficacy. • Respect child's unique identity. • Respect child's voice in personal and social issues. • Expect from child age-appropriate social contributions. • Procure basic necessities.
School personnel	• Create safe and nurturing environments; teach health education. • Enhance competencies and open doors for personal growth. • Foster meaningful involvement and afford choice in curriculum. • Educate on effects of power imbalances. • Provide social skills training. • Teach political awareness and importance of social institutions. • Afford families opportunities to become involved in school.
Professionals and community helpers	• Implement programs to prevent abuse. • Provide opportunities for training in community programs. • Empower youth and workers to have choice in programs. • Promote inclusive programs. • Model and expect respect in programs. • Advocate for preservation of vital public institutions. • Provide services in fair, equitable, and accessible manner.
Artists, journalists, and media workers	• Critique norms of violence and promote human dignity. • Convey vision of growth that includes civic duties. • Make children's issues a national priority. • Produce shows that deal with discrimination. • Eliminate violent role models from the media. • Reinforce in media benefits of participation in civic affairs. • Clarify for public the role of social justice in promoting wellness.
Policymakers and child advocates	• Establish national office to promote family wellness. • Promote and fund educational opportunities. • Establish office of ombudsperson to advocate for children's rights. • Implement legislation against discrimination. • Balance rights with obligations. • Reverse current trend of eliminating public services. • Distribute social resources not just on basis of merit but also on basis of need.

Although people's behaviours are influenced by their environments, individuals still have a measure of agency. That is, they can have a say in their personal lives and in the lives of their communities. To have agency means to be able to direct the course of events in one's life. Although there are obvious societal constraints in what one can do, there are also obvious opportunities for the exercise of self-determination.

We see the individual as having responsibility toward the self and toward others. A person can facilitate the promotion of values for himself or herself, and for those in his or her care and community. As individuals, we have the dual responsibility of looking after ourselves and looking after others. We can promote our own health by adopting better eating habits and by exercising. We can affirm our views by learning to be assertive. We can promote human diversity by accepting ourselves, with our strengths and weaknesses. But we also have a responsibility to advance these values in others. We see the role of the individual as trying to meet his or her own needs and those of the community at the same time (Dokecki, 1996; Prilleltensky, 1997). This is a balance that is very difficult to achieve because our culture socializes us to think, first and foremost, of personal interest. As Canadian thinker John Ralston Saul (1995) put it, our society 'leads to a worship of self-interest and a denial of the public good' (p. 187).

Adults have a responsibility to look after their own health and the health of their children. Youths also have a duty to care for themselves and to contribute to the well-being of the community (Damon, 1995; Flanagan & Sherrod, 1998; Youniss & Yates, 1997).

Family: The Role of Parents and Extended Family

Parents are well positioned to promote caring and the protection of health, as well as a sense of self-efficacy in their children. These benefits depend on parents' ability to interact with children in a nurturing fashion and to set for them reasonable expectations. Parental warmth, acceptance, and nurturance would seem to protect the infant from stressors early in life and to help the child cope better with challenges later in life. The absence of these qualities in the parent–child dyad can result in negative outcomes. 'Extreme coldness, open hostility, or rejection by caregivers often contributes to children's emotional distress, aggression, and delinquency' (Basic Behavioral Science Task Force of the National Advisory Mental Health Council [Task Force], 1996a, p. 623). On the other hand, a caring attitude toward the infant is a catalyst for other protective factors. As the Task Force reported, 'high levels of caregiver warmth are associated with children's elevated self-esteem, compliance with caregiver demands, internalized moral standards, cognitive competence, and social adjustment' (p. 623).

The pattern of relationship between caregiver and infant is established early in life. The quality of the attachment, the special bond between caregiver and infant, determines many of the outcomes reviewed above. The more secure infants feel in their bond with caregivers, the more willing they are to explore the world and to have new experiences (Task Force, 1996b). These findings led to successful intervention programs. Children participating in parent–child attachment programs were found to exceed controls in coping and communication skills, were better adjusted in school, and exhibited less aggression (Cowen, 1994; Task Force, 1996b).

Parenting skills are absolutely vital for the caring of children. According to a service provider, many problems '*go back to the lack of parenting ... They don't mean to do anything wrong, they just don't know how to do anything differently.*' Unfortunately, many parents are sceptical about a brighter future and lack the impetus to improve their skills. Several of our key informants told us that a sense of hopelessness pervades the lives of parents in disempowered circumstances. Parents become despondent and find themselves in a cycle of despair in which the whole family is caught. As a parent told us, '*I mean if we feel like crap, like everything is blowing up in my face, I'm not going to be all happy-happy with my kid. There is nothing you can do and the poor kid is the one that's hurting, and the cycle goes around.*' Parents and extended families have a common responsibility to look after the next generation. For some, it is easy enough; for others, it is an enormous challenge. Two proposed principles for a Canadian children's agenda read as follows:

> Children are the offspring of individual parents, but society must share responsibility for giving every child an equal start in life, and for investing in future generations of adults.
> Families have primary responsibility for the care, nurturing and support of children, but government and society must support them in these tasks.
> (Woollcombe, 1996, p. 8)

School: The Role of School Professionals

Like parents, school professionals have multiple opportunities to promote protective factors and to reduce risk factors. They are in an excellent position to advance the values of collaboration, personal development, and respect for human diversity. Classrooms are social environments in which individuals and groups face common challenges. They are a perfect place to learn and practise cooperation. There are successful social skills programs which teach children how to cooperate and resolve conflict in peaceful ways. These programs use a combination of role-play, videos, written materials, and group discussion to deal with peer pressure, interpersonal problem solving, assertiveness, and conflict mediation (Consortium on the School-Based Promotion of Social Competence, 1994; Elias & Clabby, 1992). It is unfortunate that despite their success, many school boards ignore the educational contribution of these programs (Mercer, 1989; Meyers, 1989; Weissberg & Elias, 1993).

Because of a liberal tradition of pseudo-neutrality in matters of morals and religion, most schools shy away from advancing a clear set of civic values. We say pseudo-neutrality because their proclaimed neutrality reinforces the status quo. It is just not possible to be neutral in matters of values. If you do not offer an alternate conception of values, your indifference strengthens the dominant morality. No challenge, no change. This liberal heritage, which taught a generation of educators to keep morality out of public institutions, has in effect prevented the utilization of schools for civic formation (Berman, 1997).

When the liberal pseudo-neutrality is coupled with fears of intimidation by extreme political groups, the outcome is moral silence (Berman, 1997; Damon, 1995). 'Controversy and politics are two areas that administrators and teachers are reticent to tackle for fear of community retribution or attacks from right or back-to-basics groups' (Berman, 1997, p. 181).

Educators' reluctance to become involved in moral and political issues has resulted in a narrow conception of social duties. Berman (1997) claims that

> The very conception of citizenship that teachers and students hold and that is used to frame instruction is limited. It focuses attention primarily on being a good person rather than being actively engaged in the political process, on protecting self-interest rather than promoting the common good, and on the individual as the locus of responsibility rather than institutional, systemic, or structural aspects of our political culture. (p. 174)

Schools are fertile grounds for personal development and the exploration of one's unique talents and interests. Schools are in a position to contribute not only the content but also the tools for pursuing broad intellectual and spiritual horizons. Rewarding academic experiences are conducive to the exploration of new and varied interests, and most importantly to self-efficacy and a positive intellectual self-image (Maughan, 1988). A solid education can spawn a positive chain reaction, leading to increased opportunities for employment and a higher quality of life (Rutter, 1987).

Positive exemplars of intersectoral cooperation are taking place in schools. An initiative pioneered by Edward Zigler in the United States, called *The School of the 21st Century* (21C) (Zigler, Finn-Stevenson, & Stern, 1997), illustrates the multiple gains of concentrating child and family services in schools. These schools operate from six or seven in the morning until six in the evening and integrate child care and family support programs. In addition to before- and after-school child care, the program offers vacation child care and outreach services to families. The outreach element consists of home visits to new parents designed to provide support and guidance. The visits begin in the third trimester of pregnancy and continue until children are 3 years old. Referral services, information about proper nutrition, health, and preventive care are some of the other features of the 21C.

Community: The Role of Volunteers, Paraprofessionals, and Professional Helpers

Outside the home and the school, children and youth come into contact with many caregivers. These include professionals, paraprofessionals, and volunteers in capacities such as group leaders, camp counsellors, health-care workers, therapists, youth workers, child and family services personnel, and others. These helpers are in a position to promote caring, health, self-determination, collaboration, and participation of consumers in programs affecting their lives.

Community helpers, from extracurricular instructors to child welfare workers, can increase the level of consumer involvement in programs and services. Affording consumers voice and choice can go a long way in advancing the values of collaboration, participation, and self-determination. Sharing information with clients in accessible language, fostering consumer participation in overcoming challenges, and enabling consumers to take control of their lives and communities are some of the ways community helpers can facilitate cooperation and self-determination (Dunst, Trivette, & Thompson, 1990; Schorr, 1997; Tyler, Pargament, & Gatz, 1983).

Unfortunately, children and adults alike are rarely consulted with respect to their wishes for services and programs. Professionals exert a great deal of control over services and the entire helping process, undermining the capacity of communities to solve their own problems (Durkin, 1990; Hasenfeld & Chesler, 1989; McKnight, 1995; Reiff, 1974). Although the potential for community helpers to increase protective factors exists, there is also the distinct possibility of helpers taking control away from the persons who need control the most: communities' disempowered members. A policy adviser we consulted with lamented the lack of meaningful parental voice in community programs:

> *Listening to them, valuing their contribution to any kind of thoughtfulness or input into services or anything that affects them [is important]. [However,] they are often the last people asked about it. We really do lip service to giving people who are involved in services actual input and then paying attention to it.*

Just like parents, children should also be given opportunities to participate in decisions affecting them. 'Children have a right to participate in decisions that affect them, with their informed consent and in line with their age, development, and culture.' (Woollcombe, 1996, p. 8). Health Canada's (1996b) consultations on national goals for children and youth evoked a similar sentiment:

> There are articulate, aware young people in every school, neighbourhood, and community. Instead of always talking about them and their problems, we should be talking with them. Often, they see things much more clearly than those who are trying to help. A child who has experienced the child welfare system or the juvenile system can provide valuable insights into how these systems affect them – where they hurt and where they help. (p. 15)

Culture: The Role of the Media, Artists, and Social Commentators

A change in social norms will not come about without the support of culture makers. Journalists, editorial writers, artists, academics, and social critics have enormous influence on public opinion. At present, this influence is not used to promote child and family wellness. The media are dominated by economic news. Television, a prime source of socialization, is replete with models of violence (Kohn, 1986, 1990). Dramatic changes in attention to children's issues could be achieved by cultural workers. If the nightly news or the daily papers would devote to child and family wellness a fraction of what they devote to markets and deficits, to sports, or to entertainment, there would be a tremendous rise in the national consciousness about children's rights. Child and family wellness, except for tragic and sensational cases, are not newsmakers.

The current wasted opportunities notwithstanding, the potential for culture makers to have a positive impact does exist. There are innumerable chances to model caring and compassion, to rally support for community structures, to praise acts of respect and sacrifice, to condemn gratuitous violence, and to put children first. But cultural transformation is a historical process, not a surgical procedure. The sooner we start the process, the sooner we fulfil our covenant with future generations.

Cultural workers have wonderful opportunities to clarify the role of social justice in children's well-being, to show the deleterious effects of discrimination, and to nurture civic identities based on social responsibility. Concurrently, though, norm creators will have to curtail the unrelenting communication of destructive images to children and youth. The denigration of opposite views and the degradation of the value of life are the main staples of countless television shows. Although there have been calls to restrict violence on shows for children, the entertainment industry has not been identified as a major responsible stakeholder in child and family wellness.

Missed opportunity is the best descriptor for the role of cultural forces in child welfare. Whether that will be the legacy of contemporary trendsetters for children remains to be seen. The impact of a single artist on attitudes toward children may not be readily noticeable, but the collective effort of cultural workers and norm creators is bound to have positive repercussions.

The job is for each of us who has a chance to influence public opinion to uphold the values of child and family wellness. A positive example is offered by Michael Lerner (1996), leader of the politics of meaning movement in the United States. He proposes the following declaration concerning the media:

> We will support the creation of television programs and networks aimed at providing children's entertainment that avoids excessive violence and rejects the manipulative use of sexuality that commonly appears on con-

temporary television. In addition, we will challenge the ethos of selfishness and cynicism conveyed in the media, and focus on developing media programming that strengthens ethical, spiritual, and ecological sensitivity. (p. 209)

Society: The Role of Policymakers, Legislators, Corporate Leaders, and Child Advocates

Policymakers, legislators, corporate leaders, and advocates have a crucial role to play in promoting children's physical and mental health. Much as children's emotional problems cannot be understood without knowing their families, community problems cannot be understood without studying the social, political, and economic contexts. The distribution of social resources and the protection of health depend in large measure on social policies. Politicians have enormous power to legislate changes that affect the entire population. Similarly, welfare and tax laws can affect masses of people. In some cases, how much food a child eats depends on the welfare benefits approved by politicians.

Access to valued resources such as food, shelter, and money is a social justice issue. In most capitalist and market-driven societies goods are not distributed according to people's need, but according to work or privilege (George & Wilding, 1976; Miller, 1978). A child born in privilege does not have to worry about money or food. A child born in poverty has a lot to worry about. Most capitalist societies, such as Canada and the United States, do not have fair policies to redistribute social goods so that children will not have to worry about food or rent (Barlow & Campbell, 1995; Galbraith, 1996; Kitchen, 1995; Leonard, 1997; Ross, 1996).

In Canada and the United States, coalitions and grass-roots and professional organizations do much to support the cause of children. In Canada, where this research took place, Campaign 2000, the Canadian Council on Social Development, the Child Welfare League of Canada, Voices for Children and other anti-poverty groups struggle for social and intergenerational justice, the most neglected values of all. Much can be learned from their efforts. More can be done to support them. Learning about their goals and recommendations is a good place to start.

In preparation for the second national policy conference on children in Ottawa in November 1996 (co-sponsored by the Child Welfare League of Canada, the Ontario Association of Children's Aid Societies,

Vision and Values for Child and Family Wellness   171

in partnership with the Canadian Teachers' Federation, the Children's Aid Society of Ottawa-Carleton, and the Kids Help Phone), a background paper was released (Woollcombe, 1996). The paper contained vital recommendations for Canadian social policy concerning children. Some of the recommendations consonant with our vision and values for child and family wellness are as follows:

1. To appoint a national commissioner (or ombusdman) for children, with the powers and responsibilities needed to make improvement in children's lives.
2. To always give due consideration and take into account the interests and needs of children, especially at policy-making levels of the federal, provincial, territorial and municipal governments, and to require a 'child impact statement' to determine the probable impact of any proposed legislation or regulations.
3. To invest in children and young people as a budgetary priority, so that adequate and fair resources are allocated to them in relation to spending on the needs of other sections of the population. (p. 10)

Campaign 2000, a coalition to end child poverty in Canada, published a paper in 1996 entitled *Crossroads for Canada: A Time to Invest in Children and Families*. The paper contains a blueprint for supporting disempowered children and families and for shifting national priorities to promote child and family wellness. The paper proposed the creation of a social investment fund that would have five main objectives:

1. Create a floor of decent living standards for modest and low income families.
2. Endow all young children with the stimulation and care for a healthy start in life.
3. Provide parents with family-time options during formative periods of their children's lives.
4. Protect the living standards of children when parental separation occurs.
5. Assure every academically qualified child in Canada financial access to postsecondary training and studies without having to incur massive life debts into adulthood.

In order to achieve these goals, the authors propose a comprehensive child benefit system, a national envelope for provinces to develop com-

TABLE 3.6
Questions for Assessing the Values of Programs, Practices, and Policies in Family Wellness

Domain	Questions
Caring and protection of health	Do they promote the expression of care, empathy, and concern for the physical and emotional well-being of children and families?
Self-determination	Do they promote the ability of children and adults to pursue their chosen goals without excessive frustration and in consideration of other people's needs?
Human diversity	Do they promote respect and appreciation for diverse social identities?
Collaboration and respect for the community	Do they promote peaceful, respectful, and equitable processes whereby children and adults can have meaningful input into decisions affecting their lives?
Education and personal development	Do they promote educational and personal growth?
Support for strong community structures	Do they promote vital community structures that facilitate the pursuit of personal and communal goals?
Provision of resources based on social justice	Do they promote the fair and equitable allocation of bargaining powers, obligations, and resources in society?

prehensive early development and child care systems across Canada, and a national youth education endowment plan.

We have presented a brief synopsis of what social agents can do to advance wellness values. In the next section we examine how each of us can set in motion the process of becoming more accountable, to oneself and to children, for enacting these values.

VALUES, COMMITMENT, AND ACCOUNTABILITY

Abstract values do not change the world; personal and collective actions do. The process of cultural transformation begins with small steps. When we experience small wins in our battle to promote child wellness, we feel invigorated to continue. To launch a program of personal accountability to children we can ask ourselves what small steps we can take in our personal, professional, and political lives. Inasmuch as most

Vision and Values for Child and Family Wellness 173

of us come into contact with children, directly or indirectly, as parents, relatives, workers, or just as community members, we can all do something to promote wellness values.

For the purpose of becoming more accountable to ourselves and to children, we propose a checklist of personal value interventions. Table 3.6 asks to what extent our personal, professional, and political actions reflect the seven key values of child wellness. If a particular value is promoted to a satisfactory degree, we can ask ourselves what we can do to maintain it. If a value is not promoted to a satisfactory degree, we can ask what we can do to enact it.

You will likely find that you apply some values but not others. Learning from others who found ways to address this value imbalance in their lives is a step in the right direction. We invite you to examine your work and daily interactions in light of family wellness values. We encourage you to ask to what extent your work reflects the ideals of caring and protection of health, personal growth, children's rights, collaboration and respect for others, diversity, support for community structures, and social justice.

SECTION II
Interventions

CHAPTER FOUR

Social Policies for Promoting the Well-Being of Canadian Children and Families

Ray De V. Peters, Jessica E. Peters, Marie-Claire Laurendeau, Claire Chamberland, and Leslea Peirson

INTRODUCTION

Overview

This chapter focuses on social policies that have an impact on the well-being of children and families. In examining these policies we discovered a vast array of social policies that have various effects on family wellness and child development. Therefore, to narrow the discussion we have opted to concentrate on those social policies that have been studied extensively, that are currently at the centre of public policy debates in Canada, and that show some promise of being modified to increase the well-being of Canadian children and their families.

Given these objectives, we organize the discussion into four categories, each representing a unique domain of social policy that independently and/or collectively impacts child and family functioning: (1) family benefits, (2) maternal and parental leave, (3) child care, and (4) child welfare. Permeating the discussion in each of these four areas is the issue of family poverty.

In light of the main subject area of this volume – promoting family wellness and preventing child maltreatment – we cannot ignore the issue of family and child poverty in Canada. A strong case can be made that, as we begin the twenty-first century, poverty is the predominant political and social issue affecting the well-being of children and families in Canada. This is particularly true as provincial/territorial and federal budgets appear to be facing surpluses, and debates on how to apportion the surpluses in terms of debt reductions, tax decreases, and increased social spending begin to command centre stage on all political platforms.

It is important to acknowledge major areas of social policy that are not addressed in this chapter's framework, particularly health care and education policy. Although these policy areas are critically important to the well-being of children and families, Canada has established health-care and education systems that are universally accessible to all citizens as a birthright and are among the best in the world. Therefore, without minimizing the importance of health care and education policy or entering into a discussion about the issues associated with our current structures, the chapter will not address these areas of social policy. Instead, the discussions will highlight those areas of child and family policy in which Canada shows substantial variation from other countries and, in so doing, provide examples of ways in which our policies might be strengthened to achieve better outcomes for Canadian families and their children.

What Is Child and Family Policy?

Child and family policy is a subcategory of social policy that describes what governments do to and for children and their families. More specifically, family policy is concerned with public policies (laws, regulations) that are designed to affect the quality of life for children or families with children, particularly young children (Kamerman, 1996a). Similarly, Baker (1995) suggests that family policy can be defined as a coherent set of principles about the government's role in family life that is implemented through legislation or a plan of action.

The major premise underlying family policy is that society needs children who are healthy, well educated, and socially responsible, and who will develop into productive workers, citizens, and parents (Kamerman, 1996a). The family continues to be viewed as the primary locus for child protection and socialization, and the nurture and care provided by families are essential contributors to the development of children (Daniel & Ivatts, 1998; Harris, 1996).

For the purpose of our discussion, we will view child and family policy as a field or domain that describes legislation, benefits, and services provided by governments in support of child and family well-being. Kamerman (1996a) clearly illustrates that viewing family policies as such is particularly important in those countries that do not have explicit family policies but rather a 'series of policy initiatives that are designed to achieve different and sometimes contradictory objectives and are directed toward various aspects of child and family functioning' (p. 33).

Consequently, this approach is particularly appropriate when examining social policies in the Canadian context, where family policies in the federal and provincial/territorial governments are largely implicit (Baker, 1995). Governments that use this approach to policy development imply a particular view of the role of the state in family life through a collection of independent, often contradictory policies, laws, and regulations. In comparison, governments that have developed explicit written family policies ensure that all laws and regulations impact consistently on family life. Kamerman (1996a) observes:

> In most of the OECD [Organization for Economic Co-operation and Development] countries, in particular those other than the Anglo-American countries (Australia, Canada, Great Britain, New Zealand, United States), family policy is an important social policy field and an important component of the social role of government. In other countries, family policy may be more significant as a policy perspective. For the most part, family policy in continental Europe has been universal, but supplementing the overall concern with special attention to various 'vulnerable' child and family types – in other words, targeting within a universal framework. (p. 35)

For the purpose of clarity of definition, targeted or selected policies are geared toward specified groups of people, often those with lower family incomes, one-parent households, or families experiencing abuse, neglect, or some other crisis. On the other hand, universal policies are provided to all families with dependent children, regardless of family income (Baker, 1995). In addition, as discussed in Chapter 3, European countries adopt a model of *societal or collective responsibility*, whereas in Canada and other Anglo-American countries, *individual responsibility* is the predominant model influencing social policy (Eichler, 1997). The distinctions between targeted and universal policies and between policies that reflect individual versus societal responsibility will be recurring themes in the subsequent discussion and analysis of Canadian child and family policies in comparison with those of other OECD countries.

To provide further context for the subsequent discussion, it is important to recognize that while family policy has played a major role in European social policy since the 1940s, it has more recently become an important issue in North America, fuelled by concerns that the role of the family may be threatened (Zigler, Kagan & Hall, 1996). These concerns are derived from the major social and demographic changes in the structures and composition of families and gender roles during the last few decades (Baker, 1995). These changes have been described in detail in Chapter 2 and include increases in single-parent, mother-led families headed by divorced or never-married women with young children. Other changes include fewer children, nonmarital cohabitation, divorce, and out-of-wedlock births. In addition, family policies have been strongly influenced by changes in the economy and employment patterns in industrialized countries (Harding, 1996; Zimmerman, 1995). These changes have increased concerns about the role of marriage and the family and the possible impacts on the development of children (Harris, 1996; Zigler, Kagan, & Hall, 1996). The dual focus on changes in family structure and gender roles and the balance between work and family life, while keeping sight of the consequences for children, is now at the forefront of much current debate influencing the nature of family policies in all advanced industrialized countries (Baker, 1995; Conway, 1997; Hantrais & Letablier, 1996).

CHILD AND FAMILY POLICIES IN CANADA AND OTHER OECD COUNTRIES

Social policies concerning children and families in OECD countries will be discussed under four major headings: (1) family benefits, (2) maternity and parental leave policies, (3) child care policies, and (d) child welfare policies. In the following sections, Canadian policies in each of these domains are described and compared with policies from several other industrialized countries.

Family Benefits

The first major set of family policies are a variety of child-conditional income transfer policies, referred to as economic policies, that determine the amount and eligibility of families to receive monetary supports to raise their children. The costs of raising children are high. The Canadian Council on Social Development (CCSD, 1998) recently claimed that it cost an estimated $160,000 to raise a child in Canada from birth to 18 years of age in 1998 (including the costs of child care), up from $150,000 in 1994 (CCSD, 1997). This amounts to approximately $8,800 per year for each child. Family benefits consist of a variety of cash benefits and/or tax concessions that are intended to supplement the financial costs of childrearing (Baker, 1995).

Cash Benefits

Canada

In 1989, the House of Commons unanimously passed a resolution to work toward the complete elimination of child poverty in Canada by the year 2000. Five years later, however, in 1994, over 1.3 million or about 19 per cent of all children were poor (Conway, 1997). In 1996, the child poverty rate in Canada reached 20.9 per cent, the second highest among all industrialized countries, surpassed only by the United States. During this time Canada experienced a significant change in its philosophy toward cash benefits, marking a shift away from a European model of responsibility for all children to a U.S. model of efficient delivery of benefits to only some poor children (Phipps, 1995).

Before 1993, Canada provided a universal family allowance that amounted to about $35 per month (noting various minimal provincial variations) for each child under age 18 (Baker, 1995). However, in January 1993, the federal Conservative government, led by Brian Mulroney, revoked this guaranteed income benefit and replaced it for some families with the income-tested Child Tax Benefit. The goals of the 1993 child benefit reform were fairness, effectiveness, efficiency, simplicity, and responsiveness (Woolley, Vermaeten, & Madill, 1996) and were to be achieved by increasing and targeting benefits to lower-income families, supplementing the earnings of low-income parents in the workforce, simplifying the structure of benefits, and making child benefits more responsive to changes in family needs (Phipps, 1995). In order to finance this benefit, targeted to families with middle or low incomes, the government combined money from the former family allowance and the Child Tax Credits. This benefit was nontaxable and partially indexed (when inflation is over 3 per cent) to the rising cost of living (Baker, 1995).

Therefore, in 1993, the basic child benefit available to families with incomes under $25,921 was $1,020 per child per year. For larger families, a further $75 was paid for the third and additional children. Above the income cut-off of $25,921, benefit levels were reduced by five cents for every dollar of income (Woolley et al., 1996). Families with net incomes up to $70,981 received partial benefits, while those with incomes over that amount did not receive any child benefit. In addition to this monthly benefit, a working income supplement of $500 per family per year was paid to the 'working poor,' regardless of the number of children. This benefit was not extended to nonworking families.

Because of the interaction of old and new child benefits with other elements of the tax and transfer system, the greatest gains in disposable income were experienced by families with annual incomes in the $40,000 to $50,000 range. In reality, ending universal child benefits delivered few benefits to very poor families, despite the fact that the reform was explicitly designed to 'give the greatest benefit to low income families' (Woolley et al., 1996). Furthermore, the move away from universal benefits inevitably left some parents without benefits, and without any social recognition of their contribution to society as parents (Woolley et al., 1996).

Many policy researchers argued that the new child benefit would do little to reduce child poverty in Canada because in order to create the benefit no new money was added (Kesselman, 1993; Pulkingham, Ternowetsky, & Hay, 1997). In fact, from 1994 to 1995, average after-tax income for families with children dropped slightly, except for lone-parent families, who experienced a modest increase in their incomes. The number of poor children also rose from 1.36 million to 1.47 million.

In the Speech from the Throne delivered by the federal Liberal government in 1997, a new initiative entitled the National Child Benefit (NCB) system was announced. It was the first major social policy response of the Liberal government to Parliament's 1989 resolution to fight child poverty. In this new approach to the delivery of child benefits, the federal government was to enrich and reconfigure its Child Tax Benefit/Working Income Supplement to create a single Canada Child Tax Benefit, paying the same maximum benefit to all low-income families with children while continuing to provide partial benefits to the majority of non-poor families (Battle & Mendelson, 1997).

The NCB is an innovative approach for investing in children, and was designed by the federal/provincial/territorial ministers responsible for social services and coordinated by the Council on Social Policy Renewal. As its initial contribution to this initiative, the federal government is providing an additional $850 million per year to enhance the previous Child Tax Benefit as a common income platform across the country. The objectives of the National Child Benefit system are as follows:

1. to help prevent and reduce the depth of poverty;
2. to promote attachment to the workforce by ensuring that families will always be better off as a result of working, resulting in fewer families having to rely on social assistance; and

3. to reduce overlap and duplication through closer harmonization of program objectives and benefits and through simplified administration.

In order to fulfil these objectives, the National Child Benefit system consists of three initial and simultaneous steps:

1. The federal government will increase benefits for all low-income families with children, whether or not they receive social assistance. In so doing, the government will assume more financial responsibility for providing basic income support for children. Under this system, the federal government will increase and amalgamate the current Child Tax Benefit/Working Income Supplement into one benefit: the Canada Child Tax Benefit (CCTB). The new benefit will combine:

   - the existing $5.1 billion Child Tax Benefit and Working Income Supplement;
   - the $250 million committed to increase the supplement in the 1996 budget; and,
   - the $600 million announced in the 1997 budget for the combined benefit.

   Beginning in July 1998, the maximum the Canada Child Tax Benefit provides to a family with one child is $1,625, with a further $1,425 for each additional child up to four children (i.e., $1,625, $3,050, $4,475, $5,900 for one, two, three, and four children respectively). These maximums apply to all families with a net family income up to $20,921. Families with incomes above $25,921 receive the same benefits as they did under the Child Tax Benefit, providing families with $213 per child under the age of 7 if child care expenses are not claimed on income tax returns. A sliding scale of decreased benefits exists for families with net incomes between $20,921 and $25,921.
2. Corresponding with the increased federal benefit, provinces and territories will decrease their share of social assistance payments for families with children while ensuring that these families continue to receive at least the same amount from government overall.
3. Provinces and territories have made a commitment to reinvest the money they save from welfare payments in programs that continue to target low-income families.

It must be noted that this new approach does not mean more money for Canada's poorest children, since the additional money the federal government is investing in the Canada Child Tax Benefit will be received by working-poor families – those not currently collecting welfare.

The main thrust of the new policy initiative is to break down the 'welfare wall,' which is the gap between the income earned by working parents in low-paying jobs and those collecting welfare. This has been one of the inherent problems with the Canadian welfare structure. Welfare in Canada is delivered provincially/territorially, and is an unindexed financial support to those most in need. Although provinces/territories calculate the rates of welfare differently, even the maximum amount of money provided to families is far below Statistics Canada's low-income cut-off rates. However, in addition to the money received through welfare, other subsidies and supplements are available for these families, such as dental and housing subsidies. When a family leaves welfare, they are faced not only with the loss of the income and subsidies provided to them through the welfare structure, but also with taxes payable on their new income and payments to Employment Insurance. Some, for example, lone parents, may also have to deal with the cost of child care in order to enter the workforce. Thus, the increased financial support provided by the NCB is designed to allow low-income working families to remain in the workforce, rather than resort to welfare in order to provide family resources.

One of the major criticisms of the NCB is that it pits the poorest against the poor, since those currently collecting welfare – and therefore, by assumption, Canada's poorest – will not receive any additional money from government to assist them in raising their children (Pulkingham et al., 1997). A related issue is that the money the provinces/territories are required to reinvest as part of the initiative may target working families with low incomes, not those families on social assistance. In addition, neither the benefits paid nor the family income thresholds under the CCTB are fully indexed to inflation. Indexing only occurs when the inflation rate exceeds 3 per cent. Since 1984, inflation has reduced the value of the family benefits by $800 million (in 1996 dollars), and their value continues to decline at a rate of $170 million per year.

However, Battle and Mendelson (1997) assert that it is important to start with an income stabilizer such as the CCTB. They emphasize that while the initial benefit will not directly affect welfare families, the government will need to increase the benefits for all to a level that reasonably covers the costs of raising children (similar to the government's commitment to supplying seniors with an amount of money that is reasonable to cover their costs).

Now that Canada's ratification of the Rights of the Child and its commitment to end child poverty are almost ten years old, this new initiative holds promise. However, Battle and Mendelson caution that the NCB should not be touted as a magic solution to cure child poverty. Other contributors to child poverty will also need to be addressed. To put the federal initiative into perspective, it has been estimated that the additional $850 million that has been committed will result in about 10 per cent fewer children living in poverty.

The Quebec government announced that it was consolidating family allowances into a single program in order to get families with children off social assistance, among other objectives. The program will substantially increase the allowance for low-income families and reduce benefits for families with average or high incomes. Families with average or high incomes will now be eligible for a Child Tax Credit only. Because this reform is taking place in a deficit-cutting environment, it is uncertain whether the amounts invested will be enough not only to get families with children off social assistance, but to get them out of poverty as well.

As noted above, Canada's child poverty rate reached 20.9 per cent in 1996. If the NCB attains its goal of reducing child poverty by 10 per cent, this means that 18.8 per cent of Canada's children will still live below the poverty line. Clearly, both the federal and provincial/territorial governments must do more to help poor children. Providing financial assistance is a necessary first step, but there are other ways to help low-income families. Since child poverty is always a result of family poverty, governments must also participate in job creation efforts; work to improve wages, benefits, and working conditions; and foster social support programs such as child care or advanced training for adults (CCSD, 1997). Policies and programs designed to deal with child and family poverty and well-being are discussed later in this chapter.

International Context
Since 1975, cash benefits to families have undergone a major policy shift in many industrialized countries. While these benefits were previously provided to all families, several governments, including Canada, Australia, and Germany, have introduced a means-tested, targeted benefit. The

TABLE 4.1
Family Allowances for a Family with Two Children, 1975–1990

Country	Allowances as a Percentage of Average Male Wages in Manufacturing			
	1975	1980	1985	1990
Australia	1.0	3.3	3.2	3.4
Austria	8.5	13.0	12.0	11.3
Belgium	10.4	9.8	11.0	10.4
Canada	**4.5**	**2.8**	**2.8**	**2.4**
Denmark	4.4	3.4	2.8	5.2
Finland	4.8	5.4	6.0	6.2
France	5.5	5.2	7.4	7.1
Germany	6.7	4.9	5.0	4.9
Greece	3.8	6.8	3.9	3.2
Ireland	2.7	2.5	2.9	3.0
Italy	5.9	4.6	2.3	0.0
Japan	–	–	–	0.6
Luxembourg	6.0	7.2	7.4	8.3
Netherlands	7.6	8.6	7.5	7.4
New Zealand	5.4	5.3	3.2	2.1
Norway	3.4	6.4	7.6	9.1
Portugal	7.5	3.8	3.4	4.9
Spain	2.6	1.0	0.5	0.3
Sweden	5.1	6.6	7.7	7.2
Switzerland	4.6	3.8	4.8	4.7
United Kingdom	2.7	8.9	8.8	6.3
United States	–	–	–	–

need to reduce public spending and support lower-income families are reasons given to justify this change in policy. On the other hand, countries that have retained the universal component to family allowances (e.g., France, the Netherlands, the United Kingdom, Sweden) argue that its high cost is outweighed by several advantages: no needy children are missed, administrative costs are lower, no social stigma is attached, and there are no work disincentives because income is supplemented, not replaced.

One way to compare the relative value of family allowances across various countries is to calculate the benefit in terms of the percentage of average income. Table 4.1 lists the value of family allowances across 21 countries, expressed as a percentage of average male wages in manufacturing. At 2.4 per cent, Canada is well below the average of 5.0 per cent. Both the actual and relative value of this benefit to Canadian families appear to be quite low. It is evident from this international comparison that Canada is not providing even an average amount of financial support to families. Also, the fact that Canada has abolished the universality of its support to families is of further concern, since research indicates that nations using income-tested benefits have been less successful in keeping families with children above the poverty line than have nations using universal measures (Kamerman, 1996a).

Tax Concessions

Most industrialized countries provide income tax concessions for parents with dependent children, for lone parents, or for working parents requiring child care services. There are three types of tax concessions: credits, deductions, and exemptions. Tax credits reduce the amount of income tax payable and are usually considered to be more beneficial to families because their relative value is higher for those with lower marginal tax rates. Tax deductions (which lower taxable incomes) are seen as more favourable to higher-income earners since a deduction is worth more when income is higher. Tax exemptions mean that no income tax is payable on income from a certain source. These three types of tax concessions are often referred to as negative income tax transfers or concessions.

Canada
Negative income tax transfers have become an important part of the Canadian social welfare system. Income received from the Child Tax Benefit is a credit. Other family tax concessions in Canada include:

- Married Credit – available for dependent spouses; in 1993, this was worth $915 in federal tax savings;
- Equivalent to Married Credit – worth the same as the Married Credit; attempts to treat common-law partners like married couples and prohibits lone parents from claiming the credit if they are in such a relationship;
- Goods & Services Tax Credit – a refundable tax credit for low-income filers;
- Child Care Expense Deduction – child care expenses for working parents can be deducted up to a maximum of $5,000 per child under

7 and $3,000 per child aged 7 to 14. This deduction is more useful to middle-class than to working-class families. Although subsidized child care spaces are set aside for low-income families, there are not enough spaces available for the families who need them.

International Context

While all countries use their tax systems to pursue family policy objectives, some countries focus more heavily on this form of support than others. The United States, for example, provides a variety of tax deductions (for dependants, including both children and adults, for married couples, for a head of a household, and for a single person). Because these tax concessions are deductions rather than refundable credits, families with higher marginal tax rates derive greater benefit from them than lower-income families. By comparison, Sweden delivers most family benefits through social insurance or direct state transfers rather than through tax concessions.

A Brief Review of Family Cash and Tax Benefits in Other OECD Countries

The systems of family allowances and tax concessions are well documented. Baker (1995), Gauthier (1996), and Kamerman (1996a) have examined the family policies of over twenty advanced, industrialized OECD countries. Baker (1995) used poverty rates of nonelderly families before and after taxes and transfers in the mid-1980s to illustrate the relative effectiveness of these economic transfers in alleviating child poverty (see Table 4.2). Gauthier (1996) produced the graph presented in Figure 4.1, which depicts the effect of cash transfers among 22 countries. In this figure the index represents the additional disposable income of a two-child family as a percentage of the disposable income of a single worker. The statistical information provided in these two examples explicitly illustrates the relative international position of Canada's economic policies in providing support to children and their families.

Australia

Like Canada, Australia has recently abolished universality and replaced it with an income-tested family allowance. Although the benefit is income tested, it has been more successful than the Canadian Child Tax Credit in providing more generous financial assistance to those who need it. Also interesting to note is that the benefit is still delivered as an allowance rather than through the tax system, as in Canada. In addition,

TABLE 4.2
Poverty Rates of Nonelderly Families before and after Taxes and Transfers, Mid-1980s

Country	Poverty Rate* before Taxes and Transfers**	Poverty Rate* after Taxes and Transfers**
Canada	17.4	13.9
France	20.4	9.9
Netherlands	19.9	7.6
Sweden	15.3	8.6
United Kingdom	23.2	12.5
United States	18.0	18.1
West Germany	10.7	6.8

*Percentage of all households with heads 20 to 55 years old who had incomes less than 50 per cent of the adjusted national median income.
**Includes all public assistance transfers.

Australia has added a more generous supplement for low-income families. Low-income families may qualify for rent assistance and pharmaceutical benefits, and lone parents may be eligible for a pension as well as assistance with child support. Unlike the situation in Canada, a child in Australia is worth slightly more than a dependent spouse in terms of tax concessions.

France
The present family allowance in France is paid to all families with children under 17 years of age, or under 20 if they are students. The child allowance is worth more in France than in any other country in Baker's 1995 study, and worth more than six times the former Canadian family allowance. There is also a further supplement for low-income families.

In addition to the family allowance and low-income supplement, France offers a universal young child's benefit to both employees and homemakers for nine months, from five months before birth to three months after. The idea behind this benefit is that families have greater expenses at the time of childbirth. For mothers who are also employed, the young child's allowance is combined with paid maternity leaves of sixteen weeks.

If a woman with three or more children wants to stay home to care for her children, the government may also provide a monthly parental education allowance. This allowance pays a maximum of $600 per month until the child is 3, but is income tested. A parent may also work part-time and receive partial benefits. This allowance is adjusted annually for

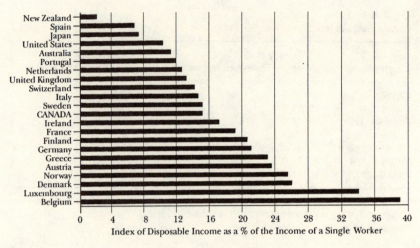

Figure 4.1 Cash Transfers to Two-Child Families, 1990

cost-of-living changes. In addition, child care is both subsidized and provided by the government. Finally, France also provides an allowance for lone parents, which is paid as a flat-rate benefit per child.

Germany

The value of family allowances in Germany varies by family size and family income. Low-income families receive a children's allowance each month worth between $22 and $101. These allowances are available to parents with children under age 16, 21 if they are unemployed and 27 if they are students.

The German tax system assumes that the husband is the economic provider and that the wife will stay at home and take care of the children. Tax credits for a financially dependent spouse may amount to the equivalent of $10,000 US. Since 1986, the German tax system has treated lone mothers the same way as married couples, in that they receive a double household deduction rather than merely one for a single person.

Netherlands

The universal child allowance in the Netherlands varies by age and number of children. For a family with two children between the ages of 6 and 12, the total benefit amounted to $2,640 per year in 1991, more than three times the value of the former Canadian family allowance.

There are no special child allowances for lone parents in the Netherlands since social assistance is relatively generous and does not require mothers with preschool children to enter the labour force. Consequently, both lone and married mothers have low employment participation rates, particularly for full-time work. There is a strong tradition of women remaining at home to care for their children, and mothers who choose this option are supported by high levels of benefits.

Sweden
As in France, Sweden's benefits for families are generous and proactive, but they are based on different philosophies. France focuses on the family as a unit, while Sweden emphasizes full employment, job training, employment equity, and individual rights. Since 1947, Sweden has provided generous economic support for all families with children under age 16 through the nontaxable child allowance, which is paid monthly to the mother or official guardian. Larger allowances are paid for third and subsequent children. While many countries were cutting back on social benefits, the child allowance was increased in Sweden in both 1982 and 1991. The 1991 allowance was worth more than four and a half times Canada's former allowance. Sweden provides numerous additional family benefits and direct services for children in addition to a child allowance. For example, housing allowances are provided for low-income parents. Most family benefits are delivered through social insurance or direct state transfers rather than tax concessions.

Both marginal and average tax rates are higher for one-earner than two-earner families. The highly progressive tax system, which expects higher-income earners to pay a larger percentage of income tax, also makes it more favourable for a woman to go out to work than for her husband to work overtime.

United Kingdom
The child benefit in the United Kingdom is nontaxable, not means tested, and is delivered to mothers or guardians weekly for children under age 16. Also, a Family Credit supplements low wages of parents working more than 24 hours per week. Universal family benefits can become a protection in times of instability, such as marriage breakdown or unemployment and when there are changes in the level and regularity of family income. All taxpayers are entitled to a basic personal tax exemption, and sole parents and sole breadwinners are entitled to additional exemptions that are comparable in value.

United States

The major family benefit in the United States is Aid to Families with Dependent Children (AFDC), which provides means-tested cash benefits to low-income parents only. AFDC is focused on moving parents from welfare to low-paying jobs and tightening up enforcement of child support orders.

The United States also provides a variety of tax deductions for dependents, including both children and adults, for married couples, for heads of households, and for single persons. Because these tax concessions are deductions rather than refundable credits, families and individuals with higher marginal tax rates derive greater benefit from them than lower-income families.

Child Support Policies

In the past two decades, most countries have experienced rising rates of marriage dissolution (Chafel, 1993; Conway, 1997; Zimmerman, 1995).

> One of the most obvious consequences of divorce is an increase in single-parent families. Where there are children, divorce creates, at least for a time, a single-parent-child(ren) household, and it is overwhelmingly the case that it is the mother who remains with the children and the father who is absent. (Harding, 1996)

Easier and more affordable access to divorce, in conjunction with society's increased acceptance of divorce, has resulted in many parents finding themselves alone in facing the task of raising their children (Baker, 1995). For many of these lone-parent families, which are predominantly headed by women, child support payments from the noncustodial parent are essential in enabling them to provide financially for their children.

> One of the salient features of childhood poverty is that it is much more prevalent among single parent families, particularly those headed by a female, whether these families are a result of separation or of birth out of wedlock. While there are many complex issues associated with the support of children in single parent families, it is apparent payments from noncustodial parents are inadequate to prevent many children from living in poverty. (Bala, 1991, p. 116)

Summarizing one of the detrimental effects of marriage dissolution,

Rickel and Becker (1997) conclude that 'the increase in single-parent families, which often receive little or no support from the absent parent, has been an important factor in the increasing numbers of children living in poverty' (p. 2). Conway (1997) confirms that for most of these sole-parent, mother-led families, the result is that women still do not experience economic justice upon family breakdown, with child support orders often contributing 'less than half the cost of raising a child and often go[ing] no higher than 20 per cent of a husband's net income' (p. 138). Although many lone parents must depend on this income, in many countries, including Canada, the default rate for these payments is extremely high. Given this reality, governments have developed child support policies aimed at ensuring that families receive these essential payments. Although these policies share a common goal, they employ different means in attempting to ensure that this support is delivered.

Private enforcement, limited advance maintenance, and advance maintenance are the most prominent child support policies (Baker, 1995). While they all maintain that both parents hold responsibility for ensuring the financial security of their children, they differ with respect to who should suffer if one parent defaults in this responsibility. The *private enforcement model*, which is the most prominent in Canada, places the onus of support on mothers because the laws are ineffective in forcing fathers to pay. With the *limited advance maintenance approach*, governments focus most of their attention on debt collection and the enforcement of noncustodial parental responsibility. However, this approach does not extend a government guarantee that the payment will be delivered, the result being that the economic security of the children is dependent on the effectiveness of the enforcement policies and on the ability to seize payments from the delinquent noncustodial parent. In contrast, the *advance maintenance approach* has focused on assuring that children receive an adequate standard of living. In this last scenario, if a parent is unwilling or unable to support his or her children, it should not be the children who suffer the consequences of the situation (i.e., poverty). Where the advance maintenance approach is used,

> a public authority, often the social security agency, guarantees a specified level of child support by advancing support payments to the custodial or caretaking parent if payment is not regularly made by the absent parent, or if payment is not made at all. In addition, the same or another public agency assumes responsibility for the collection of child support from the

absent parent, crediting what is collected against the payments advanced. (Kamerman, 1996a, p. 39)

Canada

Most provinces in Canada operate under the policy of private enforcement. With the exception of Ontario, Manitoba, and Quebec, which have implemented advance maintenance policies,

> the onus is on the custodial parent to pursue the other parent, typically with the assistance of a lawyer. If an agreement cannot be achieved in regard to child support, the matter can be brought to court, where the judge has considerable discretion in determining the amount of support. (Bala, 1991, pp. 116–17)

Exacerbating the financial inequality faced by women in Canada, custodial mothers are taxed on child support payments while separated or divorced fathers are provided with a tax concession on payments made. As is the case with many other family policies that have been examined, the Canadian experience with respect to child support payments lacks a social responsibility perspective. Instead, the focus is on keeping public expenditures low by making parents, instead of taxpayers, finance child support (Baker, 1995; Gauthier, 1996).

Netherlands

The Netherlands employs a system in which custodial parents must first sue the nonresidential parent for child support through the courts, although there is a system of limited advance maintenance. The level of child support is established by private arrangement or judicial discretion, and is related to parents' financial circumstances. Unless the recipient wishes to receive payments directly, payments are made through automatic bank account transfers. If the paying account has insufficient funds, the agency forwards money to the custodial parent and the payer is charged interest on the overdraft. Imprisonment is the final penalty for nonsupporters. Compared with other countries, the Netherlands has developed a strong administrative structure and an efficient collection system for court-awarded child support (unpaid support is less than 8 per cent).

Sweden

Both Sweden and France have advance maintenance child support policies, which share the objective of assuring more adequate provision of child support (Kamerman, 1996a). In both countries, a minimum level of child support is established. The guaranteed level of support in Sweden is set at 40 per cent of the basic needs assessment for children. If the noncustodial parent cannot pay the minimum amount or defaults on payments, the government guarantees the amount to the custodial parent. The government or appointed agency/office then takes on the task of collecting the payment from the noncustodial parent (Baker, 1995). Sweden also maintains a centralized comprehensive system to locate absent parents, establish paternity, collect child support, and disburse advance maintenance.

In Sweden, nearly 30 per cent of families are headed by lone parents, but both parents are held legally responsible for their children. The child support program is based on the assumption that mother-led families may be economically weak and that advance maintenance is, therefore, an essential service for the well-being of children and their custodial parents.

United Kingdom

The percentage of lone parents relying on social assistance in the United Kingdom rose from 38 per cent in 1979 to 70 per cent in 1992. Yet only 23 per cent of the parents in 1992 were receiving child support payments – compared with 50 per cent ten years earlier. In 1993 a limited advance maintenance program was introduced to enforce the financial responsibility of absent parents in order to reduce the financial responsibility of the state. Judges have tended to base the level of support on children's needs and the financial means of parents, who are allowed some protected income of their own. Defaulters can have their earnings or property garnished, and serious defaulting can lead to imprisonment. This new Child Support Act reduces lone mothers' reliance on social assistance by placing greater onus on fathers to pay. However, this type of support program can have the unfavourable consequence of perpetuating and reinforcing women's economic dependence on former male partners.

United States

In the United States, child support is the responsibility of state governments. In the past, most states have employed a private enforcement model. However, federal requirements are now propelling states to move in the direction of a limited advance maintenance model. The enforcement of court-awarded child support is now viewed in the United States as the strategy of choice for reducing public assistance expenditures. As more public money is being spent on lone-parent families, attempts to enforce parental support are gaining public acceptance. The calculation of support levels is the responsibility of each state and takes into consideration the needs of children and the parents' ability to pay.

Child support enforcement services are now available to all families, including those not on AFDC. Families on AFDC may keep only $64 per month of the support collected on their behalf. This indicates that the main purpose of the new enforcement system is to move families off welfare rather than improve their economic situation. Enforcement services include locating parents, establishing paternity, setting and enforcing support obligations, and collecting payments.

The primary motivation of child support reforms appears to be to reduce government expenditures rather than to assure adequate financial support to children and reduce poverty rates (Baker, 1995).

Summary

> Rigorous analyses of the effects of child-conditioned income transfer policies in several countries indicate that these family benefits are effective in redistributing income vertically, from those with more income to those with less, as well as horizontally, from those with no children to those with children. One result attributable largely to these and other child-related income transfers is significantly lower child poverty rates in such countries as Germany, the Netherlands, Norway and Sweden, than that in the United States, regardless of family structure. The success of these transfers is such that child poverty is no longer viewed as a problem in these countries. (Kamerman, 1996a, pp. 41–2)

Family allowances and tax concessions make up only a portion of the state's contribution in supporting families. In reiterating Battle and Mendelson's (1997) caution not to view the NCB as a magic solution, we move now to a discussion of several other forms of family policy: maternity and parental leave, child care, and child welfare policy. From this analysis a more complete picture of Canada's current situation as well as its relative position in an international context will emerge.

Maternity and Parental Leave Policies

With the rising cost of living, both parents in a family are finding it necessary to enter the labour force. In addition, the increase in female labour force participation since the 1960s has made maternity and parental leave benefits an important form of state support for families to help them meet the dual demands of childrearing and work (Gauthier, 1996). These cash benefits both offset some of the additional costs of having a new baby and replace wages forgone at the time of childbirth while the mother is home recovering and while both parents adjust to the new addition to the family (Kamerman, 1996a). Two types of parental leave can be distinguished: *Maternity leave* is granted to mothers at the time of birth; *parental/extended child care leaves* are granted to mothers, and in some cases fathers, for a period of time after the duration of maternity leave has expired.

Maternity Leave

Canada
Canada guarantees a working woman maternity leave of 15 weeks at 55 per cent of her wage to a maximum in 1997 of $413 weekly (Conway, 1997). To be eligible for this benefit, a female employee must have confirmed continuous employment for 20 weeks in the year prior to commencing the leave. Maternity leave benefits are paid through the federal Employment Insurance program. No benefits are available to unemployed or self-employed mothers. Some institutions and companies extend these benefits for longer periods, and/or 'top up' the salary to as much as 100 per cent (Baker, 1995).

International Context
Gauthier's (1996) analysis of maternity leave schemes indicated an increase in duration from a cross-national average (eighteen countries) of 15.5 weeks in 1975 to 22.1 weeks in 1990. The strongest increases were observed in Nordic countries. These increases were due to increased female labour force participation since the 1960s, making both maternity and parental leave important forms of state support for families (Baker, 1995). The countries providing the longest duration for maternity leave are: Denmark (28 weeks), Norway (35 weeks), Finland (53 weeks), and Sweden (65 weeks). Other countries offer similar durations of maternity leave, ranging from 14 to 20 weeks of legislated paid leave. However, Switzerland provides only 8 weeks, and Australia, United States, and New Zealand have no national maternity leave schemes.

TABLE 4.3
Maternity Leave Benefits, 1975–1990

Country	1975 Duration (weeks)	1975 Pay (%)	1980 Duration (weeks)	1980 Pay (%)	1985 Duration (weeks)	1985 Pay (%)	1990 Duration (weeks)	1990 Pay (%)
Austria	12	100	16	100	16	100	16	100
Belgium	14	60	14	80	14	80	14	80
Canada	**15**	**67**	**15**	**60**	**15**	**60**	**15**	**60**
Denmark	14	90	18	90	28	90	28	90
Finland	35	39	47	39	52	80	53	80
France	14	90	16	90	16	84	16	84
Germany	14	100	14	100	14	100	14	100
Greece	12	50	12	50	12	50	15	50
Ireland	12	65	12	65	14	70	14	70
Italy	20	80	20	80	20	80	20	80
Japan	12	60	12	60	14	60	14	60
Luxembourg	12	100	16	100	16	100	16	100
Netherlands	12	100	12	100	12	100	16	100
Norway	12	30	18	100	18	100	35	80
Portugal	9	100	13	100	13	100	13	100
Spain	12	75	14	75	14	75	16	75
Sweden	30	90	52	70	52	70	65	75
Switzerland	8	100	8	100	8	100	8	100
United Kingdom	18	30	18	30	18	30	18	45

In determining the extent of support that maternity leave benefits provide, it is important to consider the amount of pay provided during the legislated leave. This is calculated either as a flat-rate benefit (based on an average female wage in manufacturing) or as an earnings-related benefit (based on prior earnings). In addition, several countries offer a combination of these two schemes, with a portion of the leave paid as a percentage of previous earnings and the remainder as a flat-rate benefit (Baker, 1995). Many countries offer between 75 and 90 per cent wage replacement, while the United Kingdom (45 per cent), Greece (50 per cent), and Japan (60 per cent) are well below the average level of pay replacement. Austria, Germany, Luxembourg, the Netherlands, Portugal, and Switzerland all offer 100 per cent wage replacement.

In order to determine the overall extent of the support provided by maternity benefits, one must take into account both the duration of the leave and the percentage of pay during this period. Table 4.3

(from Gauthier, 1996) provides a comprehensive picture of such support internationally. As was evident in the previous discussions of family allowances and tax concessions, Canada rates poorly relative to other countries, finding itself among the bottom quarter. This results more from the limited support offered through the relatively low replacement wage of 57 per cent than from the duration of leave, which although still below the average at 15 weeks, is closer to the mean for OECD countries.

Parental and Extended Child Care Leave

Canada
The federal Employment Insurance program provides for 10 weeks of paid parental leave following the 15 weeks of maternity leave, plus an additional 17 to 18 weeks of unpaid leave under provincial jurisdiction. While 28 weeks can be taken by either parent, they cannot be taken by both parents at the same time. Therefore, the maximum available leave is 43 weeks with the last 18 weeks being unpaid. No such benefits are extended to self-employed or nonworking parents.

The Quebec government had proposed reforms to parental leave provisions that would extend these benefits to self-employed workers, who are now excluded. The benefits would be nontaxable, provide more generous income compensation, and be more attractive to fathers. However, this reform is currently on hold because Quebec has been unable to convince the federal government to increase its share of program funding.

International Context
Baker (1995) has observed that Canada and other English-speaking countries tend to view maternity and parental leave as an expense and irritant to employers, and also as a deterrent to hiring women. On the other hand, the European countries studied by Baker seem to view maternity and parental leave and benefits as maternal and child health issues, a form of employment equity for women, an inducement for reproduction, and a right for every employed woman.

The minimum childbirth-related leave among the European countries is three months in the Netherlands and a few other countries, 16 weeks in France, nine months to one year in Italy, one year in Denmark, one and one-half years in Sweden, and three years in Austria, Finland, France (for third and subsequent children), Germany, and Hungary. In

Sweden, the parental leave can be shared equally by both parents; in Austria, Canada, Denmark, Finland, Germany, Hungary, and Norway, fathers can share in some portion of the leave. In most countries the extended parental leave carries with it the right to a wage-related benefit; in some the benefit is provided at a flat rate. In most countries the benefit is funded as a contributory social insurance benefit (either a 'sickness' benefit or an unemployment insurance benefit) or a special parenting benefit. In some other countries it is funded out of general revenue.

Finland's policy is unique in that parents have a real choice following the end of the one-year, fully paid parental leave. They can choose among a guaranteed, heavily subsidized place in a child care centre, a modest subsidy to help pay for in-home child care, or a modest cash benefit to provide support for an extended two-year parental leave at home to care for a child until his or her third birthday.

Sweden also is unique in providing a one-and-one-half-year job-protected leave and a cash benefit that covers 80 per cent of wages for one year, three additional months at a minimum flat rate, and three more months as unpaid leave. The benefit is available to either parent and can be prorated so that parents may use it to cover full-time, half-time, or three-quarter-time work while children are young; this enables parents to share child care responsibilities between them for the child's first year and a half.

Policies such as these represent an attempt by society to provide time when, it is assumed, a parent needs to be at home to recover from childbirth, to provide critical child care, and to assure children a good start in life (Kamerman, 1996a).

> The overall impact of family-friendly policy measures in the Nordic states would seem to be the creation of an environment in which employment and family life are not considered to be in conflict with one another; rather, they are complementary. By the 1990s these developments extended to many of the OECD countries and seemed to characterize the major thrust of European family policy innovations for the rest of the century. These 'new' family policies suggest both the acceptance of 'working families' as a normative state for parents of young children and the value of paid time off for parenting as a social benefit. (Hantrais & Letablier, 1996, p. 127)

These policies appear to be reducing any negative effects that work might have on the family, with the result that continuity of employment can be maintained as well as the relative autonomy of family members (Hantrais & Letablier, 1996).

Summary

Maternity/parental leave policies are important components of family support. Both the legislated length of the leave and the subsidy during this period are critical to families as they plan for parenthood. In the analysis of this policy by country, it is evident that some countries go further in explicitly recognizing the importance and demands required to raise children and remain competitive in the workforce. It was shown that European countries provide longer duration of paid leave as well as a better rate of pay than many Anglo-American countries including Canada, the United Kingdom, the United States, and Australia. Also, many European countries offer additional benefits to women in raising their children, whether they are in the workforce or not.

Child Care Policy

The issue of child care is at the forefront of the debate concerning the relevant policy supports available to children and families in Canada. As with many other policies that affect the family, the root of this debate lies in the extent to which the state should be involved in the private functioning of the family. In Canada, the response to this question has been to remain silent, making the position clear that the issue is a private rather than a public responsibility. However, the rising cost of living and the question of gender equality have resulted in an increase in women's labour force participation. This has placed considerable pressure on government to reexamine the child care policy debate with a view to recognizing the need for and importance and benefits of a national child care policy.

Three prominent models of responsibility have shaped the development of child care policies in most industrialized countries (Baker, 1995): the public, social welfare, and mixed responsibility models. In the *public responsibility* model, preschool child care is seen as important for children's development and essential for enabling mothers to participate equally in the labour force. Examples of countries employing a public responsibility model of child care include France and Sweden. The *social welfare* model of child care is one in which the vast majority of services are provided by family members, neighbours, or private caregivers. Government assistance is very selective and subsidizes only the poorest and most disadvantaged children. Examples of countries that employ social welfare models include the United States and the United Kingdom. In the *mixed responsibility* approach, child care services are provided by both the private and the public sectors. Certain categories of parents, such as lone-parent families or those with low incomes, may be given priority for subsidized spaces, and fees usually vary by family income. Governments may also provide income tax deductions or credits for child care, especially for parents who are employed or are full-time students. More variation in the quality of services, costs, and subsidies is apparent in the mixed responsibility model than in the public responsibility model, and there is generally a shortage of spaces and high use of relatives as care providers. Canada, Australia, and the Netherlands follow this model.

The model selected by government reflects its philosophical beliefs as to whether nonparental child care is necessary for the well-being of children and their parents. For example, in most European countries, preschool child care is typically viewed as a citizenship right and as an important part of early childhood development regardless of the mother's employment status. It is viewed generally as a social responsibility and consequently is publicly funded, financed through payroll taxes or general revenue, with minimal or no user fees.

On the other hand, the United Kingdom and the United States have a different view of child care and hence have adopted a private/social welfare model in developing their policies. The United Kingdom, for example, has traditionally been opposed to employment for married women and mothers. The lack of a publicly funded child care policy, therefore, has kept women out of the labour force: in the 1980s, one-third of employed women did not return to their jobs after giving birth because of a lack of child care.

Canada

At present, Canada has no national child care policy. Instead, the licensing and regulation of child care fall under provincial/territorial jurisdiction. As a result of the distinct provincial/territorial responsibilities, the child care system is fragmented and the quality and availability of service vary (Baker, 1995). Although subsidized child care and family care spaces are available to low-and modest-income earners, the availability of these spaces is limited, with the demand far exceeding the supply. As a result, the majority of Canadian families make use of informal and unregulated care, which involves using sitters, relatives, and neighbours. The second most utilized form of child care is regulated daycare centres, both commercial and not-for-profit, followed by regulated family daycare with smaller child–staff ratios than child care centres. As expected, with the majority of families making use of informal child care options, concern is high with respect to the quality of the care that these children receive. The concern around quality is explained by Friendly (1994), who asserts that the quality of child care has proven effects on the developmental and social impacts on the child. Additional concerns inherent in the current Canadian child care structure are the lack of subsidized spaces in formal child care for those who need it, the lack of time parents are afforded to actually investigate and research the child care options available to them, the lack of national standards, and the low pay for child care workers, which reduces their commitment to the job and results in a high rate of turnover.

Friendly and Rothman (1995) identify four main goals for providing child care: (1) alleviating poverty, (2) fostering women's equality, (3) optimizing child development, and (4) promoting economic wellbeing. They then assess child care in Canada and conclude that the system does not meet any of these four goals.

Only a fraction of financially needy families receive assistance for child care fees. The deficiencies of the subsidy system regularly keep low-income families to whom the program is targeted out of training programs, education, and employment in much of Canada. In addition, for most modest-income families who are not eligible for subsidy, the cost of high-quality care is too high. This forces them either to pay a large percentage of their salary toward these high-quality programs (and risk falling into poverty) or to place their children in less-expensive, poorer-quality care.

The scarcity of regulated services, the weakness of legislated requirements for programs, and the shortcomings of the policy context that influences quality suggest that as the number and proportion of preschool children with mothers in the labour force increases each year, many of Canada's youngest children may be spending their preschool years in circumstances that fail to promote their healthiest development. Failure to invest in families with children has potential long-term costs to society in the form of less-healthy and more poorly functioning adults.

Friendly and Rothman (1995) conclude their analysis with a summary of policy recommendations that would enable Canada to meet the goals of child care as outlined above.

1. Child care services should be universally accessible – all children and families should be entitled to child care regardless of family income, work status, or region of the country.
2. Child care service provision should be comprehensive – to recognize the varying needs of Canadian families, programs need to be flexible and diverse and planned at the community level.
3. Child care services should be of high quality: services should be based on the best available knowledge about child development and child care practice, staff–child ratios must be acceptable and child care staff need to be adequately trained and supervised and reasonably paid.

In 1994 the National Child Care Coalition, in response to the federal government's review of Canada's social programs, developed a proposal that expanded on the above recommendations and sought federal government leadership in developing a national child care program (Friendly & Rothman, 1995). Also in 1994, the Child Care Advocacy Association of Canada (CCAAC, 1994) presented a brief entitled *Taking the First Steps – Child Care: An Investment in Canada's Future* to the House of Commons Standing Committee on Human Resources Development. The CCAAC brief put forward a plan for gradual movement toward a substantial public investment in building a system of early childhood care and education services for Canada's children (Cleveland & Krashinsky, 1998).

International Context

France and Sweden provide good examples of public models of child care responsibility.

France
The French government provides the most extensive preschool system in the world for children 3 to 6 years old (écoles maternelles). This system is funded through payroll deductions rather than through parental fees, which makes it unique in the world. Criticisms of the écoles maternelles include the fact that the hours of the preschools do not coincide with the working day, and that the staff–child ratio is high. France also

provides a cash benefit to parents who cease to work or work part-time in order to care for their children at home. This benefit is paid for a maximum of three years. The view of child care in France is that it is good for children and that it equalizes learning opportunities.

Sweden
The assumption of policy planners in Sweden is that women will work full-time and so require a full range of welfare supports to facilitate this (Rodger, 1996). Family, taxation, and labour market policies in Sweden encourage maximum labour force participation for both men and women. Development of child care services has facilitated a high rate of female labour force participation. On average, parents pay between 1 and 10 per cent of the actual cost of child care; fees are income related and cost less than 10 per cent of the average female wage. Although 73 per cent of children under the age of 6 are in publicly funded daycare, demand still exceeds supply. Priority is granted to the children of single parents, working parents, and immigrants and to children with physical disabilities. The need for additional spaces is greatest for children under 3 years of age. Parents who look after their own children at home receive no assistance.

Two days per year of parental leave from the workplace are also provided to enable parents to spend time with their children in child care facilities, to familiarize themselves with activities and get to know the staff. Also, the Swedish school system accommodates employed parents by offering children a free cooked meal at lunchtime and by providing longer school days, coinciding with the workplace hours. Publicly funded recreation centres provide before-school and after-school care for children under the age of 10 or 12. Sweden's child care system is renowned for its educational value, its strong public support, and the opportunities it provides mothers to enter the labour force.

Emerging Child Care Initiatives in Canada

Quebec has announced that it will accelerate the development of child care spaces. The government is creating educative services and reducing child care charges. It will also make early childhood centres responsible for the development of local services that respond to family needs (Gouvernement du Québec, 1997). This move runs counter to the actions of most North American governments, which are cutting child care services. By providing families with greater access to child care,

Quebec is supporting the creation of stimulating environments for preschoolers, responding to the needs of dual-earner families, and supporting community development programs to meet the needs of parents. However, the quality of services developed under this reform is threatened by budget restraints. Cutbacks may result in higher ratios adult–child ratios, which are a critical element in creating positive learning and nurturing environments in child care settings. Caution must be exercised, and the impact of ratios on the quality of child care must be carefully evaluated so that it does not hamper the development of children, especially the most disadvantaged children (Bouchard, 1997a).

In Ontario, instead of reinvesting the money that will be saved through the National Child Benefit program in universal child care, the provincial government has announced an increase in the child care expense deduction, which is most beneficial to higher-income earners. There is also some indication that the Ontario government is examining the provision of child care to parents participating in workfare programs.

Summary

Countries vary concerning who pays for child care: the users, employers (through payroll taxes), or taxpayers (through payroll or income taxes). Some try to encourage development of child care services in the private sector; others focus on providing services directly or on subsidizing not-for-profit spaces. In Canada, child care can more than double the annual cost of raising younger children and is usually the greatest single child-related expense a family incurs.

Some countries' child care policies are based on the belief that parents are performing a valuable service to all of society by providing future citizens, and deserve society's help. The provision of well-subsidized, high-quality child care to a sizeable share of parents is a way of providing that assistance. Other countries' child care policies – or lack thereof, as in Canada and the United States – appear to reflect the belief that children are the private responsibility of individual parents and it is solely the parents' responsibility to support and socialize their children, except for universal health care and education in Canada.

> In most industrialized countries, what cannot be provided in the context of home and family becomes the province of the larger society, particularly

when it comes to caring for children. Thus, most of these countries create social systems that support children as families adjust to the changes in work and marriage patterns. (Rickel & Becker, 1997, p. 21)

Although there is certainly variation among other nations, it is fair to state that generally, as compared with Americans (and Canadians, similarly), European parents enjoy far more forms of family support – including prenatal and other health care, parental leave, parental education, and, of course, child care. (Zigler & Gilman, 1996, p. 106)

Research has identified the importance of policies that support women's employment, such as affordable child care services, combined with the development of workplace flexibility relating to job sharing, sick leave, and parental leave. These aspects of family policy would, of course, help to promote qualitatively better family relationships in a changing and insecure economic and social context (Rodger, 1996).

Parents themselves differ regarding preferences for work and child care arrangements. Some prefer to work less and be more available, while others desire, and in many cases such as single mothers, require, a greater availability of formal care services in order to allow them to provide adequate economic stability for their families (Beaujot, 1997). This diversity underlies the complexity of child care and parental benefits as areas of public policy. Because of such contrasting views, the issue of child care continues to be an on-going debate at both the federal and provincial/territorial levels of government in Canada.

While the Canadian government is promoting attachment to the labour force, they are failing to provide the additional support required by families with children to balance their roles. The government's silence regarding the issue of child care seems to be consistent with its aim to reduce spending, while viewing child care expenditures as unnecessary in a time of fiscal constraints. However, the results of a recent study by Cleveland and Krashinsky (1998) suggest that universally available child care could provide significant benefits for both children and their parents. This study estimates that it would cost approximately $8,500 per year for full-time care, based on the use of adequately paid workers trained in developmentally oriented child care. The authors conclude that the benefits significantly exceed the costs with every dollar spent on such programming, generating approximately two dollars of benefits for the children and their parents.

Child Welfare Policy

Canada

Because the child welfare system in Canada is a provincial/territorial responsibility, substantial variations in legislation and practice exist across the country. These differences often result from various political/societal pressures.

Historically, child welfare practices have attempted to balance two important but sometimes conflicting roles: a protection role and a prevention role. Protecting children from abuse and neglect has been the main goal of child welfare agencies in North America for the past 100 years. However, within the past several decades, an additional mandate has emerged, namely to prevent child abuse and neglect rather than wait until cases are identified and then attempt to protect the child from further harm. This prevention focus has emphasized the importance of providing a variety of support services to families with young children and preserving the preeminent role of parents in socializing their children and preserving the family structure. Several different program approaches to family preservation and child abuse prevention are described elsewhere in this volume (see chapters 5 and 6). The focus of many of these programs and services is to strengthen the ability of parents to socialize healthy and productive children. Of course, this concern is not limited to child welfare policy and practices, but also to the health, education, and young offender sectors as well.

Although child welfare legislation in some provinces/territories specifies that a range of preventive services should be provided, in most cases these resources are only available to children and families after issues of abuse or neglect have been identified. Intensive home-based services, including family preservation programs, are one area where child welfare agencies have attempted to provide family support to prevent children coming into care.

Wolfe and Jaffe (1991) have called for a 'two-tier' system for supporting families. The first tier of services would consist of preventive activities and services for families aimed at assistance and education in child care issues and would be expected to decrease the number of children admitted into care. The second tier would consist of more familiar child welfare protection efforts that are designed to ensure that community standards are upheld and children's needs are adequately met.

However, the child welfare system is not adequately funded to provide a broad range of preventive and supportive services to families. Most services that are available are poorly coordinated and fragmented, a problem commonly acknowledged, most emphatically in the Gove Report in British Columbia (Gove, 1995). At the same time, the pressure on child welfare agencies to deal with an apparent rise in cases of child abuse and neglect has made attempts to maintain and expand preventive services extremely difficult. Given the high public visibility of child neglect, abuse, and murder over the past few years, child welfare agencies are feeling incredible pressure to substantially increase their efforts in child protection, and legislative reviews on child welfare policy are under way in many provinces (CCSD, 1997). In addition to diverting resources and attention away from more preventive efforts at supporting families in caring for their children, the increased visibility of child abuse has tended to move child welfare policy reform away from family issues to questions of child protection and children's rights.

International Context

The child welfare system as it has developed in the United States and Europe has been expected to provide, as in Canada, the same mix of two distinct functions – that of support provider and that of child protector. Some observers claim that these two roles are mutually incompatible and should be separate. For example, Pelton (1997) claims that the overlap of the two distinct roles has broadened the more intrusive functions of child welfare. Increases in child welfare funding over the last twenty years have expanded the protection function, thus diminishing the capacity to support families. Pelton observes that the protection function takes on a life of its own and will continue to grow and overshadow the supportive role. The reasons for this are many and complex. One is society's wish to protect the innocent child while not having to provide resources and support to the 'undeserving' parents. Another is the unrelenting pressure on caseworkers not to make a mistake. In a similar vein, Farrow (1997) notes that due to the unprecedented growth of the child protection system and the rapid rise in the incidence and severity of abuse among children, less serious cases of abuse and neglect are being left without service as overwhelmed staff are forced to overlook some dangers to children.

The argument has been made that, instead of one agency bearing sole responsibility for protecting children, what is required is a community partnership that is empowered with a clear accountability and that spans provincial/territorial, urban, and local players. Forensic investigation and radical state intervention would still need to occur, but only in those instances where families cannot and will not ensure a child's safety (Farrow, 1997).

A belief is emerging that current child welfare systems are fundamentally flawed. Many countries are faced with the escalating costs of maintaining child welfare investigative and supervisory infrastructures and the increased numbers of children in care (Pelton, 1997). This does not happen only in Canada. The current difficulties, however, are in no way due to lack of effort and diligence on the part of agencies. The failure is systemic and is occurring everywhere the model is in operation.

A recent paper published by the Harvard Center for the Study of Social Policy (Farrow, 1997) concludes that in order to promote children's safety, a child protection system should broaden the responsibility for child protection beyond the public child welfare agency. Such a system must include parents, neighbours, schools, health providers, child care facilities, law enforcement agencies, substance abuse treatment providers, businesses, and many other community stakeholders as partners, and must provide an array of in-home and out-of-home interventions. This expanded service system would safeguard children in many ways, by preventing maltreatment before it occurs; identifying and responding to diverse causes of child abuse and neglect; responding to the risk of maltreatment flexibly and comprehensively; and effectively prosecuting child maltreatment. However, Farrow concludes that since current child protection approaches are mandated in federal and provincial/territorial law and are deeply ingrained in policy and practice, developing a broadened child welfare system will be difficult.

These common concerns and priorities across so many social service sectors have resulted in a call for the integration and coordination of preventive services to children and their families. A common theme in many Canadian provinces/territories is the need to create a more integrated, community-based service delivery system for children and youth. Examples include the creation of integrated ministries for children and families in British Columbia and Quebec, and integrated service initiatives in Ontario (e.g., Making Services Work for People). Several examples of attempts to integrate services for children and families in Canada are described elsewhere in this volume. Similar initiatives in the United States are described by Kagan and Pritchard (1996).

A key social policy issue for child welfare is the relationship between family/child poverty and the need for child protection services. Rivers

(1998) has recently observed that as federal and provincial/territorial governments struggle to decrease deficits, spending on social programs has become a popular target for savings. What needs to be understood is that it is children who ultimately suffer when their parents lose jobs, welfare rates are cut, and family support services reduced. While children from any socioeconomic status can be abused or neglected, low-income families experience higher rates of child abuse, because poverty increases the severity and range of stresses to which these families are exposed. Thus, the issues of promoting family and child wellness and preventing child abuse and neglect become tied to economic and workplace policies that impact child poverty.

POVERTY — A CANADIAN CONUNDRUM

Given the concern about the inverse relationship between poverty and child/family well-being, questions naturally arise regarding the high rates of poverty in Canada. As mentioned earlier, child poverty in Canada is higher than in any other industrialized country except the United States, a situation which Stephen Lewis, Deputy Executive Director of UNICEF, recently described as follows:

> [It is] upsetting and unconscionable that a country as wealthy as Canada should allow that kind of festering sore on the body politic. There has never been as great a gap between rich and poor in Canada. It's time to reverse that situation. (*Toronto Star*, March 25, 1998)

Why, after ten years of advocacy for social policies to address child poverty, has the rate of child poverty increased? Further evidence of the conundrum of child poverty was provided recently by the United Nations Development Program (UNDP, 1998), which released figures on its Human Development Index (HDI), rating 174 countries on four criteria: the gross national product per capita (in 1995), life expectancy at birth, adult literacy rates, and school enrolment percentages. On these four indexes of development, Canada ranked first internationally, with France, Norway, the United States, Iceland, Finland, the Netherlands, Japan, New Zealand, and Sweden following in order.

Interestingly, however, the UNDP introduced a second index, the Human Poverty Index (HPI), which is designed to measure success in eliminating 'deprivation in human life.' The UNDP acknowledges that the so-called 'quality of life' index, the HDI, may mask barriers to opportunity that exclude many people in a given country. This new poverty index is designed as a 'relative' measure of well-being, how equitably resources are distributed in a country. The HPI is based on four criteria: the proportion of the country's population who were unemployed for more than one year; the proportion of adults exceeding a minimum literacy level; the proportion of individuals who do not reach the age of 60; and the proportion of the population living in households with disposable income below 50 per cent of that country's median family income (an indication of the relative distribution of financial resources in the country). On this poverty index, Canada ranked ninth out of seventeen of the wealthiest nations, tied with Japan and Denmark. Sweden ranked first, followed by the Netherlands, Germany, Norway, Italy, Finland, and France. The United Kingdom ranked fifteenth and the United States was seventeenth, the lowest of the wealthiest countries.

According to the UN report, Canada, France, and the United States, three of the top four countries on the HDI, have failed to ensure that all citizens have a chance to take advantage of their enviable living standards. The report cites 'significant problems of poverty' and observes that these countries' 'progress in human development has been poorly distributed.' Although these observations certainly apply to Canada, they are even more accentuated in the United States. These figures imply that it is not the overall amount of wealth, or lack thereof, that is responsible for the high rates of poverty in Canada and the United States, but rather the unequal distribution of wealth.

A number of factors have been identified as causes for the increased rates of family and child poverty in Canada during the 1990s. First, the value of income supports to families has declined. These include a decreasing median family income since 1989, cuts to the federal Child Tax Benefit in 1993, and a drop in social assistance rates throughout Canada. Also, it is increasingly difficult to achieve income security through employment. Although there has been a net increase in jobs created since 1989, there has been a decrease in full-time jobs. Many of the new jobs created are part-time, with lower wages and no benefits. Federal social program expenditures were reduced further on April 1, 1996, when the Canada Health and Social Transfer (CHST) program replaced the Canada Assistance Program (CAP). Under the CAP, provincial/territorial governments were committed to providing financial assistance to anyone in need; they were free to interpret what level of financial assistance they felt to be adequate, but they had to provide something to any person who could demonstrate need. This small protection has been lost with the CHST, as provinces/territories are now free to provide assistance only to whomever they deem to be deserving.

According to Campaign 2000, a national social movement that aims to build awareness and support for programs and policies to end child poverty in Canada, the evidence seems to indicate that both jobs with adequate wages and benefits *and* strong government income transfer programs are needed to reduce poverty and ensure income security for Canadians (Hughes, 1995).

According to many social policy analysts, the decreases in family and child supports, benefits, and services during the past decade have resulted from the ascendance of corporate ideology, with its insistence on debt and deficit reduction, as well as from the shrinking role of government in providing social programs. The result has been an increase in marginalized, especially lone-parent, families and child poverty.

Now that the federal and many provincial/territorial governments have eliminated their budget deficits, many observers have called for increases in social program spending. However, the importance of government debt reduction and personal income tax cuts continues to be emphasized by all major federal political parties, including the NDP. The issue of income tax reduction has important implications in terms of social policy. It is interesting to note that the average personal income tax paid in Canada is relatively low compared with that in many European countries. However, it is common to hear the claim that Canada must lower its taxes in order to become more competitive globally. Yet, figures for 1996 recently released by the Organization for Economic Cooperation and Development (OECD, 1998) show that Canada ranks eighteenth out of the 29 industrialized OECD countries in terms of the percentage of gross domestic product collected as tax revenue. The percentage of tax revenue that Canada receives from personal income tax is just one and a half percentage points higher than the figure for the United States, and we collect far less from corporations: 6.6 per cent of our total revenue, compared with 8.9 per cent for the United States. Our payroll taxes are about two-thirds of those in the United States and property taxes are also lower in Canada than they are south of the border. In other words, with respect to all of the taxes that are commonly identified as making us uncompetitive, we are virtually equal to the United States or actually lower. Only in consumption taxes are we significantly higher. Canada's strong competitiveness goes beyond taxation. For three years running, the Canadian accounting firm KPMG has compared cities in the United States with those in Canada to determine where it is cheapest to do business (KPMG, 1999). In all of these surveys, the cheapest American city was still more costly than the most expensive Canadian location, particularly in terms of labour, electricity, and borrowing costs. Canada's competitive advantage would only disappear if our dollar rose to 87¢ US.

The KPMG (1999) study compared Canada with six other industrial countries – the United States, France, Germany, Italy, Sweden and the United Kingdom. Again, Canada was the cheapest location in which to do business. Most significantly with respect to effective combined corporate tax rates – that is, federal plus provincial/territorial or state taxes – Canada had the lowest rate of taxes actually paid, at 27.4 per cent, while the United States came in fifth at 40 per cent. And even with their lower tax rate, Canadian companies have the advantage of not having to pay for their employees' medical insurance. These figures work against the view that corporate taxes make Canada uncompetitive with the United States. The call for tax cuts may be seen as another front in the ideological war on government. The danger in decreasing taxes is that it may result less revenue for public education, universal medicare, and a modern infrastructure – those aspects that make the Canadian economy competitive.

These figures suggest that what Canada really needs is tax reform: a shifting of the tax burden from poor working and middle-income Canadians to those who have been getting more than their fair share of Canada's collective wealth, a point highlighted by Canada's poor showing in the Human Poverty Index discussed above. It is the unequal distribution of wealth, not the lack of wealth, that generates the high rates of poverty in Canada. Tax reforms must address this problem. Implementing the type of tax system necessary to reduce income inequality and to support healthy family development will require a broad level of public understanding and support.

SUGGESTIONS FOR FAMILY POLICY REFORMS IN CANADA

In discussing the results of the comparative study of family policies in eight industrialized countries, Baker (1995) suggests several ways to measure the effectiveness of family policies. Two of these are particularly relevant to the present discussion: the first is the reduction of family and child poverty; the second is the extent to which policies reduce the conflict between earning a living and raising children. Likewise, Torjman and Battle (1995), identify two deficits in child welfare in Canada: the first is an *income deficit* for many families, resulting in, among other things, high rates of family and child poverty. The second is labelled a *time deficit*. The concept of a time deficit is relatively new in the child welfare literature (Hewlett, 1993) and refers to the difficulty in meeting work and family responsibilities, the latter including caring for children and also for sick and aging parents. These two deficits appear to be critically linked to child abuse and neglect and to low levels of family and child well-being (see also Chapter 2). The following section outlines a set of recommended changes to family policy in Canada that are designed to decrease poverty (the income deficit) and reduce work–family conflicts (the time deficit).

Decreasing Child and Family Poverty in Canada

Recommendation 1: Increase Benefits for Low-Income Families

This first step has been implemented in the new National Child Benefit described earlier in this chapter. However, it has been estimated that this increase in family benefits will result only in a minor decrease in family and child poverty in Canada, from approximately 21 per cent to 19 per cent. The reduction in poverty might be slightly greater in Quebec and British Columbia, where provincial legislation has added to the benefits of low-income families.

Although the federal government's increased benefits can be viewed as an important first step, substantially greater benefits will be required in order to make an obvious impact on poverty rates. Some have estimated that the total federal annual expenditure on child benefits would need to double, from the currently projected $6.8 billion to $13 billion. This increase may seem extremely optimistic, but it becomes more realistic when compared with the $23 billion Ottawa spends annually on cash benefits for low- and middle-income seniors. The Ontario government recently cut income taxes by $6 billion annually (benefiting mainly the wealthy); this amount is equivalent to approximately $15 billion nationally, more than enough to fund child benefits at a level that would have substantial impact on family and child poverty and overall well-being (Battle & Mendelson, 1997). It is time for Canada to increase investment in children, its most important resource.

*Recommendation 2: Restore Full Indexing to the Canadian
Child Tax Benefit*

Beginning in 1993, the federal government removed full indexing from the Child Tax Benefit. Indexing means tying the value of the benefit directly to the consumer price index (CPI); if the CPI goes up 1 per cent, the benefit goes up 1 per cent; if the CPI decreases 3 per cent, the benefit decreases 3 per cent, and so forth. Full indexing was replaced with a partial indexing formula that increases funding each year with the cost of living only when the CPI exceeds 3 per cent. Although inflation has been less than 3 per cent in recent years, it has increased enough to have dire consequences for low-income families.

The Canadian Council on Social Development estimates that over the past four years, low-income families have experienced a 13 per cent loss in purchasing power. The cumulative effect of inflation means not only that the value of child benefit payments decreases each year, but also that fewer and fewer families qualify for the maximum benefits. Billions of dollars have been silently drained from child benefits since the inflation-minus-three indexing formula was introduced (Torjman & Battle, 1995).

In 1996 the federal government recognized problems created by partial indexing of the seniors' benefit and changed its partial indexing formula to full indexing. Since then, the purchasing power of the seniors' benefit has not decreased in value, unlike the partially indexed child benefit. In the House of Commons, a majority of MPs have supported a motion that the government review its policy on partial indexing of child benefits. The federal government currently invests much more money in pension programs for elderly people than it does in child benefits (Baker, 1995; Battle & Mendelson, 1997). Reindexing child benefits may be a significant step in reducing child poverty.

Reducing Work–Family Conflicts

*Recommendation 1: Increase Work Arrangements That Respond to
Family Needs*

A variety of suggestions emerge from this chapter's review of maternity and parental leave policies in Canada and other industrialized countries. These directions include: legislation that mandates adequately compensated and fully protected leave benefits for childbearing and childrearing, including family emergencies and illness; and legislation to equalize and prorate wages and benefits associated with full- and part-time work.

Recommendation 2: Introduce Federal Child Care Policy Legislation

A new federal Child Care Act could support: (1) subsidized child care services extended to all preschool children, with fees based on a sliding scale that reflects family income; and (2) parental subsidies to offset child care fees. One of the most serious stresses for Canadian families arises from the lack of high-quality, affordable child care (Lero, Guelman, Pence, Brokman, & Nutall, 1992). Access to affordable child care is one of the greatest obstacles to participation in the workforce, particularly for lone parents, as well as participation in education and training programs. As documented earlier, in the recent study by Cleveland and Krashinsky (1998), child care not only provides important economic benefits to parents, but promotes the development and well-being of children.

The Mulroney Progressive Conservative government backed away from its promise to increase the number of high-quality affordable child care spaces when it failed to pass the Child Care Act in 1988. Although the government claimed that it could not afford the required funds for high-quality, affordable care, it did raise the value of the child care expense deduction. This deduction favours high-income families, while low- and middle-income families gain little or no benefit (Battle & Torjman, 1993), further contributing to inequality in income distribution and child poverty. Converting child care expense deductions into a refundable tax credit would assist lower-income earners.

A further recommendation is to extend public kindergarten to 4-year-olds in all provinces/territories on a noncompulsory basis. Paradoxically, the government of Ontario is backing away from its previous provision of such a service. What processes will ensure that these and other recommendations will be acted on by provincial/territorial and federal governments in order to reduce child poverty and improve child and family well-being? Another key question is, what factors explain the different values placed on children in Anglo-American countries compared with non–English-speaking European countries?

In reviewing statistics on cross-national comparisons of child and family policies, Kamerman (1996a) and Baker (1995) attempt to identify factors that may account for national differences in family policy. They both identify the importance of demographic differences between Europe and North America. After the Second World War, both the United States and Canada experienced a baby boom that did not occur in Europe. Also, the North American population has been kept relatively young through continued high rates of immigration, while European countries have experienced high rates of emigration, particularly by young people. An important consequence of this 'demographics is destiny' analysis is that advocacy groups did not form in Canada and the United States as they did in European countries to push for social policies that encourage and support childbearing and family formation.

Baker (1995) points out that the birth rate in the United States and Canada has been steadily declining in recent years, especially in Quebec. As a consequence, the Quebec government has been much more active and explicit in developing supports for childrearing families.

At the beginning of the twenty-first century, the convergence of several factors may contribute to important changes in Canadian social policies in promoting child and family well-being and preventing child poverty and abuse. These factors include: (1) the emergence of provincial/territorial and federal budget surplus dividends; (2) favourable demographic trends (i.e., continued low birth rates); (3) more powerful and politically sophisticated advocacy groups for children, women, and minorities; (4) more favourable attitudes among the Canadian electorate regarding universal, high-quality, affordable child care and progressive workplace benefits; and (5) current attempts by federal and provincial/territorial governments to coordinate a national social policy platform. Of particular interest in this regard is the current concept of 'social union,' an attempt by the Canadian federal and provincial/territorial governments to coordinate social policies throughout the country. These developments are strongly tied to issues of federal–provincial/territorial power sharing and income transfers. Current attention to social policy issues, including a National Children's Agenda, may reflect an increasing awareness of the importance of child and family well-being to a strong Canadian society.

Social policy changes that address child and family well-being would, to quote Torjman and Battle (1995),

> not only demonstrate that Canada's signature on the UN Convention on the Rights of the Child is more than a simple word on a page, but also a genuine commitment to the welfare of children ... and would represent a real investment in Canadian children and families. (p. 481)

CONCLUSIONS

This chapter has reviewed child and family policies in Canada and compared them with those in other English-speaking countries (chiefly the United States and Great Britain), where a societal model of *individual responsibility* predominates, and in non–English-speaking European countries (especially Denmark, France, Germany, the Netherlands, Norway, and Sweden), where a model of *social responsibility* strongly influences child and family policy. The comparisons yield the following conclusions regarding the current state of Canadian social policies that affect child and family well-being (O'Hara, 1998):

1. Parents in Europe receive more government help than parents in Canada.
2. Unlike Canada, European countries have a wide range of measures to support families and children. Family policies in France, Germany, the Netherlands, Norway, and Sweden include benefits for part-time workers, flexible working hours, extensive parental leave, family leave, child care, allowances, tax benefits, and income support. Meanwhile, Canada, the United Kingdom, and the United States generally leave it up to parents to choose how they want to balance their work and family life. They expect parents to deal with the difficulties of those choices privately.
3. Canada is second only to the United States in its ambivalence toward parents with young children. Family policy in the United Kingdom is somewhat more advanced than in Canada, but lags behind the European countries. Because we live next to the United States, Canadians tend to use the U.S. model without looking further abroad.
4. Canada needs to start working on a large and flexible range of options to meet the needs of families in different circumstances and with different values and behaviours. Some families prefer to have a parent at home when children are young and want government support for a stay-at-home parent. Others would prefer help paying for child care so they can work. Some parents strongly support formal, regulated child care, while others prefer child care at home. Some may want to work but may prefer part-time work, flexible hours, or parental leave options.
5. Canadians need a commitment to allocate resources to children and families and a consensus on the need for government to actively support families.

CHAPTER FIVE

A Review and Analysis of Programs to Promote Family Wellness and Prevent the Maltreatment of Preschool and Elementary-School-Aged Children

Geoffrey Nelson, Maire-Claire Laurendeau, Claire Chamberland, and Leslea Peirson

INTRODUCTION

The overarching goal of this chapter is to describe and interpret 'state of the art' programs that are designed to promote family wellness and prevent the maltreatment of children. Within this broad goal, we have several specific objectives: (1) to describe the different types of programs that have been developed to prevent child maltreatment, (2) to present a comprehensive review of the research evidence pertaining to the effectiveness of these programs, (3) to critique these programs, and (4) to note common elements of effective prevention programs.

CONCEPTUAL OVERVIEW OF PROMOTION AND PREVENTION PROGRAMS

Ecological Levels of Analysis

As was described in Chapter 1, we employ an ecological framework that focuses on multiple levels of wellness. A key notion in the ecological perspective is that smaller levels are nested within larger levels (Bronfenbrenner, 1986). In our review, we note which levels of wellness are targeted by the different program types.

Those who have conducted previous reviews of the literature have recognized that for programs to be effective in preventing child maltreatment, such programs must address the concrete daily living realities of families and parents, as well as the parent–child relationship (Cameron & Vanderwoerd, 1997a; Wolfe, 1994, 1998). Programs cannot help young mothers to stimulate their infants or manage the behaviour of their young children if the mothers lead chaotic and stressful lives characterized by a variety of risk factors. Interventions to address community and societal wellness are required to reduce such risk factors (Febbraro, 1994).

Proactive and Reactive Approaches

In our review, we focus primarily on proactive approaches (i.e., universal or high- risk), as defined in Chapter 1. We also consider some reactive (indicated) programs, which seek to prevent maltreatment from reoccurring, to prevent other family problems (e.g., out-of-home placement of the child), to prevent long-term problems for the child (e.g., emotional or behavioural problems), to prevent the maltreatment of younger siblings, or to prevent the maltreatment of the next generation of children born to those parents who have been maltreated themselves. From Chapter 2, it is clear that youth and adults who have been maltreated are at increased risk of maltreating their children. Thus, a reactive approach for one generation may be a proactive, high-risk approach for the next generation.

Conceptual Framework for the Review

These two concepts – ecological levels of analysis and proactive and reactive approaches – form the two main organizing dimensions for our review, as is visually depicted in Table 5.1. Programs are categorized by the highest ecological level addressed and the timing of the intervention. Some programs that we describe are noted in the cells as exemplars of the different program types. While not all programs fit neatly into this framework, there are general differences between the various types of programs that make this broad framework a useful tool for understanding a large number of diverse approaches.

METHODOLOGY

Defining the Literature

We used the following criteria to guide our review of the research literature: (1) proactive programs, which seek to promote family wellness and/or prevent child maltreatment, and reactive programs, which have a goal of preventing other negative outcomes (e.g., out-of-home placement); (2) inclusion of unpublished reports and book chapters as well as journal articles; (3) literature in both English and French; (4) the

TABLE 5.1
Ecological Levels, Timing, and Types of Programs for the Prevention of Child Maltreatment

Timing of the Program	Highest Ecological Level Addressed				
	Child Wellness	Family Wellness	Community Wellness		Societal Wellness
Proactive Universal	Educational and treatment programs for child sexual abuse	Parent education and training programs	Self-help/mutual aid and social support programs	Multi-component, community-based programs	Media, employment and legislative programs
High-risk	• Educational programs for children regarding sexual abuse • Programs for sexually abused boys	• Universally accessible, group-based parent training • Social learning parent training for high-risk families	• Universal home visitation • Olds's Prenatal/Early Infancy Project • Hawaii Healthy Start	• Universally accessible self-help/mutual aid and support groups • Self-help/mutual aid and support groups for high-risk families	• Better Beginnings, Better Futures • 1, 2, 3 Go! • Syracuse Family Development Project	• Media programs to educate the public about child maltreatment • Employment programs for high-risk families
Reactive Indicated	• Group treatment programs for sexually abused children	• Social learning parent training for families involved with child welfare agencies	• Family preservation programs, e.g., Homebuilders • Family treatment programs for sexually abused children	• Parents Anonymous • Parent mutual aid organization	• Project 12-Ways	• Legislative interventions regarding sexual abuse

period from 1979 through 1997; (5) programs for families with children ages zero to 12; and (6) research on programs with a prospective, controlled design.

While our review attempted to capture all of the research literature using the criteria described above, we did not limit the review to programs with a research base. We also examined innovative programs that, as yet, do not have a strong or perhaps any research foundation. We believe that part of our work in this review is to point out programs that are conceptually appealing and/or innovative but that need to be researched.

Another point that deserves some clarification is what is meant by an outcome measure related to child maltreatment. We concentrated on studies using some outcome measures related to child maltreatment. The assessment of child physical abuse and neglect ranges along a continuum from direct measures to indirect measures. At one end of the continuum are verified reports of child physical abuse, neglect, or sexual abuse from agency records or child welfare databases. Next are the various 'proxy' indicators of abuse, which include hospital admissions, use of emergency room services, and incidents of accidents, ingestions, or poisonings (MacMillan, MacMillan, Offord, Griffith, & MacMillan, 1994a). Further down the continuum are observational and self-report measures of punitive or neglectful parenting. Finally, the most indirect measures of child maltreatment are those that tap parental attitudes, such as rigid or unrealistic expectations of a child's behaviour, and that serve as indicators of child abuse potential (Azar & Rohrbeck, 1986; Milner, Gold, & Wimberly, 1986).

The assessment of child sexual abuse has followed a different route. Programs designed to prevent child sexual abuse seldom, if ever, use records of verified sexual abuse as an outcome measure. A few studies have examined children's reports of sexual abuse (Hazzard, Webb, Kleemeier, Angert, & Pohl, 1991; Kolko, Moser, & Hughes, 1989). The most commonly used outcome measures in this area are: (1) measures of knowledge of prevention concepts, and (2) measures of prevention skills in response to hypothetical or simulated situations (Daro, 1994; MacMillan, MacMillan, Offord, Griffith, & MacMillan, 1994b).

Literature Search

In our review, we employed the following search strategies. Our first step for the English literature was to locate recent review articles, book chapters, books, or unpublished reports on the prevention of child maltreatment. For the French literature, we consulted several sources that have compiled descriptive material on more than 1,000 promotion and prevention programs and activities for families and children in Quebec (Battaglini, Fortin, Heneman, Laurendeau, & Tousignant, 1997; Chamberland et al., 1996; Garant, 1992; Guay, Hamel, Brousseau, Stewart, et al., 1995, 1996, 1997; Hamel & Guay, 1996; Tourigny & Lavergne, 1995).

Next, we conducted reviews of the CHILD ABUSE AND NEGLECT and ERIC databases using the following keywords: child abuse, child neglect, incest, and prevention. We also conducted manual searches of ten journals that we had determined publish work on this topic. The manual searches of these journals were only used for the time period 1993 to 1997, as our database searches were not turning up any reports released prior to 1993 that we were not already aware of. To review the French literature, we used CD-ROM Repères (Banque de périodiques de langue française) and computerized databases (e.g., IRIS, MEDLINE, ERIC). The keywords employed in French were: abus, négligence, enfants maltraités, inceste, violence, jeunes en difficulté et prévention, intervention.

PROGRAMS TO PREVENT THE MALTREATMENT OF PRESCHOOL AND ELEMENTARY-SCHOOL-AGED CHILDREN

Programs That Focus on Child Wellness

Educational and Treatment Programs for Child Sexual Abuse

Programs that address child wellness and pay little attention to the child's social context are those that focus on child sexual abuse. The fact that most programs which strive to prevent child sexual abuse focus largely on the individual child may reflect our currently limited understanding of the risk and protective factors underlying this phenomenon, as was noted in Chapter 2.

Proactive Universal Applications
Exemplary Program. In Calgary, the Who Do You Tell? program was started by the Calgary Sexual Assault Centre in 1983 (Tutty, 1997). It has recently been updated and implemented by the Calgary Communities Against Sexual Assault in elementary schools where a request for the program has been made by the principal. Parents are invited to an information session and teachers are provided with in-service training before

the program is implemented. The program is provided in two one-hour sessions to groups of fifteen to twenty children in grades kindergarten to 6 by two trainers, with somewhat different formats for the different age groupings. In addition to providing information about unwanted touching, the program emphasizes role-playing and practice in how to respond to unwanted touches. Children also have the opportunity to talk privately with the trainers. This program has been found to enhance children's knowledge about child sexual abuse.

Programs and Research Evidence. Educational programs for young children like the Who Do You Tell? program have been implemented in preschools and elementary schools. Many programs focus solely on sexual abuse, while others focus more broadly on personal safety skills, including the prevention of abduction (Carroll-Rowan & Miltenberger, 1994). These programs aim to: (1) educate children about what constitutes sexual abuse; (2) make children aware that abusers can be family members, relatives, friends, and babysitters; (3) teach children that they are in control of their bodies; (4) differentiate between touches that are good, bad, or questionable; (5) teach resistance skills, such as saying 'no' or running away; (6) encourage children to report instances of abuse or attempted abuse to a trusted adult; and (7) let children know they are not responsible for being abused (Daro, 1994; Reppucci & Haugaard, 1989). However, as Reppucci and Haugaard (1989) point out, such knowledge and skills may be difficult for young children to grasp. Good-night kisses and being bathed by a parent are examples of situations where children may have difficulty. Also, teaching children that they have the right to say 'no' to adults flies in the face of their experiences with authority figures. Similarly, resisting and/or reporting abuse is likely to be very difficult if a child is threatened or intimidated.

The most common components of educational programs for children are instruction, including both oral presentations and videotaped material, and behavioural coaching, which can include drama and role-playing (MacMillan et al., 1994b). The former component is designed to build awareness and knowledge, while the latter is focused on prevention skills. Also, some programs provide instruction for teachers and/or parents.

There are now numerous controlled prospective evaluations of these different educational programs for elementary-school–aged children (Blumberg, Chadwick, Fogarty, Speth, & Chadwick, 1991; Conte, Rosen, Saperstein, & Shermack, 1985; Dhooper & Schneider, 1995; Fryer,

Kraizer, & Miyoshi, 1987; Harvey, Forehand, Brown, & Holmes, 1988; Hazzard et al., 1991; Hébert, Lavoie, Piché, & Poitras, 1997; Kolko et al., 1989; Kolko, Moser, Litz, & Hughes, 1987; Kraizer, Witte, & Fryer, 1989; McQuillen, O'Brien, & Schrader, 1993; Oldfield, Hays, & Megel, 1996; Saslawsky & Wurtele, 1986; Taal & Edelaar, 1997; Tutty, 1992, 1997; Vallée, Théberge, & Jobin, 1988; Wolfe, MacPherson, Blount, & Wolfe, 1986; Wurtele, Saslawsky, Miller, Marrs, & Britcher, 1986) and preschoolers (Bogat & McGrath, 1993; Nemerofsky, Carran, & Rosenberg, 1994; Peraino, 1990; Wurtele, 1990; Wurtele, Gillespie, Currier, & Franklin, 1992; Wurtele, Kast, & Meltzer, 1992; Wurtele, Kast, Miller-Perrin, & Kondrick, 1989; Wurtele & Owens, 1997). These studies and various reviews (Berrick & Barth, 1992; Daro, 1994; MacMillan et al., 1994b) have found that these programs have a clear impact on both preschoolers' and school-aged children's knowledge about child sexual abuse (Reppucci & Haugaard, 1989; Rispens, Aleman, & Goudena, 1997). Rispens et al. (1997) also found that programs that include some form of behavioural coaching to develop self-protection skills are more effective than those programs that provide only instruction.

Few studies have examined disclosures of sexual abuse, and the findings of these studies are not clear-cut (Hazzard et al., 1991; Kolko et al., 1989; Kolko et al., 1987). A concern expressed about these interventions is that they may raise children's anxiety levels. While there have been reports that most children report feeling a little worried after such programs, three controlled studies have not reported a significant impact on children's anxiety levels (Ratto & Bogat, 1990; Taal & Edelaar, 1997; Wurtele et al., 1989).

Proactive High-Risk Applications
Several authors have argued that high-risk interventions to prevent sexual abuse of children should focus on boys or men who have been sexually abused (Bagley & Thurston, 1998; Swift & Ryan-Finn, 1995; Tutty, 1991). As was reported in Chapter 2, boys and men who have been sexually abused have an increased risk of becoming perpetrators of sexual abuse themselves. At the same time, it is important to recognize that most boys who have been sexually victimized do not become perpetrators of abuse themselves.

Group interventions have been used for young children who have been sexually abused (DeLuca, Boyes, Furer, Grayson, & Hiebert-Murphy, 1992; Silovsky & Hembree-Kigin, 1994), some of which have been specifically targeted at boys (Friedrich, Luecke, Beilke, & Place, 1992;

Scott, 1992). Scott (1992) noted aggressive and sexualized behaviour in boys who had been sexually abused, which could be the precursors of sexual abuse of others. Friedrich et al. (1992) combined individual and group intervention for sexually abused boys and found significant improvement from pre-test to post-test on measures of internalizing and externalizing behaviours, depression, and social support.

Reactive Indicated Applications
Group intervention methods have been used primarily with elementary-school-aged children (DeLuca et al., 1992; Silovsky & Hembree-Kigin, 1994). These interventions address children's feelings of guilt and responsibility, reactions to the disclosure, boundary issues, peer relations, feelings of anger and fear, assertiveness, social skills, and self-esteem. Two controlled, prospective evaluations of group interventions for elementary-school-aged girls who have been sexually abused have found significant improvement for girls participating in the intervention relative to girls in the control group on measures of internalizing and externalizing behaviours (Burke, 1988; McGain & McKinzey, 1995).

There are also some group interventions for preschoolers, which usually include play and puppet activities (Oates, Gray, Schweitzer, Kempe, & Harmon, 1995).

Summary and Critique
The main findings regarding educational and treatment programs for child sexual abuse are summarized in Table 5.2. These programs tend to focus narrowly on the promotion of child wellness to the neglect of family, community, and societal wellness. In spite of this limitation, several positive findings have been reported.

The most telling criticism of educational programs in preschools or elementary schools is that there is no evidence that they prevent child sexual abuse. Critics argue that the onus for the prevention of child sexual abuse should not be on the potential victims of abuse, children, and that exclusive reliance on educational programs may lull us into a false sense of security that we have done all that is needed to prevent child sexual abuse, when much more is needed. There is a general acknowledgment in the literature that programs to prevent child sexual abuse need to go beyond the individual child to higher ecological levels of analysis (Daro, 1994; Reppucci & Haugaard, 1989).

On the other hand, Tutty (1991) defends educational programs on several grounds. First, she argues that school-based education programs

TABLE 5.2
Summary of Findings of Educational and Treatment Programs for Child Sexual Abuse

	Findings
Proactive Universal	• Educational programs for preschool and elementary-school-aged children have been widely implemented and found to significantly increase children's knowledge about child sexual abuse. • Coaching in self-protection skills and amount of instruction time are positively associated with program effectiveness. • There is no evidence that these programs prevent child sexual abuse.
High-risk	• Group programs for sexually abused boys have been developed, but there has yet to be much research on the effects of these programs.
Reactive Indicated	• Group interventions for sexually abused girls have been developed, and there is some controlled research which has reported beneficial short-term effects.

have the potential to reach large numbers of children, teachers, and parents. Second, she believes that while more attention should be focused on perpetrators, an exclusive focus on perpetrators would also be limited in potential to prevent child sexual abuse. Third, she states that increasing parent–child communication about this issue increases the potential for children to disclose abuse to their parents, which is a powerful deterrent to would-be perpetrators. In support of this argument, convicted offenders who have sexually abused children have indicated that their greatest fear is that children will report the abuse (Budin & Johnson, 1989; Conte, Wolf, & Smith, 1989). Offenders also believe that good communication between parents and children is a deterrent to potential abusers (Elliott, Browne, & Kilcoyne, 1995). Fourth, Tutty (1991) counters the accusation that such programs 'blame the victims' by arguing that such programs can also be viewed as 'empowering' children with knowledge, skills, and support for self-protection. Again this argument is supported by suggestions from convicted offenders about what children should be taught to prevent abuse: (1) disclosing abuse; (2) saying 'no'; (3) learning about proper touching of their private parts by others; (4) never getting into a stranger's car; (5) being wary of strangers who are too friendly; and (6) running away, resisting, and staying away from strangers (Budin & Johnson, 1989; Elliott et al., 1995).

It does not seem fruitful to prolong the debate about whether child-focused or ecologically focused prevention programs should be implemented. Both are potentially useful. However, greater efforts need to be made to reduce and eliminate the perpetration of abuse by adults by targeting higher ecological levels.

As far as proactive high-risk interventions are concerned, work on the identification of and intervention for sexually abused boys who are at risk of becoming perpetrators themselves is in the early stages of development. Long-term follow-up studies with control groups of such interventions are needed to determine their effectiveness in preventing the perpetration of sexual abuse in high-risk boys. With regard to reactive interventions, two controlled studies have shown positive impacts of group interventions for sexually abused elementary-school–aged girls (Burke, 1988; McGain & McKinzey, 1995). These encouraging results need to be replicated and longer-term follow-up studies need to be conducted on the efficacy of these interventions.

Programs That Focus on Family Wellness

Parent Education and Training Programs

Stakeholders spoke about the value of parent education and training programs:

> ... healthy parent, parenting resource centres ... They are very informal drop-in situations but also offer programming, parenting classes, anger management. (Parent)

> The other program I would comment on is 'Nobody's Perfect,' a parenting program which targets parents who have kids from zero to 5 ... We are very big on parenting programs, we run all sorts of them. (Adviser)

> It's a teaching module. It's not process-oriented. It's [focused on] skills in terms of dealing with acting out behaviour, how to set up routines, limits, structures, and it's narrow in its scope, but for some families that's what they need is some redirection and education. (Service provider)

Proactive Universal Applications
Parent education and training programs are available universally on a small-group basis to parents of preschool or school-aged children. These programs tend to be based on one of three theoretical perspectives on

parenting: (1) social learning theory, (2) humanistic theory, or (3) Adlerian theory (Cowan, Powell, & Cowan, 1998; Todres & Bunston, 1993). All of these approaches, when applied universally, focus on ways of improving parents' skills in managing their children's social behaviour.

The research literature on small-group-based parenting programs has been reviewed by Todres and Bunston (1993) up until 1990. A total of 62 outcome studies were reviewed, 18 social learning, 24 PET (Parent Effectiveness Training), and 20 Adlerian. While many of these studies have serious methodological flaws, the authors found that studies of the social learning and Adlerian approaches reported more positive outcomes on parents' behaviour or attitudes or children's behaviour than the studies of PET. More recent studies of Adlerian (Drapeau, Marcotte, Dupuis, & Cloutier, 1995) and social learning approaches (Spoth, Redmond, Haggerty, & Ward, 1995; Spoth, Redmond, & Shin, 1998) have reported positive impacts of universal parent training programs on measures of parents' knowledge, skill, and self-confidence.

Proactive High-Risk Applications
In this review we found only two parent education and training programs for high-risk families with young children. Je Passe Partout is an elementary-school-based program in Montreal for low-income children who have problems completing homework and who are at risk of academic failure (Saint-Pierre, 1994). Part of this program includes parent education, which focuses on parent assistance in their children's school work, including home sessions and regular phone contact with the school. Saint-Pierre (1994) found that the academic self-concept of students in the control group decreased significantly over time, while there was no comparable change for the intervention group.

Resnick (1985) conducted an intervention with low-income, single mothers with preschool children. Two different programs were compared with a matched comparison group. The first intervention, called Opportunities for Advancement, consisted of fourteen weekly group sessions, focused on goal-setting, self-esteem building, and vocational planning. The second intervention, New Directions for Mothers, consisted of the same number of sessions, but the focus of these sessions was on parent training in child management skills, which was based on social learning theory. Data were gathered from participants prior to, just after, and one year after the intervention. The two intervention groups had significantly lower scores of parental hostility-rejection toward children than the comparison group at post-test, and those who participated in the parenting program had a higher rate of play with their children at post-test than did the other two groups. However, the groups did not differ on parenting measures at the one-year follow-up.

Reactive Applications
Exemplary Program. David Wolfe and his colleagues at the University of Western Ontario have developed, implemented, and evaluated a number of behavioural parenting training programs for families with a history of physical abuse or neglect of preschool and school-aged children. In one intervention, Wolfe, Edwards, Manion, and Koverola (1988) provided interventions for low-income single mothers who were under the supervision of a child welfare agency. Most of the children were preschoolers (age range of nine months to five years). The parent training intervention consisted of coaching in child management skills and providing activities designed to promote child development. The information intervention included social activities and informal discussions about family issues. Sessions for both interventions were one and one-half hours to two hours in length and lasted approximately twenty weeks. Those in the parenting intervention attended a median of nine sessions, while those in the information intervention attended a median of twenty sessions. The group leaders were graduate students in psychology who worked in pairs.

The results of the evaluation showed a significant reduction for the parent training group in child abuse potential, maternal depression, and the frequency and intensity of child behaviour problems, relative to the information group. However, there were no significant differences on observational measures of childrearing. One year after the intervention, case workers rated the families who participated in the parenting program as managing significantly better than families who participated in the information program.

Programs and Research Evidence. Most parent education and training programs for parents who have maltreated their children are based on a social learning or cognitive-behavioural theoretical framework (Wolfe, 1994). Parents are instructed in child management and/or stress management and anger control skills. With regard to child management skills, a variety of different contingency management approaches are taught, including the use of material and social reinforcement to encourage positive behaviour and the use of ignoring, time-out, and sanctions as ways of punishing or extinguishing negative behaviours. Reading materials, role-playing with feedback, videos, and homework assignments are used to build such skills. Various cognitive techniques for problem solving and anger control have been incorporated into such interventions more recently to help parents cope with stressful situations. Most interventions are short-term, consisting of six to twelve two-hour sessions that are offered on a group basis. Some interventions have combined parent training with other components, such as in-home coaching in child management. For example, Wolfe, Kaufman, Aragona, and Sandler (1981) combined group-based parent training with home visitation.

A number of controlled evaluations of parent education and training programs for parents who have maltreated their children have been reported. Evaluations of these programs typically include outcome measures related to family wellness (e.g., parenting knowledge, attitudes, and behaviour, parental well-being) and child wellness (e.g., children's behaviour). Overall, these studies have demonstrated significant positive impacts on indicators of family and child wellness (Barth, Blythe, Schinke, & Schilling, 1983; Brunk, Henggeler, & Whelan, 1987; Burch & Mohr, 1980; Egan, 1983; Fantuzzo, Wray, Hall, Goins, & Azar, 1986; Reid, Taplin, & Lorber, 1981; Whiteman, Fanshel, & Grundy, 1987; Wolfe et al., 1981; Wolfe et al., 1988). Moreover, these positive impacts have been observed with both physically abusive and neglectful parents.

Two studies have reported on rates of out-of-home placements following a parent training intervention based on a social learning approach. Two years following a parent training intervention, placement rates were 18 per cent for the intervention group versus 30 per cent for the comparison group (significance levels were not reported) in a study by Christopherson (1979). In a randomized trial of a social learning parenting program, Szykula and Fleischman (1985) found that placement rates for 'less difficult' families (less than three reports of abuse, no serious transportation or housing problems, child's conduct not a major problem) differed significantly for the intervention (8 per cent) and control (38 per cent) groups, but there were no significant differences for 'more difficult' families between the intervention (64 per cent) and control (45 per cent) groups.

Summary and Critique
The findings regarding parent education and training programs are summarized in Table 5.3. Universally accessible social learning and Adlerian approaches to parent training have been shown to be effective in changing parents' and children's behaviour. More wide-scale imple-

TABLE 5.3
Summary of Findings of Parent Education and Training Programs

	Findings
Proactive	
Universal	• Research on educational and training programs following social learning and Adlerian approaches has reported positive impacts on parents' attitudes and behaviour and on children's behaviour. • There is no evidence that these programs prevent child maltreatment.
High-risk	• There has been very little research on parenting programs for parents at risk of maltreating their children.
Reactive	
Indicated	• Positive impacts on the behaviour of parents and children have been found in controlled studies of parent training using a social learning approach with families in which abuse and/or neglect has occurred. • There is some evidence that parent training using a social learning approach can reduce out-of-home placements of children.

mentation through family resource centres and schools is needed to promote such programs.

Parent education programs need to attend to issues of cultural diversity, power and gender roles, and parent-identified concerns. Much of the research in this area has focused on programs for middle-class parents of European ancestry. In view of different parenting practices across cultures, language barriers to accessing such programs among immigrant populations, and the increased cultural diversity in Canada, there is a need for parent education and training programs that are geared to different ethnocultural populations (Battaglini et al., 1997; Short & Johnston, 1994). When programs are implemented for families from cultures with a more collectivist orientation, the extended family could be included, especially grandparents, who play a key role in childrearing.

Parent education and training programs need to look at the important issue of gender roles in families and how power is distributed among family members. There is an important need in such programs to engage fathers more actively in their families and in the interventions that are designed to promote family wellness (e.g., Westney, Cole, & Munford, 1988). Also, many of the small-group parent education and training programs have been developed by professionals and follow a preset agenda. To promote family empowerment, it would be useful to ask parents what they would find useful in such programs (DeChillo, Koren, & Schultze, 1994).

While there has not been a great deal of program development or research on parent education and training interventions for families at risk of child maltreatment, the research on reactive applications of parent training has found that parent training programs can prevent out-of-home placement of children and have a positive impact on parents' and children's behaviour in the short term. On the other hand, there is no evidence that reactive parenting programs prevent continued abuse or neglect of children by parents.

There is no doubt that helping parents to acquire concrete skills in child management and stress management/anger control through instruction and direct coaching is a worthwhile endeavour. At the same time, however, there are several conceptual limitations to these programs. First of all, this approach assumes that parents lack skills in child management and stress management. However, it is possible that parents' skills may not be exercised because they are subject to constant stressors and social isolation. A second and related concern is that parent training programs offer a single program strategy to deal with a complex and multiply determined behaviour. The needs of parents for child care, employment, social support, and more are not addressed by parent training programs. Third, parent training programs are short-term in nature, seldom lasting longer than three months. It is not clear if such programs have enduring effects on parents and children. In summary, we believe that like any other single-focus, short-term intervention, parent training is, in itself, insufficient to prevent initial or further maltreatment of children. However, used in the context of a multi-component, community-based, long-term intervention, parent education and training is likely a very useful intervention strategy.

Family Support Programs

Proactive family support programs are geared to the parents of pre-school children, particularly during the prenatal and postnatal periods. Our key informants made the following comments about such programs:

> *When I was really young, there was this woman who used to come into our house I think once a week, because my mother needed it. She needed someone to hold her hand*

to do things. *And she would help my mother with things like budgeting, and what to buy, how to cook different things and stuff like that, and how to cope with having young children. And when she was coming, that was the happiest point in my childhood. The concrete help as opposed to the therapy stuff. I think that helped my mother and she was able to cope with being a young mother.* (Youth)

Healthy Babies is both a program and an initiative. The program provides home visits to high-risk families with children from prenatally to age 2. The Healthy Babies Initiative also includes universal screening of every newborn in Ontario with follow-up, either linkages to services or the home visiting for every family identified as high-risk. (Adviser)

Proactive Universal Applications

Home visitation programs may begin during pregnancy; the period of most intense concentration of home visiting is during the first two years of the child's life. Recent research has suggested that adequate parenting and child care during the infant's first eighteen months of life are critical to optimal brain and central nervous system development (Guy, 1997; Steinhauer, 1998). Thus, both the timing and focus of home visitation programs appear to be very important for the development of the child. Home visitors, who are usually nurses or paraprofessionals, visit women in their homes with a focus on the promotion of maternal health during pregnancy, child development, mother–child attachment, and support for mothers in their parental, social, occupational, and educational roles after the baby is born.

The relationship between the mother and the home visitor is seen as the single most critical factor in the intervention process. Home visitors strive to develop a relationship or 'working alliance' with the mother. The relationship between the home visitor and the mother provides the medium for a number of other intervention components, including education, goal-setting, problem solving, referral to community services, and mobilization of informal supports and community resources.

Home visitation programs for parents of newborns have rarely been implemented on a universal basis. In Quebec, all new mothers, after the birth of their babies, are visited once in their homes by home visitors from local community service centres. For vulnerable mothers and families, home visitation is to be offered on a more continuous and frequent basis. In Colorado, the Baby Bear Hugs program was designed to provide support to new mothers and to prevent maltreatment (Coburn, 1996). Parent volunteers are recruited and trained to visit the mothers of newborn children, with the visits beginning during pregnancy and continuing for up to three years.

In the only controlled evaluation of a universal home visitation program, Taylor and Beauchamp (1988) randomly assigned first-time mothers to a home visitation program or a control condition. Student nurses met with mothers while they were in the hospital after the birth of their babies and then for three home visits. In spite of the small sample sizes ($n = 16$ for the intervention group and $n = 14$ for the control group) and the brevity of the intervention (four home visits), the authors reported several positive findings. Compared with mothers in the control group, those in the intervention group reported significantly greater knowledge about child development and more positive attitudes about parenting and showed significantly greater amounts of verbal stimulation of their children.

Proactive High-Risk Applications
Exemplary Programs. Of the home visiting programs that have an explicit focus on preventing child physical abuse and neglect, one is particularly noteworthy: the Prenatal/Early Infancy Project developed by David Olds and colleagues (e.g., Olds & Korfmacher, 1997, 1998). This project deserves special mention for several reasons. First, Olds and colleagues have developed a well-articulated program theory that links program processes with intended outcomes (Olds, Kitzman, Cole, & Robinson, 1997). The program combines insights from ecological, self-efficacy (empowerment), and attachment theories. Second, they have described in detail challenges, successes, and issues in program implementation (see Olds & Korfmacher, 1997). Third, the research design used in the evaluation of this program has been of the highest methodological quality (see MacMillan et al., 1994a). Fourth, a fifteen-year follow-up has been completed with participants from the initial randomized trial (Olds et al., 1997). Fifth, after completing an initial randomized trial in rural New York with a sample of predominantly poor, white women in conditions in which they as investigators had a great deal of control over the implementation of the intervention (Olds et al., 1986), Olds and colleagues replicated their work in an urban community (Memphis) with a larger sample of predominantly black women under more natural conditions (the program was implemented by a public health department) (Kitzman et al., 1997). Moreover, another replication is now under way in a different urban community (Denver). Sixth, some data on cost benefits have been collected (Olds, Henderson, Phelps, Kitz-

man, & Hanks, 1993). Finally, some of the findings reported by Olds and colleagues have been very encouraging about the prevention of child physical abuse and neglect.

The original home visitation program was initiated in 1978 in Elmira, New York, a semi-rural community rated as the most economically disadvantaged in the United States. Women who were pregnant (prior to the twenty-fifth week of gestation) had no previous live births, and had at least one of three risk factors (mothers < age 19, unmarried, and low-income) were invited to participate in the study (Olds et al., 1986). Participants were randomly assigned to control conditions (which involved developmental screening and referral at ages 1 and 2 and/or free transportation for prenatal and well-child care through age 2, $n = 165$), home visitation during pregnancy plus free transportation to prenatal care ($n = 90$), and home visitation during pregnancy until the child's second birthday ($n = 99$). The home visitors were trained registered nurses who visited the mothers for just over one hour every week during the first six weeks after birth, every two weeks from six weeks to four months, every three weeks from four to fourteen months, every four weeks from fourteen to twenty months, and every six weeks from twenty to twenty-four months. The visits focused on promoting parent education, enhancing informal support, and linking with formal services.

The original study by Olds et al. (1986) reported several positive outcomes for both the mothers and the babies. Children in the control conditions were seen more often in a hospital emergency room in their first year and presented with more accidents and poisonings during their second year. For the highest-risk group (mothers < 19 years of age, unmarried, and poor), those in the control conditions had a significantly higher rate of verified physical child abuse and neglect (19 per cent), nearly five times higher than that of the nurse-home-visited group (4 per cent). Among this high-risk group, mothers in the control conditions punished/restricted and yelled at or scolded their children significantly more often than nurse-home-visited mothers.

Of the original 400 participants, 324 (> 80 per cent of the original sample) participated in a follow-up study when their children were 15 years of age (Olds, Eckenrode et al., 1997). Compared with women in the control conditions, women who were visited by nurses during pregnancy and infancy had significantly lower rates of verified child physical abuse and neglect. These results were even more clear-cut for the subgroup of low-income, unmarried women, as was the case in the two-year follow-up.

Programs and Research Evidence. The home visitation programs described in the literature differ from one another in many ways. Many home visitation programs have used nurses (e.g., Olds et al., 1986), paraprofessionals (e.g., Barth, 1991), volunteers (Jacobson & Frye, 1991), or a team of paraprofessionals, nurses, and other professionals (e.g., Gray, Cutler, Dean, & Kempe, 1979a, 1979b; Marcenko, Spence, & Samost, 1996). The length of time over which visits are conducted varies widely, with most providing home visitation until the child reaches 1 or 2 years of age. Some programs offer visits for less than six months after the baby is born (Barth, 1991; Siegel, Bauman, Schaefer, Saunders, & Ingram, 1980), while the Hawaii Healthy Start program lasts until the child is 5 years of age (Breakey & Pratt, 1991). Some programs begin the home visits during the prenatal period, but most begin at birth. Finally, the frequency of home visitation varies as well. Some programs provide weekly visitation for a period after the baby is born (e.g., Breakey & Pratt, 1991; Gray et al., 1979a; Olds et al., 1986), while others have visits only once every two to three months (Hardy & Streett, 1989). In some programs, home visitors are available for additional visits or telephone contact during periods of acute stress, but other programs follow a predetermined schedule of visits.

Several controlled studies have found significantly lower rates of abuse/neglect in the intervention group (Caruso, 1989; Center on Child Abuse Prevention Research, 1996; Hardy & Streett, 1989; Kitzman et al., 1997; Olds et al., 1986; Olds, Eckenrode et al., 1997), while others have reported no significant differences between groups (Barth, 1991; Galano & Huntington, 1997; Gray et al., 1979a, 1979b; Siegel et al., 1980). In terms of proxy measures of physical abuse and neglect (e.g., emergency room visits, reports of injuries or ingestions), several of these studies reported significantly lower rates in the intervention group than in the control group on at least one of these measures (Caruso, 1989; Center on Child Abuse Prevention Research, 1996; Gray et al., 1979a, 1979b; Hardy & Streett, 1989; Kitzman et al., 1997; Larson, 1980; Olds et al., 1986; Olds, Eckenrode et al., 1997), while two others reported no significant differences (Barth, 1991; Siegel et al., 1980). A few studies of home visitation have examined rates of out-of-home placement and have found no significant differences in placement rates for the intervention and control groups (Barth, 1991; Gray et al., 1979a, 1979b; Marcenko et al., 1996).

Evidence in support of the effectiveness of home visitation programs for high-risk families with newborn children is strongest on observational measures of parenting and parents' self-reports of their attitudes toward childrearing and child development (e.g., family wellness). With some exceptions (Barth, 1991; Booth, Mitchell, Barnard, & Spieker, 1989; Durand, Massé, & Ouellet, 1989; Larson, 1980; Marcenko et al., 1996; Van Doorninck, Dawson, Butterfield, & Alexander, 1980; Ware, Osofosky, Culp, & Eberhart-Wright, 1987), controlled prospective evaluations of home visitation programs have found significant positive impacts on parent–child interactions and parents' self-reports of their attitudes of childrearing at post-intervention and follow-up intervals of up to two years after the birth of the child (Affleck, Tennen, Rowe, Roscher, & Walker, 1989; Barnard et al., 1988; Barrera, Rosenbaum, & Cunningham, 1986; Beckwith, 1988; Black, Dubowitz, Hutcheson, Berenson-Howard, & Starr, 1995; Bromwich & Parmelee, 1979; Center on Child Abuse Prevention Research, 1996; Clinton, 1989; Field, Widmayer, Greenberg, & Stoller, 1982; Field, Widmayer, Stringer, & Ignatoff, 1980; Galano & Huntington, 1997; Gray & Ruttle, 1990; Jacobson & Frye, 1991; Kitzman et al., 1997; Lambie, Bond, & Weikart, 1974; Madden, O'Hara, & Levenstein, 1984; Olds et al., 1986; Ross, 1984; Siegel et al., 1980; Travers, Nauta, & Irwin, 1982). One longer-term follow-up (when the children were 6 to 7 years of age), however, found no lasting effects of home visitation on parent–child interaction (Epstein & Weikart, 1979).

Cost-effectiveness data on home visitation programs have been gathered in two studies. Olds et al. (1993) estimated the costs of the nurse home visitation program to be $3,300 in 1980 US dollars and $6,700 in 1997 US dollars for two and one-half years of service. In terms of government spending, these costs were recovered from the low-income families before the children reached 4 years of age. Similarly, Hardy and Streett (1989) estimated that at least $25,000 US in costs were saved in their home visitation program.

Reactive Applications
Reactive programs focus on families in which child maltreatment has already occurred. The preventive focus of such programs is often how to prevent further abuse, out-of-home placement, or abuse of younger siblings. The reader will notice that the intervention strategies are somewhat different than those described in the previous sections on proactive (universal and high-risk) family support programs. Reactive family support programs are called family preservation rather than home visitation. Another difference is that the reactive programs tend

to focus on older children. Whereas the majority of proactive programs have a focus on early infancy, many of the reactive programs focus on a wider age range of children, including elementary-school–aged children. In many respects, it appears that the families who utilize family support after maltreatment has occurred are similar to the high-risk families who have been targeted for home visitation. The difference is that the intervention does not occur until later, when the children are older and a pattern of negative parent–child relationships has taken root.

One stakeholder made the following comment about reactive family support programs:

> *I think things like family preservation, and wrap-around, and in-home child management programs have their place in terms of supporting kids to stay in families. They are not a panacea. None of them on their own are going to change the world, but they do offer a way of providing intensive support that a number of families can learn and can use. We should continue to be able to do that.* (Service provider)

Exemplary Program. Homebuilders was developed by Jill Kinney and David Haapala for implementation in the child welfare system in the state of Washington in 1974 (Fraser, Pecora, & Haapala, 1991; Kinney, Haapala, & Booth, 1991). Since its inception, the Homebuilders program has been widely disseminated and implemented in 42 states and several Canadian provinces (Dagenais & Bouchard, 1996). Homebuilders, which is the most widely used model of intensive family preservation, is a program for families of children considered to be at risk of imminent out-of-home placement. There are several key defining features of this approach: (1) families receive a variety of services in their homes, (2) the intervention is short-term (usually less than three months), and (3) the intervention is intensive (more than one day per week of face-to-face contact between the family and case worker) and is available around the clock, seven days a week.

A key assumption of this approach is that families are very open to change and intervention when they are in a state of crisis. Case workers respond immediately to family crises and provide intensive services to such families (workers have small caseloads of only two to four families at one time). The goal of the intervention is to help improve the parent–child relationship and to resolve the current crisis.

In an evaluation of Homebuilders, Pecora, Fraser, and Haapala (1991) gathered pre-test and post-test information on 453 families. The primary outcome measure was rate of out-of-home placement. Only 7 per cent of the families had a child placed out of home at the end of the intervention. One-year follow-up data were gathered from 263 of these families and were compared with a small comparison group ($n=26$). The one-year out-of-home placement rate for the intervention group was 33 per cent compared with 85 per cent of the comparison group. Since the intervention and comparison group participants differed on several characteristics, matched pairs were constructed for the one-year follow-up data and out-of-home placement rates were 44 per cent for the intervention group and 85 per cent for the comparison group.

Programs and Research Evidence. In addition to the crisis intervention approach of Homebuilders, there are two other models of intensive family preservation, according to Nelson, Landsman, and Deutelbaum (1990): (1) home-based treatment and (2) intensive family treatment. Home-based treatment is similar to Homebuilders but focuses specifically on avoiding placements for adolescents. Intensive family treatment utilizes a brief version of family systems therapy.

Intensive family preservation programs differ in terms of the ages of the children served. For example, the average age of the children in the evaluation by Yuan, McDonald, Wheeler, Struckman-Johnson, and Rivest (1990) was 6.8 years, but 13.5 years in Feldman's (1991) study. Many studies report a wide range of ages served. We have omitted studies which focus *exclusively* on adolescents in our chapter, but the reader should be aware that there are adolescents in some of the evaluations that we review. While the models of intensive family preservation reviewed by Nelson et al. (1990) differ in the ways described above, they also share several common features. All of these intervention programs are designed to: (1) prevent out-of-home placement of at-risk children, (2) enhance family functioning, and (3) protect children from further abuse.

There have been several recent reviews of the literature on the effectiveness of intensive family preservation programs (Cameron & Vanderwoerd, 1997a; Dagenais & Bouchard, 1996; Heneghan, Horwitz, & Leventhal, 1996; Rivera & Kutash, 1994b). In controlled studies of intensive family preservation, all but one (Mitchell, Tovar, & Knitzer, 1989) have found significantly lower rates of placement at the end of the intervention for the intervention groups relative to the comparison or control groups (Feldman, 1991; Lyle & Nelson, 1983; Pearson, Masnyk, & King, 1987; Raschick, 1997; Yuan et al., 1990). Of those studies that followed families at least one year after the intervention, three found no differences in placement rates (Meezan & McCroskey, 1996; Mitchell et al., 1989; Raschick, 1997), while five reported significantly lower placement rates for the intervention group than the comparison/control groups (Berquist, Szwejda, & Pope, 1993; Feldman, 1991; Pearson et al., 1987; Pecora et al., 1991; Wood, Barton, & Schroeder, 1988).

Yuan et al. (1990) found that while the rates of out-of-home placement at a six-month follow-up did not differ significantly between intervention (18 per cent) and comparison (17 per cent) groups, the number of days spent in placement was significantly higher for the control group than for the intervention group. Raschick (1997) found no significant differences between intervention and comparison groups at one-year follow-up, but at two-year follow-up, the intervention group had lower placement rates. Walton (1997) found both significantly lower rates of placement for the intervention group (15 per cent) compared with the control group (40 per cent) at a six-month follow-up and significantly fewer days that the cases were 'open' for the intervention group compared with the control group.

A somewhat different approach was taken in a study by Walton, Fraser, Lewis, Pecora, and Walton (1993), who randomly assigned children who were in foster care to a control group or a family preservation program designed to reunify the children with their families. At the end of the three-month intervention, 93 per cent of the children in the intervention program were reunited with their families compared with 28 per cent of children in the control group; this difference was statistically significant. One-year follow-up data showed 75 per cent of the intervention children living with their families, while 49 per cent of children in the control group lived with their families, which was also statistically significant.

Some studies have also examined other outcome measures pertaining to family wellness (e.g., family climate) and child wellness (e.g., social behaviour). Dagenais and Bouchard (1996) found that most of these studies reported moderate to large effects on these measures. However, in the few studies which used a comparison or control group, Dagenais and Bouchard (1996) found minimal to no changes resulting from intensive family preservation on child wellness and family wellness (Feldman, 1991; Rosenthal & Glass, 1986). In a recent randomized trial of home-based, family preservation services in Los Angeles, Meezan and McCroskey (1996) found significant improvements in the family preservation group, compared with the control group, at the end of the intervention on several areas of family wellness (e.g., interactions between parent and child) and child wellness (e.g., mothers' reports of their children's behaviour).

Dagenais and Bouchard (1996) also note that few studies have examined further abuse by parents. Hawkins (1979) found a reduction in verified cases of child maltreatment over a four-year time period (from 602 cases to 266 cases) following the introduction of the Comprehensive Emergency Services demonstration program in Nashville, Tennessee. On the other hand, Yuan et al. (1990) found no differences in rates of investigation for abuse or neglect between the intervention and control groups.

Dagenais and Bouchard (1996) have examined intervention and family characteristics that are associated with successful outcomes. They found that the number of hours of intervention provided and the extent to which concrete support is provided are inversely associated with rates of placement. With respect to family characteristics, generally speaking, low rates of placement are associated with indicators of family wellness. Families with young children who have never before been placed out of the home and who have few problems are most likely to be able to avoid placement. Families experiencing a number of risk factors (e.g., economic disadvantage, single mothers) are likely to have higher rates of placement (Bath & Haapala, 1993).

Family interventions for sexually abused children often combine a variety of program components including: court intervention; individual treatment for the child, the offender, and the nonoffending parent; marital and family therapy (Silovsky & Hembree-Kigin, 1994). Family therapists typically recommend removing the offender rather than the child from the home to prevent further abuse during treatment. A key component of family intervention is a formal session in which the offender, usually the father or step-father, apologizes to the victim and the entire family for his actions. This 'apology session' is important for breaking the pattern of keeping secrets; for beginning a reconciliation; for giving the offender the opportunity to take ownership and responsibility both for his actions and for engaging in treatment to change his behaviour; and for addressing the guilt experienced by the child. Reconciliation between the child who has been abused and the mother is also critical, as the child is often angry at and feels betrayed by the mother, while the mother feels guilty for her inaction and/or ignorance.

Giaretto (1982) evaluated the impact of a multi-component family intervention for families in which a child had been sexually abused. While further abuse was reported for the 250 families who completed

TABLE 5.4
Summary of Findings of Family Support Programs

	Findings
Proactive	
Universal	• Home visitation programs have seldom been implemented on a universal basis, and there is little research on the effectiveness of universal home visitation.
High-risk	• There are numerous examples of home visitation programs that have been implemented with high-risk parents. • There is some evidence from controlled research that such programs can prevent child maltreatment. • Controlled research has shown positive impacts of such programs on mothers' life course and parent–child relationships. • Current research suggests that home visitation is effective only if it is provided for at least one year. • The more visits provided, the better the outcomes. • There is some evidence suggesting the cost-effectiveness of such programs.
Reactive	
Indicated	• There is some evidence that intensive family preservation programs prevent out-of-home placement, but there is little evidence that they have impacts on measures of family, parent, or child wellness. • The number of hours of intervention and the availability of concrete supports are inversely associated with rates of placement. • There is very little research on family interventions for families in which child sexual abuse has been reported.

the program, the length of the follow-up interval was not specified. Similarly, Trepper and Traicoff (1983) reported only two cases of continued abuse out of 50 families who completed a family intervention program over a three-year period.

Summary and Critique
The findings regarding family support programs are summarized in Table 5.4.

Research on home visitation programs for high-risk families shows that the length of the intervention is a key factor in the prevention of child maltreatment. All of the studies that have found differences favouring the home-visited group over control/comparison groups on either verified rates of child abuse and neglect or proxy measures of abuse have provided home visitation for at least one year (Caruso, 1989; Center on Child Abuse Prevention Research, 1996; Gray et al., 1979a, 1979b; Hardy & Streett, 1989; Kitzman et al., 1997; Larson, 1980; Olds et al., 1986). The two studies that did not find an impact of home visitation on either of these outcome measures provided home visitation for only three (Siegel et al., 1980) and six months (Barth, 1991) and used paraprofessional home visitors. Of the programs that offered a small number of home visits (between nine and eleven), two have found a significant impact on either verified reports or proxy measures of child abuse or neglect (Hardy & Streett, 1989; Larson, 1980), while two have not (Barth, 1991; Siegel et al., 1980). All of the programs that have provided twenty or more home visits have reported positive impacts on either verified reports or proxy measures.

Febbraro (1994) has noted the conceptual limitations of home visitation programs for high-risk mothers. Such programs, which focus on family wellness, she argues, ignore larger social and political forces. In so doing, such interventions may inadvertently blame the victims (poor, single mothers) for their problems. Also, the goal of integrating mothers into low-wage, low-power positions in society perpetuates a system that is socially and economically unequal for women, the very conditions that threaten violence toward women and children (Albee & Perry, 1997). Febbraro (1994) argues that such micro-level interventions (which are focused on child and family wellness) should be accompanied by macro-level community development and advocacy interventions (which are focused on community and societal wellness) that are designed to change social policies to promote social, economic, and gender equality.

With regard to reactive family support programs, Dagenais and Bouchard (1996) have noted a number of problems in this research, including studies with small sample sizes, no comparison or control groups, imprecise operational definitions of key variables (e.g., 'imminent risk of placement' or 'out-of-home placement'), and a lack of attention to program implementation. While the research does indicate that various types of intensive family preservation programs can prevent out-of-home placement, the effectiveness of such programs in reducing placement rates at follow-up, in promoting family wellness, and in preventing further maltreatment of the children is less clear.

Programs That Focus on Community Wellness

There are a growing number of programs that go beyond the family to focus on the community as well. Self-help aid and social support programs not only provide family support, but they also strive to connect the family to the community. Multi-component programs often have a community development emphasis, which is designed to promote community wellness in addition to family wellness. We review programs of this nature in this section.

Self-Help and Social Support Programs

Self-help and social support programs vary in terms of professional involvement from pure self-help groups, which are run by members, to support groups, which are facilitated by professionals (Lavoie & Stewart, 1995). While there are differences among such interventions, the common thread is the focus on expanding the person's social network, increasing access to informal sources of support, and promoting social integration (helping the person to integrate into normal community settings). Parent participants in the stakeholder consultation made the following comments about self-help/mutual aid social support programs:

> *It felt good to get out of the house. We could talk to other parents of small babies.* (Parent)

> *When I first lived here and first got involved in [the self-help/mutual aid group] and Children's Aid, it was a big relief for me because I met new people. I learned that I was worth something because the way things were in life you just didn't believe that. It helped me grow emotionally, self-esteem wise to know that, 'hey, I'm okay.'* (Parent)

Proactive Universal Applications
In this review we found two evaluations of support interventions for new parents (Boger, Richter, & Weatherston, 1983; Telleen, Herzog, & Kilbane, 1989) and one report of a support program for parents with preschool or elementary-school-aged children (Home & Darveau-Fournier, 1995). Boger et al. (1983) have described a support program in which experienced parent volunteers were trained to provide first-time parents with friendship, understanding, and information. Volunteers visited new mothers once in the hospital and once in their homes after the birth of the baby. Peer support groups were then established when the infants were four to eight weeks old, and a 'Warm Line' telephone number was available for parents to call during noncrisis situa-

tions. A videotape series and written materials on parenting issues were developed and provided. Intervention mothers scored significantly better than control mothers on a measure of unrealistic expectations of the child and measures of maternal involvement and child nurturing involvement at twelve and fifteen months after the program.

Telleen et al. (1989) evaluated support groups for parents with at least one child under the age of 7. While the group was offered in a city with high levels of unemployment and high rates of child abuse, the group was universally accessible to all parents. Parents participated in either a parent education group, a social support group, or a control group. The support group met twice a week for three months, and the agenda was determined by the parents. After three months of program participation, mothers in both the parent education and the support group reported a reduced sense of isolation compared with mothers in the control group and fewer child-related stressors over time than those in the control group.

In a low-income, inner-city neighbourhood in Quebec, community workers and families formed a collective with the goals of preventing family deterioration and promoting family empowerment (Home & Darveau-Fournier, 1995). They developed Familles Gardiennes, a demonstration project that provides respite care for parents with children 12 years of age or younger on a 24-hour basis for periods of two to fifteen days, several times per year. This program is available on a universal basis to families in the neighbourhood. Group sessions and informal support are provided to families. Unfortunately, no controlled evaluation data have been reported on this program.

Proactive High-Risk Applications
Some self-help or support groups are offered only to parents of high-risk groups, including parents of premature infants (Minde et al., 1980), low-income parents (Slaughter, 1983), and teen-age mothers (De La Rey & Parekh, 1996; Henninger & Nelson, 1984). For those participating in the programs relative to parents in comparison groups, controlled evaluations of these support group interventions have found significantly enhanced satisfaction with medical care, nursing care, and information; understanding of the infant's condition; interaction with other parents; comfort with and ability to care for the baby; knowledge of community resources; more interaction with their babies (Minde et al., 1980); significantly improved maternal teaching style, child play structures, ego maturity, and expressed social values (Slaughter, 1983); significantly more

friendships, education, and/or work involvement; and significantly higher levels of emotional well-being (Henninger & Nelson, 1984). Also, Slaughter (1983) found that women participating in the discussion groups reported more change at the two-year period than women who participated in a home visitation program. Unfortunately, none of these evaluations examined rates of child maltreatment as an outcome.

There are also support interventions for high-risk children. In Montreal, the Tel-Jeunes program serves children and youth from ages 5 to 20. A telephone hotline available 24 hours a day, seven days a week is available to children and youth from across the province (there is a 1-800 number). In Montreal, the program Les Scientifines is geared to girls ages 9 to 12, primarily from low-income families. The program is a science club designed to promote skills and personal development and prevent child neglect. A healthy snack is provided by the local community service centre, and there are both structured and unstructured activities all related to scientific experiments. An evaluation of this program has found improvement in the girls' problem-solving skills relative to girls in a control group after one year of participation in the program (Chamberland, Théorêt, Garon, & Roy, 1995). Also, girls in the control group, but not those participating in the program, showed a significant increase in school absenteeism.

Reactive Applications
Exemplary Program. The largest self-help/mutual aid organization for parents that focuses on child maltreatment is Parents Anonymous. This organization was co-founded in 1970 by a social worker and a mother who had abused her child (Lieber, 1983). Currently there are more than 1,200 Parents Anonymous chapters across North America (Riessman & Carroll, 1995). Parents Anonymous chapters offer self-help/mutual aid groups, telephone help lines for parental support during crises, and written information about parenting (Paiement, 1984). Weekly two-hour meetings are held in some community setting. Anonymity and confidentiality are cornerstones to the support process, with the only exception to this condition being if and when a parent continues abusive behaviour toward a child. Parents also form friendships and get together outside of group meetings. Parents Anonymous groups typically have a chairperson (who is also a member), a sponsor (a professional who acts as a support to the chairperson), and members.

Lieber and Baker (1977) surveyed 613 members from a number of different chapters of Parents Anonymous and found statistically significant decreases in self-reported verbal and physical abuse just after joining Parents Anonymous. Also, self-esteem, social contacts, and knowledge about children's behaviour were all positively correlated with length of time in the group. In a more recent survey of 173 members of Parents Anonymous chapters in Illinois, McCray and Wolf (1997) have indicated that the majority of respondents reported improvements in several areas of life (e.g., self-esteem, family relationships, anger control, parenting skills) after joining Parents Anonymous. None of the evaluations of Parents Anonymous have used a longitudinal design or comparison groups.

Programs and Research Evidence. The parent mutual aid organization described by Cameron, Hayward, and Mamatis (1992) is an example of a reactive approach to prevention. A number of different program activities (recreation, general discussion, educational speakers, volunteer work) are offered several times a week. Parents can access a variety of supports several times a week, including parent relief, emotional support, information, guidance, and socialization/recreation, and they are also encouraged to expand their social involvements outside of the organization. Like other self-help organizations, there is a focus on parents' strengths and empowerment.

The evaluation design included an intervention group and a comparison group selected from three different sites with three different interview periods over time (an initial interview and follow-up interviews at roughly six months and one year later). There were significant differences over time for intervention participants relative to comparison group participants on the following outcome measures: rates of placement of children in care, participation in social recreational activities, parents' self-esteem and stress, and attitudes toward children. The researchers estimated that the savings to the child welfare agencies resulting from the positive impacts of the parent mutual aid organizations was between $420 and $869 Cdn per case per year.

Other support interventions focus on building a network of support around the person that includes informal supports (family, friends, neighbours) rather than an exclusive reliance on professionals. Lovell and her colleagues have conducted several evaluations of social network interventions (Lovell & Hawkins, 1988; Lovell, Reid, & Richey, 1992; Lovell & Richey, 1991, 1995; Richey, Lovell, & Reid, 1991). In all of these studies, services were provided to low-income parents who had maltreated their preschool children. One of the aims of the program was to strengthen informal supports and reduce social isolation. Group sessions focused on mutual support and skill-building (stress management, child management, etc.). Unfortunately, evaluations of this project have not found significant changes in parents' social networks or other outcome measures compared with parents in comparison groups (Lovell & Hawkins, 1988; Lovell et al., 1992; Lovell & Richey, 1991, 1995; Richey et al., 1991).

Gaudin, Wodarski, Arkinson, and Avery (1990–91) reported on a reactive intervention for low-income parents who had neglected their children. The intervention ranged from 2 to 23 months, with an average of 10 months, and included the following components: self-help/mutual aid groups, linking with volunteers ('family friends'), neighbourhood helpers, and social skills training. In contrast to the findings by Lovell and colleagues, a number of positive effects for those in the intervention group compared with the control group were found, including significant improvements in parenting skills, parenting attitudes, social network size, and perceived supportiveness of one's network. At the end of the project, 59 per cent of those in the intervention group had improved to the point where their cases were closed, as compared with 24 per cent of those in the control group (the level of statistical significance was not reported).

Éthier, Gagnier, Lacharité, and Couture (1995) have evaluated a multicomponent reactive program called Programme d'Intervention Écosystémique pour les Familles à Risque de Négligence. This project, which is carried out through a local community service centre, targets families with children aged zero to 6 who have been reported but not prosecuted for child neglect and is carried out for a period of eighteen months. Each family is paired with a support family, with whom they meet twice a week for up to two hours per visit. There are also support groups for parents on how to improve their parenting skills. While parents attend the support group meetings, which last three hours, activities to stimulate the development of the children are provided by project staff.

In a controlled evaluation of this program, Éthier et al. (1995) found no significant impacts of the program on several social network measures, parental stress, maternal depression, abuse potential of mothers, or the children's behaviour. However, the sample sizes for the groups (roughly 15 per group) were quite small.

Summary and Critique

The findings on self-help/mutual aid and social support interventions are summarized in Table 5.5. The little empirical evidence that is avail-

TABLE 5.5
Summary of Findings of Self-Help/Mutual Aid and Social Support Programs

	Findings
Proactive Universal	• There is some controlled research demonstrating that universally accessible self-help/mutual aid groups can promote family wellness and build informal social support. • There is no evidence that such programs can prevent child maltreatment.
High-risk	• There is some controlled research demonstrating that self-help/mutual aid groups for parents at risk of maltreating their children can promote family wellness and build informal social support.
Reactive Indicated	• There is some evidence that self-help/mutual aid organizations for parents who have maltreated their children have a variety of positive impacts on parents and parent–child relationships. • There is some evidence that self-help/mutual aid organizations for parents who have maltreated their children can reduce out-of-home placements and further occurrences of maltreatment.

able suggests that both universal (Boger et al., 1983; Telleen et al., 1989) and high-risk (Henninger & Nelson, 1984; Minde et al., 1980; Slaughter, 1983) self-help and support groups can promote family wellness and build informal support. More research is needed to know which type of people benefit most from these programs and what the longer-term impacts are. Also, more research is needed on the cost-effectiveness of these interventions, since they are low in cost relative to other professional services.

Reactive programs, such as Parents Anonymous and the parent mutual aid organizations described by Cameron et al. (1992), appear to be a viable and conceptually appealing alternative to professionally directed programs. The results of the controlled evaluation conducted by Cameron et al. (1992) are quite promising, in that positive impacts were found on a wide range of outcome measures.

Like parent education and training programs, self-help and support programs have not been widely implemented with different cultural groups. Thus, there is a need for adaptation of such programs to different cultural contexts. Since many of the participants in self-help and support programs are women, there needs to be greater attention to strategies to reach men and involve them in such groups.

Section II: Interventions

Multi-Component, Community-Based Programs

Recent thinking regarding the prevention of child maltreatment and the promotion of family wellness underscores the need for multi-component, community-based programs, as opposed to narrowly focused prevention programs (Cowan et al., 1998; Schorr, 1997). Such programs are often housed in a neighbourhood resource centre or a school. The following comments from stakeholders speak to the need for multi-component, community-based programs:

> *There is no single bullet that is going to solve this problem. Maltreatment and mistreatment are multiply determined. No one thing is causing abuse, so unless you have a multiply focused intervention, you are not likely to succeed.* (Adviser)

> *[There is a] public health nurse that works at [the family resource centre] monthly, who meets with a group of young parents, usually moms and their children. And I'm not sure that those same people would be a part of a program that was maybe offered by somebody else or was offered in a place that they don't already feel comfortable in. They are already attached to [the resource centre]. They feel comfortable here, so it's easy for them to come to that program. They've done different things at different times, like parenting classes and how to discipline your kids. The space is comfortable. The public health nurse has worked with us for a while, so people are comfortable with her too, but it was the space that brought them here first.* (Youth)

Proactive Universal Applications

Multi-component, community-based programs provide several different program components, including community development. Community development is a purposeful, goal-directed process that is driven by community residents to meet needs that residents have identified (Rothman & Tropman, 1987). Since research has shown a positive correlation between neighbourhood rates of poverty and rates of child maltreatment (Chamberland, Bouchard, & Beaudry, 1986; Garbarino & Sherman, 1980), community development in low-income communities may have an impact on rates of child maltreatment by building protective processes at the community level. In support of this assertion, Chamberland et al. (1986) found that mothers living in low-income communities with low rates of maltreatment had more socially cohesive networks than mothers living in low-income communities with high rates of maltreatment.

Community development interventions often create neighbourhood

Programs for Preschool and Elementary-School Children   253

organizations. Such organizations are geared to the families of preschool and/or elementary-school-aged children and offer a range of child care and family support programs (Zigler, Finn-Stevenson, & Stern, 1997). One characteristic of these interventions is the informal neighbour-to-neighbour support that is mobilized by the community development process (Garbarino & Kostelny, 1992; Korbin & Coulton, 1996; U.S. Advisory Board on Child Abuse and Neglect, 1993).

Exemplary Programs. One multi-component, universal prevention program is currently being implemented with children and families living in eight socioeconomically disadvantaged communities in Ontario. Better Beginnings, Better Futures is a twenty-five-year longitudinal prevention research project focusing on children from birth to 8 years of age and their families. The project has three major goals: (1) to prevent serious social, emotional, behavioural, physical, and cognitive problems in young children; (2) to promote the social, emotional, behavioural, physical, and cognitive development of these children; and (3) to enhance the abilities of socioeconomically disadvantaged families and communities to provide for their children (Peters, 1994).

The progress of children, their families, and their neighbourhoods will be followed until the children reach their mid-twenties in order to determine long-term program effects. Five communities are focusing their programs on children from conception to 4 years of age, and three are concentrating on the 4- to 8-year age range. Families from three communities that are not receiving program funding are also being evaluated for comparison purposes. The eight intervention communities are quite culturally diverse. All eight Better Beginnings communities are implementing a program model that consists of: (1) a multi-component, ecological model (the project is designed to address child, family, and community wellness), and (2) local responsibility and significant parent–community involvement (professionals, parents, and other local community members work collaboratively).

Although the specific program activities differ somewhat across the eight communities, they generally share the following features: (1) home visitation, (2) classroom environment, (3) child care enrichment, (4) family programs, and (5) community programs. A multidisciplinary research approach that uses both quantitative and qualitative methods is being employed to evaluate the programs and their outcomes.

Another community development project that has a focus on the prevention of child maltreatment is 1,2,3 GO!, which is being implemented in five low-income neighbourhoods and one village in the Greater

Montreal area (Bouchard, 1997b). Each neighbourhood has a local steering committee that is charged with developing an action plan to focus the energies of the community. The entire project is supported by a program committee of staff and volunteers, a partners committee with leaders from various sectors in Montreal, a supporter committee that focuses on funding, and a research team.

1,2,3 GO! is based on a multi-level, ecological framework, an emphasis on community empowerment, and sensitivity to ethnocultural diversity. The overriding goal of the project is to create a 'culture devoted to the well-being of children' (Bouchard, 1997b, p. 2). Moreover, the focus is on children from birth to 3 years of age. The research team uses a participatory approach to developing questions, designs, and methods for the project.

Programs and Research Evidence. Multi-component, community-based programs have also been implemented in the United States. Zigler et al. (1997) have described the components of one multi-component, community-based program, the School of the 21st Century (21C). 21C provides year-round care for children ages 3 to 5, from 6 a.m. to 6 p.m. Monday to Friday, and uses a curriculum that emphasizes play and social development. Also, before- and after-school programs and holiday care are provided for elementary-school-aged children with a focus on recreational activities and homework. Finally, home visitation is provided to new parents beginning in the third trimester of pregnancy. Outreach also focuses on the provision of, or referral to, community resources for health and social services and nutrition education. The services provided by 21C schools are universally available and voluntary.

Dryfoos (1994) and Holtzman (1997) have described 'full-service schools' as schools that form the centre of a spectrum of supports for neighbourhood residents. A key factor in full-service schools is the participation of parents and teachers in the planning and decision making of such services. Zigler et al. (1997) have described one program that combines the approaches of 21C and the full-service school. This project offers preschool programs for 3- and 4-year-olds, before- and after-school programs, home visitation for parents of newborns, family literacy and adult education, vacation care, and health services.

To date, there have been few evaluations of multi-component, community-based programs. Affholter, Connell, and Nauta (1983) have reported the findings of an evaluation of a universal, community-based program that focuses on child development, emphasizes family strengths, provides individualized services to families, and extends the age range for intervention from the prenatal period to age 8. Six sites were involved in the study and participants within each site were randomly assigned to intervention and control groups. The authors reported significantly more teaching interaction and parent–child activity for families in the intervention group compared with the control group. Child maltreatment outcomes were not examined.

In Syracuse, New York, Cochran and colleagues (Cochran, 1987; Cochran & Henderson, 1986) have described the Family Matters program, which was offered to families with a 3-year-old child in both low-income and middle-income neighbourhoods. Home visitation and cluster building meetings were offered to parents for two years. Follow-up data were collected from intervention families and from a control group of families who lived in comparison neighbourhoods. The researchers reported increases in the social networks of unmarried mothers participating in the intervention compared with unmarried mothers in the comparison group. Also, children in the intervention program showed significant improvement on their school report cards over time compared with control children. There were no changes in parent–child activities for program participants compared with control participants.

Proactive High-Risk Applications
Some multi-component, community-based programs target high-risk families. Like universally accessible multi-component programs, they are distinguished from other program approaches in that they are usually located in a neighbourhood and offer a range of services.

Exemplary Program. One multi-component, community-based program that was developed in 1969 is the Syracuse University Family Development Research Program (Lally, Mangione, & Honig, 1988). The program served predominantly black, low-income families, beginning during the mothers' third trimester of pregnancy. There were three major program components: (1) home visitation, (2) a children's centre, and (3) a parent-controlled organization. Home visitation was provided on a weekly basis by trained nonprofessionals who came from the same impoverished backgrounds as the families they were helping. The home visitors assisted families with childrearing, family issues, employment, and community participation; they served a liaison function with the teachers of the children's centre; and they provided families with stimulating toys and activities for the children.

Through a children's centre, the families were provided with child care for five days per week, 50 weeks per year for the first five years of the child's life! Half-time child care was provided while the children were six to fifteen months of age, and from fifteen months to sixty months, full-time child care was provided. The home visitors accompanied the parents to the centre once a week. A variety of methods were used to create a welcoming atmosphere for the parents, including all-you-can-eat spaghetti meals, once-a-month parent nights, open invitations to drop in and visit the classroom, and daily memos between the teachers and parents. At the children's centre, a variety of developmentally appropriate activities were implemented to promote children's social, emotional, and cognitive development. The centre was staffed by professionals and trained early childhood education workers. The parents also formed a parents' organization, which met monthly, had elected officers, and planned and organized family and centre events and advocacy and cooperative activities such as bulk food purchasing and child care sharing.

Outcome data were collected when the children were 3, 5, and 10 years of age (Lally et al., 1988). Children in the intervention group ($n = 65$) were compared with a matched comparison group ($n = 54$). The rate of attrition was roughly 25 per cent for both the intervention and comparison groups between 5 and 10 years. At 3 years, children in the intervention group scored significantly higher than children in the comparison group on a measure of intellectual functioning, but this difference was no longer apparent at 5 years. However, the intervention group scored significantly higher than the comparison group at both 3 and 5 years on measures of social and emotional functioning. At 10 years, there were no significant differences between boys in the intervention and comparison groups in terms of school functioning, but girls in the intervention group scored significantly better than girls in the comparison group on several different measures (grades, attendance, teacher ratings of children's behaviour). Interviews with the parents and children also showed significantly higher social and emotional development for children in the intervention group. Finally, 6 per cent of the intervention children as compared with 22 per cent of the comparison group children had been processed through the county probation department for delinquent behaviour (the level of statistical significance was not reported). This last difference translated into costs for the comparison group that were nearly ten times higher than those for the intervention group. On a negative note, Lally et al. (1988) noted that the program had very little impact on family income, employment, and housing.

Programs and Research Evidence. Like the Syracuse project, other multi-component, community-based programs often combine several different programs for the families of infants and preschool children, including home visitation, parenting education and training, health services for and assessment of the children, English-as-a-second-language classes, connection with community resources, support groups, drop-in, or respite services. In many cases, the intervention is based both within the families' homes and at a family resource centre. For example, in the Houston Parent-Child Development Center (Johnson & Breckenridge, 1982), the program begins with home visitation and then moves to centre-based activities as the children turn 2. The Family Focus program offers both home visitation and a Sharing Center simultaneously (Stilwell & Manley, 1990). The Yale Child Welfare Research Program provided several different program components at once: (1) home visitation, (2) pediatric care, (3) daycare, and (4) developmental examinations (Seitz, Rosenbaum, & Apfel, 1985). Some multi-component programs made efforts to reach out to fathers. Fathers were involved in evening sessions in the Houston Parent–Child Development Program. In the program Avancé in San Antonio, Rodriguez and Cortez (1988) have described how evening and weekend activities and community trips were held to engage fathers.

There have been several longitudinal studies with participants randomly assigned to multi-component programs or control groups. Some of these evaluations have follow-up periods as long as five to ten years after the intervention (Johnson & Walker, 1987; Seitz et al., 1985). Significant positive impacts of these multi-component, community-based programs have been reported for the parents (i.e., increased education, employment, and life satisfaction of mothers, fewer repeat pregnancies) (Andrews et al., 1982; Rodriguez & Cortez, 1988; Seitz et al., 1985); for parent–child relationships (i.e., increased affection and encouragement of the child's verbalization, a more stimulating home environment, less criticism of the child) (Andrews et al., 1982); for children (i.e., improved cognitive development, better school adjustment, less absenteeism and use of special education, fewer teacher-reported behaviour problems) (Andrews et al., 1982; Johnson & Breckenridge, 1982; Seitz et al., 1985); and for the siblings of the children who participated in the intervention (i.e., less school absenteeism, use of special education, and repeating grades) (Seitz & Apfel, 1994). Unfortunately, none of these studies examined the impacts of these programs on rates of child maltreatment.

Seitz et al. (1985) also collected some cost-benefit data. Welfare costs (excluding food stamps and medical care) were $30,000 US per year higher and education costs were $10,000 per year higher for comparison families, which 'suggests a one-year differential of approximately $40,000' (p. 389). Furthermore, in the study of younger siblings, Seitz and Apfel (1994) estimated the costs of supplemental school services to be $3,344 US for children in the intervention group compared with $29,380 US for children in the control group. Thus, this multi-faceted program not only had beneficial outcomes for the mothers and their children, but it also saved government expenditures in a very short time period.

Reactive Applications
There are several multi-component programs for families in which the parents have maltreated their children. For example, Project 12-Ways is a multi-component program for people referred by the state's child protection agency. Project 12-Ways is based on an 'ecobehavioral' model and aims to prevent repeated instances of child physical abuse or neglect (Lutzker & Rice, 1984, 1987). In-home services include the following: parenting skills, stress-reduction and self-control, social support, assertiveness training, basic life skills, use of leisure time, health promotion and nutrition, home safety, job placement, marital counselling, referral for other problems, money management, and other services.

In one evaluation of this program, Lutzker and Rice (1984) found significantly fewer verified reports of physical abuse or neglect in the intervention group compared with a matched comparison group. In a larger study, Lutzker and Rice (1987) found a significantly lower level of repeated abuse (21 per cent) for the intervention group than the comparison group (29 per cent).

In another evaluation of this program, Wesch and Lutzker (1991) collected data on out-of-home placement, adoption, abuse, and neglect across three time periods (pre-treatment, treatment, and post-treatment) for both intervention and comparison groups. Both groups showed improvement over time, but there were no significant differences reported between groups. However, focusing only on those families in which there were instances of placement, adoption, abuse, or neglect, the comparison group showed a significant increase in recidivism over time compared with the Project 12-Ways intervention group.

Jones, Neuman, and Shyne (1976) implemented an intervention for families at risk for out-of-home placement of a child under 14 years of age in three sites in New York state. An array of services was offered, including counselling, financial assistance, medical services, help with housing, family life education, education in practical aspects of home management, recreation and cultural enrichment, tutoring, vocational counselling and training, daycare, and so on. Participants were randomly assigned to intervention and control conditions. One year after the intervention began, the placement rates were 7 per cent for the intervention group and 18 per cent for the comparison group, which was statistically significant (Jones et al., 1976). Moreover, intervention families showed significantly more progress toward goals than control families. Five years after the intervention, Jones (1985) found that 34 per cent of the intervention children compared with 46 per cent of children in the control group had been placed outside of the home, a significant difference.

In another randomized trial of 120 families in New York, a similar range of services was provided to families at risk of out-of-home placement of a child (Halper & Jones, 1981). Nearly half of the children were under 3 years of age. At the end of the study period (which lasted two years) or when clients had their cases closed, the rates of placement were significantly lower for the intervention group (4 per cent) than for the control group (17 per cent). Moreover, there was significant improvement over time for intervention families on measures of the family living environment and mothers' functioning compared with control families.

Summary and Critique
Findings regarding the effectiveness of multi-component, community-based programs are summarized in Table 5.6. Multi-component, community-based programs that provide a range of universal services and supports to families in low-income, high-risk communities appear to be a very promising direction for the promotion of family wellness and the prevention of child maltreatment. Evaluations of high-risk multi-component programs have shown a number of positive impacts on family wellness and child wellness, but none of the comprehensive programs have directly examined impacts on child maltreatment.

Comprehensive programs that have been implemented with parents who have maltreated their children offer a range of program components and are available for much longer than short-term intensive family preservation or parent training programs. While evaluations of such programs have shown that they prevent out-of-home placement for some families, there is less evidence of their impact on other indicators

TABLE 5.6
Summary of Findings of Multi-Component, Community-Based Programs

	Findings
Proactive Universal	• Several multi-component, community-based programs have been implemented on a universal basis. • Research on such programs is just beginning.
High-risk	• There is some controlled research demonstrating that multi-component, community-based programs for parents at risk of maltreating their children can promote parental and child wellness. • The impacts of such programs on child maltreatment have yet to be examined.
Reactive Indicated	• There is some evidence that multi-component, community-based programs for parents who have maltreated their children can reduce out-of-home placements and further occurrences of maltreatment. • There is less evidence that such programs have an impact on other measures of family or child wellness.

of family wellness, and no evidence that they prevent further maltreatment of the children.

Programs That Focus on Societal Wellness

Media, Employment, and Legislative Programs

While critics (e.g., Febbraro, 1994) have argued that interventions that strive to promote family wellness and prevent child maltreatment need to address societal wellness, this is the least developed area of intervention. One stakeholder noted the tremendous societal obstacles that high-risk families face, even with programs that address child, family, or community wellness:

> We ask of impoverished people, who have many difficulties at the social level, at all levels, people who know they are disenfranchised, who face all kinds of prejudices, we ask them to do more than anybody would be able to, given the complexity of the situation. This becomes an added suffering. (Service provider)

In this section, we highlight some promising directions in societal-level interventions that need more attention in future research and action.

Proactive Universal Applications

Two types of proactive universal programs have focused on the societal level of analysis, both of which use the media. The first includes media programs to educate new parents about child development and child physical abuse and neglect, while the second focuses on educating the public about child sexual abuse. In their emphasis on changing attitudes, both aim to change societal norms that relate to child maltreatment.

Educational Programs for New Parents. Marie-Claire Laurendeau and her colleagues have reported on a mass media public education program for new parents in Quebec (Laurendeau, Gagnon, Desjardins, Perreault, & Kischuk, 1991). *Parents Magazine* is distributed to new parents monthly during the child's first year and then bi-monthly for the next two years. The magazine is presented in a reader-friendly format with articles covering three general areas: (1) the baby's world, (2) the parent's world, and (3) family support resources.

In an evaluation of this program after thirteen months, Laurendeau et al. found that while most parents read the magazine and reported liking it, the only clear impact of the intervention was a significant improvement in intervention parents' knowledge of and attitudes toward community resources compared with no change for comparison group parents. Kischuk, Laurendeau, Desjardins, and Perreault (1995) followed up the sample at the end of the intervention (i.e., when the children were 3 years of age) and found that mothers who received the magazine were significantly more familiar with and appreciative of community resources than mothers in the control group, but there were no significant differences between the groups on measures of knowledge of child development and critical incidents in parenting.

Other large-scale, public health interventions have focused on the dangers of shaking babies (Showers, 1992). For example, the goal of the Don't Shake the Baby Program was to educate parents about the dangers of shaking and about how to handle babies when they cry, especially colicky babies, who are at high risk of abuse.

David Riley and colleagues have developed newsletters for parents on how to promote infant development, which are distributed free of charge on a monthly basis during the child's first year of life (Riley, Meinhardt, Nelson, Salisbury, & Winnett, 1991; Riley, Salisbury, Walker, & Steinberg, 1996). One rationale for the newsletter is that it reaches socially isolated parents, who are unlikely to attend a parent training group and who are at risk of maltreating their children.

A study that compared parents who had received newsletters with parents who had not received the newsletters reported three key findings

(Riley et al., 1996). First, parents who received the newsletters scored significantly lower on a measure of child abuse potential than parents in the control group, a statistically significant difference. Second, parents who received the newsletter reported spanking or slapping their children half as much in the week prior to receiving the questionnaire than parents in the control group. Extrapolating to the 40,000 parents in Wisconsin who received the newsletter, the researchers estimated that the newsletter prevented more than one million instances of babies being struck by their parents. Third, socially isolated parents who received the newsletter were significantly more likely to offer a stimulating home environment than socially isolated parents who did not receive the newsletter.

Educational Programs Regarding Child Sexual Abuse. Daro (1994) argues that educational interventions are needed to change public perceptions and awareness of child sexual abuse and to strengthen families' capacities to foster healthy sexual development in children. Education needs to be provided to parents 'to create a context in which secrets or manipulation by another adult becomes more difficult' (Daro, 1994, p. 217). Studies that have examined the impact of child sexual abuse education programs have found that such programs can increase the knowledge of parents and teachers (Hébert, Piché, Fecteau, & Poitras, 1996; Kleemeier, Webb, Hazzard, & Pohl, 1988; Kolko et al., 1989; Kolko et al., 1987).

Child sexual abuse, which we saw in Chapter 2 is more prevalent for girls than for boys, is part of a larger societal issue of sexual exploitation of females and gender inequality (Swift & Ryan-Finn, 1995). Men have more power and privilege in society and exploitation of women is widespread (Albee & Perry, 1997).

One strategy that could be used to address sexual exploitation of females could involve programs to educate parents about the damaging impact of violence, pornography, and objectification of women and girls on children and to encourage them to not expose their children to such material. Such a program could also be used with both parents and children to help them develop media literacy about violence, pornography, and objectification. The more parents and children can become critical viewers of such material, the more likely they are to reject media violence and the degradation of women. Installing lock boxes on television sets, labelling media products for their violent and sexual content, and parents' political protests against such media materials are all ways of creating a climate that is conducive to the prevention of child sexual abuse. The importance of families and professionals becoming involved in social action to change societal norms is well captured in the following statement by Newman and Lutzker (1990):

> Our society has values and a culture that supports such axioms as 'spare the rod and spoil the child'; we even admire such lone killers as Rambo, and we laugh at such lines as Noel Coward's quip, 'women should be beaten regularly, like a gong.' In this atmosphere, which is hostile to nurturance, it is necessary for the health care professional to become an activist, to publicly boycott films, music, and books that promote violence to women and children, and to protest policies that keep a major segment of our population in despair. (pp. 243–4)

Since more than half of adult sex offenders begin their sex crimes in adolescence or earlier, Swift and Ryan-Finn (1995) argue that intervention is needed in early childhood. School-based programs that focus on changing sex-role stereotypes (e.g., Guttentag, 1977) or on the development of egalitarian relationships between boys and girls, the promotion of social skills, and the prevention of violence (Bélanger, Bowen, & Rondeau, 1997; Laurendeau, Bélanger, & Bowen, 1996; Laurendeau, Gagnon, Lapointe, & Beauregard, 1989) are strategies that can be used to promote gender equality and reduce violence and exploitation.

Proactive High-Risk Applications
A few proactive high-risk programs have focused on societal wellness by directly addressing the employment and income needs of low-income families. Field, Widmayer, Stringer, and Ignatoff (1980) randomly assigned low-income, black teen-age mothers with newborn babies to one of three conditions. The first was a home visitation program, which consisted of bi-weekly home visits by a graduate student in psychology and a black teen-age parent aide. The visits lasted for six months and focused on exercises for the mothers to do with their babies. The second was an infant nursery intervention in which the mothers were hired and trained in the same infant stimulation exercises as were provided in the home visitation. Mothers did these exercises with their own baby and with other babies in the infant nursery. These two groups were compared with a third control group. At at 4, 8, 12, and 24 months, mothers in both intervention groups interacted significantly more positively with their children; the children had significantly higher motor and mental scores and weighed more; and the mothers had returned to work or school more often and were less likely to become pregnant again. Over-

all, the greatest gains were obtained for mothers and children who participated in the infant nursery intervention.

In the Birmingham Parent–Child Development Center (Andrews et al., 1982), low-income black mothers of newborns moved from being participants in the first year to understudies to staff in the second year to staff in the third year. When the children reached four years of age, statistically significant positive impacts were found for the children (social behaviour and cognitive development), the mothers (life satisfaction), and the parent–child relationship (positive parenting behaviour) for those in the intervention group compared with those in the control group.

In Montreal, the public health department and a local community service centre initiated Au Futur, a community development project for young, black, low-income mothers (Maison d'Haïti, Association Jamaïquaine de Montréal, Direction de la santé publique de la Régie de Montréal-Centre, 1997). Project workers, who are from the black community themselves, help the women to set personal goals. A major focus is on helping women to further their education and/or obtain employment.

Reactive Indicated Applications
Swift and Ryan-Finn (1995) note that 'the legal system both reflects and shapes societal beliefs, and is a powerful tool in implementing social change' (p. 28). Legislation that makes prosecution of alleged perpetrators less intimidating for victims, the inclusion of sexual harassment and marital rape as sex offences, stiffer sentences for sex offences, and court-mandated treatment for offenders are some ways in which the legal system can change societal values related to child sexual abuse.

Pornography involving the degradation of women and children can also be addressed through legislation. In this regard, the Canadian Supreme Court ruled unanimously in 1992 that obscenity should be defined by its harmful effects on women (Hill & Silver, 1993).

Summary and Critique
Findings regarding media, employment, and legislative programs are summarized in Table 5.7. Large-scale public health approaches to parent education appear to be promising for the promotion of family wellness. For example, Daro and Gelles (1992) found that since 1988, the percentage of parents reporting that they spank, yell at, or swear at their children has declined from 64 per cent to 49 per cent.

Similarly, interventions to educate the public about child sexual abuse could help to change societal norms regarding gender inequality and the

TABLE 5.7
Summary of Findings of Media, Employment, and Legislative Programs

	Findings
Proactive Universal	• There is some evidence that the use of physical punishment as a method of discipline (i.e., spanking) is declining in society, and that public education campaigns are contributing to this decline. • More efforts are needed to educate the public about child sexual abuse and sexism.
High-risk	• There is some controlled research demonstrating that employment programs for parents at risk of maltreating their children can promote family and child wellness. • The impacts of such programs on child maltreatment have yet to be examined.
Reactive Indicated	• Legislative interventions are needed to overcome sexism and respond more humanely to victims of child sexual abuse in the legal system.

sexual exploitation of women (Daro, 1994; Swift & Ryan-Finn, 1995; Tutty, 1991). Unfortunately, at present, few of these ideas about educational intervention have been translated into practical program models.

While economic interventions to reduce child poverty can be implemented through universal income redistribution programs, as was shown in Chapter 4, community-based employment programs for low-income families can also be implemented. Research by Andrews et al. (1982) and Field et al. (1982) has shown the benefits of employing low-income women in child care roles. Finally, legislative interventions may reduce the negative impacts of sexual victimization of women and girls.

CONCLUSIONS

What Can We Conclude about the Success of Programs in Promoting Family Wellness and Preventing Child Maltreatment?

One conclusion from the literature review is that we are in different stages in our knowledge about the prevention of physical abuse and neglect of children and the prevention of child sexual abuse. Prevention program development and research regarding physical abuse and neglect are at a much more advanced stage than they are for child sexual abuse prevention. At present, child sexual abuse prevention is primarily focused on educating children about how to recognize and resist sexual abuse. More broad-based, ecological approaches targeting multiple levels of analysis and aimed at both potential perpetrators and potential victims of child sexual abuse are needed. Further research on such approaches is needed, because we do not yet know what approaches are effective in preventing child sexual abuse.

On the other hand, a wide range of approaches to preventing child physical abuse and neglect and promoting family wellness have been implemented and studied. It is clear that parent education and training, family support, self-help/mutual aid and social support groups, and a variety of multi-component, community-based programs can promote family wellness both for families in general (universal approach) and for at-risk families (high-risk approach). Moreover, some impressive longitudinal studies demonstrate the enduring impacts of such programs on family wellness (e.g., Johnson & Walker, 1987; Lally et al., 1988). However, at present, the only programs that have been shown to prevent the physical abuse and neglect of children are home visitation programs (e.g., Olds et al., 1986).

Once maltreatment has occurred, studies of intensive family preservation services have shown that out-of-home placement can be prevented (Dagenais & Bouchard, 1996). However, there is less evidence that the crisis intervention approach of intensive family preservation prevents placement over the long term, improves family wellness, or reduces rates of further maltreatment. On the other hand, more promising findings on a range of indicators of family wellness and further maltreatment have been found in studies of multi-component and long-term programs using either a self-help/mutual aid format (Cameron et al., 1992) or professional services (Halper & Jones, 1981; Jones, 1985; Jones et al., 1976; Lutzker & Rice, 1984, 1987).

Common Elements of Programs That Are Successful in Promoting Family Wellness and Preventing Child Maltreatment

In this section, we outline what we believe are the common elements of successful programs that we have reviewed. We use our own analyses of effective prevention programs that we have reviewed, the observations and analyses of previous reviews (Blanchet, Laurendeau, Paul, & Saucier, 1993; Chamberland et al., 1996; Price, Cowen, Lorion, & Ramos-

McKay, 1989; Schorr, 1997; Weissberg & Elias, 1993; Yoshikawa, 1994), and the experience and wisdom of our stakeholder key informants as the database for this section of the chapter.

Effective Prevention Programs Address Several Ecological Levels of Wellness

Effective prevention programs view child maltreatment within multiple ecological contexts. Programs that are successful in preventing child maltreatment also change a number of related domains in the family, including the life course of parents, particularly mothers, the parent–child relationship, and a variety of child outcomes. Price et al. (1989) found that effective prevention programs are based on an understanding of the risks and problems faced by the target population. Similarly, Yoshikawa (1994) found that the programs that are most effective in preventing juvenile delinquency are those that have an ecological design. Similarly, from our review, we believe that multi-component programs hold the most promise for the promotion of family wellness and the prevention of child maltreatment.

To date, sexual abuse prevention programs have not utilized an ecological framework. Since child sexual abuse is linked with physical abuse and neglect, it may be the case that more holistic interventions, such as multi-component programs, may also have an impact on rates of child sexual abuse. Child sexual abuse researchers have suggested that anything that strengthens the family and the child decreases the likelihood that sexual abuse will occur (Tutty, 1991).

Effective Prevention Programs Work with Families in Natural Settings and Strive to Strengthen the Family's Informal Support System

Effective prevention programs do not utilize the professional-clinical model in which parents and their children visit therapists in office settings. Rather, helpers provide support in natural settings, including the family home, family resource centres, preschools, schools, churches, and neighbourhood organizations. In essence, helpers take the services to families rather than wait for families to seek help (Blanchet et al., 1993; Widom, 1998):

> *Educators should visit homes more often so that people could [get] to know them well.* (Youth)

Providing help in the family's natural settings also facilitates the involvement of the family's social network (Blanchet et al., 1993). Similarly, Price et al. (1989) have argued that successful programs 'strengthen the natural support from family, community, or school settings' (p. 51). We have found that home visitation, self-help/mutual aid and social support groups, and multi-component programs have all been found to be successful in building informal social support.

Effective Prevention Programs Begin at Birth or Prenatally

The programs that have been shown to have the clearest impact on the reduction of rates of child maltreatment are home visitation programs that begin at birth or even earlier in the prenatal period. Also, multi-component programs that work with families of newborn children have been shown to promote family and child wellness.

Getting the parent–child relationship off to a good start can help to prevent chain reactions of negative events, which may occur when the parents are not adequately prepared for childrearing, and to promote parents' access to opportunities for personal development. Similarly, Blanchet et al. (1993) suggest that prevention programs be offered during key transition periods. The transition to parenthood is one such key transition for families that provides an entry point for prevention.

When a cycle of child maltreatment has begun, the best that reactive interventions can do is to prevent further abuse or out-of-home placement. One of our key informants noted how families get support only when they are in crisis and often after maltreatment has occurred:

> *There is no continuity or link within systems; we act very late and when situations have seriously deteriorated.* (Adviser)

Effective Prevention Programs Are Long-Term and Intensive

Short-term, nonintensive programs are unlikely to have a substantial impact on family wellness or child maltreatment for poor, high-risk families. It is clear from the home visitation literature that programs that last for six months or less and that provide a relatively small number of home visits do not have an impact on child maltreatment. In and of themselves, short-term educational programs, such as parent training, may be successful in imparting information and teaching skills, but their effects are likely limited to these domains. Yoshikawa (1994) found that programs that are effective in preventing juvenile delinquency last at least two years. Similarly, Blanchet et al. (1993) argue that prevention programs that are most effective are those that have a long duration and provide frequent opportunities for participation.

The nature of the intervention should change over time to meet the developmental needs of the family. For example, the Houston Parent–Child Development Center began with home visiting and a focus on the infant and then shifted to centre-based activities for parents and children as the children entered their second year of life (Johnson & Breckenridge, 1982).

Effective Prevention Programs Are Flexible, Responsive, and Owned by the Local Community

The value of partnership suggests that policymakers, service providers, parents, and community members should collaboratively develop community-based prevention programs. In the past, many programs designed to prevent the maltreatment of children have been developed and controlled by professionals (e.g., parent training programs, home visitation programs). In a community development approach, parents work side by side with professionals to decide what programs should be developed and implemented at the local level. Family resource centres and full-service schools call for substantial community participation. Programs should not be adopted as is; rather, they should be adapted to local conditions.

The very process of involving residents in the community development process can benefit the parents, their children, and the community, as Pancer and Cameron (1994) have shown in the Better Beginnings, Better Futures program. Often a strong sense of community ownership over local organizations and programs results from such an approach. There is a tension between being community-driven and using an evidence-based program model. In a successful partnership between the community and professionals, we believe that professionals should provide information on the research base for different programs, and residents would then be informed about what works and what does not. Also, in innovative approaches to prevention, professionals often do not know what works, so residents may have good ideas that turn out to be effective.

Effective Prevention Programs Are Built upon Respectful, Trusting, and Empowering Relationships between Staff and Community Members

While there is not much research on the relationships between program staff and service users, some authors (e.g., Schorr, 1997) describe this relationship as critical to the successful implementation of programs designed to promote family wellness and prevent child maltreatment. For example, the home visitation literature often mentions the importance of respectful and trusting relationships between staff and service users. Support, respect, trustworthiness, a nonjudgmental attitude, recognition and emphasis on the strengths of the people served, and commitment to egalitarian relationships are some of the qualities of professionals that are valued by community members (e.g., Blanchet et al., 1993; Chamberland et al., 1996).

Two parents from our research commented on the importance of such relationships:

> *I like the Children's Aid, especially the representative that comes to the resource centres. She doesn't put judgment over you. She doesn't make you feel like she's there butting into your life. And I can honestly feel comfortable with her ... and she made me feel good that I made the right decisions. And I was to the point of losing it and she was there and she kind of talked me down. She is really good. She has got to be the most positive woman I have ever met in my life. She's great.* (Parent)

> *We had a facilitator from CAS but she didn't tell us what to do. She didn't say this is the way it should be and this helps. She just pointed us in the right direction. We solved our problems ourselves and made decisions on how we could make things change.* (Parent)

Effective Programs Have a Sufficient Complement of Well-Trained and Competent Staff

Successful prevention programs are staffed by competent staff who are well-trained, monitored, and supervised (Blanchet et al., 1993; Chamberland et al., 1996; Schorr, 1997). Similarly, the managers of such programs are well-trained leaders who possess a variety of skills and a willingness to take risks and experiment (Chamberland et al., 1996; Schorr, 1997). Also, effective programs are characterized by a positive work climate and team spirit among the staff (Chamberland et al.,

1996). However, it is not just the training, skills, and esprit de corps of staff that is necessary for programs to be effective. There must also be organizational support for prevention, sufficient staff resources to address the issues facing families, and sufficient resources to supervise and train staff (Blanchet et al., 1993; Cameron & Vanderwoerd, 1997a; Chamberland et al., 1996; Schorr, 1997). These points were underscored by one of our key informants:

> *The staff need to be trained and the programs need to be high-quality. You can't run a good prevention program on a shoestring.* (Adviser)

Effective Programs Are Based on Research and Evaluation

Effective programs are committed to research to determine their effectiveness (Blanchet et al., 1993; Price et al., 1989; Schorr, 1997). Several of the most exemplary programs that we have reviewed have a research component built into the project (e.g., Lally et al., 1988; Olds et al., 1986). Programs that are oriented toward research and evaluation are likely to have clear and measurable outcome objectives and a theory of how the program components will have an impact on those objectives.

However, research on multi-component, community-based programs cannot be easily squeezed into the traditional paradigm of social science research. As Connell et al. (1995) have suggested, new research paradigms that utilize quasi-experimental designs and ethnographic components are needed to capture both the complex effects and the lived experiences of people who participate in such programs. Both the Better Beginnings, Better Futures project (Peters, 1994) and 1,2,3 GO! (Bouchard, 1997b) are utilizing participatory research methods, including both qualitative and quantitative data. The use of participatory methods is also consistent with the previously mentioned theme of effective programs being flexible, responsive, and owned by the local community. As one of our key informants stated:

> *Basically programs that support families at risk should be, as much as possible, evidence-based. In other words, they should be based on what we know from the literature, and a really important principle of that is that they are set up in a way that, as much as possible, duplicates the way the original program was set up. This is tied into a commitment to provide the most comprehensive service that matches whatever the original research showed. I have major concerns that people will take a project*

that worked in one place and provide it in a leaner fashion. And there are times when you need to do that, but then you need to be up front about it and you need to evaluate it. (Adviser)

Final Thoughts

We expect a great deal of programs that are designed to promote family wellness and to prevent child maltreatment. But even the best programs cannot undo the damage to families that is created by an unsupportive societal context. Within our current context, prevention programs cannot help parents to find jobs when there are few well-paying jobs to be found; they cannot help parents to further their education when English- and/or French-as-a-second-language and adult education classes are cut and university tuition and fees deregulated; they cannot help parents to access affordable housing when rent controls are lifted and no new social housing is created; they cannot help parents to obtain child care so that they can work or further their education when the costs of child care outstrip family's limited financial resources; they cannot help low-income families with financial stress when support payments are cut by government.

To be most effective in promoting family wellness and preventing child maltreatment, prevention programs need to be accompanied by social policies that address societal wellness, as was outlined in Chapter 4. We conclude our discussion of prevention programs in the macrosocial, political context with the following quote from Bouchard (1994):

> Canadian families and children suffering the consequences of poverty are growing in number. In this context, the sole use of preventive psycho-social programs to counter the consequences of poverty without an equally important global strategy to reduce economic inequality or poverty itself seems incomplete, inefficient, and even cynical. There is a danger in building a sort of prevention industry exploiting the very ones which suffer from poor living conditions. (p. 44)

CHAPTER SIX

Programming for Distressed and Disadvantaged Adolescents

Gary Cameron, Jan O'Reilly, Marie-Claire Laurendeau, and Claire Chamberland

INTRODUCTION

On your 18th birthday, they are gone.
They give you a bus ticket to the welfare office.
That's what they did to me.
You've got to do it on your own.
You can't go back to your family. (Youth)

Adolescents entering the child welfare system face unique disadvantages. Based on their review of the experiences of adolescents in the child welfare system in Ontario, Ballantyne and Raymond (1998) conclude that a 'consistent message throughout the literature and from the key informants was that whenever possible adolescents should be maintained in the family home ... more so than any other population' (p. 43). Adolescents who come into the care of the child welfare system are at high risk because of both the losses they have suffered to that point in their lives and the high probability of their experiencing one or more placement breakdowns. Indeed, there is a pattern of placing adolescents into more and more restricted settings in an attempt to control their increasing behavioural and emotional difficulties (Snow & Finlay, 1998). The National Research Council (1993) in the United States concluded that foster care has become a high-risk setting for most adolescents. Martin and Palmer (1997) present evidence that the death rate for adolescents in care is 72 per cent higher than for teens in the general population. These portraits dramatize the importance of reducing the number of adolescents entering the formal child welfare system, and into substitute care in particular.

Adolescents are at least as likely as younger children to be maltreated in their homes. A 1981 National Incidence Survey in the United States showed that 42 per cent of substantiated cases of maltreatment involved teens as victims, a rate higher than the 38 per cent of the general population who were under 18 (Garbarino, 1992; Olsen & Holmes, 1986; Youngblade & Belsky, 1990). Adolescents are victims of about one-third of all child batteries and probably an even greater percentage of sexual molestations (Barth, 1983). Between 1969 and 1996, the proportion of adolescents in care in Ontario increased from 30 to 50 per cent of the total in-care population (Ballantyne & Raymond, 1998). American statistics show a 25 per cent increase in the adolescent residential care population between 1965 and 1985 (Ballantyne & Raymond, 1998).

Despite the prevalence of maltreatment of and by adolescents, there is a consensus in the literature that adolescents are much less likely to be referred to child protection authorities than their younger counterparts, and are less likely to receive appropriate assistance if they are referred (Barth & Derezotes, 1990; Council on Scientific Affairs, 1993; National Research Council, 1993; Powers, Jaklitsch, & Eckenrode, 1989; Wolfe, 1994). In the 1981 National Incidence Study in the United States, only 24 per cent of maltreated adolescents were reported to protection services, the lowest proportion for any age group (Doueck, Hideki-Ishisaka, Love-Sweany & Gilchrist, 1987). Snow and Finlay (1998), in their qualitative investigation of the experiences of children in residential care in Ontario, raised equally strong concerns:

> The lack of support for older adolescents (age 16+) in transition from the children's service system to the adult service system presents the greatest gap in service ... Transitional age youth need the ability to access the child welfare system. Otherwise, these youth are at risk of chronic homelessness or delinquency and often end up living on the streets, in shelters or in young offender centres. (p. 40)

Adolescents at risk of maltreatment often are perceived less generously than are younger children. They are seen as more able to care for themselves when, in fact, their needs for family affiliation and protection are still great (Doueck et al., 1987). Teens are perceived as more powerful, more threatening, and even as the architects of their own misfortunes (Council on Scientific Affairs, 1993; Garbarino, 1992b; National Research Council, 1993). In addition, teens at risk in their homes, because of their acting-out behaviours and their difficulties in multiple areas of community living, frequently come to the attention of jurisdictions other than child welfare, such as corrections, school authorities, physical and mental health services, shelters, and addiction services, with their maltreatment issues often remaining hidden or secondary (National Research Council, 1993; Powers et al., 1989).

The challenges adolescents at risk of maltreatment present for programming differ substantially from those for younger children. In their review of 547 child protection cases in Ontario, Cameron and Rothery (1985) found that the concerns for families with younger children centred on the lack of parenting competence, parental delinquency, and a lack of adequate financial resources. For families with adolescents, the more common concerns were parents requesting the removal of the teen, high levels of parent–adolescent conflict, and adolescents putting themselves and others at risk through their own behaviours. The phenomenon of adolescents at risk in their own homes having difficulties in many other areas of their lives has been recognized by several other authors (Ballantyne & Raymond, 1998; Barth & Derezotes, 1990; Doueck et al., 1987; Feindler & Becker, 1994; Kagan, Reid, Roberts, & Silverman-Pollow, 1987; Werner, 1990). A reciprocal relationship exists between struggles in the home and these other problems in that each has the potential to exacerbate the other.

Age-appropriate development patterns for adolescents such as self-assertion and independence, increased interactions with peers, and greater cognitive and verbal abilities often place increased pressures on the parent–teen relationship (Feindler & Becker, 1994). The presence of power struggles between parents and teens, and parents' attempts to control the adolescents' behaviours, have been compared to the dynamics of spousal abuse (Doueck et al., 1987; Garbarino, 1992b). Mutual assault between parents and adolescents and the perception that the youth deserve their fate are part of the adolescent maltreatment profile (Doueck et al., 1987).

Another unique consideration is that a majority of the reported victims of adolescent abuse of all kinds are female and most of the perpetrators are male, the opposite of the pattern for physical abuse of younger children (Doueck et al., 1987; Feindler & Becker, 1994; Garbarino, 1992b). On the other hand, males are less likely to be reported as victims of adolescent abuse of all forms and less likely to have their cases substantiated (Barth & Derezotes, 1990). However, there is a lack of detail about how the types and prevalence of maltreatment differ for male and female adolescent populations.

When designing programs for adolescents at risk of requiring child welfare services, one needs to take into account three general characteristics of this population: (1) adolescents experience conflict and dangers of maltreatment in their own homes; (2) teens pose a risk to themselves because of self-defeating behaviours – they are likely to be experiencing difficulties in important aspects of community living, with important consequences for their own well-being and integration into their families; and (3) some will be a danger to other adults and children around them because of their aggression and other dysfunctional behaviours. For example, many acquaintance assaults, about 20 per cent of forcible rapes, and about half of sexual molestations of young children are perpetrated by adolescents (Barth & Derezotes, 1990; Wolfe, Wekerle, Reitzel, & Gough, 1995).

A strong consensus in the literature is that responding to the issue of adolescent maltreatment cannot focus exclusively on the experiences of youth in their homes. Youth maltreatment, as a precipitating factor, a co-occurring phenomenon, or both, is associated with many other difficulties in adolescents' lives (Ballantyne & Raymond, 1998; Barth, 1983; Cameron & Vanderwoerd, 1997a; Cicchetti, Toth, & Hennessy, 1993; Council on Scientific Affairs, 1993; Emery & Laumann-Billings, 1998; Feindler & Becker, 1994; Kagan et al., 1987; National Research Council, 1993; Powers & Eckenrode, 1988; Rickel & Allen, 1987; Schorr, 1997; Snow & Finlay, 1998; Spaid & Fraser, 1991). For example, Garbarino (1992b) concludes that

> abuse and neglect are embedded in a wide range of adolescent problems – delinquency, parricide, running away, and prostitution to name but four that are mentioned frequently in research and clinical reports, with the degree of coincidence being in excess of 65 per cent in some samples. (p. 94)

In Snow and Finlay's (1998) study of youth in Ontario's residential and secure care facilities, many youths describe having had multiple child welfare placements prior to their entry into the young offender system; in fact, 57.2 per cent of the youth self-reported five or more placements. In a review of follow-up studies, Lewis, Mallough, and Webb (1989) estimated that about 20 per cent of abused children go on to become delinquent, compared with a base line of about 5 per cent in the general population. Many other authors have commented on the relatively high prevalence of maltreatment among delinquent youths (Briggs, Miller, Sayles, Tovar, & Davenport Dozier, 1997; Feindler &

Becker, 1994; National Research Council, 1993; Watts & Ellis, 1993; Werner, 1990; Wolfe et al., 1995).

The association between maltreatment and a higher risk of youths living on the streets is well known (Farber, McCoard, Kinast, & Baum-Falkner, 1984; Fischer and Birdie, 1978; National Research Council, 1993; Martin & Palmer, 1997; Powers et al., 1989). Alleva (1998) found that 70 per cent of sheltered youth had child welfare experience. In their study of 489 Calgary street kids, Kufeldt and Nimmo (1987) note that 53 per cent of 'runners' and 30 per cent of the 'in and outers' said that they were on the streets primarily because of their experiences with child welfare agencies and, secondarily, because of their experiences with their biological parents.

In a stratified random sample of 602 youths from ten public health clinics, a history of physical abuse, sexual abuse, or rape was related to participation in more HIV risk behaviours and to the increase of these behaviours between adolescence and young adulthood (Cunningham, Stiffman, Dore, & Earls, 1994). On a more cautionary note, the National Research Council (1993) concludes that although victims of childhood abuse may be more vulnerable to sexual promiscuity and at increased risk of teenage pregnancy as well as substance abuse, the available research on the nature of these relationships is not conclusive.

Martin and Palmer (1997) present evidence that many studies of children and youths in care show that they experience serious school difficulties before, during, and after care. This is consistent with the findings of a study of 223 abused and neglected youths served by runaway and homeless youth programs in New York State during 1986–7. One of the most common problems for these teens was school difficulties in the form of truancy and poor academic performance, both of which were likely to lead to dropping out (Powers & Jaklitsch, 1989).

A second consensus in the literature is that many of the difficulties experienced by adolescents in high-risk circumstances occur at the same time. Several longitudinal studies have shown that parent–adolescent struggles and adolescent behaviour difficulties will cluster together for many teens and often will continue from adolescence through young adulthood (Jessor, Donovan, & Costa, 1991; Jessor & Jessor, 1977; Werner, 1990). In addition, many of these difficulties will be strongly and negatively affected by economic, social, and community deterioration, especially in its more extreme manifestations (Coley & Chase-Larsdale, 1998; Garbarino, 1992b; Schorr, 1997). Werner (1990) describes this phenomenon as a stacking of problems from childhood through adolescence. Many other authors have noted the tendency for these types of behaviour problems to co-occur (Botvin & Tortu, 1988; Briggs et al., 1997; Bruene-Butler, Hampson, Elias, Clabby, & Schuyler, 1997; Danish, 1997; Hamberg, 1992; Hawkins, Catalano, & Miller, 1992; Karabanow, 1998; Powers & Jaklitsch, 1989; Powers et al., 1989; Watts & Ellis, 1993; Werner, 1990).

Organizing Principles for This Review

This chapter not only focuses on the experiences of the adolescent in the home; it also considers the support needs of parents as well as the challenges that adolescents face in their lives outside of the home. There is substantial mutual influence among these various areas of activity. In a similar vein, attention should be given to adolescent behaviours that pose a risk to teens themselves and to others.

In our opinion, a clear demarcation between prevention and remediation is not helpful when looking at programming for adolescents. For example, while our attention may be focused on a desire to prevent out-of-home placements for adolescents, in most instances, struggles in the home, difficulties in community living, and coping with the personal pain of past and current transgressions will be well established. Often, there is a progression from early childhood experiences to difficulties as an adolescent. This is not to suggest that purely preventive programs are not appropriate for adolescents (for example, see the discussion of competence and skill development programs later in this chapter). Nonetheless, as with many populations, prevention/promotion of future outcomes requires attention to well-established troubles.

Our review of the literature found relatively few programs created specifically for maltreated youths. As a result, there is a need to draw lessons from a broad range of programming for adolescents (Barth & Derezotes, 1990). Our review draws information from adolescent programming that focuses on substance abuse, teen pregnancy, delinquency, school failure, and runaways, as well as adolescent maltreatment. Because of the broad sweep of our search for useful ideas, we rely on others' reviews of the evidence for effective programming as well as assessments of specific programs.

As a foundation, we situate our deliberations within the context of the particular developmental challenges of adolescence as well as the major risk and protective factors relevant to designing programs for these

Programming for Adolescents 279

teens. This is supplemented by a consideration of the priority foci gleaned from previous general reviews of programming. Together, these form a lens through which to consider the nature and effectiveness of particular program models in the balance of the chapter. They also provide the framework used to group program models for our discussions: adolescent competence and skill development programs, family- and parent-focused programs, social integration programs, multiple component programs, and neighbourhood transformation programs.

DEVELOPMENTAL CONTEXT

The transitions of adolescence can be a struggle even for a youth growing up in a nurturing family. For those who have been maltreated, there is the added requirement of redressing the consequences of earlier losses with diminished access to supportive resources. Feelings of aloneness and anger, fears of abandonment, physiological reactions, acting out, and regressive behaviour are common among maltreated teens (Powers et al., 1989).

The following developmental tasks for youth are those most commonly identified in the literature reviewed (Ballantyne & Raymond, 1998; Barth, 1983; Coley & Chase-Larsdale, 1998; Dusenbury & Botvin, 1990; Fuchs, 1990; Gibson, 1993; Hamberg, 1992; Hopkins & Emler, 1990; Jaffe, Sudermann, & Reitzel, 1992; Kazdin, 1993; Martin & Palmer, 1997; Masten & Coatsworth, 1998; Pitman, Wolfe, & Wekerle, 1998; Powers et al., 1989; Straus,1994; Turner, Norman, & Zunz, 1995):

- Sexuality – moving from the onset of puberty to positive sexual intimacy;
- Family – completing a process of greater independence from parents and the renegotiation of attachments within the family;
- Cognitive – emergence and consolidation of more advanced reasoning abilities;
- Peers – expanding relations with peers, increasing social skills, and developing the capacity for emotional intimacy outside the family;
- Social integration – beginning and expanding their own prosocial connections with adults outside the family as well as in the worlds of education, work, and social institutions;
- Education – moving from primary education through high school and preparing for postsecondary education or the world of work;

- Employment – making initial decisions about future work and preparing for a career;
- Ethics – expanding and consolidating a prosocial system of values;
- Identities – developing healthy identities for the beginnings of young adulthood; and
- Legal – preparing for and assuming legal responsibilities for driving, voting, self-care, and other statuses as an adult.

RISK FACTORS

Understanding, and developing good programs for, adolescents at risk of entering the child protection system requires a clear articulation of the pressures pushing teens toward this outcome. Because of the co-occurrence of maltreatment and other difficulties for adolescents, and the substantial overlap of risk factors for many problems, the risk factors below are synthesized from a review of the literature for *maltreatment* (Ballantyne & Raymond, 1998; Barth & Derezotes, 1990; Cameron & Vanderwoerd, 1997a), *teen pregnancy* (Dryfoos, 1990; National Research Council, 1993; Stevens-Simm & Reichert, 1994), *juvenile delinquency* (Dryfoos, 1990; Gendreau, 1996; National Research Council, 1993; Palmer & Liddle, 1996; Werner, 1990), and *school failure* (Carnahan, 1994; Dryfoos, 1990; Hymel, Comfort, Schonert-Reichel, & McDougall, 1996; Srebank & Elias, 1993). Several discussions of commonalities in risk factors across problem areas were also reviewed for our summary (Dryfoos, 1990; National Research Council, 1993; Werner, 1990; Yoshikawa, 1994).

Childhood and Adolescent Problem Behaviours

'The greater the variety, frequency and seriousness of childhood antisocial behavior, the more likely [these difficulties are] to persist into adulthood' (Fergusson & Lynskey, 1996, p. 81). Many authors have identified early and persistent acting-out behaviours by the child as a concern both for adolescent difficulties in the home and in many parts of youths' lives (Blythe, Hodges, & Guterman, 1990; Briggs et al., 1997; Fuchs, 1990; Hawkins, Catalano, & Miller, 1992; Wolfe, 1994). Dryfoos (1994) believes that a 'strong case can be made for targeting for immediate and powerful interventions those youngsters "who do it all" or at least do most of it. Almost one in three adolescents fall into this category' (p. 37). Early sexual activity, substance abuse, and/or academic failure as well as a low commitment to school have all been singled out as important early warning signs (Ballantyne & Raymond, 1998; Barth, 1983; Briggs et al., 1997; Coley & Chase-Larsdale, 1998; Fuchs, 1990; Hawkins, Catalano, & Miller, 1992; Kazdin, 1993; Rae Grant, 1994; Rickel & Allen, 1987; Sandberg, 1989; Snow & Finlay, 1998; Wolfe, 1994).

Difficulties with Peers

'Over two decades of research has established peer relations as the most reliable and sensitive predictor ... of problems during childhood and later life' (Bruene-Butler et al., 1997, p. 240). Poor social skills, problems with peers, and early rejection by peers have all been identified as reasons for concern (Blythe et al., 1990; Briggs et al., 1997; Fuchs, 1990; Garbarino, 1992; Hawkins, Catalano, & Miller, 1992; Rickel & Allen, 1987; Turner et al., 1995; Willis, Holden, & Rosenberg, 1992). Children showing early psychosocial development difficulties have been suggested as appropriate beneficiaries of prevention programming (Garbarino, 1992; Rickel & Allen, 1987; Wolfe, 1994).

Parents' Substance Abuse and History of Maltreatment

Parental substance abuse is a common correlate of maltreatment and many serious adolescent behaviour difficulties (Allison, Leone, & Rowse-Spero, 1990; Ballantyne & Raymond, 1998; Briggs et al., 1997; Doueck et al., 1987; Hawkins, Catalano, & Miller, 1992; Sandberg, 1989; Wolfe, 1994). In addition, the parents' history of being abused in their families of origin is an important consideration. Feindler and Becker (1994) suggest that the rate of intergenerational transmission of maltreatment is approximately 30 per cent, arguing that the treatment of abused adolescents is important to help break the cycle of abuse.

Family Problems

The quality of relationships within the home is a major consideration in assessing the risk of adolescent maltreatment and various adolescent behaviour problems (Allison et al., 1990; Ballantyne & Raymond, 1998; Barth & Derezotes, 1990; Briggs et al., 1997; Cloutier, Champoux, Jacques, & Chamberland, 1994; Coley & Chase-Larsdale, 1998; Dishion, 1990; Doueck et al., 1987; Garbarino, 1992; Hawkins, Catalano, & Miller, 1992; Hirschi, 1995; McLoyd, 1998; Werner, 1990; Wolfe, 1994). In particular, on-going conflict between parents and teenagers, as well as interparental conflict and/or violence, are very common in maltreating families. Harsh, rigid, or inconsistent parenting, and low attachment between parents and teens, increase the risk of maltreatment and adolescent behaviour problems. Inadequate parental supervision and monitoring also place teens at risk. Deviant family norms increase the likelihood of antisocial adolescent behaviours.

Step-Parents

Step-parents and parents' lovers are overrepresented in all kinds of adolescent abuse, particularly of teenage girls, suggesting that step-parent families deserve a specific focus for maltreatment prevention programming (Ballantyne & Raymond, 1998; Barth & Derezotes, 1990; Garbarino, 1992; National Research Council, 1993; Wolfe, 1994).

Lack of Social Integration

Well-documented indicators of higher potential for a variety of adolescent problems include involvement with a delinquent peer network and a lack of positive connections to schools or to employment. The absence of positive involvements with prosocial adults outside of the home and early rejection by peers also place adolescents at risk (Ballantyne & Raymond, 1998; Briggs et al., 1997; Bruene-Butler et al., 1997; Fergusson & Lynskey, 1996; Hawkins, Catalano, & Miller, 1992; Hawkins & Fraser, 1983; Hopkins & Emler, 1990; Pelton, 1994; Rickel & Allen, 1987; Sandberg, 1989; Wolfe, 1994; Wolfe et al., 1995).

Neighbourhood Disintegration

The disintegration of positive social ties among neighbours and the collapse of community institutions increases the likelihood of breakdown for all families (Ballantyne & Raymond, 1998; Barth & Derezotes, 1990; Coley & Chase-Larsdale, 1998; Garbarino & Kostelny, 1992, 1994; Garbarino, Kostelny, & Dubrow, 1991; Hawkins, Catalano, & Miller, 1992; McLoyd, 1998; National Research Council, 1993; Sandberg, 1989).

Lack of Economic Resources

In contrast to the situation of younger children, there are deep disagreements in the literature about the importance of poverty in the etiology of adolescent maltreatment. Drawing mainly on the 1981 National

Incidence Study of maltreatment in the United States, some authors (Garbarino, 1992b; Olsen & Holmes, 1986) conclude that poverty is not a major risk factor in the maltreatment of adolescents. This incidence study found that families of maltreated adolescents had similar employment patterns to the general population and were much less likely to be on welfare and to be in the lowest income categories than maltreating families with younger children. Using the same data, Barth and Derezotes (1990) argue that while the data are less than conclusive, the evidence is that poor adolescents are more likely to be victims of abuse than their non-poor counterparts. Ballantyne and Raymond (1998) are more adamant in their position:

> Even though socio-economic status is not significantly related to difficult parent/adolescent relationships, it does co-relate with out-of-home placements. Studies indicate that adolescents who come into foster care or move into residential treatment are often from socio-economically disadvantaged families. In fact, one study indicates that the most relevant factor predicting which youth will come into foster care is family income ... [Also, family income impacts] on other factors that influence family breakdown ... [such as] maternal depression, paternal substance abuse and paternal anti-social behaviour. (pp. 81–82)

Our interpretation of the evidence is that poverty is an important risk consideration in the maltreatment of adolescents. There is a consensus in the literature that extreme conditions of family and neighbourhood poverty increase the likelihood of family breakdown. In addition, poverty is associated with higher frequencies of other important risk factors for adolescent maltreatment, as well as with various adolescent problems that can follow or co-occur with maltreatment. Finally, there may be important differences between the broader population of families where parent–adolescent conflict is a serious concern and those families with a relatively high probability of involvement with formal child protection and other restrictive services. The evidence is that poor teens are more likely to be placed in foster care as well as in residential and juvenile detention settings (Ballantyne & Raymond, 1998).

PATTERNS ACROSS PROGRAM MODELS

A variety of program models have shown promise for working with adolescents from conflicted homes. Some of these approaches endeavour to bridge multiple areas of living; others focus on particular issues. Some rely on one central approach to helping; others combine strategies. In this section, we examine the literature on adolescent programming principles that cut across specific program models.

Our purpose is to provide a framework or a perspective to orient the discussion of the nature and effectiveness of the specific program models discussed later in the chapter. As mentioned earlier, this framework is built on both our prior discussions of population characteristics, as well as general lessons identified in reviews of programming for maltreated youth and for teens at risk of pregnancy, school failure, delinquency, substance abuse, and running away/homelessness (Astroth, 1993; Ballantyne & Raymond, 1998; Barth, 1983; Barth & Derezotes, 1990; Bogenschneider, 1996; Cicchetti et al., 1993; Council on Scientific Affairs, 1993; Dryfoos, 1990, 1993, 1994, 1997; Durlak, 1995; Dusenbury & Falco, 1997; Eccles et al., 1993; Elias, Gager, & Leon, 1997; Emery & Laumann-Billings, 1998; Feindler & Becker, 1994; Gendreau, 1996; Gottfredson, Fink, Skroban, & Gottfredson, 1997; Kagan et al. 1987; Kazdin, 1993; Lerner, 1995; Miller & Paikoff, 1992; National Research Council, 1993; Ostrom, Lerner, Richard, & Freel, 1995; Palmer, 1996; Peterson, 1995; Powers et al., 1989; Pransky, 1991; Rae Grant, 1994; Rickel & Allen, 1987; Rothery & Cameron, 1985; Sagrestano & Paikoff, 1997; Scales, 1990; Schorr, 1989, 1997; Snow & Finlay, 1998; Spaid & Fraser, 1991; Srebank & Elias, 1993; Straus, 1994; Takanishi, 1993; Turner et al., 1995; Weissberg, Barton, & Schriver, 1997; Werner, 1990). There is a fair amount of agreement on the lessons to be drawn from programming for these various populations. The patterns identified here should be understood as having been associated with positive outcomes in a variety of adolescent programming initiatives rather than as characteristics that must be present in every program model.

Priority Foci

Populations

There is no clear agreement in the literature about the groups that should receive priority attention for programming. Some argue that while there is a need for universal as well as focused programs, given the realities of limited resources, most of our efforts should go into helping those at greatest risk (Barry, 1994; Barth & Derezotes, 1990; Werner, 1990). Dryfoos (1994) suggests focusing on 'youth who do it all.' Garbarino (1992) recommends that adolescents who demonstrate developmental problems be a principal group for prevention and protection efforts. He also argues that programming should not be exclusively for low-income populations and that early childhood programming alone will not be sufficient. Late elementary schools and junior high schools have been seen as priority settings for prevention programming (Garbarino, 1992a, 1992b; Pransky, 1991).

Social Competencies

Feelings of self-worth and personal competence as well as the possession of relevant social skills all foster resiliency in adolescents (Ballantyne & Raymond, 1998; Schorr, 1997). Programming to augment life skills and social competence has been used to good effect with teens in many settings.

Family

More so than with younger children, programming for youths needs to pay attention to internal family functioning. Parent-adolescent conflict is a common reason why youths enter out-of-home placements. While they are experimenting with their new-found power and increasing independence, teens have a continuing need for supportive family relations, at a time when these connections often experience their greatest strains. Indeed, a positive relationship with at least one parent is an important protective factor for endangered adolescents (Ballantyne & Raymond, 1998; Fergusson & Lynskey, 1996; Hawkins, Catalano, & Miller, 1992). Teens present new and daunting parenting challenges for many families. Mediating conflict, ameliorating family relations, improving parenting competencies, providing emotional and practical supports to parents, and creating opportunities for parent and/or adolescent relief from pressures in the home have all been identified as useful helping strategies for families of adolescents.

Social Connections

The disintegration of socially acceptable values and bonds is a common correlate of antisocial and self-destructive tendencies for adolescents. Positive connections with prosocial peers and with one or more adults outside of the home are important protective factors for teens. Along with commitment to school, academic achievement, participation in church and other civic engagements, they are critical resources in teens' struggles to forge new identities (Ballantyne & Raymond, 1998; Barth & Derezotes, 1990; Fergusson & Lynskey, 1996; Freeman, 1993; Hawkins, Catalano, & Miller, 1992; National Research Council, 1993; Putnam, 1993; Sandberg, 1989; Schorr, 1997; Srebank & Elias, 1993; Straus, 1994; Wolfe et al., 1995). Programming with the potential to foster these types of social involvements and to build positive personal and social values is an important resource in working with adolescents. Adolescents benefit from having safe places to go, experiencing a sense of belonging to a larger collectivity, and feeling that they have their own contributions to make in these engagements.

Economic Resources

Resources such as recreational services, family counselling, parent or teen relief, and academic supports are more available to those with adequate discretionary income. Many families of adolescents seeking out child welfare services will have limited access to these kinds of supports. Others will be struggling with poor housing, inadequate diets, and a limited availability of other vital tangible resources. While not mentioned frequently by other reviewers, our contention is that fostering access to the support services and to the basic necessities of daily living that are available to families with adequate incomes will be important programming considerations for a meaningful proportion of endangered adolescents and their families.

MAJOR PROGRAM STRATEGIES

This section reviews specific program approaches for disadvantaged adolescents and the evidence for their effectiveness. Building on our earlier examination of contextual factors and general programming patterns, this discussion of program models is grouped into five broad categories: adolescent competence and skill development programs, family- and parent-focused programs, social integration programs, multiple-component programs, and neighbourhood transformation programs. Programs focused on other teen groupings are also included in this discussion, when they are relevant to understanding and improving programming for adolescents at risk of maltreatment. For similar reasons, a few programs are discussed that involve younger children.

Adolescent Competence and Skill Development Programs

Competence and skills development programs are the most commonly used prevention strategy with adolescents. In our review, these were the only programs that were used extensively with general adolescent populations, rather than with identified high-risk groups. Weissberg, Caplan, and Harwood (1991) found that school-based, classroom training was the most common competence and skill development approach and that most of these programs have been brief (one year or less), single-method, single-level intervention strategies. The authors conclude that there is little evidence to suggest that these types of programs promote behavioural improvements that last for several years after the intervention. The presentation of information given in these programs is inadequate, by itself, to modify behaviours (Barth & Derezotes, 1990; Dusenbury & Botvin, 1990; Hawkins, Catalano, & Miller, 1992). In their review of adolescent maltreatment programs, Barth and Derezotes (1990) argue that the most effective programs include role-play practice of the skills both inside and outside of the classroom. The best programs pay attention to affective, cognitive, and social skills as well as to the family, school, and community contexts of the problems in living (Barth & Derezotes, 1990; Rickel & Allen, 1987).

Barth and Derezotes (1990) also suggest that the most powerful competence and skill development programs may be those that include a focus on changing the culture of the peer group. Srebank and Elias (1993) propose that cross-age peer tutoring may be a particularly powerful way to increase the engagement of low-achieving youth who are at risk of becoming uninterested in school and alienated from peers. While many programs use a combination of types of teachers, taking advantage of the influence of peers has been a major component of many competence and skill development program models. The National Research Council (1993) points out that 'the almost universal use of small groups, flexible grouping practices, symbols of membership (uniforms, t-shirts), and clear structures (regular meetings, codes of conduct) reflect on organizational and programmatic recognition of the importance of group membership' in working with adolescents (pp. 219–220).

Longer programs allow for more time to practise skills and for change in group culture to occur. Also, there is reason to believe that competence and skill development approaches will work best for multiply disadvantaged teens if combined with other approaches to helping

(Cameron & Vanderwoerd, 1997a; Wolfe, 1994). Weissberg and colleagues (1991) summarize their review of the characteristics of good competence and skill development programming for adolescents:

1) The most efficacious programs enhance students' cognitive, affective, and behavioral skills, promote prosocial attitudes, values and perceptions of norms, and provide accurate, socio-culturally relevant information about targeted social and health domains.
2) They employ teaching methods that ensure student engagements, foster applications of positive behavior in real-life situations, and transform the ways in which children and adolescents communicate about problem situations.
3) To address adequately the widespread social and health problems of children, multi-year, multi-level, multi-component interventions – in which peers, parents, the school, and community members reinforce classroom instruction – are realistically needed. (p. 273)

Straus (1994) concurs, stating that 'social skills training is most effective when it is used in conjunction with other approaches' (p. 174).

Durlak (1995) presents the results of a meta-analysis of 261 school-based programs for the prevention of behavioural and social problems. This study found that problem-solving programs significantly increased competencies but were the only type of intervention not effective in changing problems. He concludes that the link between the promotion of problem-solving skills and the prevention of problems has not been demonstrated. Yet, he points out that problem-solving training has been incorporated into several multi-component programs that have had positive results.

Durlak and Wells (1994) conducted a meta-analysis of 130 controlled outcome studies of person-centred prevention programs, 94 per cent of which were in schools. Behavioural and cognitive-behavioural interventions were equally effective in producing moderately strong effects, almost two times as high as nonbehavioural interventions. Programs that targeted the externalization of problems achieved the highest effects.

A meta-analysis by Durlak, Fuhrman, and Lampman (1991) on the effectiveness of cognitive-behavioural interventions in producing behaviour changes in adolescents showed the highest rates of positive change in youths aged 11 to 13 years of age. Hawkins, Catalano, and Miller (1992) present evidence of the effectiveness of problem-solving skills training for reducing drug use at three-year follow-up for boys who received the training at age 11; however, they suggest that more investigation of the relationship between age and the efficacy of problem-solving training is required before firm conclusions can be drawn.

The published research on competence and skill development programs for adolescents is too vast to be completely documented in this review. Instead, the programs presented below have been selected from a much larger pool to illustrate the nature and the potential of these types of interventions.

School-Based Skill Development Programs

Barth and Derezotes (1990) evaluated various approaches to child abuse prevention programs in California. Programs were selected that served tenth grade students, and six types of programs were included in the study: (1) a peer-tutoring approach, (2) a skill-based curriculum, (3) a nationally recognized program that emphasizes student self-defence, (4) a program based on a feminist, rape-prevention curriculum, (5) a program that was particularly interactive with the school system, and (6) an eclectic curriculum. The study covered a two-year period and was based on student self-reports at pre-test, post-test, and follow-up at three to five months. Also included were interviews with students, parents, and professionals plus a survey of key informants. Program group ($n = 251$) and control group ($n = 200$) participants were selected from participating high schools. In general, post-test results showed that program participants made statistically significant gains in knowledge, attitudes, and intentions. The peer-taught group did have significantly higher scores on the overall summary scale than the adult-taught and control groups. Students who received the training had higher scores at follow-up than at post-test. However, Barth and Derezotes (1990) caution:

> Although statistically significant gains were found, the effect sizes were small. Only 23% of students who took the class learned more than they would have had they not taken it, and only one of six students ... learned at least ten percent more than students who did not ... There was no evidence that students who took the classes disclosed abuse more often or actually used the skills they were taught to protect themselves. (pp. 121–122)

The Postponing Sexual Involvement Program (Howard & McCabe, 1992) serves low-income African-American children in eighth grade, ages 13 to 14. It has two components: a human sexuality curriculum taught by nurses and counsellors over five class periods and a five-class postponing sexual involvement curriculum led by older adolescents in the eleventh and twelfth grades. Using a quasi-experimental design, the researchers found that program youths were more likely to delay sexual involvement and were less likely to report being sexually active at the end of the ninth grade. There were one-third as many pregnancies for girls in the program group as for girls in the comparison group.

The Life Skills Training Program (LST) (Dusenbury & Botvin, 1990) is a competence-enhancement program designed to be implemented with seventh grade students from 12 to 13 years of age. This age is selected because it is considered to be a critical period for the initiation of substance abuse as well as other problem behaviours. The program focuses on preventing the use of gateway substances such as tobacco, alcohol, and marijuana. The training program provides for eighteen sessions in grade 7 as well as for ten and five booster sessions in grades 8 and 9 respectively. The curriculum has three general components: information and skills specific to resisting social influences to smoke, drink, or use drugs; a focus on personal coping skills; and an emphasis on general social skills. The program has been implemented using three different types of program providers: project staff, older peer leaders, and regular classroom teachers. The importance of proper training and support of these program providers is emphasized. Promising program outcomes are reported by the study authors:

> In a total of eight separate studies, the LST program has been demonstrated to be effective at reducing new cigarette smoking from between 40%–75% in the experimental group at the end of the intervention ... the program was demonstrated to reduce problem behaviors and marijuana use ... Most of the studies ... have involved predominantly white, middle-class samples. (pp. 472–473)

More recent studies of LST with Hispanic and African-American students have also shown positive results.

The Social Competence Promotion Program for Young Adolescents (Weissberg, Barton, & Schriver, 1997) teaches students cognitive, behavioural, and affective skills. This program has been implemented across the New Haven, Connecticut, public school system. Forty-five sessions provide instruction in class. Environmental supports are offered to promote social competencies, to enhance communication between school staff and students, and to prevent antisocial and aggressive behaviour, substance abuse, and high-risk sexual behaviours. The classroom program has three modules: 27 lessons in social problem-solving skills, and two nine-lesson sessions to apply these skills to the prevention of substance abuse and high-risk sexual behaviours. Teachers are trained to model problem solving to students outside of the formal sessions and to encourage the use of these methods in everyday situations. Several controlled studies have assessed the program. In one study, the frequency of antisocial behaviour remained stable for the program group, but increased 36.8 per cent for the control group from pre-test to post-test assessments, and self-reports indicated that program participants felt less inclined to use drugs or alcohol. In a one-year follow-up study, students with two years of program intervention maintained improvements in problem-solving skills, prosocial values, and teacher-rated peer relations and behavioural conduct.

The Skills for Adolescents version of the Quest Program focuses on health and the promotion of positive relationships and aims to prevent drug abuse. Expressions of feelings are encouraged and protected in conversation circles and role-plays, as well as in participation-culminating projects. The program is designed to build on the Skills for Growing Program for younger children. A 1988 study of 553 seventh graders in three randomly selected schools reported significant reductions in absences, disciplinary actions, and visits to school counsellors. Other studies have reported improvement in student knowledge about alcohol and drugs, and less use of these substances in the month prior to assessment (all studies reported in Elias et al., 1997).

The Social Decision-Making and Social Problem-Solving Program uses a comprehensive curriculum focused on the transition periods for junior-high-school students. It emphasizes social readiness skills, confidence building, the promotion of positive health development, critical thinking, self-control, group participation, social awareness, and problem solving (Elias et al., 1997). Findings of several studies show improvements in teacher and student ratings of social decision-making abilities, prosocial and coping behaviours, and in sensitivity toward others (findings reported in Elias et al., 1997).

Pitman and colleagues (1998) describe the Youth Relationship Project, which focuses on the prevention of violence in dating relationships. Youths aged 14 to 16 participate in an eighteen-week program designed to provide awareness and interpersonal skill development. Participants examine the role of media in enhancing and glamorizing violence and explore issues of power and control in familial, societal, and relationship contexts. Both young men and women participate in weekly two-hour groups with a male and female facilitator. Participants are referred from child protective services or from high schools if the adolescent is considered to be at risk based on their history of maltreatment and other selection criteria. For 58 youths who were receiving services from child protection services, weekly co-facilitator ratings suggested considerable growth in youth interest and in support given and received. Compared with a group receiving regular child welfare services, an interpersonal coercion scale showed a statistically significant advantage for the program group at follow-up.

According to Durlak (1995), the research on drug programming offers some of the strongest evidence for the effectiveness of school-based, competence, and skill development programming, particularly in delaying the early onset of drug use and in reducing the number of children who use drugs and how often they do so. He claims that the most successful programs train children systematically in understanding and resisting pressures, provide booster sessions to help maintain the short-term gains over time, create public media campaigns, and involve the broader community in expanding the school-based efforts. Barth and Derezotes (1990) suggest that 'reviews of evaluations of adolescent drug prevention programs indicated that peer-taught programs generally had more successful outcomes than adult-taught programs' (p. 29). Tobler (1986) reviewed the evaluations of 143 adolescent drug prevention programs and found that peer programs focused on social life skills and refusal of drugs were the only approach that actually reduced drug-abusing behaviours among general school populations. A more pessimistic conclusion was reached by Bangert-Drowns (1988) based on a meta-analysis of 33 school-based drug prevention programs. This author concludes that these competence and skill development programs had positive effects on knowledge and attitudes, but did not impact on actual use of drugs.

Community and After-School Skill Development Programs

Feindler and Becker (1994) describe a parent–adolescent, social skills development program. After separate training in discrete skills, the parents and adolescents practise the new skills while interacting with each other. Results indicated that social skills improved for both parents and youth and were maintained at a ten-month follow-up. Feindler and

Becker (1994) also present the results of an assessment of a comprehensive skill development program for adolescents and their families. In addition to skills training, parents and adolescents practise the new methods during sessions focusing on salient issues between them. Results show an improvement in problem solving, family cohesiveness, and attitudes about family relationships. No data on the occurrence of adolescent abuse or out-of-home placements were provided in these two studies.

The Nurturing Program for Parents and Adolescents (Bavolek, 1988; as cited in Barth & Derezotes, 1990) has shown a capacity to reduce parental approval of corporal punishment, to increase parental knowledge of appropriate behaviour management methods, and to decrease parent–adolescent conflict. No measures of actual impacts on rates of adolescent abuse or placements were provided in this assessment.

The Going for the Goal Program (Danish, 1997) is an after-school program intended to help adolescents develop a sense of personal control and confidence about the future. Ten one-hour skill development workshops are taught by two or three trained high-school student leaders per fifteen younger students. An evaluation showed program participants had better school attendance, fewer health-compromising behaviours, and a decrease in violent and other problem behaviours compared with a control group.

The Teen Education and Employment Network (Bauman et al.,1997) aims to improve the competencies of adolescents with chronic health problems. It is a twelve-session social and communication skills program coupled with a four-month part-time internship in a community agency in a helping role. Many of the participants come from minority and low-income families. Twenty to 35 adolescents are trained as a cohort and are paid $4.75 per hour to participate with $1.75 withheld until graduation. An experimental design was used to evaluate the program with 278 in the program group and 150 in the control group. Of the 278 program participants, 140 finished the training and 109 completed the internship. The intervention group showed enhanced self-esteem compared with the control group. While all kinds of participants benefited, the intervention impact was much stronger for girls and for younger adolescents (14 to 15 years old). Most self-esteem and mental health gains were maintained over the one-year follow-up period.

Family- and Parent-Focused Programs

Family-focused programs seek to reduce parent–teen conflict, enhance parent–teen attachment, increase the consistency and appropriateness of parental rewards and sanctions, maintain the adolescents' exposure to prosocial adult role models, and support parents practically and emotionally with their parenting (Hawkins & Fraser, 1883). Ballantyne and Raymond (1998) suggest that a family focus is more successful than an individual focus in avoiding out-of-home placements for youth, in decreasing antisocial behaviours, and in addressing adolescent behavioural and emotional problems. Tolan and Loeber (1993) conclude that the relatively good outcomes of family interventions with antisocial youths suggest that they should be the treatment of choice when dealing with antisocial behaviours. Nichols and Schwartz (1995) state that 'with conduct disordered children ... there seems to be a consensus among reviewers that effective treatments should be family based' (p. 563).

Family Therapy

Hawkins, Catalano, and Miller (1992) conclude from their review that family therapy has reduced delinquency among juvenile offenders and prevented it among their siblings. A meta-analysis by Hazelrigg, Cooper, and Borduin (1987) suggested that family therapy does not have as positive an effect on changing behaviours in adolescents as do some other program models; however when compared with other forms of therapy, it is more effective. Straus (1994) concurs, stating that 'family therapy has proven effective for a range of adolescent problems and compared to other (psychotherapy) approaches, it has been shown to be equal or superior in effectiveness in several studies' (p. 28).

Bank, Hicks Marlowe, Reid, Patterson, and Weinrott (1991) randomly assigned participants to family-based parent training or to a control group receiving weekly family therapy sessions (type of family therapy unspecified). All adolescents were repeat offenders referred by the juvenile court; the families were described as 'extremely distressed,' experiencing frequent external crises and marital discord. Many of the parents were considered to be very antisocial and often depressed, and much treatment time was devoted to these issues. Program sessions were conducted separately with each family typically with both the adolescents and parents present for these sessions. Parents were trained to concretely identify prosocial and antisocial behaviours and to chart these behaviours to facilitate weekly supervision. Efforts were made to help parents develop close communications with the youths' schools. Parent cards were filled out by teachers on a daily basis noting trouble in school. Behavioural contacts were negotiated between the teens and their parents. Participants received about 45 hours of face-to-face and phone contact compared with about 50 hours for the control group. There was a greater reduction in serious crimes for the experimental group during the treatment year and a similar reduction for the control group in the first of the three follow-up years. These reductions persisted during follow-up for both groups. However, youths in the experimental group spent significantly less time in institutional settings than those in the control group (an average of 96.7 days compared with 152.4 days), resulting in a savings of nearly $100,000 US over the three-year period. One caveat was that 'the clinical work with these families was extremely difficult. It took tremendous effort to prevent staff burnout and, in the end, it appeared that a still more powerful intervention would have been appropriate' (p. 31). While both approaches to family work produced benefits, there were advantages for the expanded family-based parent training model over more traditional family therapy.

The Oregon Social Learning Center's (OSLC) program of research has implemented social learning principles in family treatment, specifically targeting parent management practices. Researchers at the Learning Center, based on twenty years of work with families with antisocial children, have found promising results of parent management techniques with a variety of antisocial child behaviours, including substance abuse (Palmer & Liddle, 1996). Alexander, Holtzworth-Munroe, and Jameson (1994) observe that the OSLC's program of research demonstrates 'the absolute and comparative efficiency of social learning-based parent training interventions' (p. 621). Nichols and Schwartz (1995) summarize the results of the OSLC work as demonstrating that:

> (1) parent management training has been found effective for the treatment of conduct disorders and to produce long-term results; (2) there is a system-wide impact from this type of family-oriented treatment, even though interventions were directed toward the conduct disordered child; and, (3) there is evidence that successful treatment can be conducted through nonsymptomatic members. (p. 564)

A structural family approach with an emphasis on issues such as leadership, system organization, communication flow, and conflict resolution was used with families of drug-abusing Hispanic children and adolescents with behaviour problems (Alexander et al., 1994; Kazdin, 1994). One study of this population (Szapocznik, Kurtines, Santistebon,

& Rio, 1990) found that at a one year follow-up, families receiving structural family therapy had improved their internal functioning greatly, family functioning of youths who had received individual psychodynamic treatment had deteriorated, and family functioning of youths who had participated in small-group recreational activities was unchanged. While family functioning improved, there was no discernible impact on child or adolescent antisocial behaviour from the family therapy (Kazdin, 1994).

Barkley, Guevremont, Anastopoulos, and Fletcher (1992) compared the efficacy of parent management training, structural family therapy, and problem-solving and communication training with adolescents with attention deficit hyperactivity disorder. All three approaches produced statistically significant improvements in parent–youth communication, number of conflicts, and anger intensity during conflicts. Improvements in overall adolescent symptoms and in functioning at school also occurred (Kazdin, 1994). However, only a minority of these changes for the youths were judged to be clinically significant – from 5 to 30 per cent depending on the outcome measure used (Kazdin, 1994).

A study by Lewis, Piercy, Sprenkle, and Trepper (1990) compared brief family therapy with drug education showing significant pre–post-intervention decreases in drug use for family therapy, but not for drug education. Similarly, research by Joanning, Quinn, Thomas, and Mullen (1992) showed greater reduction in drug use following family therapy than after drug education or peer group therapy.

Kagan et al. (1987) assessed a program in which short-term foster home placement was combined with outreach family counselling during crises and with opportunities for long-term family work. Cases came from referrals from family court judges, and consisted of those where the goal was reunification with families, where severe abuse and neglect were involved, or where youths were likely to need adoptive families. Many of the youths displayed serious behavioural problems, such as substance abuse, school avoidance, running away from home, destructive and aggressive behaviour, and sexual acting out, or had experienced sexual abuse. Most were troubled by chronic uncertainty about where and with whom they would be living. Sixty-two per cent of the youths had had a prior out-of-home placement. Families were described as chronically unstable with inter-parent and parent–teen conflicts being common. Behavioural problems of the youths decreased over the study period. Generally, the youths were functioning adequately in school, and the incidence of running away dropped from 66 to 17 per cent.

Fifty-five per cent of the 29 youths returned to their parents or relatives, or to the care of an adequate family. The lack of a comparison group for this study suggests caution in interpreting these findings.

Despite strong arguments for including the improvement of family functioning as part of programming for adolescents, both the quantity and quality of research on family therapy approaches uncovered in this review suggest the need for caution in drawing conclusions about their effectiveness. The evidence suggests that various approaches to family therapy have produced positive changes in family functioning, especially in the area of parent–teen conflict. However, it is not clear that family therapy has produced meaningful changes in youth symptomology or behaviour outside of the home. This is an area where conceptualizing and demonstrating the value of family therapy requires greater clarity. In addition, it would be useful to explore how family therapy complements other program strategies for adolescents and their families. It is likely that in a situation of great and persistent disadvantage, family therapy will not prove to be credible as a stand-alone model.

Intensive Family Preservation Services

In this program model, in-home services, often provided by a primary worker, allow for high levels of weekly contact with families but for relatively short periods of time, typically between six and twelve weeks. Some programs allow booster sessions for families. In theory at least, connecting families with community resources is an important component of the approach (Cameron & Vanderwoerd, 1997a).

Schorr (1997) presents evidence that Michigan's state-wide Families First program co-occurred with a 28 per cent decrease in out-of-home placements between 1993 and 1995, a period when the number of children in care increased in almost every other state. However, she also describes serious problems with 'model drift,' the formidable task of getting local organizations to adopt the program, and the difficulties in maintaining program quality across settings.

The Early Offender Program (Howitt & Moore, 1991) provided intensive, in-home interventions for youths who were 13 years of age or younger at the time of their first adjudication and who had two or more prior police contacts. Caseloads were restricted to twelve to fifteen cases per worker, and paid paraprofessionals provided expanded coverage by monitoring youths on weekends and evenings, transporting youngsters, and providing tutoring and other supports. Some youths were referred for outside counselling, and program youngsters had the opportunity to perform community service. School attendance and performance were emphasized. Direct supports to parents were provided. A comparison group of youths who would have been eligible for the program between 1980 and 1985 was compared with 145 program participants between 1985 and 1989. For youngsters who were 17 as of 1 June 1990, 38 per cent of the program group and 72 per cent of the comparison group had new adjudications. Out-of-home placements were used for 30 per cent of the program participants, with an average stay of 177 days, in contrast with placements for 67 per cent of the comparison group averaging 257 days.

Schwartz, AuClair, and Harris (1990) assessed an intensive family preservation services program for seriously disturbed adolescents who had been approved for placement. Participants ($n = 116$) were selected from a pool of eligible adolescents and randomly assigned to the program or placed in foster homes, hospitals, group homes, or residential treatment centres. Of the 58 youths assigned to the program, 25 remained in their own homes for the entire twelve- to sixteen-month study period. The total number of days in placement were 4,777 for the program participants and 12,037 for the comparison group.

In another study, young offenders ($n = 84$) receiving in-home family preservation services that used a multisystemic family therapy orientation had about half as many arrests as youths who received traditional services (Henggler, Melton, & Smith, 1992). At 2.4 years after referral, 39 per cent of those in the multisystemic family preservation sample had not been rearrested, compared with 20 per cent for those using traditional services.

In the Missouri Delinquency Project, two hundred chronic juvenile offenders were randomly assigned to a multisystemic in-home family preservation program or to individual counselling. Four year follow-up data revealed that recidivism rates were 22 per cent for the program group and 71 per cent for those who completed individual therapy. The program youths also showed less parent–adolescent conflict and less inter-parent conflict than the comparison group (Henggler et al., 1994).

A quasi-experimental design was employed to compare juvenile offenders in the Family Ties family preservation program ($n = 93$) with randomly selected youths ($n = 40$) who had been adjudicated in family court and placed in a state youth facility. The rate of rearrest for the program group was 20 per cent, compared with 42 per cent for the comparison group. Reincarceration rates were 18 per cent and 40 per cent respectively (Rivera & Kutash, 1994a).

Rivera and Kutash (1994a) conclude from their review of intensive family preservation services that:

> while it appears that many family preservation programs have proven effective at keeping families intact and preventing or delaying the placement of children deemed at risk for substitute care, the effects do not appear to be long-lasting and families continue to be at risk following service termination. (pp. 71–72)

Cameron and Vanderwoerd (1997a) come to similar conclusions:

> There is convincing evidence that, when they are focused in fact on 'high-risk' populations, IFPS [intensive family preservation services] programs often reduce both the frequency that children need to be placed outside their homes and the amount of time children spend in care ... [consequently] IFPS programs can result in substantial cost savings for the host agencies ... While research evidence is scarce, because of their ability to bring professional expertise to bear on selected personal and family concerns, it seems reasonable to expect limited positive changes in these areas ... There is some research evidence that IFPS benefits attenuate with the passage of time after program involvement ends. Finally, there are no reasons to expect IFPS involvement to lessen families' reliance on professional services, after IFPS participation ends. (p. 125)

Ballantyne and Raymond (1998) add that:

> practitioners and parents both indicated that crisis intervention is a very important component in an overall strategy to assist families with keeping adolescents at home ... [However, crisis intervention] is rarely satisfactory to meet the needs of most families if used in isolation ... This is especially true for families with severe and chronic risk factors ... [where it] should be used in combination with other forms of intervention that can provide more ongoing supports. (pp. 133–134)

While the results from the research have been inconsistent, intensive family preservation services have demonstrated their capacity to prevent family breakdown and to reduce the need for out-of-home placements of adolescents in several studies. The evidence is less clear that the benefits from this intervention are sustained over time without other kinds of continuing supports. In this review, some encouraging results were associated with intensive family preservation services that incorporated a multisystemic therapy orientation. Precisely how this orientation differs from more traditional intensive family preservation services models is not clear from this research.

Parent-Focused Programs

Adolescents, with their increased abilities to resist parents' initiatives and their need for more independence, present unique parenting challenges. Some good results have been reported from program strategies focused on supporting parents of adolescents with these challenges. Hawkins, Catalano, and Miller (1992) state:

> Randomized experimental tests of parental skills training have shown significant reductions in pre-adolescents' problem behaviors when compared to controls ... [T]he existing evidence suggests the promise of parenting skills training and involvement for preventing adolescent drug abuse ... [However, the] problems of nonparticipation, attrition and implementation in parenting skills training programs have been well documented. (pp. 92–93)

On the other hand, Cameron and Vanderwoerd (1997a) raise several important caveats about parent effectiveness training. Some studies in their review suggest that the gains in parent–child relations and in child behaviours become less evident over time after program involvement ends. Equally of concern, three studies in their review suggested that the benefits of parent training were less evident when parents were coping with high levels of stress and multiple difficulties in their lives. Several other studies suggested that parent training was more effective with multiply disadvantaged families when joined with other supports and services.

Other promising, albeit less frequently used, support strategies are the building of informal support networks and mutual aid organizations for parents of adolescents. Turcotte (1990) reports on a retrospective study on the experiences of the parents of difficult adolescents who participated in an intervention based on Tough Love's mutual aid principles and methods. Groups were led by two professional social workers, and each group consisted of eight to ten parents. Participation in the program lasted on average about nine months. Turcotte reports that participation helped parents regain confidence and take actions that led to changes in their teens' behaviours. The most significant positive effect noted was on parents' experiences of parenthood.

Ballantyne and Raymond (1998), in their review of resources for maltreated teens in Ontario, found few mutual aid or support networks for their parents. But the evidence that was available indicated that parents of difficult adolescents found great relief in talking to others in similar circumstances and appreciated the assistance provided in managing their difficulties with their adolescents. Cameron and Vanderwoerd (1997a) identified informal helping in general, and mutual aid organizations and support networks in particular, as very promising yet extremely underdeveloped resources for all child welfare populations. They also present evidence that program models incorporating these informal support and mutual aid elements are the only ones that have shown a long-term potential to lessen reliance on professional services for various populations.

Social Integration Programs

Having positive involvements with community institutions, with adults outside of the home, as well as with friends and peers, has been identified as a valuable resource for adolescent development and as a buffer against troubles inside and outside of the home (Ballantyne & Raymond, 1998; Hawkins, Catalano, & Miller, 1992; Hawkins & Fraser, 1983). Despite the agreement about the centrality of these prosocial connections for healthy teen development, programs using these insights as core helping strategies for adolescents are comparatively rare. This is consistent with the earlier recognition by Cameron and Vanderwoerd (1997a) of the substantial neglect of the power of informal helping and social integration strategies in the social services in general. This is an area where there are strong justifications and ample scope for experimentation with programming for adolescents.

Connections with Adults

The National Research Council (1993) states:

> Perhaps the most serious risk facing adolescents in high-risk settings is isolation from the nurturance, safety, and guidance that comes from sus-

tained relationships with adults. Parents are the best source of support, but for many adolescents, parents are not particularly involved in their lives. (p. 213)

An early evaluation of the YouthBuild program highlighted the importance of creating relationships between participating youths and program adults that are based on trust and using these relationships to challenge the youths to perform and persevere in their pursuit of conventional goals (Schorr, 1997).

Partners in Denver (Hawkins & Fraser, 1983; Wall, Hawkins, Lishner, & Fraser, 1981) creates one-to-one relationships between youth and adults. Voluntary participants referred from the juvenile justice system are expected to spend at least three hours a week with their matched adult. Several evaluations of the program suggest a reduced likelihood of participating youth getting into trouble more serious than the actions that initially brought them to the program.

Project Wincroft in Manchester, England (Hawkins & Fraser, 1983; Smith, Farrant, & Marchant, 1972), matched delinquent youths with adult community volunteers and the pair were offered a variety of recreational and vocational activities. Nondelinquent friends of the participating youth could be invited to these activities. At the end of two and one-half years of service, 37 per cent of the program youths and 54.4 per cent of a matched control youths had a subsequent court appearance.

LoSciuto and colleagues (Gottfredson et al., 1997; LoSciuto, Rajala, Townsend, & Taylor, 1996) conducted a recent study of a program pairing high-risk grade 6 students with elderly mentors. The program demonstrated positive effects on attitudes toward school, community service, the elderly, and intentions to use drugs.

Polit, Quint, and Riccio (1988) reported on a program matching pregnant teens with mature women. In addition to mentoring, this program included regularly scheduled peer group sessions, workshops, counselling, and individualized brokering for health, education, employment, and employability development. Recreational activities, transportation, and child care assistance were also available (Davis & Tolan, 1993). Five years later, the participants in the program were doing better on a variety of indicators than their peers who had not been involved – for example, mean weekly income, length of time employed, fewer subsequent children, higher vocabulary scores for children, and per cent of children enrolled in Head Start.

As a caution, Davis and Tolan (1993) point out that in the previous program for pregnant teens, the turnover of mentors was high and the teenagers reported great difficulty in transferring loyalties. Straus (1994) also emphasizes the difficulties in implementing mentoring programs. Straus points out that for these programs to be successful, mentors and youth generally need to share racial and cultural characteristics, develop their relationship carefully, and have the association endure for a lengthy period of time. The National Research Council (1993) argues that mentoring relationships with young people can be successful if they extend over time and if the mentors themselves have clear goals, adequate training, and adequate support from the sponsoring organization. Marjorie Wilkes of New York Mentoring (quoted in Schorr, 1997) adds that:

> effective mentoring requires program structures that support mentors in their own efforts to build trust and develop positive relationships with youth ... Programs must provide the infrastructure – including screening, training and ongoing supervision – to foster the development of effective relationships. (p. 12)

Freeman (1993) found in a study that Big Brothers/Big Sisters had 40,000 families on their waiting list. In reference to the I Have a Dream Program, Hamilton and Hamilton (1992) said that:

> recruiting, training, and matching mentors proved much more difficult than we had anticipated and required more time and resources than we had expected ... Only about half the pairs met regularly ... [T]he natural way for [a caring relationship] to happen is that an adult and a youth gradually become close through contact in their daily lives. (pp. 547–550)

Given the difficulties of finding and sustaining long-term volunteer mentorships, it may prove easier to foster positive adult–youth connections through relationships that develop naturally through participation in other kinds of social activities and programming.

Peer Tutors, Mediators, and Counsellors

In the Kauai longitudinal study, the resilient children had good peer relationships (Fergusson & Lynskey, 1996). In Tobler's (1986) meta-analysis of 240 drug abuse programs, peer influence programs were 'dramatically more effective than all the other programs' (p. 167). Nonetheless, peer relationships are a two-edged sword. Antisocial peer involvements are one of the strongest correlates with difficulties in many areas of adolescents' lives. Programming stressing the use of peers as helpers emphasizes the prosocial nature of these engagements and often complements peer supports with involvements with adults.

The School Transition Project (Jason et al., 1992) involved high-risk multi-ethnic middle-school youth (grades 4 to 6) who were entering new inner-city schools. Students at risk of academic failure based on low standardized achievement scores received an orientation program from sixth-grade students and in-school academic tutoring from college students or home tutoring from trained parents. Program students improved their achievement scores significantly and 50 per cent more moved out of the academic at-risk category. At one-year follow-up, the program academic gains were maintained. However, the parent tutors produced more positive change than the college tutors.

In the Study Buddy Program (Cowen, Hightower, Pedro-Carroll, & Work, 1989; Srebank & Elias, 1993) students in fourth through sixth grades were paired and met twice weekly. Participants showed improved adjustment and social skills, higher standardized test scores, and fewer tardy or truant days.

The Valued Youth Program (Supik, 1991) used students with limited English proficiency and who were themselves at risk of school failure as tutors for younger children who were having difficulties. In addition to improved academic performance for the younger students, the tutors showed less absenteeism and disciplinary problems, higher grades, improved self-concepts, and a reduced dropout rate.

A meta-analysis reported in Davis and Tolan (1993) found that in 33 of 39 studies, students who served as tutors performed better academically than did control students. Straus (1994) makes this overall assessment:

> Overall, the evaluations of tutoring suggest a reciprocal effectiveness for elementary- and secondary-school recipients, as well as for adolescent providers. All show small but significant gains in academic and personal functioning, even in studies of older youth [as tutors] who have themselves evidenced problems ... Like youth volunteers, peer helpers are aided by being positioned to help others. However, the additional success in peer-helper programs also argues persuasively for the curative power of being needed and respected by other children and adolescents. (p. 167)

Srebank and Elias (1993) note that both same-age and cross-age tutoring have been effective.

When a program of combined individual and group peer counselling was conducted with middle-school students considered to be severely disruptive, the program led to a 14 per cent decrease in school absences, a 16 per cent increase in self-concept, and a 26 per cent increase in positive school attitude (Nenortas, 1987). Ballantyne and Raymond (1998) report that mediation programs in schools select and train students to mediate peer disputes. Assessments of these programs have reported less violence in schools and enhanced conflict resolution skills of students. They also describe similar programs for delinquent youth which increased the participants' conflict resolution skills. The National Research Council (1993) supports these conclusions, stating that an 'emerging body of research indicates that various forms of peer counselling and instruction, when conducted with adult guidance, can serve as supports for coping with the influences of high-risk settings' (p. 217).

Mutual Aid Groups/Networks, Alternative After-School Activities

Few programs for adolescents have mutual aid or alternative forms of involvement as their key helping strategies. Yet there are strong arguments for experimenting with these types of support strategies for teens, for both their potential benefits to participating teens and their potential to relieve pressure on families. Because of the demands these kinds of participation make on teens' willingness to participate and on their abilities to interact positively with other youths, extra assistance may be required to support some youths in such endeavours (Cameron & Vanderwoerd, 1997a).

Fashimpar (1991) describes a program for delinquent males from 11 to 16 years of age that involved participation in a mini-bike club – bike maintenance, trail riding, and group meetings for six hours a week are offered contingent on good behaviour, regular school attendance, and maintaining a 2.0 grade point average – in addition to regular probation services. Compared with a control group receiving regular probation services, the mini-bike group had more positive change on all five measures of personal functioning as well as on measures of academic performance and absenteeism.

Nonetheless, Hawkins, Catalano, and Miller (1992) suggest that the evidence for the effectiveness of involvement in alternative activities with delinquent youths is mixed. They argue that, when provided at high levels of frequency, participation in alternative activities can help youths to develop new skills useful in their daily lives. For example, they suggest that Outward Bound programs, which provide risk-taking challenges as opportunities to learn new skills, could be combined with ongoing efforts focused on mastery of the adolescents' routine environments. The National Research Council (1993) suggests that:

> street-based outreach [is] the most effective strategy for reaching [vulnerable and isolated youth]. However, this strategy for adolescents from high-risk settings requires aggressive outreach by talented providers who know and are trusted in the community ... For example, midnight basketball leagues in New York City appear to be effective settings for conducting outreach to populations at risk for health problems. (p. 204)

Straus (1994) argues that:

> among lower income male youth, those involved with sports display significantly less delinquent activity than non-athletic counterparts ... However, this finding does not hold true for middle-class adolescents, and the debate over the merits of organized sports as a mental health tool persists. (p. 164)

Debrusk and Hellison (1989) evaluated a physical education program for fourth-grade delinquency-prone youths. Student self-reports and teacher observations suggested positive affective behaviour change for the participating youths. In reference to community youth organizations, Davis and Tolan (1993) argue that:

> the natural fit of the programs with the goals of adolescent development, especially social responsibility; the programs' accessibility to many otherwise unreachable youth; and the positive impact found among the few evaluated programs suggest that they deserve carefully designed programming and evaluation. Their enhancement may provide one of the more effective means of primary prevention. (p. 433)

Ballantyne and Raymond (1998) reported that parents, interviewed for their review of child welfare services for adolescents in Ontario,

> stated that activities after school are very helpful because the period following school is a very stressful time. Parents indicated that these activities should be well supervised ... Youth indicated that they would like a program that promoted interaction with peers, and included such activities as recreational activities and homework support. (p. 138)

Les Scientifiques (Chamberland, Théorêt, Garon, & Roy, 1995) is an extracurricular science club for girls from 9 to 12 at two primary schools in a disadvantaged district in Montreal. Activities take place from Monday to Thursday from 3:30 to 5:30 P.M. A healthy snack is provided and the group has both structured and unstructured activity time. Compared with a control group, active program participants showed improvements in problem-solving abilities, more motivation in school, less absenteeism, and more interest in nontraditional careers.

Cameron and Rothery (1985) evaluated two after-school programs for adolescents who were receiving child protection service and who were considered to be at risk of out-of-home placements. Located in community settings, they provided the youths with a safe place to go three or four times a week for the late afternoon and early evening. These programs provided structured group activities, a variety of recreational and social activities, expectations of youth involvement in planning the program and maintaining the premises, as well as regular homework times and supports. In comparison with regular child welfare services to adolescents, the programs showed moderate effectiveness in preventing out-of-home placements. The after-school program with the higher level of weekly contact with youth, the lower worker-to-youth ratio, and the longer time of average program involvement had clearer impacts on prevention of out-of-home placement. However, the authors suggested that because of the relatively small sample of program cases ($n = 42$) and the nonrandom assignment to program and comparison conditions, these findings should be considered suggestive rather than conclusive.

Pransky (1991) describes an after-school truancy prevention program for 11- to 15-year-old youths. The program runs for eleven hours each week after school as well as on weekends and focuses on role modelling, esteem building, job-skill training, tutoring, athletic activities, and neighbourhood enrichment projects. A comparison of 141 program participants with 50 youths in a comparison group showed significantly less truancy in the program group. There was also a 72.6 per cent improvement in the program participants' mean grade point average as well as a 55.6 per cent drop in the number of days absent from school.

A study of Alateen (Hughes, 1977), a twelve-step mutual aid organization for adolescents who have an alcoholic parent, typically sponsored by a twelve-step Alanon group for partners of alcoholics or for adult children of alcoholics, revealed positive changes in self-esteem for members ($n = 25$) in contrast to a comparison group of teens who had an alcoholic parent but were not members of Alateen. The Alateen members also had fewer problems at school or with law enforcement officials. Alateen groups are low-cost resources for teens and exist across North America. Mutual aid organizations and support networks have been successfully created for a variety of disadvantaged and distressed populations (Cameron & Vanderwoerd, 1997a) and in our opinion merit adaptation for greater inclusion in demonstration programs for helping adolescents. Strong support for these types of options was voiced by youths who were involved with child welfare agencies and who were interviewed in our qualitative study:

> *When I'm asked this question [What was the most helpful?], always the same answer comes up. The only ... thing that worked for me is [the youth network]. Relating to other people who have been through the same thing as I have.*
>
> *It wasn't just me alone, it was a group of kids ... Even though we had counsellors, I didn't feel safe going to counsellors, but I did with my peers.*
>
> *Peer groups. If you're 12 years old, having a 35-year-old tell you that they understand ... you're just like, yeah, whatever. But if you have somebody who's 15 and you're 12, it's different because you can relate to them better and they've been through it closer to you. It sounds more real, and you look up to them.*

The Positive Peer Culture Program (Vorrath & Brendtro, 1985) forms groups of nine youths under the guidance of a group leader. The focus is on changing youth subculture and mobilizing the power of a peer group in a productive manner. Specific procedures are used to foster caring behaviours, and youths are responsible for helping one another. There is an attempt to set expectations high to challenge youths to do all they are capable of accomplishing. Originally developed for residential treatment settings, the challenge of transferring the approach to school and community settings has proved to be formidable. Yet in public school settings, the program has demonstrated a capacity to reduce delinquent behaviour and school suspensions, and improve school attendance and attitudes toward school.

Connections to Community

Keeping distressed and disadvantaged youths positively attached to schools is an important priority (Ballantyne & Raymond, 1998; Dryfoos,

1990; Schorr, 1997). Youths regularly involved with religious institutions and other prosocial community organizations are much less vulnerable to negative peer influences (Hawkins, Catalano, & Miller, 1992).

In addition, youths 'need opportunities to succeed and to be rewarded for success. They need opportunities to contribute, to feel in control, and to demonstrate competencies ... to develop and use their interpersonal, academic and vocational skills' (National Research Council, 1993, p. 223). Community service either as volunteers or through paid internships have proven to be useful parts of several program models for adolescents (Davis & Tolan, 1993). Straus (1994) concurs, stating that studies of volunteer service opportunities, while scarce, 'consistently indicate that voluntary service reduces feelings of isolation and alienation, increases understanding and connection to the community, and develops a sense of competence and self-worth in participants' (p. 166). Fostering social integration and positive community connections, and helping adolescents make positive contributions to the community are, in our opinion, underutilized areas in programming for adolescents.

The Teen Outreach Program (Philliber & Allen, 1992) is designed to facilitate school progress and pregnancy prevention through a focus on alternative life options. It is an after-school program for seventh to twelfth grade students aged 11 to 19. It has been implemented in both Canada and the United States and emphasizes two components: weekly small-group discussions regarding life planning and goal setting as well as structured community service volunteering for at least one hour a week. The expectation is that improved social competence and connections to adults will lead to enhanced psychological functioning and decreased problem behaviours (Coley & Chase-Larsdale, 1998). The program has been evaluated using experimental and quasi-experimental designs. Program students were found to have fewer pregnancies, failed courses, and school suspensions and lower rates of school dropout and sexual intercourse.

Multiple-Component Programs

The clearest consensus in the literature is that for many adolescents at risk of entering the child protection or other restrictive service system, one-shot, unidimensional interventions will not suffice (Ballantyne & Raymond, 1998; Cameron & Vanderwoerd, 1997a; Chung & Elias; 1996; Davis & Tolan, 1993; Hawkins, Catalano, & Miller, 1992; Henggler et al., 1992; Lerner, 1995; National Research Council, 1993; Pransky, 1991;

Schorr, 1989, 1997; Straus, 1994; Weissberg, Barton, & Schriver, 1997; Werner, 1990). The common prescription is multi-component helping strategies focused on important sources of stress as well as wellness for adolescents and their families. These strategies call for high levels of support at any one point in time and often over a period of years. These comprehensive approaches typically are proposed for youth confronting multiple developmental disadvantages rather than for general teen populations.

Within the general pattern of inclusiveness, there is a great deal of variance in the nature and the number of elements included in these programs. On average, these programs are the most expensive of those reviewed; on the other hand, they often produce the most substantial and enduring positive changes for the most disadvantaged participants (Cameron & Vanderwoerd, 1997a). These broad strategies also represent more demanding implementation and replication challenges; they do not fit easily with service delivery and control procedures in established agencies. Perhaps it should not be surprising that this review found relatively few programs clearly following this prescription. In the remainder of this section, examples of multiple-component programs are presented as illustrations of the characteristics and the potential of these strategies.

The Quantum Opportunities Program (QOP) (Dugger, 1995; Schorr, 1997) involved teens ages 13 to 15 over four years. These were children from low-income communities where the risk of school dropout, early pregnancy, substance abuse, and criminal activity were high. The teens were paid small stipends ($1.00/hr), which were matched in a college fund for them, for the hours they spent studying mathematics and vocabulary on the program's computers; being tutored; doing volunteer work; going to plays, ballets, and museums; visiting college campuses; and listening to guest speakers. Students had contact with the program on weekends and during the summer, and expectations of students were purposefully high. If students missed school, program staff actively looked for them. After-school tutoring help was available (Dugger, 1995). The reported outcomes are encouraging:

> In each of four cities, significantly more participants ended up graduating from high school, avoiding teenage pregnancy, and not in trouble with the law than a control group ... In one city, the QOP group had one fifth as many high school dropouts as the control group and three times as many youngsters in college. In another, only 7 percent of the participants had

babies as teenagers; the control group, over four times as much. (Schorr, 1997, p.3)

In Missouri's Walbridge Caring Communities Project (Schorr, 1997), modified state budgeting and financing procedures allowed local officials the flexibility to create programs that matched their specific requirements. Local inter-agency steering committees were created to cut through red tape and 'to make happen whatever needed to happen for this to be successful' (p. 98). The project provided intensive family preservation services, academic tutoring, after-school programs, and summer camps. Older youths had access to fitness classes, martial arts lessons, homework help, Saturday night dances, and other activities. Supports such as short-term financial assistance, pre-employment training, and respite nights were available. A school–parent organization was built and the projects provided 'a refuge and a comfortable place to spend time' (p. 98). Community campaigns to purge the neighbourhoods of drugs were organized. Services to prevent unnecessary out-of-home placements were established in addition to a school-based team to intervene early with families of children having difficulties. No data were provided on the outcomes from this initiative.

In the Iowa Patch Approach (Schorr, 1997), both public and private agencies work together in neighbourhood family resource centres. These resource centres emphasize working with local natural helping networks, and neighbourhood partners are sought out to act as mentors. Public health nurses, social workers from a local settlement house, as well as housing inspectors work in the resource centres. Someone from the local child protection agency works as part of the Patch team. No outcome data were available on this approach.

The Center for Family Life (Kahn & Kamerman, 1996) was created as part of a child welfare services reform project. It has a basic community infrastructure including child care, day camp, summer and after-school recreation, teen evening programs, parent workshops, summer youth employment, and so on. It also makes available a variety of individual, family, and group counselling opportunities as well as community-based foster care. Once again, no outcome data were available on this project.

The Johns Hopkins Pregnancy Prevention Program (Coley & Chase-Larsdale, 1998; Dryfoos, 1994; Durlack, 1995; Zabin, 1992) offers sexuality and contraceptive education, medical and contraceptive services, along with individual and group counselling to junior and senior high-school students. The clinics are adjacent to the schools and the education and counselling are provided in the schools, while the medical and contraceptive services are available in the clinics. Compared with students in schools without the program, and in the program schools before the creation of the program, program participants showed an increase in contraceptive and sexual knowledge, postponed first sexual involvement about seven months, increased use of contraception when sexually active, and substantially reduced levels of teen pregnancy (Zabin, 1992). The pregnancy rate in program schools fell by 30 per cent, while in comparison schools the rates rose by 58 per cent (Coley & Chase-Larsdale, 1998; Hardy & Zabin, 1991).

Dryfoos (1994) reviewed the data on school-based health clinics and concluded that they were being used by the highest-risk students who report the greatest number of problems. She suggests that they reduce school absences and increase access to psychosocial counselling. She also concludes that they lower teen pregnancy rates and improve sexual self-protective behaviours, but only in programs offering comprehensive family planning services.

Kagan et al. (1987) describe a program that has been effective in keeping delinquent youths out of custody. 'The full range of components of care in this program have been well integrated into the community enhancing its effectiveness' (p. 185). The program offers individual, family, and group counselling; communication and problem-skills training for parents and youth; identification and involvement of support networks; interventions with schools on behalf of the teens; access to special education teachers; short-term respite care; plus a 24-hour crisis telephone line and outreach service. A single practitioner coordinates the help provided to a family. There is contact with the family at least once per week and intensive involvement with the program can continue as long as needed.

The Wraparound approach has been described as more of a process than a program. It is built around a strengths focus, a philosophy of unconditional care, individualized service planning, interdisciplinary teams, proactive planning for crises, and respect for family values and cultures (Yoe, Santarcangelo, Atkins, & Burchard, 1996). In addition to professional involvements, many of the supports are provided by community volunteers. The model was created to work with families whose youth are at the highest risk of out-of-home placement, or where there is an interest in returning an already-placed youth to less-restrictive community living. Yoe et al. (1996) suggest that seven to ten hours a week of coordinating services and supports for a multiply challenged child is required in this model and case managers' caseloads need to be kept to four to seven children at a time. While the research base is limited, initial studies suggest that in the Wraparound approach, more youths with serious behaviour difficulties have been maintained successfully in their families or communities, and their behavioural difficulties have been reduced (Ballantyne & Raymond, 1998).

Many comprehensive programs are located in schools. These programs typically provide an array of services and supports to students, or they focus on transforming the environment of the school itself to provide a more appropriate learning experience for disadvantaged youth. Examples of these programs include: Career Academies (Olsen, 1994), School Transition Environment Project (Felner et al., 1993), Seattle Social Development Project (O'Donnell, Hawkins, Catalano, Abbott, & Day, 1995), Success for All (Madden, Slavin, Karweit, Dolan, & Weisit, 1993), Cormer Process (Cormer, 1988), and CoZi Schools (Schorr, 1997). The scope of this review does not allow for a discussion of all of these efforts. Rather, we examine a few approaches that are germane to our interests.

Beacon Schools in New York City (Schorr, 1997) attempt to join school-based services to a community-building effort. As an example, a Beacon School in central Harlem is open seven days a week from 9 A.M. to 11 P.M. or midnight. Youth workers help with homework and animate after-school sports and recreation activities for about two hundred children from 3 P.M. to 6 P.M. The program staff provide an atmosphere of predictability and the youth are expected to show responsibility toward their community. Conflict-resolution skills are taught to the youths. Parents can take part in parent support groups and there is a family dinner night. Programs for adults include Alcoholics Anonymous, Narcotics Anonymous, aerobics, and educational workshops. Youth leadership activities begin at 7 P.M. 'Activities for adolescents in the late evenings and on weekends have turned out to be particularly important ... classes [are offered] in drama, dance, video, community-service, job readiness ... and computer skills ... [There is also] Boy Scouts ... Friday is teen movie night' (pp. 51–52). Program staff often mediate between parents and teachers. 'Academic performance at the school has improved dramatically ... [from 580th of 620 schools in reading in 1991 to 319th three years later] ... Attendance has improved and police report fewer felony arrests among neighborhood youth' (p. 51).

Dryfoos (1994) describes the creation of a settlement house in a New York middle school: 'The vision was a school building open all days and evenings, weekends and summers with a challenging educational program matched with after-school enrichment, health and social services, and community education' (p. 100). At 7 A.M. there is a dance and recreation plus breakfast for about 100 students. After school about 500 students take part in a variety of activities. In the evening, there are programs for teenagers, parents, and other community residents. English as a second language is taught to about 400 people. There is a family resource centre, which is open from 8:30 A.M. to 8:30 P.M., offering help with issues such as immigration, housing, welfare assistance, drug prevention, adult education. and so on. Dental and medical services are also available.

The School Bullying Project (Durlak, 1995; Olweus, 1992) involved a general school population in 112 grade 4 through 7 classes in 42 primary and junior high schools in Bergin, Norway. The program stressed careful monitoring of youth behaviour and immediate nonphysical sanctions for rule violations as well as reinforcement from adults for positive behaviours. School assemblies and teacher conferences were held to identify possible solutions to the problem. Children who bullied were counselled and support was offered to their parents. Class rules were established and class meetings were held to discuss problems (Durlak, 1995). The project research team collected and reported back information about the nature of the bullying problem in each of the participating schools. They also prepared a 32-page booklet for school personnel offering suggestions about what they could do, plus a twenty-minute video, and a four-page folder with information and advice for parents (Olweus, 1992). Substantial reductions in incidents of bullying were reported in participating schools, a state of affairs that remained evident twenty months after the formal intervention ended.

Neighbourhood Transformation Projects

Recently, while visiting a well-attended program for new mothers in one of the Better Beginings, Better Futures Prevention Project's demonstration communities in Ontario, the research team had to pass by the drug dealers 'doing business' outside the front door of the community centre where the new moms' program was housed. In their study of the impact on children of growing up in violent areas, Garbarino, Kostelny and Dubrow (1991) used living in a tumultuous neighbourhood in inner-city Chicago as one of their case studies. A recent concession in the literature on helping disadvantaged populations is that in some communities the devastation facing residents is so extreme that it will overpower any program strategy for children and families (McLoyd, 1998; Schorr, 1997). While these conclusions have been grounded in perceptions of realities in the worst of inner-city neighbourhoods in the United States, there are certainly communities in Canada in which such portraits would be recognized.

In language reminiscent of the 'war on poverty' in North America in the 1970s, and grounded in a deep pessimism about the potential of current public service delivery systems, there is a call for neighbourhood transformation initiatives that join public and private resources, as well as local residents and external experts, in locally controlled human service, economic, and community development (Barry, 1994; Garbarino & Kostelny, 1994; Halpern, 1996; Nelson, 1996; Schorr, 1997). However, there are some cautioning voices. Kahn and Kamerman (1996) point out that neighbourhoods, no matter how successfully organized, simply do not have control over critical economic development resources. Kubisch (1996) highlights the many obstacles to collaboration, even when only the human services are involved.

The standard vehicle for many of these neighbourhood transformation initiatives has been a community development corporation. Schorr (1997) describes these as:

> free-standing, community-based organizations dedicated to the revitalization of a discrete – usually distressed – geographic area ... Their activities typically include the construction and rehabilitation of housing, but most also provide housing-related services, and some do community advocacy and organizing and provide some social services. Some develop commercial real estate and try to bring capital into the neighborhood in support of neighborhood small business. Many have also become vehicles for residents to enter into social networks and address both neighborhood and individual needs. (p. 316)

As examples, the Newark New Community Corporation (Schorr, 1997) has refurbished or built about 2,500 apartments, provides transitional housing, and organizes an array of social services for homeless families, teen moms, victims of domestic violence, and abused or neglected children awaiting permanent placement. They have a credit union; a scholarship fund; after-school, summer, and teen-parent programs; as well as health services, employment training, and intensive family support services.

A Ford Foundation initiative in Milwaukee, Detroit, Hartford, and Memphis (Kahn & Kamerman, 1996) seeks to create broad community partnerships in local neighbourhoods. The approach is intended to be inclusive, involving economic development, job training, education, housing, child care, public safety, and social services. One of its goals is to allow local participatory processes to define the shape of projects.

The Savannah Youth Futures Authority (Schorr, 1997) uses a series of family resource centres as the physical manifestation of their community-building vision. These centres provide a range of health, mental health, educational, and recreational supports as well as opportunities for resident participation. 'Promising data [are] beginning to come in. Black infant mortality has dropped by nearly 45 percent since 1992. Births to Black teens have dropped 12 percent. Foster care placements are down almost 25 percent over the past two years' (p. 343).

MOVING BEYOND PROGRAMS

The pessimism sometimes noted in the literature about the potential of programming for disadvantaged youth is not supported by this review. Rather, we found promising approaches that focused on ameliorating parent–teen relationships, supporting the parents of teenagers, building the social competences of youth, and connecting teens to peers, adults, and the community. Many of the more powerful programs concentrate on several of these areas. Nonetheless, the level of distress in some communities is so high that even the most comprehensive and intensive programs are likely to be overwhelmed. Neighbourhood transformation strategies are being tried in some of these communities.

While many of these promising approaches merit emulation, Cameron and Vanderwoerd (1997a) raise the spectre of a program trap. 'There is no one size fits all program. As we have seen, all ... programs have their strengths and limitations. Thinking in terms of discrete programs is limiting. It creates false choices between one helping system and another' (p. 240). In addition, even the wealthiest of service organizations can create only a small number of stand-alone programs in addition to their core activities.

The best demonstration projects, no matter how good the evidence for superior outcomes and costs, have had little effect on how mainstream service organizations do business. And almost all of the resources currently available for helping youth, or likely to become available in the near future, are invested in these established service organizations. The true challenge of building on what we have learned about helping disadvantaged youth and families becomes one of service organization and delivery system transformation. Cameron and Vanderwoerd (1997a) call for demonstration organizations or delivery systems as the next vital step. Many have identified the broad replication of promising programs and their incorporation into mainstream ways of working as daunting obstacles but as obstacles that should be faced now. The current interest in prevention or empowerment zones (see Chapter 7) reflects this interest in service system transformations.

Part of the difficulty in bringing about change is that we do not want to devalue what is being done well now as we try to incorporate new ways of helping. It is wise to remember that we have no clear blueprints to follow in constructing these new realities. Also, planned organizational change is a slow and complex process and one where skilled help can be an asset. These are very big challenges; however, if we can begin to think creatively about these questions, and to experiment in an informed fashion, more of what we have learned about better ways to help can become available to youth and their families.

CHAPTER SEVEN

Program Implementation and Diffusion

Gary Cameron, Jeff Karabanow, Marie-Claire Laurendeau, and Claire Chamberland

Ziggy's Law: For every complex problem, there is a very simple solution! And it is always wrong!

T. Wilson

INTRODUCTION

No issue is more fundamental in improving benefits than bringing what we have learned into everyday ways of working in the human services. Schorr (1997, p. xiii) sums up the challenge: 'We have learned to create the small exceptions that can change the lives of hundreds. But we have not learned to make the exceptions to the rule to change the lives of millions.' Dryfoos (1997) calls for 'much more intensive and large-scale replication of effective prevention programs, using proven components that cut across categorical domains' (p. 19). Cameron and Vanderwoerd (1997a) argue that we need to disconnect our idea of good child welfare practice from images that standardize agencies and often make their efforts more expensive and less productive. They state that, at present, demonstration organizations and service delivery systems may be more useful than demonstration programs.

Whether programs have proven to be effective or not seems to have little bearing on their ability to survive in recognizable form. For example, the home health visitor program in Elmira, New York, developed by David Olds, despite strong evidence for its effectiveness, 'on the day the program went from university-sponsored to a Medicaid-funded health department program, the nurses' caseloads were doubled, the duration of their visits curtailed, and the families dropped from the rolls when the baby was four months old ... all of the nurses in the original program left' (Schorr, 1997, p. 4). Lerner (1995) reports that about 50 per cent of the programs described by Schorr (1989) as effective were not in existence one year after she visited them. Cameron and Rothery (1985), in their assessment of eight child welfare family support programs, observed that ineffective programs can and do survive and that there was little guidance to help agencies to distinguish promising from less useful efforts. In reviewing programming for adolescents, Dryfoos (1993) points out some interventions that have long since been found not to have any effects are still heavily utilized in the field. Durlack (1995) concurs: 'many seemingly effective programs have never been used in schools ... some programs have simply faded away or been replaced by others for unknown or vague reasons' (p. 71).

Program model drift – or inadvertent movement away from original intentions and basic operating requirements – is a common phenomenon. Cameron and Rothery (1985) discovered that family support programs, particularly in their early stages of development, were under great pressure to gain legitimacy and frequently had difficulty generating appropriate referrals, creating the temptation to work with whatever participants could be recruited. Despite early indications of success, when the Families First Program was replicated across Michigan, deviations from the requirements of the model were seen as posing serious threats to the safety of children. Some intensive family preservation services have shown an ability to reduce the need for out-of-home placements of children and adolescents, yet the difficulty these programs have targeting their services on families at risk of breakdown are well known (Cameron & Vanderwoerd, 1997a; Hayward, Cameron, & Brown, 1998; Hayward, Cameron, & Peirson, 1995; Schorr, 1997).

Many of the programs reporting superior outcomes in the literature received unusual levels of attention and support during the time of their assessment. For example, in Dryfoos's (1993) review of promising programs for disadvantaged adolescents, half of the exemplar programs were implemented by the people who designed them. Schorr (1997) describes the challenge of adapting exemplary programs to everyday settings as finding ways that 'ordinary people can achieve the ends it once took a miracle worker to achieve' (p. xxvii).

Based on her work as a short-term consultant providing training to 186 separate programs, Julia W. Chambliss (April 1998, personal communication on Internet discussion group) argues that 'while local prevention boards may recognize and support the need to implement empirically-validated programs, they have faced almost insurmountable difficulties in doing so.' Rothery and Cameron (1985) use an analogy of small businesses started by local entrepreneurs to describe the program implementation environment in Ontario's child welfare agencies:

> Programs are developed through the independent initiatives of these entrepreneurs (often front-line service professionals). Little guidance is available and difficult decisions must be based on their own best judgement. These individuals invest tremendous energy and commitment into their programs. Program survival, which is often tenuous, depends on their ability to convince the controllers of needed resources of the value of their programs. These people have limited access to technical expertise and few opportunities to benefit from the experiences of other innovators. Like all small business initiatives, some are 'successful' and some 'fail.' However, unlike small businesses, ineffective programs can and do survive and there is currently no practical way for decision makers to distinguish between the more successful and less promising programs. (p. 82)

While the rationale for large-scale replications of promising program approaches with child welfare populations is convincing, the obstacles facing such efforts are formidable, even daunting. Current services have constituencies of tens of thousands of workers trained in traditional methods, and existing legislative and funding frameworks mitigate against experimentation (Cameron & Vanderwoerd, 1997a; Schorr, 1997). The challenge of protecting innovations within bureaucracies frequently wears out their champions (Schorr, 1997). Notwithstanding the magnitude of these challenges, practitioners and scholars are beginning to devote more attention to the requirements of good program implementation and replication. Clarifying what has been learned about good program implementation and replication from these efforts is the purpose of this chapter.

Organization of the Chapter

This discussion focuses on the implementation requirements for single programs as well as the challenges of replicating successful programs in diverse settings or bringing them into established service organizations. The paper is organized around major issues or themes that emerged from this review of the program implementation and program replication literature. It has been supplemented by insights drawn from the project development research in five Canadian projects in which the principal author of this paper has been involved.[1] The emphasis will be on identifying some of the major requirements for good program development and program replication. While the creation of a single program and the replication of a program model in multiple settings are different undertakings, this review found that the requirements for success in both areas have many elements in common. Both processes will be discussed within each theme area. The purpose is not to present a complete model of program development/replication nor a step-by-step manual about how to proceed. Rather, the intent is to identify and discuss key issues and processes that need understanding and attention if we hope to increase the usefulness of prevention programming.

THEME ONE: BALANCING CLARITY AND ADAPTATION

There is a deep tension at the heart of prevention program development. On the one hand, there is a convincing rationale for building on what we have learned about what works best with various populations. The best programs have solid theoretical and empirical foundations, supplying them with a clarity of purpose and methods. Pulling equally strongly is the deeply held conviction in the power and propriety of empowering, participatory program development processes, coupled with the need for programs to be sensitive to cultural and other community differences.

These forces frequently pull programs in different directions. Indeed, participatory processes are a major source of program model drift. On the other hand, lack of professional and local participant acceptance often seriously impedes program development progress, and lack of fit with particular settings or populations can lead to ineffective helping. The debate between these competing requirements can evoke a good

---

1 The five projects are:
   (1) the Family Support Services in Child Welfare Project, which included an assessment of eight family support programs;
   (2) the Parent Mutual Aid Organizations in Child Welfare Project, which created and assessed mutual aid programs in three communities;
   (3) an investigation of five intensive family preservation service programs in four communities;
   (4) the Better Beginnings, Better Futures Prevention Project's program model/project development research for seven communities;
   (5) the Promising Programs and Organizational Realities Project focusing on the issue of bringing promising programs into child welfare agencies.

deal of passion, and finding an appropriate compromise is seldom easy. Yet finding a workable balance is at the heart of good program development and replication.

The Need for a Program Model

A truism in the prevention literature is that future programming should have solid conceptual and empirical underpinnings – there must be clearly articulated reasons why the proposed interventions should be expected to produce the projected results with the populations of interest (Cameron & Vanderwoerd, 1997a; Elias, 1997; Ontario Ministry of Community and Social Services, 1990; Schorr, 1989, 1997). Pure evolutionary processes are not sufficient. Difficult as it may be, there is a need to articulate which program elements are vital to good outcomes and which can be adapted in particular settings (Elias, 1997; Schorr, 1997). These assumptions should be tested empirically.

Many promising programs have such rationales. For example, the Healthy Families America's home health visitor programs 'share a common core. Critical program elements include a standardized assessment tool, intensive services over three to five years with well-defined criteria for increasing or decreasing the frequency of services, limited caseloads, and intensive training and supervision of service providers' (Schorr, 1997, p. 44). Parent Mutual Aid Organizations for child welfare families (Cameron, Hayward, & Mamatis, 1992) incorporate helping elements from informal created networks/mutual aid groups as well as from formal programs with disadvantaged populations requiring scheduled formal activities at least three times a week, supports for consistency of participation, between-meeting member contacts, educational and emotional support resources for members, and member responsibilities for organizational functioning.

The Primary Mental Health Project (Hightower, 1997) is 'best seen as a structural model with four basic elements ... [providing] an overarching emphasis ... Although the PMHP structural model has remained consistent, program implementation has varied ... reducing school adjustment difficulties in a variety of settings' (p. 193). YouthBuild (Schorr, 1997) 'depends on having a set of program ideas that are sound and well-developed through experience, on being able to teach these ideas, and being able to inspire local leadership of very high quality with these ideas' (p. 36). The Prenatal/Early Infancy Project (Olds, 1997a,b) builds on insights from human ecology theory, self-efficacy theory, and attachment theory and specifies operating parameters such as the duration and frequency of program participation as well as the helping processes to be emphasized with families.

The Conservation Company and Public/Private Ventures (1994) conclude from their study of program replication experiences that 'like any new product seeking to build a market, a social prototype worthy of replication must be clear in concept and able to show that it works well' (p. 20). Cowen, Hightower, Johnson, Sarno, and Weissberg (1989) highlight the need for a clear articulation of project goals, philosophy, and procedures as a guide for successful replications. Van der Vegt and Knip (1988) argue that project replication requires clarity about project goals and methods and how these are connected to implementation issues that will have to be faced. In studying replication experiences with the British Burglary Prevention Project, Tilley (1996) stresses the importance of specifying causal mechanisms that lead to program outcomes – in this case, removing parking meters, establishing home watch groups, and targeting already victimized dwellings, resulting in increased perceived risk of apprehension and more difficult entry into houses.

Many family support programs in child welfare agencies are justified by very general and ambiguous program rationales, and program developers have little access to empirical evidence or technical support to guide their efforts (Cameron and Rothery, 1985). Schorr (1997) highlights the costs of this pattern: 'Leaving local initiatives to painstakingly make these discoveries on their own, or to never make them at all, has been a wasteful process and will interfere with further progress in spreading these initiatives ... What these fragile initiatives need is "friendly technical assistance," just as they need friendly research and evaluation' (p. 370). Cameron and Vanderwoerd (1997a) argue that a minimum requirement for credible program development/replication is the use of an explicit program impact framework in which programs have a plausible rationale that is grounded conceptually and empirically and that explains why projected outcomes are reasonable.

The Value of Participation

Participatory processes contribute to good program development/replication in two ways: as a healing factor in prevention helping strategies and as a vehicle to increase the appropriateness and acceptance of prevention projects in local settings. Arguments about the primacy of participatory processes in prevention can be powerfully persuasive for many participants, and accommodating the need for sound program rationales is seldom simple (Cameron & Cadell, 1998). The following view of the role of participatory processes in prevention expressed at a Better Beginnings, Better Futures demonstration site illustrates the value of participation (Cameron & Vanderwoerd, 1997b):

> The involvement and participation of community leaders was the vehicle by which primary prevention objectives were possible ... Prevention programs were developed and evolved because of this continuing process of community involvement. The experience of people working on the front lines in this project is of an intimate connection between resident involvement and prevention outcomes; one becomes possible because of the other. (p. 87)

Empowering participation of neighbourhood residents and program participants in project/program actualization can bring substantial, sometimes transforming, benefits to those for whom such opportunities are created. Occupying valued social roles, learning new skills, receiving recognition for what they are doing, acquiring an expanded network of social connections, and participating in a greater diversity of settings, relating to professionals, public officials, and other power holders on a more equal footing, and enjoying one's influence over important decisions can have a powerful and beneficial impact on the self-images and the daily experiences of active participants, particularly those from disadvantaged settings (Cameron & Vanderwoerd, 1997a). For example, in both the Parent Mutual Aid Organizations in Child Welfare and Better Beginnings, Better Futures demonstration projects, active participants reported great satisfaction with these kinds of opportunities in addition to improvements in their self-confidence and self-esteem (Cameron, Hayward, & Mamatis, 1992; Pancer & Cameron, 1993; Pancer & Foxall, 1998).

Empowering participation of a substantial number of people has been described as an essential ingredient in transforming conditions for disadvantaged groups and communities (Biklen, 1983; Kemp, Whittaker, & Tracy, 1997; Labonté, 1990). In addition, some argue that a prime objective of prevention is to foster self-determination in a fashion that promotes greater fairness and equity (Cochran, 1987; Prilleltensky & Laurendeau, 1994).

Many have emphasized the contribution of program adaptability and local commitment to good program development and replication. For example, in the Improving Social Awareness–Social Problem-Solving

Project (Bruene-Butler, Hampson, Elias, Clabby, & Schuyer, 1997) 'much of the success of this initiative can be attributed to the use of action research methods that allow for multi-year collaboration and direct input from teachers and students' (p. 245). Blumenkrantz (1992), referring to the process of creating a Rites of Passage Experience (ROPE) Program, observes that 'acceptance and participation in a process for program development and implementation is the last critical element. Viable prevention strategies are born and sustained from an ongoing process of collaboration' (p. 92). Weissberg, Kussler, and Gullota (1997) argue that 'a sense of ownership and contribution to the intervention is important not only for adults but also for targeted children. Programs that involve their target audience in the intervention design are more likely to set appropriate ... goals and ... are more likely to flourish than those that adhere to rigid criteria – that is, fidelity' (p. 18).

The developers of the Better Beginnings, Better Futures demonstration sites became convinced that respectful partnerships between local residents and formal service providers, created by getting to know each other personally, having safe environments in which to interact, and possessing a commitment to see things through, were critical contributors to their success in fostering resident participation, cooperation between service organizations, and the development of acceptable prevention programming (Cameron, Vanderwoerd, & Peters, 1995; Pancer & Cameron, 1993).

Others argue that participatory processes augment participants' interest in and commitment to programs (Goldberg, 1995; Goodman, Steckler, Hoover, & Schwartz, 1993). Blumenkrantz (1992) suggests that participatory processes recognize the evolving nature of social interactions and the need to establish structures to guide continuing evaluation and modification of the interventions to respond to changing needs in communities. Abatena (1997) stresses that local participation is essential for community problem-solving in three areas: (1) proper problem diagnosis and needs assessment; (2) sound decision making about relevant and feasible goals and solutions; and (3) successful program implementation. Lerner (1995) suggests that building local commitment and capacities can help to reduce the unfortunate pattern of effective programs not surviving over time.

On the other hand, several recent accounts describe the costs and the difficulties of participatory approaches to project/program development. Participatory processes usually increase the time, expenses, and complexity of decision making (Cameron & Vanderwoerd, 1997b; Goldberg, 1995; Validiserri, Ronald, Aultman, & Curran, 1995). In addition, conflict between nonprofessional and professional participants and among various professional groupings is a common theme in reports describing participatory program development processes (Annie E. Casey Foundation, 1995; Goodman, Steckler, Hoover, & Schwartz, 1993; Pancer & Cameron, 1993; Valdiserri et al., 1995). For example, White and Wehlage (1995), in their discussion of the New Futures Project, describe how front-line workers as well as consumers of services were unable to influence policymaking structures of projects dominated by agency managers and senior public officials. In Better Beginnings, Better Futures, a great emphasis has been given to participatory processes for project development and management. Notwithstanding the benefits that have accrued from these processes, they have absorbed a substantial amount of time and energy at most demonstration sites and have required the modification of 'traditional' methods of administrative decision making to enable the participation of local residents. Negotiating relationships between residents and service providers has been a demanding and frequently controversial challenge at most demonstration sites (Cameron & Vanderwoerd, 1997b; Cameron, Vanderwoerd, & Peters, 1995; Pancer & Cameron, 1993).

Local influences and participatory processes are also a major source of program 'drift' or deviation from prescribed aspects of programs. Hayward, Cameron, and Peirson (1995), in their investigation of intensive family preservation services program development processes at five child welfare and children's mental health settings, discovered that the discretion of individual professionals over referrals to programs resulted in the programs not focusing on families with children at immediate risk of out-of-home placement as originally intended. They also found substantial deviation from the program's intended service delivery parameters from site to site.

Despite the investment of about $10 million in each demonstration community over five years, the New Futures Project's emphasis on locally controlled development processes has not resulted in either greater integration of local service networks or the creation of services and supports that reduced the incidence of problems such as teen pregnancies (Nelson, 1996; Annie E. Casey Foundation, 1995; White & Wehlage, 1995). In her examination of neighbourhood-transformation initiatives in disadvantaged communities, Schorr (1997) observed that projects that relied exclusively on 'bottom-up' or locally determined processes were less successful in creating useful resources than those stressing local-external partnerships and informed oversight of program development processes.

Transactive Structures and Partnerships

The creation of transactive structures and partnerships to guide planned change (Friedmann, 1973) has been suggested as a way to manage the tension between the need for a credible model and the importance of local adaptation. Transactive structures are venues where formal knowledge and local wisdom meet and better decisions are predicted from an on-going process of debate and adaptation. In Better Beginnings, Better Futures, the creation of respectful partnerships developed over time between local residents and service professionals, along with structures fostering on-going dialogue between different types of participants, have been repeatedly identified as an essential project development characteristic (Cameron & Vanderwoerd, 1997b; Cameron, Vanderwoerd, & Peters, 1995; Pancer & Cameron, 1993).

Notwithstanding the merits of partnerships and structures that enable on-going dialogue, some constraints on these participatory processes are suggested. The need for defining a credible program model must be respected, as should clarity about the place of participatory processes in program helping as well as in project/program development. Some effective programs require a minimal amount of local determination, for example, the Elmira home health visitor project (Olds, 1997); while others have empowering participation at the heart of their helping processes – for example, Parent Mutual Aid Organizations (Cameron, Hayward & Mamatis, 1992) – or of their project/program development requirements, such as Better Beginnings, Better Futures (Ontario Ministry of Community and Social Services, 1990).

THEME TWO: TIME, COMPLEXITY, RESOURCE, AND EXPERTISE REQUIREMENTS

Understanding of and respect for the sophisticated demands of good program development and dissemination processes have been relatively absent from our deliberations about how to better help disadvantaged children and families. Scholarship has focused on the conceptual underpinnings of interventions along with evidence of their outcomes, but has given less credence to considerations of the messy challenges of putting these ideas into practice in everyday settings. Equally disturbing is the oft-repeated pattern of investing substantial resources in promising programs yet making little provision to ensure their proper development. The expectation is that these challenges can be solved with existing resources and expertise. Yet the evidence of the dire consequences of this lack of attention is accumulating.

Consequences of Inattention

An exploration of family support programs in child welfare agencies in Ontario (Cameron & Rothery, 1985; Rothery & Cameron, 1985) painted a portrait of program drift and precariousness: some programs responded to the pressures of nonuse by accepting any and all referrals; others were pushed to accept only high-risk families or families in a state of crisis; there was a loss of control over important service parameters (e.g., frequency and duration of service) in some programs; none of these programs were built on formal needs assessments or from reviews of existing theory and evidence but, rather, were based on general impressions of what was needed; program documentation capacity was almost nonexistent; most programs did not have clear guidelines for the kinds of referrals they should accept; program budgets were small and precarious and required constant negotiation; and very few resources were allocated to program development, management, or documentation processes.

A more recent assessment of intensive family preservation programs in three child welfare and two children's mental health settings in Ontario uncovered an inability to involve originally designated populations in these programs and, in one program, substantial drift in prescribed service delivery parameters (Hayward, Cameron, & Brown, 1998; Hayward, Cameron, & Peirson, 1995). Preliminary outcomes suggest that these implementation problems contributed to a lack of superior benefits from involvement in these programs – contrary to what might have been predicted from the outcome evidence for intensive family preservation services in other settings (see the discussion in chapters 5 and 6 in this volume).

Commenting on the lack of success of the Youth Policy Group in New York City, Gray (1995) identified five issues: '(1) inattention to structures during implementation; (2) failure of group members to understand their different institutional cultures; (3) pervasive historical tensions; (4) institutional disincentives for implementation; (5) failure to build a constituency' (pp. 84–85).

The New Futures initiative, despite a five-year development time frame and the investment of an average of $10 million in each participating city, did not produce either deep transformations in service delivery systems or better outcomes for children as anticipated. In explaining these findings, the Center for the Study of Social Policy (1995) observed that 'no one had a recipe that spelled out how to implement cross-agency reforms ... Perhaps the single biggest lesson from New Futures is how little is known about the nuts and bolts of restructuring service systems in a way that cuts across single programs and individual agencies ... Our collective rhetoric about cross-system change is far ahead of any operational knowledge of how to get from here to there' (pp. xii–xiii).

One of the strongest messages from the program development and replication literature is the importance of preparing for the substantial time and effort required by almost all program creation initiatives. A parallel message is that program development and replication are very complex challenges. A focus on intervention content is not sufficient; specialized knowledge and experience in project/program creation and management processes are required.

Time and Effort

Schorr (1997) observed that 'most successful school reforms emphasize the long-term nature of successful staff development efforts and the importance of feedback, trial and error, and problem-solving over time' (p. 255). Similarly, developers of the Sandtowne Community Development Corporation commented that 'no one realized how hard and time consuming it would be to nurture the neighborhood leadership and build the capacity of existing community organizations and service providers to implement radically new program activities in ways that could sustain them over time' (Schorr, 1997, p. 324).

Better Beginnings, Better Futures demonstration sites needed from three to five years to have most of their required project development elements – such as administrative structures, resident participation, service provider involvement, and prevention programs – in place in a reasonably stable fashion (Cameron & Vanderwoerd, 1997b, Cameron, Vanderwoerd, & Peters, 1995; Pancer & Cameron, 1993). In the Parent Mutual Aid Organizations (PMAO) in Child Welfare Project, sites required between one and two years to create a minimum level of program activities and participatory management structures. By the end of the third

330   Section II: Interventions

year, the member control elements of the PMAO were just beginning to become important (Cameron, Hayward, & Mamatis, 1992).

In his examination of the requirements for successful organizational change, Michael Beer (1980) estimates that a major change process requires about five years from initiation to stable acceptance. Bruene-Butler and colleagues (1997), based on their experiences with replicating the Improving Social Awareness–Social Problem-Solving Project, estimated that 'institutionalizing a comprehensive program generally takes 3 to 7 years' (p. 256). From his efforts with the Rites of Passage Experience (ROPE) Program, Blumenkrantz (1992) states that 'for the most part, nothing in our educational experience prepares us for understanding the time it takes for anything new to take hold and become embedded in a community ... you cannot count on it being engineered according to a calendar' (pp. 100–101).

Demanding Complexity

A complementary theme in the literature is the complex and demanding requirements of successful program development and replication processes. For example, Cowen, Hightower, Johnson, Sarno, and Weissberg (1989), drawing from their work with the Primary Mental Health Project, suggest that 'state-level program dissemination requires time and effort, a comprehensive planning framework, a strong emphasis on training, consultation, and program monitoring procedures' (p. 314). Project coordinators/managers in Better Beginnings, Better Futures articulated the pressures they felt, along with the tremendous effort required of them and others, to pull the diverse aspects of the projects together – such as gaining community acceptance, fostering resident involvement, coordinating work with existing service organizations, building administrative structures and procedures, and developing new programs (Cameron & Vanderwoerd, 1997b). Project developers with the Parent Mutual Aid Organizations echoed these sentiments: 'It's been very easy to lose faith with this ... we worked for two years ... and basically in the last six or eight months I've seen what makes it all worthwhile ... and I almost left three times in the middle of it' (Cameron & Cadell, 1998).

Pressures of Start-Up

The early stages of project/program creation have been compared to 'building an airplane and flying it' at the same time (Mickelson, Yon, &

Carlton-Lalley, 1995). Everything is being built at the same time and for the first time. In many instances, participants will be entering new areas of responsibility and learning as they go – often with minimal support or guidance. The first few years of development are times of trial and error and high levels of stress and struggle before basic organizational and program components have attained some definition and stability. In both the Better Beginnings, Better Futures (Cameron & Vanderwoerd, 1997b) and the Parent Mutual Aid Organizations (Cameron, Hayward, & Mamatis, 1992) projects, the first years where characterized by both creativity and struggle as project development teams' talents and convictions were stretched by new challenges (Cameron & Cadell, 1998).

Nelson (1996) emphasizes that New Futures initiatives require a great deal of front-end time to accomplish initial developmental tasks. The Annie E. Casey Foundation (1995) pointed to 'the difficulty of simultaneously running programs and pursuing the systems analysis, policy evaluation, public education, planning and advocacy necessary' (p. 2) to initiate a New Futures project.

Creating Legitimacy

Many program developers stress the importance of selling and building support for new initiatives. For instance, three studies of replication experiences with the Social Decision-Making and Problem-Solving Project confirmed that 'long-term, high-fidelity institutionalization was more likely when there was an active group consisting of those who implemented the program and who were closest to its impacts ... Essential among the activities of such groups were providing a sustaining vision of the program, offering encouragement, and setting up in-house procedures to monitor its progress and improve its effectiveness' (Elias 1997, p. 276).

In their study of eight family support programs, Cameron and Rothery (1985) found that 'a dominant theme in the development of these programs was the need for continuous efforts to explain and sell the new approach to child protection personnel' (p. 273). 'Program informants saw the need to properly explain the family support programs to management and to work at assuring their continued support of the program' (p. 290). The Conservation Company and Public/Private Ventures (1994) propose that 'to work best, replication needs a champion, convinced of the program's goals and committed to its expansion' (p. 32). Cowen, Hightower, Johnson, Sarno, and Weissberg's (1989) analysis of the Primary Mental Health Project identified the importance of influential leadership in project dissemination. They also saw a need for a full-time coordinator who would be involved in recruiting, gaining funding, consulting, visiting sites, and active networking. Heller and Firestone's (1995) analysis of the replication and institutionalization of the Social Problem-Solving Program in multiple school districts emphasized the importance of both champions and project managers providing and selling a vision, obtaining resources, providing encouragement and recognition, adapting standard operating procedures, monitoring change, and handling disturbances.

The Importance of Initial Personnel Selection

The critical importance of initial personnel choices for a program has been demonstrated repeatedly. In the Parent Mutual Aid Organizations in Child Welfare Project, the personality and talents of the program developer at each site had a dramatic effect on the pace and content of accomplishments:

> Certain worker traits and aptitudes did appear to be associated with more successful program development in the Demonstration Project. It was clear that the biases the program workers brought with them to the job largely determined how they worked with members. Workers were generally not able to modify the main ingredients of their preferred approach to program development. (Cameron, Hayward, & Mamatis, 1992, p. 119)

Similarly, in the Better Beginnings, Better Futures Project, the different characteristics of the project managers/coordinators at each site had a great impact on site priorities and ways of working (Cameron & Vanderwoerd, 1997b). This perception is supported by Hightower's (1997) analysis of the Primary Mental Health Project: 'An extremely important step in the start-up process is selection of the personnel who are central to the program's operation ... Selecting the right child associates with the right characteristics is absolutely critical' (pp. 195–196).

Struggle and Resistance Are Normal

The strength of the emotions expressed and the vehemence of the struggles that surface in many community development or organizational change processes shock the uninitiated. Conflict and confusion are not uncommon in project/program creation and dissemination; they are normal occurrences that require skilled attention to minimize serious disruptions.

The power of resistence in established service systems, and in some neighbourhoods, is enormous and has often stopped the introduction of programs or deformed them in an essential fashion. For example, Arella (1993) describes directing the Multi-Service Adolescent Program: 'This is an extremely difficult program to manage ... multiple missions and differing professional traditions required substantially more staff training and higher level decision making than might have been originally anticipated' (p. 242). In New Futures, 'an array of programs was proposed to reduce the number of dropouts. These had to be negotiated in a process that was inevitably conflict ridden and political ... The difficulty of building consensus in communities was almost always underestimated' (White & Wehlage, 1995, p. 28).

In the Parent Mutual Aid Organizations in Child Welfare Project (Cameron, Hayward, & Mamatis, 1992), resistance by a senior manager successfully impeded the growth of a local PMAO until she moved on and was replaced by a more receptive manager. Conflict between members and differences with professionals from the host child welfare agency were challenging parts of project development at each site. In Better Beginnings, Better Futures, relations between local residents and service professionals required on-going negotiation. One Better Beginnings demonstration site experienced persistent tension with the expectations of its host board of education, eventually resulting in the project seeking an alternative host organization (Cameron & Jeffey, 1999).

THEME THREE: THE CENTRALITY OF SUPPORT AND DIRECTION

It is no accident that so many of the successful programs in the literature are demonstration projects (Cameron & Vanderwoerd, 1997a; Dryfoos, 1997). These projects receive the careful attention of the people who conceived them and typically have a level of development support and monitoring not available to on-going programs. The program development literature is unequivocal about the pivotal importance of a development infrastructure in building and replicating programs. Two broad functions have been identified for these infrastructures. The first is encouragement and expert guidance to deal with the myriad of organizational challenges involved in creating a complex program/project, along with training and consultation about intervention procedures.

The second is direction to assure that quality conditions are maintained in developing the project and working with program participants. This includes the responsibility and ability to intervene if concerns arise.

The Need for Infrastructure

Lizbeth Schorr (1997) provides numerous illustrations of the role of a support and direction infrastructure in the creation and dissemination of promising programs. For the YouthBuild programs, a formalized network of existing sites was created to set standards and protect the core vision against destabilizing influences. She argues that 'new programs must develop a sense of mission, of belonging to something larger than one's own isolated efforts, and must have access to people who have successfully implemented programs' (p. 36). The National Council for the Prevention of Child Abuse in the United States established Healthy Families America (HFA) to create a strategic plan and initial training capabilities to foster replications of Hawaii's Healthy Start successful home visiting program. 'As with most conscientious replication efforts ... [there was a need for] designing a strong system of quality controls ... [as well as] certifying programs by granting or withdrawing the use of HFA trademarked name' (Schorr, 1997, pp. 44–45). For the successful Beacon Schools initiatives, 'none was left to its own devices to start from scratch and to cope in isolation with the difficulties that came up ... [the] Youth Development Institute [was created and] became a continuing source of support, technical assistance, and documentation to the Beacons' (Schorr, 1997, p. 53).

Elias (1997) reaches a similar conclusion based on experiences with the Social Decision-Making and Problem-Solving Project:

> To the extent to which an innovation is operator dependent and has few technical features, guidelines for making the proper adaptation without rendering key elements of a program ineffective are quite scarce. This validates ... the benefits that derive from having on-site consultants experienced with implementing one's innovation in related settings to assist with the kinds of configural decision making and anticipation that will be necessary if the effort is to proceed. (p. 270)

In the Life-Skills Training Program, project staff observe randomly chosen classroom implementations of the program and, if appropriate, offer feedback and advice to prevent program drift in the early stages of development (Dusenbury & Botvin, 1990).

Training of Program Providers

A special focus of the need for a support and direction infrastructure is the importance of good training of program delivery personnel in the helping methods central to the program model. Schorr (1997) observes that 'staff of successful programs are trained and supported to provide high-quality, responsive services ... discretion requires excellent training' (p. 10). For example, the Primary Mental Health Project has created, and refined numerous times, a comprehensive training program for its new child associates (Hightower, 1997). In the Rites of Passage Experience Program, training of a core group 'provides a critical foundation, with their support and understanding of the requirements and complexity of the primary prevention initiative; this core group is then able to become committed to and take responsibility for the implementation of this promising prevention strategy' (Blumenkrantz, 1992, pp. 90–91). The evaluation by Olds, Henderson, Chamberlin, and Tatelbaum (1986) of Olds's home-health visitor program for new mothers emphasizes the importance of training home visitors to foster close relationships with participating mothers and to ensure that the theory underpinning service content and service-delivery methods are understood and respected.

THEME FOUR: THE POWER OF ESTABLISHED PROCEDURES

It is much more likely for established systems to transform promising programs to fit their expectations than for the innovations to influence everyday ways of working in established settings. Whoever has the responsibility for the day-to-day delivery of the intervention, or determines its acceptance into established relationships, exercises great power over whether a new program will be implemented as required for its effectiveness or, in some instances, at all. Accordingly, the program development and dissemination literature places great emphasis on the importance of both host organization and community selection as well as on negotiating acceptance and modifying existing procedures to allow innovations a chance to prosper.

Schorr (1997) argues that successful dissemination of promising programs into established agencies involves 'not ignoring the institutional context, and ... not leaving the responsibility for creating a more hospitable context to the front-line people, who are not in a position to change the wider environment' (p. 30). She identifies three basic defusion strategies: (1) choose a setting welcoming to the innovation; (2) look for a niche for development that has fewer rules and other constraints; and (3) invest time and resources to modify existing procedures and attitudes to be more receptive to the innovation. She adds that 'no one should underestimate how fundamentally discretion in program design and front-line practice goes against the bureaucratic grain' (p. 78). Morrill (1996) concurs: 'The character of the existing delivery system includes significant interconnected and self-reinforcing features, such as categorical program fragmentation and categorical funding. The reformers are continually faced with a never-ending set of issues that forces them back towards the status quo and eventually exhausts them' (p. 192).

Selecting and Negotiating Host Settings

Not every organization or neighbourhood is an appropriate host for a new approach to helping children and families. For example, in the Parent Mutual Aid Organizations in Child Welfare Demonstration Project, the demonstration site with the most active support by senior managers, the most receptive agency niche (a family resource centre affiliated with the agency), and the highest investment of additional resources from the host agency developed much quicker than the other sites and the demands placed on project developers were less stressful (Cameron, Hayward, & Mamatis, 1992). In Better Beginnings, Better Futures, one site with a local board of education as its host reported chronic difficulties finding suitable flexibility within the board's administrative procedures and marshalling consistent support for the continuation of the project under the board's auspices (Cameron & Vanderwoerd, 1997b). In the Promising Programs and Organizational Realities Project, feedback from front-line child protection personnel from three local child welfare agencies, as well as from agency liaison personnel from the local Ministry of Community and Social Services, made it evident that bringing promising programs into the everyday world of child welfare would encounter significant resistance and would require careful planning and implementation (Cameron & Vanderwoerd, 1997a).

Commins and Elias (1991) identify characteristics that should be sought in a host school for an innovative program: (1) disincentives external to the school are at least balanced by external incentives; (2) relationships among teachers are good; (3) the values of school personnel are congruent with those of the innovation; (4) there is an active group within the school who can serve as champions and leaders for the innovation; (5) there is consistent support from the principal for the innovation; and (6) there is top-level support from the school district for the innovation and a willingness to make plans for its long-term continuance.

Lessons drawn from the New Futures Project about selecting host communities for neighbourhood service delivery system transformations are similar: (1) core leadership is required; (2) there is capacity to manage a complex initiative; (3) key actors are convinced about the need to transform existing arrangements and committed to the goals of the innovation project; and (4) there is a lead agency with credibility and adequate authority (Nelson, 1996, p. 174).

The importance of identifying and supporting credible local leadership receives strong emphasis in the literature on program creation and replication (Commins & Elias, 1991; Dryfoos, 1993; Mickelson, Yon, & Carlton-Lalley, 1995; Pentz, 1996; Zetlin, 1995). For example, Gottfredson, Fink, Skroban, and Gottfredson (1997) state that having appropriate leaders was one of the most consistent findings from the educational change research. In the replications of the Primary Mental Health Project, Cowen, Hightower, Johnson, Sarno, and Weissberg (1989) stress the importance of having the support, and continued involvement, of government representatives with appropriate authority. For the Social Decision-Making and Problem-Solving Project, implementation studies show 'that full institutionalization was related primarily to leadership roles being filled consistently and by multiple individuals usually from varied roles' (Elias, 1997, p. 276).

In a case study of a prevention initiative in an educational setting, Gottfredson and colleagues (1997) attribute the lack of successful program implementation to the resistance of teachers and counsellors to attempts to modify their practices and to a lack of continuity of key managers in the school during this time. In their study of a project to educate homeless children, Mickelson, Yon, and Carlton-Lalley (1995) lament the negative consequences of receiving little support from policymakers or from educators within the school system. White and Wehlage (1995) document the resistance to the New Futures Projects by those who perceived them as challenging their professional expertise and discretion.

The general lesson is that innovative projects do not survive in hostile environments. Investments in selecting a welcoming setting, in creating receptive conditions for the initiative, as well as in sustaining this support over time are critical components of sound program creation and dissemination strategies. Resistance is a normal reaction to innovations that are perceived as threats to existing ways of working or prerogatives. It is essential to anticipate such reactions and to intervene to neutralize their impact on new ways of working. This underlines the importance of investing in appropriate development infrastructures for new program creation and diffusion.

THEME FIVE: CROSSING BOUNDARIES AND FOSTERING INNOVATION

Participants in our study claimed that there needs to be more investment in intersectoral cooperation. On the other hand, despite the undeniable importance of crossing professional and formal service boundaries, the available research outlines four reasons for caution in accepting the immediate relevance of broad service integration strategies to improved helping:

1. To date, research does not show a close connection between formal service integration and better outcomes for children and families.
2. Many promising programs and helping strategies differ substantially from those used in mainline services systems, suggesting a need for creating new ways of helping in addition to streamlining established bureaucracies.
3. The rigidities and the large number of existing rules and regulations, as well as the bureaucratic cultures of government departments and many human service organizations, have been identified as major obstacles to improved services for children and families. It is unclear how formal service integration projects might resolve problems of excessive rigidity and territoriality (Schorr, 1997).
4. Service integration initiatives have proved to be extraordinarily complex and to incorporate priority focuses of their own – such as reducing costs or elaborating new control procedures – which often have little to do with nurturing innovation or supporting promising programming.

Multiple Impediments

Some of the loudest laments in the literature decry the often insurmountable impediments that existing systems – legislative mandates, funding criteria, operating rules and procedures, professional cultures, and organizational/bureaucratic self-interests – represent for even the best-justified and amply supported program innovations. One of our study's informants from British Columbia observed that 'child welfare ... tends to produce specialization among the practitioners. While specialist skills are needed, they tend to produce rigidities within the services which are not easily modified. The Gove Report's Mathew's Story provides many examples of such rigidities.' Another respondent in our study complained that 'much of the declaration of principles that deal with family enhancing and family support and prevention, when translated into legislation, become things the agency MAY do, and all the things that deal with protection are things the agency SHALL do.'

As mentioned, in the Promising Programs and Organizational Realities Project, one of the strongest sources of resistence to experimentation within child welfare came from regional government representatives who were adamant that agencies under their supervision adhere to existing rules and regulations. More recently, concerns about the safety of children under the supervision of child welfare agencies in Ontario have resulted in more detailed rules and procedures about how to conduct risk assessments, coupled with higher levels of central monitoring of conformance to these prescriptions. Whether or not these procedures have the potential to more adequately protect children living in extremely dangerous circumstances, they are apt to lessen discretion and to increase rigidity in child welfare responses.

Our analysis indicates a need to expand the vision of child welfare from the current legalistic and investigative emphasis on child protection to a broader and more helpful purpose of improving child well-being (Lindsey, 1995). For a large majority of families coming to child welfare agencies, child, family, and community well-being are inseparable. In order to prevent the worst from happening, we are making it increasingly difficult for most families to receive the positive supports that would be both helpful and appreciated.

Talking about the nature of public bureaucracies in general, Schorr (1997) states bluntly that in order to 'eliminate the possibility that public servants will do anything wrong ... we make it virtually impossible for them to do anything right' (p. 65). She adds that many of the solutions currently in vogue – services integration, privatization, contracting out, reliance on market discipline, reliance on private charities – will not solve the bureaucracy problem. What will be required is a taming of bureaucratic constraints and a renewed commitment to public services. Morrill (1996) dramatizes these concerns: 'Few from prior waves [of reforms] ... have survived in any form, and the objectives that they embodied remain as distant from the common practice – particularly of public agencies – as ever' (p. 187). Kelman (1990) concludes that 'the case must be made that the maze of rules, clearances, and limits on discretion and judgement that compromise the bureaucratic paradigm exact a terrible toll ... If we are to begin changing the public sector, we need to argue that the cost is too high' (p. 57).

Service Integration

Impressive claims have been made about the potential benefits of greater formal service integration, including less waste of scarce resources, easier access to services, more-responsive service systems, greater consistency and fairness in responses to requests for help, and more effective services (Beatrice, 1990; Gans & Horton, 1975; Taylor, Brooks, Phanindis, & Rossmo, 1991). Nonetheless, there is a lack of agreement about the nature of service integration, how to best implement it, and whether the benefits warrant the effort (Cameron, Vanderwoerd, & Peters, 1995).

Pandiani and Maynard (1993) conclude from their review of the research that 'despite the intuitive and common sense appeal of interagency collaboration, the results reported in the literature on its effectiveness are checkered at best' (p. 87). While a few studies suggest some positive effects on service delivery and costs (Bruner, 1991; VanderSchie, Wagenfield, & Worgress, 1987), there are more studies and reviews questioning service integration's impact, particularly on improved services and better outcomes for service participants (Aiken, Dewar, DiTomaso, Hage, & Zeitz, 1975; Deber, Rondeau, & Beatty, 1990; Frumkin, Imershein, Chackerian, & Martin, 1983; Gans & Horton, 1975; Oliver, 1990; Pandiani & Maynard, 1993; Redburn, 1997; Runkle-Hooyman, 1976; Weiss, 1981; Wharf, 1994). Rotheram-Borus (1997) concludes that 'the data [on service integration] have not supported the importance of this factor for improving children's outcomes ... [it] does appear to be a strategy for cutting the costs of delivering mental health services' (p. 139).

Stories of the difficulties confronted in efforts to foster cross-organizational collaborations in the human services are common. Early in the Better Beginnings, Better Futures Project, local demonstration site representatives expressed their frustration with the ambiguity of the service integration concept and the lack of guidelines for creating greater service integration in their communities. While their efforts did result in more cooperative undertakings, and in new resources being created in each demonstration community, there were no examples of the merging or the transfer of long-term administrative control over agency mandates or resources (Cameron, Vanderwoerd, & Peters, 1995).

Similarly, seven years after the inception of the New Futures Project, the sponsoring foundation concluded that 'comprehensive reform of service systems is the path of most resistance ... vested interests in current practice, fiscal constraints and political risks [were able to undermine and minimize system change]' (Schorr, 1997, p. 316). The sponsoring Annie E. Casey Foundation (1995) concluded that 'if real authority to collectively allocate resources, decategorize program rules, and delegate authority across systems is not given upfront to collaborative governing bodies, this power will not emerge. Collaboratives that begin as information sharing will stay information sharing' (p. 12).

Transforming Organizations and Delivery Systems

The literature is clearer about the impediments to service systems change than about how to move ahead. Yet there is increasing recognition that a fundamental challenge is how to transform existing ways of working.

What follows are some preliminary conjectures about the process of moving toward a more powerful and responsive system for helping disadvantaged children, families, and neighbourhoods:

1. We need to support bounded organizational and delivery system experiments that focus on bringing helping principles from promising programs into everyday ways of helping disadvantaged children and families.
2. For such experiments, we require procedures to circumvent or waive existing rules and procedures governing funding allocations and service delivery.
3. Barriers between agencies and service sectors have to be bridged to enable more holistic helping to take place.

4. Professional, bureaucratic, and political cultures must be constrained to allow more empowering partnerships to be created between paid helpers and other project participants, including those using helping programs.
5. In some experiments, there has to be an integration of economic, political, and social concerns.
6. Powerful supporters and champions for these experiments are needed to overcome obstacles and to maintain momentum.
7. Ample time (perhaps from five to ten years) must be allocated for such experiments, and appropriate and adequate resources to support the planned change process is essential to success.

There are several reasons for the urgency of bounded organization and delivery system experiments. First, it is essential to move beyond specific program models, no matter how promising. The broader and more important puzzle is what helping elements should be available in a given neighbourhood, organization, or delivery system and how these elements can be marshalled on behalf of children, families, or groups. Second, experience has taught us that too broad a scope for reform increases the strength of opposition to the changes and easily overwhelms what we know how to do. The struggles of the New Futures and, to a lesser extent, the Better Beginnings, Better Futures Projects illustrate some of the costs of a focus for planned change that is too ambitious. Third, despite what has been learned about promising programs, we do not know what reformed organizations and delivery systems might include or how they might operate. In particular, there is no clarity about the proper balance and relationship between the supportive programming reviewed in this volume and the investigative/apprehension services currently central to child welfare. Nor is there any consensus about what service systems should be involved or what the appropriate organizational or community host settings would be. Fourth, there is much that we do not know about creating partnerships between divergent formal helpers as well as between paid helpers and program participants/community representatives. Finally, the details of good helping strategies will need to vary across populations and settings. An unequivocal lesson from the past twenty years is to beware of single solutions to complex problems, notwithstanding their political and emotional appeal. The time, resource, and knowledge demands of these undertakings require a healthy respect and some humility about what we know how to do.

In a bounded experiment, an organization, a coalition of organizations, or a community would apply for waivers from existing rigid procedures. Such a proposal must include adequate consideration of the time and expert support needed for the planned change process, and of to the requirements of the new program and helping strategies. Assistance, generally in the form of a coalition of selected power holders who are strongly committed to the experiment, will be required to overcome the bureaucratic obstacles to working differently, to trouble-shoot, and to maintain support for the experiment. In addition, there must be ample provision for a credible process and outcome assessment of the experiment and assurance of a wide diffusion of what is learned from the demonstration project. Finally, past experiences indicate the value of a prior commitment to continuing and building on the demonstration model, at least in the host settings, should it prove to be superior to previous ways of working. Without protection, even the most successful of projects will be transformed quickly by established interests, once the special focus on the demonstration period ceases.

In the Families First Program in Michigan, 'a Barriers Busters board [was created] to grant waivers to remove regulations that hinder collaborative service delivery and [there was] a requirement that every community create a multipurpose board to coordinate all human services in the county' (Schorr, 1997, p. 112). Schorr (1997) also describes the Los Angeles Family Preservation and Family Support Networks, 25 networks of churches, boys' and girls' clubs, daycare centres, and neighbourhood organizations created in communities where the child welfare statutory placement rates were the highest. The roles and responsibilities of each member of a network are defined and each network must identify a lead agency. Networks are held accountable to a set of standards, and changes have been made to how money and resources are allocated. Local networks are also supported to increase their management capabilities.

The United States Advisory Board on Child Abuse and Neglect's 'top priority recommendation was for the creation of Prevention Zones – model neighbourhoods in which intensive efforts are made to facilitate neighbours helping neighbours and to promote economic and social development for the purpose of preventing child abuse and neglect' (Melton & Barry, 1994a, p. 8). The endorsement of prevention/empowerment zones as a focus for experimentation and intensive investments in children and families is relatively new in the literature (Fuchs & Thompson, 1994; Garbarino & Kostelny, 1994; Kahn & Kamerman, 1996).

Cameron and Vanderwoerd (1997) caution that it is not yet clear how desirable or feasible it would be to put the ideas from promising programs into everyday practice. Yet, they add, 'if we cannot begin to think creatively about these questions and to experiment in an informed fashion, much of what has been learned about helping disadvantaged children and families over the past twenty years must remain marginal to the daily work of child welfare' (p. 246).

BEGINNING LESSONS

Program implementation that produces desired results presents complicated understanding and application challenges. In practice, even the most rudimentary requirements of sound implementation are too often neither understood nor accepted. To begin to take more than marginal advantage of promising programming for disadvantaged children and families, much greater attention and investment in credible program creation and replication processes are essential. As a beginning point in this process, the following points merit careful attention:

1. Articulating a program model: Whenever possible, programs should build on available theory and research. At a minimum, deliberate use should be made of a program impact framework linking the life circumstances of program participants, program service content and operating parameters, and program outcomes. An attempt should be made to identify those program elements vital to success and those characteristics open to adaptation. The role of participatory processes in the program helping model should be described.
2. Identifying participatory development processes: There should be a clear description of the role of local adaptation and legitimacy building in project/program creation and how these processes are to be managed. This should include a consideration of how participatory processes are to be balanced with the need for a credible intervention model.
3. Allowing adequate time: Experience demonstrates that even moderately complex program/project creation and organizational/delivery system change require from three to seven years from initiation to stability. In addition, particular provisions have to be made for higher levels of stress and difficulties during the first few years of development.
4. Creating a support and overseeing infrastructure: Good project/pro-

gram development/replication processes demand an adequate investment in planned-change expertise. Informed guidance from staff and others familiar with the development processes will be instrumental in increasing success. Training support, technical assistance, and help with obtaining and maintaining legitimacy are required. Structures and processes to sustain a project/program vision, to set standards, and to monitor and assure proper development, including a capacity to correct deviations that threaten effectiveness, promote good project/program development and diffusion. Of particular impact is the selection and support of initial project/program personnel.

5. Selecting receptive settings: Projects/programs will not prosper in hostile or ill-prepared environments. Not all organizations or communities will be willing or able to welcome and sustain an innovation. Care should be taken in selecting host organizations and communities. Factors identified as important in making choices about host settings include having values congruent with those of the project/program; possessing adequate management capacities; receiving support from key power holders as well as from staff and others who will have to implement the change; demonstrating a history of productive relations between the partners involved in the change; and identifying a credible lead agency. In addition, investments have to be made in negotiating acceptance and creating legitimacy for the projects/programs in the host settings.

6. Facilitating innovation: Existing procedures and self-interests typically represent imposing barriers to new methods of working. Time and effort are required to create space in which experimentation is possible. Procedures for waiving existing rules and regulations need to be put in place along with strategies to cross professional and agency boundaries. Teams of strategically placed managers and public officials have been effective in some projects in breaking down such barriers. Demonstration or prevention zones have been proposed as focuses for experimentation and intensive investment in helping disadvantaged children and families.

This chapter has emphasized the importance of moving from demonstration programs to demonstration organizations and delivery systems; from discrete exemplary programs benefiting small numbers of participants to the transformation of mainline services where almost all of the potentially available resources are to be found. A caveat is that reforms of great scope increase the resistance to change and can easily overtax our capacity to successfully manage change. Well-planned and bounded systems experiments have been suggested as appropriate focuses for our energies at this point.

Promising programs typically differ substantially from common helping methods in established service organizations. It is equally true that the methods of project/program creation and replication associated with success bear little resemblance to everyday ways of promoting new initiatives. Achieving better outcomes for disadvantaged children and families will require credible helping strategies in partnership with adequate development structures and procedures.

SECTION III

Aboriginal Context and Interventions

CHAPTER EIGHT

A Circle of Healing: Family Wellness in Aboriginal Communities

Ed Connors and Frank Maidman

The prophecies of Aboriginal peoples told them that they would encounter the people from Europe, that they would be introduced to a new way of living, and that they would lose their way of life for a period of time. These teachings also told them that they would experience many forms of ill health and that many of their people would die before this time ended. However, these prophecies also offer hope because they tell them that a time of healing will come when they will once again find their way and begin again to walk the path of health. At this time Aboriginal peoples will begin to thrive in a true state of health and will lead the way for many other races to recapture their original knowledge about how to live in peace, balance, and harmony with all of Creation. We will then have come full circle to health and healing.

First Nations communities on reserves constitute the largest number of tribal communities in Canada at present. While these reserve communities differ from one another in many ways, they are similar in that they are all examples of tribal communities. The tribal community offers an environment which is different socially, economically, and politically from most other communities in Canada. Although First Nations people in Canada do not commonly refer to their communities as tribal, this term will be used in the context of this chapter to reflect the relationships between First Nations communities in Canada and tribal communities around the world.

From the time of sustained contact with Europeans five hundred years ago, Aboriginal communities in North America have been transformed in varying degrees by the experiences of acculturation (Berry, 1990). Some communities remain closely attached to traditional lifestyles while others co-exist with non-Native society, considerably distanced from their tribal roots. However, even the most assimilated communities maintain connections with their tribal roots and continue to be influenced by traditional beliefs.

THE ROOTS OF TRIBAL CULTURE: HOLISTIC THOUGHT

There is a growing acceptance within the behavioural sciences that culture is influential in shaping our present-day perceptions and behaviours (McGoldrick, Pearce, & Giordano, 1982). Some of the most convincing evidence for this can be found within the Native cultures. In the case of North American Indians, culture has been responsible for shaping a shared world-view or form of thought that is quite different from the world-view of most people of European descent. In brief, Aboriginal people have viewed the world from a holistic perspective for thousands of years.

When one examines the world-views of the Aboriginal peoples, it becomes clear that these philosophies have emerged from tribal experiences. These experiences have been translated to explain the interdependence between the environment, people, and the spirit. These understandings have instructed Aboriginal peoples on how to maintain a balanced co-existence with all of Creation in order that all may survive. This form of thought is often symbolized by the sacred circle or medicine wheel, which contains the teachings about the interconnection among all of Creation. The circle is a symbol that represents the knowledge offered by holistic world-views shared by Aboriginal peoples. From this perspective, elements that affect change in a person are simultaneously seen as impacting on the person's family, community, nation, and surrounding environment.

Our ancestors evolved these understandings over thousands of years of observation of interdependent relationships that were:

> based upon a very simple and pragmatic understanding of their presence on this earth. If they failed to consider what the environment had to offer, how much it could give, and what times it was prepared to do this – they would simply die. (Clarkson, Morrissette, & Regallet, 1992, p. 4)

It is around this basic understanding of interdependence that an entire system of beliefs has evolved. These beliefs serve to inform individuals of their purpose for existence and the part that they are to play in order to preserve and maintain a state of balance or equilibrium within the universe. The state of balance is also a central characteristic of Aboriginal beliefs about health and healthy development.

Tribal societies offer an organizational structure that promotes supportive, mutually protective relationships that are based on the seven commonly held values of wisdom, love, respect, bravery, honesty, humility, and truth, as explained in the following Aboriginal proverb:

SEVEN SACRED GIFTS
To Cherish Knowledge is to Know WISDOM
To Know LOVE is to Know Peace
To Honour All of the Creation is to Have RESPECT
BRAVERY is to Face the Foe with Integrity
HONESTY in Facing a Situation is to be Brave
HUMILITY is to Know Yourself as a Sacred Part of Creation
TRUTH is to Know all of These Things.

(Anonymous)

These gifts are understood to be the core values or teachings from the Creator. The image of the Creator within First Nations is one of a Great Kind Spirit, or in the Ojibway language, Kitchi-Manitou.

Respectful, sharing, caring environments ensure that all members of the tribal group are part of an interdependent system of relationships that provides maximum protection for its members. The beliefs that provide the social order for these communities establish environments of total inclusion. In other words, everything that has been created has a purpose within the circle of creation. These communities, usually numbering less than 1,000 members, value all of their members equally and recognize their unique contributions to the survival of the group. Their values support respectful relationships in which no one uses power to interfere with the choices an individual makes regarding her or his own life.

Based on what we know about tribal societies, it would appear that self-destructive behaviours and aggression toward other members of the tribal group are minimized by the social structures that are designed to ensure the survival of the group. Obviously, within interdependent communities any uncontrolled aggressive behaviour expressed within the community is viewed by all members as a threat to the entire group and is therefore checked by its members.

It is not a coincidence that we chose to maintain our tribal lifestyles for the majority of the time that we have existed on this planet. There is considerable evidence that supports the belief that tribal societies in their natural state offer healthier environments than civilized societies. The social organization provided within civilized society does not offer the degree of protection and safeguards from internal violence that tribal society once did. In comparison to civilized societies, tribal societies that have remained relatively untouched by civilized society have remained comparatively nonviolent and protective of their members.

To develop an accurate understanding of Aboriginal people one must throw away many of the Hollywood images. Obviously, no one mould describes all Aboriginal people. While there are many shared beliefs and practices among Indian tribes that stem from the holistic view of the world, there are many more differences than similarities. However, the similarities are what have become most salient and consequently serve to bind Aboriginal people together with all tribal people on Mother Earth.

TRADITIONAL TRIBAL FAMILY LIFE

The healthy tribal family provides support, security, and encouragement by being sensitive to the needs of its members. Within the tribal family the ability to communicate needs effectively is crucial for survival because everyone depends on one another. If one person's needs go unmet the resulting ill effects are felt by the entire group.

The following descriptions represent some features that are characteristic of healthy tribal families. These characteristics have evolved from the beliefs and values that emanate from the holistic world-view of tribal people. The information that follows has been developed from *In the Spirit of the Family* (National Native Association of Treatment Directors, 1989), a manual for training First Nations therapists to work with families. While the characteristics presented are admittedly not a conclusive list, they do represent some of the most salient features of healthy tribal families.

Tribal families and communities operate as cooperative, interdependent units. These families are designed for survival in what are often very harsh and hostile environments. In such circumstances it is necessary that everyone's role be well defined and carried out as best as possible because the survival of the community is dependent upon everyone carrying through with their responsibilities. In this way the family is interdependent. It is also crucial that family members learn to work cooperatively with each other, because if conflict were to get out of hand, the survival

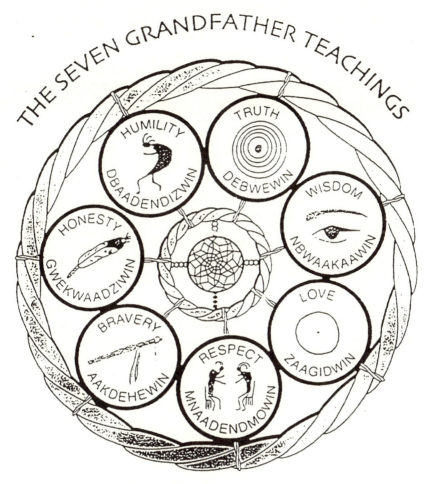

Figure 8.1 The Seven Sacred Gifts

of the entire family would be at risk. Therefore, the values promote behaviours that minimize conflict and maximize cooperative, peaceful relationships.

Tribal families encourage the development of unique identity. The tribal family organization promotes both group identity and individual identity. Tribal groups allow people to identify with a group of people who share language and customs. Within the tribal grouping people further identify themselves as members of clans. A clan helps to identify an entire extended family as it has formed through many generations. As such, it also defines the boundaries of relationships, responsibilities, and expectations for each member. A clan also creates a large, sophisticated network of social relationships that serves to exert pressure for conformity and social control.

Despite having these large group affiliations to define identity, individuals are also encouraged to recognize and value their unique gifts and abilities, and to express these within the group. While adhering to the established parameters of group behaviour, the individual is encouraged to contribute his or her refinement of the shared perceptions. In this way each individual leaves his or her unique mark on the shared experience and thus the tribal community evolves collectively.

Tribal families teach and grow through children. Children are seen as the most valuable resource, for without these gifts from the Creator the family would not continue to exist. These gifts are treasured, loved, protected, and nurtured by the entire extended family. All members of the family have, as their responsibility, the task of nurturing the young to learn and grow into their next roles. Thus, within the tribal family: (1) older siblings provide protection, love, and teaching; (2) parents provide love, teaching, food, and shelter; (3) elders/grandparents provide love, care, and teaching; (4) aunts and uncles often act as additional parental figures; and (5) clan members and community members monitor and provide expectations for socially appropriate behaviour.

In the tribal family children are taught life skills for independent living. While the ability to live cooperatively as part of a group is highly valued, one of the main tasks of parenting and nurturing is to foster the ability to survive and function independently of others. This means that children are supported to take on new tasks as soon as they demonstrate the ability to do so. This style of parenting usually produces self-reliant, self-confident young adults who can function independently from their family unit, if necessary.

Tribal families promote mutual respect for the individuality of members. It is recognized that strong families are built on strong individuals and that strong communities require strong families. To meet this objective, all members of the family are encouraged to express their ideas and opinions within the context of respect for the Creator, themselves, and one another. It is also considered important not to interfere with an individual's actions as this may show disrespect for their rights of self-determination. Noninterference is enacted within environments in which children are constantly monitored by the entire community and encouraged by expectation to emit socially appropriate behaviour.

Tribal families maintain a separation of generations and flexibility of roles. The boundaries or divisions between infancy, childhood, young adulthood, parenthood, and elderhood are well defined. Usually the transition to each new stage is recognized by a community or family ceremony. Further, each of the roles is well defined, and one of the family functions is to ensure that its members learn and fulfil their responsibilities. From this experience individual identity forms within the context of the larger community. While the boundaries are well defined, there is also room for flexibility as members. For short periods of time family members may serve in different roles as required. For example, grandparents or an older child might temporarily assume total parenting functions while the parents are away.

The tribal family continues to grow in spite of whatever trouble comes along and has the ability to use crisis as an opportunity for growth. The tribal family is adaptable and resilient in that it has the capacity to encounter crisis and use the discoveries from these experiences to become stronger. Problems are perceived as challenges and opportunities for learning. These perceptions have provided Aboriginal people with the capacity to survive numerous challenges from the environment and the European settlers. However depleted abilities may be, Aboriginal people have remained strong enough to survive tremendous crises over the past five hundred years.

The tribal family initiates and maintains growth-producing relationships and experience within and outside of the family. While the tribal family recognizes that it is important to develop a close-knit, supportive family unit, it is equally important that its members have exposure to and experiences with different families, clans, and tribes. This thinking is what prompts arranged marriages between members of different tribes. This principle generally acknowledges that for a family to continue to grow and develop, it is necessary that it promote behaviour that allows for a continuous flow of new, healthy ideas and experiences into and out of the family.

THE CARE OF CHILDREN AND CHILD DEVELOPMENT IN TRIBAL COMMUNITIES

The holistic world-view shapes the beliefs and values that guide the structure of the tribal family. These, in turn, inform the patterns of parenting practices. This can be seen within the examples of common Aboriginal parenting practices presented in Table 8.1. These examples of traditional parenting practices demonstrate how the traditional beliefs and values emanating from a holistic world-view shape the interaction between adults and children within tribal communities.

The Emergence of 'Civilized Thought'

Approximately 5,000 years ago civilized society was born when the idea to cultivate and farm some particularly fertile regions of the world began. This led to the settlement of populations larger than one thousand people in certain geographic regions and accompanying changes in the social structures that these people lived within. To begin with, Native families became more self-reliant than they had been in tribal societies because they were able to produce food for the family unit independent of the community. In addition, the development of the concept of property ownership was a central part of the new social structure and value system. As Natives relinquished their nomadic lifestyles, they also changed their perception of their relationship with the land.

It appears as though the influence of women in socializing males to check their aggressive tendencies declined as the evolving social structures began to support and promote male dominance on the basis of their greater aggressive tendencies. These social structures tended to be hierarchical in design, allowing males to exert power and control over women, children, and all other life forms that are viewed as lesser beings. The accompanying value system supported competition, independence, and the accumulation of property. In turn, the amount of property accumulated was an indication of one's position in the social hierarchy, thus determining one's degree of power and control. The principles from tribal society of sharing, caring, and equality[1] were replaced in civilized society with the accumulation of property, independence from the group, and dominance by the most aggressive members.

World-View Options

When civilized society emerged, a completely new way of thinking and behaving evolved. This created new lifestyle options for humans. We can

---

[1] Rupert Ross (1992) offers an excellent description of tribal thought in his book *Dancing with a Ghost: Exploring Indian Reality*.

TABLE 8.1
Beliefs and Values That Guide Aboriginal Parenting Practices

Beliefs and Values	Examples of Adult–Child Interaction
Children are special gifts on loan from the Creator. They are new spirits who are tenuously attached to this world and can be taken back if they are treated disrespectfully.	• Caring and respectful actions toward children prevent them from being taken back. • Expectant mothers relate to their child from conception with respect and appreciation. • Adults are very thoughtful when correcting children's behaviour. • Adults use primarily teasing and shunning to draw children's attention to their inappropriate behaviour and to teach them to exercise self-control over modification of behaviour. • Spirit beings are also involved by parents as guides to oversee and assist their children to correct their own behaviour. • Adults do not respond to children's intervening demands.
Uncontrolled anger leaves a person's Spirit vulnerable to be taken over by evil spirits.	• Children are taught to exercise self-control over open displays of anger.
Each child has been sent with gifts to enhance and benefit the community.	• Prior to or at birth, a child's name is selected which identifies some of the gifts that child carries. • Children are treated as valuable contributing community members. • Children are carefully listened to and observed in order to understand their points of view. Their input is considered in both family and community matters.
The Creator has determined and directs the unique course of development of each child's gifts. Adults support the unfolding of these gifts.	• Each child's unique developmental pattern is respected with little or no comparison to their peers. Parents' expectations of their children's development are minimal. • Adults do not interfere with children's activities out of respect for their divinely directed learning process and growing self-determination.
It is best to provide the Creator's teachings, such as respectful behaviour, through your actions. Your actions are more truthful than your words.	• Adults avoid interrupting a child's play until they are finished. • Adults avoid forcing a child to comply.
The Creator always knows when we have done our best as we are supposed to.	• Praise is used to encourage excellence and positive development in each individual without comparison to peer performance. In this way, children are taught to be humble.

think in a holistic manner and live as if everything in Creation is interdependent and of equal importance. Or we can think linearly and live as if the world is ordered in hierarchies based on one's ability to exert control over lesser beings. Between these two options are at least two additional alternatives. Like many multilingual persons, people can attempt to integrate both forms of thought in ways that employ the world-view in their environment. Or they can become totally disconnected from both world-views. This has been the experience of many Aboriginal people.

Acculturation with Euro-Western culture has produced a new breed of Aboriginal people. Among full-blooded Indians, there exists a spectrum of persons – ranging from those totally faithful to traditional ways, to those who practise exclusively the traditions of the dominant culture. Some of the latter persons are products of boarding and residential schools and cross-cultural adoptions and fostering. A variety of alternate and institutional care arrangements resulted in children being assimilated into Euro-Western culture. Another influential factor in shaping the identity of the present-day Native person is mixed tribal and interracial marriages. When persons from different tribal affiliations mate, their offspring become the products of, at times, very different Indian traditions. The offspring of interracial marriages are another form of new-breed Native persons, Canada's Métis people.

We must examine our history since contact with Europeans if we are to understand and appreciate how Canada's First Nations families and communities have been separated from holistic thinking and lifestyles. It is this holistic world-view that has produced beliefs and values to guide relatively healthy childrearing practices within tribal communities.

HISTORY OF NATIVE CHILD WELFARE

**Assaults on Tribal Communities' Lifestyles and Families:
The Early Years**

Historical evidence supports the fact that, from the point of contact between Europeans and Aboriginal people, the ethnocentric world-view of the new settlers led them to perceive the original inhabitants as obstacles in the way of their plans for colonization. Initially, First Nations' knowledge allowed the new settlers to adapt to this land and survive. Later, the value of the Aboriginal people to the colonizers quickly diminished as they became confident in their ability to sustain their own lives. From that point forward, the colonizers began to view the Native people as problematic and expendable.

Recorded Canadian history from the 1600s to the mid-1800s is full of events enacted by the colonizers that can be identified as acts of genocide against Aboriginal people. These included the elimination of people through warfare, starvation, disease, and the introduction of addictive substances such as alcohol (Dickason, 1992; Farb, 1978; Morrison & Wilson, 1995). The estimated Native population of North America at the time of contact varies from 1.5 to 12 million people. Even if the lower figure is used as an estimate, the decline in Native population to less than 250,000 by the late 1800s is an indication of the devastating impact of colonization on the Native family.

Establishment of Reserves

By the 1850s the Canadian government began a less overtly violent method of dealing with the remaining Aboriginal population. It was determined that they could be better controlled and monitored if they were confined within particular tracts of land. Clearly the establishment of reserves was seen not only as a way to gain control of the land and to monitor and control the Aboriginal people, but also as a step toward further assimilation of the Native people to the 'civilized' lifestyle and world-view of the colonizer.

In the years following the signing of the treaties and the establishment of reserves, many Aboriginal people were forcibly removed from their traditional territories and detained within the confines of their new reserve homelands. They were no longer free to travel on the land and often required the written permission of the Indian agent, who, much like a jailer, had the responsibility to monitor the coming and going of the reserve population. This person also had the final decision-making power for the reserve as the Canadian government's official responsible for carrying out the agreements within the treaties to meet the needs for food, shelter, education, medical care, and other basic needs of the Aboriginal people. However, shortly after the reserves were established, it became apparent that most of the agreements were not being fulfilled and that the Indian agent's role was mainly to control and monitor the Native people. This shift to a reserve lifestyle separated Aboriginal people from the land, and became a major step toward separating them from their traditional lifestyles.

As the Native people moved from living a nomadic hunting-gathering lifestyle to a sedentary agriculture lifestyle, the roles of men and women began to change, as did the family structures. Men's roles as providers for their families began to decrease; self-destructive behaviour and family violence began to increase. In addition, the increased dependence on the Canadian government to meet the basic needs of life began the development of a dependent welfare lifestyle. It was at this point that the Canadian government began to step up its policies of assimilation as it enacted laws to further control the lifestyles of First Nations peoples. This included laws that prohibited the expression of traditional spiritual ways and healing practices.

The Canadian government also began to forcibly impose their democratic system of government on reserve communities. This replaced traditional systems of government that had evolved from holistic thought and were based on principles of equality. Their traditional governing structures tended to reinforce decision making by consensus as opposed to majority rule. As this new democratic system was imposed on reserve communities, fundamental principles that had previously maintained peaceful, balanced relationships were violated. This change impacted severely on family relationships and structure, as clan members became pitted against each other over decision making that often determined positions of power and control within the community. With this new system of government, factions formed within communities that were now formed around the purpose of gaining control over the decision-making powers for the community through positions of elected office.

As adults began experiencing the frustrations of oppression within their own communities, similar patterns began establishing themselves within family structures. Parents, especially fathers who had become disenfranchised of their roles, began acting in oppressive and abusive manners within their own families. This often became the only place that males felt any degree of control or influence. Never before had the tribal family and community experienced such division, internal conflict, and lack of balance.

Residential Schools

Before the late 1800s First Nations children lived within the confines of the reserve community. Here, they continued to be raised with traditional holistic beliefs and values and parenting styles that had been modified somewhat to adapt to reserve living. However, in 1879 Canada adopted the model of aggressive assimilation that the Americans had initiated with Aboriginal people living in the United States. Nicholas Davin, who had been appointed by Ottawa to study this policy, reported: 'If anything is to be done with the Indian, we must catch him very young' (as cited in Teichroeb, 1997, p. 27). This began the establishment of the residential school system that between 1879 and the 1940s saw the development of 76 schools across Canada. Between 1920 and 1940, when it was made law that status Indian children attend residential school, more than 50 per cent of Native youths were raised away from their families and communities during most of their formative years. It is now obvious that the purpose of these schools was to ensure that Native youths were separated from the holistic world-view of their families and indoctrinated into the linear, reductionistic world-views of the colonizer.

Within the residential schools, children were prohibited from using their languages and practising any of their cultural ways. They became fully immersed within a regimented and controlling environment that taught beliefs and values that often stood in stark contrast to the holistic world-view of their families and communities. 'Missionaries, horrified at the relaxed approach to parenting adopted by Natives, set about correcting the children's uncivilized manners with rigid schedules and harsh discipline' (Teichroeb, 1997, p. 27).

By the time the Canadian government began to abandon the residential school policy in the 1960s,[2] several generations of children had been raised without the beliefs and values that had formerly guided their holistic approaches to parenting. As well, many generations of parents had limited experience with parenting, because their children had been raised in residential schools. The accumulated experiences of separation, loss, and abuse led to people entering parenthood who had limited capacity to form healthy emotional bonds and who were therefore often unable to offer nurturing environments to their children. In fact, many graduates of residential schools repeated the oppressive, controlling, and abusive relationship patterns that they had been exposed to as children in these schools. Many of their children were raised in foster care, adoptive care, group homes, reform schools, training schools, and correctional facilities. Most of those who experienced residential schooling suffered from the long-term effects of unresolved grief associated with multiple losses, and the effects of this unresolved grief have been passed on through several generations. Today the core of healing efforts

---

2 The final closure of residential schools did not occur until the 1970s.

within Aboriginal communities is focused on lifting the symptoms related to unresolved multigenerational grief.

Child Welfare on Reserves

The residential school experience set the stage for the next level of assault on the Native family. The new form of assimilation became known as child welfare, a system that the civilized state had created for protecting children from harm by their family members. The close-knit interdependent structure of First Nations families and communities had previously served to ensure the protection and safety of its members. However, as the hierarchical power structures began to be implemented within the social structures of reserve communities, women and children became increasingly vulnerable to abuse. Civilized society's new solution to this problem was to remove children permanently from their families and communities and adopt them, most often to non-Native families. This was thought to be a sure way to fully assimilate Aboriginal children to the 'civilized' world-view.

It was no coincidence that as the Indian Act was being amended to phase out residential schools and to allow for the integration of First Nations children into the public school system, another amendment in 1951 allowed for the provision of child welfare services on reserves (Johnston, 1983). While it was stated that this amendment was made to ensure equal quality of care to Native and non-Native children, the consequences of this action can be understood as yet another act of assimilation. As non-Native social workers entered reserve environments, they were ill-equipped to understand and assist with the devastation that they encountered. In addition to not understanding the culture and history of the people they were to serve, these people also did not receive specific training in child welfare. It was not until the 1980s that many schools of social work began offering training in child welfare. To make matters worse, the poorly developed and ill-defined government policies surrounding child welfare offered minimal guidelines for effective child welfare practice (Johnston, 1983).

By this time the patriarchal welfare state and the residential school system had badly damaged the ability of families and reserve communities to offer the healthy nurturing environments that they had provided only several generations earlier. Poverty, coupled with dysfunctional parenting, the lack of understanding of Native culture, racist attitudes, and policies of apprehension resulted in the permanent removal of thousands of First Nations children from their families and communities. One-quarter of the children who were removed from their families were taken primarily because of the state of poverty their families were experiencing. During the 1960s some reserve communities were almost emptied of children, who had been apprehended and placed for adoption. In 1983 a survey by the Canadian Council on Social Development found that in Manitoba 60 per cent of the children in care were Aboriginal. For Alberta and Saskatchewan, the figures were 50 per cent and 70 per cent respectively (Johnston, 1983).

The Effects of Acculturation on Aboriginal Families

As a consequence of the acculturation process, Aboriginal communities and families, who have not remained separated from the dominant culture, have undergone transformations for over five hundred years since contact occurred with European people. Despite these changes, the following features of family structure and kinship appear to have remained relatively constant.

The Remaining Strengths in Aboriginal Families

While non-Native families have been moving steadily toward smaller nuclear-family units, Native families have continued to retain large extended-family networks. Many First Nations communities consist of two or three large extended-family networks that have become interconnected through couple unions over the past several generations, and inter-marriage between First Nations communities has created extremely large family networks within treaty regions. In addition, First Nations people use terms analogous to father, mother, daughter, and son to identify relationships that are determined by clan and generation as opposed to bloodline alone (Campbell, 1989). In many First Nations communities, children are raised by their grandparents or other extended-family members who then become identified as parents and are often referred to as such. Generally speaking, there is a more extensive and intensive experience of kinship in Native families than in the larger Canadian society.

The Harmful Effects of Acculturation

The process of disconnection from cultural identities and lifestyles, as a consequence of colonization, threw First Nations families into disarray within a few generations. In many communities, healthy parenting styles that once promoted close, cohesive, and nurturing families have been replaced by approaches that often encourage the development of low self-esteem and hopelessness. For example, large kinship networks have become more complex because stable, long-term, committed relationships have become less common over the last few generations. This has followed the weakening of traditional ethical guidelines which once provided guidance for committed, lifelong marriages. As a result, men have sired numerous children, few of whom carry their surnames, and many children have not been parented by their biological fathers.

Since the 1960s, First Nations families began to move to urban centres in search of employment. During the early stages of migration, most Natives had minimal education and therefore were eligible for menial labour positions that were most often seasonal employment. As a result, many Native families moved between urban and reserve settings. This migration pattern has continued for status Indians. In cities such as Regina many Native families spend the winter months in the city and the summer at their reserve. Today it is estimated that more than 30 per cent of the status Native population lives off-reserve (Waldman, 1985).

The movement from reserve to urban communities has also produced a shift from the extended family of grandparents, aunts, uncles, and other relatives attending to and meeting the needs of its members, to small single-parent families. Small, one-parent family units are often unable to fulfil roles of support, security, and encouragement for their members. Certainly, the fact that relatives live in separate homes or communities means that their roles related to meeting the needs of family members have changed. For example, grandparents often are not involved in parenting their grandchildren. Therefore, the nurturing relationships that once existed between grandparents and grandchildren have become more emotionally distant. Many children have not learned the lesson of respecting their elders; elders are losing their ability to teach and nurture the young. As First Nations communities have moved away from the extended-family structure, tremendous pressures have been placed on a few caregivers to meet the parenting responsibilities.

With the shift to Euro-Western values, First Nations families have become disconnected from their traditional beliefs and the roles of family members have become poorly defined, or not defined at all. As a result, the boundaries between childhood and adulthood, for example, may lack definition. Consequently, children often perform parental functions, and parents at times act as children. This confusion of roles contributes significantly to self-abuse and abuse of others. This role confusion is also evident when grandparents assume the full parenting role with their grandchildren because the parents are unable to parent.

Many Native family resources have been so severely weakened that the crises families now face place enormous burdens on their ability to survive. Obviously, for those who have chosen to take their own lives, their strengths have been totally depleted. It appears that the families of these individuals have lost the ability to instil the traditional perception of crisis as an opportunity for growth and the resources necessary to support the accompanying survival behaviours. Unfortunately, many Aboriginal people lack a strong sense of cultural and/or personal identity because of all of the aforementioned assaults on Native families. Also, many Aboriginal families have lost the capacity for healthy exchange with others. Consequently, they live alienated and isolated lives. Therefore, the potential for self-destructive and abusive behaviour is often high.

> For Indians in Canada, overall life expectancy is 10 years less than the national average. Perinatal and neonatal Indian mortality are almost twice as high. Violent deaths and suicides occur among Indians at more than six times the national rate. Indians are jailed at more than three times the national rate. Over 50 percent of Indian health problems are alcohol-related. One out of three Indian families lives in crowded conditions. Only 50–60 percent of Indian housing has running water, and sewage disposal. Although participation in elementary schools has recently approached the national level, secondary school participation is still 12 percent with a completion rate of about 20 percent, as compared to a national rate of 75 percent. University participation is less than half the national level. Participation in the labor force is less than 40 percent.
>
> And with employment at only about 30 percent of the working age group, and average income well below national levels, about 50 percent of the Indian population has to resort to governmental social assistance. Even for off-reserve Indians who have attempted to enter the economic mainstream, the levels of unemployment and governmental dependency stand at about 25–30 percent. (Waldman, 1985, p. 209)

Virtually the same statistics were reported by the Royal Commission on Aboriginal Peoples in 1995.

Today, as many Aboriginal families let go of traditional practices to follow the civilized path, it has become increasingly difficult for Native children to define their identities on the group or the individual level. Without a well-defined identity, Native youths become confused about their purpose or role in life. The road maps that once helped them plot their course in life have been removed. In some cases, they have adopted road maps from 'civilized' society. Others have relatively nothing and are wandering lost, feeling frightened, hopeless, and angry.

HEALING OURSELVES

> I believe that healing for us as human beings will be hard to do unless we become humble and honest and straightforward in all our dealings with women and children and men. What we are searching for is harmony and balance again. The way that it was before the strangers came to this sacred land, and messed things up for us with their strange ways. They came with an unbelievable greed and arrogance. They came to a paradise and they turned it into a living hell upon earth. (Solomon, 1994, p. 73)

Aboriginal Child Welfare

During the 1960s First Nations communities became alarmed that non-Native child welfare actions were leading to almost certain complete destruction of their communities. By then, a large number of children had been permanently separated from their families and communities. Between 1969 and 1974, 80 per cent of the Indian children in care were adopted to non-Native families within Canada and the United States. At present 40 per cent of permanent wards are Aboriginal children. Within regions with higher concentrations of Native people that percentage rises to 70 per cent (Webber, 1998).

After an Alberta Blackfoot band signed an agreement with the province and federal government in 1973 for the provision of child welfare services in their community, a number of First Nations bands across Canada began efforts to exercise more control over the provision of child welfare services in First Nations communities. In Manitoba this began in 1982, when a moratorium was placed on the adoption of First Nations children outside of their communities and the country. Up until 1986, when the Department of Indian Affairs began a moratorium on new negotiations and funding arrangements, 152 agreements were signed with First Nations to provide child welfare services to their own communities. In the 1980s, as First Nations communities established increasing numbers of locally controlled child welfare agencies, Indian

Affairs responded by creating policy for the establishment of new agencies requiring a minimum of 1,000 children per agency, excluding child care costs from agreements. Also, they insisted that provincial legislation and standards be applied. Finally, it was stipulated that agreements would only be possible as resources became available. Since then, only a few new First Nations child welfare agencies have been initiated. However, full support of and confidence in these agencies by non-Native agencies and governments have not been established.

The numbers of Aboriginal children in the care of child protection agencies can only be estimated. Statistics are inconsistent, definitions vary, or information is unavailable (Timpson, 1994). However, it is clear that since the 1960s, Aboriginal children have been disproportionately represented in care. For example, in 1980, 4.6 per cent of all status Indian children were in care – four and one-half times the rate of all Canadian children (Johnston, 1983). By 1990, 4 per cent of Aboriginal children were in care compared, with an estimated 0.4 per cent of the general population (Timpson, 1994). In Manitoba, one-quarter of children placed for adoption are Métis, though they comprise only 5.6 per cent of the population.

Facilitating the Healing

For Aboriginal communities, the establishment of child welfare agencies and various family support and healing programs marks a return to carrying responsibility for the development of healthy families and healthy communities. Some consider this healing movement to be the backbone to rebuilding the state of health that many believe First Nations peoples enjoyed in pre-contact days. Others believe that rebuilding healthy families and communities is the essence of self-government.

As these new Aboriginal agencies and programs have evolved, it has become incumbent upon them to define how they can improve the child welfare policies and practices of the non-Native society that had promoted assimilation and community destruction. Simply replacing non-Native social workers with First Nations workers who speak the Native language and know the culture is obviously insufficient. Even the practices of some Aboriginal child welfare agencies that continue to follow the policies and practices dictated by provincial child welfare mandates appear to do nothing more than replicate destructive processes. The only apparent difference is that now First Nations people act in often oppressive ways toward First Nations families and communities.

Aboriginal agencies also report that the non-Native agencies, institutions, and government branches that they must interact with or depend on continue to express racist and oppressive attitudes toward them. Although they wish to exert self-control over child welfare matters, government policies and oppressive attitudes continue to prevent real self-government from being implemented. It appears that creating Aboriginal agencies and programs requires that Aboriginal people once again define what has enabled them to live in healthy relationships with self, others, all of Creation, and the Creator. They must redefine health from the context of the holistic world-view and translate this into principles for healthy living in our current reality. In the process perhaps it will be discovered that First Nations peoples had far more to offer to the colonizers than was originally appreciated or understood. In fact, what was discovered, discouraged, and destroyed may prove to be the keys to survival for all peoples on Mother Earth.

As Aboriginal programs have evolved, the following guidelines (McKenzie & Morrissette, 1993) have generally served to define culturally appropriate services:

- Recognition of the importance of control over and provision of services by Aboriginal people.
- Recognition of the effects of the processes of colonization on Aboriginal people and the need to provide services consistent with an individual's identification with Aboriginal identity.
- Recognition of a distinct traditional First Nations world-view and set of beliefs, values, and customs, and the importance of incorporating these into models of healing. Appreciation of values of respect, sharing, family and group cooperation, and holism.
- Recognition of the role of elders, women, and children in community life.
- Recognition of the importance of traditional knowledge and languages.
- Recognition of the importance of building culturally appropriate services through an adaptive process of policy development and implementation that involves community and staff consultation in a continuous and comprehensive fashion.
- Recognition of the importance of well-managed organizations and well-trained staff that incorporate a commitment to culturally appropriate services and working with other informal and formal helping services in a more holistic fashion.

Further elaboration of what Aboriginal people recognize as important elements of the healing process were identified by McCormick (1995) through interviews with 50 Aboriginal people. In addition to understanding the problem, setting goals, obtaining help from others, engaging in challenging activities, learning from a role model, and helping others, the research indicated that healing should facilitate: expression of emotion, participating in ceremony, anchoring self in tradition, connection with nature, establishing social connection, exercise, establishing spiritual connection, and self-care. McCormick claims that 'the aim of healing for First Nations people is concerned with attaining and maintaining balance between the four dimensions of the person: physical, emotional, mental and spiritual' (p. 312). He later concludes that healing in First Nations communities focuses on reestablishing interconnectedness through actions that support and encourage enhanced connections with family, community, culture, nation, and spirituality. This work is significant because it begins to define holistic healing in Aboriginal communities from the perspective of Aboriginal people.

The large extended-family networks within First Nations require large-scale interventions. Individually focused models of treatment, such as behavioural therapy approaches, fall short of addressing the complex relationship issues that must be addressed if significant and lasting changes are to be affected. Assisting the healing of multigenerational extended-family problems within First Nations communities requires a holistic or ecological approach to treatment. All other therapeutic interventions can be considered as merely band-aid solutions that often fail to acknowledge the sources contributing to the illness that lie within the extended family, community, and environment.

The majority of destructive behaviours directed at self and others within tribal society are associated with the period of transition when families are lost between the tribal and 'civilized' lifestyle. While this may be true, there is also considerable evidence to support the belief that families within civilized society do less to promote healthy lifestyles and life-enhancing behaviour than tribal families. If the Aboriginal prophecies are correct, we are now awakening to this realization.

Visions of Family Wellness

Aboriginal people think holistically when discussing visions for the most appropriate ways of assuring their children's safety, health, and well-being. They understand the child's growth and well-being as a product of interaction with the family as a whole. Strengthening the child requires strengthening the family. Increasingly, Aboriginal communities are returning to traditional culture as a source of values, principles, and specific practices for the 'good life.' Traditional beliefs concerning children are at the centre of this movement. These are conveyed by traditional leaders and elders to provide the motivational and emotional momentum for everyday parenting and program development.

Recent studies (Maidman, 1995; Native Child and Family Services of Toronto, 1990) identify a number of 'shoulds' concerning family life. For example, intact families should include elders and relatives. Family unity should be based on quality time, harmony, stability, love, good communication, and mutual respect. A stable material foundation should exist that includes a home, sufficient money, and employment. Skilled and knowledgeable parents should express love, discipline appropriately, offer a respectful environment free of physical and sexual abuse, and appropriately role model with sound values. Respect for children, and the notion that Aboriginal families should grow with and through children, are reflected in the idea that children have important teaching roles within the family and community. The community care principle encourages all members to share childrearing and support the nuclear family as principal caregiver. Further, family relationships, values, beliefs, and parenting should be influenced by Native culture and pride. Families should be involved with the community *as a family*, for recreation, socialization, community growth, and healing. Families should also grow and solve problems with available sources of help. Finally, families should develop the capacity and values to improve physical well-being through nutrition, exercise, and health values. Such qualities rule out the abusive and destructive behaviours of physical and sexual assault, substance abuse, and neglect (Maidman, 1995).

We know, however, that the emerging visions are not fully realized in daily life. For a glimpse of what may contribute to family problems and child maltreatment, we turn to an examination of current realities of Aboriginal family life.

ABORIGINAL FAMILY LIFE: CURRENT REALITIES

Arguably, we may never understand why and how maltreatment occurs. Even so, we begin to grasp a context by fitting together the demographic puzzle. Although not exhaustive, the points listed in Table 8.2, which are drawn from action research conducted in First Nations communities, consulting experience, the Royal Commission on Aboriginal Peoples (1997), and other sources (e.g., Frank Maidman Associates, 1998; Health Canada, 1997b; Indian and Northern Affairs Canada, 1987; Maidman, 1982, 1995; Native Child and Family Services of Toronto, 1990; Statistics Canada, 1993, Timpson, 1994) serve to illustrate some of the current realities impacting Aboriginal family life and childrearing practices.

PREVENTION IN ABORIGINAL COMMUNITIES: MODELS AND PRACTICE

Aboriginal people are critical of the mainstream child protection approach of removing children from their homes without attention to restoring the family as the natural caregiver. Recently, several prevention initiatives have evolved. These are the subject of this section. The following categories may create an impression that Aboriginal programs and practices follow the linear program assumptions of non-Aboriginal programming, in which changes are targeted in isolation from the whole. However, one of our themes is that in the implementation of these practices, the complex, holistic nature of causality is taken into account and guides actual program delivery. Hence, program planning and delivery of prevention practices are encouraging the development of holistic thought.

Practices for Children and Youth

Practices targeting children and youth take short- and long-range prevention perspectives. In the short run, some recognize that young people are active players in current or potentially abusive and neglecting environments. They have the potential to recognize and respond to challenges to their well-being. Such practices empower children, through the development of self-esteem, safety skills, and awareness of community resources (Maidman, 1996a). Preventive practices for children and youth also build supportive relationships within the peer group. These have an immediate protective benefit, while implicitly exposing Aboriginal children to early holistic ideas and experiences of how individuals depend on others in a caring community. In the long run, other practices prepare children and youth for their future adult roles in society, teaching the values, attitudes, and opportunities to develop in a healthy way. These socialization experiences supplement

TABLE 8.2
Aboriginal Family Life: Current Realities

Realities	Childrearing Practices
Unemployment	• A primary concern for Aboriginal people and a problem facing many families. • Rates of unemployment for Native people are higher than for the general population.
Community-wide issues	• Issues of concern vary across communities but include: negative attitudes, community divisions, gossip, long-standing conflict between families, lack of community participation and program support, general dissatisfaction with local leadership and band office staff, lack of social and recreational opportunities, crime/vandalism, loss of culture/identity, and multigenerational loss.
Urban setting	• In addition to the other realities in this table, families in urban settings also contend with: cultural conditions (cultural differences, urban culture shock), economic factors (low-paying jobs, discrimination, turnover), insufficient or inadequate housing, broken or transient family life, limited support within the family, alienation, and social isolation.
Family structure	• Almost one-third of all Aboriginal children under age 15 live with a single parent, with the proportion rising to almost one-half of the families in urban settings. • More than 10% of Aboriginal children under age 15 do not live with either parent.
Family problems	• More than one-third of Aboriginal people surveyed in several studies report that family violence against both partners and children is a serious problem in First Nations families. • Other family problems include fighting, communication problems, emotional neglect, and difficulty expressing love and affection.
Parenting problems	• Problems associated with parenting (e.g., difficulties controlling and disciplining children, problems with communication, a lack of involvement and commitment to parenting) are a primary concern in First Nations communities. • Linked to single parenting, unemployment, alcohol abuse, family conflict, social isolation, lack of familiarity with helping resources, and impacts of residential school experiences.
Alcohol abuse	• Alcohol and drug abuse, though reported to be declining, is a problem that continues to plague First Nations communities. • Linked to stressful family relationships, poor parenting, and parent–child role reversals, and is often concurrently present in situations of maltreatment.

TABLE 8.2 (*concluded*)
Aboriginal Family Life: Current Realities

Realities	Childrearing Practices
Physical health	• Parents with limited knowledge of health and giving birth are less likely to look after themselves prenatally and their infant babies. • Mothers who abuse alcohol may give birth to babies with fetal alcohol syndrome or fetal alcohol effect. • Families with on-going health problems and health-care needs may not have the time or energy to give appropriate attention to their growing children.
Problems of youth	• Concerns regarding youth vary across First Nations communities (e.g., substance abuse, teen sexual behaviour, low self-esteem, school dropout, fighting, disrespect, and suicide).

current, sometimes highly dysfunctional, environments, developing strengths and resilience.

Finally, practices associated with social and recreational programming are particularly important for Aboriginal children and youth. Most First Nations communities lack the facilities and programming skills for recreational development. Many are isolated from urban centres, and experience boredom and temptation (Frank Maidman Associates, 1998). Early attraction to an unhealthy lifestyle of drugs, alcohol, and promiscuity is the precursor to an adult lifestyle detrimental to the care and safety of children. Whatever the focus of educational practices for Aboriginal youth and children, programs aspire to create safe learning environments.

Early Child Development

Early child development opportunities are provided through such programs as Aboriginal Head Start; Better Beginnings, Better Futures; and (formerly) the L'il Beavers Program (Ontario Federation of Indian Friendship Centres, 1986). Early-intervention projects integrate the American Head Start experience concerning the importance of whole-family intervention, with their unique application of culture-based content and organization (Aboriginal Head Start Subcommittee on National Principles and Guidelines, 1996).

Early child development practices are preventive in three ways. First, they socialize children for an adulthood that is respectful toward self and others, free of abuses, and contributes to the material stability of family life. At-risk children are surrounded with positive and nurturing experiences, increasing their resiliency against their current situations and providing the emotional foundations for growth. Through cultural education they develop pride in themselves as Aboriginal childre and become a meaningful part of the Aboriginal community. Second, these programs offer parents opportunities to learn parenting and other life skills. As well, they socialize, increase their pride and self-esteem, and become integrated into the community. Finally, the Head Start versions of early childhood education link to a network of social support services. Through these programs, staff identify high-risk situations (e.g., alcohol abuse) and refer families to appropriate supports or remedial services.

Aboriginal Head Start

Aboriginal Head Start (AHS) is a promising national program. Local communities are encouraged to develop unique program designs. Each is expected to provide services in education, culture and language, health promotion, nutrition, and social support. As well, parents are expected to contribute to program design, development, operations, and evaluation (Aboriginal Head Start Subcommittee on National Principles and Guidelines, 1996). The program recognizes that children's success in school, and indeed the development of lifelong learning, reflects strengths within the individual child *and* the supportive and adaptive characteristics of the family. Preschool programs, through supportive social networks, often benefit parents as well in their relationships with children, life satisfaction, psychological well-being, and parenting and other skills. Since the family's economic circumstances also affect the child's mental and physical health, some programs provide learning and career development opportunities for parents. Long-term studies have found that children who participated in American Head Start programs have better health, immunization rates, and nutrition. They also display greater social and emotional stability than non-participating peers (Washington & Bailey, 1995).

Preliminary evaluation results of Canadian Aboriginal Head Start initiatives are available (Becker & Galley, 1996). One pilot study reinforced what we have learned from American evaluation of child development programs for disadvantaged children. *Involving families in the program is important.* Home visits, involvement in learning with children, and outreach personnel are all emerging as important features of quality programs. For example, parents believe that the program positively affected their children's verbalization, self-confidence, and socialization skills (Becker & Galley, 1996).

Practices for Children's Empowerment and Healing

Children can acquire the tools or life skills to increase their emotional resiliency against abuse trauma and enhance their ability to cope with emotional or physical threats. Children need socialization experiences in order to feel good about themselves and to learn the skills they need to help themselves and others. They may also learn their rights as children. They learn to recognize harmful situations, behaviours, and substances. As well, they receive early exposure to cultural beliefs and attitudes that support the concept of a caring, responsive Aboriginal community. Finally, children may learn to respect and link with their local Aboriginal community, thereby reducing their isolation.

Children's Circle Program
One such children's initiative in an urban setting is the Children's Circle Program. Under the auspices of Native Child and Family Services of Toronto, this program responds to the needs of children from multiproblem, addictive, high-risk families. The program assumes that children have needs related to bonding, emotionality, socialization, education, and physical health (Maidman, 1996a). They need to increase their self-esteem while learning the dangers of alcohol and drugs and understanding the value of a lifestyle based on sobriety. Such children may benefit from mixing with children in similar circumstances, with opportunities to express their feelings about their situations. Also, they need to familiarize themselves with community resources and acquire protective attitudes and skills.

Staff pursue these objectives through structured learning activities and interaction, based on cultural and contemporary knowledge and techniques. These include: education about Native culture through teachings, traditional ceremonies, and rituals; alcohol and drug abuse education; group work; and safety and self-help skill development. Like the Aboriginal Head Start Program, needy parents and children are referred for special services.

The Children's Circle Program has a strong cultural base. Native women plan, prepare, and provide all program activities. A talking-circle format is used. Native values, beliefs, and traditions are core to cultural education. Elders participate in special teaching and ceremonies. Traditional medicines, resources, and symbols are used. For easy access, the program is offered in school and community locations close to Aboriginal populations.

A formative evaluation of the Children's Circle Program (Maidman, 1996a) concluded that school-aged children, ages 9 to 11, participating in both school-based and agency children's circles, had indeed become empowered. Participants improved or maintained their Native pride and self-esteem. They were less likely to feel responsible for helping their alcoholic abusive parents. They expressed attitudes and beliefs that were conducive to safety and self-protection. However, some participating children did not change in their reluctance to talk about their parents' problems. This drew attention to the strength of 'family rules' against discussing family problems, prompting a recommendation for more holistic family-focused program activities.

The Integration of Prevention and Healing

Some children's programs empower through play, culture, and safety learning. Others respond to serious problems by integrating mainstream therapy, traditional healing, and cultural learning. According to the intergenerational transmission of abuse hypothesis, children who have been sexually or physically abused are more likely to abuse as adults. The preventive challenge, then, is to restore their health and well-being well before adulthood. Another dimension of the preventive challenge is to help the family members heal when their personal pain is a threat to the safety and well-being of their present and unborn children. This more holistic perspective recognizes the interdependence of dysfunctional family problems. The implication is that *integrated practices are needed to move the whole family toward health*.

Mooka'am Sexual Abuse Treatment Program
The Mooka'am Sexual Abuse Treatment Program takes up these prevention challenges (Maidman & Beedie, 1994). It blends specific traditional healing and contemporary practices. Recognizing that sexual abuse may be intergenerational, Mooka'am offers services to adult victims *and* their families, adolescents, and children, including suspected abuse victims. The following description focuses on the children's component only.

Children may enter the program with low self-esteem and feelings of inadequacy, reflected in their relationships and schooling. Although healing work with children is similar in some ways to that of other clients (cultural learning and participation in summer camp), it also involves age-appropriate approaches. Children usually do not have the words to express their experiences or how they feel. Talking and writing about abuse is unrealistic. Accordingly, the core practices in the program include nondirective and directive play therapy, blended with traditional healing.

The work with children also helps them avoid future abuse. To achieve this goal, staff integrate preventive education and traditional teachings. For example, a poster combined traditional ideas and symbols with contemporary ideas concerning 'good touch, bad touch.'

Coming from multiple-abuse backgrounds, participating children may be troubled with matters other than sexual abuse. Depending on their immediate needs, staff focus on other issues, including those of the adult parents. This reinforces the holistic principle that programs should not focus on problems in ways that artificially serve the program but neglect the client (Maidman & Beedie, 1994).

A formative evaluation of the Mooka'am Program demonstrated that troubled children from highly dysfunctional families strengthened their resilience and knowledge of threatening situations. They developed positive self-esteem, increased Native pride, and acquired safety and other prevention knowledge. Qualitative information suggested that particularly dysfunctional family dynamics may have affected the progress of some children (Maidman & Beedie, 1994).

Child Care

As a child welfare service, child care provided privately or in community centres is used when family care of the child must be supplemented. Ideally, it can also strengthen and support positive parenting. Child care practitioners provide quality group care and supervision when parents are unable to care for children due to employment, sickness, and the like. Such circumstances call for the child care to supplement, but not substitute for, parental care.

In addition to providing food, shelter, and adult supervision, most Aboriginal centre-based child care facilities provide cultural education, basic language learning, and simple school readiness teaching (Frank Maidman Associates, 1998). *To create preventive community structures, cen-*

tre-based Aboriginal child care is organized to strengthen the supportive and protective community network around children. This is realized by forging strong relationships with the community at large: involving seniors in planning, teaching, and other program activities; organizing field visits; encouraging community participation; and participating in community festivities.

Many Aboriginal child care centres incorporate cultural teachings and practices. These include general ceremonies, seasonal ceremonies, regular circles, and spiritual activities. The cultural component contributes to prevention in many ways. Cultural teachings introduce or reinforce the values and beliefs associated with the caring tribal community. The social organization of cultural practice (e.g., ceremonies, elder involvement, circles) builds community relationships in children's lives.

Potentially, child care may also service families with children who, because of mental, physical, or emotional challenges, are demanding and stressful. Relief to overburdened parents for part of the day may help avoid institutionalization. Ideally, staff will have the abilities to work with special-needs children. As well, group-based child care encourages normal contact between peers and isolated special-needs children. Child care may also offer temporary relief when the parent–child relationship is disturbed, allowing the parent to become emotionally reorganized for more positive contact. Thus, child care supports parental capacity to care for the child, reduces tension or conflict, and increases the likelihood that the child will be maintained in the home.

Child care may also be an alternative to a homemaker service when the parents have died or deserted, or during prolonged hospitalization. Child care facilities may also be used as remedial measures for deprived home environments, such as housing shortages. Of growing importance is a belief that child care prevents the placement of children in substitute care and also acts as a respite in protective services.

Evaluation of the national First Nations/Inuit Child Care Initiative (Martin Spigelman Research Associates, The Project Group, & Terriplan Consultants, 1997) suggests that Aboriginal centre-based child care had positive effects. These directly impacted the high-risk elements of child maltreatment, while strengthening protective mechanisms. Many parents participated in educational, employment, and other opportunities, knowing that their children were safe and well. Child care provided services to many families at risk of child maltreatment: working parents, young people returning to school, families on assistance, single parents, families with special-needs children, and families involved with family services. Child care also helped integrate families into community life, reducing the social isolation typical of troubled and maltreating families. A majority felt that the initiative increased their community participation, making them more aware of child care issues. Regional committee contacts and staff believed that child care was a cost-effective approach to community social and economic development. All study centres developed linkages with human service programs, particularly in the health sector.

Several child care practices provided learning opportunities and resources for parents that enhanced their skills and self-esteem. Parents became active in centre activities, particularly management and governance. Some centres offered parenting courses and other ancillary resources or activities such as a library, or play groups for other community children. Finally, staff successfully incorporated community values and traditions into their operations, primarily through community and elder participation.

Youth Work Practices

Aboriginal youth services exemplify prevention programming for future generations. Today's Aboriginal youth are tomorrow's parents; many already have children. Some are involved in dysfunctional and unsafe family relationships. Their behaviour has the potential to contribute to the quality of family life. As community members, they are role models for young children and generally contribute to the quality of the family's social environment. Finally, they are the potential carriers of Aboriginal culture (Frank Maidman Associates, 1998).

Effective practices for Aboriginal youth provide them with the learning and growth experiences that help reduce the later risks of child maltreatment. Generally, such practices prepare young men and women for adulthood, particularly family roles. Preventive practices address the risk factors associated with substance abuse, unemployment and poverty, inadequate parenting skills and knowledge, family abuse, social isolation, and marital conflict. Preventive practices also help youth become aware of the dangers of certain lifestyle excesses (e.g., substance abuse) that may affect later family life. They facilitate their commitment and involvement in education or training, as steps to meaningful employment and enjoyment of lifelong learning. They support their involvement into Aboriginal community life, where they can secure access to supportive resources, friendship, and growth opportunities, and participate in a collective self-esteem. Prevention practices also help youth learn values for positive sexuality and gender relations. They provide social and recreational opportunities, which keep youth out of trouble at an early age, prevent the onset of a troubled life, and strengthen the values related to physical health and social relationships. In addition they provide respite experiences and parenting education for young parents.

Youth identity issues present a special challenge. This is true for all Aboriginal youth. It may be so for urban and Métis youth. Urban youth are away from their family and community cultural reinforcements of their identity. They are less exposed to traditional Aboriginal culture, and may be targets of racism (Frank Maidman Associates, 1998). Those from adoptive families or multiple foster placements likely missed the consistent nurturing of stable family life. As well, they may have experienced family violence and emotional abuse. With these socialization experiences, they struggle to form close attachments with others. Métis youth, like other Aboriginal youth, share similar backgrounds and current circumstances. For some, identity issues are further affected by: (1) their being of mixed heritage; (2) having lived near a First Nations community, and possibly having been exposed to traditional culture; and (3) not being integrated into an urban Métis community. Practices for Métis and Aboriginal youth living in cities may be particularly effective when they reduce isolation, build lasting relationships with others, and perhaps help them connect with their original families.

Knowledge of effective preventive practices for Aboriginal youth comes primarily from the Community Action Program for Children (CAPC) evaluation project (Obonsawin-Irwin Consulting, 1997). The CAPC projects targeted younger children, but included some programs for Aboriginal youth. Most were educational, although some provided direct service. Teen-oriented preventive practices included the distribution of educational brochures, workshops, traditional ceremonies, elder teachings, circles, one-to-one education and counselling, referrals, and the distribution of condoms.

An oft-repeated cultural objective is to restore elders' traditional community roles in relation to young people. Off-reserve cultural development projects have successfully created positive attitudes toward elders. Workshops and elder teachings may have been particularly effective. All participating teens said they had learned the importance of developing relationships with elders. They learned how to relate to them and to use their knowledge from elders in daily life (Obonsawin-Irwin Consulting,

1997). Elder teachings, workshops, ceremonies, and circles comprised the core cultural education and development practices. Although the effects of *each* practice cannot be assessed, strong evidence speaks to the aggregated impact. All participants reported a new appreciation of how cultural learning increased their pride. Feeling better about themselves also helped them make appropriate decisions affecting their well-being (Obonsawin-Irwin Consulting, 1997).

Aboriginal youth also need specific learning opportunities on sexuality. CAPC projects successfully enhanced teen knowledge of their sexuality and helped them apply this knowledge. Participants reported an increased respect for their sexual selves, as they became knowledgeable about safe-sex practices, birth control, and sexually transmitted diseases. Some left abusive relationships. Others became better able to access prenatal health care services (Obonsawin-Irwin Consulting, 1997).

Practices for Parents and Families

Aboriginal wisdom suggests that the following families are more likely to neglect or abuse their children: single parents, the unemployed, parents with residential school and other institutional backgrounds, families living in communities with high concentrations of residential school backgrounds, those living unhealthy lifestyles, multi-problem families, the socially isolated, and parents who were abused or neglected as children. Such factors undermine the quality of parenting by fostering inadequate parenting skills, stress, and the inability to cope or seek help; family conflict; low self-esteem; negative lifestyles (e.g., gambling); and insufficient quality time with children. The following practices are preventive by (1) directly targeting the high-risk factors or (2) modifying the negative consequences of the risk factors. They promote change through program activities *and* the organization of practice (e.g., parents as volunteers) (Health Canada, 1996a).

Healing Practices for Adult Family Members

Much as they reflect public issues and social contexts, the private problems of parents need to be addressed in preventive actions against child maltreatment. Personal issues such as alcohol or drug abuse are targeted by clinical or traditional healing. These issues contribute to maltreatment through their impact on partner relationships, the perception and response to children, or the incapacity to seek or use helping services. Healing practices *restore personal health and well-being, thereby lowering the risk of parents maltreating children and other adults.* As well, they promote healthy interaction with children. Even though focusing on individual parent needs, most Aboriginal healing practices incorporate holistic principles.

Individual help, through counselling, therapy, or traditional healing, is available in a variety of private and program settings. Such treatments are often holistic in scope, targeting several life domains. For example, alcohol and drug abuse treatment programs for Aboriginal people offer workshops or circles in life skills and communications, cultural education and spirituality, as well as alcohol treatment (Beauvais, 1992; Brady, 1995; Edwards & Edwards, 1988; Edwards, Seaman, Drews, & Edwards, 1995; Jilek, 1994; Oetting, Beauvais, & Edwards, 1988). Sexual abuse treatment programs are also important settings for prevention work. With new programming initiatives and freer discussions of sexuality, more sexual abuse disclosures have surfaced.

The following are either effective or promising practices and principles for helping Aboriginal adults.

Professional Counselling/Therapy
These practices address the emotional needs of clients, enhance their self-esteem, and resolve inner conflicts. They address the psychological effects of victimization, oppression, poverty, abusive or stressful relationships, present or previous involvements with the child welfare system, and the like. Most of these issues are related to their situation and identity as Aboriginal people, and require the understanding and empathy of Aboriginal counsellors.

Lay Counselling
Lay counselling by community staff or natural helpers (e.g., elders) is also available. Local Aboriginal counsellors are familiar with community conditions and how they affect private lives. Peer counselling may be provided by those in similar circumstances, such as single parents or sexual abuse victims. This encourages self-help, lasting friendships, and a sense of community.

Traditional Healing
Traditional healing practices are also available. These include: (1) counselling by spiritual healers, (2) healing circles, and (3) cultural events and spiritual ceremonies. Sweat lodges and other traditional ceremo-

nies are major healing activities for clients as they address all four aspects of self – physical, emotional, psychological, and spiritual. Ceremonies cleanse the body, help release deep feelings such as sadness, and develop social and emotional connections with others. They clear and relax the mind, and connect clients to the Creator and their own spiritual power through prayer, offerings, and song. Cultural education helps build self-esteem and restore lost dignity. Elders participate in program development, spiritual ceremonies, healing circles and group work, and staff direction and support. They provide traditional teachings about gender relationships and healthy sexuality. Other adult healing practices include storytelling, expressive therapy (journal or diary keeping, poetry writing, storytelling, and visual expression), life skills training, and teaching lifestyle alternatives to self-destructive coping behaviours (Maidman & Beedie, 1994).

The above practice principles are consistent with the previously discussed British Columbia mental health study that probed the sources of healing for Aboriginal people (McCormick, 1995). A recent study of an urban program combining contemporary clinical or social work practices and traditional Aboriginal healing methods also reinforces many of the British Columbia study results (Maidman & Beadie, 1994). Mooka'am Healing and Treatment Services (Native Child and Family Services of Toronto) offers sexual abuse treatment for abuse victims who have maltreated their children or who are at risk of doing so. Some are already involved with child protection authorities. Evaluation indicated that participants developed a more positive sense of themselves generally and as victims. They established trusting attitudes, becoming more comfortable in social and intimate situations. Sustaining their pride as Native people, they participated in more communal cultural activities. Mooka'am participants also improved their lifestyle by relaxing more, becoming more community-oriented, and developing insight into substance and food abuses. They became more self-protective, resourceful, and active in coping and created stronger systems of support from different sources. Finally, the program helped participants develop a more positive sense of their parenting and assisted with material circumstances such as housing, jobs, and income (Maidman & Beedie, 1994).

Parent Education

Many Aboriginal people believe that inadequate parenting places their children at risk (Frank Maidman Associates, 1998), a perception that has spawned numerous parent education programs across the country. At particularly high risk are single Aboriginal women who become pregnant early and who lack adequate income and social supports. Although parent education programs focus primarily on developing skills and knowledge, planners are aware that parenting difficulties are associated with a host of historical and contemporary community and family issues. As one key informant[3] urged, the 'root causes' and holistic forces affecting poor parenting must be kept in mind. Parent–child interaction does not occur in a vacuum.

Parent education provides a range of skills, knowledge, and values. Programs help parents learn specific techniques for raising children. Parent education also imparts coping skills to pregnant women, easing the transition to parenthood. Program participants learn other relevant life skills, such as budgeting and nutritious meal preparation (Sauve & Miller, 1998). Some programs also provide coping and stress management techniques (Sauve & Miller, 1998). Above all, traditional parent education reinforces the sacred values of respecting the child as a gift from the Creator, and honouring the parenting function. Many parenting programs utilize prepackaged programs designed for Aboriginal people, including Raising the Children (Frank Maidman Associates, 1998) and Positive Indian Parenting (Northwestern Indian Child Welfare Institute, 1986). These combine traditional beliefs and values with contemporary techniques. The effective ones acknowledge the roles of wider family system and community dynamics. Parent education is also an important component of the CAPC projects for off-reserve Aboriginal communities. Practices consist of parenting circles (self-help support), classes, moms and tots activities, drop-in or sharing circles, one-on-one counselling, home visits, cultural workshops, teaching of traditional crafts to parents and children, drop-in activities, and the distribution of materials, such as clothing (Obonsawin-Irwin Consulting, 1997). In some communities, elders provide parenting workshops from a traditional perspective.

Parent education targets three different categories. As universal prevention, workshops provide learning opportunities that are available to the whole community. Selective events target high-risk parents such as single-mothers or teenagers. Finally, parenting education may be

---

3 In this chapter the term 'key informant' refers to various individuals who reviewed draft materials, not to participants in the qualitative study.

required through customary care agreements or court orders. These are examples of indicated prevention in which the parenting-related conditions for future maltreatment are minimized through education.

There is enormous support for the idea of strengthening parenting in Aboriginal families (Frank Maidman Associates, 1998). Many culture-based parent education programs are in place across Canada (Maidman, 1998). Even so, we lack cumulative evidence for their effectiveness. Recent evaluation of parent education in urban settings reinforces the perception that parent education is important and effective (Obonsawin-Irwin Consulting, 1997). The projects that were evaluated demonstrated several positive impacts. Parents improved parenting practices: they began to use positive disciplinary practices and communication, they became more patient with children, they refrained from hitting or yelling, they spent more time with their children, and they praised good behaviour. Other projects benefited children's health and well-being by helping mothers develop healthy habits, knowledge about nutrition, and practical food-buying habits. They learned how food and nutrition affect behaviour. Pregnant women stopped smoking, drinking, and using drugs, and new parents began to exercise and diet. Expectant mothers learned anxiety-reducing coping skills for the transition to parenthood (Obonsawin-Irwin Consulting, 1997).

Customary Care

Customary care has its roots in traditional community and tribal family life. It is a set of beliefs, principles, and practices through which Aboriginal communities assume child care responsibility. As an arrangement for child care using community resources and processes, customary care is legitimized by a traditional belief that communities are responsible for the care and well-being of children. Typically, an alternative family and living arrangement is made in which extended-family members care for the child, temporarily or indefinitely. The community makes this arrangement when quality parenting is undermined by family circumstances such as parental illness, absence, or child maltreatment. Ideally, customary care is a consensual co-parenting relationship. Should extended-family members not be willing, available, or appropriate, other local Aboriginal customary care parents are chosen. Traditionally, the decision was informal. Today, such arrangements are structured according to the policies and procedures of local community or regional Aboriginal authorities (Maidman, 1988).

Contemporary Adaptations

In some parts of Canada, efforts are underway to codify customary care into contemporary beliefs and principles (Payukotayno James and Hudson's Bay Family Services, & Tikinagan Child and Family Services, 1988). From consultation with 38 First Nations, the following ideas establish a bridge to contemporary realities. Customary care emphasizes: (1) prevention and support; (2) participation of community members in decision-making concerning child maltreatment cases; (3) voluntary admission to care and placement within the community; (4) involvement of extended-family members; (5) involvement of other services; (6) a holistic view of the family as a unit, and the concept of the person as a unity of physical, spiritual, mental, and emotional parts; (7) a nonjudgmental and supportive approach to parents, reflected in the priority given to home-based family support, parent participation in decision making, the reinforcement of parental roles, and the concept of co-parenting; and (8) case planning involving family members. Elders believe that today's application should blend with modern helping methods while avoiding mainstream options for child protection. Counselling, therapy, or traditional healing should be available to troubled families, but children should never be removed from their family or community. Finally, for appropriate customary care family practice, staff also need cultural competence, including cultural, ceremonial, and customary therapeutic methods (Jourdain, n.d.).

Customary care has numerous potential preventive benefits for the wider community as well as for high-risk or troubled families. It can restore the traditional values, beliefs, and principles of the community as child care agent. It teaches that caring, safety, and well-being are the community standard. Because child maltreatment evokes a community response (e.g., alternative living arrangements), customary care is also socially controlling. By mobilizing extended family and local community members, customary care strengthens family support and co-parenting networks. These networks are sources of learning for families who need parenting ideas and skills.

Customary care is widely valued by Aboriginal people as a community arrangement for assuring the safety and well-being of children (Frank Maidman Associates, 1998; Jourdain, n.d.). Although effectiveness studies are unavailable, early assessments are promising. They suggest that appropriately developed and supported customary care creates healthy community dynamics. After the first few years of bands assuming responsibility for children, the number of children in care of outside agencies began to drop (Indian and Northern Affairs Canada, 1987; Maidman, 1988). Placements were consensually supported by parents in 50 to 95 per cent of cases.

A recent Australian study documented benefits to children and customary caregivers. The program included Aboriginal staff, local involvement in assessments, policy agreements from the community, training for caregivers, and adequate financial support. Success was indicated by improved children's health and school attendance, and by the children's attendance at school with shoes and lunches. Caregivers secured better housing, and the children's families utilized local community resources (Durst, 1996).

Family Support

Services to support families are available from most Aboriginal child and family service agencies across Canada (ARA Consulting Group, 1993; Beck, n.d.; Dilico Ojibway Child and Family Services, 1996; Graff, 1987; Grand Council Treaty #3, Anishinaabe Family Support Services Committee, 1992; Hudson & McKenzie, 1984; Hunter, 1998; James N. Docherty & Associates, 1992; Maidman, 1988; Native Child and Family Services of Toronto, 1990; Organization and Systems Development, 1996; Weechi-It-Te-Win Family Services Inc. & Ontario Ministry of Community and Social Services, 1995). Supporting families involves strengthening their capacity for independent functioning, lessening their dependency on professionals, and keeping them intact (Canadian Socio-Telich Ltd., 1984). Specifically, family support may involve material aid, physical assistance, emotionally supportive interaction, guidance, advice and information, feedback concerning family behaviour, and facilitation of social participation. In Aboriginal communities, family support is provided primarily by family service or family support workers and by other service providers. They support through direct actions or by encouraging help from relatives, friends, other community members, and elders (Maidman, 1988). Family support is provided through organized programs (e.g., parent education) and through office or home visits. It is also provided during contacts with other resources, facilities, or larger institutions, such as courts.

There are several distinctive features of Aboriginal family support in First Nations communities. First, family boundaries may be broadened to include extended family, close friends, household members, or whomever contributes to family functions and parenting. Reinforcing traditional helping roles is important. Second, the community as a whole may receive help to bolster the family environment. In some sense, the community *is* family, since so many people are related. Third, some family support programs minimize the role distinction between natural community resources and formal family services. Staff are trained as caring community members – modelling the extended family and using local helping knowledge, customs, and resources. Child protection authorities may be an important part of this network. Finally, this holistic scope of First Nations' family support is mirrored in cities. For example, The Ontario Federation of Indian Friendships Centres' Aboriginal Family Support Program pursues eight objectives. Friendship centres provide a variety of support initiatives: early job development, parent education, cultural education and events, crisis intervention or stress relief, material support, community education, community development and events, and services to facilitate access to resources (Frank Maidman Associates, 1998).

Aboriginal family support programs concentrating on strengthening family relationships have demonstrated success in establishing more positive relationships between partners, as well as parent–child, sibling, and playmate relationships. Those focusing on help-seeking practices made positive differences in families looking for assistance with substance abuse and medical problems (Obonsawin-Irwin Consulting, 1997). Also, liaison between urban family support workers and child protection authorities may have effectively prevented child protection interventions, or perhaps accelerated the return of children to their natural parents (Obonsawin-Irwin Consulting, 1997).

In some family support projects, child welfare clients were involved through supervision orders or placements. They began to show positive health, parenting, and career changes. Family support projects also made changes in the mothers' personal well-being and socioeconomic circumstances (Obonsawin-Irwin Consulting, 1997), effects that either directly reduce risk factors or help the parents better cope with stressful circumstances.

Home Visitations

The home visitation is a core family support practice, particularly in First Nations communities. Once a widely used practice, recent budget cutbacks may have reduced its frequency in urban programs. Even so, in small First Nation communities, easier travel and privacy make home visits a viable choice. In the small ccommunities, and to some extent in cities, community staff use approaches that are consistent with tradition, local customs, and their own familiarity with clients.

As child maltreatment prevention, home visitations allow workers to help reduce risks by reaching out to socially isolated families and assessing parent–child interaction and parenting skills through observation. They respond immediately to stress-producing family crises, helping families avoid maltreatment by facilitating access to community resources. In the process, staff offer a customized advocacy and resource brokerage relationship. The focus of home visitations is typically the parent and the parent–child relationship. A potential additional advantage, particularly in First Nations, is that workers may engage others close to the family.

In First Nations communities, the effectiveness of home visitations may also be related to privacy, since many centralized programs are provided near busy band offices. Home visits for parent education avoid the 'bad parent' stigma. As well, they allow staff to customize their teaching according to their perceptions of a family's specific needs. Finally, workers find it easier to establish a trusting relationship with clients through natural means, such as helping with dishes or carrying wood.

Home visitations in urban settings overcome the clients' difficulty in accessing other locations, because of distance and expense. Even so, staff travel costs, limited client coverage, and the need to reduce social isolation are all noteworthy limitations.

In many cases, high-risk parents are isolated and lack interactional skills and confidence to seek informal support. They struggle to negotiate their needs with institutions or simply to make friends. Where this is evident, home visitations may supplement parent circles or other networking and social events. Home visitations may be transitional or parallel services. The transition can be facilitated gradually through accompanying visits by other parents or volunteers.

Evaluations of the home visit as a prevention tool are underway (Lam and Associates, 1997). Estimates concerning home visitation effectiveness in Aboriginal communities are based on an evaluation of Healthy Families Arizona, an American Indian study (Honahni, 1998). Families receiving home visitations were less likely to abuse their children. Several abuse-related factors were reduced, including stress and unemployment. More than 95 per cent of the infants were immunized, and parents sought help from primary care physicians. Parents became more skilful at solving problems and providing health care to children.

Participants also improved their ability to cope with problems and stress, giving each other support. They were happy, their living situations improved, and they became more patient with their children (Honahni, 1998).

Advocacy

Families at risk of maltreating their children experience enormous stress from socioeconomic or family conditions. Contacts with community authorities or institutions may be culturally alien and stressful. Isolated and generally lacking in the capacity to use community resources, these families may benefit from advocacy work.

Recent research documents the perceived effectiveness of advocacy work. Family advocates support clients who are involved with child protection agencies, courts, social assistance, landlords, and schools (Frank Maidman Associates, 1998; Maidman, 1988). Advocates undertake different tasks as they pursue a variety of goals. Advocacy work is effective for prevention work when it helps reduce a build-up of client frustration and stress. Also, it facilitates access to community resources (e.g., housing) before problems escalate. Advocacy presents opportunities to negotiate potentially detrimental child welfare decisions. Through role modelling, advocates help families become their own advocates (Maidman, 1988). Some Aboriginal family workers support families by liaising with protection authorities in urban settings and First Nations communities.

Family Counselling and Therapy

Many models for counselling or providing therapy to entire Aboriginal families have been described in the literature (Connors, 1993b; Dykeman, Nelson, & Appleton, 1995; Morrissette, 1994; Morrissette, McKenzie, & Morrissette, 1993; National Native Association of Treatment Directors, 1989; O'Connell, 1985; Pennell & Burford, 1994). Generally, family-centred work assumes that individual symptoms or dysfunctional interactions, as well as thinking, feeling, and bodily states are interrelated with larger family, group, or community patterns. Such patterns may include role relationships, dysfunctional communications, and the like. For Aboriginal problems, an ecological family therapy that recognizes the contributions of disturbed extended-family relationships, community dynamics (e.g., family scapegoating), and institutional factors (e.g., child welfare decisions, local housing policy) may be most effective. Family counselling or therapy has been used to deal with problems such as marital violence or conflict directly associated with child maltreatment. Family intervention is offered before serious abuse or neglect occurs, or as part of a treatment plan to stop reoccurrence.

Details of family practice vary. Reflecting an ecological perspective (Connors, 1993b), Aboriginal or non-Aboriginal therapists working with Aboriginal clients attend to cultural and community issues. Thus, effective family therapy or counselling understands family and community belief systems concerning problems, wellness, and healing. Such practice considers family structure and function and respects traditional roles of immediate and extended-family members (O'Connell, 1985).

Ecological family counsellors work with the culture-based helping style of families, possibly integrating culturally wise elders, helpers, and other traditional practices. Equally important is their practice of working within a community context, always remaining sensitive to how dynamics from long-standing community structures (e.g., power inequities) and events may reinforce problems. In assessment and intervention, some ecological family workers consider intergenerational effects of historical events (e.g., oppression, residential schools), paying attention to how these contribute to family and childrearing patterns (Morrissette et al., 1993). They use cultural methods (e.g., teachings, medicine wheel) to empower whole families and family members by encouraging holistic thinking, balance, and a positive, culture-based identity. Consistent with ecological family work is family networking, which is described next.

Family Networking

One type of family intervention practice that may be particularly effective for Aboriginal communities is family networking, or social network intervention (Speck & Attneave, 1973). Consistent with holistic thinking, it uses extended-family and community resources. One of the above authors, an American Indian, described this practice as retribalization and healing in family crises. Family network interventions energize the family's natural and community supports, including helpful relatives, friends, or neighbours. Network intervention aims to stimulate, reflect, and focus the group's potential to deal with specific problems. To facilitate, the intervention team avoids a therapeutic function, keeping the responsibility within the network.

Experience with family networking indicates that healing processes may have little to do with the presenting problem or the facilitator's initial intentions. By unleashing varied perspectives and synergistic energy, networking effects help solve problems at other levels of family and community life such as alcohol abuse, isolation of families, or oppressive power structures.

Family networking initially evolved as a set of principles and techniques for helping troubled families. These principles are evident in two specific models – Family Group Conferencing and the Wraparound process.

Family Group Conferencing
Family group conferencing (or family group decision making) was originally conceived in New Zealand. This is a practice that, when supported by the community and child welfare authorities and well-timed, could help many families without apprehending children (Pennell & Burford, 1994; Ross, 1996). The aims of this model are (1) to keep children and adults safe, and (2) to promote their well-being. This method builds partnerships between immediate and extended-family members, the community at large, and the government. At a family group conference, the abusive or neglecting family meets with relatives, friends, and other close supporters to develop a plan for resolving concerns. The plan may entail formal resources, but it may also involve natural community supports and traditional healing. As each new intervention animates natural helping, the traditional tribal community comes to life. By receiving approval from the referring authority, the plans have contemporary legitimation and support.

Fortunately, the Family Group Conferencing Model has been evaluated in three Inuit rural and urban communities in Newfoundland and Labrador (Pennell & Burford, 1997). Family group conferencing produced positive changes in family unity, as members talked openly, were motivated to change, and became mutually supportive. They also became more resourceful and improved their care for children and youth by establishing closer relationships and more positive parenting. Other family problems such as drinking were lessened. As well, there was formal evidence of reduced family violence, decreases in substantiated child abuse or neglect, fewer emergency responses to crises, and reduced indicators of woman abuse (Pennell & Burford, 1997). Most project children made positive gains in their development, though they still lagged behind other children in the community. Changes were noted in identity, family, and social relationships, and in emotional and behavioural development. Family group conferencing was *least effective* in helping the most chaotic families and in reducing mother abuse by adolescents.

Assessment of Family Group Conferencing in New Zealand also shows promising results. Children admitted to social welfare department residences dropped from 2,712 in 1988 to 923 in 1992-3. Also, prosecuted cases against young people dropped 27 per cent (Ross, 1996).

Wraparound
Another family-focused community networking process that is being tried in various parts of Canada (Ottawa-Carleton Wraparound, 1999), Australia, and New Zealand (New Zealand Government, 1997) and that has been adopted by several American Indian communities (Frank Maidman Associates, 1998) is the Wraparound process. This model reflects family networking principles and is somewhat similar to Family Group Conferencing. Wraparound is a family-focused community-wide process to help families develop individualized service plans. It undertakes standardized assessment of family strengths and weaknesses in all aspects of family life, and makes extensive use of local formal helping resources. Unlike earlier family network techniques, it relies less on the family's natural helping network. Finally, the Wraparound process insists upon the flexible use of existing resources, rather than the forcing of family needs into existing programmatic solutions.

The Wraparound process is facilitated by a four- to ten-member child and family team of professionals and volunteers, broadly representing the community. The family and children are integral team members, as are relatives or other community members recommended by the family and children. Team service providers represent various agencies and programs. This guarantees that plans, services, and supports cut across traditional agency or program boundaries. Ideally, there is access to flexible noncategorized funding.

The process works toward a needs-driven, multifaceted service plan that typically integrates existing, new, or modified services, with informal or natural community help. The plan typically includes withdrawal of formalized services in favour of natural support. It builds on families' and children's strengths, and is compatible with the values, norms, and preferences of the family, the child, and the community. Culturally competent service plans holistically address the needs of all family life domains: financial, educational, vocational, cultural, social and recreational, behavioural and emotional, health, legal, safety, and others.

The process helps the family to reframe 'problems' as needs. The Wraparound process incorporates a serious monitoring and evaluation component. Service outcomes must be measured for individual cases. If the service plan doesn't work, it must be modified. Family needs remain at the centre of unconditional adaptable services.

Both of the above models involve working with individual families in their natural community environments. As described below, other interventions gather family members together with other families in healing lodges.

Family Healing Lodges

Family-centred practices are also provided in healing lodges. Lodges accept families for extended treatment. Interventions are selective or indicated, since lodge participants either are troubled high-risk families or have already abused or neglected their children. Typically, healing lodges aspire to create wellness in the family while reducing risks of new or continuing patterns of child maltreatment. Some families participate through a court order.

One common feature of healing lodges is the 'healing setting.' As a context for specific practices, the physical setting is designed to create opportunities for healthier experiences. As well, the setting requires social arrangements and tasks for families requiring new skills and knowledge. Each setting characteristically has evolved its unique internal culture based on traditional holistic thought, which becomes a foundation for change. Healing settings are somewhat controlled and structured, with elements of the traditional tribal community. Self-help processes, for example, are encouraged. Specifically, the healing setting consists of: physical structures, policies, rules, routines, program activities, and resources. Each contributes to the healing process. Some physical structures – individual family cottages, for example – will promote a closer interaction within the family. Other structures promote stronger 'community' relationships through wider interaction with others. For isolated families, this may be the first time that close contacts are encouraged.

Lodge practices stress the association between nature, natural rhythms, and healing. There are traditional knowledge and practices, such as smudging, sweat lodges, fasting, ceremonies, and teachings. Most promote reflection and change in lifestyle, and facilitate change in individuals, families, and communities. Reflecting the holistic philosophy, practices heal the four parts of the person and target all life-cycle stages (Sioux Lookout Area Family Treatment Centre, 1990).

Community Prevention Practice

This section reviews practices that aim for changes in the community as a whole. The assumption is that community-wide characteristics contribute to patterns of family wellness or dysfunction, appropriate childrearing or maltreatment (Coulton, Korbin, Su, & Chow, 1995; Garbarino, Stocking, & Associates, 1980; Vondra, 1990). The historical context of Aboriginal community dysfunction has been documented in major reviews, both nationally (Royal Commission on Aboriginal Peoples, 1997) and provincially (Community Panel, Family and Children's Legislation Review in British Columbia, Aboriginal Committee, 1992). Policies mandating residential schools, community relocation, the apprehension of children from their families and communities, and limits on Aboriginal economic opportunities have all been linked to the disruption of communities, family life, and childrearing.

In general, community prevention practices seek to empower communities. Some practices seek to avoid child maltreatment by creating community well-being or health. Others build local resources for responding to troubled family situations that threaten children's safety and health. Still others offer healing opportunities for serious emotional or relational issues that may affect the well-being of children. These practices are organized to educate and reinforce the traditional values and community norms for positive relationships. For the most part, the various practices create opportunities for: awareness and learning, interaction and bonding between people, mutual helping, controlling unacceptable behaviour, developing a collective positive self-esteem, and promoting emotional healing.

Community Development

Community development practices have been used by Aboriginal communities to improve the quality of family life and childrearing, and are acknowledged in public policy. Community development empowers communities to recognize and utilize their strengths in creating change. Some say that community development may be an important preliminary step for the successful implementation of other prevention programs, such as healing lodges (Frank Maidman Associates, 1998).

Typically, community development specialists do not provide direct service; they help communities to help themselves.

Aboriginal communities across Canada have adopted community development practices to develop well communities, meet family needs, and solve problems affecting family life and parenting (Awasis Agency of Northern Manitoba, 1997; Bopp & Bopp, 1985; Maidman, 1995). In cities, strong collectivist movements are beginning to emerge, as Aboriginal communities begin to pool their resources and strengthen their partnerships toward common goals. For example, in a downtown Vancouver community, the following themes pertaining to community values emerged from an action research project (Van Uchelen, Davidson, Quressette, Brasfield, & Demerais, 1997). Community participants believed that collective community action should strive for: achieving a sense of community, identity, and spirituality; avoiding illness; coming through hardship; and living in a good way. In other urban communities, community development initiatives include organizing family resource libraries; networking with community agencies; sensitizing mainstream organizations to cultural differences; and developing youth groups, fundraising, referrals, and program information sessions (Obonsawin-Irwin Consulting, 1997).

Community Education

Community education in Aboriginal communities aims for the development of better parenting standards and practices, awareness of serious issues affecting family life and child development, and the encouragement of healthier lifestyles. These objectives are facilitated through elder teachings, media practices, and community action research.

Elder Teachings. In traditional Aboriginal communities, elders were important and revered carriers of wisdom about families, childrearing, and the quality of life. Such information covered practical tips, as well as deep, fundamental values, beliefs, and morality concerning how to live in a good way. Aboriginal communities once again seek guidance from elders in recovering core culture to energize community renewal. They contribute to community education at all levels, providing teachings in specific programs or at open community events. They regularly contribute to staff training and offer individual support. Elder teachings are valued in circles, workshops, board meetings, and healing events.

We should be clear about the various types of elders and the roles they play. Those who teach the traditions should be distinguished from traditional healers, traditional counsellors, and life skills teachers. Traditional healers are 'medicine men and women' who have acquired a body of traditional skills and knowledge, including the knowledge of traditional medicines and their use. Traditional counsellors may or may not be recognized as elders, but their methods include traditional healing. Depending on their training and background, they may also offer contemporary methods. Elders who are 'life skills teachers' are often Aboriginal seniors, who share their life experience and wisdom to young parents, children, and other community members.

Media Practices. Some educational work is accomplished through the dissemination of literature throughout Aboriginal communities, addressing such issues as sexual abuse, the dangers of smoking and drinking, and fetal alcohol syndrome. Some materials offer traditional cultural content: how to use traditional values and modern methods to prevent child abuse and neglect. Others encourage seeking advice from elders, teaching traditional parenting values and child care methods, and involving extended-family members in respite care (National Indian Child Welfare Association, 1990a, 1990b).

Depending on program resources and strategy, promotional materials target particular community groups, such as new parents, teens, or recent arrivals to the city. Materials for new parents have the advantage of providing age-specific parenting information in an interesting, colourful, and traditional style. The advantage of using promotional materials to educate communities and parents lies in the potential of reaching people who are hesitant to attend helping programs but who obtain materials at social agencies, such as friendship centres. Even so, extremely isolated families in urban settings may not establish contact with any community. Also, they may not be influenced by written materials.

Whereas written educational materials provide specific factual information to isolated passive audiences, other possibly more effective Aboriginal community educational initiatives occur as part of holistic community-based projects. These appeal to the audience's emotional, spiritual, and physical selves, and are typically provided in groups. The recipient is actively involved with factual material – presented in written or visual form, or through teachings, talking circles, and workshops. Participants have opportunities to raise questions, comment, share practical difficulties, and the like.

The Aboriginal Healing and Wellness Strategy, for example, funds several projects incorporating promotional work. Through this program, Aboriginal people seek to change health conditions in their communities by increasing health promotion and education to improve health status. The promotional components strive to stimulate: family violence awareness, prevention program education, healthy lifestyles, and accessibility to health services. Unlike many promotional practices, this strategy uses media-based promotional materials more comprehensively. Projects integrate promotional activities with a variety of other health and wellness activities, such as talking circles or workshops. These involve the person more holistically, and are provided by Aboriginal staff, working face-to-face with community members, incorporating cultural content and resources. Elders, for example, are frequently used in educational workshops.

The Community Healing and Intervention Program (CHIP) is another example of a more holistic approach to promotion (Fournier & Crey, 1997; Health Canada, 1997b). Developed initially for Inuit communities, CHIP was designed primarily to respond to community needs related to fetal alcohol syndrome (FAS) or fetal alcohol effects (FAE). The promotion of healthy lifestyles is part of a comprehensive approach, combining with other prevention activities to minimize risk behaviour, help those living with FAS/FAE, and teach afflicted persons how to avoid risk behaviour.

Community Action Research. Community action research is another practice that facilitates community education. Sometimes used for needs assessment for community or program development, it facilitates community-wide dialogue on family values, principles, issues, and solutions. Essentially, this practice is a catalyst for tapping, sharing, and organizing local community knowledge.

Community action research entails the collection and sharing of information for learning, problem solving, and change. Through dialogue with researchers, community members confront their way of life and establish a foundation for change. Action research is educational and preventive, for it evolves new community lifestyles. As universal prevention, it benefits all members. The community dialogue is an opportunity for members to reflect on their way of life in a positive and creative way, possibly reviving the tacit culture that is outside of awareness. It offers a collective way to consider the implications of traditional culture for modern life (Bopp & Bopp, 1985). Further, the dialogue is a catalyst for the identification of shared values and community action themes (Van Uchelen et al., 1997).

One variant of action research, *participatory research,* involves local community members in the research process. They are trained to identify a research focus, gather information, discuss the information with other members, analyse information, and draw change implications (Maidman, 1995; Maidman & Conchelos, 1991). In addition to community educational accomplishments, participatory research can develop resource people and materials for new programs or other solutions. Because participatory research is empowering for the individuals and the community, it promotes wellness and helps to reduce risk. As well, it benefits future generations and incorporates traditional and local community culture. Depending on the scope and objectives, participatory research can resolve specific issues, or transform local cultures and conditions.

Little research is available to assess the effectiveness of community education initiatives in Aboriginal communities. Public education to raise awareness, change cultural norms, or teach positive parenting skills may result from small-group formats. This has been confirmed in recent evaluations of the CAPC projects (Obonsawin-Irwin Consulting, 1997), most of which use the group, workshop, or circle as vehicles to promote learning. Participants reported increased knowledge of such topics as nutrition, budgeting, and breast feeding. Teens reported increased awareness of sexuality and gender relationships.

Case studies are the best sources of information concerning action research effects. These document how community action research mobilizes local leaders and other community members to share their family and parenting values, perceptions of issues, and conditions for community development. Specific strategies have evolved, as well as locally appropriate service models, implementation strategies, and policy recommendations (Maidman, 1982, 1995; Maidman & Conchelos, 1991). Action research has also proven useful in the local production of educational materials. For example, the process has created specific educational resources, including local histories, biographies, and information about traditional life ways for language and culture programs, as well as parenting and educational practice (Bopp & Bopp, 1985).

Self-Help: Mobilizing the Natural Helping Resources
Community development initiatives drawing upon local natural helping resources are consistent with the values and beliefs of traditional tribal communities. In the past, families turned to relatives, friends, and other community members for daily help. In tribal communities, interdependence fostered by community norms of reciprocity helped organize a social order for survival. Today, First Nations family agencies and urban programs encourage the unpaid contributions of volunteers in different program roles. Relatives, elders, service providers, and other commu-

nity members are recruited for program planning, governance, assistance with program activities, and program evaluation.

Voluntarism. The objectives in a community participation philosophy include a need to secure assistance in program tasks. Well-designed volunteer programming, training, and support potentially establish a broad community-based commitment to child and family well-being. Through program participation, community members become educated on family life issues, parenting, and child maltreatment. By securing community ownership and support of particular programs, voluntarism helps programs stay responsive and compatible with community needs and local conditions. Volunteer recruitment in Aboriginal communities empowers the community to share the tasks of building a supportive climate for children's health, safety, and well-being. It strengthens local relationships and the collective identity. Finally, volunteers may have the opportunity for on-the-job development of skills and self-esteem, which are transferable to education, training, or employment.

Across Canada, many urban community members now participate in community and parent councils in Aboriginal Head Start programs. The Community Watch Program mobilized volunteers in an Aboriginal housing complex to raise sensitivity and responsiveness to violence, substance use, child abuse and neglect, and various environmental threats to families and children (Maidman, 1996b). CAPC Aboriginal prevention projects also involve volunteers in nearly all projects, mostly in program delivery (Obonsawin-Irwin Consulting, 1997).

Parent Circles. Parent circles are networking initiatives that bring parents together informally or within specific programs. As arrangements that contribute to the prevention of child maltreatment, parent networking increases the knowledge and skills of parents in relation to specific practical concerns. In the process, parent circles help alleviate social isolation. They provide opportunities for mutual help as participants exchange tangible resources, practical information, and emotional support. New supportive relationships may be established that endure beyond the program. The parent circle may also contribute to the planning and carrying out of useful community activities.

Effectiveness of natural helping is demonstrated by the sheer numbers of unpaid community personnel in Aboriginal family and children's programs. Consultations with service providers and evaluation studies reveal that unpaid personnel contribute to program activities, planning, support activities, and the on-going monitoring of programs (Frank Maidman Associates, 1998). For example, Family Support Committees in fourteen First Nations communities comprised well over 70 volunteers. Over 200 local community members volunteered for unpaid family support activities. These included customary child care, emotional support, counselling to troubled families, workshops, fundraising, and program assistance (Maidman, 1988).

Community Control
Some community development interventions incorporate specific community control measures to reduce the risks to families and children. Such approaches assume that children are maltreated because of a breakdown in community norms and sanctions. Prevention involves strengthening the informal or natural sources of control against unacceptable behaviour, and making arrangements for identifying and taking action against wrongdoers. Such actions might include: (1) reporting family violence to the police, (2) making referrals to child protection authorities, (3) expressing concern to neighbours or the perpetrators, and (4) protecting young girls from pimps. These measures are provided by community watch and community protection initiatives, sometimes organized by warrior societies.

Community control interventions may be most effective when accompanied by measures to encourage the inner control of behaviour, supported by changing relationships and local culture. One study documented and assessed a program for an urban Aboriginal community (Maidman, 1996b). The community development model included establishment of a system for reporting incidents of violence, abuse, and threats to safety. However, it also included actions to mobilize untrained local volunteer leaders and provided community-wide education concerning issues affecting family life and childrearing. Overall, the model balanced community control with efforts to change local behaviour through awareness and commitment to new standards of community and family behaviour. In the process, new relationships were established.

Community Healing

Healthy, responsive communities are populated by emotionally healthy individuals, energized by strong relationships. Such communities have a strong sense of community, nurtured by collective pride, ownership of programs, and mutual responsibility. The traditional tribal community previously enjoyed all of these qualities. However, historical factors and the colonial relationship destroyed much of the integrity of community life. These qualities, though, are gradually being restored through community healing.

Aboriginal people regard community healing practices as effective and promising for alleviating the personal pain related to past injustices, family and community problems, and current issues. Consistent with collectivist values, community healing seeks to restore harmony between people and groups. As a preventive intervention, community healing strengthens caregivers. It helps build: (1) community standards for acceptable and unacceptable behaviour for family life, childrearing, and community living; (2) stronger role models within the community; and (3) more responsive and caring support persons for families in need. At the community level, healed communities have the capacity to build social and economic arrangements for healthy family life and child development.

Aboriginal healing emerges from a different world-view and principles than Euro-Canadian thinking. This world-view is symbolized by the circle and the concept of interdependence and balance within all aspects of life. Returning to a balanced state involves a person's present and past relationships. A complete healing journey involves restoring balance to the family and the community.

Abuse is also viewed differently by Aboriginal people. Many non-Aboriginals see abuse as a quality of interaction between one individual (the perpetrator) and another (the victim). From this perspective, healing may be individualistic, focusing on one or the other. For Aboriginal people, the offender's actions radiate outwardly, disturbing victim, self, and the lives of countless community members. The forces of balance and harmony are replaced by negative emotions and disturbed relationships. Hate, anger, blame, and mutual alienation hover in and around the children's life-space. From this perspective, an important healing goal is to restore and protect the community, by rebalancing relationships. As one key informant noted, conflict is a prevailing characteristic of many First Nations communities and help with conflict resolution is most needed.

Community healing practices are increasingly being documented (Awasis Agency of Northern Manitoba, 1997; Connors & Oates, 1997; Health Canada, 1997a; Krawll, 1994; McCormick, 1995; Ross, 1996; Van Uchelen et al., 1997) and are elements in most Aboriginal preventive practices. Because of the holistic perspective, the *community at large* potentially benefits from problem-solving practice. Practices directed to specific issues of child maltreatment are organized in ways that benefit larger circles of people. Healing (or sentencing circle) models (Awasis Agency of Northern Manitoba, 1997), for example, bring together extended family members, victims, and offenders to determine what injustice has occurred, and what processes should correct the harm.

Specific practices contributing to community healing include community healing circles, mediation and peace making, and traditional healing practices such as sweat lodges and ceremonies. Many are family-focused, yet benefit the larger community. Others, like traditional healing, are important components of many interventions. To paraphrase a key informant, having traditional healing activities, even on a small scale, promotes a gradual awakening and community acceptance of culture.

The Hollow Water Model
The Hollow Water Model, known also as Community Holistic Circle Healing, is organized around the following healing steps. First, there is initial disclosure, followed immediately by protection of the child, usually through placement in a community home. This is followed by confronting the victimizer, assisting the nonoffending partner as well as all concerned families. Friends of the families are involved as allies. A team approach is coordinated, in which the victimizer is assisted to admit and accept responsibility. The team prepares the victim, victimizer, and all families to attend a special community gathering, and commit to a special healing contract. Following implementation of the healing contract, a community cleansing ceremony is held to mark the completion of the healing contract, the restoration of balance, and a new beginning (Connors & Oates, 1997; Ross, 1996; Solicitor General of Canada, 1997).

This process is linked to the child protection and justice system in the following ways. A group of volunteer and interdisciplinary interagency people form an assessment team that includes the appropriate child protection and justice authorities. This team creates a plan of action and monitors the plan. The perpetrator is immediately charged and asked to plead guilty. The court is asked to delay sentencing, pending choice of the court or community healing process. Should the perpetrator accept healing, he is placed on probation and healing begins. Should he refuse, he proceeds through the court process.

An assessment of the Hollow Water Model, although exploratory, has provided rather impressive results. Only five of 45 offenders chose the court process. Of those completing the healing circle, only two repeated abuses (Ross, 1996). Within the community, there were increased numbers of disclosures of child sexual abuse, even though community members had little awareness of the model (Taylor-Henry & Hill, 1990). Community helpers viewed the holistic process as effective and culturally relevant. If these impacts are consistent across all communities, the community healing model may be an economically viable alternative to court.

The Hollow Water Model has been adapted to urban settings. Evaluation of The Circle of Harmony Healing Society in Terrace, British Columbia, reveals a contrast to the models implemented in First Nations. Adaptation to the urban environment leads to closer links with formal urban services, less reliance on close extended-family networks, and an extensive use of volunteer mental health workers (Connors, 1993a). The impact of the program cannot be estimated from this evaluation, other than apparent client satisfaction.

Social and Recreational Opportunities

Consultations with elders and service providers suggest that social and recreational activities could provide enormous preventive opportunities (Frank Maidman Associates, 1998). They keep people busy and discourage unhealthy activities such as substance abuse or gambling. Well-designed opportunities strengthen bonds between families and between parents and children. By encouraging helping networks and friendships, they promote informal, natural counselling. Finally, social and recreational opportunities help build a collective self-esteem and a strong sense of community. Many Aboriginal people believe that the most effective community-wide initiatives will: bring children together with elders, provide high visibility for elders, encourage whole-family participation, recover the traditional pattern of parental visiting, and keep children and youth meaningfully occupied (Frank Maidman Associates, 1998).

On another level, social and recreational opportunities may reverse *anomic* trends in neighbourhoods or communities (Garbarino & Kostelny, 1992). In such communities, people go their own ways and do not see much of each other. Without a sense of community, the community lacks a focal point. There is no meaningful centre for active people, and no cohesion to the structure of influence. Anonymity prevails, making it difficult to mobilize for common interests. Anomic communities lack qualities for problem solving, and information does not circulate freely. Initial individual responses to problems are evident, but they lack coordinated collective response. Promising practices for building more socially integrated communities include social gatherings and recreational opportunities, organized children's programs that include social play and cultural learning, traditional gatherings, arts and crafts for everyone, and social and recreational activities for the entire family.

Repatriation

The need for repatriation services is indirectly related to past mainstream provincial child protection policies and practices in which children deemed in need of protection could be placed in homes away from their original families and communities. Three assumptions lead to the designation of repatriation as a prevention service. First, children's well-being is affected by the quality of life of their families and communities and by the consistency of the various socializing environments. If child protection decisions lead to children moving around varied child care settings (Johnston, 1983), their emotional well-being is at risk. A second assumption is that some children growing up outside of their original families and communities experience emotional and identity stress in culturally alien environments. Third, past child welfare decisions are viewed by Native people as highly disruptive to their communities and families, creating unhealthy environments for children left behind. Many First Nations Aboriginal service providers report cases where alcohol abuse by parents is partly explained by the loss of their children to the child protection system.

With these assumptions, then, repatriation services aim to restore family and community relationships and stability for those who have lost their children. They give repatriated children the opportunity to be part of their families and community, to learn their culture, and to experience a stable family life. Finally, repatriation aims to bring children out of difficult circumstances as they struggle to adjust in alien families and communities.

As prevention, repatriation is a universal strategy for strengthening families and whole communities. Also, by reducing the risk of maltreatment in specific high-risk Aboriginal populations, it may also be deemed 'selective.' Finally, if previously maltreating families receive support after their children are returned, repatriation may also qualify as 'indicated' prevention.

PREVENTION THEMES IN FIRST NATIONS CHILD WELFARE INITIATIVES: A SUMMARY

Preventive practices typically include cultural learning as part of the change strategy. Prevention services aim to prevent problems or limit their impact. Depending on their goals and their target groups, prevention services may be of different types. Some are directed to *whole communities* or even larger populations. These aim to create the information, resources, relationships, and community structures so that family life is strong and so that parent–child relationships support the safe, healthy development of children.

Other prevention initiatives focus on *specific target populations* (e.g., single parents, previously abused women, teens, or communities with high residential mobility or conflict) where there is a risk of child maltreatment or evidence of early problems. These prevention strategies aim to *create strengths* (e.g., parent education), *build resourcefulness* (e.g., building natural helping networks, voluntarism), *limit the seriousness of early problems* (e.g., family support services), help *alleviate the stress* of urban living (also family support), and *advocate* for families needing access to other services. As well, such interventions will *alert the clients to their parenting obligations and rights* according to legislation and perhaps Aboriginal beliefs. In these initiatives, therapy or healing may be used as a *tool* for preventing later child maltreatment.

The final set of preventions involve *direct interventions* into troubled lives for the purpose of avoiding more serious problems (e.g., injury or death) and setting the stage for changing troubled family situations. Removing children from abusive homes through foster or customary care arrangements while parents receive help is one example.

Stepping back from the previous program details, this section presents a summary of themes marking unique features of Aboriginal prevention approaches.

Focus on Strong Communities and Families through Cultural Recovery

The various initiatives to restore well-being to families and children are best understood within a broad social and healing movement, as Aboriginal communities establish their rightful place in Canadian society through cultural recovery and self-determination.

Focus on Vision, Philosophy, Values, and Principles

Aboriginal program planners stress the articulation of vision, values, and principles as the heart and soul of their prevention programs. These are grounded in traditional cultural ideas such as holism, the roles of extended families, customary care, and the like.

Focus on the Family

Most Aboriginal prevention services take the *family unit* as the main focus in understanding matters of children's maltreatment and well-being. By identifying the family unit as an important focal point for their work, programs typically recognize the impact of external influences, from the family's immediate network (e.g., relatives, friends, neighbours) to more distant sets of influences like community behaviours, resources, opportunities, or indeed public policies. Rather than reducing complex problems in living to simplistic explanations, a holistic understanding incorporates physical health and the spiritual, emotional, and psychological aspects of living. All of these are nested within interdependent contexts of relationships, family groups and networks, communities, and society at large.

Focus on the Life Cycle

Healing and prevention programs respect the Aboriginal notion of the wheel of life or life cycle. The ages and stages of life from birth to death are recognized as infants, toddlers, children, youth, young adults, parents, grandparents, and elders.

Focus on Cultural Learning

Through cultural learning, prevention programs aim to create a sense of pride and self-esteem by building a social and helping community that shares a common sense of belonging and by teaching specific knowledge and practices for living and healing. A close analysis of Aboriginal prevention programs and practices shows that cultural learning involves the four processes of: (1) knowing and understanding various parts of culture; (2) valuing and respecting culture as important; (3) wanting to live in a good way and to adapt the culture to modern living; and (4) incorporating culture into a valued individual and collective identity as a Native person and as a community (Taylor, 1997).

Focus on Culture-Based Practice

Aboriginal programs also incorporate traditional cultural principles into staff service roles. How staff provide services through specific relationships with their clients reflects important beliefs and norms from

Native culture. For example, unlike contemporary social work practice, service staff typically supplement scientific and professional knowledge and practice with resources from Native culture. The Native holistic principle also applies to staff development. Staff are regarded as more than a bundle of skills and knowledge. Most programs recognize that emotional dimensions of helping, including staff needs, are as important as professional and cultural excellence. Because Aboriginal staff may have dysfunctional backgrounds, their experiences with clients may evoke negative memories or feelings. Agency opportunities (e.g., staff circles) to deal with these issues may contribute to staff development and stress management. Staff roles are often centred around informal care, common-sense wisdom, community involvement, role modelling, and teaching. Service staff may also be expected to function like extended-family members (Maidman, 1988).

Focus on Natural Support Systems

The Aboriginal community is deemed an important partner in the care of children. This principle is implemented through the use of natural sources of support to aid in crises. Of the various sources of support identified in mainstream publications, the most important for Aboriginal communities are the extended-family members; friends; neighbours and other local community members; role-related helpers; and persons with similar problems. In theory, mobilization refers to recruiting, orienting, training, and providing follow-up support to these natural helpers. Should all of these activities happen in practice, mobilizing natural support systems then becomes a way of strengthening the community as whole.

Themes in Urban Aboriginal Communities

Aboriginal-controlled human services exist in many urban centres across Canada. Central to most programs are efforts to build Aboriginal community relationships and help break down social isolation. As well, such programs give family members the confidence and skills for urban survival. Related to this is cultural recovery, and the adaptation of traditional values and norms to an urban environment. The culture base of urban prevention programs is an important principle. Heterogeneous urban populations render program planning and delivery particularly challenging. Because so many urban Aboriginal clients are acculturated, the principles of program diversity, client choice of services, and program adaptability, are very important. In content, the learning of traditional values, beliefs, and family practices seems as important in cities as in traditional reserve communities. Even so, finding traditional teachers is enormously challenging.

CHALLENGES OF PROGRAM IMPLEMENTATION IN FIRST NATIONS COMMUNITIES

Thus far, we have summarized various examples of Aboriginal prevention and protection initiatives. Consultation, research, and evaluation experience reveal that putting into practice the visions of what communities hope to achieve has been a complex process. This process may be best understood as one of integration of vision, resources, organizational support, and community circumstances. However, the social problems and general conditions affecting the introduction of new programs have been little understood and documented. Table 8.3 does not provide definitive statements based on a comprehensive knowledge of the growing pains of Aboriginal prevention programs across Canada. Rather, it presents complications. Because these complications were so challenging to those programs with which we were involved, they are worth being treated as 'working ideas' by program planners, community leaders, and consultants.

ACTION SUGGESTIONS

The following suggestions are organized according to the categories of individuals who might implement the recommendation. To be useful for various kinds of prevention programs, the following suggestions are general in nature. Hopefully, these action principles will be adapted to various initiatives in diverse local circumstances. Each suggestion grows out of the challenges faced by First Nations communities in their innovative efforts. They also respond to the issues raised by community members in recent community action research studies.

Aboriginal World-View

- Funders are gradually learning and respecting the Aboriginal holistic world-view. This must continue.
- Culture-based development and implementation requires 'resource slack.'

TABLE 8.3
Challenges of Program Implementation in Aboriginal Communities

Themes	Challenges
Contexts of program implementation	• The quality of program delivery cannot be separated from larger processes such as community expectations, program resources, inter-agency cooperation, planning processes, the overall health of the community, and historical factors.
Establishing a traditional culture base	• Inadequate understanding of the meaning of abstractions such as "holism" particularly in relation to management and service practices. • Conflict between the understanding of values and principles and actual practice. • Difficulties of acting according to principles due to local community conditions. • Local disagreements concerning values.
Engaging community support	• Public legitimation and support of new prevention programs is precarious in some communities, evidenced by poor turnout to meetings or program activities and critical comments about the program informally or during evaluation. • Unfavourable responses have been ascribed to limited opportunities for initial consultation, negative past history with child welfare in general, lack of faith in Aboriginal capacity to be successful, limited tolerance for growth and experimentation, and limited initial or on-going public education about programs.
Training	• Self-government means that many new Aboriginal organizations and programs are quickly coming into being without a gradual evolution, human resources, or organizational culture. • Lack of professionally trained management and service staff. • Trained staff educated in mainstream institutions; inappropriate fit between training curriculum, training styles and methods, and the needs of First Nations service providers. • Local staff often have suffered the same abuses and misery brought by clients; care for service providers is important. • Extraordinarily high turnover in Aboriginal organizations.
Pressure to deliver services	• Communities granting legitimacy to front-line service actions, not to developmental activities such as team-building, policy development, and training. • Action-oriented management and staff with limited focus on program/organizational development. • Insufficient funding to cover developmental costs such as training. • Policy and organizational development conducted by outside technical consultants that is neither understood nor supported by key community players.

TABLE 8.3 (*continued*)
Challenges of Program Implementation in Aboriginal Communities

Themes	Challenges
Implementing community education	• Lack of facilities, equipment, and funding for prevention. • Difficulty of encouraging community involvement through volunteer organizations and general participation. • Inadequate leadership and organizational skills. • Differences of opinion within some communities concerning the importance of Native cultural awareness and spirituality. • Pressures to respond to family crises at the expense of coaching and participating in proactive activities.
Working with troubled families	• Clients who resist help, refuse to acknowledge problems, blame others, are reluctant to talk, and manipulate.
Supporting the natural helpers	• Despite the commitment to energizing the natural helpers in many First Nations communities, there may be insufficient attention given to how this should be done.
Unanticipated consequences	• Abuse of programs by some families such as use of short-term child placements as "baby-sitting." • Misuse of programs in the absence of alternative community resources. • Augmenting statistics to improve chances for continued or increased funding.
Integration of services	• Tension between the staff of various local programs evidenced by lack of attendance at meetings, communication problems, and mutual ignorance of programs. • Larger systems problems manifested in preexisting community relations and divisive bureaucratic structures and funding.
Engaging mainstream institutions	• Difficulties in negotiating culture contacts; management, workers and clients must interact with people in non-Native workplaces and conduct their affairs according to the rules, policies, procedures, and customs of mainstream institutions that may lack the patience and organizational flexibility to accommodate the style of First Nations services.
Funding limitations	• Many First Nations communities lack appropriate facilities and equipment for prevention work. • Limited funding slack to accommodate unanticipated development expenses. • Alternative parenting arrangements for at-risk children incur enormous direct service costs, which are often covered through primary prevention budgets. • The focus on crisis management absorbs funding that could be spent on hiring community development specialists.

TABLE 8.3 (*concluded*)
Challenges of Program Implementation in Aboriginal Communities

Themes	Challenges
Local political control	• Interventions sometimes require decisive actions and hard-hitting educational programs, but in some small communities with entrenched political structures, such actions may disturb the status quo and offend self-interests.
Narrowing of service delivery	• Despite holistic ideals, pressure for counselling services, budget cutbacks, and pressures from political leaders all narrow the focus of actual service delivery to isolated symptomatic problems. • Little attention to small remote areas where there are serious issues such as alcohol abuse, family conflict, and child maltreatment.
Customary care	• Some communities lack sufficient customary care families who are willing or able to take children, particularly babies or special-needs children. • Some families fear retaliation from natural parents. • Some families expect financial support at the level of provincial child welfare to meet their needs. • Difficulties providing post-placement follow-up work with natural families. • Inadequate staff training for providing customary care services.
Other relevant themes	• Familiarity with clients and community; necessity of working with relatives. • Role conflicts as staff helper and community member. • Confusion over the appropriate knowledge base for helping. • Nonacceptance of authority and/or "legal" authority from Chief and council. • Clients' knowledge of practitioners' private lives, past and present. • Lack of acceptance of problems due to prevalence in community subculture.

Consultation and Training

- First Nations communities should be consulted broadly in planning new prevention initiatives. Aboriginal regional agencies should support rather than supersede local community development.
- Detailed knowledge of the prevention program and its practices should be facilitated and documented, covering: community problems for which the program exists, what the program will address,

organizational support, core program activities, techniques, resources, and the like.
- In-service training should be a key strategy in implementing new prevention programs in First Nations communities. Training should: (1) meaningfully link with other developmental activities, including resource development, formative evaluation, community feedback, and education concerning the program; (2) respond directly to the problems of implementing the program; (3) avoid prepackaged curriculum materials developed elsewhere, in favour of locally relevant ideas and resources; (4) use trainers who are familiar with technical aspects of the training *and* with the community conditions in which new skills and knowledge will be used; and (5) incorporate personal development training.
- Some management, staff, and board members should take responsibility for planning and monitoring the *early* implementation of a new program, and develop problem-solving procedures. Consideration should be given to a formative (i.e., process) evaluation to assist the *fine-tuning* of a new program during early stages.
- To minimize communication problems, community planners should: (1) give special attention to the significant communication networks surrounding the program innovation; (2) identify appropriate internal and community communication structures for information-sharing concerning innovation challenges and successes and instil community and organizational norms supporting feedback; (3) assure opportunities for staff and community feedback (e.g., staff meetings, training, evaluation) concerning problems in implementing new programs; and (4) allow for communication concerning negative emotions.
- To manage the time challenges of implementing new programs, there should be: (1) clarity about various key stages of the implementation process, (2) avoidance of tight time lines during the early period to allow flexibility to respond to challenges, and (3) opportunities for service providers to engage in group reflection about new role requirements and tasks.
- The Aboriginal leaders such as executive directors or program coordinators, should take active roles in promoting an organizational culture that supports new prevention programs and practices. Support for a new prevention program or service comes from the sponsoring organization's environment, its formal organizational structure and internal processes, and its organizational culture.

Community Harmony and Child Maltreatment Prevention

We recommend that prevention programs seriously attempt to build broad community harmony within First Nations communities. Local divisiveness is created by numerous factors: family conflicts, local politics, jealousy, or disagreements over the place of traditional spirituality. Disharmony in First Nations communities is relevant to prevention programs related to child maltreatment in at least three ways. First, community disharmony contributes to the breakdown of community norms and controls against alcohol abuse, family violence, and inappropriate childrearing. Second, disharmony is a negative social environment for introducing new prevention initiatives and contributes to the undermining of success through such dynamics as mistrust, lack of cooperation, inadequate volunteer spirit, and pessimism. Third, community disharmony weakens the psychological sense of community, an important ingredient for natural helping. For these reasons, community-healing initiatives should be an essential part of any new prevention programming. Understanding and breaking down the social and psychological barriers between individuals and groups should be an important part of all program development phases, starting with the needs assessment and ending with the celebration of success.

Again, a comprehensive holistic perspective emerges as the most appropriate starting point. Programs that isolate small areas of family life or personal functioning will undoubtedly make some difference. But, more often than not, they will leave root causes untouched, causing problems to emerge symptomatically in other ways. Children are protected through the natural healthy functioning of well communities. Taking children away from dysfunctional families in unhealthy communities, without addressing the larger pains, will reinforce the dysfunctions of family and community. Intrusive child protection measures must go hand-in-hand with family preservation and community healing.

First Nations Leadership and the Culture of Family Well-Being

Within healthy communities, First Nations leaders have important roles in building a community cultural climate that values children while creating and sustaining conditions for safety and well-being. Part of this requires family life and family well-being to be front and centre of the community agenda.

It is beyond the scope of this work to address the various challenges or successes of Aboriginal leadership. We shall focus instead on ideas and issues flowing from prevention program evaluations. As well, our comments are energized by the tremendous importance given to children in traditional Aboriginal community life. From this, we argue that a First Nation's community culture must be organized around the value of children. Local leaders can help shape that culture. By local leaders, we refer to chiefs, council members, elders, the heads of programs and agencies, and others with community visibility and influence.

Local leaders must be committed to family well-being and the safety of children. They must demonstrate this commitment through actions, not simply feelings and words. Such actions should include shared initiatives with other leaders across the provinces and territories, and indeed across Canada. Of extreme importance for shaping a family-oriented local culture are *actions visible to community members*. The small size of most First Nations communities lends itself to enormous impacts from leaders. Their actions must convey a message that family violence and child maltreatment are not tolerable.

VALUES AND BELIEFS FOR A HEALTHIER FUTURE

As we face the unfolding of the prophecies of healing, we have much to do to assist families to find their paths to healing. In particular, we need to look very carefully and critically at where the values and beliefs that we have adopted from civilized society are taking us. Are they assisting us to develop the type of family and community environment that we seek? Are they leading us to live in peace and balance with each other and all of Creation? Are they leading us on a path of health? We are now challenged to evaluate the values and beliefs that we have evolved and compare them with those from tribal societies. This may lead us to recognize that many of the values and beliefs from tribal societies guide us to live healthier lifestyles.

Despite the many assaults that have occurred on the Aboriginal families of North America during the past five hundred years, Native people have survived and are beginning their recovery from their state of ill health. While it is a travesty that some First Nations did not survive to see this time of healing, it is a testament of the resilience and strength of the tribal family that so many Aboriginal families remain. Today, many Aboriginal people are beginning to realize that most of the strengths that enabled their survival lie within their culture. Those ways that the colonizers regarded as primitive and from which they attempted to separate Native people are what many First Nations and non-Native people now realize contain the tools that will likely ensure the survival of all peoples and all of Creation on this planet. This is why today there is a strong resurgence of Native culture and Native pride. Aboriginal families are now coming full circle to redefine the principles from their past that will help them to form a healthier future.

SECTION IV
Conclusion

CHAPTER NINE

Beyond the Boundaries: Themes for Thinking and Action in the Promotion of Family Wellness and the Prevention of Child Maltreatment

Geoffrey Nelson, Isaac Prilleltensky, and Leslea Peirson

INTRODUCTION

The purpose of this concluding chapter is to reflect on what we have learned regarding the promotion of family wellness and the prevention of child maltreatment (fundamentals for thinking). In addition, this chapter focuses on what can be done to enhance Canada's ability to improve the lives of children (fundamentals for action). In so doing, we consider key themes that we have identified throughout the book. Some of these themes relate to our conceptual framework that we described in Chapter 1 and that we have used throughout the book, while other themes have emerged over the course of this project. In many ways, these themes are quite consistent with the world-view of Aboriginal people, which was described in Chapter 8. All together we have identified six themes, which we describe in the sections that follow.

In suggesting directions for the future, we are proposing not so much changing what we do as going beyond the boundaries of current practice. The current crises in child maltreatment and child welfare agencies clearly indicate that change is needed. If Canadians are serious about reducing child maltreatment, we believe that we can make significant headway towards this goal if different stakeholder groups attend to the directions that we identify. These directions focus on expanding the frontiers of what we are currently doing. As we noted in Chapter 3, all segments of Canadian society have a role to play in reducing this social problem, and each stakeholder group's role is different but complementary. Thus, some of the directions for action that we suggest relate more to one stakeholder group than to others. For example, our suggested directions for social policy changes are obviously directed more at policymakers than at any other stakeholder group. But policymakers are influenced by political pressure, so citizens can organize and exert such pressure on government to take the problem of child maltreatment seriously. The directions that we recommend all relate to the themes that we have identified.

THEMES

Theme 1: Beyond the Individual – The Ecological Perspective

By now it is clear that a narrow focus on individual children or parents is not a useful guide for policy or programs to promote family wellness and to prevent child maltreatment. In Table 9.1, we outline where we are now, where we need to go, and what we need to do to move beyond a focus on the individual to an ecological focus on people in context.

Fundamentals for Thinking

We know from Chapter 2, and similar reviews (Belsky, 1993; Emery & Laumann-Billings, 1998), that child maltreatment is multiply determined, and that the probability of abuse and neglect escalates with an increase in risk factors. Although the literature related to wellness is not as developed as the literature on maltreatment, it is quite apparent that there are also multiple pathways to wellness. However, despite our knowledge of the etiological complexity of maltreatment and wellness, current attempts at remediation, prevention, and promotion have not fully reflected the diversity in contributing factors.

As described in chapters 4 through 6, many policies and programs offer single-focused supports (e.g., cash and tax benefits, parenting skills courses, self-help groups) or assistance in a few select areas (e.g., home visiting and peer support groups for new parents; crisis intervention and concrete supports for high-risk families). Multi-component programs addressing a variety of contributing factors and family needs are less common in practice, but there is evidence that these approaches are gaining popularity. Better Beginnings, Better Futures in Ontario, 1,2,3 GO! in the greater Montreal area, and the Community Action Program for Children, which is implemented in high-risk communities across the country, are some examples of recent initiatives to provide multi-component programming in Canada. In general, however, most interventions are more narrowly focused.

TABLE 9.1
Theme 1: Beyond the Individual – The Ecological Perspective

Fundamentals for Thinking Lessons Learned		Fundamentals for Action Future Directions
Where We Are Now	Where We Need to Go	What We Need to Do
• Family wellness and child maltreatment are multiply determined phenomena. • Proactive and reactive approaches have tended to be focused on the micro level.	• There is a need for multi-focused interventions that address the diversity of factors that contribute to child maltreatment and family wellness. • There is a trend toward ecologically focused interventions that address several levels of analysis.	• Promote multi-focused interventions that address the diversity and expanse of difficulties and opportunities facing children and families. • Promote action at all ecological levels to enhance child, parental and family, community, and societal wellness.

We learned in the Interventions section of this volume that policies and programs targeting single contributing factors are unlikely to be instrumental in reducing maltreatment. What is missing from these models is a holistic focus and a practical recognition of the cumulative and sometimes interacting nature of factors contributing to maltreatment and wellness. While it is true that families may have a variety of needs met through an assortment of resources, there is often little integration of services. We tend to disconnect people's needs when we provide fragmented supports. Some of our consultation participants said that this separation (dealing with different agencies or ministries, meeting with multiple case workers, going to appointments in various locations) contributes added stress to families who are already experiencing difficulty. Contrary to these mainstream methods of helping, we learned in Chapter 8 that Aboriginal practices support holistic beliefs of health and healthy development, emphasizing an interrelated yet balanced connection between the individual, the family, the community, society, and Creation. It should be noted, however, that holistic thinking and action are not new; they are an integral part of the traditional worldview of Aboriginal communities. We are at a point now where we must begin to relearn how to apply this form of thinking and action in the current context.

Our attempts to assist high-risk families and to support families who are functioning well are restricted not only by the narrow focus on selected determinants of maltreatment and wellness but also by the pervasive concentration on individuals and families to the neglect of community- and societal-level structures. Our fixation with the micro level predominates despite convincing evidence that factors occurring at the meso and macro levels (e.g., availability of resources, social cohesion, income security and stability, social norms and values) have an incredible influence on the incidence of maltreatment and states of wellness. Where we are now is really a context in which interventions focus on addressing the concrete needs of individuals and families and/or changing their behaviour. Other than a few studies (e.g., Blyth & Roehlkepartian, 1993; Coulton, Korbin, Su, & Chow, 1995; Garbarino & Kostelny, 1992; Korbin & Coulton, 1996), we have done little to acknowledge and examine community- and societal-level contributions to prevention and promotion.

Multi-focused interventions that respond to the range and number of contributing factors and that adapt to the realities of families as they move through developmental phases are likely to have a greater impact on reducing the incidence of maltreatment and fostering healthy family functioning than are single-focused programs. While there are examples of these types of initiatives in practice, there is much more that needs to be done to facilitate the diffusion of successful models. Multicomponent interventions are less prevalent, and perhaps less appealing from an organizational standpoint, because they are often horizontally and vertically complex (many sectors are often involved in services and multiple ecological levels are engaged), they may require adaptation to varying community contexts, and they can be difficult to evaluate. At the same time, we should remember that in trying to prevent child maltreatment we are not dealing with a simple problem; thus we can hardly expect a simple solution to suffice.

Even the most promising multi-focused efforts may be overpowered by larger economic, cultural, and environmental conditions. A truly comprehensive approach to preventing child maltreatment and promoting family wellness would include more than micro-level, band-aid solutions to social problems (e.g., food banks are not an effective strategy for reducing poverty); it would focus on reducing social risks by improving conditions in areas such as employment, income supports, housing standards, child care, and so on. We need more ecological balance in our attempts to prevent maltreatment and promote family wellness. The roles of meso- and macro-level structures in the creation of vulnerable contexts or the enhancement of wellness have long been neglected. It is time to break a new trail, to expand the obligation and potential for prevention and promotion into the community and societal domains. This is not to say that interventions targeting individuals and families should be abandoned; rather, they should be complemented by other interventions.

Fundamentals for Action

To further an ecological perspective on preventing child maltreatment and promoting family wellness, we propose the following:

1. Promote multi-focused interventions that address the range and number of difficulties and opportunities facing children and families; this may require the participation and cooperation of multiple sectors (refer to Theme 5 on the issue of partnerships later in this chapter) and may take substantial time.
2. Promote action at all ecological levels: from interventions that aim to

strengthen individual capacities to policies that are enacted to counteract or compensate for unjust social conditions; from programs that work to improve family dynamics to community development initiatives that cultivate strong and cohesive neighbourhoods and foster a culture of caring.
3. Promote empirical research to establish more comprehensive inventories of vulnerabilities, protective mechanisms, and promoting mechanisms; to advance our understanding of the relationships among contributing factors; and to improve our actions (programs and organizational systems) to alleviate difficulties that can lead to maltreatment.

Theme 2: Beyond Individualism and Self-Interest – Values for a Just and Caring Society

One of the unique contributions of our work is our articulation of a value base that can inform policies and programs. In Table 9.2, we provide an overview of fundamentals for thinking and action related to the values that we believe characterize a just and caring society.

Fundamentals for Thinking

Child wellness, as we saw in Chapter 1, is defined as a state of affairs in which children's needs for love, care, and protection are met. For these needs to be met, children require the right combination of values, resources, policies, and programs. Children's wellness depends on the actions of parents and the availability of external supports and societal resources. The individual actions of parents are influenced by the presence of formal and informal supports. Children need their parents and parents need resources.

If we think of children's needs in terms of what parents and communities can do for them, we see that parents are assigned the primary responsibility and that the state is withdrawing its helping functions. If we think of values as principles that guide the allocation of rights and responsibilities, we see that our society assigns more importance to individual rights and responsibilities than to public obligations. This creates a state of imbalance whereby individuals are expected to care for their own children without many supports, supports that are crucial for raising healthy children. Powerful trends in society accord preference to individual rights and responsibilities and undermine the role of public

TABLE 9.2
Theme 2: Beyond Individualism and Self-Interest – Values for a Just and Caring Society

Fundamentals for Thinking Lessons Learned		Fundamentals for Action Future Directions
Where We Are Now	Where We Need to Go	What We Need to Do
• Societal values of individualism, self-interest, and survival of the fittest lead to "victim-blaming" and to the philosophy of individual responsibility. • Child maltreatment is viewed as an individual or family problem, disconnected from societal forces and power dynamics.	• Societal values of justice, collectivism, and cooperation lead to solidarity and philosophy of social responsibility. • Social responsibility posits that family wellness and child maltreatment are universal concerns in which everyone has a stake, including the government.	• Resist pressure to pathologize families and individualize social problems and reformulate solutions in terms of parental, communal, *and* government responsibility. • Support individuals *and* social structures by paying *equal attention* to personal, collective, and relational values in programs and policies.

institutions in caring for its citizens. As a result, we live in a state of imbalance. But if balance between individual and social responsibility is so important, why do we neglect it?

The answer is complicated, but part of it lies in the fact that most societies are run not necessarily on the basis of everyone's needs but mostly on the needs of those who run them. If those who run society benefit from individualistic philosophies, we can expect a neglect of the state. If those who run society benefit from collectivist philosophies, we can expect a neglect of individual needs. In conservative eras, as Levine and Levine (1992) and Prilleltensky (1994a) have shown, personal and social problems are framed and defined in intrapsychic terms. In conservative times, the role of the state in creating and solving difficulties is undermined and minimized. Leaders are under pressure by corporations to cut taxes and public expenditures (Allahar & Côté, 1998; Evans & Wekerle, 1997). To avoid investments in public agencies, a victim-blaming discourse is fostered. This discourse assigns responsibility for the problem and the solution to individual people, 'suggesting that present inequalities are justified because if people really wanted to work hard and improve themselves they could do so. No systemic injustice explains their inequality; instead, those who do not get ahead have failed themselves' (Allahar & Côté, 1998, p. 15). If all problems are personal problems, then there is no need for the state to intervene. Fix people not society – that is the central motto of this mentality.

We live in conservative times, times in which collective values are largely neglected in favour of individual responsibility (Eichler, 1997; Evans & Wekerle, 1997). Individualism, which dominates the public agenda, finds its way into child and family problems – it influences how we define and deal with child maltreatment. Maltreatment tends to be defined in mother-, father-, or family-blaming terms (Febbraro, 1994), in large disregard of societal factors such as unemployment, a culture of self-indulgence, and structural violence. While maltreatment is played out in the family, and parents cannot be absolved of responsibility, parents are subject to negative social forces that distort their abilities to strive for a balance between their personal well-being and the well-being of their children. Eichler (1997) refers to the tendency to blame families as the *microstructural bias*, according to which there is 'a tendency to treat families as encapsulated units. Behaviours are then explained by simply looking at what happens within the unit rather than by trying to understand how familial behaviours are partially affected by extraneous factors' (p. 9).

Just as individualism overshadows interdependence, intolerance prevents diversity. Despite a rhetoric of diversity and acceptance of varied family constellations, conservative values still reject nontraditional families (Leonard, 1997). Nontraditional families struggle for recognition and continue to suffer from discriminatory policies and cultural norms (Eichler, 1997; Lindeman Nelson, 1997; Nicholson, 1997). Nicholson (1997) claims that nontraditional families are made to feel ashamed that they don't fit the traditional family mould:

> Not only gay and lesbians but also heterosexuals living alone; unmarried heterosexuals living together; married couples with husbands at home caring for children or wives working outside of the home; and children living in single-parent, step family, or alternating households are either 'in the closet' or somewhat embarrassed about how they live. (p. 27)

In light of this picture, where the needs of the powerful carry the day, we ask ourselves what can be done. The answer can already be gleaned from the present state of value imbalance.

We have established that we need a balance between individual and community rights and responsibilities. We propose to balance the scale by *temporarily* pushing individualist values to the background and by placing collectivist values in the foreground. We emphasize *temporarily* because we strive to reach an equilibrium, not another state of imbalance where communal goals overshadow personal needs. The ideal state of affairs is a balanced state of affairs. As Midgley and Hughes (1997) put it:

> Individual and communal ideals cannot simply fight a war here ... The problem is not to get rid of one aspect or the other but to find new ways of trying to reconcile them, to achieve a balance between them which does justice to both kinds of need. (pp. 62-63)

The balance we need to achieve applies not only to the dialectic between individuals and communities, but also to the tension between rights and obligations. It seems that we live in an era of entitlements. Corporations demand a favourable business climate, members of Parliament don't want to give up their pensions, the middle-class expects less taxes, and lobbying groups claim their rights. This is understandable; constituencies seek to empower themselves. This is where we are. But this state of affairs caused the excesses of individualism that many have already documented (Saul, 1995). Allahar and Côté (1998) remind us that our social system 'encourages one to be "selfish": to explore one's self indefinitely, to be concerned or even obsessed with feeding one's self-esteem' (p. 159). The current preoccupation with rights has to be balanced with obligations – the obligations of individuals, governments, and corporations. This is where we need to go. To get there, Eichler (1997) proposes a model of social responsibility for family policies.

Eichler's (1997) model of social responsibility toward the family and children embodies the notion of equality in the context of families, communities, and societies. She tries to reach a balance between the role of parents and the role of the state in looking after children and the family unit. According to her model, 'adult members of an interdependent unit are responsible for their own and each other's economic well-being. Fathers and mothers are both responsible for their children's well-being, whether or not they live with them' (p. 16). Eichler recognizes not only the shared responsibility of parents, but also the role of government in supporting children: 'The public shares the responsibility with both parents for the care of dependent children. If one parent is genuinely absent or unable to contribute his or her share, society will pay the cost of his or her contribution' (p. 16).

Eichler's model of social responsibility is consistent with our ecological model of wellness: a child's well-being is co-determined by dynamics operating at all levels of analysis. Communities, for instance, affect children in a very direct way. The chapter on Aboriginal people illustrated how communities can be mobilized to support and to impose norms of caring and respect at the same time. The examples given by Connors and Maidman concerning customary care, family networking, and healing circles point to the dual role of community supports. Relatives and friends provide moral support and enforce cultural norms of respect at the same time.

Fundamentals for Action

We need to engage in two concurrent tasks: on the one hand, we need to resist oppressive family practices; on the other, we need to promote wellness. To resist oppressive policies and practices we need to be aware of what we are doing wrong. Eichler (1997) maintains that there are seven biases that permeate values, thinking, and action. We recommend familiarizing ourselves with these biases in order to resist them.

The *monolithic bias* consists of viewing the traditional family as representing the entire spectrum of families, thereby neglecting family diversity. This tendency implies not only that there is 'one' kind of family, but also that this is the 'best' kind of family. The *conservative bias* refers to a romantic view of the family whereby past forms of family relationships are glorified and ugly aspects such as spousal and child abuse are ignored. The *sexist bias* draws attention to policies and programs that expect women to do most of the caring work and that, at the same time, blame women when things go wrong. The *ageist bias* is present when the voices of children and the elderly are muted in favour of perspectives of middle-aged adults. The *microstructural bias*, which we already reviewed, leads to a neglect of social factors in explaining and solving problems. The *racist bias* devalues families who are from ethnic minorities; the *heterosexist bias* discriminates against families that are based on gay or lesbian relationships.

A pernicious outcome of these biases is the search for pathology in the 'other,' in those deemed different or incapable of forming a 'traditional' family. It is crucial to resist the pressure to pathologize single mothers, the poor, or homosexuals. None of us is immune to cultural pressures to reproduce the biases identified by Eichler.

But in addition to resisting negative practices, we need to engage in positive steps. Positive steps entail the promotion of personal, collective, and relational values for the benefit of children *and* communities. To promote *personal values* for children we suggest the following:

1. Promote caring and protection of health by facilitating access to health care through universal and outreach programs, and by establishing networks of support for parents.
2. Promote education and personal development by establishing national policies for accessible and affordable child care, by incorporating into schools social and emotional learning, and by providing parents with opportunities for occupational growth.
3. Promote self-determination and empowerment by affording children and adults voice and choice in selection and administration of programs and policies affecting their lives.

To foster *collective values*, we suggest these ideas:

1. Promote social justice in the provision of resources by ensuring fair allocation of bargaining powers, resources, and obligations in society and by providing families with comprehensive supports that meet their needs for housing and economic security.

2. Promote strong community structures by preserving and creating new sources of formal and informal support.

To advance *relational values*, we propose the following:

1. Promote respect and appreciation for families' diverse identities by promoting inclusive policies that do not discriminate.
2. Promote collaboration and respect for the community by balancing policies for personal responsibility with policies that promote obligations toward the community at large.

Theme 3: Beyond Programs – Social Policies for a Just and Caring Society

A third theme that we have identified is the current overemphasis on prevention programs as *the* answer to the problem of child maltreatment. As Febbraro (1994) has argued, prevention programs cannot address macrosocial and political factors that contribute to child maltreatment. A potentially big part of the answer to child maltreatment lies in changing social policies that can address such macrosocial and political factors. Table 9.3 provides an overview of this theme.

Fundamentals for Thinking

Most programs to promote family wellness and prevent maltreatment are directed toward families at risk. We need to move beyond single programs to comprehensive policies that support all families, including those considered to be at risk. The problem is that in the current political climate comprehensive policies are being weakened, not strengthened. Although a few new initiatives have been introduced in Canada to help children, such as the National Child Benefit announced in 1997, the federal and provincial/territorial governments in Canada have been dismantling the welfare system at a rapid pace. 'Against a background of economic restructuring, globalization, and the overriding imperative of deficit reduction, the Canadian "welfare state" is in retreat' (Evans & Wekerle, 1997, p. 3).

Instead of promoting models of social responsibility, the current climate promotes individual responsibility as the solution to social and family problems. Despite massive evidence concerning the interdependence of personal and social factors in abuse and maltreatment –

TABLE 9.3
Theme 3: Beyond Programs – Social Policies for a Just and Caring Society

Fundamentals for Thinking Lessons Learned		Fundamentals for Action Future Directions
Where We Are Now	Where We Need to Go	What We Need to Do
• Individual responsibility model leads to programs that are only for families at risk. • Such programs do not address social and economic determinants of maltreatment and wellness, but instead emphasize adjusting people to unjust social conditions.	• Social responsibility model leads to social policies that support all families, including those considered to be at risk. • Such policies, which are prominent in some European countries, address some of the social and economic determinants of child maltreatment and emphasize family support.	• Resist corporate agenda that pursues "hollowing out of the welfare state" and promote universal and accessible policies that support all families according to their needs. • Support coalitions and social movements that strive to restore the role of public sector, that promote social and intergenerational justice, and that fight child poverty.

evidence available to all who want to see it – government policies and programs continue to focus on individual-level solutions. The pressure of corporations is too great for child advocates in governments to resist the tide against the provision of adequate welfare. 'The dominant discourse in Canada in the 1990s reframes societal problems in terms of market forces, global competitiveness, and individualism' (Evans & Wekerle, 1997, p. 13).

Children and families in Canada, especially the economically disadvantaged, are facing a very difficult reality. 'The progressive notion that the state should be responsible for how well its citizens fare has degenerated to a sense that "welfare" means government handouts to the unfortunate or the lazy' (Griffin Cohen, 1997, p. 48). People in need face a shaming mentality that points a finger at their inadequacies as parents and as providers. There is no longer a sense that the collective should look after those who require temporary assistance. 'With depressing uniformity governments in Canada have rejected a sense that collectively providing services is good for everybody and that social institutions are necessary so that people are in a position to care for themselves' (Griffin Cohen, 1997, p. 48).

As Eichler (1997) pointed out, a social responsibility model would do much to address the lack of universal programs and policies to support families according to their needs. Under a social-responsibility covenant, governments would not cave in to the demands of big business to slash government programs (Barlow & Campbell, 1995; Korten, 1995; McQuaig, 1995). Instead, parents, communities, and the private and public sectors would become partners in supporting citizens in need, just like many European countries do. As we saw in Chapter 4, child poverty is no longer a problem in many European countries.

'If we had a social responsibility model of the family, first and foremost, we would not have children living below the poverty line,' Eichler writes (1997, p. 147). She goes on to demonstrate that welfare reforms in the provinces/territories and the federal devolution of powers have harmed welfare recipients, '38 per cent of whom are children' (p. 147).

Proper financing of the welfare state is important, but it is by no means the only component of a social responsibility model. Formal supports cannot replace informal helping. The chapter on Aboriginal people includes many examples of community involvement in family issues. The kind of help offered by relatives and friends cannot be replaced by bureaucratized forms of aid. Similarly, the chapters on programs indicate the necessity of informal sources of help. Our research in Cuba indicates that despite material deprivation, communities play a large role in child wellness. Formal and informal community structures are in place to provide before- and after-school child care, full child care for infants, breakfast programs, home visitation by professionals, as well as respite and support for families with special needs.

All children and families require both strong public services and vibrant informal supports. The idea of community and informal support should not be used, however, to absolve government of its legitimate role in providing universal programs and policies.

Fundamentals for Action

Professional helpers and managers may feel uncomfortable with the idea of joining social movements as a means of helping children and families. Their professional training goes against the idea of mixing politics and work. This mentality is unfortunate because it creates artificial divisions between our roles as professional helpers and our civic duties. There comes a time, however, when nothing less than social change will help people in need; and there comes a time when nothing but social action will generate social change. We believe that time is now. Powerful lobbying groups are invested in dismantling the welfare state (Barlow & Campbell, 1995; McQuaig, 1995, 1998). Going quietly about our business while they promote their agenda is not acceptable. While welfare workers struggle with increasing numbers of children at risk, interest groups are urging government to slash spending. As food bank workers scramble with increased demands, some people are pushing government to reduce welfare payments. We can either wait for what remains of the welfare state to vanish, or we can join social movements to rescue what is left of it and revive a sense of collective duty.

It is crucial for child advocates to see beyond their narrow occupational difficulties and locate family problems in the context of poverty. Allahar and Côté (1998) write about what it means to be poor in Canada:

> There are over two million poor households in Canada. Those hardest hit by the course of poverty are the young, the elderly, Aboriginals, visible minorities, and women. What is worse, poverty is a vicious circle from which few people ever escape on their own. Poor people are generally at greater risk of random violence than better-off Canadians. They also tend to be sick more often, receive lower quality medical care, and take longer to recover than non-poor Canadians ... they are less likely to do well at

school, less likely to have good jobs, and less likely to feel optimistic about their long-term chances of success. (p. 58)

Welfare for the poor has to be compared with welfare for the rich. While the former suffer the problems documented above, the latter enjoy high standards of living. 'Poverty in Canada exists in a social system where government bails out and gives massive subsidies to big business, creates tax loopholes for the wealthy, [and] grants tax holidays and other incentives to foreign investors' (Allahar & Côté, 1998, p. 58). Yet, most commentators lament how welfare to the poor is a burden on the state and neglect to mention welfare to the rich.

Anti-poverty, women's, labour, and citizens' coalitions offer alternatives to the business agenda, while children's rights groups pressure the federal government to live up to its commitment to end child poverty by the year 2000. Suggesting radical changes to our taxation system and an increase in transfer payments to the provinces, specifically designated for poor children, is not a heretical proposition. When the entire House of Commons voted in 1989 to end child poverty by the year 2000, parliamentarians acknowledged that a profound problem requires a profound solution.

We suggest joining Campaign 2000, the Child Welfare League of Canada, the Canadian Council on Social Development, the Council of Canadians, and similar organizations in order to promote children's economic and social-emotional wellness. Following their lead (Campaign 2000, 1996; Woollcombe, 1996), we propose to foster *economic wellness* by:

1. investing in children and youth as a budgetary priority;
2. allocating resources to children in proportion to spending on other age groups;
3. creating a minimum decent living standard for modest and low-income families;
4. increasing benefits for low-income families and restoring full indexing to the Canadian Child Tax Benefit; and,
5. protecting the living standards of children when parental separation occurs.

We suggest promoting *social-emotional wellness* by:

1. appointing a national commissioner (or ombudsperson) for chil-

dren, with the powers and responsibilities needed to make improvements in children's lives;
2. giving due consideration to the interests and needs of children and requiring a child impact statement in any proposed legislation or regulation at the federal, provincial, territorial, or municipal level of government;
3. introducing legislation to provide all young children high-quality and affordable child care; and,
4. offering parents family-time options during formative periods of their children's lives.

As we have seen in Chapter 4, several European countries have already implemented similar initiatives, with great success. The time has come for Canada to follow suit.

Theme 4: Beyond Child Protection – Promotion and Prevention Programs

Another theme that we have identified is the need to move beyond child protection to a greater emphasis on the promotion of family wellness and the prevention of child maltreatment. In Table 9.4, we provide an overview of this theme.

Fundamentals for Thinking

Child protection is the mandate of child welfare agencies across Canada. This is a necessary and important function. However, with funding cuts, child welfare agencies are struggling to meet their basic mandate, let alone think about how maltreatment can be prevented in the first place. On the prevention continuum described in Chapter 1, child protection services are at the reactive end of the continuum. Investigations of alleged maltreatment lead to either the removal of children from the home to ensure their safety or the provision of family counselling to restore family functioning. These are the services most commonly provided by child welfare agencies. By definition, such actions cannot possibly prevent child maltreatment.

The most innovative services typically provided by child welfare agencies are intensive family preservation services, which were described in detail in chapters 5 and 6. Even these intensive support programs are provided after maltreatment has occurred, and their primary objective is to

TABLE 9.4
Theme 4: Beyond Child Protection – Promotion and Prevention Programs

Fundamentals for Thinking Lessons Learned		Fundamentals for Action Future Directions
Where We Are Now	Where We Need to Go	What We Need to Do
• Currently, child protection and reactive programs are emphasized in the field of child welfare.	• Proactive early-intervention programs are needed to promote family wellness and prevent child maltreatment.	• Maintain funding for child protection services. • Increase innovation in child welfare agencies through intensive family preservation programs and self-help/mutual aid organizations. • Increase proactive programs to promote family wellness and prevent child maltreatment. • Encourage further research and development to develop sound approaches to the prevention of child sexual abuse.

prevent out-of-home placements. Another promising reactive approach is self-help/mutual aid organizations, such as the Parent Mutual Aid Organizations described by Cameron, Hayward, and Mamatis (1992). Within the context of three child welfare agencies, these organizations were developed to provide peer support and promote community integration. A variety of positive outcomes were reported in an initial evaluation of these organizations (Cameron et al., 1992). While this seems to be a promising approach, it is also a reactive application that cannot prevent maltreatment. Thus we now have a system of child welfare agencies struggling to fulfil their mandate of child protection. Even the most successful innovations in such settings are reactive in nature. Like many other helping systems, the child welfare system is not oriented toward wellness promotion or the prevention of maltreatment.

From the literature reviewed in chapters 5 and 6, it is clear that a variety of proactive program approaches have been developed with the goals of promoting family wellness and preventing child maltreatment. Most of these programs have been implemented on a high-risk as opposed to a universal basis. While several types of prevention models have been developed, those that research has shown to have the most promise are home visitation programs; multi-component, community-based programs; and self-help/mutual aid programs.

Also in Chapter 5, we identified several key characteristics of effective prevention programs. From this review, it is clear that the most successful proactive prevention approaches to child maltreatment begin at birth or prenatally and provide support on a regular basis over a period of years. However, it is important to keep in mind that child maltreatment can first appear during a child's elementary-school years or even when the child enters adolescence. Thus, prevention programs should continue to be provided throughout elementary school and high school. Several promising approaches to the prevention of adolescent maltreatment were identified in Chapter 6. Multi-component programs, school-based programs, community-based programs, and family programs are needed to promote adolescent wellness.

From the reviews in chapters 5 and 6, we also know that there is no evidence that any program model has been successful in preventing child sexual abuse. Current efforts focus on educating children in how to recognize and resist sexual abuse. While this is a valid approach that can be universally implemented, it is, by itself, quite limited. There needs to be greater attention paid to the potential perpetrators of child sexual abuse. We know child sexual abuse is strongly tied to gender. Boys and men constitute the overwhelming majority of perpetrators, and girls constitute the vast majority of victims of sexual abuse.

A variety of universal program strategies that would impact on the potential perpetrators of child sexual abuse have been suggested, including: (1) educational programs (those that encourage equal gender relationships and those that promote the message that child sexual abuse is a crime and is damaging to children); (2) legislative interventions (legislation that would make the prosecution of alleged perpetrators less intimidating for victims); and (3) media interventions (reducing the sexual exploitation of women and children in movies, videos, television, and magazines).

Fundamentals for Action

First, we must maintain and enhance child protection services and reactive intervention programs provided by child welfare agencies. Second, we must go beyond the boundaries of child protection into the area of proactive promotion and prevention programs; only these programs have the potential to prevent child maltreatment. Three concrete suggestions are:

1. It is important to maintain funding for child protection services. The protection of children from imminent risk is a basic value that needs to be upheld. Child welfare agencies must have adequate funding to ensure that they are able to fulfil this important mandate.
2. There needs to be an increase in innovation in child welfare agencies through intensive family preservation programs and self-help/mutual aid organizations. These programs offer a solid approach to reactive intervention that can help to keep children in their homes and restore and enhance family functioning. The self-help/mutual aid approach, in which professionals assist the users of child welfare services to develop their own peer supports and programs, is a particularly innovative approach.
3. To prevent child maltreatment, there needs to be an increase in proactive programs. Such programs should start at birth or prenatally and be offered on a regular basis over a period of years, as is the case with some home visitation and multi-component, community-based programs. Also, preventive interventions during elementary school and high school should continue to be provided.

Theme 5: Beyond Child Welfare – Partnerships and Community

To expand our vision beyond child protection toward promotion and prevention, we need to shift our focus from the child welfare system to an emphasis on partnerships and community. Key dimensions of this theme are highlighted in Table 9.5.

Fundamentals for Thinking

We cannot expect the child welfare system, by itself, to promote family wellness and prevent child maltreatment. The child welfare system is legally responsible for child protection; communities, governments, and Canadian society need to share some responsibility for child protection and also assume responsibility for promotion and prevention. Professionals and agencies do not hold all the answers to problems such as child maltreatment. In fact, some formal 'helping' systems have done more harm than good. One clear-cut example of this is the residential schools for Aboriginal people that have left a legacy of misuse of power, child physical and sexual abuse, and other ill effects of colonialism.

Many different sectors need to be involved in the promotion of family wellness and the prevention of child maltreatment. Health, child care, preschool, and education sectors need to be involved. Since all families are different, no one service system can meet all of their needs. Service integration is required to address multiple needs. A key concept in this regard is that of partnership. As we indicated in Chapter 1, we believe that partnerships should enhance the status of disadvantaged people in society and promote values that guide promotion and prevention efforts.

Informal sectors, including neighbourhood associations, self-help organizations, and other voluntary groups, have an important role to play in the promotion of family wellness and the prevention of child maltreatment. In our view, it is important to build a bridge between the formal and informal sectors and to involve a variety of different stakeholders in developing promotion and prevention programs. In this regard, there is a need for partnerships between professionals and community residents, partnerships that focus on developing the capacity of the community to achieve some goal (Chavis, 1995; Labonté, 1993; Nelson, Amio, Prilleltensky, & Nickels, 2000).

As we indicated in Chapter 7, on implementation issues, there needs to be some balance between community participation in program devel-

TABLE 9.5
Theme 5: Beyond Child Welfare – Partnerships and Community

Fundamentals for Thinking Lessons Learned		Fundamentals for Action Future Directions
Where We Are Now	Where We Need to Go	What We Need to Do
• The child welfare system cannot, by itself, promote family wellness and prevent child maltreatment. • Professionals and agencies cannot, by themselves, promote family wellness and prevent child maltreatment.	• There is a need for partnerships between different organizations at different levels to promote family wellness and prevent child maltreatment. • There is a need for partnerships between professionals and agencies, on the one hand, and citizens and the community, on the other hand, to promote family wellness and prevent child maltreatment.	• Involve the community in identifying local issues and problems. • Provide information and education to community members regarding prevention alternatives. • Professionals and agencies need to be sensitized and trained in alternative approaches to working with disadvantaged communities. • Involve the community in program design, planning, and implementation. • Involve community members in community research and evaluation on program implementation and effectiveness. • Tailor the program to the unique needs and strengths of the community and be sensitive to the ethnic and cultural diversity of the community.

opment and evidence-based programs. Heller (1996) has asserted that 'citizen groups do not always choose wisely, so community coalitions also have been known to champion popular programs that have no empirical support' (p. 1126). In contrast, McKnight (1995) argues that the wisdom of the community is superior to the knowledge of professionals. Our view is that both professionals and community members can contribute to the development of effective promotion and prevention programs. Professionals can bring information about successful programs so that community members can 'choose wisely,' while community members have insight as to what might work in their community. A synergy of ideas can result from bridging these different perspectives.

Fundamentals for Action

Nelson et al. (2000) have suggested that partnerships between different professional agencies and community members bring together two diverse approaches to the development of promotion and prevention programs: (1) deductive/nomothetic approaches, which are most often associated with scientific and professional approaches to knowledge, and (2) inductive/experiential approaches, which are associated with community development approaches. An emphasis on partnerships and community seems like a desirable way to merge these two perspectives. However, as Lord and Church (1998) have asserted, partnerships that bridge professional agencies and disadvantaged community members can be very challenging and conflict-laden.

Some research has examined the types of relationships that disadvantaged people and professionals would like to have with one another (Constantino & Nelson, 1995; MacGillivary & Nelson, 1998). It is clear that disadvantaged people want to have power, respect, and support from professionals; they do not want to be labelled, patronized, or used in a token way. In short, people want authentic and egalitarian relationships in any partnership. This requires a shift in roles for professionals from that of expert to that of collaborator and resource person. Such relationships form the basis for performing a variety of tasks and strategies in the development of promotion and prevention programs (Bogenschneider, 1996). We provide some concrete examples of partnership tasks for program development below:

1. Professionals must involve the community in identifying local issues and problems. This is a vital first step in deciding whose agenda will

be served. Governments can offer some broad parameters for program development (e.g., age groups targeted, type of prevention), but community members need to be involved in assessing their community's needs.
2. Professionals need to provide information and education to community members regarding prevention alternatives so that the community can make informed decisions about which approach might work best in their circumstances.
3. Professionals and agencies should be sensitized and trained in alternative approaches to working with disadvantaged communities. 'Partnership shock' can be reduced and more desirable relationships forged when professionals are sensitized to the circumstances of disadvantaged people and trained in alternative professional roles, attitudes, and behaviours.
4. The community should be involved in program design, planning, implementation, and evaluation. Involving stakeholders in the program development process builds community ownership and can lead to potentially innovative programs.

Theme 6: Beyond Outcomes and Model Programs – Implementation and Diffusion

Many of the best programs described in the literature are demonstration projects that do not extend beyond the involvement of the professionals and researchers who created them. It is not sufficient to document positive outcomes. We must also know the factors involved in program implementation that give rise to positive outcomes, and we must learn how to diffuse programs to other communities. A brief synopsis of this theme is provided in Table 9.6.

Fundamentals for Thinking

In Chapter 7, the authors pointed out Schorr's (1997) observation about promotion and prevention programs: 'We have learned to create the small exceptions that can change the lives of hundreds. But we have not learned to make the exceptions to the rule to change the lives of millions' (p. xiii).

Knowledge transfer is not a straightforward, rational process of taking what has been shown to work and then implementing it on a wider scale. Model programs are often implemented under ideal conditions:

TABLE 9.6
Theme 6: Beyond Outcomes and Model Programs – Implementation and Diffusion

Fundamentals for Thinking Lessons Learned		Fundamentals for Action Future Directions
Where We Are Now	Where We Need to Go	What We Need to Do
• There are some excellent research demonstration projects, but also many barriers to their diffusion. • Research has focused more on the demonstration of positive outcomes than on implementation processes.	• Evidence-based programs need to be diffused to other settings so they are implemented on a larger scale. • Greater emphasis needs to be paid to implementation processes in promotion and prevention programs.	• Articulate a program model. • Develop partnerships that balance participatory processes and adherence to an evidence-based program model. • Allow adequate time for program planning and implementation. • Create an infrastructure that provides support and guidance. • Diffuse the program to receptive settings. • Break down bureaucratic barriers to innovation. • Devote more research to implementation and diffusion processes.

they are well-funded (albeit usually on a time-limited basis); there is excellent leadership – staff are carefully selected and well trained; and the host settings are receptive to the innovation. More often than not, there is considerable slippage in these conditions when such model programs are transferred to other settings, or there is no intention or plan for diffusing the intervention beyond the original setting. Some of the barriers to diffusion of innovations are: (1) existing professional ideology and practices that run counter to the innovation, (2) resistance from a variety of different stakeholders, (3) inadequate funding mechanisms, (4) lack of knowledge about successful diffusion strategies, (5) failure to involve relevant stakeholders in the implementation process, and (6) failure to tailor the program to the unique circumstances of the community and its members (Gager & Elias, 1997; Johnson, Malone, & Hightower, 1997).

To date, more attention has been devoted to outcome research on promotion and prevention programs than to issues of implementation and diffusion. More recently, prevention researchers have exhorted their colleagues to examine implementation and diffusion processes (Durlak, 1998; Gager & Elias, 1997; Johnson et al., 1997; Peirson & Prilleltensky, 1994; Winett et al., 1995).

Evidence-based programs need to be diffused to other settings so that they are implemented on a larger scale. At the same time, there needs to be a greater research emphasis on implementation processes in promotion and prevention programs. We need to know under what conditions promotion and prevention programs are likely to be effective. Research on 'intervention integrity,' 'treatment fidelity,' or 'implementation evaluation' needs to have a higher priority than is currently the case (Durlak, 1998; Lynch, Geller, Hunt, Galano, & Dubas, 1998). As Durlak (1998) has shown in his review of several prevention programs for children and youth, the quality of program implementation is positively associated with outcomes for participants. We also need to know more about the process of knowledge transfer and diffusion of innovation (Gager & Elias, 1997; Kress, Cimring, & Elias, 1997; Winett et al., 1995). What are the conditions associated with successful diffusion of an innovative program?

Fundamentals for Action

Several authors have suggested guidelines for implementation and diffusion (Durlak, 1998; Johnson et al., 1997; Nelson et al., 2000). From the literature reviewed in Chapter 7, we synthesize these guidelines into some concrete steps that can be taken to promote high-quality implementation and diffusion:

1. Articulate a program model that clearly specifies program activities and intended outcomes and that provides a rationale for linking activities and outcomes. There need to be rational-empirical program models that make sense and have been shown to work.
2. Develop partnerships that balance participatory processes and adherence to an evidence-based program model. Researchers, professionals, and community members can all contribute to the development and/or adaptation of a program model. It is equally important to build community ownership of a program and to adhere to conditions that are associated with positive outcomes.
3. Allow adequate time for program planning and implementation. Pressures to begin programming immediately need to be eliminated so that thoughtful planning and a positive working climate can be established.
4. Diffuse the program to receptive settings. Settings vary in their receptiveness to change. Since organizational and staff resistance to change is a major obstacle to successful diffusion of innovation, it makes sense to carefully screen settings for their receptiveness to the innovation. A partnership agreement with clear expectations and a commitment to implement the program might be helpful in this regard.
5. Break down bureaucratic barriers to innovation. Implementation and diffusion sometimes die because of intransigent bureaucracies that are more interested in maintaining traditional ways of doing business than in creating innovation. Decision makers who have the clout to eliminate some of these barriers need to be involved in implementation and diffusion to cut through red tape.

LISTENING TO CHILDREN AND YOUTH: VOICES OF THE FUTURE

An eight-year-old child suffering from a rare blood disease was in need of a transfusion. But no match could be found. The girl's doctor and mother then asked her six-year-old brother if he would be willing to give his blood to save his sister's life. He said he would have to think about it, and eventually said 'Okay, I'll do it.' A couple of days later, the brother and sister laid down beside one another in the hospital while the blood was successfully transferred. After a few minutes, the little boy called the doctor over to his bed and whispered in the physician's ear, 'Will I start to die right away?'

This true story was told by Bob Glossop, Director of the Vanier Institute of the Family at the conference 'Canada's Children, Canada's Future' in Ottawa in 1996. His closing remarks after telling this story were the following: 'This is what a child was willing to give for the sake of love. And it leaves me with the question: What are we willing to give to our children for the sake of tomorrow?'

Throughout this book, we have heard from researchers, professionals, and policymakers about the promotion of family wellness and the prevention of child maltreatment. Stories like the one cited above remind us that we have much to learn from children and youth. Thus, it seems only fitting that we end this volume with the voices of children and youth who were interviewed for this project. It is important to hear their hopes, dreams, and aspirations about what life could be and should be.

Interviewer: What is important in the lives of children and families?

Safety. Safety is a big issue, that the child is provided for and that the parents offer an environment that the child is able to speak when they want to, have their views, and not feel threatened.

Communication ... Just being able to sit down and talk about what I expect of you [as a parent] and what you expect of me.

To talk to your family every day. Having some interaction.

Family time ... To do things together ... Spend time together. Set a time to have fun and play.

Respect is a big factor ... If they show they respect you as much as you respect them.

Parents need to get involved and to be interested in what the child is doing, particularly in terms of education.

Education. School.

Encouragement from your family and friends.

Three square meals a day ... A place to live, a home.

Money ... Enough income.

Emotional stuff is more important [than practical needs]. Food and stuff, it was important at the time, but it wasn't as important as just being able to feel comfortable.

I would say that a lot of children would rather have a parent that will hug you and read you a bedtime story rather than a parent that will buy you the latest toys or give you name-brand cereal.

Love.

You just want to hear it, ['I love you'], or you just want a hug or something ... It's supposed to be understood that parents will love you no matter what, but they don't say that, and you need to hear it.

Every child should grow up with two parents ... Having both parents together ... You need to have your family. You need both parents. You need to have a strong family.

Interviewer: What are some of your thoughts on preventing problems and promoting wellness?

I think there are big problems that need to be solved to keep families from getting into trouble, things like being poor and not having child care. Big basic problems to relieve the stress on parents.

More counselling at home and doing stuff with families before problems occur ... Little things add on to little things and it becomes so big. So trying to get somebody in to help with the little things before problems get so big.

I think it's everybody's role to assess the problem before it becomes bigger. Children's aid is having problems of its own right now. In order to assess the problem before it becomes bigger, solve the little problems ... More community development.

It's everybody's problem because it's all the systems working together ... So it's not just children's aid, it's education, it's social welfare, it's health, it's everything. They need to work together. It's everybody's problem, but sometimes, it's nobody's responsibility.

I think there needs to be more focus on prevention, but on long-term prevention. I think because services tend to be focused on where there are already problems, you need that, but you are forever going to be fixing problems instead of keeping them from happening in the first place. So prevention needs to be a key. But it has to be long-term prevention ... Like even welfare I think is a short-term prevention thing, and it doesn't work because you just keep on bandaging it month after month, or year after year instead of forever.

I think prevention shouldn't just be preventing the bad things. It should be prevention with the point of view of having people be healthy and happy, and not so much that they just squeak by, but for them to have the best life they can have.

References

Abatena, H. (1997). The significance of planned community participation in problem solving and developing a viable community capability. *Journal of Community Practice*, 4(2), 13–25.

Aber, J.L., & Allen, J.P. (1987). The effects of maltreatment on young children's socioemotional development: An attachment theory perspective. *Developmental Psychology*, 23, 406–414.

Aboriginal Head Start Subcommittee on National Principles and Guidelines. (1996). *Aboriginal Head Start program principles and guidelines*. Unpublished manuscript.

Affholter, D.P., Connell, D., & Nauta, M.J. (1983). Evaluation of the Child and Family Resource Program: Early evidence of parent–child interaction effects. *Evaluation Review*, 7, 65–79.

Affleck, G., Tennen, H., Rowe, J., Roscher, B., & Walker, L. (1989). Effects of formal support on mothers' adaptation to the hospital-to-home transition of high-risk infants: The benefits and costs of helping. *Child Development*, 60, 488–501.

Aiken, M., Dewar, R., DiTomaso, N., Hage, J., & Zeitz, G. (1975). *Coordinating Human Services*. Washington, DC: Jossey-Bass.

Ainsworth, M., & Marvin, R. (1995). On the shaping of attachment theory and research: An interview with Mary D.S. Ainsworth. In E. Waters, B. Vaughn, G. Posada, & K. Kondo-Ikemura (Eds.), *Caregiving, cultural, and cognitive perspectives on secure-base behavior and working models: New growing points of attachment theory and research* (pp. 3–24). Monographs of the Society for Research in Child Development. (Serial No. 244, Vol. 60, Nos. 2–3).

Albee, G.W. (1980). *Social sciences and social change: The primary prevention of disturbance in youth*. Burlington, VT: University of Vermont.

Albee, G.W. (1985). The argument for primary prevention. *Journal of Primary Prevention*, 5, 213–219.

Albee, G.W. (1986). Toward a just society: Lessons from observations on the primary prevention of psychopathology. *American Psychologist, 41*, 891–898.

Albee, G.W. (1990). The futility of psychotherapy. *Journal of Mind and Behavior, 11*(3/4), 369–384.

Albee, G.W., & Gullotta, T.P. (Eds.). (1997a). *Primary prevention works*. London: Sage.

Albee, G.W., & Gullotta, T.P. (1997b). Primary prevention's evolution. In G.W. Albee & T.P. Gullotta (Eds.), *Primary prevention works* (pp. 3–22). London: Sage.

Albee, G.W., & Perry, M. (1997). Economic and social causes of sexism and the exploitation of women. *Journal of Community and Applied Social Psychology, 8*, 145–160.

Alexander, J.F., Holtzworth-Munroe, A., & Jameson, P. (1994). The process and outcome of marital and family therapy: Research review and evaluation. In A. Bergin, & S. Garfield (Eds.), *Handbook of psychotherapy and behavior change* (4th ed., pp. 595–630). New York: John Wiley & Sons, Inc.

Allahar, A.L., & Côté, J.E. (1998). *Richer and poorer: The structure of inequality in Canada*. Toronto: Lorimer.

Allard-Dansereau, C., Hebert, M., Tremblay, C., & Bernard-Bonnin, A.C. (1998, June). *Family environment and the impact of sexual abuse*. Poster session presented at the Ontario Prevention Congress, Hamilton, Ontario, Canada.

Allen, D., & Tarnowski, K. (1989). Depressive characteristics of physically abused children. *Journal of Abnormal Child Psychology, 17*, 1–11.

Allen, R.E., & Oliver, J.M. (1982). The effects of child maltreatment on language development. *Child Abuse and Neglect, 6*, 299–305.

Alleva, F. (1998). *Youth at risk, systems in crisis: A dialogue with youth who needed shelter*. Unpublished doctoral dissertation, Boston University, MA.

Allison, K., Leone, P.E., & Rowse-Spero, E. (1990). Drug and alcohol use among adolescents. In P.E. Leone (Ed.), *Understanding troubled and troubling youth* (pp. 173–193). Newbury Park, CA: Sage Publications.

Altemeier, W., O'Connor, S., Vietze, P., Sandler, H., & Sherrod, K. (1982). Antecedents of child abuse. *Behavioral Pediatrics, 100*, 823–829.

Altemeier, W., O'Connor, S., Vietze, P., Sandler, H., & Sherrod, K. (1984). Prediction of child abuse: A prospective study of feasibility. *Child Abuse and Neglect, 8*, 393–400.

Altemeier, W., Vietze, P., Sherrod, K., Sandler, H., Folsey, S., & O'Connor, S. (1979). Prediction of child maltreatment during pregnancy. *Journal of the American Academy of Child Psychiatry, 42*, 205–218.

American Association for Protecting Children. (1987). *Highlights of official child neglect and abuse reporting 1986*. Denver, CO: American Human Association.

Anderson, K., Lytton, H., & Romney, D. (1986). Mother's interactions with normal and conduct disordered boys: Who affects whom? *Developmental Psychology, 22*, 604–609.

Andrews, S.R., Blumenthal, J.B., Johnson, D.L., Kahn, A.J., Ferguson, C.J., Lasater, T.M., Malone, P., & Wallace, D.B. (1982). The skills of mothering: A study of the Parent–Child Development Centers. *Monographs of the Society for Research in Child Development, 47*(6, Serial No. 198).

Annie E. Casey Foundation. (1995). *The path of most resistance: Reflections on lessons learned from New Futures.* Baltimore, MD: Author.

Anthony, E.J. (1987). Risk, vulnerability, and resilience: An overview. In E.J. Anthony & B.J. Cohler (Eds.), *The invulnerable child* (pp. 3–48). New York: The Guilford Press.

Antonovsky, A., & Sourani, T. (1988). Family sense of coherence and family adaptation. *Journal of Marriage and the Family, 50*, 79–92.

ARA Consulting Group. (1993). *Ojibway Tribal Family Services operational review.* Unpublished report.

Aragona, J.A. (1983). Physical child abuse: An interactional analysis (Doctoral dissertation. University of South Florida. 1983). *Dissertations Abstracts International, 44*, 1225B.

Arella, L.R. (1993). Multiservice adolescent programs: Seeking institutional partnership alternatives. *Journal of Youth and Adolescence, 22*(3), 283–295.

Armitage, A. (1993). The policy and legislative context. In B. Wharf (Ed.), *Rethinking child welfare in Canada* (pp. 37–63). Toronto: McClelland & Stewart.

Association des centres d'accueil du Québec (ACAQ). (1991). *Commission des centres de réadaptation pour mères en difficulté d'adaptation. La clientèle des centres de réadaptation pour mères en difficulté d'adaptation.* Montreal: Author.

Astroth, K.A. (1993). Youth at risk? Reevaluating the deficit model of youth development. *Extension Journal, 31*(3), 10–18.

Avard, D. (1995, Winter). Canadian Institute of Child Health report confirms inequalities in health for Canada's children. *Rights now: Promoting the U.N. Convention on the Rights of the Child,* 1.

Awasis Agency of Northern Manitoba. (1997). *First Nations family justice: Mee-noo-stah-tan Mi-ni-si-win.* Thompson, MB: Author.

Azar, S.T. (1986). A framework for understanding child maltreatment: An integration of cognitive, behavioural and developmental perspectives. *Canadian Journal of Behavioural Science, 18*, 340–355.

Azar, S.T. (1989). Training parents of abused children. In C.E. Schaefer & J.M. Briesmeister (Eds.), *Handbook of parent training* (pp. 414–441). New York: John Wiley.

Azar, S.T. (1997). A cognitive behavioral approach to understanding and treating parents who physically abuse their children. In D.A. Wolfe, R.J. McMahon, & R. De V. Peters (Eds.), *Child abuse: New directions in prevention and treatment across the lifespan* (pp. 79–101). London: Sage.

Azar, S.T., Robinson, D.R., Hekimian, E., & Twentyman, C.T. (1984). Unrealistic expectations and problem-solving ability in maltreating and comparison mothers. *Journal of Consulting and Clinical Psychology, 52*, 687–691.

Azar, S.T., & Rohrbeck, C.A. (1986). Child abuse and unrealistic expectations: Further validation of the Parent Opinion Questionnaire. *Journal of Consulting and Clinical Psychology, 54*, 867–868.

Badgley, R.F., et al. (Committee on Sexual Offences Against Children and Youth). (1984). *Sexual offences against children.* (Catalogue No. J2–50/1984E). Ottawa: Department of Supply and Services Canada.

Bagley, C. (1989). Prevalence and correlates of unwanted sexual acts in childhood in a national Canadian sample. *Canadian Journal of Public Health, 80*, 295–296.

Bagley, C., & Thurston, W.E. (1998). Decreasing child sexual abuse. In *Canada health action: Building on the legacy – Determinants of health, Vol. I – Children and youth* (pp. 133–173). Ste-Foy, PQ: Éditions Multimondes Inc.

Baker, M. (1995). *Canadian family policies: Cross national comparisons.* Toronto: University of Toronto Press.

Baker, M. (1997, Spring). Entre le pain et les soins: Les pères et la loi canadienne sur le divorce. *Politiques du père – Lien Social et Politiques (Revue International en Action Communautaire), 37*, 63–73.

Bala, N. (1991). Justice issues. In L.C. Johnston & D. Banhort (Eds.), *Children, families and public policy in the 90's* (pp. 105–131). Toronto: Thompson Educational Publishing.

Baladerian, N.J. (1991). Abuse causes disabilities. *Disability and the Family.* Culver City, CA: Spectrum.

Ballantyne, M., & Raymond, L. (1998, April). *Effective strategies for adolescents at risk of out-of-home placement.* Toronto: Ontario Association of Children's Aid Societies.

Bandura, A. (1977). Self-efficacy: Toward a unifying theory of behavioral change. *Psychological Review, 84*, 191–215.

Bangert-Drowns, R.L. (1988). The effects of school-based substance abuse education: A meta-analysis. *Journal of Drug Education, 18*, 243–264.

Bank, L., Hicks Marlowe, J., Reid, J.B., Patterson, G.R., & Weinrott, M.R. (1991). A comparative evaluation of parent-training interventions for families of chronic delinquents. *Journal of Abnormal Child Psychology, 19*(1), 20–31.

Barkley, R.A., Guevremont, D.C., Anastopoulos, A.D., & Fletcher, K.E. (1992).

A comparison of three family therapy programs for treating family conflicts in adolescents with attention deficit hyperactivity disorder. *Journal of Consulting and Clinical Psychology, 60,* 450–462.

Barlow, M., & Campbell, B. (1995). *Straight through the heart: How the liberals abandoned the just society.* Toronto: HarperCollins.

Barnard, K.E., Magyary, D., Sumner, G., Booth, C.L., Mitchell, S.K., & Spieker, S. (1988). Prevention of parenting alterations for women with low social support. *Psychiatry, 51,* 248–253.

Barnett, W.S., & Boocock, S.S. (Eds.). (1998). *Early care and education for children in poverty.* Albany, NY: State University of New York Press.

Barrera, M.E., Rosenbaum, P.L., & Cunningham, C.E. (1986). Early home intervention with low-birth-weight infants and their parents. *Child Development, 57,* 20–33.

Barry, F.D. (1994). A neighborhood-based approach: What is it? In G.B. Melton & F.D. Barry (Eds.), *Protecting children from abuse and neglect: Foundations for a new national strategy* (pp. 15–34). New York: The Guilford Press.

Barth, R.P. (1983). Social support networks in services for adolescents and their families. In J.K. Whittaker & J. Garbarino (Eds.), *Social support networks: Informal helping in the human services* (pp. 299–330). New York: Aldine de Gruyter.

Barth, R.P. (1991). An experimental evaluation of in-home child abuse prevention services. *Child Abuse and Neglect, 15,* 363–375.

Barth, R.P., Blythe, B.J., Schinke, S.P., & Schilling, R.F. (1983). Self-control training with maltreating parents. *Child Welfare, 62,* 313–322.

Barth, R.P., & Derezotes, D.S. (1990). *Preventing adolescent abuse: Effective intervention strategies and techniques.* Lexington, MA: Lexington Books.

Basic Behavioral Science Task Force of the National Advisory Mental Health Council. (1996a). Basic behavioral science research for mental health: Family processes and social networks. *American Psychologist, 51,* 622–630.

Basic Behavioral Science Task Force of the National Advisory Mental Health Council. (1996b). Basic behavioral science research for mental health: Vulnerability and resilience. *American Psychologist, 51,* 22–28.

Bath, H.I., & Haapala, D.A. (1993). Intensive family preservation services with abused and neglected children: An examination of group differences. *Child Abuse and Neglect, 17,* 213–225.

Battaglini, A., Fortin, S., Heneman, B., Laurendeau, M.-C., & Tousignant, M. (1997). *Bilan des interventions en soutien parental et en stimulation auprès des clientèles pluriethniques.* Montréal: Régie régionale de la Santé et des Services Sociaux de Montréal-Centre.

Battle, K., & Mendelson, M. (1997). *Child benefit reform in Canada: An evaluative framework and future directions.* Ottawa: Caledon Institute of Social Policy.

Battle, K., & Torjman, S. (1993). *Federal social programs: Setting the record straight.* Ottawa: The Caledon Institute of Social Policy.

Bauer, W.D., & Twentyman, C.T. (1985). Abusing, neglectful, and comparison mothers' responses to child-related and non–child-related stressors. *Journal of Consulting and Clinical Psychology, 53*, 335–343.

Bauman, L.J., Coupey, S.M., Koeber, C., Lauby, J.L., Silver, E.J., & Stein, R.E. (1997). Teen education and employment network. In G.W. Albee & T.P. Gullotta (Eds.), *Primary prevention works* (pp. 313–340). Thousand Oaks, CA: Sage Publications.

Baumrind, D. (1989). Rearing competent children. In W. Damon (Ed.), *Child development today and tomorrow* (pp. 349–378). San Francisco, CA: Jossey-Bass.

Beardslee, W., & Podorefsky, M. (1988). Resilient adolescents whose parents have serious affective and other psychiatric disorders: Importance of self-understanding and relationships. *American Journal of Psychiatry, 145*, 63–68.

Beatrice, D.F. (1990). Inter-agency coordination: A practitioner's guide to a strategy for effective social policy. *Administration in Social Work, 14*, 45–59.

Beaujot, R. (1997). Parental preferences for work and childcare. *Canadian Public Policy, 23*(3), 275–288.

Beauvais, F. (1992). An integrated model for prevention and treatment of drug abuse among American Indian youth. *Journal of Addictive Diseases, 11*(3), 63–80.

Beavers, W.R., & Hampson, R.B. (1990). *Successful families: Assessment and intervention.* New York: W.W. Norton.

Beck, E.C. (n.d.). *Organizational review of Kunuwanimano Child & Family Services.* Unpublished manuscript.

Becker, J., & Galley, V.J. (1996). *Aboriginal Head-Start summer pilot program: Evaluation & final report.* Unpublished manuscript.

Beckwith, L. (1988). Intervention with disadvantaged parents of sick pre-term infants. *Psychiatry, 51*, 242–247.

Beer, M. (1980). *Organizational change and development: A systems view.* Glenview, IL: Scott, Foresman and Company.

Bélanger, J., Bowen, F., & Rondeau, N. (1997). *Évaluation d'un programme visant le développement de la compétence sociale à la maternelle.* Montréal: Direction de la santé publique de Montréal-Centre et Département de psychopédagogie et d'androgogie de l'Université de Montréal.

Belsky, J. (1980). Child maltreatment: An ecological integration. *American Psychologist, 35*(4), 320–335.

Belsky, J. (1993). Etiology of child maltreatment: A developmental-ecological analysis. *Psychological Bulletin, 114*, 413–434.

Belsky, J., Youngblade, L., & Pensky, E. (1990). Childrearing history, marital quality and maternal affect: Intergenerational transmission in a low-risk sample. *Development and Psychopathology, 1*, 294–304.

Benedict, M.I., White, R.B., & Cornely, D.A. (1985). Maternal perinatal risk factors and child abuse. *Child Abuse and Neglect, 9*, 217–224.

Benson, P.L. (1997). *All kids are our kids: What communities must do to raise caring and responsible children and adolescents.* San Francisco, CA: Jossey-Bass Publishers.

Benson, P.L., Galbraith, J., & Espeland, P. (1998a). *What kids need to succeed: Proven, practical ways to raise good kids.* Minneapolis, MN: Free Spirit Publishing.

Benson, P.L., Galbraith, J., & Espeland, P. (1998b). *What teens need to succeed: Proven practical ways to shape your own future.* Minneapolis, MN: Free Spirit Publishing.

Berkowitz, D.J. (1983). Aversively stimulated aggression: Some parallels and differences in research with animals and humans. *American Psychologist, 38*, 1135–1144.

Berliner, L. (1991). The effects of sexual abuse on children. *Violence Update, 1*, 1–10.

Berman, S. (1997). *Children's social consciousness and the development of social responsibility.* Albany, NY: State University of New York Press.

Berquist, C., Szwejda, D., & Pope, G. (1993). *Evaluation of Michigan's Families First Program: Summary report.* Lansing, MI: Michigan Department of Social Services, University Associates.

Berrick, J.D., & Barth, R.P. (1992). Child sexual abuse prevention: Research review and recommendations. *Social Work Research and Abstracts, 28*, 6–15.

Berry, J. (1990). Acculturation and adaptation: Health consequences of cultural contact among circumpolar peoples. *Arctic Medical Research, 49*, 142–150.

Bertrand, J. (1996). Enriching the preschool experiences of children. In National Forum on Health (Ed.), *What determines health?* (pp. 8–11). (Ministry of Public Works and Government Services of Canada, Catalogue No. H21–126/3–1996E). Ottawa: National Forum on Health.

Besharov, D.J. (1996, December 1). When home is hell: We are too reluctant to take children from bad parents. *The Washington Post*, pp. C1, C5–6.

Better Beginnings, Better Futures: An integrated model of primary prevention of emotional and behavioural problems. (1989). Toronto: Queen's Printer for Ontario.

Biklen, D.P. (1983). *Community organizing: Theory and practice.* Englewood Cliffs, NJ: Prentice Hall Inc.

Black, M.M., Dubowitz, H., Hutcheson, J., Berenson-Howard, J., & Starr, R.H. (1995). A randomized clinical trial of home intervention for children with failure to thrive. *Pediatrics, 95*, 807–814.

Blanchet, L., Laurendeau, M.-C., Paul, D., & Saucier, J.-F. (1993). *La prévention et la promotion en santé mentale: Préparer l'avenir.* Boucherville, PQ: Gaëtan Morin Éditeur.

Blumberg, E., Chadwick, M., Fogarty, L., Speth, T., & Chadwick, D. (1991). The touch discrimination component of sexual abuse prevention training: Unanticipated positive consequences. *Journal of Interpersonal Violence, 6,* 12–28.

Blumberg, M. (1974). Psychopathology of the abusing parent. *American Journal of Psychotherapy, 28,* 21–29.

Blumenkrantz, D.G. (1992). *Fulfilling the promise of children's services: Why primary prevention efforts fail and how they can succeed.* San Francisco, CA: Jossey-Bass Publishers.

Blyth, D.A., & Roehlkepartian, E.C. (1993). *Healthy communities, healthy youth: How communities can contribute to positive youth development.* Minneapolis, MN: Search Institute.

Blythe, B., Hodges, V., & Guterman, N. (1990). Interventions for maltreated adolescents. In M. Rothery & G. Cameron (Eds.), Child maltreatment: Expanding our concept of helping (pp. 33–48). Hillsdale, NJ: Lawrence Erlbaum Associates Inc.

Bogat, G.A., & McGrath, M.P. (1993). Preschoolers' cognitions of authority and its relationship to sexual abuse education. *Child Abuse and Neglect, 17,* 651–662.

Bogenschneider, K. (1996). An ecological risk/protective theory for building prevention programs, policies and community capacity to support youth. *Family Relations, 45,* 127–138.

Boger, R., Richter, R., Weatherston, D. (1983). Perinatal positive parenting: A program of primary prevention through support of first-time parents. *Infant Mental Health Journal, 4,* 297–308.

Bond, L.A. (1984). From prevention to promotion: Optimizing infant development. In J.M. Joffe, G.W. Albee, & L.D. Kelly (Eds.), *Readings in primary prevention of psychopathology: Basic concepts* (pp. 286–307). Hanover, NH: University Press of New England.

Booth, C.L., Mitchell, S.K., Barnard, K.E., & Spieker, S.J. (1989). Development of maternal social skills in multiproblem families: Effects on the mother–child relationship. *Child Development, 25,* 403–412.

Bopp, J., & Bopp, M. (1985). *Taking the time to listen: Using community-based research to build programs.* Lethbridge, AB: Four Worlds Development Press.

Botvin, G.J., & Tortu, S. (1988). Preventing adolescent substance abuse through life skills training. In R.H. Price, E.L. Cowen, R.P. Lorion, & J. Ramos-McKay (Eds.), *14 ounces of prevention: A casebook for practitioners* (pp. 98–110). Washington, DC: American Psychological Association.

Bouchard, C. (1991). *Un Québec fou de ses enfants: Rapport du groupe de travail pour les jeunes.* Québec: Ministère de la Santé et des Services Sociaux, Gouvernement du Québec.

Bouchard, C. (1994). Discours et parcours de la prévention de la violence: Une réflexion sur les valeurs en jeu. *Revue Canadienne de Santé Mentale Communautaire, 13*(2), 37–45.

Bouchard, C. (1995). *Un monde d'adultes à la hauteur des enfants.* Groupe de recherche et d'action sur la victimisation des enfants. Université du Québec à Montréal.

Bouchard, C. (1997a). Québec makes children a priority. In *The progress of Canada's children 1997.* Ottawa: Canadian Council on Social Development.

Bouchard, C. (1997b, février). *The community as a participative learning environment: The case of Centraide of Greater Montréal 1,2,3 GO! project.* Conférence prononcée devant l'Institut canadien de recherches avancée (Human Development Program) lors de la 14ième biennale de l'International Society for the Study of Behavioural Development, Québec.

Bouchard, C., Chamberland, C., & Beaudry, J. (1988). *Prédire et prévenir les mauvais traitements envers les enfants.* Montréal: Laboratoire de recherche en écologie humaine et sociale (LAREHS), Université du Québec à Montréal.

Bouchard, C., & Defossé, E. (1989). Utilisation des comportements coercitifs envers les enfants: Stress, conflits et manque de soutien dans la vie des mères. *Apprentissage et Socialisation, 12,* 19–28.

Bouchard, C., Le Bossé, Y., & Dumont, M. (1995). Contexte écologique des signalements retenus en protection de la jeunesse: Une étude comparative des régions Laurentides-Lanaudière et Chaudière-Appalaches. *Les cahiers d'analyse du GRAVE, 2*(5).

Bouchard, C., & Tessier, R. (1996). Conduites à caractère violent à l'endroit des enfants. In C. Lavalléem, M. Clarkson, & L. Chénard (Eds.), *Conduites à caractère violent dans la résolution de conflits entre proches* (pp. 21–76). Montréal: Gouvernement du Québec, Santé Québec.

Bouchard, C., Tessier, R., Fraser, A., & Laganière, J. (1996). La violence familiale envers les enfants: Prévalence dans la Basse-Ville et étude de validité de la mesure. In R. Tessier & G. Tessier (Eds.), *Enfance et famille: Contextes de développement.* Ste-Foy, PQ: Presses de l'Université du Québec.

Boudreau, F. (1991). Stakeholders as partners: The challenges of partnership in Quebec mental health policy. *Canadian Journal of Community Mental Health, 10*(1), 7–28.

Bourassa, J., Couture, L., et al. (1986). *L'éclosion du devenir parent: Éléments théoriques suivis d'un programme pilote de formation des intervenants en périnatalité auprès des familles à risque.* Québec: Département de santé communautaire du Centre hospitalier universitaire de Laval.

Bousha, D., & Twentyman, C. (1984). Mother–child interactional style in abuse, neglect, and control groups. *Journal of Abnormal Psychology, 93*, 106–114.

Bowden, P. (1997). *Caring: Gender-sensitive ethics*. London: Routledge.

Bowlby, J. (1969). *Attachment and loss: Vol. 1. Attachment*. New York: Basic Books.

Bradley, E.J., & Peters, R.D. (1991). Physically abusive and nonabusive mothers' perceptions of parenting and child behavior. *American Journal of Orthopsychiatry, 61*, 455–460.

Brady, M. (1995). Culture in treatment, culture as treatment: A critical appraisal of development in addictions programs for indigenous North Americans and Australians. *Social Science and Medicine, 41*(11), 1487–1498.

Breakey, G., & Pratt, B. (1991, April). Healthy growth for Hawaii's 'Healthy Start': Toward a systematic statewide approach to the prevention of child abuse and neglect. *Zero to Three*, 16–22.

Briggs, H.E., Miller, D.B., Sayles, R., Tovar, D.D., & Davenport Dozier, C. (1997). Correlates of substance abuse among youth: A note for professionals, service providers and families. *Community Alternatives: International Journal of Family Care, 9*(2), 110–116.

Bromwich, R., & Parmelee, A. (1979). An intervention program for pre-term infants. In T. Field, A. Sostek, S. Goldberg, & H. Schuman (Eds.), *Infants born at risk* (pp. 389–411). New York: Spectrum Publishers.

Bronfenbrenner, U. (1979). *The ecology of human development*. Cambridge, MA: Harvard University Press.

Bronfenbrenner, U. (1986). Ecology of the family as a context for human development: Research perspectives. *Developmental Psychology, 22*, 723–742.

Bronfenbrenner, U., & Neville, P.R. (1994). America's children and families: An international perspective. In S.L. Kagan & B. Weissbourd (Eds.), *Putting families first* (pp. 3–27). San Francisco, CA: Jossey-Bass.

Brooks, R.B. (1991). *The self-esteem teacher*. Circle Pines, MN: American Guidance Service.

Brooks, R.B. (1992). Self-esteem during the school years: Its normal development and hazardous decline. *Pediatric Clinics of North America, 39*, 537–550.

Brooks, R.B. (1994). Children at risk: Fostering resilience and hope. *American Journal of Orthopsychiatry, 64*(4), 545–553.

Broussard, E.R. (1997). Infant–family resource program. In G.W. Albee & T.P. Gullotta (Eds.), *Primary prevention works* (pp. 87–119). London: Sage.

Brown, C.J. (1997). Child abuse survey stuns Ontarians. *Canadian Medical Association Journal, 157*, 867.

Brown, G.W., & Harris, T.O. (1978). *Social origins of depression: A study of psychiatric disorders in women*. London: Tavistock Publications.

Brown, S.E. (1984). Social class, child maltreatment, and delinquent behavior. *Criminology, 22,* 259–278.

Browne, K., & Herbert, M. (1997). *Preventing family violence.* New York: Wiley.

Browne, K., & Saqi, S. (1988). Mother–infant interaction and attachment in physically abusing families. *Journal of Reproductive and Infant Psychology, 6,* 163–182.

Bruene-Butler, L., Hampson, J., Elias, M.J., Clabby, J.F., & Schuyler, T. (1997). The Improving Social Awareness–Social Problem-Solving Project. In G.W. Albee & T.P. Gullotta (Eds.), *Primary prevention works* (pp. 239–267). Thousand Oaks, CA: Sage Publications.

Bruner, C. (1991). *Thinking collaboratively: Ten questions and answers to help policy makers improve children's services.* Washington, DC: Education and Human Services Consortium.

Brunk, M., & Henggeler, S. (1984). Child influences on adult controls. *Developmental Psychology, 20,* 1074–1081.

Brunk, M., Henggeler, S.W., & Whelan, J.P. (1987). Comparison of multisystemic therapy and parent training in the brief treatment of child abuse and neglect. *Journal of Consulting and Clinical Psychology, 55,* 171–178.

Budin, L.E., & Johnson, C.F. (1989). Sex abuse prevention programs: Offenders' attitudes about their efficacy. *Child Abuse and Neglect, 13,* 77–87.

Bugental, D., Blue, J., & Lewis, J. (1990). Caregiver beliefs and dysphoric affect directed to difficult children. *Developmental Psychology, 26,* 631–638.

Bugental, D.B., Mantyla, S.M., & Lewis, J. (1989). Parental attributions as moderators of affective communication to children at risk for physical abuse. In D. Cicchetti & V. Carlson (Eds.), *Child maltreatment: Theory and research on the causes and consequences of child abuse and neglect* (pp. 254–279). Cambridge, MA: Cambridge University Press.

Burch, G., & Mohr, V. (1980). Evaluating a child abuse intervention program. *Social Casework, 61,* 90–99.

Burgdoff, K. (1980). *Natural study of the incidence and severity of child abuse and neglect.* Washington, DC: National Center on Child Abuse and Neglect, U.S. Department of Health and Human Services.

Burgess, R.L., & Conger, R.D. (1978). Family interaction in abusive, neglectful, and normal families. *Child Development, 49,* 1163–1173.

Burgess, R.L., Garbarino, J., & Gilstrap, B. (1983). Violence to the family. In E.J. Callahan & K. McCluskey (Eds.), *Life span developmental psychology: Nonnormative life events.* San Diego, CA: Academic Press.

Burke, M. (1988). Short-term therapy for sexually abused girls: A learning theory based treatment for negative affect. *Dissertation Abstracts International, 49*(5-B), 1935 (University Microfilms No. 88-12052).

Burton, S. (1997). *When there's a will there's a way: Reinforcing child care practice.* London: National Children's Bureau.

Butterfoss, F.D., Goodman, R.M., & Wandersman, A. (1993). Community coalitions for prevention and health promotion. *Health Education Research, 8,* 315–330.

Bycer, A., Breed., L.D., Fluke, J.E., & Costello, T. (1984). *Unemployment and child abuse and neglect reporting.* Denver, CO: American Humane Association.

Caliso, J., & Milner, J. (1992). Childhood history of abuse and child abuse screening. *Child Abuse and Neglect, 16,* 647–659.

Cameron, G., & Cadell, S. (1998). *Empowering participation in prevention programs: Lessons from 10 demonstration sites.* Manuscript under review.

Cameron, G., Hayward, K., & Mamatis, D. (1992). *Mutual aid and child welfare: The parent mutual aid organizations in child welfare demonstration project.* Waterloo, ON: Centre for Social Welfare Studies, Wilfrid Laurier University.

Cameron, G. & Jeffey, H. (1999). *Finding a balance: Project development in Better Beginnings, Better Futures.* Kingston, ON: Better Beginnings Research Coordination Unit, Queen's University.

Cameron, G., & Rothery, M. (1985, May). *The use of family support in children's aid societies: An exploratory study.* Toronto: Ontario Ministry of Community and Social Services.

Cameron, G., & Vanderwoerd, J. (with L. Peirson). (1997a). *Protecting children and supporting families: Promising programs and organizational realities.* New York: Aldine de Gruyter.

Cameron, G., & Vanderwoerd, J. (1997b). *Values, process and commitment: Better Beginnings, Better Futures project organization and management.* Kingston, ON: Better Beginnings Research Coordination Unit, Queen's University.

Cameron, G., Vanderwoerd, J., & Peters, R. (1995). *Building bridges: Service providers' involvement in Better Beginnings, Better Futures.* Kingston, ON: Better Beginnings Research Coordination Unit, Queen's University.

Campaign 2000. (1996, November). *Crossroads for Canada: A time to invest in children and families.* Toronto: Author. (Available from Campaign 2000, c/o Family Service Association, 355 Church Street, Toronto, Ontario, Canada, M5B 1Z8).

Campaign 2000. (1997a). *Perspectives on a national agenda for Canada's children: Options for national consideration at the meeting of Canada's Premiers.* Toronto: Author. (Available from Campaign 2000, c/o Family Service Association, 355 Church Street, Toronto, Ontario, Canada, M5B 1Z8).

Campaign 2000. (1997b). *Report card 1997: Child poverty in Canada* [Brochure]. Toronto: Author. (Available from Campaign 2000, c/o Family Service Association, 355 Church Street, Toronto, Ontario, Canada, M5B 1Z8).

Campbell, J. (1989). *Historical atlas of world mythology: Vol. 2. The way of the seeded earth. Part 2: Mythologies of the primitive planters: The Northern Americas.* New York: Harper & Row.

Canada Health and Social Transfers – An unhealthy prospect for healthy development. (1997). *Voices for Children, 1.*

Canadian Council on Social Development. (1996). *The progress of Canada's children 1996.* Ottawa: Author.

Canadian Council on Social Development. (1997). *The progress of Canada's children 1997.* Ottawa: Author.

Canadian Council on Social Development. (1998). *The progress of Canada's children 1998: Focus on youth.* Ottawa: Author.

Canadian Institute of Child Health. (1994). *The health of Canada's children: A statistical profile.* Ottawa: Author.

Canadian Public Health Association. (1996). *Action statement for health promotion in Canada.* Ottawa: Author.

Canadian Socio-Telich Ltd. (1984). *The nature and effectiveness of family support measures in child welfare.* Unpublished report to Ontario Ministry of Community and Social Services.

Caplan, G. (1964). *Principles of preventive psychiatry.* New York: Basic Books.

Carnahan, S. (1994). Preventing school failure and dropout. In R.J. Simeonsson (Ed.), *Risk, resilience, and prevention: Promoting the well-being of all children.* Baltimore, MD: Paul H. Brookes Publishing Company.

Carroll-Rowan, L.A., & Miltenberger, R.G. (1994). A comparison of procedures for teaching abduction prevention to preschoolers. *Education and Treatment of Children, 17,* 113–128.

Carter, B., & McGoldrick, M. (Eds.). (1989). *The changing family life cycle: Framework for family therapy.* Boston, MA: Allyn & Bacon.

Caruso, G.-A.L. (1989). Optimum Growth Project: Support for families with young children. *Prevention in Human Services, 6*(2), 123–139.

Caruso Whitney, G. (1997). Early intervention for high-risk families: Reflecting on a 20-year old model. In G.W. Albee & T.P. Gullotta (Eds.), *Primary prevention works* (pp. 68–86). London: Sage.

Center for the Study of Social Policy. (1995, May). *Building new futures for at-risk youth: Findings from a five-year multi-site evaluation.* Washington, DC: Author.

Center on Child Abuse Prevention Research, National Committee to Prevent Child Abuse. (1996). *Intensive home visitation: A randomized trial, follow-up, and risk assessment study of Hawaii's Healthy Start program.* Chicago, IL: Author.

Chafel, J.A. (1993). *Child poverty and public policy.* Washington, DC: The Urban Institute Press.

Chamberland, C. (1996). Écologie et prévention: Pertinence pour la santé cinnybaytaure. In R. Tessier & G. Tessier (Eds.), *Enfance et famille: Contextes de développement* (pp. 61–79). Ste-Foy, PQ: Presses de l'Université du Québec.

Chamberland, C., Bouchard, C., & Beaudry, J. (1986). Conduites abusives et négligentes envers les enfants: Réalités canadienne et américaine. *Revue canadienne des sciences du comportement, 18,* 391–412.

Chamberland, C., Dallaire, N., Fréchette, L., Lindsay, J., Hébert, J., Cameron, S., & Beaudoin, G. (1996). *Promotion du bien-être et prévention des problèmes sociaux chez les jeunes et leur famille: Portrait des pratiques et analyse des conditions de réussite.* Montréal: Université de Montréal.

Chamberland, C., & Fortin, A. (1995). Preventing violence towards children: Overview of the research evidence and a perspective from Quebec. *Revista Interamericana de Psicologia/Interamerican Journal of Psychology, 29*(2), 143–157.

Chamberland, C., Théorêt, M., Garon, R., & Roy, D. (1995). *Les scientifines en action: Conception, implantation, et évaluation – Rapport de recherche.* Montréal: Université de Montréal, Faculté des arts et des sciences, École de service social.

Chambliss, J. (1998). Personal Communication via Internet.

Charbonneau, J., & Oxman-Martinez, J. (1996). Abus sexuels et négligence: Mêmes causes, mêmes effets, mêmes traitements? *Santé Mentale au Québec, 21*(1), 249–270.

Chavis, D.M. (1995). Building community capacity to prevent violence through coalitions and partnerships. *Journal of Health Care for the Poor and Underserved, 6,* 234–244.

Cheal, D. (1996). Stories about step-families. In *Growing up in Canada: National Longitudinal Survey of Children and Youth* (pp. 93–101). (Catalogue No. 89-550-MPE, no.1). Ottawa: Human Resources Development Canada and Statistics Canada.

Chénard, L., Cadrin, H., & Loiselle, J. (1990). *État de la santé des femmes et des enfants victimes de violence conjugale: Rapport de recherche.* Centre Hospitalier Régional de Rimouski, Département de Santé Communautaire.

Chess, S. (1989). Defying the voice of doom. In T. Dugan & R. Coles (Eds.), *The child in our times: Studies in the development of resilience* (pp. 179–199). New York: Brunner/Mazel.

Chilamkurti, C., & Milner, J.S. (1993). Perceptions and evaluations of child transgressions and disciplinary techniques in high- and low-risk mothers and their children. *Child Development, 64,* 1801–1814.

Child Care Advocacy Association of Canada. (1994). *Taking the first steps. Child care: An investment in Canada's future.* A brief to the Standing Committee on Human Resources Development. Halifax, NS: Author.

A choice of futures: Canada's commitment to its children, Fact sheet #4: Poverty and the child welfare system. (1989). (Available from Canadian Council on Social Development, 55 Parkdale Ave., Ottawa, Ontario, K1Y 4G1, or from Vanier Institute of the Family, 120 Holland Ave., Suite 300, Ottawa, Ontario, K1Y 0X6).

Christopherson, E.R. (1979). The family training program: Intensive home-based family-centered parent training. *Education and Treatment of Children, 2,* 287–292.

Chung, H.H., & Elias, M. (1996). Patterns of adolescent involvement in problem behaviors: Relationship to self-efficacy, social problems and life events. *American Journal of Community Psychology, 24*(6), 771–784.

Cicchetti, D., & Carlson, V. (1989). *Child maltreatment: Theory and research on the causes and consequences of child abuse and neglect.* Cambridge, MA: Cambridge University Press.

Cicchetti, D., & Lynch, M. (1993). Toward an ecological/transactional model of community violence and maltreatment: Consequences for children's development. *Psychiatry, 56,* 96–118.

Cicchetti, D., Rogosch, F.A., Lynch, M., & Holt, K.D. (1993). Resilience in maltreated children: Processes leading to adaptive outcomes. *Development and Psychopathology, 5,* 629–647.

Cicchetti, D., & Toth, S.L. (1995). A developmental psychopathological perspective on child abuse and neglect. *Journal of the American Academy of Child and Adolescent Psychiatry, 34,* 541–565.

Cicchetti, D., Toth, S.L., & Hennessy, K. (1993). Child maltreatment and school adaptation: Problems and promises. In D. Cicchetti & S.L. Toth (Eds.), *Child abuse, child development and social policy* (pp. 300–322). Norwood, NJ: Ablex Publishing Corporation.

Clabby, J.F., & Elias, M.J. (1990). Competence enhancement and primary prevention as core functions of CMHCs: A case study and blueprint for the future. *Prevention in Human Services, 7*(2), 3–15.

Clarke, M. (1992). *Fighting poverty through programs: Social and health programs for Canada's poor children and youth.* Report prepared for Campaign 2000. Ottawa: Children•Enfants•Jeunesse•Youth (CEJY). (Available from CEJY, 55 Parkdale Ave., Ottawa, Ontario, K1Y 1E5).

Clarkson, L., Morrissette, V., & Regallet, G. (1992). *Our responsibility to the seventh generation: Indigenous peoples and sustainable development.* Winnipeg, MB: International Institute for Sustainable Development.

Claussen, A.H., & Crittenden, P.M. (1991). Physical and psychological maltreatment: Relations among types of maltreatment. *Child Abuse and Neglect, 15,* 5–18.

Cleveland, G., & Krashinsky, M. (1998). *The benefits and costs of good child care: The economic rationale for public investment in young children.* Toronto: Centre for Urban and Community Studies, University of Toronto.

Clinton, B. (1989). *Maternal and Infant Health Outreach Worker Project: Final technical report.* Nashville, TN: Vanderbilt University, Center for Health Services.

Cloutier, R., Champoux, L., Jacques, C., & Chamberland, S. (1994). *Enquête: Ados, familles et mileau de vie: La parole aux ados!* Québec: Association de centres jeunesses du Québec et Centre de recherche sur les services communitaires, Université Laval.

Coburn, N. (1996). Universal home visitation in Colorado. *Protecting Children, 12*(1), 5–11.

Cochran, M. (1987). Empowering families: An alternative to the deficit model. In K. Hurrelmann, F.-X. Kaufmann, & F. Lösel (Eds.), *Social intervention: Potential and constraints* (pp. 105–119). Berlin: Walter de Gruyter.

Cochran, M., & Henderson, C.R. (1986, February). *Family matters: Evaluation of the parental empowerment program – A summary of a final report to the National Institute of Education.* Ithaca, NY: Cornell University.

Cohen-Schlanger, M., Fitzpatrick, A., Hulchanski, J.D., & Raphael, D. (1995). Housing as a factor in admissions of children to temporary care: A survey. *Child Welfare, 74*(3), 547–562.

Cohler, B.J. (1987). Adversity, resilience, and the study of lives. In E.J. Anthony & B.J. Cohler (Eds.), *The invulnerable child* (pp. 363–424). New York: The Guilford Press.

Coleman, J.S. (1987). Families and schools. *Educational Researcher, 16,* 32–38.

Coles, R. (1997). *The moral intelligence of children.* New York: Random House.

Coley, R.L., & Chase-Larsdale, P.L. (1998). Adolescent pregnancy and parenthood. *American Psychologist, 53*(2), 153–165.

Colletta, N.D. (1983). At risk for depression: A study of young mothers. *Journal of Genetic Psychology, 142,* 301–310.

Commins, W.W., & Elias, M.J. (1991). Institutionalization of mental health programs in organizational contexts: The case of elementary schools. *Journal of Community Psychology, 19,* 207–220.

Commission on Prevention of Mental-Emotional Disabilities. (1987). Report of the Commission on Prevention of Mental-Emotional Disabilities. *The Journal of Primary Prevention, 7*(4).

Community Panel, Family and Children's Legislation Review in British Columbia. Aboriginal Committee. (1992). *Liberating our children, liberating our nations.* Unpublished document.

Concerted Action on the Prevention of Child Abuse in Europe. (1997, April). *An overview of child maltreatment prevention strategies in Europe: Vol. 1.* European Commission grant BMH4–CT96–0829.

Connell, J.P., Kubisch, A.C., Schorr, L.B., & Weiss, C.H. (Eds.). (1995). *New approaches to evaluating community initiatives: Concepts, methods, and contexts.* New York: The Aspen Institute.

Connelly, C., & Straus, M. (1992). Mother's age and risk for physical abuse. *Child Abuse and Neglect, 16,* 709–718.

Connors, E. (1993a). *Evaluation of the Circle of Harmony Healing Society.* Report to Mental Health Services, British Columbia. Unpublished manuscript.

Connors, E. (1993b). Healing in First Nations: The spirit of family. In M.R. Rodway & B. Trute (Eds.), *The ecological perspective in family-centered therapy* (pp. 51–65). Queenston, ON: The Edwin-Mellen Press.

Connors, E.A., & Oates, M.L.B. Jr. (1997). The emergence of sexual abuse treatment models within First Nations communities. In D. Wolfe, R. McMahon, & R. DeV. Peters (Eds.), *The emergence of sexual abuse treatment models in child abuse: New directions in prevention and treatment across the lifespan* (pp. 224–242). Thousand Oaks, CA: Sage Publications

Conseil de la famille. (1996). *Choix et soutien ... telles sont les exigences des familles québécoises au regard d'une éventuelle politique à la petite enfance.* Québec: Gouvernement du Québec.

Conseil permanent de la jeunesse. (1993). *'Dites à tout le monde qu'on existe...' Avis sur la pauvreté des jeunes.* Québec: Gouvernement du Québec.

Conservation Company and Public/Private Ventures. (1994). *Building from strength: Replication as a strategy for expanding social programs that work.* Philadelphia: Replication and Program Services, Inc.

Consortium on the School-Based Promotion of Social Competence. (1994). The school-based promotion of social competence: Theory, research, practice, and policy. In R.J. Haggerty, L.R. Sherrod, N. Garmezy, & M. Rutter (Eds.), *Stress, risk, and resilience in children and adolescents: Processes, mechanisms, and interventions* (pp. 268–316). New York: Cambridge University Press.

Constantino, V., & Nelson, G. (1995). Changing relationships between self-help groups and mental health professionals: Shifting ideology and power. *Canadian Journal of Community Mental Health, 14*(2), 55–70.

Conte, J.R., Rosen, C., Saperstein, L., & Shermack, R. (1985). An evaluation of a program to prevent the sexual victimization of young children. *Child Abuse and Neglect, 9,* 319–328.

Conte, J.R., Wolf, S., & Smith, T. (1989). What sexual offenders tell us about prevention strategies. *Child Abuse and Neglect, 13,* 293–301.

Conway, J.F. (1997). *The Canadian family in crisis.* Toronto: James Lorimer & Co.

Coohey, C., & Braun, N. (1997). Toward an integrated framework for understanding child physical abuse. *Child Abuse and Neglect, 21*(11), 1081–1094.

Corey, E.J.B., Miller, C.L., & Widlak, F.W. (1975). Factors contributing to child abuse. *Nursing Research, 24,* 293–295.

Cormer, J.P. (1988). Educating poor minority children. *Scientific American, 259*, 42–48.

Corse, S., Schmid, K., & Trickett, P. (1990). Social network characteristics of mothers in abusing and nonabusing families and their relationships to parenting beliefs. *Journal of Community Psychology, 18*, 44–59.

Coulton, C.J., Korbin, J.E., Su, M., & Chow, J. (1995). Community level factors and child maltreatment rates. *Child Development, 66*, 1262–1276.

Council on Scientific Affairs, American Medical Association. (1993). Adolescents as victims of family violence. *Journal of the American Medical Association, 270*(15), 1850–1856.

Cowan, P.A., Powell, D., & Cowan, C.P. (1998). Parenting interventions: A family systems perspective. In W. Damon, I.E. Sigel, & K.A. Renninger (Eds.), *Handbook of child psychology*, Vol. 4 (5th ed., pp. 3–72). New York: John Wiley and Sons.

Cowen, E.L. (1977). Baby-steps toward primary prevention. *American Journal of Community Psychology, 5*(1), 1–22.

Cowen, E.L. (1980). The wooing of primary prevention. *American Journal of Community Psychology, 8*(3), 258–284.

Cowen, E.L. (1991). In pursuit of wellness. *American Psychologist, 46*, 404–408.

Cowen, E.L. (1994). The enhancement of psychological wellness: Challenges and opportunities. *American Journal of Community Psychology, 22*, 149–179.

Cowen, E.L. (1996). The ontogenesis of primary prevention: Lengthy strides and stubbed toes. *American Journal of Community Psychology, 24*, 235–249.

Cowen, E.L., Hightower, A.D., Johnson, D.B., Sarno, M., & Weissberg, R.P. (1989). State-level dissemination of a program for early detection and prevention of school maladjustment. *Professional Psychology: Research and Practice, 20*(5), 309–314.

Cowen, E.L., Hightower, A.D., Pedro-Carroll, J.A., & Work, W.C. (1989). School-based models for primary prevention programming with children. *Prevention in Human Services, 7*(1), 133–160.

Cowen, E.L., Wyman, P., Work, W., & Parker, G. (1990). The Rochester Child Resilience Project: Overview and summary of first-year findings. *Development and Psychopathology, 2*, 193–212.

Creighton, S. (1985). Epidemiological study of abused children and their families in the United Kingdom between 1977 and 1982. *Child Abuse and Neglect, 9*, 441–448.

Crittenden, P.M. (1981). Abusing, neglecting, problematic, and adequate dyads: Differentiating by patterns of interaction. *Merrill-Palmer Quarterly, 27*, 1–18.

Crittenden, P.M. (1985). Social networks, quality of childrearing, and child development. *Child Development, 56*, 1299–1313.

Crittenden, P.M. (1992). Children's strategies for coping with adverse home environments: An interpretation using attachment theory. *Child Abuse and Neglect, 16,* 329–343.
Crittenden, P.M., & Ainsworth, M.D.S. (1989). Child maltreatment and attachment theory. In D. Cicchetti & V. Carlson (Eds.), *Child maltreatment: Theory and research on the causes and consequences of child abuse and neglect* (pp. 432–463). Cambridge, MA: Cambridge University Press.
Crockenberg, S. (1987). Predictors and correlates of anger toward and punitive control of toddlers by adolescent mothers. *Child Development, 58,* 964–975.
Cryan, J.R. (1985). Intellectual, emotional and social deficits of abused children: A review. *Childhood Education, 61,* 388–392.
Culp, R.E., Culp, A.M., Soulis, J., & Letts, D. (1989). Self-esteem and depression in abusive, neglecting, and nonmaltreating mothers. *Infant Mental Health Journal, 10,* 243–251.
Cunningham, R.M., Stiffman, A.R., Dore, P., & Earls, F. (1994). The association of physical and sexual abuse with HIV risk behaviors in adolescence and young adulthood: Implications for public health. *Child Abuse and Neglect, 18*(3), 233–245.
Curran, D. (1983). *Traits of a healthy family.* San Francisco, CA: Harper & Row.
Curtis, L.C., & Hodge, M. (1994). Old standards, new dilemmas: Ethics and boundaries in community support services. *Psychosocial Rehabilitation Journal, 18*(2), 13–33.
Curwin, R.L. (1992). *Rediscovering hope: Our greatest teaching strategy.* Bloomington, IN: National Educational Service.
Dagenais, C., & Bouchard, C. (1996). Recension des écrits concernant l'impact des programmes de soutien intensif visant à maintenir les enfants et adolescents dans leur famille. *Revue Canadienne de Santé Mentale Communautaire, 15*(1), 63–82.
Daly, M., & Wilson, M. (1980). Discriminative parental solicitude: A biological perspective. *Journal of Marriage and the Family, 42,* 277–288.
Daly, M., & Wilson, M. (1985). Child abuse and other risks of not living with both parents. *Ethology and Sociobiology, 6,* 197–210.
Daly, M., & Wilson, M. (1988). Evolutionary social psychology and family homicide. *Science, 242,* 519–524.
Daly, M., & Wilson, M. (1994). Some differential attributes of lethal assaults on small children by stepfathers versus genetic fathers. *Ethology and Sociobiology, 15,* 318–389.
Damon, W. (1995). *Greater expectations: Overcoming the culture of indulgence in America's homes and schools.* New York: The Free Press.

Daniel, P., & Ivatts, J. (1998). *Children and social policy.* London: Macmillan Press Limited.

Danish, S.J. (1997). Going for the goal: A life skills program for adolescents. In G.W. Albee & T.P. Gullotta (Eds.), *Primary prevention works* (pp. 291–312). Thousand Oaks, CA: Sage.

Danish, S.J., & D'Augelli, A.R. (1984). Promoting competence and enhancing development through life development intervention. In J.M. Joffe, G.W. Albee, & L.D. Kelly (Eds.), *Readings in primary prevention of psychopathology: Basic concepts* (pp. 308–325). Hanover, NH: University Press of New England.

Daro, D. (1994). Prevention of child sexual abuse. *The Future of Children, 4,* 198–223.

Daro, D., & Gelles, R. (1992). Public attitudes and behaviors with respect to child abuse prevention. *Journal of Interpersonal Violence, 7,* 517–531.

Daro, D., & McCurdy, K. (1990). *Current trends in abuse reporting and fatalities: The results of the 1990 annual fifty-state survey.* Chicago, IL: National Committee for the Prevention of Child Abuse.

Davis, L., & Tolan, P.H. (1993). Alternative and preventive interventions. In P.H. Tolan & B.J. Cohler (Eds.), *Handbook of clinical research and practice with adolescents* (pp. 429–447). New York: John Wiley & Sons Inc.

Davy, D. (1997, July 8). To witness violence is child abuse: Our CAS first to link police domestic calls to children's trauma. *The Hamilton Spectator,* pp. A1, A4.

Deber, R.B., Rondeau, K.V., & Beatty, M. (1990). *The integration and coordination of health and social service delivery: Evaluation of models, an annotated literature review.* Unpublished manuscript.

Debrusk, M., & Hellison, D. (1989). Implementing a physical education self-responsibility model for delinquency-prone youth. *Journal of Teaching in Physical Education, 8,* 104–112.

DeChillo, N., Koren, P.E., & Schultze, K.H. (1994). From paternalism to partnership: Family and professional collaboration in children's mental health. *American Journal of Orthopsychiatry, 64,* 564–576.

De La Rey, C., & Parekh, A. (1996). Community-based peer groups: An intervention programme for teenage mothers. *Journal of Community and Applied Social Psychology, 6,* 373–381.

Delisle, J.R. (1984). *Gifted children speak out.* New York: Walker.

Delozier, P.P. (1982). Attachment theory and child abuse. In M. Parkes & J. Stevenson-Hinde (Eds.), *The place of attachment in human behavior* (pp. 95–117). New York: Basic Books.

DeLuca, R.V., Boyes, D.A., Furer, P., Grayson, A.D., & Hiebert-Murphy, D. (1992). Group treatment for child sexual abuse. *Canadian Psychology, 33,* 168–176.

dePaul, J., & Arruabarrena, M.I. (1995). Behavior problems in school-aged physically abused and neglected children in Spain. *Child Abuse and Neglect*, *19*(4), 409–418.

Dhooper, S., & Schneider, P. (1995). Evaluation of a school-based child abuse prevention program. *Research on Social Work Practice*, *5*, 36–46.

Dickason, O. (1992). *Canada's First Nations*. Toronto: McClelland & Stewart.

Dietrich, D., Starr, R.H., Jr, & Weisfield, G.E. (1983). Infant maltreatment: Caretaker-infant interaction and developmental consequences at different levels of parenting failure. *Pediatrics*, *72*, 532–540.

Dilico Ojibway Child and Family Services. (1996). *Work plan for the development and enhancement of intervention services under the Child and Family Services Act*. Unpublished manuscript.

Direction de la santé publique. (1996). *Partenaires pour la santé et le bien-être des tout-petits. État de la situation pour la région de Montréal-Centre*. Montréal: Régie Régionale de la Santé et des Services Sociaux de Montréal-Centre.

Disbrow, M.A., Doerr, H., & Caulfield, C. (1977). Measuring the components of parents' potential for child abuse and neglect. *International Journal of Child Abuse and Neglect*, *12*, 279–296.

Dishion, T.J. (1990). The peer context of troublesome child and adolescent behavior. In P.E. Leone (Ed.), *Understanding troubled and troubling youth* (pp. 128–153). Newbury Park, CA: Sage Publications.

Docherty, J. (1997, June 6). Blessed are the poor, for they can be labelled. *The Globe and Mail*, p. A18.

Dodge, K.A., Bates, J.E., & Pettit, G. (1990). Mechanisms in the cycle of violence. *Science*, *250*, 1678–1683.

Dokecki, P. (1996). *The tragi-comic professional: Basic considerations for ethical reflective-generative practice*. Pittsburgh, PA: Duquesne University Press.

Dooley, M.D. (1994). Women, children, and poverty in Canada. *Canadian Public Policy*, *20*(4), 430–443.

Doueck, H.S., Hideki-Ishisaka, A., Love-Sweany, S., & Gilchrist, L.D. (1987). Adolescent maltreatment: Themes form the empirical literature. *Journal of Interpersonal Violence*, *2*(2), 139–153.

Doyle, V. (1992). *Housing and children in Canada*. Ottawa: Children•Enfants•Jeunesse•Youth (CEJY). Report prepared for Campaign 2000. (Available from CEJY, 55 Parkdale Ave., Ottawa, Ontario, K1Y 1E5).

Drapeau, S., Marcotte, R., Dupuis, F., & Cloutier, R. (1995). *Développement et évaluation du programme soutien aux parents 'Vie de famille, de la discipline à l'amour.'* Québec: Centre de recherche sur les services communautaires de l'Université Laval.

Drotar, D. (1992). Prevention of neglect and nonorganic failure to thrive. In

D.J. Willis, E.W. Holden, & M. Rosenberg (Eds.), *Prevention of child maltreatment: Developmental and ecological perspectives* (pp. 115–149). New York: John Wiley and Sons.

Dryfoos, J.G. (1990). *Adolescents at risk: Prevalence and prevention.* Oxford: Oxford University Press.

Dryfoos, J.G. (1993). Common components of successful interactions with high-risk youth. In N.J. Bell & R.W. Bell (Eds.), *Adolescent risk taking* (pp. 133–155). Newbury Park, CA: Sage Publications.

Dryfoos, J.G. (1994). *Full-service schools: A revolution in health and social services for children, youth, and families.* San Francisco, CA: Jossey-Bass.

Dryfoos, J.G. (1997). The prevalence of problem behaviors: Implications for programs. In R.P. Weissberg, T.P. Gullotta, R.L. Hampton, B.A. Ryan, & G.R. Adams (Eds.), *Healthy children 2010: Enhancing children's wellness* (pp. 17–46). Thousand Oaks, CA: Sage Publications.

Dubowitz, H., Hampton, R.L., Bithoney, W.G., & Newberger, E.H. (1987). Inflicted and noninflicted injuries: Differences in child and familial characteristics. *American Journal of Orthopsychiatry, 57,* 525–535.

Dubowitz, H., & Newberger, E. (1989). Pediatrics and child abuse. In D. Cicchetti & V. Carlson (Eds.), *Child maltreatment: Theory and research on the causes and consequences of child abuse and neglect* (pp. 76–94). Cambridge, MA: Cambridge University Press.

Dugan, T., & Coles, R. (Eds.). (1989). *The child in our times: Studies in the development of resiliency.* New York: Brunner/Mazel.

Dugger, C.W. (1995, March 9). Guiding hand to college for ghetto youth. *New York Times National,* p. A1.

Dulac, G. (1993). La paternité: Les transformations sociales récentes. In Conseil de la Famille, *Collection Études et recherches.* Québec: Gouvernement du Québec.

Dunst, C.J., Trivette, C.M., & Thompson, R.B. (1990). Supporting and strengthening family functioning: Toward a congruence between principles and practice. *Prevention in Human Services, 9,* 19–43.

Durand, D., Massé, R., & Ouellet, F. (1989). *De la Visite: Experimentation et évaluation d'une intervention en prévention de l'enfance maltraitée – Rapport synthèse.* Montréal: Département de santé communautaire Lakeshore, Verdun, et Sacré Cœur.

Durkin, R. (1990). Competency, relevance, and empowerment: A case for the restructuring of children's programs. *Children and Youth Services, 13,* 105–117.

Durlak, J.A. (1995). School-based prevention programs for children and adolescents. In E. Peled, P.G. Jaffe, & J.L. Edelson (Eds.), *Ending the cycle of violence: Community responses to children of battered women.* Thousand Oaks, CA: Sage Publications.

Durlak, J.A. (1998). Why program implementation is important. *Journal of Prevention and Intervention in the Community, 17,* 5–18.

Durlak, J.A., Fuhrman, T., & Lampman, C. (1991). Effectiveness of cognitive-behavior therapy for maladapting children: A meta-analysis. *Psychological Bulletin, 110*(2), 204–214.

Durlak, J.A., & Wells, A.M. (1994, October). *An evaluation of primary prevention mental health programs for children and adolescents.* Paper presented at the First Annual Kansas Conference on Child Clinical Psychology, Laurence, KS.

Durlak, J.A., & Wells, A.M. (1997). Primary prevention of mental health programs for children and adolescents: A meta-analytic review. *American Journal of Community Psychology, 25,* 115–152.

Durlak, J.A., & Wells, A.M. (1998). Evaluation of indicated preventive intervention (secondary prevention) mental health programs for children and adolescents. *American Journal of Community Psychology, 26,* 775–802.

Durst, D. (1996). *First Nations self-government of social services: An annotated bibliography.* Regina, SK: University of Regina.

Dusenbury, L., & Botvin, G.J. (1990). Competence enhancement and the prevention of adolescent problem behavior. In K. Hurrelmann & F. Losel (Eds.), *Health hazards in adolescence* (pp. 460–475). New York: Walter de Gruyter.

Dusenbury, L., & Falco, M. (1997). School-based drug abuse prevention strategies: From research to policy and practice. In R.P. Weissberg, T.P. Gullotta, R.L. Hampton, B.A. Ryan, & G.R. Adams (Eds.), *Healthy children 2010: Enhancing children's wellness* (pp. 47–77). Thousand Oaks, CA: Sage Publications.

Dykeman, C., Nelson, J.R., & Appleton, V. (1995). Building strong working alliances with American Indian families. *Social Work in Education, 17*(3), 148–155.

Eccles, J., Midgley, S., Wigfield, C., Buchanan, A., Miller, C., Reuman, D., Flanagan, C., & MacIver, D. (1993). Development during adolescence: The impact of stage–environment fit on young adolescents' experiences in schools and families. *American Psychologist, 48*(2), 90–101.

Edwards, E.D., & Edwards, M.E. (1988). Alcoholism prevention/treatment and Native American youth: A community approach. *Journal of Drug Issues, 18*(1), 103–114.

Edwards, E.D., Seaman, J.R., Drews, J., & Edwards, M.E. (1995). A community approach for Native American drug and alcohol prevention programs: A logic model framework. *Alcoholism Treatment Quarterly, 13*(2), 43–62.

Egan, K.J. (1983). Stress management and child management with abusive parents. *Journal of Clinical Child Psychology, 12,* 292–299.

Egeland, B., Breitenbucher, M., & Rosenberg, D. (1980). Prospective study of the significance of life stress in the etiology of child abuse. *Journal of Consulting and Clinical Psychology, 48,* 195–205.

Egeland, B., & Brunnquell, D. (1979). An at-risk approach to the study of child abuse: Some preliminary findings. *Journal of the American Academy of Child Psychiatry, 18*, 219–235.

Egeland, B., & Jacobvitz, D. (1984, April). *Intergenerational continuity in parental abuse: Causes and consequences.* Paper presented at the Conference on Biosocial Perspectives in Abuse and Neglect, York, ME.

Egeland, B., Jacobvitz, D., & Papatola, K. (1987). Intergenerational continuity of abuse. In R. Gelles & J. Lancaster (Eds.), *Child abuse and neglect: Biosocial dimensions* (pp. 255–276). Chicago: Aldine.

Egeland, B., Jacobvitz, D., & Sroufe, A. (1988). Breaking the cycle of abuse. *Child Development, 59,* 1080–1088.

Egeland, B., & Sroufe, A. (1981). Developmental sequelae of maltreatment in infancy. *New Directions for Child Development, 11,* 77–92.

Egeland, B., Sroufe, A., & Erickson, M. (1983). The developmental consequences of different patterns of maltreatment. *Child Abuse and Neglect, 7,* 459–469.

Egeland, B., & Vaughn, B. (1981). Failure of 'bond formation' as a cause of abuse, neglect, and maltreatment. *American Journal of Orthopsychiatry, 51,* 78–84.

Egley, L.C. (1991). What changes the societal prevalence of domestic violence? *Journal of Marriage and the Family, 53,* 885–897.

Eichler, M. (1997). *Family shifts: Families, policies, and gender equality.* Toronto: Oxford University Press.

Elder, G. (1977). Family history and the life course. *Journal of Family History, 2,* 279–304.

Elias, M. (1987). Establishing enduring prevention programs: Advancing the legacy of Swampscott. *American Journal of Community Psychology, 15,* 539–553.

Elias, M.J. (1997). Reinterpreting dissemination of prevention programs as widespread implementation with effectiveness and fidelity. In R.P. Weissberg, T.P. Gullotta, R.L. Hampton, B.A. Ryan, & G.A. Adams (Eds.), *Healthy children 2010: Establishing preventive services* (pp. 253–289). Thousand Oaks, CA: Sage Publications.

Elias, M.J., & Clabby, J.F. (1992). *Building social problem-solving skills: Guidelines from a school-based program.* San Francisco, CA: Jossey-Bass.

Elias, M.J., Gager, P., & Leon, S. (1997). Spreading a warm blanket of prevention over all children: Guidelines for selecting substance abuse and related prevention curricula for use in the schools. *The Journal of Primary Prevention, 18*(1), 41–69.

Elliott, M., Browne, K., & Kilcoyne, J. (1995). Child sexual abuse prevention: What offenders tell us. *Child Abuse and Neglect, 19,* 579–594.

Elmer, E. (1977). *Fragile families, troubled children: The aftermath of infant trauma.* Pittsburgh, PA: University of Pittsburgh Press.

Emery, R.E., & Laumann-Billings, L. (1998). An overview of the nature, causes, and consequences of abusive family relationships. *American Psychologist, 53,* 121–135.

Engfer, A., & Gavranidou, M. (1988, June). *Prospective identification of violent mother–child relationships.* Paper presented at the Third European Conference on Developmental Research, Budapest.

Epp, J. (1988). *Mental health for Canadians: Striking a balance.* Ottawa: Minister of Supply and Services.

Epstein, A., & Weikart, D. (1979). *The Ypsilanti-Carnegie Infant Education Project: Longitudinal follow-up.* Ypsilanti, MI: High/Scope Educational Research Foundation.

Epstein, T. (1977). Alcohol and family abuse. In *Alcohol casualties and crime,* NIAAA Report. Rockville, MD: U.S. Department of Health and Human Services, National Institute on Alcohol Abuse and Alcoholism.

Éthier, L.S., Gagnier, J.-P., Lacharité, C., & Couture, G. (1995). *Évaluation de l'impact à court terme d'un programme d'intervention écosystémique pour familles à risque de négligence.* Trois-Rivières, PQ: Groupe de recherche en développement de l'enfant et de la famille, Université du Québec à Trois-Rivières.

Éthier, L.S., & LaFrenière, P. (1991). *Le stress des mères monoparentales en relation avec l'agressivité de l'enfant d'âge préscolaire.* Unpublished manuscript.

Éthier, L., Palacio-Quintin, E., & Couture, G. (1992). *Les enfants maltraités et leur famille évaluation et intervention.* Rapport de recherche présenté à la Direction de la Protection de la Jeunesse (région 04), Groupe de recherche en développement de l'enfant. Trois-Rivières, PQ: Département de Psychologie, Université du Québec à Trois-Rivières.

Éthier, L.S., Palacio-Quintin, E., & Jourdan-Ionescu, C. (1991). *À porpos du concept de maltraitement: Abus et négligence, deux entités distinctes?* Unpublished manuscript.

Éthier, L.S., & Piché. C. (1989). Facteurs multidimensionnels reliés au maltraitement des enfants en milieu familial. *Actes du Colloque du CQEJ 'La violence et les jeunes,'* 37–47.

Etzioni, A. (1993). *The spirit of community.* New York: Touchstone.

Etzioni, A. (1996). *The new golden rule.* New York: Basic Books.

Evans, A.L., (1980). Personality characteristics and disciplinary attitudes of child-abusing mothers. *Child Abuse and Neglect, 4,* 179–187.

Evans, P.M., & Wekerle, G.R. (1997). The shifting terrain of women's welfare: Theory, discourse, and activism. In P.M. Evans & G.R. Wekerle (Eds.), *Women and the Canadian welfare state* (pp. 3–27). Toronto: University of Toronto Press.

Famularo, R., Fenton, T., Kinscherff, R., Ayoub, C., & Barnum, R. (1994). Maternal and child posttraumatic stress disorder in cases of child maltreatment. *Child Abuse and Neglect, 18,* 27–36.

Fantuzzo, J.W., Wray, L., Hall, R., Goins, C., & Azar, S. (1986). Parent and social-skills training for mentally retarded mothers identified as child maltreaters. *American Journal of Mental Deficiency, 91,* 135–140.

Farb, P. (1978). *Man's rise to civilization.* Toronto: Fitzhenry & Whiteside.

Farber, E.A., & Egeland, B. (1987). Invulnerability among abused and neglected children. In E.J. Anthony & B.J. Cohler (Eds.), *The invulnerable child* (pp. 253–288). New York: The Guilford Press.

Farber, E., McCoard, D., Kinast, C., & Baum-Falkner, D., (1984). Violence in families of adolescent runaways. *Child Abuse and Neglect, 8,* 295–299.

Farrow, F. (1997). *Building community partnerships for child protection.* Cambridge, MA: Harvard Center for the Study of Social Policy.

Fashimpar, G.A. (1991). From probation to mini-bikes: A comparison of traditional and innovative programs for community treatment of delinquent adolescents. *Social Work with Groups, 14*(2), 105–119.

Febbraro, A.R. (1994). Single mothers 'at risk' for child maltreatment: An appraisal of person-centred interventions and a call for emancipatory action. *Canadian Journal of Community Mental Health, 13*(2), 47–60.

Federal, Provincial and Territorial Advisory Committee on Population Health. (1994). *Strategies for population health: Investing in the health of Canadians.* (Minister of Supply and Services Canada, Catalogue No. H39-316/1194-E). Ottawa: Health Canada Communications Directorate.

Federal, Provincial and Territorial Advisory Committee on Population Health. (1996). *Report on the health of Canadians.* (Minister of Supply and Services Canada, Catalogue No. H39-385/1996–1E). Ottawa: Health Canada Communications and Consultation Directorate.

Federal-Provincial Working Group on Child and Family Services Information. (1998, February). *Child and Family Services Statistical Report 1994–95 to 1996–97* (2nd ed.). Hull, PQ: Author.

Feindler, E.L., & Becker, J.V. (1994). Interventions in family violence involving children and adolescents. In L.D. Eron, J. Gentry, & P. Schlegel (Eds.), *Reason to hope: A psychosocial perspective on violence and youth* (pp. 405–430). Washington, DC: American Psychological Association.

Feldman, L.H. (1991). Evaluating the impact of intensive family preservation services in New Jersey. In K. Wells & D.E. Biegel (Eds.), *Intensive family preservation services: Research and evaluation* (pp. 47–71). Newbury Park, CA: Sage.

Felner, R.D., Brand, S., Adan, A.M., Mulhall, P.F., Flowers, N., Sartain, B., & Dubois, D.L. (1993). Restructuring the ecology of the school as an approach to prevention during school transitions: Longitudinal follow-ups and extensions of the School Transition Environment Project (STEP). *Prevention in Human Services, 10,* 103–136.

Fergusson, D.M., & Lynskey, M.T. (1996). Adolescent resiliency to family adversity. *Journal of Child Psychology and Psychiatry, 37*(3), 281–292.

Field, T.F., Widmayer, S.M., Greenberg, R., & Stoller, S. (1982). Effects of parent training on teenage mothers and their infants. *Pediatrics, 69,* 703–707.

Field, T.F., Widmayer, S.M., Stringer, S., & Ignatoff, E. (1980). Teenage, lower-class, black mothers and their preterm infants: An intervention and developmental follow-up. *Child Development, 51,* 426–436.

Finkelhor, D. (1994a). Current information on the scope and nature of child sexual abuse. *Future Child, 4,* 31–53.

Finkelhor, D. (1994b). The international epidemiology of child sexual abuse. *Child Abuse and Neglect, 18,* 409–417.

Finkelhor, D., & Browne, A. (1985). The traumatic impact of child sexual abuse: A conceptualization. *American Journal of Orthopsychiatry, 55,* 530–541.

Finkelhor, D., & Dziuba-Leatherman, J. (1994). Victimization of children. *American Psychologist, 49,* 173–183.

Fischer, B., & Birdie, J. (1978). Adolescent abuse and neglect: Issues of incidence, intervention and service delivery. *Child Abuse and Neglect, 2*(3), 173–192.

Flanagan, C.A., & Sherrod, L.R. (Eds.). (1998). Political development: Youth growing up in a global community [Special issue]. *Journal of Social Issues, 54,* 447–627.

Fortin, A. (1992). Le mauvais traitement psychologique: Une réalité encore mal connue. *Prisme, 3,* 88–100.

Fortin, A., & Chamberland, C. (1995). Preventing the psychological maltreatment of children. *Journal of Interpersonal Violence, 10*(3), 275–295.

Fournier, S., & Crey, E. (1997). *Stolen from our embrace: The abduction of First Nations children and the restoration of Aboriginal communities.* Vancouver: Douglas & McIntyre.

Fox, D., & Prilleltensky, I. (Eds.). (1997). *Critical psychology: An introduction.* London: Sage.

Fox, J. (1981). Social work ethics and children: Protection versus empowerment. *Children and Youth Review, 6,* 319–328.

Frank Maidman Associates. (1998). *Anishnaabe Mno-Taagok: The learning circle.* Unpublished report to Ontario Federation of Indian Friendship Centres/Ontario Ministry of Community and Social Services, Toronto, Ontario.

Fraser, M.W., Pecora, P., & Haapala, D.A. (Eds.). (1991). *Families in crisis: The impact of intensive family preservation services.* New York: Aldine de Gruyter.

Freeman, M. (1993). *The kindness of strangers: Adult mentors, urban youth and the new volunteerism*. San Francisco, CA: Jossey-Bass Publishers.

Freire, P. (1997). *Pedagogy of hope*. New York: Continuum.

Friedmann, J. (1973). *Retracking America: A theory of transactive planning*. New York: Anchor Press/Doubleday.

Friedrich, W.N., Luecke, W.J., Beilke, R.L., & Place, V. (1992). Psychotherapy outcome of sexually abused boys: An agency study. *Journal of Interpersonal Violence, 7*, 396–409.

Friedrich, W.N., & Wheeler, K.K. (1982). The abusing parent revisited: A decade of psychological research. *Journal of Nervous and Mental Disease, 10*, 577–587.

Friendly, M. (1994). *Child care policy in Canada: Putting the pieces together*. Don Mills, ON: Addison-Wesley Ltd.

Friendly, M., & Rothman, L. (1995). Miles to go … The policy context of child care in Canada. *Child Welfare, 74*(3), 503–524.

Frodi, A.M. (1981). Contribution of infant characteristics to child abuse. *American Journal of Mental Deficiency, 85*, 341–349.

Frodi, A.M., & Lamb, M.E. (1980). Child abusers' responses to infant smiles and cries. *Child Development, 51*, 238–241.

Frumkin, M., Imershein, A., Chackerian, R., & Martin, P. (1983). Evaluating state level integration of human services. *Administration in Social Work, 7*, 13–24.

Fryer, G., Kraizer, S., & Miyoshi, T. (1987). Measuring actual reduction of risk to child abuse: A new approach. *Child Abuse and Neglect, 11*, 173–179.

Fuchs, D.M. (1990). Programs for preventing placement of adolescents. In M. Rothery & G. Cameron (Eds.), *Child maltreatment: Expanding our concept of helping* (pp. 49–62). Hillsdale, NJ: Lawrence Erlbaum Associates Inc.

Fuchs, E.R., & Thompson, J.P. (1994). Urban community initiatives and shifting federal policy: The case of empowerment zones. In A. Kahn & S. Kamerman (Eds.), *Children and their families in big cities* (pp. 241–255). New York: Cross-National Studies Research Program, Columbia University School of Social Work.

Fullan, M., & Pomfret, A. (1977). Research on curriculum and instruction implementation. *Review of Educational Reform, 47*(1), 335–397.

Furstenberg, F.F. (1993). How families manage risk and opportunity in dangerous neighborhoods. In W.J. Wilson (Ed.), *Sociology and the public agenda* (pp. 231–258). Newbury Park, CA: Sage.

Furstenberg, F.F., Brooks-Gunn, J., & Morgan, S.P. (1987). *Adolescent mothers in later life*. New York: Cambridge University Press.

Gabinet, L. (1983). Child abuse treatment failures reveal need for redefinition of the problem. *Child Abuse and Neglect, 7*, 395–402.

Gadd, J. (1996, November 28). Romanow says cuts affecting children. *The Globe and Mail*, p. A5.

Gager, P.J., & Elias, M.J. (1997). Implementing prevention programs in high-risk environments: Application of the resiliency paradigm. *American Journal of Orthopsychiatry, 67*, 363–373.

Gaines, R., Sandgrund, A., Green, A., & Power, E. (1978). Etiological factors in child maltreatment: A multivariate study of abusing, neglecting, and normal mothers. *Journal of Abnormal Psychology, 87*, 531–540.

Galano, J., & Huntington, L. (1997). *Year V evaluation of the Hampton, Virginia Healthy Families Partnership, 1992–1997.* Hampton, VA: Healthy Families Partnership.

Galbraith, J.K. (1996). *The good society.* New York: Houghton Mifflin.

Galdston, R. (1965). Observations on children who have been physically abused and their parents. *American Journal of Psychiatry, 122*, 440–443.

Gallup, G.H., Moore, D.W., & Schussel, R. (1995). *Disciplining children in America: A Gallup Poll report.* Princeton, NJ: The Gallup Organization.

Gans, S.P., & Horton, G.T. (1975). *Integration of human services: The state and municipal levels.* New York: Praeger.

Garant, L. (1992). Les programmes de soutien familial – Une alternative au placement des jeuncs? Québec: Services de l'évaluation prévention et services communautaires, Collection études et analyses no. 15, Direction générale de la planification et de l'évaluation Ministère de la Santé et des Services Sociaux, Gouvernement du Québec.

Garbarino, J. (1976). A preliminary study of some ecological correlates of child abuse. *Child Development, 47*, 178–185.

Garbarino, J. (1977a). The human ecology of child maltreatment: A conceptual model for research. *Journal of Marriage and the Family, 39*, 721–735.

Garbarino, J. (1977b). The price of privacy: An analysis of the social dynamics of child abuse. *Child Welfare, 56*, 565–575.

Garbarino, J. (1989). The incidence and prevalence of child maltreatment. In L. Ohlin & M. Tonry (Eds.), *Family violence* (pp. 219–261). Chicago: University of Chicago.

Garbarino, J. (Ed.). (1992a). *Children and families in the social environment* (2nd ed.). New York: Aldine de Gruyter.

Garbarino, J. (1992b). Preventing adolescent maltreatment. In D.J. Willis, W.E. Holden, & M. Rosenberg (Eds.), *Prevention of child maltreatment: Developmental and ecological perspectives* (pp. 94–112). New York: John Wiley and Sons.

Garbarino, J. (1996). A vision of family policy for the 21st century. *Journal of Social Issues, 52*(3), 197–203.

Garbarino, J., & Crouter, A. (1978). Defining the community context for parent–child relations: The correlates of child maltreatment. *Child Development, 49,* 604–616.

Garbarino, J., Dubrow, N., Kostelny, K., & Pardo, C. (1992). Resilience and coping in children at risk. In *Children in danger: Coping with the consequences of community violence* (pp. 100–114). San Francisco, CA: Jossey-Bass.

Garbarino, J., Guttman, E., & Seeley, J. (1986). *The psychologically battered child: Strategies for identification, assessment and intervention.* San Francisco, CA: Jossey-Bass.

Garbarino, J., & Kostelny, K. (1992). Child maltreatment as a community problem. *Child Abuse and Neglect, 16,* 455–464.

Garbarino, J., & Kostelny, K. (1994). Neighborhood-based programs. In G.B. Melton & F.D. Barry (Eds.), *Protecting children from abuse and neglect: Foundations for a new national strategy* (pp. 304–352). New York: The Guilford Press.

Garbarino, J., Kostelny, K., & Dubrow, N. (1991). *No place to be a child: Growing up in a war zone.* Lexington, MA: Lexington Books.

Garbarino, J., & Sherman, D. (1980). High risk neighborhoods and high risk families: The human ecology of child maltreatment. *Child Development, 51,* 188–198.

Garbarino, J., Stocking, H., & Associates. (1980). *Protecting children from abuse and neglect.* San Francisco, CA: Jossey-Bass.

Gardner, R.C., & Esses, V.M. (Eds.). (1996). Ethnic relations in a multicultural society [Special issue]. *Canadian Journal of Behavioural Science, 28,* 145–251.

Garmezy, N. (1987). Stress, competence, and development: Continuities in the study of schizophrenic adults, children vulnerable to psychopathology, and the search for stress-resistant children. *American Journal of Orthopsychiatry, 57,* 159–174.

Garmezy, N. (1991). Resiliency and vulnerability to adverse developmental outcomes associated with poverty. *American Behavioral Scientist, 34*(4), 416–430.

Gaudin, J.M., Wodarski, J.S., Arkinson, M.K., & Avery, L.S. (1990–91). Remedying child neglect: Effectiveness of social network interventions. *The Journal of Applied Social Sciences, 15*(1), 97–123.

Gauthier, A.H. (1996). *The state and the family: A comparative analysis of family policies in industrialized countries.* Oxford: Clarendon Press.

Gayford, J.J. (1975). Wife battering: A preliminary survey of 100 cases. *British Medical Journal, 25,* 194–197.

Gelles, R. (1973). Child abuse as psychopathology: A sociological critique and reformulation. *American Journal of Orthopsychiatry, 43,* 611–621.

Gelles, R. (1975). The social construction of child abuse. *American Journal of Orthopsychiatry, 45,* 363–371.

Gelles, R. (1976). Demythologizing child abuse. *Family Coordinator, 25,* 135–141.

Gelles, R.J. (1992). Poverty and violence toward children. *American Behavioral Scientist, 35*, 258–274.

Gelles, R.J., & Hargreaves, E.F. (1981). Maternal employment and violence toward children. *Journal of Family Issues, 2*, 509–530.

Gelles, R., & Harrop, J. (1991). The risk of abusive violence among children with nongenetic caretakers. *Family Relations, 40*, 78–83.

Gendreau, P. (1996). The principles of effective intervention with offenders. In A.T. Harland (Ed.), *Choosing correctional options that work: Defining the demand and evaluating the supply.* Thousand Oaks, CA: Sage Publications.

George, V., & Wilding, P. (1976). *Ideology and social welfare.* Boston, MA: Routledge & Kegan Paul.

Giaretto, H. (1982). Humanistic treatment of father–daughter incest. In National Institute of Mental Health, *Sexual abuse of children* (pp. 39–46). (DHHS Publication No. 78–30161). Washington, DC: United States Department of Health and Human Services.

Gibson, C.M. (1993). Empowerment theory and practice with adolescents of color in the child welfare system. *Families in Society: The Journal of Contemporary Human Services, 74*(7), 387–396.

Gil, D.G. (1970). *Violence against children: Physical child abuse in the United States.* Cambridge, MA: Harvard University Press.

Gil, D. (1971). Violence against children. *Journal of Marriage and the Family, 33*, 637–648.

Gil, D. (1973). *Violence against children.* Cambridge, MA: Harvard University Press.

Gil, D. (1976). Primary prevention of child abuse: A philosophical and political issue. *Journal of Pediatric Psychology, 1*, 54–57.

Giles-Sims, J., & Finkelhor, D. (1984). Child abuse in step-families. *Family Relations, 33*, 407–413.

Giovannoni, J.M., & Billingsley, A. (1970). Child neglect among the poor: A study of parental adequacy in families of three ethnic groups. *Child Welfare, 84*, 196–214.

Glossop, B. (1996, March). Bailing out on future generations: Erosion of social programs jeopardizes prospects of future generations. *Transitions, 26*(1), 12–13.

Goldberg, G.S. (1995). Theory and practice in program development: A study of the planning and implementation of fourteen social programs. *Social Service Review, 69*, 614–655.

Goldston, S.E. (1991). A survey of prevention activities in state mental health authorities. *Professional Psychology: Research and Practice, 22*, 315–321.

Gomes-Schwartz, B., Horowitz, J.M., Cardarelli, A.P., & Sauzier, M. (1990). The aftermath of child sexual abuse: 18 months later. In B. Gomes-Schwartz,

J.M. Horowitz, & A.P. Cardarelli (Eds.), *Child sexual abuse: The initial effects* (pp. 132–152). Newbury Park, CA: Sage.

Goodman, R., Steckler, A., Hoover, S., & Schwartz, R. (1993). A critique of contemporary community health promotion approaches: Based on a qualitative review of six programs in Maine. *American Journal of Health Promotion, 7*(3), 208–221.

Goodwin, C. (1997, December 10). Child welfare workers fear disaster near. *The Kitchener-Waterloo Record*, pp. A1, A2.

Gore, S., & Eckenrode, J. (1994). Context and process in research on risk and resilience. In R.J. Haggerty, L.R. Sherrod, N. Garmezy, & M. Rutter (Eds.), *Stress, risk, and resilience in children and adolescents: Processes, mechanisms, and interventions* (pp. 19–63). New York: Cambridge University Press.

Gottfredson, D.C., Fink, C.M., Skroban, S., & Gottfredson, G.D. (1997). Making prevention work. In R.P. Weissberg, T.P. Gullotta, R.L. Hampton, B.A. Ryan, & G.R. Adams (Eds.), *Healthy children 2010: Establishing preventive services* (pp. 219–252). Thousand Oaks, CA: Sage Publications.

Gottlieb, B.H. (1987). Using social support to protect and promote health. *Journal of Primary Prevention, 8*(1–2), 49–70.

Gottlieb, B.H. (1998). Strategies to promote the optimal development of Canada's youth. In *Canada health action: Building on the legacy. Papers commissioned by the National Forum on health. Determinants of health: Vol. 1. Children and youth* (pp. 235–273). Sainte-Foy, PQ: Éditions MultiMondes.

Goulet, L. (1995). *Learning from children in difficult circumstances*. Ottawa: Canadian Coalition for the Rights of Children.

Gouvernement du Québec. (1991). *Un Québec fou de ses enfants*. Ministère de la Santé et des Services Sociaux.

Gouvernement du Québec. (1997). *Familles en tête: Nouvelles dispositions de la politique familial. Les enfants au coeur de nos choix*. Québec: Gouvernement du Québec.

Gove, T.J. (1995). *Report of the Gove inquiry into child protection in British Columbia*. Victoria, BC: Ministry of Social Services.

Graff, J. (1987). Strength within the circle [Special issue]. *Journal of Child Care*. Calgary, AB: The University of Calgary Press.

Graham-Bermann, S.A., & Levendosky, A.A. (1998). Traumatic stress symptoms in children of battered women. *Journal of Interpersonal Violence, 13*(1), 111–128.

Grand Council Treaty #3, Anishinaabe Family Support Services Committee. (1992). *Anishinaabe way: Community care of families and children*. Unpublished manuscript.

Gray, B. (1989). *Collaborating: Finding common ground for multiparty problems*. San Francisco, CA: Jossey-Bass.

Gray, B. (1995). Obstacles to success in educational collaboration. In L.C. Rigsky, M.C. Reynolds, & M.C. Wang (Eds.), *School-community connections: Exploring issues for research and practice* (pp. 75–95). San Francisco, CA: Jossey-Bass Publishers.

Gray, J.D., Cutler, C.A., Dean, J.G., & Kempe, C.H. (1979a). Prediction and prevention of child abuse. *Seminars in Perinatology, 3,* 85–90.

Gray, J.D., Culter, C.A., Dean, J.G., & Kempe, C.H. (1979b). Prediction and prevention of child abuse and neglect. *Journal of Social Issues, 35,* 127–139.

Gray, S.W., & Ruttle, K. (1990). The family-oriented home visiting program: A longitudinal study. *Genetic Psychology Monographs, 102,* 299–316.

Gribble, P., Cowen, E., Wyman, P., Work, W., Wannon, M., & Raoof, A. (1993). Parent and child views of parent–child relationship qualities and resilient outcomes among urban children. *Journal of Child Psychology and Psychiatry and Allied Disciplines, 34,* 507–519.

Griffin Cohen, M. (1997). From the welfare state to vampire capitalism. In P.M. Evans & G.R. Wekerle (Eds.), *Women and the Canadian welfare state* (pp. 28–67). Toronto: University of Toronto Press.

Grizenko, N., & Pawliuk, N. (1994). Risk and protective factors for disruptive behavior disorders in children. *American Journal of Orthopsychiatry, 64,* 534–544.

Guay, D., Hamel, M., Brousseau, L., Stewart, B., et al. (1995, 1996, 1997). *Prévention de l'abus et de la négligence envers les enfants: Répertoire des activités et programmes Québécois.* Montréal: Directions de la santé publique de Montréal et du Bas Saint-Laurent, 15 volumes (un par région sociosanitaire du Québec).

Guay, J. (1984). *L'intervenant professionnel face à l'aide naturelle.* Chicoutimi, PQ: Gaëtan Morin.

Gullotta, P. (1997). Operationalizing Albee's incidence formula. In G.W. Albee & T.P. Gullotta (Eds.), *Primary prevention works* (pp. 23–37). London: Sage.

Guttentag, M. (1977). The prevention of sexism. In G. Albee & J. Joffe (Eds.), *Primary prevention of psychopathology,* Vol 1: The issues (pp. 238–253). Hanover, NH: The University Press of New England.

Guy, K.A. (Ed.). (1997). *Our promise to children.* Ottawa: Health Canada.

Habermas, J. (1990). *Moral consciousness and communicative action.* Cambridge, MA: MIT Press.

Haggerty, R.J., Sherrod, L.R., Garmezy, N., & Rutter, M. (Eds.). (1994). *Stress, risk and resilience in children and adolescents: Processes, mechanisms, and interventions.* Cambridge, MA: Cambridge University Press.

Halper, G., & Jones, M.A. (1981). *Serving families at risk of dissolution: Public preventative services in New York City.* New York: Children's Bureau of the Administration of Children, Youth and Families, Department of Health and Human Services.

Halpern, R. (1996). Neighborhood-based strategies to address poverty-related social problems: An historical perspective. In A. Kahn & S. Kamerman (Eds.), *Children and their families in big cities* (pp. 60–88). New York: Cross-National Studies Research Program, Columbia University School of Social Work.

Hamberg, D.A. (1992). *Today's children: Creating a future for a generation in crisis.* New York: Time Books, Random House, Inc.

Hamel, M., & Guay, D. (1996). *Prévention de l'abus et de la négligence envers les enfants: État de la situation au Québec – Rapport final.* Québec: Directions de la santé publique – Régie régionale et de la Santé et des Services Sociaux de Bas Saint-Laurent et Direction de la santé publique – Régie régionale et de la Santé et des Services Sociaux de Montréal-Centre.

Hamilton, N., & Bhatti, T. (1996). *Population health promotion: An integrated model of population health and health promotion.* Ottawa: Health Canada, Health Promotion Development Division.

Hamilton, S.F., & Hamilton, M.A. (1992, March). Mentoring programs: Promise and paradox. *Phi Delta Kappan,* 546–550.

Hample, N. (1979). *Hugging, hitting and other family matters: Children talk about their families.* New York: The Dial Press.

Hampton, R.L. (1987). Race, class, and child maltreatment. *Journal of Comparative Family Studies, 18,* 113–126.

Hantrais, L., & Letablier, M.-T. (1996). *Families and family policy in Europe.* New York: Longman Publishing.

Harding, L.F. (1996). *Family state and social policy.* London: Macmillan Press imited.

Hardy, J.B., & Streett, R. (1989). Family support and parenting education in the home: An effective extension of clinic-based preventive health care services for poor children. *Journal of Pediatrics, 115,* 927–931.

Hardy, J.B., & Zabin, L.S. (1991). *Adolescent pregnancy in an urban environment: Issues, programs and evaluation.* Baltimore, MD: Urban & Schwarzenberg.

Harris, I. (1996). *Children in jeopardy: Can we break the cycle of poverty?* New Haven, CT: Yale University Press.

Hart, S.N., Binggeli, N.J., & Brassard, M.R. (1998). Evidence for the effects of psychological maltreatment. *Journal of Emotional Abuse, 1*(1), 27–58.

Hart, S.N., Gelardo, M., & Brassard, M. (1986). Psychological maltreatment. In J. Jacobsen (Ed.), *The psychiatric sequelae of child abuse* (pp. 133–168). Springfield, IL: Charles C. Thomas.

Hart, S.N., Germain, R.B., & Brassard, M. (1987). The challenge: To better understand and combat psychological maltreatment of children and youth. In M.R. Brassard, R. Germain, & S.N. Hart (Eds.), *Psychological maltreatment of children and youth* (pp. 2–24). New York: Pergamon.

Harvey, J. (1991). *La protecton sur mesure, un projet collectif.* Groupe de travail sur l'application des mesures de protection de la jeunesse, Ministère de la Santé et des Services Sociaux, Gouvernement du Québec.

Harvey, P., Forehand, R., Brown, C.F., & Holmes, T. (1988). The prevention of sexual abuse: Examination of a program with kindergarten age children. *Behavior Therapy, 19,* 429–435.

Hasenfeld, Y., & Chesler, M.A. (1989). Client empowerment in the human services: Personal and professional agenda. *The Journal of Applied Behavioral Science, 25,* 499–521.

Haste, H. (1996). Communitarianism and the social construction of morality. *Journal of Moral Education, 25,* 47–55.

Hawkins, J.D., Catalano, R.F., & Miller, J.Y. (1992). Risk and protective factors for alcohol and other drug problems in adolescence and early adulthood: Implications for substance abuse prevention. *Psychological Bulletin, 112*(1), 64–105.

Hawkins, J.D., & Fraser, M.W. (1983). Social support networks in delinquency prevention and treatment. In J.K. Whittaker & J. Garbarino (Eds.), *Social support networks: Informal helping in the human services* (pp. 333–352). New York: Aldine de Gruyter.

Hawkins, R. (1979). Developing comprehensive emergency services. In S. Maybanks & M. Bryce (Eds.), *Home-based services for children and families: Policy, practice, and research* (pp. 103–111). Springfield, IL: C.C. Thomas.

Hayward, K., Cameron, G., & Brown, J. (1998). *Intensive family preservation services: A review of the literature.* Waterloo, ON: Faculty of Social Work, Wilfrid Laurier University.

Hayward, K., Cameron, G., & Peirson, L., (1995). *A different approach: Program development and service delivery in intensive family preservation services.* Waterloo, ON: Centre for Social Welfare Studies, Faculty of Social Work, Wilfrid Laurier University.

Hazelrigg, M.D., Cooper, H.M., & Borduin, C.M. (1987). Evaluating the effectiveness of family therapies: An integrative review and analysis. *Psychological Bulletin, 101*(3), 428–442.

Hazzard, A., Webb, C., Kleemeier, C., Angert, L., & Pohl, J. (1991). Child sexual abuse prevention: Evaluation and one-year follow-up. *Child Abuse and Neglect, 15,* 123–138.

Health Canada. (1996a). *Family violence in Aboriginal communities: An Aboriginal perspective* (Catalogue No. H72-21/150-1997-E). Ottawa: Author.

Health Canada. (1996b). *Turning points: Canadians from coast to coast set a new course for healthy child and youth development. The national goals for healthy child and youth development.* (Family and Child Health Unit, Catalogue No. H21-125/1995E). Ottawa: Author.

Health Canada. (1997a). *Beginning a long journey: A review of projects funded by the family violence prevention division.* (Catalogue No. H72–21/150–1997–E). Ottawa: Author.

Health Canada. (1997b). *It takes a community: A resource manual for community-based prevention of fetal alcohol syndrome and fetal alcohol effects.* (Catalogue No. H34–84/1997E). Ottawa: Ministry of Health, Medical Services Branch.

Hearn, B. (1995). *Child and family support and protection: A Practical approach.* London: National Children's Bureau.

Heatherington, E.M. (1989). Coping with family transitions: Winners, losers and survivors. *Child Development, 60,* 1–14.

Hébert, M., Lavoie, F., Piché, C., & Poitras, M. (1997). Évaluation d'un programme de prévention des abus sexuels chez les élèves du primaire. *Revue Québécoise de Psychologie, 8*(3), 1–23.

Hébert, M., Piché, C., Fecteau, M.-F., & Poitras, M. (1996). Parents' participation in a child sexual abuse prevention programme. *Journal of Child Centred Practice, 41,* 59–81.

Heller, K. (1996). Coming of age of prevention science: Comments on the 1994 National Institute of Mental Health-Institute of Medicine reports. *American Psychologist, 51,* 1123–1127.

Heller, M., & Firestone, W. (1995). Who's in charge here? Sources of leadership in change in eight schools. *The Elementary School Journal , 96*(1), 65–86.

Heneghan, A.M., Horwitz, S.M., & Leventhal, J.M. (1996). Evaluating intensive family preservation programs: A methodological review. *Pediatrics, 97,* 535–542.

Henggler, S.W., Melton, G.B., & Smith, L. (1992). Family preservation using multisystemic therapy: An effective alternative to incarcerating serious juvenile offenders. *Journal of Consulting and Clinical Psychology, 60*(6), 953–961.

Henggler, S.W., Schoenwald, S.K., Borduin, C.M., Pickrel, S., Brondino, M.J., Rowland, M.D., & Scherer, D.G. (1994). Family preservation using multisystemic treatment with adolescent offenders and substance abusers: Long-term outcome, current projects, and interagency collaboration. In C.J. Liberton, K. Kutash, & R.M., Friedman (Eds.), *The sixth annual research conference proceedings for a system of care for children's mental health: Expanding the research base.* Tampa, FL: University of South Florida, Florida Mental Health Institute, Research and Training Center for Children's Mental Health.

Henninger, C., & Nelson, G. (1984). Evaluation of a social support program for young unwed mothers. *Journal of Primary Prevention, 5,* 3–16.

Hepworth, H.P. (1980). *Foster care and adoption in Canada.* Ottawa: Canadian Council on Social Development.

Hernández, A. (1997). *Pedagogy, democracy, and feminism: Rethinking the public sphere.* Albany, NY: State University of New York Press.

Herrenkohl, E., & Herrenkohl, R. (1979). A comparison of abused children and their nonabused siblings. *Journal of the American Academy of Child Psychiatry, 18,* 260–269.

Herrenkohl, E.C., Herrenkhol, R.C., & Egolf, B. (1994). Resilient early school-age children from maltreating homes: Outcomes in late adolescence. *American Journal of Orthopsychiatry, 64*(2), 301–309.

Herrenkohl, E., Herrenkohl, R., & Toedtler, L. (1983). Perspectives on the intergenerational transmission of abuse. In D. Finkelhor, R. Gelles, G. Hotaling, & M. Straus (Eds.), *The dark side of families* (pp. 305–316). Beverly Hills, CA: Sage.

Herrenkohl, R.C., Herrenkohl, E.C., & Egolf, B.P. (1983). Circumstances surrounding the occurrences of child maltreatment. *Journal of Consulting and Clinical Psychology, 51,* 424–431.

Hewlett, S. (1993). *Child neglect in rich nations.* New York: United Nations Children's Fund.

Hightower, A.D. (1997). Primary Mental Health Project. In G.W. Albee & T.P. Gullotta (Eds.), *Primary prevention works* (pp. 191–212). Thousand Oaks, CA: Sage Publications.

Hill, S., & Silver, N. (1993). Civil rights antipornography legislation: Addressing harm to women. In E. Buchwald, P. Fletcher, & M. Roth (Eds.), *Transforming a rape culture* (pp. 282–299). Minneapolis, MN: Milkweed Editions.

Hirschi, T. (1995). The family. In J.A. Wilson & J. Petersilia (Eds.), *Crime.* San Francisco, CA: ICS Press.

Hoffman-Plotkin, D., & Twentyman, C.T. (1984). A multimodal assessment of behavioral and cognitive deficits in abused and neglected preschoolers. *Child Development, 55,* 794–802.

Holden, G.W. (1998). Introduction: The development of research into another consequence of family violence. In G.W. Holden, R. Geffner, & E.N. Jouriles (Eds.), *Children exposed to marital violence: Theory, research and applied issues* (pp. 1–18). Washington, DC: American Psychological Association.

Holtzman, W.H. (1997). Community psychology and full-service schools in different cultures. *American Psychologist, 52,* 381–389.

Home, A., & Darveau-Fournier, L. (1995). Respite child care: A support and empowerment strategy for families in a high-risk community. *Prevention in Human Services, 12*(1), 69–88.

Honahni, T. (1998). Healthy families Arizona: A prevention program. *Pathways Child Abuse Prevention: A Practical Forum for Services to Indian Children & Families, 13*(1), 10.

Hopkins, N., & Emler, N. (1990). Social network participation and problem behavior in adolescence. In K. Hurrelmann & F. Losel (Eds.), *Health hazards in adolescence* (pp. 390–400). New York: Walter de Gruyter.

Howard, M., & McCabe, J.A. (1992). An information and skills approach for younger teens. Postponing sexual involvement program. In B.C. Miller, J.J. Card, R.L. Paikoff, & J.L. Peterson (Eds.), *Preventing adolescent pregnancy: Model programs and evaluations* (pp. 83–109). Newbury Park, CA: Sage Publications.

Howes, C., & Espinosa, M.P. (1985). The consequences of child abuse for the formation of relationships with peers. *Child Abuse and Neglect, 9,* 397–404.

Howitt, P.S., & Moore, E.A. (1991). The efficiency of intensive early intervention: An evaluation of the Oakland County Probate Court Early Offender Program. *Juvenile and Family Court Journal,* 23–30.

Hudson, P., & McKenzie, B. (1984). *Evaluation of Dakota Ojibway Child and Family Services: Final report.* Prepared for Dakota Ojibway Child and Family Services & Evaluation Branch, Corporate Policy Department of Indian Affairs and Northern Development, Ottawa, Ontario.

Hughes, C. (1995). Child poverty, Campaign 2000, and child welfare practice: Working to end child poverty in Canada. *Child Welfare, 74*(3), 779–794.

Hughes, J. (1977). Adolescent children of alcoholic parents and the relationship of Alateen to these children. *Journal of Consulting and Clinical Psychology, 45*(5), 946–947.

Hunter, A. (1998). *Kunuwanimano child and family services proposal for funding increase for the First Nations family support programs.* Unpublished manuscript.

Hunter, R., & Kilstrom, N. (1979). Breaking the cycle in abusive families. *American Journal of Psychiatry, 136,* 1320–1322.

Hunter, R.S., Kilstrom, N., Kraybill, E.N., & Loda, F. (1978). Antecedents of child abuse and neglect in premature infants: A prospective study in a newborn intensive care unit. *Pediatrics, 61,* 629–635.

Hymel, S., Comfort, C., Schonert-Reichel, K., & McDougall, P. (1996). Academic failure and school dropout: The influence of peers. In J. Juvonen & K.R. Wentzel (Eds.), *Social motivations: Understanding children's school adjustment.* Cambridge, MA: Cambridge University Press.

Indian and Northern Affairs Canada. (1987). *Indian child and family services in Canada.* (QS-5236–000–EE-A1). Ottawa: Minister of Indian Affairs and Northern Development.

Institute of Medicine. (1994). *Reducing risks for mental disorders: Frontiers for preventive intervention research.* Washington, DC: National Academy Press.

Jacobson, S.W., & Frye, D.F. (1991). Effect of maternal social support on attachment: Experimental evidence. *Child Development, 62,* 572–582.

Jaffe, P.G., Sudermann, M., & Reitzel, D. (1992). Working with children and adolescents to end the cycle of violence: A social learning approach to intervention and prevention programs. In R. DeV. Peters, R.J. McMahon, & V.

Quinsey (Eds.), *Aggression and violence throughout the lifespan* (pp. 90–110). Newbury Park: CA: Sage Publications.
Jaffe, P., Wolfe, D., & Wilson, S. (1990). *Children of battered women*. Thousand Oaks, CA: Sage.
Jaffe, P., Wolfe, D.A., Wilson, S.K., & Zak, L. (1986). Family violence and child adjustment: A comparative analysis of girls' and boys' behavioral symptoms. *American Journal of Psychiatry, 143,* 74–77.
James N. Docherty and Associates. (1992). *A comprehensive review of Payukotayno: James and Hudson Bay family services*. Unpublished manuscript.
Jasmin, M. (1992). *La protection de la jeunesse ... plus qu'une loi*. Groupe de travail sur l'évaluation de la Loi sur la protection de la jeunesse et sur l'application de la Loi sur les Jeunes contrevenants. Ministère de la Santé et des Services Sociaux, Governement du Québec.
Jason, L.A., Weine, A.M., Johnson, J.H., Warren-Sohlberg, L., Filippelli, L.A., Turner, E.Y., & Lardon, C. (1992). *Helping transfer students: Strategies for educational and social readjustment*. San Francisco, CA: Jossey-Bass Publishers.
Jessor, R., Donovan, J.E., & Costa, F.M. (1991). *Beyond adolescence: Problem behavior and young adult development*. New York: Cambridge University Press.
Jessor, R., & Jessor, S.L. (1977). *Problem behavior and psychological development: A longitudinal study of youth*. New York: Academic Press.
Jilek, W.G. (1994). Traditional healing in the prevention and treatment of alcohol and drug abuse. *Transcultural Psychiatric Research Review, 31,* 219–258.
Joanning, H., Quinn, W., Thomas, F., & Mullen, R. (1992). Treating adolescent drug abuse: A comparison of family systems therapy, group therapy, and family drug abuse. *Journal of Marital and Family Therapy, 18,* 345–356.
Johnson, D.L., & Breckenridge, J.N. (1982). The Houston Parent–Child Development Center and the primary prevention of behavior problems in young children. *American Journal of Community Psychology, 10,* 305–316.
Johnson, D., Malone, P., & Hightower, A.D. (1997). Barriers to primary prevention efforts in the schools. *Applied and Preventive Psychology, 6,* 81–90.
Johnson, D.L., & Walker, T. (1987). Primary prevention of behavior problems in Mexican-American children. *American Journal of Community Psychology, 15,* 375–385.
Johnston, P. (1983). *Native children and the child welfare system*. Toronto: James Lorimer & Co.
Jones, E.D., & McCurdy, K. (1992). The links between types of maltreatment and demographic characteristics of children. *Child Abuse and Neglect, 16,* 201–215.
Jones. L. (1990). Unemployment and child abuse. *Families in Society, 71,* 579–588.
Jones, M.A. (1985). *A second chance for families: Five years later follow-up of a program to prevent foster care*. New York: Child Welfare League of America.

Jones, M.A., Neuman, R., & Shyne, A.W. (1976). *A second chance for families: Evaluation of a program to reduce foster care.* New York: Child Welfare League of America.

Jourdain, L.W. (n.d.). *Customary care: Cultural perspectives for Aboriginal child welfare.* Weechi-It-Te-Win Family Services Inc., Fort Francis, Ontario. Unpublished presentation.

Kagan, S.L., & Pritchard, E. (1996). Linking services for children and families: Past legacy, future possibilities. In E.F. Zigler, S.L. Kagan, & N.W. Hall (Eds.), *Children, families and government: Preparing for the twenty-first century* (pp. 373–393). Cambridge, MA: Cambridge University Press.

Kagan, R.M., Reid, W.J., Roberts, S.E., & Silverman-Pollow, J. (1987). Engaging families of court-mandated youths in an alternative to institutional placement. *Child Welfare, 66*(4), 365–376.

Kahn, A., & Kamerman, S. (1996). *Children and their families in big cities.* New York: Cross-National Studies Research Program, Columbia University School of Social Work.

Kamerman, S.B. (1996a). Child and family policies: An international perspective. In E.F. Zigler, S.L. Kagan, N.W. Hall (Eds.), *Children, families and government: Preparing for the twenty-first century* (pp. 31–48). Cambridge, MA: Cambridge University Press.

Kamerman, S.B. (1996b). The new politics of child and family policies. *Social Work, 41,* 453–465.

Kamerman, S.B., & Kahn, A. (1988, Fall). What Europe does for single-parent families. *Public Interest, 93,* 70–86.

Kamerman, S.B., & Kahn, A. (1991). Trends, issues, and possible lessons. In S.B. Kamerman & A. Kahn, (Eds.), *Child care, parental leave and the under 3's* (pp. 201–224). New York: Auborn House.

Kandel, E., Mednick, S.A., Kirkegaard-Sorensen, L., Hutchings, B., Knop, J., Rosenberg, R., & Schulsinger, F. (1988). IQ as a protective factor for subjects at high risk for antisocial behavior. *Journal of Consulting and Clinical Psychology, 56,* 224–226.

Kane, R. (1994). *Through the moral maze: Searching for absolute values in a pluralistic world.* New York: Paragon.

Kantor, G.K., & Straus, M.A. (1990). The 'drunken bum' theory of wife beating. In M.A. Straus & R.J. Gelles (Eds.), *Physical violence in American families* (pp. 203–224). New Brunswick, NJ: Transaction Press.

Karabanow, J. (1998). *A place to sleep: Exploring the relationship between the voluntary shelter and the child welfare system.* Waterloo, ON: Faculty of Social Work, Wilfrid Laurier University. (Unpublished doctoral comprehensive paper.)

Kasarda, J.D., & Janowitz, M. (1974). Community attachment in mass society. *American Sociological Review, 39,* 328–339.

Katz, K. (1992). Communication problems in maltreated children: A tutorial. *Journal of Childhood Communication Disorders, 14*(2), 147–163.

Katz, M. (1994, May). From challenged childhood to achieving adulthood: Studies in resilience. *Chadder,* 8–11.

Kaufman, J., & Zigler, E. (1987). Do abused children become abusive parents? *American Journal of Orthopsychiatry, 57,* 186–192.

Kavanagh, K., Youngblade, L., Reid, J., & Fagot, B. (1988). Interactions between children and abusive versus control parents. *Journal of Clinical Child Psychology, 17,* 137–142.

Kazdin, A.E. (1993). Adolescent mental health prevention and treatment programs. *American Psychologist, 48*(2), 127–141.

Kazdin, A.E. (1994). Psychotherapy for children and adolescents. In A. Bergin & S. Garfield (Eds.), *Handbook of psychotherapy and behavior change* (4th ed., pp. 543–594). New York: John Wiley & Sons, Inc.

Kazdin, A., Moser, J., Colbus, D., & Bell, R. (1985). Depressive symptoms among physically abused and psychiatrically disturbed children. *Journal of Abnormal Psychology, 94,* 298–307.

Keating, D.P., & Mustard, J.F. (1996). The National Longitudinal Survey of Children and Youth: An essential element for building a learning society in Canada. In *Growing up in Canada: National Longitudinal Survey of Children and Youth* (pp. 7–13). (Statistics Canada, Cat. No. 89–550–MPE, no. 1). Ottawa: Human Resources Development Canada and Statistics Canada.

Kekes, J. (1993). *The morality of pluralism.* Princeton, NJ: Princeton University Press.

Kelleher, K., Chaffin, M., Hollenberg, J., & Fischer, E. (1994). Alcohol and drug disorders among physically abusive and neglectful parents in a community-based sample. *American Journal of Public Health, 84,* 1586–1590.

Kelman, S. (1990, Summer). The renewal of the public sector. *The American Prospect,* 50–57.

Kemp, S., Whittaker, J.K., & Tracy, E.M. (1997). *Rethinking environment for empowerment practice. Empowerment practice in social work: Developing richer conceptual foundations.* Toronto: University of Toronto, Faculty of Social Work.

Kempe, C., Silverman, F., Steele, B., Broegemueller, W., & Silver, H. (1962). The battered child syndrome. *Journal of the American Medical Association, 181,* 17–24.

Kendall-Tackett, K.A., Meyer Williams, L., & Finkelhor, D. (1993). Impact of sexual abuse on children: A review and synthesis of recent empirical studies. *Psychological Bulletin, 113*(1), 164–180.

Kennedy, M. (1998, January 17). Teen pregnancies on rise. *The Kitchener-Waterloo Record,* p. A8.

Kesselman, J.R. (1993). The Child Tax Benefit: Simple, fair, responsive? *Canadian Public Policy, 19,* 109–132.

Kinney, J., Haapala, D., & Booth, C. (1991). *Keeping families together: The Homebuilders model.* New York: Aldine de Gruyter.

Kischuk, N., Laurendeau, M.-C., Desjardins, N., & Perreault, R. (1995). Parental support: Effects of mass-media intervention. *Canadian Journal of Public Health, 86,* 128–132.

Kiser, L.J., Heston, J., Millsap, P.A., & Pruitt, D.B. (1991). Physical and sexual abuse in childhood: Relationship with post-traumatic stress disorder. *Journal of the American Academy of Child and Adolescent Psychiatry, 30,* 776–783.

Kitchen, B. (1995). Children and the case for distributive justice between generations in Canada. *Child Welfare, 74,* 430–458.

Kitzman, H., Olds, D.L., Henderson, C.R., Hanks, C., Cole, R., Tatelbaum, R., McConnochie, K.M., Sidora, K., Luckey, D.W., Shaver, D., Engelhardt, K., James, D., & Barnard, K. (1997). Effect of prenatal and infancy home visitation on pregnancy outcomes, childhood injuries, and repeated childbearing: A randomized controlled trial. *Journal of the American Medical Association, 278,* 644–652.

Kleemeier, C., Webb, C., Hazzard, A., & Pohl, J. (1988). Child sexual abuse prevention: Evaluation of a teacher training model. *Child Abuse and Neglect, 12,* 555–561.

Klein, M., & Stern, L. (1971). Low birth weight and the battered child syndrome. *American Journal of Diseases of Childhood, 122,* 15.

Klodawsky, F., & Spector, A. (1988). New families, new housing needs, new urban environments: The case of single parent families. In C. Andrew & B.M. Milroy (Eds.), *Life spaces: Gender, household, employment* (pp. 141–158). Vancouver: University of British Columbia Press.

Kobasa, S. (1985). Stressful life events, personality, and health: An inquiry into hardiness. In A. Monat & R. Lazarus (Eds.), *Stress and coping* (2nd ed., pp. 174–188). New York: Columbia University Press.

Kohn, A. (1986). *No contest: The case against competition.* Boston, MA: Houghton Mifflin.

Kohn, A. (1990). *The brighter side of human nature.* New York: Basic Books.

Kolko, D.J., Moser, J.T., & Hughes, J. (1989). Classroom training in sexual victimization awareness and prevention skills: An extension of the red flag/green flag program. *Journal of Family Violence, 4,* 25–45.

Kolko, D.J., Moser, J.T., Litz, J., & Hughes, J. (1987). Promoting awareness and prevention of child sexual victimization using the red flag/green flag program: An evaluation with follow-up. *Journal of Family Violence, 2,* 11–35.

Korbin, J. (1994). Sociocultural factors in child maltreatment. In G.B. Melton & F.D. Barry (Eds.), *Protecting children from abuse and neglect: Foundations for a new national strategy* (pp. 182–223). New York: The Guildford Press.

Korbin, J.E., & Coulton, C.J. (1996). The role of neighbors and the government in neighborhood-based child protection. *Journal of Social Issues, 52,* 163–176.

Korten, D.C. (1995). *When corporations rule the world.* San Francisco, CA: Berret-Koehler.

Kotelchuck, M. (1982). Child abuse and neglect: Prediction and misclassification. In R.H. Starr, Jr. (Ed.), *Child abuse prediction: Policy implications* (pp. 67–104). Cambridge, MA: Ballinger.

KPMG. (1999). *The competitive alternatives.* Toronto: Author.

Kraemer, S., & Roberts, J. (Eds.). (1996). *The politics of attachment: Towards a secure society.* London: Free Association Books.

Kraizer, S., Witte, S.S., & Fryer, G.E. (1989). Child sexual abuse prevention programs: What makes them effective in protecting children? *Children Today, 18,* 23–28.

Krawll, M.B. (1994). *Understanding the role of healing in Aboriginal communities.* Ministry of Solicitor General of Canada, Ottawa, Ontario.

Kress, J.S., Cimring, B.R., & Elias, M.J. (1997). Community psychology consultation and the transition to institutional ownership and operation of intervention. *Journal of Educational and Psychological Consultation, 8,* 231–253.

Krishnan, V., & Morrison, K.B. (1995). An ecological model of child maltreatment in a Canadian province. *Child Abuse and Neglect, 19*(1), 101–113.

Krugman, R.D. (1995). Future directions in preventing child abuse. *Child Abuse and Neglect, 19,* 273–279.

Krugman, R.D., Lenherr, M., Betz, L., & Fryer, G.E. (1986). The relationship between unemployment and physical abuse of children. *Child Abuse and Neglect, 10,* 415–418.

Kruttschnitt, C., McLeod, J.D., & Dornfeld, M. (1993). The economic environment of child abuse. *Social Problems, 41*(2), 299–315.

Kubisch, A.C. (1996, January/February). Comprehensive community initiatives: Lessons in neighborhood transformation. *Shelterforce,* 7–12.

Kufeldt, K., & Nimmo, M. (1987). Youth on the street. *Child Abuse and Neglect, 11*(4), 531–543.

Kurtz, P.D., Gaudin, J.M., Wodarski, J.S., & Howing, P.T. (1993). Maltreatment and the school-aged child: School performance consequences. *Child Abuse and Neglect, 17*(5), 581–589.

Kymlicka, W. (1990). *Contemporary political philosophy.* New York: Oxford.

Labonté, R. (1990). Empowerment: Notes on professional and community dimensions. *Canadian Review of Social Policy, 26,* 64–75.

Labonté, R. (1993). Community development and partnerships. *Canadian Journal of Public Health, 84,* 237–240.

Lahey, B.B., Conger, R.D., Atkeson, B.M., & Treiber, F.A. (1984). Parenting behavior and emotional status of physically abusive mothers. *Journal of Consulting and Clinical Psychology, 52,* 1062–1071.

Lally, J.R., Mangione, P.L., Honig, A.S. (1988). The Syracuse University Family Development Research Program: Long-range impact on an early intervention with low-income children and their families. In D.R. Powell (Ed.), *Parent education as early childhood intervention: Emerging directions in theory, research, and practice* (pp. 79–104). Norwood, NJ: Ablex Publishing Corporation.

Lam and Associates. (1997). *Healthy Families Arizona: Evaluation report, 1992–96.* Prepared for the Arizona Department of Economic Security, Phoenix, Arizona.

Lambie, D., Bond, J.T., & Weikart, D. (1974). *Home teaching with mothers and infants.* Ypsilanti, MI: High/Scope Educational Research Foundation.

Landy, S., & Tam, K.K. (1996). Yes, parenting does make a difference to the development of children in Canada. In *Growing up in Canada: National Longitudinal Survey of Children and Youth* (pp. 103–118). (Catalogue No. 89–550–MPE, no.1). Ottawa: Human Resources Development Canada and Statistics Canada.

Lane, T.W., & Davis, G.E. (1987). Child maltreatment and juvenile delinquency: Does a relationship exist? In J.D. Burchard & S.N. Burchard (Eds.), *Prevention of delinquent behavior: Primary prevention of psychopathology* (pp. 122–138). Newbury Park, CA: Sage.

Larrance, D.T., & Twentyman, C.T. (1983). Maternal attributions and child abuse. *Journal of Abnormal Psychology, 92,* 449–457.

Larson, C.P. (1980). Efficacy of prenatal and postpartum home visits on child health and development. *Pediatrics, 66,* 191–197.

Laurendeau, M.-C., Bélanger, J., & Bowen, F. (1996). Prévenir la violence à l'école: Un point de vue Québécois. *Les Cahiers de la Sécurité Intérieure, 25,* 185–196.

Laurendeau, M.-C., Gagnon, G., Desjardins, N., Perreault, R., & Kischuk, N. (1991). Evaluation of an early, mass media parental support intervention. *Journal of Primary Prevention, 11,* 207–225.

Laurendeau, M.-C., Gagnon, G., Lapointe, Y., & Beauregard, F. (1989). Sensibilation à la violence en milieu scolaire: Évaluation d'un programme pilote. *Apprentissage et Socialisation, 12,* 89–98.

Lavoie, F., & Stewart, M. (1995). Mutual-aid groups and support groups: The Canadian context. *Canadian Journal of Community Mental Health, 14*(2), 5–12.

Layzer, J.I., Goodson, B.D., & DeLange, C. (1986). Children in shelters. *Response, 9,* 2–5.

Leonard, K.E., & Jacob, T. (1988). Alcohol, alcoholism, and family violence. In V.B. Van Hasselt, R.L. Morrison, A.S. Bellack, & M. Hersen (Eds.), *Handbook of family violence* (pp. 383–406). New York: Plenum.

Leonard, P. (1997). *Postmodern welfare: Reconstructing and emancipatory project.* London: Sage.

Lerner, M. (1995). *America's youth in crisis: Challenges and options for programs and policies.* Thousand Oaks, CA: Sage Publications.

Lerner, M. (1996). *The politics of meaning.* New York: Addison-Wesley.

Lero, D., Guelman, H., Pence, A., Brokman, L., & Nutall, S. (1992). *Canadian national child care study: Parental work patterns and child care needs.* (Catalogue No. 89-529E). Ottawa: Minister of Supply and Services.

Leventhal, J.M. (1981). Risk factors for child abuse: Methodologic standards in case-control studies. *Pediatrics, 68,* 684–690.

Levesque, R.J. (1996). International children's rights: Can they make a difference in American family policy? *American Psychologist, 51,* 1251–1256.

Levine, M., & Levine, A. (1992). *Helping children: A social history.* New York: Oxford University Press.

Levinson, D. (1989). *Family violence in cross-cultural perspective.* Newbury Park, CA: Sage.

Levitt, M.J., Weber, R.A., & Clark, M.C. (1986). Social network relationships as sources of maternal support and well-being. *Developmental Psychology, 22,* 310–316.

Lewis, D.O. (1992). From abuse to violence: Psychological consequences of maltreatment. *Journal of the American Academy of Child and Adolescent Psychiatry, 31,* 383–391.

Lewis, D.O., Mallough, C., & Webb, V. (1989). Child abuse and violent criminality. In D. Cicchetti & V. Carlson (Eds.), *Child maltreatment: Theory and research on the causes and consequences of child abuse and neglect* (pp. 707–720). Cambridge, MA: Cambridge University Press.

Lewis, R.A., Piercy, F.P., Sprenkle, D.H., & Trepper, T. (1990). Family-based interventions for helping drug-abusing adolescents. *Journal of Adolescent Research, 5,* 82–95.

Lichtenstein, K. (1983, May). *Prediction based on census data and economic indicators.* Paper presented at the 3rd National Conference on Research, Demonstration, and Evaluation in Public Social Services, American Public Welfare Association, Washington, DC.

Lieber, L.L. (1983). The self-help approach: Parents Anonymous. *Journal of Clinical Child Psychology, 12,* 288–291.

Lieber, L.L., & Baker, J.M. (1977). Parents Anonymous – Self-help treatment for child abusing parents: A review and evaluation. *Child Abuse and Neglect, 1,* 133–148.

Limber, S.P., & Wilcox, B.L. (1996). Application of the U.N. Convention on the Rights of the Child to the United States. *American Psychologist, 51,* 1246–1250.

Lindeman Nelson, H. (1997). Introduction. In H. Lindeman Nelson (Ed.), *Feminism and families* (pp. 1–12). London: Routledge.

Lindsey, D. (1995). *The welfare of children*. New York: Oxford University Press.

Lipman, E.L., Offord, D.R., & Dooley, D. (1996). What do we know about children from single-mother families? Questions and answers from the National Longitudinal Survey of Children and Youth. In *Growing up in Canada: National Longitudinal Survey of Children and Youth* (pp. 83–91). (Catalogue No. 89-550-MPE, no. 1). Ottawa: Human Resources Development Canada and Statistics Canada.

Lipsitt, L. (1991). Childhood experience and subsequent resiliency. *Brown University Child and Adolescent Behavior*, 7(8), 8.

Lochhead, C., & Shillington, R. (1996). *A statistical profile of urban poverty*. Ottawa: Centre for International Statistics, Canadian Council on Social Development.

Loeber, R., Felton, D.K., & Reid, J.B. (1984). A social learning approach to the reduction of coercive processes in child abusive families: A molecular analysis. *Advances in Behavior Research and Therapy*, 6, 29–45.

Loizou, A. (1996). Social justice and social policy. In M. Lavalette & A. Pratt (Eds.), *Social policy* (pp. 163–181). London: Sage.

Lord, J., & Church, K. (1998). Beyond 'partnership shock': Getting to 'yes,' living with 'no.' *Canadian Journal of Rehabilitation*, 12, 113–122.

Lord, J., & Hutchison, P. (1993). The process of empowerment: Implications for theory and practice. *Canadian Journal of Community Mental Health*, 12, 5–22.

LoSciuto, L., Rajala, A.K., Townsend, T.N., & Taylor, A.S., (1996). An outcome evaluation of Across Ages: An intergenerational mentoring approach to drug prevention. *Journal of Adolescent Research*, 11, 116–129.

Lovell, M.L., & Hawkins, D.J. (1988). An evaluation of a group intervention to increase the personal social networks of abusive mothers. *Children and Youth Services Review*, 10, 175–188.

Lovell, M.L., Reid, K., & Richey, C.A. (1992). Social support training for abusive mothers. In J. Garland (Ed.), *Social group work reaching out: People, places, and power* (pp. 95–107). New York: The Haworth Press.

Lovell, M.L. & Richey, C.A. (1991). Implementing agency-based social-support skill training. *Families in Society: The Journal of Contemporary Human Services*, 72, 563–572.

Lovell, M.L., & Richey, C.A. (1995). The effectiveness of social-support skill training with multi-problem families at risk for child maltreatment. *Canadian Journal of Community Mental Health*, 14(1), 29–48.

Lung, C.T., & Daro, D. (1996). *Current trends in child abuse reporting and fatalities: The results of the 1995 annual fifty state survey*. Chicago, IL: National Committee to Prevent Child Abuse.

Luthar, S. (1991). Vulnerability and resilience: A study of high-risk adolescents. *Child Development, 62,* 600–616.

Luthar, S.S., & Zigler, E. (1991). Vulnerability and competence among high-risk adolescents. *Development and Psychopathology, 4,* 287–299.

Lutzker, J.R., & Rice, J.M. (1984). Project 12–Ways: Measuring outcome of a large in-home service for treatment and prevention of child abuse and neglect. *Child Abuse and Neglect, 8,* 519–524.

Lutzker, J.R., & Rice, J.M. (1987). Using recidivism data to evaluate Project 12-Ways: An ecobehavioral approach to the treatment and prevention of child abuse and neglect. *Journal of Family Violence, 2,* 283–290.

Lyle, C.G., & Nelson, J. (1983, July). *Home based vs. traditional child protection services: A study of the home based services demonstration project in the Ramsey County Community Human Services Department.* Unpublished paper.

Lynch, K.B., Geller, S.R., Hunt, D.R., Galano, J., & Dubas, J.S. (1998). Successful program development using implementation evaluation. *Journal of Prevention and Intervention in the Community, 17,* 51–64.

Lynch, M.A., & Roberts, J. (1982). *Consequences of child abuse.* San Diego, CA: Academic Press.

Lyons-Ruth, K., Connell, D.B., Zoll, D., & Stahl, J. (1987). Infants at social risk: Relations among infant maltreatment, maternal behavior, and infant attachment behavior. *Developmental Psychology, 23,* 223–232.

MacGillivary, H., & Nelson, G. (1998). Partnership in mental health: What is it and how to do it. *Canadian Journal of Rehabilitation, 12,* 71–84.

Mackie, R. (1998, January 21). Cuts hurt children's aid. *The Globe and Mail,* p. A8.

MacMillan, H.L., & Finkel, K.C. (1995, June). Maltreatment of children. *Medicine North America,* 571–572, 587–589.

MacMillan, H.L., Fleming, J.E., Trocmé, N., Boyle, M.H., Wong, M., Racine, Y.A., Beardslee, W.R., & Offord, D.R. (1997). Prevalence of child physical and sexual abuse in the community: Results from the Ontario Health Supplement. *Journal of the American Medical Association, 277,* 131–135.

MacMillan, H.L., MacMillan, J.H., Offord, D.R., Griffith, L., & MacMillan, A. (1994a). Primary prevention of child physical abuse and neglect: A critical review. Part I. *Journal of Child Psychology and Psychiatry, 35,* 835–856.

MacMillan, H.L., MacMillan, J.H., Offord, D.R., Griffith, L., & MacMillan, A. (1994b). Primary prevention of child sexual abuse: A critical review. Part II. *Journal of Child Psychology and Psychiatry, 35,* 857–876.

MacMillan, H.L., Niec, A.C., & Offord, D.R. (1995). Child physical abuse: Risk indicators and prevention. In T.J. David (Ed.), *Recent advances in paediatrics* (pp. 53–67). Edinburgh, Scotland: Churchill, Livingston.

Macpherson, A.S. (1984). *Housing and health: Public health implications of the affordable housing crisis.* Toronto: City of Toronto Department of Public Health, Mimeo.

Madden, J., O'Hara, J., & Levenstein, P. (1984). Home again: Effects of the mother–child home program on mother and child. *Child Development, 55,* 636–647.

Madden, N.A., Slavin, R.F., Karweit, N.K., Dolan, L.J., & Weisit, B.A. (1993). Success for all: Longitudinal effects of a restructuring program for inner-city elementary schools. *American Educational Research Journal, 30,* 123–148.

Maden, M.F., & Wrench, D.F. (1977). Significant findings in child abuse research. *Victimology, 2,* 196–224.

Maidman, F. (1982). *Native people in the urban setting.* Report to the Task Force on Urban Native People. Toronto, Ontario.

Maidman, F. (1988). *The experience of growth.* Unpublished manuscript.

Maidman, F. (1995). *Gzaa-Gaah-Naah-Nig Child and Family Services: Service descriptions and proposals.* Unpublished planning papers.

Maidman, F. (1996a). *Mooka'am Children's Circle Program: An evaluation.* Unpublished manuscript.

Maidman, F. (1996b). *Working towards community well-being at Gabriel Dumont: An evaluation of the community watch program.* Unpublished report.

Maidman, F. (1998). *The Aboriginal Prenatal Nutrition Program: An evaluation.* Unpublished report.

Maidman, F., & Beedie, M. (1994). *Mooka'am Sexual Abuse Treatment Program: Evaluation of impact.* Unpublished report.

Maidman, F., & Conchelos, G. (1991). *Towards a valued life-style: A needs assessment and planning paper for Native people in Simcoe County and York Region.* Unpublished report.

Main, M., & George, D. (1985). Response of abused and disadvantaged toddlers to distress in agemates: A study in the daycare setting. *Developmental Psychology, 21,* 407–412.

Maison d'Haïti, Association Jamaïquaine de Montréal, Direction de la santé publique de la Régie de Montréal-Centre. (1997). *Rapport annuel, Avril, 1996–Mars, 1997: Au Futur – Project de promotion du développement de l'enfant et insertion sociale des jeunes mères de la communauté noire de Montréal.*

Malinosky-Rummell, R., & Hansen, D.J. (1993). Long-term consequences of child abuse and neglect. *Psychological Bulletin, 114,* 68–79.

Malkin, C.M., & Lamb, M.E. (1994). Child maltreatment: A test of sociobiological theory. *Journal of Comparative Family Studies, 25,* 121–133.

Marcenko, M.O., Spence, M., & Samost, L. (1996). Outcomes of a home visitation trial for pregnant and postpartum women at risk for child placement. *Children and Youth Services Review, 18,* 243–259.

Marcil-Gratton, N. (1995, December). To become couples and parents – New answers to an old challenge: Québec as a showcase. In *Transition* (pp. 10–11, 15). Ottawa: Vanier Institute of the Family.

Marsden, L. (Chair). (1991). Canada, Standing Senate Committee on Social Affairs, Science and Technology, *Children in poverty: Toward a better future.* Second Session, 34th Parliament (Catalogue No. XC28–342/1–01). Ottawa: Minister of Supply and Services Canada.

Martin, F.E., & Palmer, T. (1997, Fall). Transitions to adulthood: A child welfare youth perspective. *Community Alternatives: International Journal of Family Care, 9*(2), 29–60.

Martin, M.J., & Walters, J. (1982). Familial correlates of selected types of child abuse and neglect. *Journal of Marriage and the Family, 44,* 267–276.

Martin Spigelman Research Associates, The Project Group, & Terriplan Consultants. (1997). *Investing in the children's future: An evaluation of the First Nations/Inuit child care initiative.* Unpublished report prepared for the Aboriginal Relations Office, Human Resources Development Canada.

Mash, E.J., Johnston, C., & Kovitz, K. (1983). A comparison of the mother–child interactions of physically abused and nonabused children during play and task situations. *Journal of Clinical Child Psychology, 12,* 337–346.

Mash, E.J., & Wolfe, D.A. (1991). Methodological issues in research on physical child abuse. *Criminal Justice and Behavior, 18,* 8–29.

Massé, R., & Bastien, M.-F. (1995). *Isolement social, pauvreté et maltraitance: Une étude castémoin.* Montréal: Équipe écologie humaine et sociale, Direction de la santé publique, Montréal.

Masten, A.S. (1982). *Humor and creative thinking in stress-resistant children.* Unpublished doctoral dissertation, University of Minnesota.

Masten, A., Best, K., & Garmezy, N. (1990). Resilience and development: Contributions from the study of children who overcome adversity. *Development and Psychopathology, 2,* 425–444.

Masten, A.S., & Coatsworth, J.D. (1998). The development of competence in favorable and unfavorable environments. *American Psychologist, 53*(2), 205–220.

Masten, A.S., Garmezy, N., Tellegen, A., Pellegrini, D.S., Larkin, K., & Larsen, A. (1988). Competence and stress in school children: The moderating effects of individual and family qualities. *Journal of Child Psychology and Psychiatry, 29,* 745–764.

Mattaini, M.A., McGowan, B.G., & Williams, G. (1996). Child maltreatment. In M.A. Mattaini & B.A. Thyer (Eds.), *Finding solutions to social problems: Behavioral strategies for change* (pp. 223–266). Washington, DC: American Psychological Association.

Maughan, B. (1988). School experiences as risk/protective factors. In M. Rutter (Ed.), *Studies of psychosocial risk* (pp. 200–220). Cambridge, MA: Cambridge University Press.

Maxwell, J. (1993). Globalization and family security. In National Forum on Family Security (Ed.), *Family security in insecure times* (pp. 19–55). Ottawa: Canadian Council on Social Development.

Mayer, M. (1997). *Les contextes écologiques d'incidence de mauvais traitements à l'égard des enfants de la région de Montréal.* Unpublished doctoral dissertation, Faculté des études supérieures en sciences humaines appliquées, Université de Montréal, Québec.

Mayer-Renaud, M. (1990a). *Les enfants négligés sur le territoire du CSSMM, Vol. 1, Les manifestations de la négligence et leurs chevauchements.* Montréal: Centre des Services Sociaux du Montréal métropolitain.

Mayer-Renaud, M. (1990b). *Les enfants négligés sur le territoire du CSSMM Vol. 2, Leurs caractéristiques personnelles, familiales et sociales.* Montréal: Centre des Services Sociaux du Montréal métropolitain.

Mayer-Renaud, M. (1991). Le phénomène de la négligence. Montréal: Centre des Services Sociaux du Montréal métropolitain.

Mayer-Renaud, M. (1993). *La problématique de la négligence à l'égard des enfants: Une synthèse des causes et des conséquences.* Montréal: Centre de protection de l'enfance et de la jeunesse du Montréal métropolitain.

Mayton, D.M., Ball-Rokeach, S.J., & Loges, W.E. (1994). Human values and social issues: An introduction. *Journal of Social Issues, 50*(4), 1–8.

McClain, P., Sacks, J., & Frohlke, R., & Ewigman, B.G. (1993). Estimates of fatal child abuse and neglect, United States, 1979–1988. *Pediatrics, 91,* 338–343.

McCloskey, L.A., Figueredo, A.J., & Koss, M.P. (1995). The effects of systemic family violence on children's mental health. *Child Development, 66,* 1239–1261.

McCormick, R.M. (1995). The facilitation of healing for the First Nations people of British Columbia. *Canadian Journal of Native Education, 21,* 249–322.

McCoy, C.W. (1996). Reexamining models of healthy families. *Contemporary Family Therapy, 18*(2), 243–256.

McCray, J.S., & Wolf, L. (1997, March). *1996 Illinois Parents Anonymous parent survey report.* Chicago: Children's Home and Aid Society.

McCubbin, H.I., McCubbin, M.A., & Thompson, A.I. (1992). Resiliency in families: The role of family schema and appraisal in family adaptation to crises. In T.H. Brubaker (Ed.), *Family relations: Challenges for the future* (pp. 153–177). Newbury Park, CA: Sage.

McGain, B., & McKinzey, R.K. (1995). The efficacy of group treatment in sexually abused girls. *Child Abuse and Neglect, 19,* 1157–1169.

McGee, R., & Wolfe, D. (1991). Psychological maltreatment: Towards an operational definition. *Development and Psychopathology, 3,* 1–27.

McGee, R., Wolfe, D., Yuen, S., Wilson, S., & Carnochan, J. (1993, March). *The measurement of maltreatment: Which method is best?* Paper presented at the biennial meetings of the Society for Research in Child Development, New Orleans, LA.

McGoldrick, M., Pearce, J., & Giordano, J. (1982). *Ethnicity and family therapy.* New York: The Guilford Press.

McIntyre, L. (1996). Starting out. In *Growing up in Canada: National Longitudinal Survey of Children and Youth* (pp. 47–56). (Catalogue No. 89–550–MPE, no. 1). Ottawa: Human Resources Development Canada and Statistics Canada.

McKenzie, B., & Morrissette, V. (1993). *Aboriginal child and family services in Manitoba: Implementation issues and the development of culturally appropriate services.* Paper presented to 6th Conference on Social Welfare Policy, St. John's, Newfoundland.

McKnight, J. (1989, Summer). Do no harm: Policy options that meet human needs. *Social Policy,* 5–15.

McKnight, J. (1995). *The careless society: Community and its counterfeits.* New York: Basic Books.

McLaughlin, M.A. (1988). Homelessness in small-town and rural Canada. *Perception, 12*(1), 33–36.

McLeer, S.V., Deblinger, E., Hentry, D., & Orvaschel, H. (1992). Sexually abused children at high risk for post-traumatic stress disorder. *Journal of the American Academy of Child and Adolescent Psychiatry, 31,* 875–879.

McLoyd, V.C. (1990). The impact of economic hardship on black families and children: Psychological distress, parenting, and socioemotional development, *Child Development, 61,* 311–346.

McLoyd, V.C. (1998). Socioeconomic disadvantage and child development. *American Psychologist, 53*(2), 185–204.

McQuaig, L. (1995). *Shooting the hippo.* Toronto: Penguin.

McQuaig, L. (1998). *The cult of impotence.* Toronto: Viking.

McQuillen, J.S., O'Brien, P.E., & Schrader, D.C. (1993, May). *Testing the effectiveness of intervention programs on children's compliance-resisting behaviors.* Paper presented at the Annual Meeting of the International Communication Association, Washington, DC.

Meezan, W., & McCroskey, J. (1996, Winter). Improving family functioning through family preservation services: Results of the Los Angeles experiment. *Family Preservation Journal,* 9–29.

Meier, J.H. (1985). *Assault against children: Why it happens, how to stop it.* San Diego, CA: College-Hill Press.

Melnick, B., & Hurley, J. (1969). Distinctive personality attributes of child abusing mothers. *Journal of Consulting and Clinical Psychology, 33*, 746–749.

Melton, G.B. (1991). Preserving the dignity of children around the world: The UN Convention on the Rights of the Child. *Child Abuse and Neglect, 15*, 343–350.

Melton, G.B. (1996). The child's right to a family environment: Why children's rights and family values are compatible. *American Psychologist, 51*, 1234–1238.

Melton, G.B., & Barry, F.D. (1994a). Neighbors helping neighbors: The vision of the U.S. Advisory Board on Child Abuse and Neglect. In G.B. Melton & F.D. Barry (Eds.), *Protecting children from abuse and neglect: Foundations for a new national strategy* (pp. 1–13). New York: The Guilford Press.

Melton, G.B., & Barry, F.D. (Eds.). (1994b). *Protecting children from abuse and neglect: Foundations for a new national strategy*. New York: The Guilford Press.

Mercer, J.R. (1989). Why haven't schools changed the focus from pathology to prevention?: Conceptual and legal obstacles. In L.A. Bond & B.E. Compas (Eds.), *Primary prevention and promotion in schools* (pp. 345–360). London: Sage.

Messier, C., & Toupin. J. (1994). *La clientèle multiethnique des centres de réadaptation pour les jeunes en difficulté*. Québec: Commission de protection des droits de la jeunesse, Gouvernement du Québec.

Meyers, J. (1989). The practice of psychology in the schools for the primary prevention of learning and adjustment problems in children: A perspective from the field of education. In L.A. Bond & B.E. Compas (Eds.), *Primary prevention and promotion in schools* (pp. 391–420). Newbury Park, CA: Sage.

Mickelson, R.A., Yon, M.G., & Carlton-Lalley, I. (1995). Slipping through the cracks: The education of homeless children. In L.C. Rigsby, M.C. Reynolds, & M.C. Wang (Eds.), *School-community connections: Exploring issues for research and practice* (pp. 374–387). San Francisco, CA: Jossey-Bass Publishers.

Midgley, M., & Hughes, J. (1997). Are families out of date? In H. Lindeman Nelson (Ed.), *Feminism and families* (pp. 55–68). London: Routledge.

Miller, B.C., & Paikoff, R.L. (1992). Comparing adolescent pregnancy prevention programs: Methods and results. In B.C. Miller, J.J. Card, R.L. Paikoff, & J.L. Peterson (Eds.), *Preventing adolescent pregnancy: Model programs and evaluations* (pp. 265–284). Newbury Park, CA: Sage Publications.

Miller, D. (1978). *Social justice*. Oxford: Clarendon.

Milner, J.S. (1988). An ego-strength scale for the Child Abuse Potential Inventory. *Journal of Family Violence, 3*, 151–162.

Milner, J.S. (1993). Social information processing and physical child abuse. *Clinical Psychology Review, 13*, 275–294.

Milner, J.S., Gold, R.G., & Wimberly, R.C. (1986). Prediction and explanation of child abuse: Cross-validation of the child abuse potential inventory. *Journal of Consulting and Clinical Psychology, 54,* 865–866.

Milner, J.S., Halsey, L.B., & Fultz, J. (1995). Empathic responsiveness and affective reactivity to infant stimuli in high- and low-risk for physical child abuse mothers. *Child Abuse and Neglect, 19,* 767–780.

Milner, J.S., & Robertson, K.R. (1990). Comparison of physical child abusers, intrafamilial sexual child abusers, and child neglecters. *Journal of Interpersonal Violence, 5,* 37–48.

Minde, K., Shosenberg, N., Marton, P., Thompson, J., Ripley, J., & Burns, S. (1980). Self-help groups in a premature nursery. *Journal of Pediatrics, 96,* 933–940.

Ministère de la Santé et des Services Sociaux. (1998). *Rapports statsitiques annuels des Centres Jeunesse. Rapport 'S' 480.* Québec: Gouvernement du Québec.

Mitchell, A. (1998a, January 17). Teen-age pregnancy on rise again. *The Globe and Mail,* pp. A1, A7.

Mitchell, A. (1998b, February 13). More children running away younger, Statscan says. *The Globe and Mail,* p. A3.

Mitchell, C., Tovar, P., & Knitzer, J. (1989). *The Bronx Homebuilders Program: An evaluation of the first 45 families.* New York: Bank Street College of Education, Division of Research, Demonstration and Policy.

Mitchell, R.E., Billings, A.G., & Moos, R.H. (1982). Social support and well-being: Implications for prevention programs. *Journal of Primary Prevention, 3,* 77–98.

Moisan, M. (1997, Spring). Les hommes et l'utilisation du congé parental au Québec: Faits saillants d'une recherche. *Politiques du père – Lien social et Politiques (Revue International en Action Communautaire), 37,* 111–119.

Moore, M., Sixsmith, J., Knowles, K., Kagan, C., Lewis, D., Beazley, S., & Rout, U. (1996). *Children's reflections on family life.* Washington, DC: The Falmer Press.

Moran, P.B., & Eckenrode, J. (1992). Protective personality characteristics among adolescent victims of maltreatment. *Child Abuse and Neglect, 16,* 743–754.

Morrill, W.A. (1996). Getting beyond the micro 'GeeWhiz': Can innovative service change the service system? In A. Kahn & S. Kamerman (Eds.), *Children and their families in big cities* (pp. 186–210). New York: Cross-National Studies Research Program, Columbia University School of Social Work.

Morrison, R., & Wilson, C. (1995). *Native peoples: The Canadian experience.* Toronto: McClelland & Stewart.

Morrison, S. (1997, July 9). Abuse a huge problem: Study shows. *The Hamilton Spectator,* p. A1.

Morrissette, P.J. (1994). The holocaust of First Nation people: Residual effects on parenting and treatment implications. *Contemporary Family Therapy, 16*(5), 381–394.

Morrissette, V., McKenzie, B., & Morrissette, L. (1993). Towards an Aboriginal model of social work practice: Cultural knowledge and traditional practices. *Canadian Social Work Review, 10*(1), 91–108.

Muir, R.C., Monaghan, S.M., Gilmore, R.J., Clarkson, J.E., Crooks, T.J., & Egan, T.G. (1989). Predicting child abuse and neglect in New Zealand. *Australia and New Zealand Journal of Psychiatry, 23,* 255–260.

Mulhall, S., & Swift, A. (1996). *Liberals and communitarians* (2nd ed.). Oxford: Blackwell.

Muñoz, R., Mrazek, P.J., & Haggerty, R.J. (1996). Institute of Medicine report on prevention of mental disorders: Summary and commentary. *American Psychologist, 51,* 1116–1122.

Murphy, L.B. (1987). Further reflections on resilience. In E.J. Anthony & B.J. Cohler (Eds.), *The invulnerable child* (pp. 84–105). New York: The Guilford Press.

Murphy, L.B., & Moriarty, A.E. (1976). *Vulnerability, coping, and growth.* New Haven, CT: Yale University Press.

Murphy, S., Orkow, B., & Nicola, R. (1985). Prediction of child abuse and neglect: A prospective study. *Child Abuse and Neglect, 9,* 225–235.

National Center on Child Abuse and Neglect, Office of Human Development Services, Department of Health and Human Services. (1988). *Study findings: Study of national incidence and prevalence of child abuse and neglect.* Washington, DC: U.S. Government Printing Office.

National Center on Child Abuse and Neglect. (1993). *National child abuse and neglect data system: 1991 summary data component.* Washington, DC: U.S. Government Printing Office.

National Center on Child Abuse and Neglect. (1994). *Child maltreatment 1992: Reports from the States to the National Center on Child Abuse and Neglect.* Washington, DC: U.S. Government Printing Office.

National Crime Prevention Council. (1996). *Preventing crime by investing in families: An integrated approach to promote positive outcomes in children.* Ottawa: Author.

National Forum on Health. (Ed.). (1996). *What determines health?* (Ministry of Public Works and Government Services of Canada, Catalogue No. H21–126/3–116E). Ottawa: Author.

National Indian Child Welfare Association, Inc. (1990a). *Walking in your child's moccasins: A booklet about child abuse and child neglect for parents and care givers of Indian children.* Portland, OR: Author.

National Indian Child Welfare Association, Inc. (1990b). *Watchful eyes: Community involvement in preventing child abuse and child neglect of Indian children.* Portland, OR: Author.

National Longitudinal Survey of Children and Youth. (1996). *Growing up in Canada.* (Catalogue No. 89–550–MPE, no. 1). Ottawa: Human Resources Development Canada and Statistics Canada.

National Longitudinal Survey of Children and Youth. (1998). *Workshop paper series from Investing in children: A national research conference*, October 27 to 29, 1998, Ottawa, Ontario. (Available from Applied Research Branch, Human Resources Development Canada, 7th Floor, Narono Building, 360 Laurier Ave., Ottawa, Ontario, K1A 0J9).

National Native Association of Treatment Directors. (1989). *In the spirit of the family: Native alcohol & drug counselors' family systems treatment intervention handbook.* Calgary, Alberta.

National Research Council. (1993). *Losing generations: Adolescents in high-risk settings.* Washington, DC: National Academy Press.

Native Child and Family Services of Toronto. (1990). *Native family well-being in urban settings: A culture based child and family services model.* Toronto: Author.

Nelson, D.W. (1996). The path of most resistance: Lessons learned from 'New Futures.' In A. Kahn & S. Kamerman (Eds.), *Children and their families in big cities* (pp. 160–184). New York: Cross-National Studies Research Program, Columbia University School of Social Work.

Nelson, G., Amio, J., Prilleltensky, I., & Nickels, P. (2000). Partnerships for implementing and evaluating school and community prevention programs. *Journal of Educational and Psychological Consultation, 11,* 121–146.

Nelson, G., Prilleltensky, I., Laurendeau, M.-C., & Powell, B. (1996). A survey of prevention activities in mental health in the Canadian provinces and territories. *Canadian Psychology, 37,* 161–172.

Nelson, G., Prilleltensky, I., & McGillivary. (in press). Value-based partnerships: Toward solidarity with oppressed groups. *American Journal of Community Psychology.*

Nelson, G., Prilleltensky, I., & Peters, R. DeV. (1999). Mental health promotion and the prevention of mental health problems in the community. In W. Marshall & P. Firestone (Eds.), *Abnormal psychology* (pp. 461–478). Scarborough, ON: Prentice-Hall.

Nelson, K., Landsman, M.J., & Deutelbaum, W. (1990). Three models of family-centered placement prevention programs. *Child Welfare, 114,* 1–21.

Nemerofsky, A.G., Carran, D.T., & Rosenberg, L.A. (1994). Age variation in performance among preschool children in a sexual abuse prevention program. *Journal of Child Sexual Abuse, 3,* 85–102.

Nenortas, G.V. (1987). *A dropout prevention program utilizing peer group counseling with middle school alternative students.* Ft Lauderdale, FL: Nova University Center for the Advancement of Education.

Newman, M.R., & Lutzker, J.R. (1990). Prevention programs. In R.T. Ammerman, & M. Hersen (Eds.), *Children at risk: An evaluation of the factors contributing to child abuse and neglect* (pp. 225–248). New York: Plenum Press.

New Zealand Government. (1997). *Wraparound Programme provider announced.* [On-line] www.newsroom.co.nz/stories/PO9710/S00190.htm.

Ney, P.G. (1989). Child mistreatment: Possible reasons for its transgenerational transmission. *Canadian Journal of Psychiatry, 34,* 371–378.

Nichols, M.P., & Schwartz, R.C. (1995). *Family therapy: Concepts and methods* (3rd ed.). Boston, MA: Allyn and Bacon.

Nicholson, L. (1997). The myth of the traditional family. In H. Lindeman Nelson (Ed.), *Feminism and families* (pp. 27–42). London: Routledge.

Norman, E., & Turner, S. (1991). *Adolescent substance abuse prevention programs.* New York: New York State Division of Substance Abuse Services.

Northwestern Indian Child Welfare Institute. (1986). *Positive Indian parenting.* Portland, OR: Author.

Novick, M. (1994). Foreword. In J. O'Neill (Author), *The missing child in liberal theory.* Toronto: University of Toronto Press.

Oates, R.K., & Forrest, D. (1985). Mothers of abused children: A comparison study. *Clinical Pediatrics, 24,* 9–13.

Oates, R.K., Gray, J., Schweitzer, L., Kempe, R.S., & Harmon, R.J. (1995). A therapeutic preschool for abused children: The Keepsafe project. *Child Abuse and Neglect, 19,* 1379–1386.

Obonsawin-Irwin Consulting. (1997). *Findings report for an evaluation of Ontario's off-reserve Community Action Program for Children, and the Canadian Pre-natal Nutrition Program.* Unpublished report.

O'Connell, J.C. (1985). A family systems approach for serving rural, reservation native American communities. *Journal of American Indian Education, 24*(2), 1–6.

O'Donnell, J., Hawkins, J.D., Catalano, R.F., Abbott, R.D., & Day, L.E. (1995). Preventing school failure, drug use, and delinquency among low-income children: Long-term intervention in elementary schools. *American Journal of Orthopsychiatry, 65,* 87–100.

Oetting, E.R., Beauvais, F., & Edwards, R. (1988). Alcohol and Indian youth: Social and psychological correlates and prevention. *The Journal of Drug Issues, 18*(1), 87–101.

Offord, D.R., Boyle, M.H., & Szatmari, P. (1987). Ontario Child Health Study, II: Six month prevalence of disorder and rates of service utilization. *Archives of General Psychiatry, 44,* 832–836.

O'Hara, C. (1998). *Comparative family policy: Eight countries' stories.* Toronto: Canadian Policy Research Networks.

O'Keefe, M. (1995). Predictors of child abuse in maritally violent families. *Journal of Interpersonal Violence, 10,* 3–25.

Oldershaw, L., Walters, G.C., & Hall, D.K. (1986). Control strategies and noncompliance in abusive mother–child dyads: An observational study. *Child Development, 57,* 722–732.

Oldfield, D., Hays, B.J., & Megel, M.E. (1996). Evaluation of the effectiveness of Project Trust: An elementary school-based victimization prevention strategy. *Child Abuse and Neglect, 20,* 821–832.

Olds, D. (1997a). The Prenatal Early Infancy Project: Preventing child abuse and neglect in the context of promoting maternal and child health. In D.A. Wolfe, R.J. McMahon, & R.De V. Peters (Eds.), *Child abuse: New directions in prevention and treatment across the lifespan* (pp. 157–176). London: Sage.

Olds, D. (1997b). The Prenatal/Early Infancy Project: Fifteen years later. In G.W. Albee & T.P. Gullotta (Eds.), *Primary prevention works* (pp. 41–67). London: Sage.

Olds, D.L., Eckenrode, J., Henderson, C.R., Kitzman, H., Powers, J., Cole, R., Sidora, K., Morris, P., Pettitt, L.M., & Luckey, D. (1997). Long-term effects of home visitation on maternal life course and child abuse and neglect: Fifteen-year follow-up of a randomized trial. *Journal of the American Medical Association, 278,* 637–643.

Olds, D.L., Henderson, C.R., Chamberlin, R., & Tatelbaum, R. (1986). Preventing child abuse and neglect: A randomized trial of nurse home visitation. *Pediatrics, 78,* 65–78.

Olds, D.L., Henderson, C.R., Phelps, C., Kitzman, H., & Hanks, C. (1993). Effects of prenatal and infancy nurse home visitation on government spending. *Medical Care, 31,* 155–174.

Olds, D.L., Kitzman, H., Cole, R., & Robinson, J. (1997). Theoretical foundations of a program of home visitation for pregnant women and parents of young children. *Journal of Community Psychology, 25,* 9–25.

Olds, D.L., & Korfmacher, J. (1997). Prenatal and early childhood home visitation I: Evolution of a program of research [Special issue]. *Journal of Community Psychology, 25*(1).

Olds, D.L., & Korfmacher, J. (1998). Prenatal and early childhood home visitation II: Findings and future directions [Special issue]. *Journal of Community Psychology, 26*(1).

Oliver, C. (1990). Determinants of interorganizational relationships: Integration and future directions. *Academy of Management Review, 15,* 214–265.

Olsen, L. (1994, February 23). On the career track. *Education Week,* 25–33.

Olsen, L.J., & Holmes, W.M. (1986). Youth at risk: Adolescents and maltreatment. *Children and Youth Services Review, 8,* 13–35.

Olweus, D. (1992). Bullying among school children: Intervention and prevention. In R. Peters, R.J. McMahon, & V.L. Quensey (Eds.), *Aggression and violence throughout the life span* (pp. 110–121). Newbury Park, CA: Sage Publications.

O'Neill, J. (1994). *The missing child in liberal theory.* Toronto: University of Toronto Press.

Ontario Federation of Indian Friendship Centres, Ministry of Community and Social Services. (1986). *Provincial evaluation of the L'il Beavers Program.* Unpublished report.

Ontario Ministry of Community and Social Services. (1990). *Better Beginnings, Better Futures: An integrated model of primary prevention of emotional and behavioural problems.* Toronto: Queen's Printer for Ontario.

Organization for Economic Co-operation and Development. (1998, June/July). OECD in figures: Statistics on the member countries. Supplement to *The OECD Observer,* No. 212. Paris: Author.

Organization and Systems Development Inc. (1996). *Nog-Da-Win-Da-Min family and community services: Organizational review.* Unpublished manuscript.

Orme, T.C., & Rimmer, J. (1981). Alcoholism and child abuse: A review. *Journal of Studies on Alcohol, 42,* 273–287.

Ostrom, C., Lerner, W., Richard, M., & Freel, M.A. (1995). Building on the capacity of youth and families through university community collaborations: The development-in-context (DICE) evaluation model. *Journal of Adolescent Research, 10*(4), 427–448.

Ottawa-Carleton Wraparound. (1999). *What is the wraparound process?* [On-line] www.ysb.on.ca./wpproc.htm.

Oxman-Martinez, J. (1993). *La négligence faite aux enfants: Une problématique inquiétante.* Les Centres jeunesse de la Montérégie. Centre de protection de l'enfance et de la jeunesse de la Montérégie, Longueuil.

Paiement, J. (1984). Parents Anonymous: A resource for troubled parents. *Canada's Mental Health, 32*(2), 7–9.

Palacio-Quintin, E. (1995). Les mauvais traitements envers les enfants: Facteurs sociaux et dynamique familiale. *Liens entre violence physique, psychologique et sexuelle faite aux enfants et aux femmes: Actes du séminaire tenu à Drummondville le 11 novembre 1994.* Cri-Viff, Collection Réflexions, *3,* 5–14.

Palmer, R.B., & Liddle, H.A. (1996). Adolescent drug use: Contemporary perspectives on etiology and treatment. In G.M. Blau & T.P. Gullotta (Eds.), *Adolescent dysfunctional behavior: Causes, interventions and prevention* (pp. 113–148). Thousand Oaks, CA: Sage Publications.

Palmer, T. (1996). Programmatic and non-programmatic aspects of successful intervention. In A.T. Harland (Ed.), *Choosing correctional options that work: Defining the demand and evaluating the supply.* Thousand Oaks, CA: Sage Publications.

Pan, H.S., Neidig, P.H., & O'Leary, K.D. (1994). Predicting mild and severe husband to wife physical aggression. *Journal of Consulting and Clinical Psychology, 62,* 975–981.

Pancer, S.M., & Cameron, G. (1993). *Better Beginnings, Better Futures resident participation report.* Kingston, ON: Better Beginnings, Better Futures Research Coordination Unit, Queen's University.

Pancer, S.M., & Cameron, G. (1994). Resident participation in the Better Beginnings, Better Futures prevention project: I. The impact of involvement. *Canadian Journal of Community Mental Health, 13*(2), 197–211.

Pancer, S.M., & Foxall, K. (1998). *Our journey from Better Beginnings to Better Futures: The personal stories of community residents.* Kingston, ON: Better Beginnings, Better Futures Research Coordination Unit, Queen's University.

Pandiani, J.A., & Maynard, A.G. (1993). Vermont's local interagency teams: An evaluation of service coordination and system change. *Community Alternatives International Journal of Family Care, 5,* 85–97.

Parker, G.R., & Hazdi-Pavlovic, D. (1984). Modification of levels of depression in mother-bereaved women by parental and marriage relationships. *Psychological Medicine, 14,* 125–135.

Payukotayno James and Hudson's Bay Family Services, Tikinagan Child and Family Services. (1988). *As long as the sun shines ... from generation to generation.* Unpublished report.

Pearce, D. (1978). The feminization of poverty: Women, work and welfare. *Urban and Social Change Review, 2,* 1, 2.

Pearson, C.L., Masnyk, K., & King, P.A. (1987). *Intensive family services: Evaluation of foster care prevention in Maryland – Final report.* Baltimore, MD: Maryland Department of Human Resources, Social Services Administration.

Pecora, P.J., Fraser, M.W., & Haapala, D.A. (1991). Client outcomes and issues for program design. In D.E. Biegel & K. Wells (Eds.), *Family preservation services: Research and evaluation* (pp. 3–32). Newbury Park, CA: Sage.

Peirson, L., Laurendeau, M.-C., Chamberland, C., & Lefort, L. (1998, March). *114 Voices.* Technical working document prepared for the Family Wellness Project Team based on qualitative research.

Peirson, L., & Prilleltensky, I. (1994). Understanding school change to facilitate prevention: A study of change in a secondary school. *Canadian Journal of Community Mental Health, 13*(2), 127–144.

Pelton, L. (1978). Child abuse and neglect: The myth of classlessness. *American Journal of Orthopsychiatry, 48,* 608–617.

Pelton, L.H. (1981). *The social context of child-abuse and neglect.* New York: Human Services Press.

Pelton, L.H. (1994). The role of material factors in child abuse and neglect. In

G.B. Melton & F.D. Barry (Eds.), *Protecting children from abuse and neglect: Foundations for a new national strategy* (pp. 131–181). New York: The Guilford Press.

Pelton, L.H. (1997). Child welfare policy and practice: The myth of family preservation. *American Journal of Orthopsychiatry, 67*, 545–553.

Pennell, J., & Burford, G. (1994). Widening the circle: Family group decision making. *Journal of Child and Youth Care, 9*(1), 1–11.

Pennell, J., & Burford, G. (1997). *Family group-decision making: After the conference – Progress in resolving violence and promoting well-being. Outcome report summary.* St. John's, NF: Memorial University of Newfoundland School of Social Work.

Pentz, M.A. (1996). Community organization and school liaisons: How to get programs started. *Journal of School Health, 56*(9), 382–388.

Peraino, J.M. (1990). Evaluation of a preschool antivictimization program. *Journal of Interpersonal Violence, 5*, 520–528.

Peters, R. DeV. (1994). Better Beginnings, Better Futures: A community-based approach to primary prevention. *Canadian Journal of Community Mental Health, 13*(2), 183–188.

Peterson, G. (1995). The need for common principles in prevention programs for children, adolescents and families. *Journal of Adolescent Research, 10*(4), 470–485.

Peterson, L., & Brown, D. (1994). Integrating child injury and abuse-neglect research: Common histories, etiologies, and solutions. *Psychological Bulletin, 116*, 293–315.

Pharand, S. (1995, November). *Burning out earning a living: The experiences of non-unionized, working parents in the service sector.* Report prepared for the Child Care Advocacy Association of Canada.

Philliber, S., & Allen, J.P. (1992). Life options and community service: Teen Outreach Program. In B.C. Miller, J.J. Card, R.L. Paikoff, & J.L. Peterson (Eds.), *Preventing adolescent pregnancy: Model programs and evaluations* (pp. 139–155). Newbury Park, CA: Sage Publication.

Phipps, S. (1995). Canadian child benefits: Behavioral consequences and income adequacy. *Canadian Public Policy, 21*(1), 20–30.

Pianta, R., Egeland, B., & Erickson, M.F. (1989). The antecedents of maltreatment: Results of the mother–child interaction research project. In D. Cicchetti & V. Carlson (Eds.), *Child maltreatment: Theory and research on the causes and consequences of child abuse and neglect* (pp. 203–253). Cambridge, MA: Cambridge University Press.

Pitman, A.L., Wolfe, D.A., & Wekerle, C. (1998). Prevention during adolescence: The Youth Relationships Project. In J. Luzker (Ed.), *Handbook on research and treatment in child abuse and neglect* (pp. 341–356). New York: The Guilford Press.

Polansky, N.A., Chalmers, M.A., Buttenwieser, E., & Williams, D.P. (1981). *Damaged parents.* Chicago: University of Chicago Press.

Polansky, N.A., Gaudin, J.M., Ammons, P.W., & Davis, K.B. (1985). The psychological ecology of the neglectful mother. *Child Abuse and Neglect, 9,* 265–275.

Polit, D., Quint, J.C., & Riccio, J.A. (1988). *The challenges of serving teenage mothers: Lessons from Project Redirection.* New York: Manpower Demonstration Research Corporation.

Powers, J.L., & Eckenrode, J. (1988). The maltreatment of adolescents. *Child Abuse and Neglect, 12,* 189–199.

Powers, J.L., & Jaklitsch, B.W. (1989). *Understanding survivors of abuse: Stories of homeless and runaway adolescents.* Lexington, MA: Lexington Books.

Powers, J.L., & Jaklitsch, B., & Eckenrode, J. (1989). Behavioral characteristics of maltreatment among runaway and homeless youth. *Early Child Development and Care, 42,* 127–139.

Pransky, J. (1991). *Prevention: The critical need.* Springfield, MO: Burnell Foundation and Paradigm Press.

Price, R.H., Cowen, E.L., Lorion, R.P., & Ramos-McKay, J. (Eds.). (1988). *14 ounces of prevention: A casebook for practitioners.* Washington, DC: American Psychological Association.

Price, R.H., Cowen, E.L., Lorion, R.P., & Ramos-McKay, J. (1989). The search for effective prevention programs; What we learned along the way. *American Journal of Orthopsychiatry, 59,* 49–58.

Prilleltensky, I. (1994a). *The morals and politics of psychology: Psychological discourse and the status quo.* Albany, NY: State University of New York Press.

Prilleltensky, I. (1994b). The UN Convention on the Rights of the Child: Implications for children's mental health. *Canadian Journal of Community Mental Health, 13*(2), 77–93.

Prilleltensky, I. (1997). Values, assumptions, and practices: Assessing the moral implications of psychological discourse and action. *American Psychologist, 47,* 517–535.

Prilleltensky, I., & Gonick, L. (1996). Polities change, oppression remains: On the psychology and politics of oppression. *Political Psychology, 17,* 127–147.

Prilleltensky, I., & Laurendeau, M.-C. (1994). Introduction: Prevention and the public good. *Canadian Journal of Community Mental Health, 13*(2), 5–9.

Prilleltensky, I., & Nelson, G. (1997). Community psychology: Reclaiming social justice. In D. Fox & I. Prilleltensky (Eds.), *Critical psychology: An introduction* (pp. 166–184). London: Sage.

Prino, C.T., & Peyrot, M. (1994). The effect of child physical abuse and neglect on aggressive, withdrawn, and prosocial behavior. *Child Abuse and Neglect, 18*(10), 871–884.,

Pritchard, M.S. (1996). *Reasonable children: Moral education and moral learning.* Lawrence, KS: University Press of Kansas.

Pulkingham, J., Ternowetsky, G., & Hay, D. (1997). The new Canada Child Tax Benefit: Eradicating poverty or victimizing the poorest? *CCPA Monitor, 4*(1), 6–7.

Putnam, R.D. (1993, Spring). The prosperous community: Social capital and public life. *The American Prospect,* 35–42.

Putnam, R.W. (1996). Creating reflective dialogue. In S. Toulmin & B. Gustavsen (Eds.), *Beyond theory: Changing organizations through participation* (pp. 41–52). Philadelphia: John Benjamins North America.

Quinton, D., & Rutter, M. (1988). *Parenting break down: The making and breaking of intergenerational links.* Avebury: UJA.

Quinton, D., Rutter, M., & Liddle, C. (1984). Institutional rearing, parenting difficulties, and marital support. *Psychological Medicine, 14,* 107–124.

Radke-Yarrow, M., & Sherman, T. (1990). Hard growing: Children who survive. In J. Rolf, A.S. Masten, D. Cicchetti, K.H. Nuechterlein, & S. Weintraub (Eds.), *Risk and protective factors in the development of psychopathology* (pp. 97–119). Cambridge, MA: Cambridge University Press.

Rae Grant, N.I. (1994). Preventive interventions for children and adolescents: Where are we now and how far have we come? *Canadian Journal of Community Mental Health, 13*(2), 17–29.

Ramey, C.T., & Ramey, S.L. (1998). Early intervention and early experience. *American Psychologist, 53,* 109–120.

Rappaport, J. (1981). In praise of paradox: A social policy of empowerment over prevention. *American Journal of Community Psychology, 9,* 1–25.

Rappaport, J. (1987). Terms of empowerment/exemplars of prevention: Toward a theory for community psychology. *American Journal of Community Psychology, 15,* 121–148.

Raschick, M. (1997). A multi-faceted, intensive family preservation program evaluation. *Family Preservation Journal, 2*(2), 33–52.

Rattcliffe, J., & Wallack, L. (1985/86). Primary prevention in public health: An analysis of some basis assumptions. *International Quarterly of Community Health Education, 6,* 216–239.

Ratto, R., & Bogat, G. (1990). An evaluation of a preschool curriculum to educate children in the prevention of sexual abuse. *Journal of Community sychology, 18,* 289–297.

Redburn, F.S. (1997). On human services integration. *Public Administration Review, 37,* 264–269.

Reid, J.B., & Kavanagh, K. (1985). A social interactional approach to child abuse: Risk, prevention, and treatment. In M. Chesney & R. Rosenman Eds.),

Anger and hostility in behavioral and cardiovascular disorders (pp. 44–59). New York: Hemisphere/McGraw-Hill.

Reid, J.B. Kavanagh, K., & Baldwin, D.V. (1987). Abusive parents' perceptions of child problem behaviors: An example of parental bias. *Journal of Abnormal Child Psychology, 15,* 457–466.

Reid, J., Taplin, P., & Lorber, R. (1981). A social interactional approach to the treatment of abusive families. In R.B. Stuart (Ed.), *Violent behavior: Social learning approaches to prediction, management, and treatment* (pp. 83–101). New York: Brunner/Mazel.

Reiff, R. (1974). The control of knowledge: The power of the helping professions. *Journal of Applied Behavioral Science, 10,* 451–461.

Reiss, D. (1981). *The family's construction of reality.* Cambridge, MA: Harvard University Press.

Reiss, D., & Oliveri, M.E. (1980). Family paradigm and family coping: A proposal for linking the family's intrinsic adaptation capacities to its responses to stress. *Family Relations, 29,* 431–444.

Reiss, D., & Price, R.H. (1996). National research agenda for prevention research: The National Institute of Mental Health report. *American Psychologist, 51,* 1109–1115.

Reppucci, N.D., & Haugaard, J.J. (1989). Prevention of child sexual abuse: Myth or reality. *American Psychologist, 44,* 1266–1275.

Resnick, G. (1985). Enhancing parental competencies for high risk mothers: An evaluation of prevention effects. *Child Abuse and Neglect, 9,* 479–489.

Rhodes, W., & Brown, W. (Eds.). (1991). *Why some children succeed despite the odds.* New York: Praeger.

Richey, C.A., Lovell, M.L., & Reid, K. (1991). Interpersonal skill training to enhance social support among women at risk for child maltreatment. *Children and Youth Services Review, 13,* 41–59.

Richters, J.E., & Martinez, P.E. (1993). Violent communities, family choices, and children's chances: An algorithm for improving the odds. *Development and Psychopathology, 5,* 609–627.

Rickel, A.U., & Allen, L. (1987). Preventing maladjustment from infancy through adolescence. Newbury Park, CA: Sage Publications.

Rickel, A.U., & Becker, E. (1997). *Keeping children from harm's way.* Washington, DC: American Psychological Association.

Riessman, F., & Carroll, D. (1995). *Redefining self-help: Policies and practices.* San Francisco, CA: Jossey-Bass.

Riley, D., Meinhardt, G., Nelson, C., Salisbury, M.J., & Winnett, T. (1991). How effective are age-paced newsletters for new parents? A replication and extension of earlier studies. *Family Relations, 40,* 247–253.

Riley, D., Salisbury, M.J., Walker, S.K., & Steinberg, J. (1996, November). *Parenting the first year: Wisconsin statewide impact report.* Madison, WI: University of Wisconsin-Extension and School of Human Ecology, University of Wisconsin.

Rispens, J., Aleman, A., & Goudena, P.P. (1997). Prevention of child sexual abuse victimization: A meta-analysis. *Child Abuse and Neglect, 21,* 975–987.

Rivera, V.R., & Kutash, K. (1994a). *Components of a system of care: What does the research say?* Tampa, FL: University of South Florida, Florida Mental Health Institute, Research and Training Center for Children's Mental Health.

Rivera, V.R., & Kutash, K. (1994b). Family preservation services. In V.R. Rivera & K. Kutash, *Components of a system of care: What does the research say?* Tampa, FL: University of South Florida, Florida Mental Health Institute, Research and Training Center for Children's Mental Health.

Rivera, V., & Widom, C.S. (1992). Childhood victimization and violent offending. *Violence and Victims, 5,* 19–35.

Rivers, B. (1998, Fall/Winter). Stacey and Canada's children deserve better. *The Communicator: Faculty of Social Work Alumni Association Newsletter.* Toronto: University of Toronto Faculty of Social Work.

Robichaud, J.-B., Guay, L., Colin, C., Pothier, M., & Saucier, J.-F. (1994). *Les liens entre la pauvreté et la santé mentale de l'exclusion à l'équité.* Le Comité de la santé mentale du Québec, Gaëtan Morin, Éditeur.

Rodger, J. (1995). Family policy or moral regulation? *Critical Social Policy, 15,* 5–25.

Rodger, J.J., (1996). *Family life and social control: A sociological perspective.* London: MacMillan Press Limited.

Rodriguez, G.G., & Cortez, C.P. (1988). The evaluation of the Avancé Parent–Child Education Program. In H.B. Weiss & F.H. Jacobs (Eds.), *Evaluating family programs* (pp. 287–302). New York: Aldine de Gruyter.

Rogeness, G., Amrung, S., Macedo, C., Harris, W., & Fisher, C. (1986). Psychopathology in abused and neglected children. *Journal of the American Academy of Child Psychiatry, 25,* 659–665.

Rolf, J., Masten, A., Cicchetti, D., Nuechterlein, K.H., & Weintraub, S. (Eds.). (1990). *Risk and protective factors in the development of psychopathology.* New York: Cambridge University Press.

Rolland, J.S. (1994). *Families, illness, and disability: An integrative treatment model.* New York: Basic Books.

Rosen, B. (1978). Self-concept disturbance among mothers who abuse their children. *Psychological Reports, 43,* 323–326.

Rosenthal, J.A., & Glass, G.V. (1986). Impacts of alternatives to out-of-home placement: A quasi-experimental study. *Children and Youth Services Review, 8,* 305–321.

Ross, D.P. (1996, November). *Measuring social progress, starting with the well-being of Canada's children, youth and families.* Paper presented at Canada's children ... Canada's future, Ottawa, Ontario.

Ross, D.P., Scott, K., & Kelly, M. (1996a). *Child poverty: What are the consequences?* Ottawa: Centre for International Statistics, Canadian Council on Social Development.

Ross, D.P., Scott, K., & Kelly, M.A. (1996b). Overview: Children in Canada in the 1990s. In *Growing up in Canada: National Longitudinal Survey of Children and Youth* (pp. 15–45). (Catalogue No. 89–550–MPE, no. 1). Ottawa: Human Resources Development Canada and Statistics Canada.

Ross, D.P., & Shillington, R. (1989). *The Canadian fact book on poverty.* Ottawa: Canadian Council on Social Development.

Ross, D.P., Shillington, E.R., & Lochhead, C. (1994). *The Canadian fact book on poverty – 1994.* Ottawa: Canadian Council on Social Development.

Ross, G.S. (1984). Home intervention for premature infants of low-income families. *American Journal of Orthopsychiatry, 54,* 263–269.

Ross, R. (1992). *Dancing with a ghost: Exploring Indian reality.* Markham, ON: Octopus Publishing Group.

Ross, R. (1996). *Returning to the teachings: Exploring Aboriginal justice.* Toronto: Penguin Books.

Rotheram-Borus, M.J. (1997). Mental health services for children and adolescents. In R.P. Weissberg, T.P. Gullotta, R.L. Hampton, B.A. Ryan, & G.A. Adams (Eds.), *Healthy children 2010: Establishing preventive services* (pp. 124–153). Thousand Oaks, CA: Sage Publications.

Rothery, M., & Cameron, G. (1985, September). *Understanding family support in child welfare: A summary report.* Toronto: Ontario Ministry of Community and Social Services.

Rothman, J., & Tropman, J.E. (1987). Models of community organization and macro practice perspectives: Their mixing and phasing. In F.M. Cox, J.L. Erlich, J. Rothman, & J.E. Tropman (Eds.), *Strategies of community organization* (4th ed., pp. 3–26). Itasca, IL: Peacock Publishers.

Royal Commission on Aboriginal Peoples. (1995). *Choosing life. Special report on suicide among Aboriginal people.* Ottawa: Canada Communication Group – Publishing.

Royal Commission on Aboriginal Peoples. (1997). *For seven generations.* Ottawa: Libraxus. [On-line] www.Libraxus.com.

Runkle-Hooyman, N. (1976). The practice implications of interorganizational theory for services integration. *Journal of Sociology and Social Welfare, 3,* 558–564.

Rutter, M. (1979). Protective factors in children's response to stress and disadvantage. In M.W. Kent & J. Rolf (Eds.), *Primary prevention of psychopathology:*

Vol. III. Social competence in children (pp. 49–74). Hanover, NH: University Press of New England.

Rutter, M. (1980). School influences on children's behavior and development. *Pediatrics, 65,* 208–220.

Rutter, M. (1985). Resilience in the face of adversity: Protective factors and resistance to psychiatric disorder. *British Journal of Psychiatry, 147,* 598–611.

Rutter, M. (1987). Psychosocial resilience and protective mechanisms. *American Journal of Orthopsychiatry, 57*(3), 316–331.

Rutter, M. (1988). *Studies of psychosocial risk: The power of longitudinal data.* Oxford: Cambridge University Press.

Rutter, M. (1989). Intergenerational continuities and discontinuities in serious parenting difficulties. In V. Carlson & D. Cicchetti (Eds.), *Child maltreatment: Theory and research on the causes and consequences of child abuse and neglect* (pp. 317–348). Cambridge, MA: Cambridge University Press.

Rutter, M. (1990). Psychosocial resilience and protective mechanisms. In J. Rolf, A.S. Masten., D. Cicchetti, K.H. Nuechterlein, & S. Weintraub (Eds.), *Risk and protective factors in the development of psychopathology* (pp. 181–214). New York: Cambridge University Press.

Rutter, M. (1994). Stress research: Accomplishments and tasks ahead. In R.J. Haggerty, L.R. Sherrod, N. Garmezy, & M. Rutter (Eds.), *Stress, risk, and resilience in children and adolescents: Processes, mechanisms, and interventions* (pp. 354–386). New York: Cambridge University Press.

Rutter, M., Maugham, B., Mortimore, P., & Ouston, J. (1979). *Fifteen thousand hours.* Cambridge, MA: Harvard University Press.

Rutter, M., & Quinton, D. (1984). Long-term follow-up of women institutionalized in childhood: Factors promoting good functioning in adult life. *British Journal of Developmental Psychology, 18,* 225–234.

Sagrestano, L.M., & Paikoff, R.L. (1997). Preventing high-risk sexual behavior, sexually transmitted diseases, and pregnancy among adolescents. In R.P. Weissberg, T.P. Gullotta, R.L. Hampton, B.A. Ryan, & G.R. Adams (Eds.), *Healthy children 2010: Enhancing children's wellness* (pp. 76–104). Thousand Oaks, CA: Sage Publications.

Saint-Pierre, A. (1994). *'Je Passe Partout et les parents': Évaluation du programme d'intervention familiale – Rapport de recherche.* Montréal: Je Passe Partout.

Sampson, R.J. (1991). Linking the micro- and macrolevel dimensions of community social organization. *Social Forces, 70,* 43–64.

Sampson, R.J., & Groves, W.B. (1989). Community structure and crime: Testing social-disorganization theory. *American Journal of Sociology, 94,* 775–802.

Sandberg, D.N. (1989). *The child abuse delinquency connection.* Lexington, MA: Lexington Books.

Sandel, M. (Ed.). (1984). *Liberalism and its critics.* New York: New York University Press.

Sandel, M. (1996). *Democracy's discontent.* Cambridge, MA: Harvard University Press.

Saslawsky, D., & Wurtele, S. (1986). Educating children about sexual abuse: Implications for paediatric intervention and possible prevention. *Journal of Paediatric Psychology, 11,* 235–245.

Saul, J.R. (1995). *The unconscious civilization.* Concord, ON: Anansi.

Sauve, A., & Miller, R. (1998). *Kognaasowin program report.* Unpublished report.

Scales, P. (1990). Developing capable young people: An alternative strategy for prevention programs. *Journal of Early Adolescence, 10*(4), 420–438.

Scheper-Hughes, N., & Hoffman, D. (1997). Brazil: Moving targets. *Natural History, 106*(6), 34–43.

Schmidt, E., & Eldridge, A. (1986). The attachment relationship and child maltreatment. *Infant Mental Health Journal, 7,* 264–273.

Schneider-Rosen, K., Braunwald, K.G., Carlson, V., & Cicchetti, D. (1985). Current perspectives in attachment theory: Illustrations from the study of maltreated infants. In I. Bretherton & E. Waters (Eds.), *Monographs of the Society for Research in Child Development, 50*(1–2 Serial No, 209), 194–210.

Schorr, L. (1989). *Within our reach: Breaking the cycle of disadvantage.* New York: Doubleday.

Schorr, L. (1997). *Common purpose: Strengthening families and neighborhoods to rebuild America.* New York: Doubleday/Anchor Books.

Schwartz, I.M., AuClaire, P., & Harris, L. (1990, March). *Family preservation service as an alternative to the out of home placement of seriously emotionally disturbed adolescents: The Hennepin County experience.* Ann Arbor, MI: Center for the Study of Youth Policy, School of Social Work, University of Michigan.

Schwartz, S.H. (1994). Are there universal aspects in the structure and contents of human values? *Journal of Social Issues, 50*(4), 19–46.

Scott, W. (1992). Group therapy with sexually abused boys: Notes toward managing behavior. *Clinical Social Work Journal, 20,* 488–490.

Seagull, E.A.W. (1987). Social support and child maltreatment: A review of the evidence. *Child Abuse and Neglect: The International Journal, 11,* 41–52.

Sedlak, A.J., & Broadhurst, D.D. (1996). *Third national incidence study on child abuse and neglect.* Washington, DC: U.S. Department of Health and Human Services.

Segal, J. (1988). Teachers have enormous power in affecting children's self-esteem. *Brown University Child Behavior and Development Newsletter, 4,* 1–3.

Seitz, V., & Apfel, N.H. (1994). Parent-focused intervention: Diffusion effects on siblings. *Child Development, 65,* 677–683.

Seitz, V., Rosenbaum, L.K., & Apfel, N.H. (1985). Effects of family support intervention: A ten-year follow-up. *Child Development, 56*, 376–391.

Shapiro, D. (1995). Liberalism and communitarianism. *Philosophical Books, 36*, 145–155.

Shaw, D., & McKay, H. (1942). *Juvenile delinquency in urban areas.* Chicago: University of Chicago Press.

Sherrod, K.B., O'Connor, S., Vietze, P.M., & Altemeier, W.A. (1984). Child health and maltreatment. *Child Development, 55*, 1174–1183.

Shields, C. (1995). Improving the life prospects of children: A community systems approach. *Child Welfare, 74*, 605–618.

Shillington, R. (1990). Estimates of the extent of Native child poverty: 1986 Census. In M. Novick & R. Volpe (Eds.), *Perspectives on social practice.* Toronto: Laidlaw Foundation.

Shorkey, C.T., & Armendariz, J. (1985). Personal worth, self-esteem, anomia, hostility, and irrational thinking of abusing mothers: A multivariate approach. *Journal of Clinical Psychology, 41*, 1409–1414.

Short, K.H., & Johnston, C. (1994). Ethnocultural parent education in Canada: Current status and directions. *Canadian Journal of Community Mental Health, 13*(1), 43–54.

Showers, J. (1992). 'Don't shake the baby': The effectiveness of a prevention program. *Child Abuse and Neglect, 16*, 11–18.

Siegel, E., Bauman, K.E., Schaefer, E.S., Saunders, M.M., & Ingram, D.D. (1980). Hospital and home support during infancy: Impact on maternal attachment, child abuse and neglect, and health care utilization. *Pediatrics, 66*, 183–190.

Silovsky, J.F., & Hembree-Kigin, T.L. (1994). Family and group treatment for sexually abused children: A review. *Journal of Child Sexual Abuse, 3*(3), 1–20.

Silvers, J., & Hagler, J. (1997, December 6). Eugenics: The children's executioner. *The Globe and Mail,* pp. D1, D4.

Simeonsson, R. (1995). *Risk, resilience, and prevention: Promoting the well-being of all children.* Baltimore, MD: Brookes.

Simmons, R. (Chair, Standing Committee on Health). (1997, April). *Towards well-being: Strategies for healthy children.* Ottawa: Public Works and Government Services Canada.

Simone, R. (1995, February 27). Some teen pregnancies deliberate, experts say. *The Kitchener-Waterloo Record,* pp. A1, A2.

Sioux Lookout Area Family Treatment Centre. (1990). *Program design.* Unpublished report.

Slaughter, D. (1983). Early intervention and its effects on maternal and child development. *Monographs of the Society for Research in Child Development, 48*(4).

Smith, C., Farrant, M., & Marchant, M. (1972). *The Wincroft youth project: A social-work programme in a slum area.* London: Tavistock.

Snow, K., & Finlay, J. (1998, April). *Voices from within: Youth speak out.* Toronto: Office of the Child and Family Service Advocacy, Queen's Printer for Ontario.

Solicitor General of Canada. (1997). *The four circles of hollow water. Aboriginal people's collection.* (Catalogue No. JS5-1/15-1997E). Ottawa.

Solomon, A. (1994). *Eating bitterness: A vision beyond the prison walls.* Toronto: N.C. Press/ University of Toronto Press.

Spaid, W.M., & Fraser, M. (1991). The correlates of success/failure in brief and intensive family treatment: Implications for family preservation services. *Children and Youth Services Review, 13,* 77–99.

Spearly, J.L., & Lauderdale, M. (1983). Community characteristics and ethnicity in the prediction of child maltreatment rates. *Child Abuse and Neglect, 7,* 91–105.

Speck, R.V., & Attneave, C.L. (1973). *Family networks: A way toward retribalization and healing in family crises.* United States: Pantheon Books.

Spoth, R., Redmond, C., Haggerty, K., & Ward, T. (1995). A controlled parenting skills outcome study: Examining individual difference and attendance effects. *Journal of Marriage and the Family, 57,* 449–464.

Spoth, R., Redmond, C., & Shin, C. (1998). Direct and indirect latent-variable parenting outcomes of two universal family-focused preventive interventions: Extending a public health-oriented research base. *Journal of Consulting and Clinical Psychology, 66,* 385–399.

Srebank, D.S., & Elias, M.J. (1993). An ecological, interpersonal skills approach to drop out prevention. *American Journal of Orthospsychiatry, 63*(4), 526–535.

Stack, C.B. (1974). *All our kin: Strategies for survival in a black community.* New York: Harper & Row.

Standing Committee on Health. (1997). *Towards well-being: Strategies for healthy children – Report of the Standing Committee on Health respecting consideration of a study on preventative strategies for healthy children.* House of Commons. Ottawa: Canada Communication Group – Publishing, Public Works and Government Services Canada.

Stark, E., & Flitcraft, A. (1988). Women and children at risk: A feminist perspective on child abuse. *International Journal of Health Sciences, 18,* 97–118.

Starr, R.H., Jr. (1982). A research-based approach to the prediction of child abuse. In R.H. Starr, Jr (Ed.), *Child abuse prediction: Policy implications* (pp. 105–134). Cambridge, MA: Ballinger.

Starr, R.H., Dubowitz, E.O., & Bush, B.A. (1990). The epidemiology of child maltreatment. In R.D. Ammerman & M. Herson (Eds.), *Children at risk: An evaluation of factors contributing to child abuse and neglect* (pp. 23–54). New York: Plenum.

Statistical profile of Canada's children. (1997, Winter/Spring). *Applied Research Bulletin, 3*(1), 3.

Statistics Canada. (1993). *Language, tradition, health, lifestyle and social issues (Aboriginal Peoples Survey)*. Ottawa: Ministry of Industry, Science and Technology.

Statistics Canada. (1998). *1996 Census tabular data*. [On-line] www.statcan.ca.

Steele, B.F., & Pollack, C.B. (1968). A psychiatric study of parents who abuse infants and small children. In R.E. Helfer & C.H. Kempe (Eds.), *The battered child* (pp. 89–133). Chicago: University of Chicago Press.

Steinberg, L., Catalano, R., & Dooley, D. (1981). Economic antecedents of child abuse and neglect. *Child Development, 52,* 975–985.

Steinhauer, P. (1996, April). *The primary needs of children: A blueprint for effective health promotion at the community level.* Working paper for the Promotion/Prevention Task Force, Sparrow Lake Alliance.

Steinhauer, P. (1998). Developing resiliency in children from disadvantaged populations. In *Canada health action: Building on the legacy – Determinants of health, Vol. I – Children and youth* (pp. 103–131). Ste Foy, PQ: Éditions Multimondes Inc.

Steinhauer, P.D., Santa-Barbara, J., & Skinner, H. (1984). The process model of family functioning. *The Canadian Journal of Psychiatry, 29,* 77–88.

Sternberg, K.J., Lamb, M.E., Greenbaum, C., Cicchetti, D., Dawud, S., Cortes, R.M., Krispin, O., & Lorey, F. (1993). Effects of domestic violence on children's behavior problems and depression. *Developmental Psychology, 29,* 44–52.

Stevens-Simm, C., & Reichert, S. (1994). Sexual abuse, adolescent pregnancy, and child abuse. A developmental approach to an intergenerational cycle. *Archives of Pediatric and Adolescent Medicine, 148,* 23–27.

Stilwell, E., & Manley, B.B. (1990). A family focus approach to child abuse prevention. *Journal of Primary Prevention, 10,* 333–341.

Stinnett, N., & DeFrain, J. (1985). *Secrets of strong families.* Toronto: Little, Brown, & Company.

Stinnett, N., DeFrain, J., King, K., Knaub, P., & Rowe, G. (Eds.). (1981). *Family strengths 3: Roots of well-being.* Lincoln, NE: University of Nebraska Press.

Straker, G., & Jacobson, R.S. (1981). Aggression, emotional maladjustment, and empathy in the abused child. *Developmental Psychology, 17,* 762–765.

Straus, M.A. (1994). *Violence in the lives of adolescents.* New York: W.W. Norton & Company.

Straus, M.A., Gelles, R.J., & Steinmetz, S.K. (1980). *Behind closed doors: Violence in the American family.* Newbury Park, CA: Sage.

Supik, J. (1991). Partners for valued youth: The final report. *Intercultural Development Research Association (INDRA) Newsletter, 18,* 1–4.

Susman, E.J., Trickett, P.K., Iannotti, R.J., Hollenbeck, B.E., & Zahn-Waxler, C. (1985). Child rearing patterns in depressed, abusive, and normal mothers. *American Journal of Orthopsychiatry, 55*, 237–251.

Suttles, G. (1968). *The social order of the slums.* Chicago: University of Chicago Press.

Swift, C.F., & Ryan-Finn, K. (1995). Perpetrator prevention: Stopping the development of sexually abusive behavior. *Prevention in Human Services, 12*(2), 13–44.

Szapocznik, J., Kurtines, W., Santistebon, D.A., & Rio, A.T. (1990). Interplay of advances between theory, research, and applications in treatment interventions aimed at behavior problem children and adolescents. *Journal of Consulting and Clinical Psychology, 58*, 696–703.

Szykula, S.A., & Fleischman, M.J. (1985). Reducing out-of-home placements of abused children: Two controlled field studies. *Child Abuse and Neglect, 9*, 277–283.

Taal, M., & Edelaar, M. (1997). Positive and negative effects of a child sexual abuse prevention program. *Child Abuse and Neglect, 21*, 399–410.

Takanishi, R. (1993). The opportunities of adolescence: Research, interventions and policy. *American Psychologist, 48*(2), 85–87.

Tappan, M.B., & Brown, L.M. (1996). Envisioning a postmodern moral pedagogy. *Journal of Moral Education, 25*, 101–109.

Tatara, T. (1994). The recent rise in the U.S. child substitute care population: An analysis of national child substitute care flow data. In R.P. Barth, J.D. Berrick, & N. Gilbert (Eds.), *Child welfare research review. Vol 1* (pp. 126–145). New York: Columbia University Press.

Taylor, B., Brooks, J., Phanindis, J., & Rossmo, K. (1991). Services for Vancouver street youth: An integrated delivery model. *Journal of Child and Youth Care, 6*, 49–61.

Taylor, C. (1992). *Multiculturalism and 'the politics of recognition.'* Princeton, NJ: Princeton University Press.

Taylor, D.K., & Beauchamp, C. (1988). Hospital-based primary prevention strategy in child abuse: A multi-level needs assessment. *Child Abuse and Neglect, 12*, 343–354.

Taylor, D.M. (1997). The quest for collective identify. *Canadian Psychology, 38*(3), 184–189.

Taylor-Henry, S., & Hill, E. (1990). *Treatment and healing, an evaluation: Community holistic circle healing.* Unpublished manuscript.

Teichroeb, R. (1997). *Flowers on my grave.* Toronto: HarperCollins.

Telleen, S., Herzog, A., & Kilbane, T.L. (1989). Impact of a family support program on mothers' social support and parenting stress. *American Journal of Orthopsychiatry, 59*, 410–419.

Thompson, R.A. (1994). Social support and the prevention of child maltreatment. In G.B. Melton & F.D. Barry (Eds.), *Protecting children from abuse and neglect: Foundations for a new national strategy* (pp. 40–130). New York: The Guilford Press.

Tilley, N. (1996). Demonstration, exemplification, duplication and replication in evaluation research. *Evaluation, 2*(1), 35–50.

Timpson, J. (1994). Aboriginal families and child welfare: Challenges for First Nations and family services. In *Royal Commission on Aboriginal Peoples, 1997.* Ottawa: Libraxus. [On-line] www.Libraxus.com.

Tobler, N.S. (1986). Meta-analysis of 143 adolescent drug prevention programs: Quantitative outcome results of program participants compared to a control or comparison group. *Journal of Drug Issues, 16,* 537–568.

Todres, R., & Bunston, T. (1993). Parent education program evaluation: A review of the literature. *Canadian Journal of Community Mental Health, 12*(1), 225–257.

Tolan, P.H., & Guerra, N. (1998). Societal causes of violence against children. In P.K. Trickett & C.J. Schellenbach (Eds.), *Violence against children in the family and the community* (pp. 195–209). Washington, DC: American Psychological Association.

Tolan, P.H., & Loeber, R. (1993). Antisocial behavior. In P.H. Tolan & B.J. Cohler (Eds.), *Handbook of clinical research and practice with adolescents* (pp. 307–331). New York: John Wiley & Sons Inc.

Torjman, S., & Battle, K. (1995). Cutting the deficits in child welfare. *Child Welfare, 74*(3), 459–485.

Toronto Star. (1998, March 25). Child poverty 'lamentable' Lewis says.

Tourigny, M., & Lavergne, C. (1995). *Les agressions à caractère sexuel (ACS): État de la situation, efficacité des programmes de prévention, et facteurs associés à la dénonciation.* Montréal: Laboratoire de recherche en écologie humaine et sociale (LAREHS), Université du Québec à Montréal.

Tourigny, M., Péladeau, N., & Bouchard, C. (1993). Abus sexuel et dévoilement chez les jeunes Québécois. *Revue Sociologique, 1*(2), 13–34.

Tower, C.C. (1993). The neglect of children. In *Understanding child abuse and neglect* (2nd ed., pp. 95–122). Boston: Allyn & Bacon.

Travers, J., Nauta, M., & Irwin, N. (1982). *The effects of a social program: Final report of the Child and Family Resource Program's infant/toddler component.* Cambridge, MA: Abt Associates.

Trepper, T.S., & Traicoff, M.E. (1983). Treatment of intrafamily sexuality: Issues in therapy and research. *Journal of Sex Education and Therapy, 4,* 14–18.

Trickett, E.J., Watts, R.J., & Birman, D. (Eds.). (1994). *Human diversity: Perspectives on people in context.* San Francisco, CA: Jossey-Bass.

Trickett, P.K., & Kuczynski, L. (1986). Children's misbehaviors and parental discipline strategies in abusive and nonabusive families. *Developmental Psychology, 22*, 115–123.

Trickett, P.K., & Susman, E.J. (1988). Parental perceptions of child-rearing practices in physically abusive and nonabusive families. *Developmental Psychology, 24*, 115–123.

Trickett, P.K., & Weinstein, R. (1991). Physical abuse of adolescents. In R. Lerner, A. Petersen, & J. Brooks-Gunn (Eds.), *Encyclopedia of adolescence, Vol II* (pp. 780–784). New York: Garland.

Trocmé, N., McPhee, D., & Tam, K.K. (1995). Child abuse and neglect in Ontario: Incidence and characteristics. *Child Welfare, 74*, 563–586.

Trocmé, N., McPhee, D., Tam, K.K., & Hay, T. (1994). *Ontario incidence study of reported child abuse and neglect*. Toronto: Institute for the Prevention of Child Abuse.

Trocmé, N., Michalski, J.H., McPhee, D., Tam, K.K., & Scarth, S. (1995). *Canadian incidence study of reported child maltreatment: Methodology and feasibility review*. Final report prepared for Family Violence Prevention, Health Canada. Toronto: Centre for Applied Social Research, Faculty of Social Work, University of Toronto.

Turcotte, D. (1990, March). Intervention based on principles of mutual aid: Process and impact on parents of adolescents. *Canada's Mental Health, 38*(1), 16–19.

Turner, S., Norman, E., & Zunz, S. (1995). Enhancing resiliency in girls and boys: A case for gender specific adolescent prevention programming. *The Journal of Primary Prevention, 16*(1), 25–38.

Tutty, L.M. (1991). Child sexual abuse: A range of program options. In B. Thomlison & C. Bagley (Eds.), Child sexual abuse: Expanding the research base on program and treatment outcomes [Special issue]. *Journal of Child and Youth Care*, 23–41.

Tutty, L.M. (1992). The ability of elementary school children to learn child sexual abuse prevention concepts. *Child Abuse and Neglect, 16*, 369–384.

Tutty, L.M. (1997). Child sexual abuse prevention programs: Evaluating Who Do You Tell. *Child Abuse and Neglect, 21*, 869–881.

Twentyman, C.T., & Plotkin, R.C. (1982). Unrealistic expectations of parents who maltreat their children: An educational deficit pertaining to child development. *Journal of Clinical Psychology, 38*, 497–503.

Tyler, F.B., Pargament, K.I., & Gatz, M. (1983). The resource collaborator role: A model for interactions involving psychologists. *American Psychologist, 38*, 388–398.

Tyler, T.R., Boeckmann, R.J., Smith, H.J., & Huo, Y.J. (1997). *Social justice in a diverse society*. Boulder, CO: Westview Press.

United Nations. (1991). *United Nations Convention on the Rights of the Child.* (Minister of Supply and Services Canada, Catalogue No. S2-210/1991E). Hull, PQ: Communications Branch, Human Rights Directorate, Department of Canadian Heritage.

United Nations Development Program. (1998). *Human development report 1998.* New York: Oxford University Press.

U.S. Advisory Board on Child Abuse and Neglect. (1993, September). *Neighbors helping neighbors: A new national strategy for the protection of children.* Washington, DC: Department of Health and Human Services, Administration for Children and Families.

Validiserri, R., Ronald, O., Aultman, T., & Curran, J. (1995). Community planning: A national strategy to improve HIV prevention programs. *Journal of Community Health, 20*(2), 87–100.

Vallée, F., Théberge, Y., & Jobin, L. (1988). *Évaluation d'un programme de prévention des abus sexuels en scolaire.* CLSC de la Guadeloupe et Département de santé communautaire de Centre Hospitalier Régional de Beauce, La Guadeloupe.

Van der Vegt, R., & Knip, H. (1988). The role of the principal in school improvement. *Journal of Research and Development in Education, 22*(1), 60–68.

Van Doorninck, W., Dawson, P., Butterfield, P., & Alexander, A. (1980). *Parent–infant support through lay health visitors: Final report to the Bureau of Community Health Services.* Denver, CO: University of Colorado Health Sciences Center.

Van Uchelen, C.P., Davidson, S.F., Quressette, S.V.A., Brasfield, C.R., & Demerais, L.H. (1997). What makes us strong: Urban Aboriginal perspectives on wellness and strength. *Canadian Journal of Community Mental Health, 16*(2), 37–50.

Vander-Schie, R.A., Wagenfield, M.O., & Worgress, B.L. (1987). Reorganizing human services at the local level: The Kalamazoo county experience. *New England Journal of Human Services, 7,* 29–33.

Vanier Institute of the Family. (1996, March). Youth crime – What do we know? *Transition, 26*(1), 11.

Vaux, A. (1988). *Social support: Theory, research, and intervention.* New York: Praeger Publishers.

Vissing, Y.M., Straus, M.S., Gelles, R.J., & Harrop, J.W. (1991). Verbal aggression by parents and psychosocial problems of children. *Child Abuse and Neglect, 15,* 223–238.

Vondra, J.I. (1990). The community as place: The community context of child abuse and neglect. In D.G. Unger & M.B. Sussman (Eds.), *Families in community settings: Interdisciplinary perspectives. Marriage and Family Review, 15,* 19–38.

Vorrath, H.H., & Brendtro, L.K. (1985). *Positive peer culture* (2nd ed.). New York: Aldine de Gruyter.

Waldman, C. (1985). *Atlas of the North American Indian*. New York: Fact on File Publications.

Wall, J., Hawkins, J., Lishner, D., & Fraser, M. (1981). *Juvenile delinquency prevention: Compendium of thirty-six program models*. Washington, DC: U.S. Government Printing Office.

Walsh, F. (1996). The concept of family resilience: Crisis and challenge. *Family Process, 35*(3), 261–281.

Walton, E. (1997). Enhancing investigative decisions in child welfare: An exploratory use of intensive family preservation services. *Child Welfare, 76*, 447–461.

Walton, E., Fraser, M.W., Lewis, R.E., Pecora, P.J., & Walton, W.K. (1993). In-home family focused reunification: An experimental study. *Child Welfare, 72*, 473–487.

Ware, L., Osofosky, J., Culp, A., & Eberhart-Wright, A. (1987). *A preventive mental health program for adolescent mothers and infants*. Unpublished paper from the Menninger Infant Project presented at the American Academy of Child and Adolescent Psychiatry Meeting, Washington, DC.

Washington, V., & Bailey, U. (1995). *Project Head Start*. New York: Garland Publishing Inc.

Watts, D.W., & Ellis, A.M. (1993). Sexual abuse and drinking and drug use: Implications for prevention. *Journal of Drug Education, 23*(2), 183–200.

Webber, M. (1998). *As if kids mattered*. Toronto: Key Porter.

Webster-Stratton, C. (1985). Comparison of abusive and nonabusive families with conduct-disordered children. *American Journal of Orthopsychiatry, 55*, 59–69.

Weechi-It-Te-Win Family Services Inc., & Ontario Ministry of Community and Social Services. (1995). *Building healthier communities: A report of the operational review of Weechi-It-Te-Win Family Services, prepared by the operational review team*. Unpublished report.

Weick, A., & Saleebey, D. (1995, March). Supporting family strengths: Orienting policy and practice toward the 21st Century. *Families in Society: The Journal of Contemporary Human Services*, 141–149.

Weikart, D.P., & Schweinhart, L.J. (1997). High/Scope Perry Preschool Program. In G.W. Albee & T.P. Gullotta (Eds.), *Primary prevention works* (pp. 146–166). London: Sage.

Weiss, J.A. (1981). Substance vs. symbol in administrative reform: The case of human services coordination. *Policy Analysis, 7*, 21–45.

Weissberg, R.P., Barton, H.A., & Shriver, T.P. (1997). The Social-Competence Promotion Program for young adults. In G.W. Albee & T.P. Gullotta (Eds.), *Primary prevention works* (pp. 268–290). Thousand Oaks, CA: Sage Publications.

Weissberg, R.P., Caplan, M., & Harwood, R.L. (1991). Promoting competent young people in competence-enhancing environments: A systems-based perspective on primary prevention. *Journal of Consulting and Clinical Psychology, 59*(6), 830–841.

Weissberg, R.P., & Elias, M.J. (1993). Enhancing young people's social competence and health behavior: An important challenge for educators, scientists, policymakers, and funders. *Applied and Preventive Psychology, 2,* 179–190.

Weissberg, R.P., Gullotta, T.P., Hampton, R.L., Ryan, B.A., & Adams, G.R. (Eds.). (1997). *Enhancing children's wellness.* London: Sage.

Weissberg, R.P., Kusler, C.B., & Gullotta, T.P. (1997). Introduction and overview: Prevention services – From optimistic promise to widespread, effective practice. In R.P. Weissberg, T.P. Gullotta, R.L. Hampton, B.A. Ryan, & G.R. Adams (Eds.), *Healthy children 2010: Establishing preventive services* (pp. 1–26). Thousand Oaks, CA: Sage

Weisz, V., & Tomkins, A.J. (1996). The right to a family environment for children with disabilities. *American Psychologist, 51,* 1239–1245.

Wekerle, C., & Wolfe, D.A. (1993). Prevention of child physical abuse and neglect: Promising new directions. *Clinical Psychology Review, 13,* 501–540.

Werner, E.E. (1985). Stress and protective factors in children's lives. In A.R. Nicol (Ed.), *Longitudinal studies in child psychology and psychiatry: Practical lessons from research experience* (pp. 335–355). New York: John Wiley & Sons.

Werner, E.E. (1989). High-risk children in young adulthood: A longitudinal study from birth to 32 years. *American Journal of Orthopsychiatry, 59,* 72–81.

Werner, E.E. (1990). Antecedents and consequences of deviant behavior. In K. Hurrelmann & F. Losel (Eds.), *Health hazards in adolescence* (pp. 210–225). New York: Walter de Gruyter.

Werner, E.E. (1993). Risk, resilience, and recovery: Perspectives from the Kauai Longitudinal Study. *Development and Psychopathology, 5,* 503–515.

Werner, E.E., Bierman, J.M., & French, F.E. (1971). *The children of Kauai.* Honolulu, HI: University of Hawaii Press.

Werner, E.E., & Smith, R.S. (1977). *Kauai's children come of age.* Honolulu, HI: University of Hawaii Press.

Werner, E.E., & Smith, R.S. (1982). *Vulnerable but invincible: A longitudinal study of resilient children and youth.* New York: McGraw-Hill.

Werner, E.E., & Smith, R.S. (1992). *Overcoming the odds: High risk children from birth to adulthood.* Ithaca, NY: Cornell University Press.

Wesch, D., & Lutzker, J.R. (1991). A comprehensive 5–year evaluation of Project 12–Ways: An ecobehavioral program for treating and preventing child abuse and neglect. *Journal of Family Violence, 6,* 17–35.

Westney, O.E., Cole, O.J., & Munford, T.L., (1988). The effects of prenatal education intervention on unwed prospective adolescent fathers. *Journal of Adolescent Health Care, 9,* 214–218.

Wharf, B. (1993). Rethinking child welfare. In B. Wharf (Ed.), *Rethinking child welfare in Canada* (pp. 210–230). Toronto: McClelland & Stewart.

Wharf, B. (1994, April). *Research on organizing and delivering child welfare services.* Victoria, BC: School of Social Work, University of Victoria.

Wharf, B., & McKenzie, B. (1998). *Connecting policy to practice in the human services.* Toronto: Oxford University Press.

Whipple, E.E., & Webster-Stratton, C. (1991). The role of parental stress in physically abusive families. *Child Abuse and Neglect, 15,* 279–291.

White, J.A., & Wehlage, G. (1995). Community collaboration: If it is such a good idea, why is it so hard to do? *Educational Evaluation and Policy Analysis, 17*(1), 23–38.

White, J.L., Moffitt, T.E., & Silva, P.A. (1989). A prospective replication of the protective effects of IQ in subjects at high risk for juvenile delinquency. *Journal of Consulting and Clinical Psychology, 57,* 719–724.

Whiteman, M., Fanshel, D., & Grundy, J.F. (1987). Cognitive-behavioral interventions aimed at anger of parents at risk of child abuse. *Social Work, 32,* 469–474.

Whiting, B., & Whiting, J. (1975). *Children of six cultures.* Cambridge, MA: Harvard University Press.

Whittaker, J.K., & Garbarino, J. (1983). *Social support networks: Informal helping in the human services.* New York: Aldine Publishing Co.

Widom, C.S. (1989a). Does violence beget violence? A critical examination of the literature. *Psychological Bulletin, 106*(1), 3–28.

Widom, C.S. (1989b). The cycle of violence. *Science, 244,* 160–166.

Widom, C.S. (1992, June). *Child abuse and alcohol use.* Paper prepared for the Working Group on Alcohol-Related Violence: Fostering Interdisciplinary Perspectives, convened by the National Institute on Alcohol Abuse and Alcoholism, Washington, DC.

Widom, C.S. (1998). Child victims: Searching for opportunities to break the cycle of violence. *Applied and Preventive Psychology, 7,* 225–234.

Wilkins, R., Sherman, G.J., & Best, P.A.F. (1991). Birth outcomes and infant mortality by income in urban Canada, 1986. In *Health Reports.* Vol. 3. No. 1. Ottawa: Industry, Science and Technology Canada.

Williams-Meyer, L., & Finkelhor, D. (1992). *The characteristics of incestuous fathers.* Washington, DC: Report to the National Center on Child Abuse and Neglect.

Williamson, J.F., Borduin, C.M., & Howe, B.A. (1991). The ecology of adolescent maltreatment: A multilevel examination of adolescent physical abuse, sexual abuse and neglect. *Journal of Consulting and Clinical Psychology, 59,* 449–459.

Willis, D.J., Holden, E.W., & Rosenberg, M. (Eds.). (1992). *Prevention of child maltreatment: Developmental and ecological perspectives.* New York: John Wiley & Sons.

Willis, D.J., & Silovsky, J. (1998). Prevention of violence at the societal level. In P.K. Trickett & C.J. Schellenbach (Eds.), *Violence against children in the family and the community* (pp. 401–416). Washington, DC: American Psychological Association.

Wilson, M. (1996). Citizenship and welfare. In M. Lavalette & A. Pratt (Eds.), *Social policy* (pp. 182–195). London: Sage.

Wilson, M., & Daly, M. (1987). Risk of maltreatment of children living with stepparents. In R.J. Gelles & J.B. Lancaster (Eds.), *Child abuse and neglect: Biosocial dimensions* (pp. 215–232). Hawthorne, NY: Aldine de Gruyter.

Wilson, T. (1981). *Ziggy faces life.* New York: Signet Books.

Winett, R.A., Anderson, E.S., Desiderato, L.L., Solomon, L.J., Perry, M., Kelly, J.A., Sikkema, K.J., Roffman, R.A., Norman, A.D., Lombard, D.N., & Lombard, T.N. (1995). Enhancing social diffusion theory as a basis for prevention intervention: A conceptual and strategic framework. *Applied and Preventive Psychology, 4,* 233–245.

Wolfe, D.A. (1985). Child-abusive parents: An empirical review and analysis. *Psychological Bulletin, 97,* 462–482.

Wolfe, D.A. (1987). *Child abuse: Implications for child development and psychopathology.* Thousand Oaks, CA: Sage.

Wolfe, D.A. (1991). *Preventing physical and emotional abuse of children.* New York: The Guilford Press.

Wolfe, D.A. (1994). The role of intervention and treatment services in the prevention of abuse and neglect. In G.B. Melton & F.D. Barry (Eds.), *Protecting children from abuse and neglect: Foundations for a new national strategy* (pp. 224–303). New York: The Guilford Press.

Wolfe, D.A. (1998). Prevention of child abuse and neglect. In *Canada health action: Building on the legacy – Determinants of health, Vol. I – Children and youth* (pp. 103–131). Ste Foy, PQ: Éditions Multimondes Inc.

Wolfe, D.A., Edwards, B., Manion, I., & Koverola, C. (1988). Early intervention for parents at risk of child abuse and neglect: A preliminary investigation. *Journal of Consulting and Clinical Psychology, 56,* 40–47.

Wolfe, D.A., Fairbank, J.A., Kelly, J.A., & Bradlyn, A.S. (1983). Child abusive parents' physiological responses to stressful and nonstressful behaviour in children. *Behavioural Assessment, 5,* 363–371.

Wolfe, D.A., & Jaffe, P. (1991). Children in care of the state: Policy issues for the 1990's. In L.C. Johnson & R. Banhort (Eds.), *Children, families and public policy in the 90's.* Toronto: Thompson Educational Publishing.

Wolfe, D.A., Kaufman, K., Aragona, J., & Sandler, J. (1981). *The child management program for abusive parents: Procedures for developing a child abuse intervention program.* Winter Park, FL: Anna Publishing.

Wolfe, D.A., MacPherson, T., Blount, R., & Wolfe, V.V. (1986). Evaluation of a brief intervention for educating school children in awareness of physical and sexual abuse. *Child Abuse and Neglect, 10,* 85–92.

Wolfe, D.A., Sas, L., & Wekerle, C. (1994). Factors associated with the development of posttraumatic stress disorder among child victims of sexual abuse. *Child Abuse and Neglect, 18,* 37–50.

Wolfe, D.A., Wekerle, C., Reitzel, D., & Gough, R. (1995). Strategies to address violence in the lives of high-risk youth. In E. Peled, P.G. Jaffe, & J.L. Edleson (Eds.), *Ending the cycle of violence: Community responses to the children of battered women* (pp. 235–251). Thousand Oaks, CA: Sage Publications.

Wolfner, G.D., & Gelles, R.J. (1993). A profile of violence toward children: A national study. *Child Abuse and Neglect, 17,* 197–212.

Wood, S., Barton, K., & Schroeder, C. (1988). In-home treatment of abusive families: Cost and placement at one year. *Psychotherapy, 25,* 409–413.

Woodward, K. (1996). Feminist critiques of social policy. In M. Lavalette & A. Pratt (Eds.), *Social policy* (pp. 83–100). London: Sage.

Woollcombe, S. (1996, November). *Canada's children ... Canada's future: A background paper for the second national policy conference on children.* Ottawa.

Woolley, F., Vermaeten, A., & Madill, J. (1996). Ending universality: The case of child benefits. *Canadian Public Policy, 22*(1).

Wurtele, S.K. (1990). Teaching personal safety skills to four-year-old children: A behavioral approach. *Behavior Therapy, 21,* 25–32.

Wurtele, S.K., Gillespie, E.I., Currier, L.L., & Franklin, C.F. (1992). A comparison of teachers vs. parents as instructors of a personal safety program for preschoolers. *Child Abuse and Neglect, 16,* 127–137.

Wurtele, S.K., Kast, L.C., & Meltzer, A.M. (1992). Sexual abuse prevention for young children: A comparison of teachers and parents as instructors. *Child Abuse and Neglect, 16,* 865–876.

Wurtele, S.K., Kast, L.C., Miller-Perrin, C.L., & Kondrick, P.A. (1989). Comparison of programs for teaching personal safety to preschoolers. *Journal of Consulting and Clinical Psychology, 57,* 505–511.

Wurtele, S.K., & Owens, J.S. (1997). Teaching personal safety skills to young children: An investigation of age and gender across five studies. *Child Abuse and Neglect, 21,* 805–814.

Wurtele, S.K., Saslawsky, D.A., Miller, C.L., Marrs, S.R., & Britcher, J.C. (1986). Teaching personal safety skills for potential prevention of sexual abuse: A comparison of treatments. *Journal of Consulting and Clinical Psychology, 54,* 688–692.

Yates, M., & Youniss, J. (1998). Community service and political identity development in adolescence. *Journal of Social Issues, 54,* 495–512.

Yoe, J.T., Santarcangelo, S., Atkins, M., & Burchard, J.D. (1996). Wraparound care in Vermont: Program development, implementation and evaluation of a statewide system of individualized services. *Journal of Child and Family Studies, 5*(1), 23–39.

Yoshikawa, H. (1994). Prevention as cumulative protection: Effects of early family support and education on chronic delinquency and its risks. *Psychological Bulletin, 115,* 28–54.

Young, L. (1964). *Wednesday's children: A study of child neglect and abuse.* New York: McGraw-Hill.

Youngblade, L.M., & Belsky, J. (1990). Social and emotional consequences of child maltreatment. In R.T. Ammerman & M. Hersen (Eds.), *Children at risk: An evaluation of factors contributing to child abuse and neglect* (pp. 109–148). New York: Plenum Press.

Youniss, J., & Yates, M. (1997). *Community service and social responsibility.* Chicago: University of Chicago Press.

Yuan, Y.Y.T., McDonald, W.R., Wheeler, C.E., Struckman-Johnson, D., & Rivest, M. (1990). *Evaluation of AB 1562 in-home care demonstration projects, Vol. I: Final report.* Sacramento, CA: Office of the Child Abuse Prevention Department of Social Services.

Zabin, L.S. (1992). School-based reproductive health services: The Johns Hopkins Program. In B.C. Miller, J.J. Card, R.L. Paikoff, & J.L. Petersen (Eds.), *Preventing adolescent pregnancy: Model programs and evaluations* (pp. 156–184). Newbury Park, CA: Sage Publications.

Zetlin, A. (1995). Commentary: Lessons learned about integrating services. In L.C. Rigsby, M.C. Reynolds, & M.C. Wang (Eds.), *School-community connections: Exploring issues for research and practice* (pp. 422–443). San Francisco, CA: Jossey-Bass Publishers.

Ziegart, K.A. (1983). The Swedish prohibition of corporal punishment: A preliminary report. *Journal of Marriage and the Family, 45,* 917–926.

Zigler, E.F., Finn-Stevenson, M., & Stern, B.M. (1997). Supporting children and families in the schools: The school of the 21st Century. *American Journal of Orthopsychiatry, 67,* 396–407.

Zigler, E.F., & Gilman, E. (1996). Not just any care: Shaping a coherent child care policy. In E.F. Zigler, S.L. Kagan, & N.W. Hall (Eds.), *Children, families and government: Preparing for the twenty-first century* (pp. 94–116). Cambridge, MA: Cambridge University Press.

Zigler, E., & Hall, N.W. (1989). Physical child abuse in America: Past, present, and future. In D. Cicchetti & V. Carlson (Eds.), *Child maltreatment: Theory and research on the causes and consequences of child abuse and neglect* (pp. 38–75). New York: Cambridge University Press.

Zigler, E.F., Kagan, S.L., & Hall, N.W. (1996). *Children, families and government: Preparing for the twenty-first century.* Cambridge, MA: Cambridge University Press.

Zill, N., Moore, K.A., Wolpow Smith, E., Stief, T., & Coiro, M.J. (1995). The life circumstances of children in welfare families: A profile based on national survey data. In P.L. Chase Landsdale & J. Brooks-Gunn (Eds.), *Escape from poverty: What makes a difference for children?* (pp. 38–59). New York: Cambridge University Press.

Zimmerman, S.L. (1995). *Understanding family policy: Theories and applications.* Thousand Oaks, CA: Sage Publications.

Zunz, S.J., Turner, S., & Norman, E. (1993). Accentuating the positive: Stressing resiliency in school-based substance abuse prevention programs. *Social Work in Education, 15*(3), 169–176.

Zuravin, S.J. (1988). Fertility patterns: Their relationship to child physical abuse and child neglect. *Journal of Marriage and the Family, 50,* 983–993.

Zuravin, S.J. (1989). The ecology of child abuse and neglect: Review of the literature and presentation of data. *Violence and Victims, 4,* 101–120.

Zuravin, S.J. (1991). Unplanned childbearing and family size: Their relationship to child neglect and abuse. *Family Planning Perspectives, 23,* 155–161.

Zuravin, S.J., & Grief, G.L. (1989). Normative and child-maltreating AFDC mothers. *Social Casework: The Journal of Contemporary Social Work, 74,* 76–84.

Zyblock, M. (1996, December). *Why is family market income inequality increasing in Canada? Examining the effects of aging, family formation, globalization and technology.* (W-96-11E). Working paper prepared for the Applied Research Branch, Strategic Policy, Human Resources Development Canada, Hull, Quebec.

Index

Aboriginal, 28
  advocacy, 390
  challenges in program implementation, 409–13
  child care, 377–9
  child maltreatment prevention, 414
  children, 354–5, 371, 373–4
  community prevention practice, 395–405
  consultation and training, 412–14
  contemporary adaptations, 386–7
  customary care, 385–6
  family support, 387–8, 390–3, 394–5
  government, 366–8
  healing, 394–5, 401–3
  Hollow Water Model, 403
  home visitation, 388–90
  leadership and family well-being, 414
  parent education, 383–5
  parents and families, 381
  policies, 367, 395
  prevention in communities, 371–7
  prevention themes, 405–9
  programs, 371
  repatriation, 405
  Seven Sacred Gifts, 351, 353
  values and beliefs for a healthier future, 415–16
  Wraparound, 393–4
  youth, 379–81
Aboriginal communities, 28–9
  acculturation, 358, 363–6
  beliefs and values that guide parenting practices, 357
  care of children and child development, 355–6
  child welfare, 366–7
  family life, 370–3
  family wellness, 349–416
  history of Native child welfare, 358
  roots of tribal culture, 350–2
  schools, 360–2
  traditional family life, 352–5
  visions of family wellness, 369–70
Aboriginal Headstart, 373–5
Aboriginal Healing and Wellness Strategy, 397–8
abuse, 238, 244, 247, 252, 381. *See also* maltreatment
  rates, 5
  spousal, 275
accountability, 172–3
acute stressors, families with, 84–5

addictions, 91–2
Adlerian theory, 230, 232
adolescents
  abuse rates, 273–4
  beyond programs, 316
  competence and skill development programs, 287
  developmental context, 279–80
  family- and parent-focused programs, 293
  major program strategies, 286
  neighbourhood transformation projects, 314–16
  priority foci, 284–6
  problem behaviours, 280–3
  social integration programs, 301–9
age, 98–9
agents of values, children as, 147–9
approaches
  case management, 15
  community development, 15
  ecological, 369
  indicated reactive, 221, 227, 231, 239–44, 248–50, 258–9, 264
  proactive high-risk, 226–7, 230–1, 236–9, 247–8, 255–8, 263–4
  proactive universal, 221, 224–6, 229–30, 235–6, 246–7, 252–5, 261–3
  self-help/mutual aid, 15
artists, 168–70
at-risk families, 64
attachment, 282, 323
  secure, 113, 138
  theory, 62
Australia, 179, 185, 188–9, 197, 201, 393
Austria, 124, 197, 199, 200

Badgley Report, 44

behaviour
  children, difficult, 96–7
  children, positive, 118
Belgium, 132
benefits, 213
  cash, 181
  Child Tax, 181, 184, 187
  maternity leave, 198
  National Child, 182–4
Better Beginnings, Better Futures, 26, 253, 269, 271, 314, 324, 327, 329, 330, 331, 332, 333, 336, 341, 342, 373, 420
biological predisposition, 93–4
blaming the victim, 127, 228
Brazil, 124
budget
  Canada, 3
  cost, 5–6, 24, 57
  funding, 4
  government saving, 6
  United States, 3

Campaign 2000, 170–1, 213, 434
Canada, 12, 34, 44–50, 63, 65, 124, 128, 132, 158–9, 165, 170–2, 177–81, 187–94, 197, 199, 200–2, 204, 206, 208–20, 272, 315, 349, 358, 359, 366, 393, 400, 420
  children in care, 57
  poverty, 64–9
Canadian Council on Social Development, 170, 180, 216, 363, 434
Canadian Incidence Study of Reported Child Abuse and Neglect, 50
Canadian Public Health Association, 4
Canadian Teachers Federation, 170
caregivers, 71–2, 167

caring and protection of health, 134, 138, 152, 154, 156, 172
change agents, 161, 163
child advocates, 162, 163, 170–2, 433
child care, 143, 167, 202, 272, 312
    cost, 75–6
    initiatives, Canada, 205–6
    options, 74–6
    policy, 201–8
children, 445–8
    as agents of values, 152
    as beneficiaries and agents of values, 147–9
    cognitive functioning, 96
    families, 139
    maltreatment of, 5
    as recipients of values, 152
    rights of, 124, 126, 133, 140–1, 163, 169, 185, 209
Children's Aid Society of Ottawa-Carleton, 170
Children's Circle Program, 375–6
child welfare
    partnerships and community, 439–42
    workers, 129
Child Welfare League of Canada, 170, 434
civic duties, 166
civic identity, 146
collaboration and respect for the community, 134, 145–7, 152–6, 172
Colorado, 235
commitment, 172–3
communication, 115–16
communitarian philosophy, 135–7
community, 29, 167–8
    climate, positive, 110

contribution of, 4
    structures, 134, 143–4, 172
consequences, 50–8
    of maltreatment, 43
    on children's functioning, 51–6
conservatism, 126–7
context, 16, 20–1, 31, 35, 37, 41–50
contradictions, 158
contributing factors, 57–100
coping, 113, 116
corporate leaders, 170–2
cost-effectiveness, 6, 239, 251, 258, 379
countries, international, 186
Cuba, 132
culture, 12, 14, 71, 143, 168–70, 233
    background, children, 99
    First Nations, 28, 370, 407–8
    media, 168–70
    religion, 166

databases, 34
Denmark, 132, 197, 199, 200, 212
Department of Indian Affairs, 366
divorce, 72, 85, 180, 192
document review, 34

ecological hierarchy, 59
ecological perspective, 7, 9, 10, 62, 138, 149, 150, 420–4
economic insecurity, 85
education, 134
    parental, 90–1
    personal development, 134, 140, 172
    training programs, 229–34
emotional abuse, 3, 46–50, 80
employment, 85
empowerment, 31, 162
    children, 375

family, 234
parents, 249
England, 132
entertainment industry, 169. *See also* media
epidemiology, of child maltreatment, 42–50
etiology, 16, 20–1, 31, 35, 43
Europe, 179, 181, 199, 201, 209, 217, 219, 233

family
  allowance, 181, 186, 188–90
  alternative, 62
  benefits, 180–96
  blended, 62, 81, 364
  climate, positive and supportive, 114–15
  cohabitation, 62
  cohesion, 112–14
  environment, 137
  grandparent, 62, 364
  homosexual, 62
  lack of time, 84
  privacy, 71
  reconstituted, 62
  resources, 76–8
  role of, 164–5
  single-parent, 62, 68, 81, 181, 207, 364
  size and structure, 81–4
  step-, 81
  structure, 111–12
  therapy, 294–7
  work conflicts, 216–18
Finland, 197, 199, 200, 211, 212
First Nations, 27, 43. *See also* Aboriginal
France, 186, 189–90, 194–5, 199, 201, 204, 211, 212, 214, 219

Gallup poll, 44
gender
  and children, 97–8
  roles, 78, 180, 233
Germany, 185, 190, 198, 199, 200, 211, 214, 219
Ghana, 132
government, 179, 202
Great Britain, 179
Greece, 198

health, caring and the protection of, 138–40
Health Canada, 4
helpers, 167
High/Scope Perry Preschool, 6
Holland, 132. *See also* Netherlands
homebuilders, 240–1
home visitation, 269
housing
  adequacy, 78–9, 85
  appropriate, 107
  cost, 79
human diversity, 134, 136, 142, 144–5, 152–6, 158, 164, 166, 172
humanistic theory, 230
Hungary, 200

Iceland, 211
immigration, 69–71
implementation, 27, 39
  diffusion, 442–5
impoverishment, 73–4, 75
incidence of maltreatment, 6, 20, 32, 44–5, 73–4
Indians, 350, 352, 358, 361–2, 364–7. *See also* Aboriginal
individual, 11, 162
individualism, 128, 426
individualistic values, 127

intelligence, children's, 118–20
international statistics, 44–50
interventions, 17, 27, 38
  collective, 128
  definition, 7
  personal, 128–9
  situational, 129
interview guide, 35
intrapsychic, 126–7, 426
  mode of help, 126
Israel, 132
Italy, 199, 212, 214

Japan, 198, 211, 212

key informants, 34
kibbutz, 136
Kids Help Phone, 171

legislators, 162, 170–2
levels of analysis, 8, 11, 38, 60, 150
  ecological, 220–2, 227
liberal philosophy, 135
low birth weight, 63, 94–6
Luxembourg, 198

macrosystem, 11, 60, 62
maltreatment, child, 5, 57, 139
  definition, 11
  ecological perspective on, 7–12
  ecology of, 77
  incidence/prevalence, 44–5, 71, 275
  parental history of, 87–8
  physical, 223
  prevention of, 50, 60, 161, 218, 220, 235, 245, 272, 423
  prevention of, themes for thinking and action, 419–48
  probability of, 58, 60
  psychological, 46–50, 63
  rate, 58
  statistics, 44–5
  vulnerabilities associated with, 63–100
media, 168–70, 397
mental health, 145
  child, 96
  parental, 93
  workers, 129
mentor, 108
mesosystem, 11, 60, 62
methodology, 33
Metropolitan Toronto Children's Aid Society, 66
microsystem, 11, 60, 62
  level, 59
Montreal, 230, 248, 254, 264, 273
moral expectations, 147, 149
myths, 159

National Crime Prevention Council, 4
National Forum on Health, 4
National Incidence Study, 44, 274, 283
native child welfare, 28
needs, 59, 134, 137, 147
  collective, 134
  personal, 134
  relational, 134
neglect, 45–50, 63–4, 223, 237–8, 265, 370, 381
Netherlands, 132, 186, 190–1, 194, 198–9, 202, 211–12, 219
networks, social, 81
New Zealand, 179, 197, 211, 393
North America, 128, 144, 205, 207, 217,
Norway, 197, 200, 211, 212, 219

objectives, 16, 29
Ontario, 5, 26, 206, 210, 217, 231, 276
Ontario Association of Children's Aid Societies, 170
Ontario Health Supplement, 44
Organization for Economic Co-operation and Development, 179

parental history of positive relationship with parent, 117
parent effectiveness training, 230
parenting skills, 165, 250
  poor or underdeveloped, 89–90
  positive parenting practices, 117–18
parents
  history of maltreatment, 281–2
  lovers, 282
  step-, 282
Parents Anonymous, 248–9
participants, 34
partner relationship, positive, 116–17
partnerships, 14, 136–7, 269
  definition, 15
  values, 138
personality factors, parental, 92–3
philosophy
  liberal, 133, 135
  moral, 129–31
  political, 129–31
physical abuse, 46–50, 63, 237–8, 265, 272, 275, 370, 376
physical health, children, 96
plan of action, 29–32
policies, 21, 23, 27, 32, 35, 38, 59, 151, 156–7, 161
  child, 8–12
  child care, 201–8
  child and family, 178–96
  child support, 192–6
  child welfare, 208–11
  community, 8–12
  definition, 178
  economic, 184, 188
  essential factors, 23
  evaluation, 160
  family policy reforms, 214–15
  high-risk, 12, 25, 32
  indicated, 12, 25
  just and caring society, 430–5
  maternity and parental leave, 196–201
  parental and family, 8–12
  proactive, 12, 25, 32
  promoting well-being of children and families in Canada, 177–219
  reactive, 12, 25, 32
  social, 8–12, 104–5, 130
  supportive, 104–5
  universal, 12, 25, 32, 179
policymakers, 157, 162, 163, 170–2, 420
Portugal, 198
poverty, 3, 4, 64–9, 73, 78, 83, 151, 170, 184–5, 189, 203, 215, 252, 265, 282–3, 315, 362–3, 379, 382, 433–4
  as Canadian conundrum, 211–14
  decreasing child and family, 215–18
power, 233, 275, 356, 391
  professional, 14
Prenatal/Early Infancy Project, 6, 236–7, 322
prevalence of maltreatment, 43–4, 56
prevention, 25, 32, 40–1, 162, 208, 252
  budget, 3
  types, 25

prevention of child maltreatment, 8, 40–1. *See also* maltreatment
  framework for, 3
prevention programs, effectiveness, 6
Prevention Task Force of the American Psychological Association, 26
priorities, 157
problem
  scope of, 43–50
  skills for solving, 116, 120
professional, role of, 15
programs, 24, 27, 32, 36, 38, 39, 77, 146, 156, 151, 157
  adolescents, 273–317
  balancing clarity and adaptation, 321–7
  centrality of support and direction, 333–5
  child, 8–12
  child wellness, 224–9
  community, 8–12
  community wellness, 245–60
  consequences of inattention, 328–9
  creating legitimacy, 331–2
  crossing boundaries and fostering innovation, 338–44
  demanding complexity, 330
  early intervention, 158–9
  educational, 227–9
  evaluation, 160
  family support, 234–45
  family wellness, 229–45
  home visitation, 235–9, 253, 255
  implementation, beginning lessons, 344–5
  implementation and diffusion, 318–46
  importance of initial personal struggle, 332
  long-term, 268
  media, employment, legislative, 260–5
  model, need for, 322–3
  multi-component community-based, 252–60
  multiple impediments, 339–40
  need for infrastructure, 334–5
  1,2,3, Go!, 253–4, 271
  parental and family, 8–12
  patterns, 283–4
  power of established procedures, 335–6
  preschool/elementary-age children, 220–72
  pressures of start-up, 330–1
  prevention, 159, 161
  prevention of maltreatment
    common elements, 266–72
    preschool/elementary-age children, 220–72
    success of, 265–6
Primary Mental Health Project, 322, 332, 335, 337
program model drift, 319, 321
promote family wellness
  common elements, 266–72
  preschool/elementary-age children, 220–72
  success of, 265–6
protection-promotion-prevention, 435–8
selecting and negotiating settings, 336–8
self-help, 246–51
service integration, 340–1
social, 8–12, 159
social support, 246–51
societal wellness, 260–5
struggle and resistance, 332–3

time, complexity, resource, and expertise requirements, 327–33
time and effort, 329–30
training of program providers, 335
transactive structures and partnerships, 327
transforming organizations and delivery systems, 341–4
treatment-oriented, 25
value of participation, 323–7
Project 12-Ways, 258
promotion, 162
promotion of child wellness, 177
basic values, 131–8, 162
value-driven actions, 163
promotion of family wellness, 161, 162, 177, 423
basic values, 131–8
framework for, 3
themes for thinking and action, 419–48
promotion mechanisms, 59, 61, 62
associated with resilience and wellness, 100–22
definition, 102
promotion–prevention–protection continuum, 12, 13, 16, 32, 42, 59, 62
protective factors, 11, 20, 162, 168, 278
protective mechanisms, 21, 42, 58, 60–2
associated with resilience and wellness, 100–22
definition, 102
protective/promoting mechanisms
community-level 105–10
family and parental level, 110–18
infant/child/adolescent level, 118–22

societal level, 103–5
provision of resources, 141–3
public concern, 5
Quebec, 34, 78, 205–6, 210, 235, 247

research framework, 18–19
resilience, 42, 56–8, 60–1, 373
perspective, 121–2
protective and promoting mechanisms associated with, 100–22
resources, 81, 83, 107–9
child, 8–12
community, 8–12
parental and family, 8–12
societal, 8–12
risk factors, 11, 20, 63, 69, 145, 166, 278, 280, 329
Royal Commission on Aboriginal Peoples, 365, 371

school, 165–7
environments, 109–10
School of the 21st Century, 254
self-abuse, 365
self-determination, 134, 140–2, 144, 145, 150, 152, 153, 156, 157, 164, 167–8, 172, 406
self-efficacy, 21, 140, 146, 164, 167, 322
theory, 62
self-esteem, 145, 160, 165, 230, 249, 364, 371, 382
service recipients, 15
sexual abuse, 46–50, 99–100, 101, 223, 224–9, 243, 262, 264, 265, 267, 277, 376–7, 382, 397, 403, 438
situational mode of help, 126
social awareness, 105

social challenge, 160-1
social cohesion, 73, 80-1
social competence, 120
social isolation, 80-1
social justice, 134, 136, 141-3, 152-6, 161, 169, 170, 172
social learning theory, 230, 232
social networks, 80-1
social skills, 21
    training, 250
social support, 107-9, 267-8
social values, strong, 105
stakeholders/groups, 14, 15, 42, 130, 252, 260
    consultation process, 34
Standing Committee on Health, 68
Standing Committee on Health of the House of Commons, 4
substance abuse, 281, 370, 372, 381
support networks, 80-1
    emotional, 80
    family, 80
Sweden, 132, 159, 186, 188, 191, 194-5, 197, 199, 200, 201, 205, 211-12, 214, 219
Switzerland, 197, 198
Syracuse University Family Development Research Program, 255-6

tax concessions, 187-8
Technical Advisory Group to the Ontario Ministry of Community and Social Services, 26
teen parenthood, 88-9
teen pregnancy, 278, 280, 310, 312, 316
temperament
    negative children, 96-7
    positive children, 118

Toronto, 6

unemployment, 64, 69, 73-4, 247, 365, 372, 379, 381
United Kingdom, 186, 191, 195, 198, 201, 202, 212, 214, 219
United Nations Convention on the Rights of the Child, 125, 131-3, 137, 139, 140, 146, 150
United States, 12, 26, 34, 44-50, 124, 132, 159, 167, 169, 170, 179, 181, 187, 192, 195-6, 197, 201-2, 206-7, 209, 211-12, 214, 219, 254, 273-4, 315, 361, 366
United States National Incidence Studies of Child Abuse and Neglect, 44

values, 16, 22-3, 31, 35, 38, 125-6, 160, 370
    agents of, 147
    beneficiaries of, 147
    challenging myths and misconceptions, 159-60
    child, 8-12
    child and family wellness, 124-73
    choice and definition of, 131-2
    collective, 22, 126-7, 131, 133, 151, 161, 429
    collective wellness, 141-4
    commitment and accountability, 172-3
    community, 8-12
    context, 130
    contradictions, 158-9
    definition, 21-3
    historical context, 125-7
    just and caring society, 424-30
    parental and family, 8-12
    personal, 22, 61, 131, 133, 151, 429

personal wellness, 138–41
relational, 22, 133, 151, 430
relational wellness, 144–7
role of wellness, 151–61
seeking balance, 161–2
social, 8–12, 144, 247
sources, 129–31
victim blaming. *See* blaming the victim
violence, 85, 169, 262, 263, 316
community, 79–80
neighbourhood, 162
spousal, 85–7
tolerance of, 70–1
vision, 16, 21, 31, 35, 38, 125, 149, 152–4
child and family wellness, 124–73
definition, 22
Voices for Children, 170
volunteers, 130, 146, 159, 167, 235–8, 249, 250, 309–10, 312, 400
vulnerabilities, 42–3, 58–63, 179, 424
associated with child maltreatment, 63–100
community-level, 72–81
definition, 58
family/parental-level, 81–94
infant/child/adolescent-level, 94–9
sexual abuse, 99–101

societal-level, 65, 69

wellness, 147, 391
child, 4, 10, 148, 232, 245, 424
child and family vision of, 149–50
community, 10, 148, 164, 245
definition, 7–8
ecological and hierarchical, 43, 57, 59, 60
ecological level of, 267
ecological perspective on, 7–12
economic, 434
family, 42, 148, 229, 232–3, 245, 251
parent, 232
parental, 148
parent and family, 10
personal, 138
priorities, 157–8
promotion of, 8, 21, 168, 218, 252, 264, 272
protective and promoting mechanisms, 100–22
social-emotional, 434–5
societal, 10, 148, 150, 245
youth, 4
Who Do You Tell?, 224–5

youth, 445–8